HOUGHTON MIFFLIN HARCOURT

WRITE SOURCE

TEACHER'S EDITION

Grade 7

Authors

Dave Kemper, Patrick Sebranek, and Verne Meyer

Illustrator

Chris Krenzke

GREAT SOURCE.

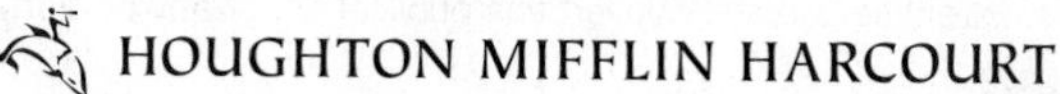

Teacher Consultants

Patty Beckstead
St. George, Utah

Amy Goodman
Anchorage, Alaska

Debra McConnell
Williston, Vermont

Steve Mellen
Temple Hills, Maryland

Reviewers

Ilene R. Abrams
Cobb County School District
Marietta, Georgia

Doreen A. Caswell
Mary G. Montgomery
Semmes, Alabama

Marilyn Erbentraut
Randall Consolidated
Bassett, Wisconsin

Mary M. Fischer
Arlington Public Schools
Arlington, Massachusetts

Michelle Gallagher
Pinellas County Schools
Largo, Florida

Cullen Hemstreet
Jefferson Parish Schools
Metairie, Louisiana

Alberta Lantz
School District of Waukesha
Waukesha, Wisconsin

Rita Martin
Jenks Public Schools
Jenks, Oklahoma

Inge Noa
Unified School District 475
Junction City, Kansas

Mary Osborne
Pinellas County Schools
Largo, Florida

Tamara Jo Rhomberg
Rockwood School District
St. Louis, Missouri

Deborah Richmond
Ferry Pass Middle School
Pensacola, Florida

Robert Wright
Sebastian River Middle School, Indian River S.D.
Sebastian River, Florida

Printed in the U.S.A.

ISBN 978-0-547-48450-1

5 6 7 8 9 10 0877 19 18 17 16 15 14

4500483539 B C D E F G

In the Front Matter

Program Overview

Professional Development for Writing

THE FORMS, THE PROCESS, AND THE TRAITS

WRITING WORKSHOP AND GRAMMAR

WRITING ACROSS THE CURRICULUM, ACADEMIC VOCABULARY, AND TEST PREPARATION

DIFFERENTIATION

RESEARCH

Teacher Resources

In the Wraparound

The Writing Process

USING THE WRITING PROCESS

The Forms of Writing

DESCRIPTIVE WRITING

NARRATIVE WRITING

EXPOSITORY WRITING

PERSUASIVE WRITING

RESPONSE TO LITERATURE

In the Wraparound

How does *Write Source* work?

Write Source is a complete language arts curriculum focused on writing and grammar in print and digital formats.

With writing instruction at the core, grammar, usage, and mechanics are taught in an authentic writing context.

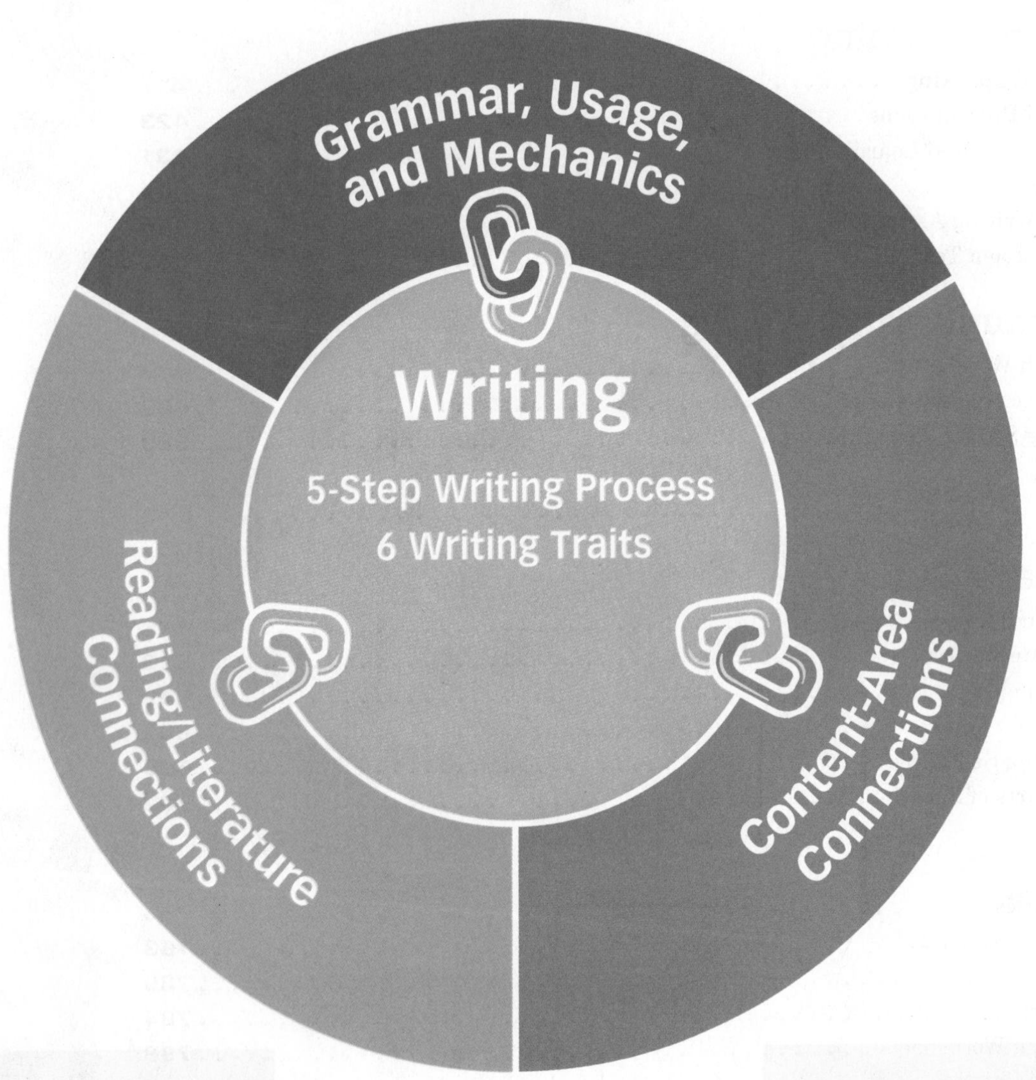

The Six Traits of Effective Writing
- Ideas
- Organization
- Voice
- Word Choice
- Sentence Fluency
- Conventions

Steps of the Writing Process
- Prewriting
- Writing
- Revising
- Editing
- Publishing

Introduce the writing form:

- Analyze a model paragraph.
- Preview the form by responding to questions about the model and by writing a paragraph.
-  Reflect on how revising for the six traits and editing for **conventions** can improve writing.

Each core form of writing unit follows the same instructional path—a consistent writing curriculum across all grade levels.

Explore the writing form:

- Analyze a model story or essay.
-  **Read authentic real-world fiction and nonfiction** that models the writing form.
- Use the writing process to write a story or essay.
-  Use the six traits to revise and then edit the writing for **conventions.**
- Repeat these steps for an additional writing assignment.

Write in the content areas:

-  Write a piece in the same writing form **across the major content areas**—science, social studies, math, and the arts.

Write for the assessment:

- Write a piece in the same writing form for assessment.

Write Source prepares students for success in the 21st century.

What are the main components of *Write Source*?

The *Write Source* **Student Edition** reflects the latest research on writing instruction. The **Teacher's Edition** has all the support you need to help students become confident, proficient writers.

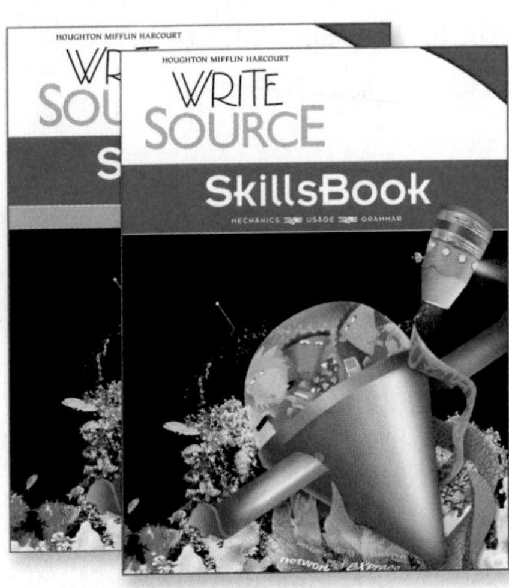

The **SkillsBook** helps students practice and improve grammar, usage, and mechanics skills.

The **Assessment** book provides a pretest, progress tests, and a post-test.

The **Daily Language Workouts** build student grammar skills through quick, daily editing and proofreading activities.

Write Source Online
www.hmheducation.com/writesource

- Discover the power of writing instruction with **Net-text**, an interactive, collaborative online worktext.
- Engage students in grammar through **GrammarSnap**, the grammar practice Web application.
- Transform writing instruction through high-functioning **Interactive Whiteboard Lessons**.
- Support instruction with a searchable **File Cabinet** teacher resource.
- Score essays accurately and efficiently with **Online Essay Scoring**.

How does the Teacher's Edition support instruction?

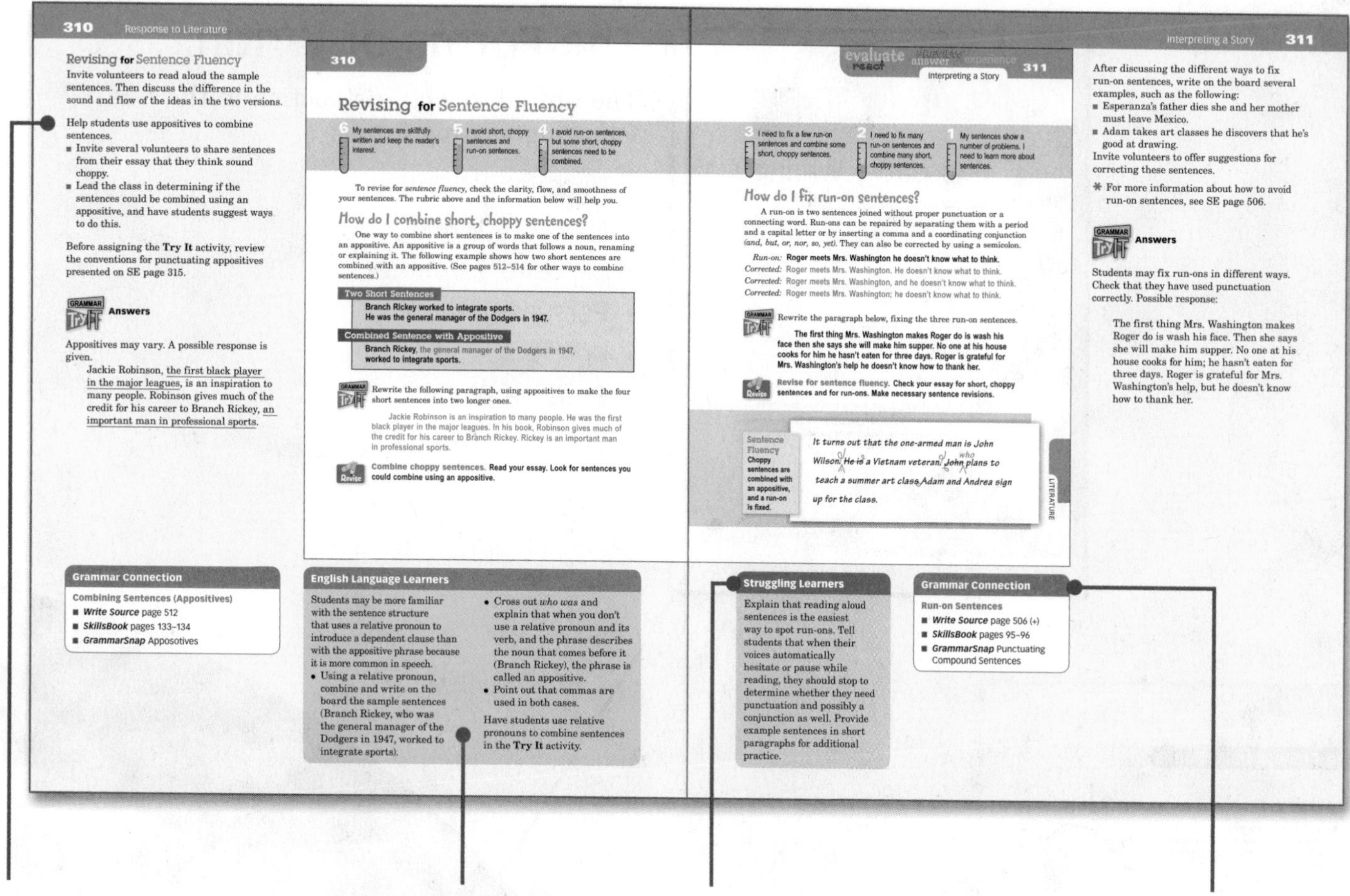

310 Response to Literature

Revising for Sentence Fluency
Invite volunteers to read aloud the sample sentences. Then discuss the difference in the sound and flow of the ideas in the two versions.

Help students use appositives to combine sentences.
- Invite several volunteers to share sentences from their essay that they think sound choppy.
- Lead the class in determining if the sentences could be combined using an appositive, and have students suggest ways to do this.

Before assigning the **Try It** activity, review the conventions for punctuating appositives presented on SE page 315.

GRAMMAR Try It **Answers**

Appositives may vary. A possible response is given.

Jackie Robinson, the first black player in the major leagues, is an inspiration to many people. Robinson gives much of the credit for his career to Branch Rickey, an important man in professional sports.

310

Revising for Sentence Fluency

6 My sentences are skillfully written and keep the reader's interest.
5 I avoid short, choppy sentences and run-on sentences.
4 I avoid run-on sentences, but some short, choppy sentences need to be combined.

To revise for *sentence fluency*, check the clarity, flow, and smoothness of your sentences. The rubric above and the information below will help you.

How do I combine short, choppy sentences?

One way to combine short sentences is to make one of the sentences into an appositive. An appositive is a group of words that follows a noun, renaming or explaining it. The following example shows how two short sentences are combined with an appositive. (See pages 512–514 for other ways to combine sentences.)

Two Short Sentences
Branch Rickey worked to integrate sports.
He was the general manager of the Dodgers in 1947.

Combined Sentence with Appositive
Branch Rickey, the general manager of the Dodgers in 1947, worked to integrate sports.

GRAMMAR Try It: Rewrite the following paragraph, using appositives to make the four short sentences into two longer ones.

Jackie Robinson is an inspiration to many people. He was the first black player in the major leagues. In his book, Robinson gives much of the credit for his career to Branch Rickey. Rickey is an important man in professional sports.

Revise: **Combine choppy sentences.** Read your essay. Look for sentences you could combine using an appositive.

evaluate react answer experience 311 Interpreting a Story

3 I need to fix a few run-on sentences and combine some short, choppy sentences.
2 I need to fix many run-on sentences and combine many short, choppy sentences.
1 My sentences show a number of problems. I need to learn more about sentences.

How do I fix run-on sentences?

A run-on is two sentences joined without proper punctuation or a connecting word. Run-ons can be repaired by separating them with a period and a capital letter or by inserting a comma and a coordinating conjunction (*and, but, or, nor, so, yet*). They can also be corrected by using a semicolon.

Run-on: Roger meets Mrs. Washington he doesn't know what to think.
Corrected: Roger meets Mrs. Washington. He doesn't know what to think.
Corrected: Roger meets Mrs. Washington, and he doesn't know what to think.
Corrected: Roger meets Mrs. Washington; he doesn't know what to think.

GRAMMAR Try It: Rewrite the paragraph below, fixing the three run-on sentences.

The first thing Mrs. Washington makes Roger do is wash his face then she says she will make him supper. No one at his house cooks for him he hasn't eaten for three days. Roger is grateful for Mrs. Washington's help he doesn't know how to thank her.

Revise: **Revise for sentence fluency.** Check your essay for short, choppy sentences and for run-ons. Make necessary sentence revisions.

Sentence Fluency: Choppy sentences are combined with an appositive, and a run-on is fixed.

It turns out that the one-armed man is John Wilson. He is a Vietnam veteran. John plans to teach a summer art class Adam and Andrea sign up for the class.

LITERATURE

Interpreting a Story 311

After discussing the different ways to fix run-on sentences, write on the board several examples, such as the following:
- Esperanza's father dies she and her mother must leave Mexico.
- Adam takes art classes he discovers that he's good at drawing.

Invite volunteers to offer suggestions for correcting these sentences.

* For more information about how to avoid run-on sentences, see SE page 506.

GRAMMAR Try It **Answers**

Students may fix run-ons in different ways. Check that they have used punctuation correctly. Possible response:

The first thing Mrs. Washington makes Roger do is wash his face. Then she says she will make him supper. No one at his house cooks for him; he hasn't eaten for three days. Roger is grateful for Mrs. Washington's help, but he doesn't know how to thank her.

Grammar Connection
Combining Sentences (Appositives)
- *Write Source* page 512
- *SkillsBook* pages 133–134
- *GrammarSnap* Appositives

English Language Learners
Students may be more familiar with the sentence structure that uses a relative pronoun to introduce a dependent clause than with the appositive phrase because it is more common in speech.
- Using a relative pronoun, combine and write on the board the sample sentences (Branch Rickey, who was the general manager of the Dodgers in 1947, worked to integrate sports).
- Cross out *who was* and explain that when you don't use a relative pronoun and its verb, and the phrase describes the noun that comes before it (Branch Rickey), the phrase is called an appositive.
- Point out that commas are used in both cases.

Have students use relative pronouns to combine sentences in the **Try It** activity.

Struggling Learners
Explain that reading aloud sentences is the easiest way to spot run-ons. Tell students that when their voices automatically hesitate or pause while reading, they should stop to determine whether they need punctuation and possibly a conjunction as well. Provide example sentences in short paragraphs for additional practice.

Grammar Connection
Run-on Sentences
- *Write Source* page 506 (+)
- *SkillsBook* pages 95–96
- *GrammarSnap* Punctuating Compound Sentences

Teaching suggestions and activity answers provide the support you need to implement writing instruction.

The Teacher's Edition provides consistent support for **English language learners.**

Differentiated Instruction for struggling learners and advanced learners is provided throughout the core instructional units.

Grammar Connections support grammar, usage, and mechanics instruction.

Additional Resources

- Common Core State Standards Correlation
- Yearlong Timetable
- Professional Development for Writing
- Reading–Writing Connection
- Benchmark Papers
- Graphic Organizers

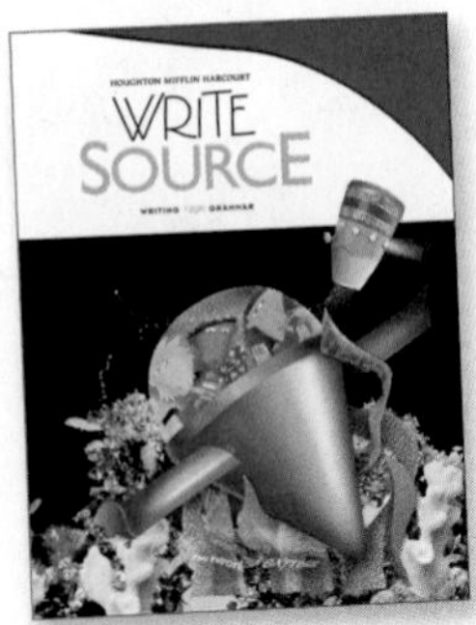

How is *Write Source* organized?

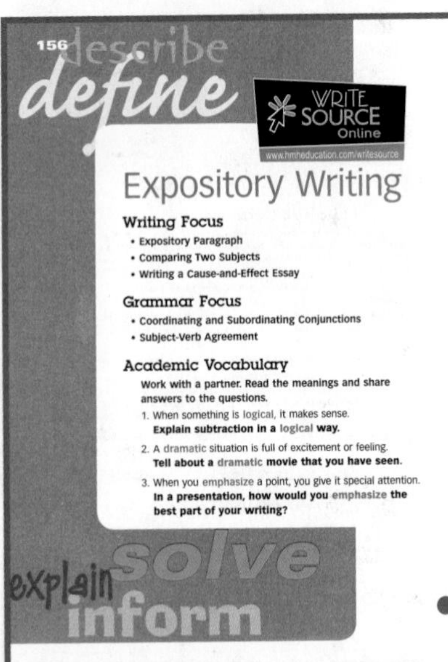

156

describe
define

WRITE SOURCE Online
www.hmheducation.com/writesource

Expository Writing

Writing Focus
- Expository Paragraph
- Comparing Two Subjects
- Writing a Cause-and-Effect Essay

Grammar Focus
- Coordinating and Subordinating Conjunctions
- Subject-Verb Agreement

Academic Vocabulary

Work with a partner. Read the meanings and share answers to the questions.

1. When something is logical, it makes sense.
   Explain subtraction in a logical way.
2. A dramatic situation is full of excitement or feeling.
   Tell about a dramatic movie that you have seen.
3. When you emphasize a point, you give it special attention.
   In a presentation, how would you emphasize the best part of your writing?

explain solve inform

The Forms of Writing

The units focus on instruction in the following writing forms:

- Descriptive Writing
- Narrative Writing
- Expository Writing
- Persuasive Writing
- Response to Literature
- Creative Writing
- Research Writing

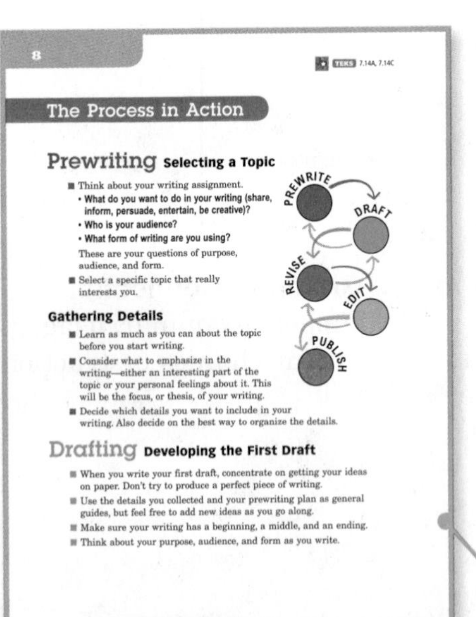

8

TEKS 7.14A, 7.14C

The Process in Action

Prewriting **Selecting a Topic**

- Think about your writing assignment.
  - **What do you want to do in your writing (share, inform, persuade, entertain, be creative)?**
  - **Who is your audience?**
  - **What form of writing are you using?**

  These are your questions of purpose, audience, and form.
- Select a specific topic that really interests you.

Gathering Details

- Learn as much as you can about the topic before you start writing.
- Consider what to emphasize in the writing—either an interesting part of the topic or your personal feelings about it. This will be the focus, or thesis, of your writing.
- Decide which details you want to include in your writing. Also decide on the best way to organize the details.

Drafting **Developing the First Draft**

- When you write your first draft, concentrate on getting your ideas on paper. Don't try to produce a perfect piece of writing.
- Use the details you collected and your prewriting plan as general guides, but feel free to add new ideas as you go along.
- Make sure your writing has a beginning, a middle, and an ending.
- Think about your purpose, audience, and form as you write.

The Writing Process

This unit introduces students to the steps in the writing process and integrates instruction on the six traits of effective writing.

The Tools of Learning

The third section helps students improve important classroom skills: listening and speaking, note taking, critical reading, summarizing, and test taking.

Basic Grammar and Writing

This section covers the fundamental building blocks of writing: words, sentences, and paragraphs.

A Writer's Resource

This section is a writing guide with information about development and presentation of writing.

Proofreader's Guide

This section addresses the conventions of standard English: punctuation, mechanics, spelling, grammar, and usage.

How does *Write Source* support today's digital-age learners?

Write Source Online taps into the power of interactivity, collaboration, and motivation to deliver a coordinated, comprehensive technology program for writing and grammar.

With ***Write Source Online***, teachers and students:

- personalize their writing experience through a **customizable dashboard**, **community network**, and **electronic portfolios**
- easily transition from reading to build a **solid foundation in writing and grammar**
- experience **interactive guided instruction** using Net-text, an online worktext with comprehensive writing support, tools for peer-to-peer collaboration, and point-of-use grammar practice

Preparing students and teachers
for success in the 21st century.

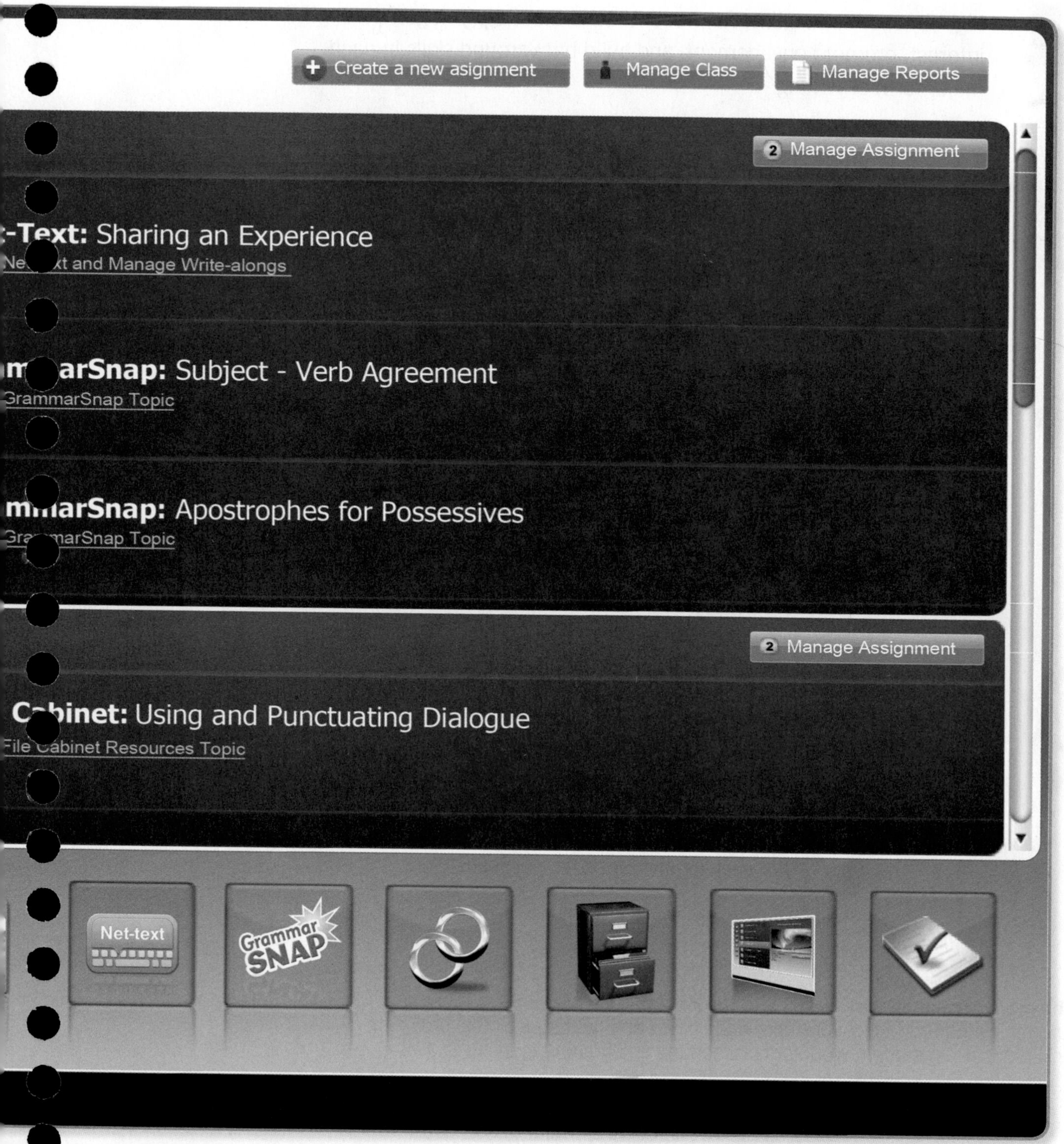

Create a new asignment
Manage Class
Manage Reports
Manage Assignment
-Text: Sharing an Experience
Ne xt and Manage Write-alongs
m arSnap: Subject - Verb Agreement
GrammarSnap Topic
mmarSnap: Apostrophes for Possessives
Gra marSnap Topic
Manage Assignment
C binet: Using and Punctuating Dialogue
File Cabinet Resources Topic
Net-text
Grammar SNAP

What are the components of *Write Source Online*?

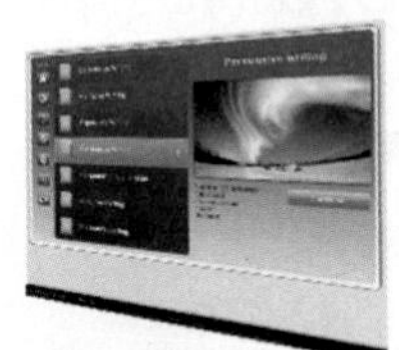

Set the stage for success with Interactive Whiteboard Lessons, high-functioning multimedia presentations that help you generate interest, promote engagement, and build background skills in each major form of writing.

Transform students into writers with Net-text, an innovative online worktext that features interactive instruction, online document creation, peer-to-peer commenting, and integrated grammar—all supported by tools that help you monitor progress and give feedback.

Engage students in grammar with GrammarSnap, a multimedia application that reinforces and extends understanding of key topics through videos, games, and quizzes that make learning about grammar fun.

Students are motivated to earn **SkillSnap points to unlock a variety of accessories** for their avatar character.

Tap into the power of publishing with the *Write Source Online* Portfolio, a customizable resource that gives students an authentic forum for sharing and reflecting on their writing.

Students and classrooms can connect in **My Network** to share and comment on each other's published portfolios.

Simplify the management of daily work with the Assignment Manager, a tool that delivers automatic student notifications about due dates and next steps while providing you with linked access to student work for commenting and grading.

Energize instruction with an innovative, integrated online writing program.

plays
literature connections
instructional videos
satire
graphic organizers
presentation
creative writing
online peer reviewing
process
grammar
writing
writing in the arts
poetry
descriptive writing
collaboration
voice
mechanics
prewriting
paragraph
expository writing
assessment
stories
rubric
publishing
traits

Write Source Online
www.hmheducation.com/writesource

editing
ideas
writing across the curriculum
interactive instrucion
essay scoring
revising
narrative writing
essay
organization
sentence fluency
conventions
informative
writing forms
benchmark papers
games
writing in math
persuasive writing

Additional Resources

- **Bookshelf** *Write Source* print component eBooks
- **Essay Scoring** Prompts for additional writing practice with automatic scoring and evaluation
- **File Cabinet** Thousands of printable teacher resources, such as blackline masters and additional assessments, that help you minimize planning time and differentiate instruction

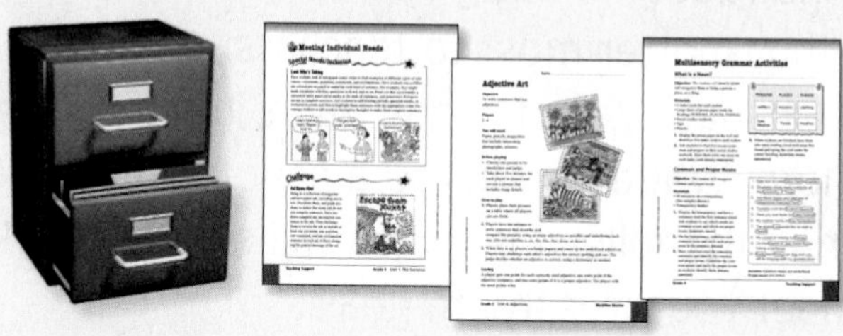

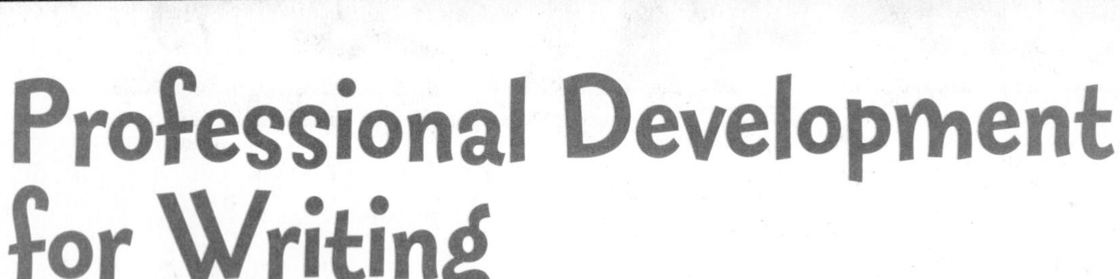

Professional Development for Writing

This section of the *Write Source* Teacher's Edition provides information to help you make the most of *Write Source* in your classroom. The program's instructional design includes comprehensive support for the topics that matter most to teachers: grammar, writing workshops, academic vocabulary, test preparation, the use of technology, and so much more. Whether you are a new teacher or a veteran, the information in the following pages will show how *Write Source* can help you meet your classroom goals.

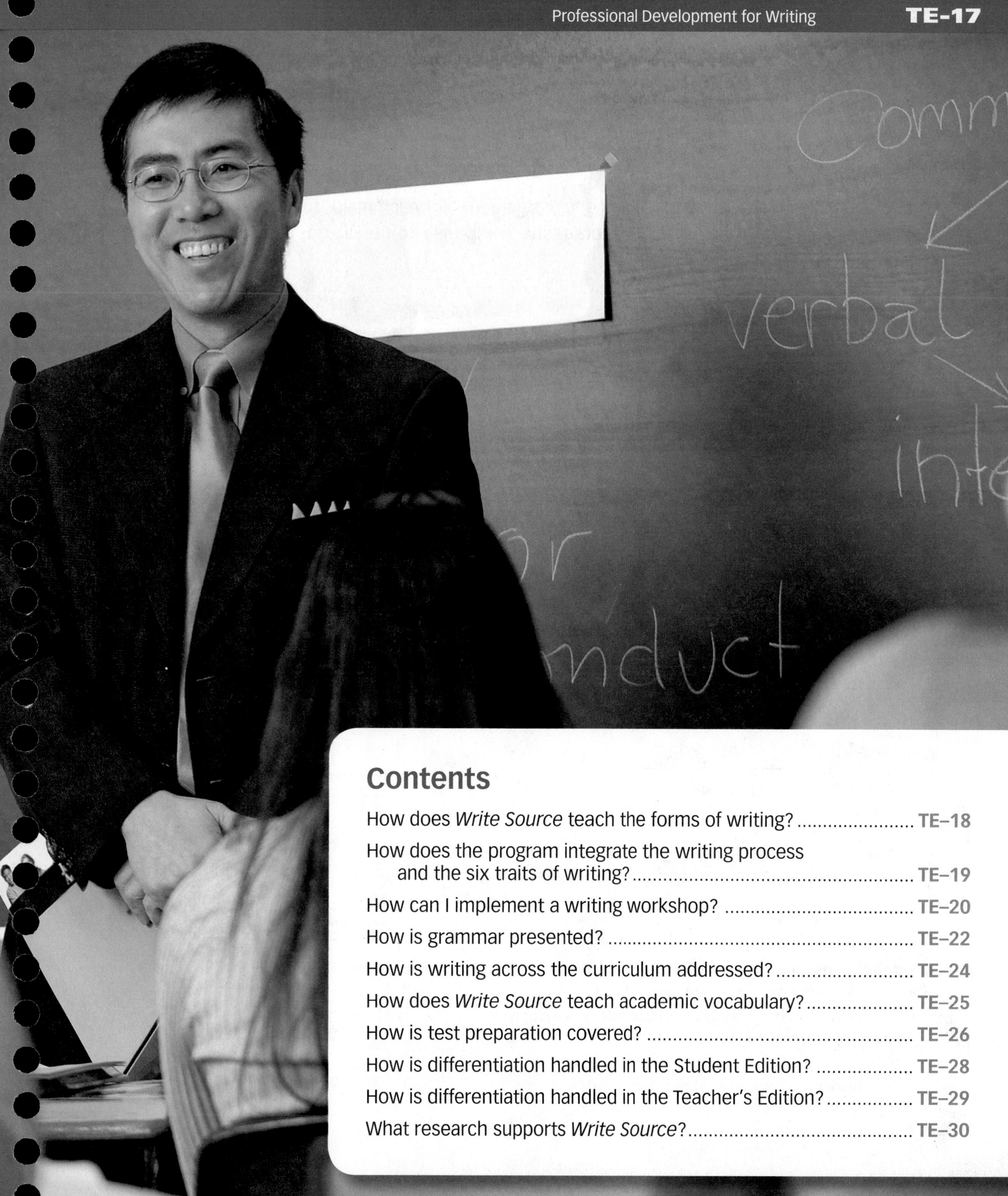

Contents

How does *Write Source* teach the forms of writing?

Write Source provides numerous models and assignments for each major form of writing: **descriptive, narrative, expository, persuasive, response to literature, creative,** and **research**.

Writing Assignments

The core writing units provide students with comprehensive, research-based exploration of the narrative, expository, persuasive, and literary response forms of writing. Each of these units employs the following instructional sequence:

- a **start-up paragraph assignment**—complete with a writing model and step-by-step writing guidelines
- one or more **multiparagraph assignments**—complete with writing models, in-depth step-by-step guidelines, and integration of traits and grammar instruction
- **Writing Across the Curriculum assignments**—complete with writing models and writing tips
- one **assessment writing assignment**—complete with a model response to a prompt plus writing tips

persuade convince support argue reason 223

Persuasive Writing

Proposing a Solution

It's easy to see problems. Maybe your city has a problem with litter or noise pollution or congestion. Maybe your school needs a new gymnasium or more computers or better wheelchair access. Everyone can see problems, but people who see solutions can make a real difference in the world around them.

In this chapter, you will be writing a persuasive problem-solution essay. First, you'll need to convince the reader the problem is serious. Then you must show that you have the best solution. With a well-written problem-solution essay, perhaps you can solve a problem in your school or community.

Writing Guidelines

Subject: A problem in your school or community
Form: Persuasive essay
Purpose: To propose a solution
Audience: Classmates and community members

LITTER

Writing Skills and Strategies

As students develop their compositions in each unit, they use the following skills and strategies in a variety of contexts:

- reading and responding to texts (writing models)
- **integrating the traits of writing into the writing process**
- using graphic organizers
- developing beginnings, middles, and endings
- **practicing grammar skills in context**
- publishing (presenting) writing
- **assessing with an analytical, mode-specific scoring rubric**
- reflecting on writing
- **responding to an assessment prompt**

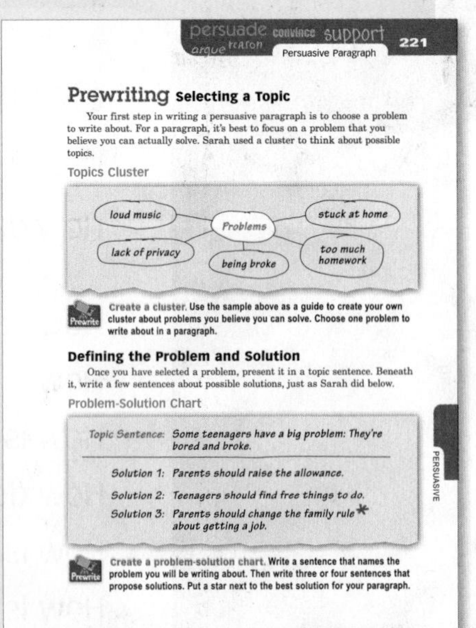
persuade convince support argue reason Persuasive Paragraph 221

Prewriting Selecting a Topic

Your first step in writing a persuasive paragraph is to choose a problem to write about. For a paragraph, it's best to focus on a problem that you believe you can actually solve. Sarah used a cluster to think about possible topics.

Topics Cluster

Create a cluster. Use the sample above as a guide to create your own cluster about problems you believe you can solve. Choose one problem to write about in a paragraph.

Defining the Problem and Solution

Once you have selected a problem, present it in a topic sentence. Beneath it, write a few sentences about possible solutions, just as Sarah did below.

Problem-Solution Chart

Topic Sentence: Some teenagers have a big problem: They're bored and broke.
Solution 1: Parents should raise the allowance.
Solution 2: Teenagers should find free things to do.
Solution 3: Parents should change the family rule * about getting a job.

Create a problem-solution chart. Write a sentence that names the problem you will be writing about. Then write three or four sentences that propose solutions. Put a star next to the best solution for your paragraph.

PERSUASIVE

How does the program integrate the writing process and the traits?

Throughout each core forms of writing unit, the six traits of effective writing are integrated into the steps of the writing process. As students develop their writing, they develop an understanding of and appreciation for each trait of writing. In addition, a rubric, checklists, guidelines, and activities are used to ensure that each piece of writing is completely traits based.

The Process and the Traits in the Core Units

Understanding Your Goal

This page helps students understand the goal of their writing. It lists expectations for each trait as it relates to the writing form.

Focus on the Traits

As students develop each writing, they will find valuable discussions of the six traits at different steps in the writing process.

Revising and Editing for the Traits

When students are ready to revise and edit, they will find traits-based guidelines, strategies, and checklists to help them improve their writing.

Rubrics for the Core Units

A traits-based rubric concludes each unit. This rubric ties directly to the goal chart at the beginning of the unit and the rubric strips presented on the revising and editing pages.

Special Note: For more information about the writing traits, we recommend *Creating Writers Through 6-Trait Writing Assessment and Instruction*, 4th ed., by Vicki Spandel (Addison Wesley Longman, 2005) and *Write Traits®* by Vicki Spandel and Jeff Hicks (Houghton Mifflin Harcourt, 2011).

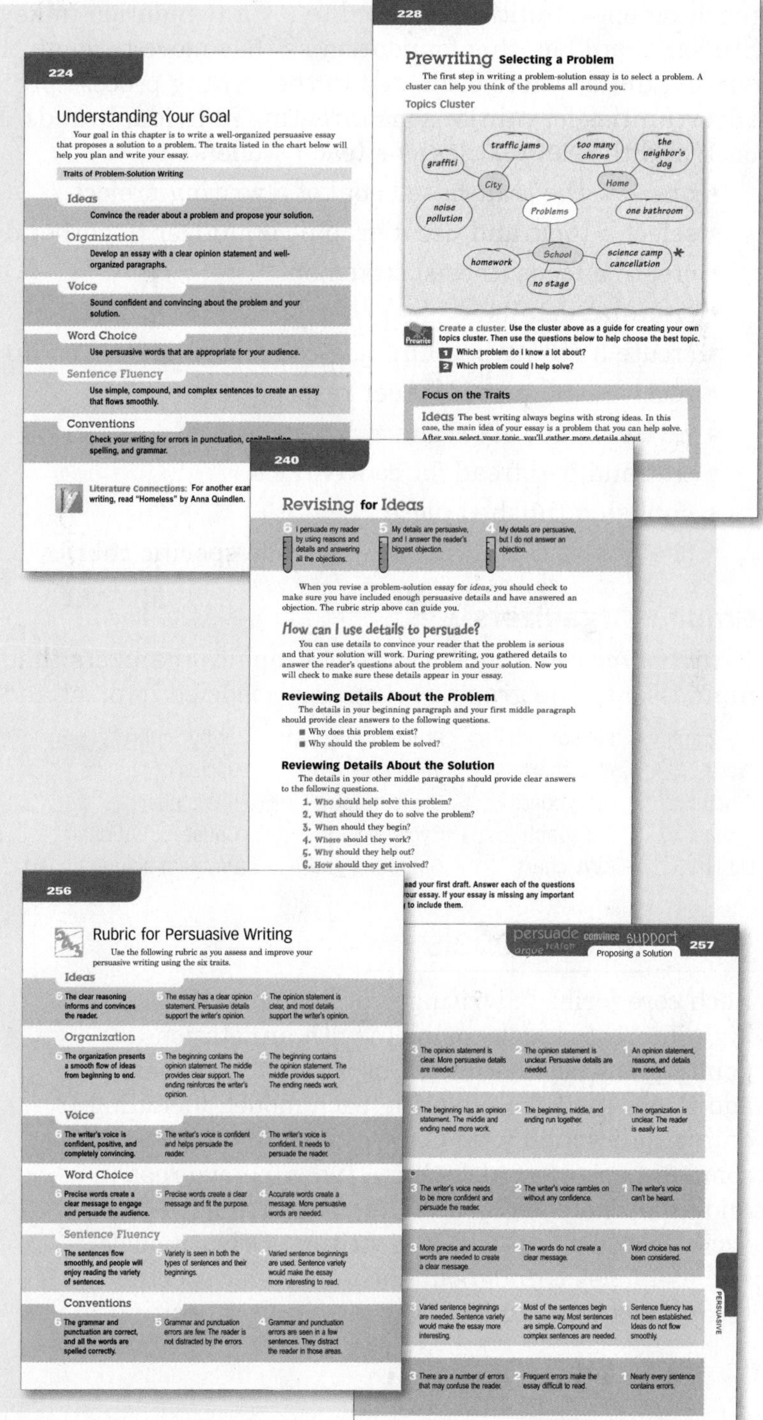

228

Prewriting Selecting a Problem

The first step in writing a problem-solution essay is to select a problem. A cluster can help you think of the problems all around you.

Topics Cluster

Create a cluster. Use the cluster above as a guide for creating your own topics cluster. Then use the questions below to help choose the best topic.

1 Which problem do I know a lot about?

2 Which problem could I help solve?

Focus on the Traits

Ideas The best writing always begins with strong ideas. In this case, the main idea of your essay is a problem that you can help solve.

224

Understanding Your Goal

Your goal in this chapter is to write a well-organized persuasive essay that proposes a solution to a problem. The traits listed in the chart below will help you plan and write your essay.

Traits of Problem-Solution Writing

Ideas

Convince the reader about a problem and propose your solution.

Organization

Develop an essay with a clear opinion statement and well-organized paragraphs.

Voice

Sound confident and convincing about the problem and your solution.

Word Choice

Use persuasive words that are appropriate for your audience.

Sentence Fluency

Use simple, compound, and complex sentences to create an essay that flows smoothly.

Conventions

Check your writing for errors in punctuation, capitalization, spelling, and grammar.

Literature Connections: For another example ... writing, read "Homeless" by Anna Quindlen.

240

Revising for Ideas

6	5	4
I persuade my reader by using reasons and details and answering all the objections.	My details are persuasive, and I answer the reader's biggest objection.	My details are persuasive, but I do not answer an objection.

When you revise a problem-solution essay for *ideas*, you should check to make sure you have included enough persuasive details and have answered an objection. The rubric strip above can guide you.

How can I use details to persuade?

You can use details to convince your reader that the problem is serious and that your solution will work. During prewriting, you gathered details to answer the reader's questions about the problem and your solution. Now you will check to make sure these details appear in your essay.

Reviewing Details About the Problem

The details in your beginning paragraph and your first middle paragraph should provide clear answers to the following questions.

- Why does this problem exist?
- Why should the problem be solved?

Reviewing Details About the Solution

The details in your other middle paragraphs should provide clear answers to the following questions.

1. Who should help solve this problem?
2. What should they do to solve the problem?
3. When should they begin?
4. Where should they work?
5. Why should they help out?
6. How should they get involved?

256

Rubric for Persuasive Writing

Use the following rubric as you assess and improve your persuasive writing using the six traits.

	6	5	4
Ideas	The clear reasoning informs and convinces the reader.	The essay has a clear opinion statement. Persuasive details support the writer's opinion.	The opinion statement is clear, and most details support the writer's opinion.
Organization	The organization presents a smooth flow of ideas from beginning to end.	The beginning contains the opinion statement. The middle provides clear support. The ending reinforces the writer's opinion.	The beginning contains the opinion statement. The middle provides support. The ending needs work.
Voice	The writer's voice is confident, positive, and completely convincing.	The writer's voice is confident and helps persuade the reader.	The writer's voice is confident. It needs to persuade the reader.
Word Choice	Precise words create a clear message to engage and persuade the audience.	Precise words create a clear message and fit the purpose.	Accurate words create a message. More persuasive words are needed.
Sentence Fluency	The sentences flow smoothly, and people will enjoy reading the variety of sentences.	Variety is seen in both the types of sentences and their beginnings.	Varied sentence beginnings are used. Sentence variety would make the essay more interesting to read.
Conventions	The grammar and punctuation are correct, and all the words are spelled correctly.	Grammar and punctuation errors are few. The reader is not distracted by the errors.	Grammar and punctuation errors are seen in a few sentences. They distract the reader in those areas.

257 Proposing a Solution

3	2	1
The opinion statement is clear. More persuasive details are needed.	The opinion statement is unclear. Persuasive details are needed.	An opinion statement, reasons, and details are needed.
The beginning has an opinion statement. The middle and ending need more work.	The beginning, middle, and ending run together.	The organization is unclear. The reader is easily lost.
The writer's voice needs to be more confident and persuade the reader.	The writer's voice rambles on without any confidence.	The writer's voice can't be heard.
More precise and accurate words are needed to create a clear message.	The words do not create a clear message.	Word choice has not been considered.
Varied sentence beginnings are needed. Sentence variety would make the essay more interesting.	Most of the sentences begin the same way. Most sentences are simple. Compound and complex sentences are needed.	Sentence fluency has not been established. Ideas do not flow smoothly.
There are a number of errors that may confuse the reader.	Frequent errors make the essay difficult to read.	Nearly every sentence contains errors.

How can I implement a writing workshop?

Write Source supports a writing workshop through both print and technology resources. The program includes minilessons for instruction, high-quality models to encourage writing, support for whole-class sharing, and much more.

Integrated Minilessons

As a starting point, **Interactive Whiteboard Lessons** provide short, focused teaching opportunities designed to lay a foundation in key concepts. Students build on this foundation as they move through the core forms of writing units, where each step in the writing process presents additional opportunities for minilessons targeting individual needs. Both the print book and the **Net-text** lessons teach students to:

- preview the trait-based goal of a writing project
- select a topic and use a graphic organizer to gather details
- create a focus (thesis) statement
- organize details
- create a strong beginning, a coherent middle, and an effective ending
- receive (and provide) peer responses
- revise for the six traits
- edit and proofread for conventions
- publish a finished piece
- use analytical (traits-based), mode-specific rubrics

Mon	Tues	Wed	Thurs	Fri
Writing Minilessons (10 minutes as needed)				
Status Checks (2 minutes) Find out what students will work on for the day.				
Individual Work (30 minutes) Writing, Revising, Editing, Conferencing, or Publishing				
Whole-Class Sharing Session (5 minutes)				

Graphic Organizers

Write Source contains a wealth of graphic organizers that can serve as the subjects of minilessons. The graphic organizers modeled in print and technology include the following:

Pie graph	Sensory chart	Process diagram	"Why" chart	Topic list
Web	Plot chart	Venn diagram	Basics of life list	Character chart
Cluster	Storyboard	Circle graph	5 W's chart	Picture diagram
T-chart	Bar graph	Cycle diagram	Cause-effect chart	Comparison-contrast chart
Outline	KWL chart	Gathering grid	Problem-solution chart	Time line

High-Quality Models

Each core forms of writing unit begins with a high-interest model, complete with annotations pointing out key features. The **Net-text** provides additional tools for exploring each model, including online interaction with classroom peers to rate and comment on the model. Once students have read and analyzed each model, they will be ready—and excited—to begin their own writing. Other models and examples throughout each unit offer specific techniques that students can use in their writing.

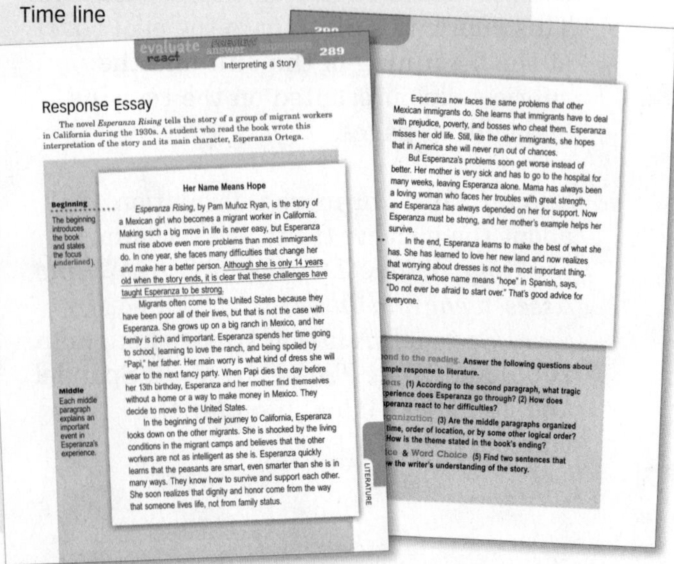
evaluate react answer 289
Interpreting a Story

Response Essay

The novel *Esperanza Rising* tells the story of a group of migrant workers in California during the 1930s. A student who read the book wrote this interpretation of the story and its main character, Esperanza Ortega.

Beginning The beginning introduces the book and states the focus (underlined).

Her Name Means Hope

Esperanza Rising, by Pam Muñoz Ryan, is the story of a Mexican girl who becomes a migrant worker in California. Making such a big move in life is never easy, but Esperanza must rise above even more problems than most immigrants do. In one year, she faces many difficulties that change her and make her a better person. Although she is only 14 years old when the story ends, it is clear that these challenges have taught Esperanza to be strong.

Middle Each middle paragraph explains an important event in Esperanza's experience.

Migrants often come to the United States because they have been poor all of their lives, but that is not the case with Esperanza. She grows up on a big ranch in Mexico, and her family is rich and important. Esperanza spends her time going to school, learning to love the ranch, and being spoiled by "Papi," her father. Her main worry is what kind of dress she will wear to the next fancy party. When Papi dies the day before her 13th birthday, Esperanza and her mother find themselves without a home or a way to make money in Mexico. They decide to move to the United States.

In the beginning of their journey to California, Esperanza looks down on the other migrants. She is shocked by the living conditions in the migrant camps and believes that the other workers are not as intelligent as she is. Esperanza quickly learns that the peasants are smart, even smarter than she is in many ways. They know how to survive and support each other. She soon realizes that dignity and honor come from the way that someone lives life, not from family status.

LITERATURE

Esperanza now faces the same problems that other Mexican immigrants do. She learns that immigrants have to deal with prejudice, poverty, and bosses who cheat them. Esperanza misses her old life. Still, like the other immigrants, she hopes that in America she will never run out of chances.

But Esperanza's problems soon get worse instead of better. Her mother is very sick and has to go to the hospital for many weeks, leaving Esperanza alone. Mama has always been a loving woman who faces her troubles with great strength, and Esperanza has always depended on her for support. Now Esperanza must be strong, and her mother's example helps her survive.

In the end, Esperanza learns to make the best of what she has. She has learned to love her new land and now realizes that worrying about dresses is not the most important thing. Esperanza, whose name means "hope" in Spanish, says, "Do not ever be afraid to start over." That's good advice for everyone.

ond to the reading. Answer the following questions about mple response to literature.

(1) According to the second paragraph, what tragic perience does Esperanza go through? (2) How does peranza react to her difficulties?

ganization (3) Are the middle paragraphs organized time, order of location, or by some other logical order? How is the theme stated in the book's ending?

ice & Word Choice (5) Find two sentences that w the writer's understanding of the story.

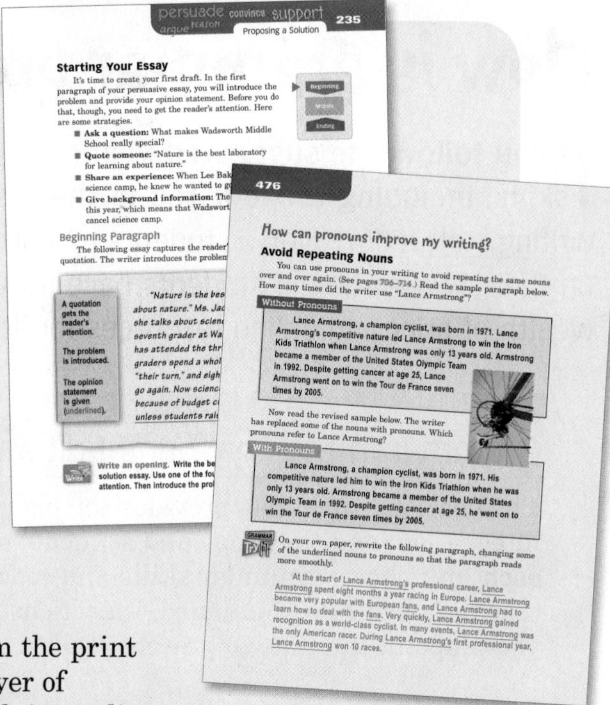

persuade convince support argue reason 235
Proposing a Solution

Starting Your Essay

It's time to create your first draft. In the first paragraph of your persuasive essay, you will introduce the problem and provide your opinion statement. Before you do that, though, you need to get the reader's attention. Here are some strategies.

- **Ask a question:** What makes Wadsworth Middle School really special?
- **Quote someone:** "Nature is the best laboratory for learning about nature."
- **Share an experience:** When Lee Bak science camp, he knew he wanted to g
- **Give background information:** The this year, which means that Wadswort cancel science camp.

Beginning Paragraph

The following essay captures the reader' quotation. The writer introduces the problem

A quotation gets the reader's attention.

The problem is introduced.

The opinion statement is given (underlined).

"Nature is the bes about nature." Ms. Jac she talks about scienc seventh grader at Wa has attended the thr graders spend a whol "their turn," and eigh go again. Now scienc because of budget c unless students rai

Write an opening. Write the be solution essay. Use one of the fou attention. Then introduce the pro

476

How can pronouns improve my writing?

Avoid Repeating Nouns

You can use pronouns in your writing to avoid repeating the same nouns over and over again. (See pages 706–714.) Read the sample paragraph below. How many times did the writer use "Lance Armstrong"?

Without Pronouns

Lance Armstrong, a champion cyclist, was born in 1971. Lance Armstrong's competitive nature led Lance Armstrong to win the Iron Kids Triathlon when Lance Armstrong was only 13 years old. Armstrong became a member of the United States Olympic Team in 1992. Despite getting cancer at age 25, Lance Armstrong went on to win the Tour de France seven times by 2005.

Now read the revised sample below. The writer has replaced some of the nouns with pronouns. Which pronouns refer to Lance Armstrong?

With Pronouns

Lance Armstrong, a champion cyclist, was born in 1971. His competitive nature led him to win the Iron Kids Triathlon when he was only 13 years old. Armstrong became a member of the United States Olympic Team in 1992. Despite getting cancer at age 25, he went on to win the Tour de France seven times by 2005.

GRAMMAR Try It On your own paper, rewrite the following paragraph, changing some of the underlined nouns to pronouns so that the paragraph reads more smoothly.

At the start of Lance Armstrong's professional career, Lance Armstrong spent eight months a year racing in Europe. Lance Armstrong became very popular with European fans, and Lance Armstrong had to learn how to deal with the fans. Very quickly, Lance Armstrong gained recognition as a world-class cyclist. In many events, Lance Armstrong was the only American racer. During Lance Armstrong's first professional year, Lance Armstrong won 10 races.

Individual Writing

Write Source makes it easy for writing-workshop students to work on their own. It also provides specific help whenever students have questions about their writing. Here are some of the areas that are addressed:

- catching the reader's interest
- providing background information
- developing strong paragraphs
- elaborating on ideas
- organizing ideas by time, location, importance, logic
- quoting, paraphrasing, and summarizing
- using transitions
- drawing conclusions
- calling the reader to act

In addition to supporting these and other key concepts from the print components, the *Write Source* **Net-text** provides an extra layer of scaffolding for independent writing, including exercises with immediate feedback, at-a-click support for grammar and conventions concepts, ready access to such resources as a dictionary and thesaurus, and an application for creating and managing work online.

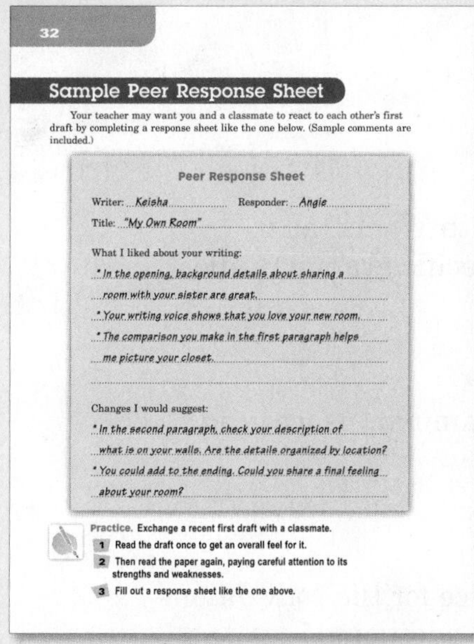

32

Sample Peer Response Sheet

Your teacher may want you and a classmate to react to each other's first draft by completing a response sheet like the one below. (Sample comments are included.)

Peer Response Sheet

Writer: *Keisha* Responder: *Angie*

Title: *"My Own Room"*

What I liked about your writing:

** In the opening, background details about sharing a room with your sister are great.*

** Your writing voice shows that you love your new room.*

** The comparison you make in the first paragraph helps me picture your closet.*

Changes I would suggest:

** In the second paragraph, check your description of what is on your walls. Are the details organized by location?*

** You could add to the ending. Could you share a final feeling about your room?*

Practice. Exchange a recent first draft with a classmate.

1. Read the draft once to get an overall feel for it.
2. Then read the paper again, paying careful attention to its strengths and weaknesses.
3. Fill out a response sheet like the one above.

Peer and Teacher Response

Write Source teaches peer responding and provides a peer response sheet. Consistent integration of the traits into the writing process allows students and teachers to speak a common language as they conduct response sessions. Traits-based checklists help pinpoint just what is working—and what could work better—in each piece of writing. The *Write Source* **Net-text** provides additional support for teacher-to-student and student-to-student response, including a commenting tool and commenting notifications.

Whole-Class Sharing

Write Source helps students prepare their work for whole-class sharing— whether in a traditional presentation or in the public section of the **Online Portfolio**. In addition, the program provides a wealth of suggestions for publishing in a variety of forms and for a variety of audiences.

How is grammar presented?

If you follow the suggested yearlong timetable, you will cover all the key grammar skills, including those listed in the state standards. Grammar instruction integrated into writing instruction allows students to learn about grammar in context when they are working on their own writing. If students have trouble with a particular concept, you can refer to a wealth of print and online resources for additional support.

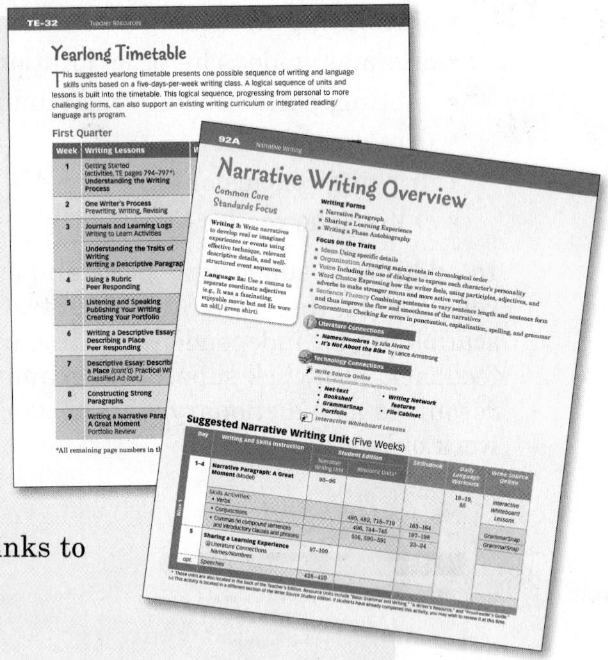

Grammar in the Teacher's Edition

The yearlong timetable provides the big picture of grammar integration, and the scope and sequence at the beginning of each unit shows grammar skills and concepts to teach while teaching writing. Grammar Connections at point of use help you pinpoint the time to present skills and concepts.

Grammar in the Student Edition

Forms of Writing

During the development of the main composition in each core forms of writing unit, grammar instruction is integrated within the revising and editing steps. Grammar instruction includes examples, practice, and application activities; and it links to students' writing.

Basic Grammar and Writing

For more grammar in the context of writing, refer to "Working with Words" and "Building Effective Sentences." Use these minilessons to teach specific grammar and style topics that students can apply to their writing.

Proofreader's Guide

This section serves as a complete conventions guide, providing grammar, usage, and mechanics rules, instruction, examples, and practice.

Write Source Online

The *Write Source* **Net-text** offers interactive instruction and practice for the conventions topics embedded in the core writing units. **GrammarSnap** provides additional instruction, practice, and basic skills reinforcement through videos, minilessons, games, and quizzes.

Grammar in Other Program Components

The *SkillsBook* provides more than 130 grammar, usage, punctuation, mechanics, spelling, and sentence-construction activities. The *Assessment* book contains a pretest, benchmark tests, and a post-test for basic writing and editing skills. *Daily Language Workouts* includes a year's worth of sentences (daily) and paragraphs (weekly) for editing practice.

Planning Grammar Instruction

Should I implement *all* of the suggested basic grammar activities?

In the course of the year, if you assigned every grammar exercise listed in the unit scope and sequence charts (located in the unit overviews of your Teacher's Edition), your students would complete **all** of the "Basic Grammar and Writing," "Proofreader's Guide," *SkillsBook*, and **GrammarSnap** activities.

Because the most effective teaching of grammar happens in context, grammar instruction appears at appropriate times during the revising and editing of the core writing forms units. As the teacher, you must choose the type and amount of instruction that will best meet the needs of your students.

How are all the grammar resources related?

The *SkillsBook* grammar activities parallel and expand on the rules and exercises found in the "Proofreader's Guide" of the Student Edition. In the "Basic Grammar and Writing" section, brief exercises function well as minilessons and may be assigned on an as-needed basis. **GrammarSnap** offers additional support for key grammar topics in an engaging, interactive format.

How do I use the Unit Overview charts?

The sample below from the persuasive writing unit is followed by an explanation of how to read and use the charts.

Suggested Persuasive Writing Unit (Five Weeks)

	Day	Writing and Skills Instruction	*Student Edition* Persuasive Writing Unit	*Student Edition* Resource Units*	*SkillsBook*	*Daily Language Workouts*	*Write Source Online*
Week 1	1–5	**Persuasive Paragraph: Problem/Solution**	219–222			38–39, 95	*Interactive Whiteboard Lessons*
		Skills Activities: • Apostrophes		604–605, 606–607	37		
		• Using the Right Word		668–676	64		
	opt.	*Speeches*	428–429				
Week 2	6	**Persuasive Essay: Problem/Solution** (Model) Literature Connections "Homeless"	223–226			40–41, 96	
	7–8	(Prewriting)	227–232				*Net-text*

1. The Resource Units column indicates the Student Edition pages that cover rules, examples, and exercises for corresponding skills activities.
2. The *SkillsBook, Daily Language Workouts*, and **Write Source Online** columns indicate pages and information from those particular resources.

How do I use *Daily Language Workouts*?

Daily Language Workouts is a teacher resource that provides a high-interest sentence for each day of the year and weekly paragraphs for additional editing and proofreading practice. This regular practice helps students develop the objectivity they need to effectively edit their own writing.

How is writing across the curriculum addressed?

Write Source program provides a wide variety of writing across the curriculum activities and assignments. It promotes *writing to show learning, writing to learn new concepts,* and *writing to reflect on learning.*

Writing to Show Learning

Writing to show learning is the most common type of writing that content-area teachers assign. The following forms of writing covered in the program are commonly used for this purpose.

- descriptive paragraph and essay
- narrative paragraph and essay
- expository paragraph and essay
- persuasive paragraph and essay
- response paragraph and book review
- response to nonfiction
- summary paragraph
- research report

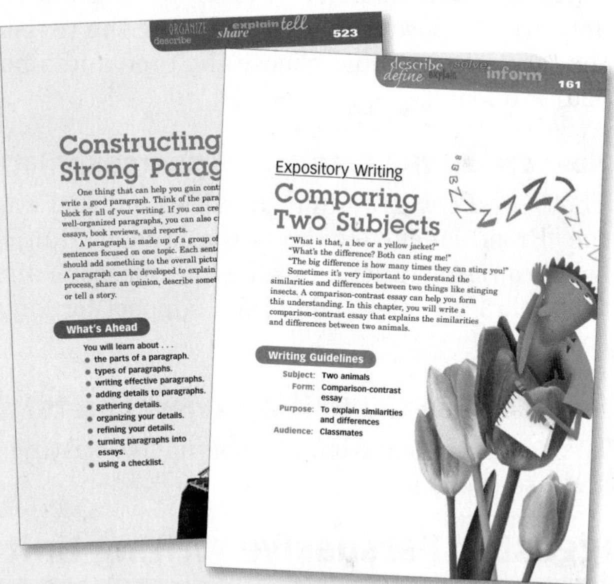
ORGANIZE describe share explain tell 523

Constructing
Strong Parag

One thing that can help you gain cont
write a good paragraph. Think of the para
block for all of your writing. If you can cre
well-organized paragraphs, you can also c
essays, book reviews, and reports.

A paragraph is made up of a group of
sentences focused on one topic. Each sent
should add something to the overall pictu
A paragraph can be developed to explain
process, share an opinion, describe somet
or tell a story.

What's Ahead

You will learn about . . .
- the parts of a paragraph.
- types of paragraphs.
- writing effective paragraphs.
- adding details to paragraphs.
- gathering details.
- organizing your details.
- refining your details.
- turning paragraphs into essays.
- using a checklist.

describe define solve explain inform 161

Expository Writing

Comparing Two Subjects

"What is that, a bee or a yellow jacket?"
"What's the difference? Both can sting me!"
"The big difference is how many times they can sting you!"

Sometimes it's very important to understand the similarities and differences between two things like stinging insects. A comparison-contrast essay can help you form this understanding. In this chapter, you will write a comparison-contrast essay that explains the similarities and differences between two animals.

Writing Guidelines

Subject: Two animals
Form: Comparison-contrast essay
Purpose: To explain similarities and differences
Audience: Classmates

Sample Writing-Across-the-Curriculum Assignments

Descriptive Writing

Social Studies: Describing a Famous Place
Math: Writing a Geometric Riddle
Science: Writing a Lab Report

Narrative Writing

Social Studies: Writing a Letter About a Cultural Experience
Math: Writing a Learning-Log Entry
Science: Writing a TV Script

Expository Writing

Social Studies: Writing a Business Letter
Math: Writing Explanations
Science: Writing an Extended Definition

Persuasive Writing

Social Studies: Writing a Campaign Speech
Math: Creating a Graph
Science: Writing a Proposal

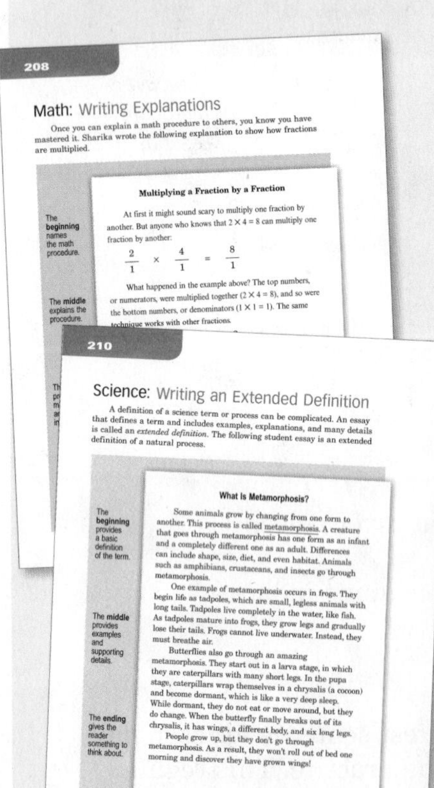
208

Math: Writing Explanations

Once you can explain a math procedure to others, you know you have mastered it. Sharika wrote the following explanation to show how fractions are multiplied.

The beginning names the math procedure.

The middle explains the procedure.

Multiplying a Fraction by a Fraction

At first it might sound scary to multiply one fraction by another. But anyone who knows that 2 × 4 = 8 can multiply one fraction by another:

$$\frac{2}{1} \times \frac{4}{1} = \frac{8}{1}$$

What happened in the example above? The top numbers, or numerators, were multiplied together (2 × 4 = 8), and so were the bottom numbers, or denominators (1 × 1 = 1). The same technique works with other fractions.

210

Science: Writing an Extended Definition

A definition of a science term or process can be complicated. An essay that defines a term and includes examples, explanations, and many details is called an *extended definition*. The following student essay is an extended definition of a natural process.

What Is Metamorphosis?

The beginning provides a basic definition of the term.

Some animals grow by changing from one form to another. This process is called metamorphosis. A creature that goes through metamorphosis has one form as an infant and a completely different one as an adult. Differences can include shape, size, diet, and even habitat. Animals such as amphibians, crustaceans, and insects go through metamorphosis.

The middle provides examples and supporting details.

One example of metamorphosis occurs in frogs. They begin life as tadpoles, which are small, legless animals with long tails. Tadpoles live completely in the water, like fish. As tadpoles mature into frogs, they grow legs and gradually lose their tails. Frogs cannot live underwater. Instead, they must breathe air.

Butterflies also go through an amazing metamorphosis. They start out in a larva stage, in which they are caterpillars with many short legs. In the pupa stage, caterpillars wrap themselves in a chrysalis (a cocoon) and become dormant, which is like a very deep sleep. While dormant, they do not eat or move around, but they do change. When the butterfly finally breaks out of its chrysalis, it has wings, a different body, and six long legs.

The ending gives the reader something to think about.

People grow up, but they don't go through metamorphosis. As a result, they won't roll out of bed one morning and discover they have grown wings!

How does *Write Source* teach academic vocabulary?

Write Source gives students the opportunity to learn and use academic vocabulary terms so essential for success in school.

Academic Vocabulary in *Write Source*

Academic vocabulary refers to the words students must know in order to understand the concepts they encounter in school. Academic vocabulary terms such as *element, analyze, substantial*, and *consistent* are not specific to any one subject but rather denote key ideas and skills relevant to many subject areas. In a sense, academic vocabulary is the language of school. To be successful in school, students must understand and be able to use academic vocabulary as they write about and discuss what they learn in class.

The *Write Source* Academic Vocabulary feature gives students the opportunity to learn and practice using new academic vocabulary in a collaborative activity. This feature, which appears at the beginning of each unit of the Student Edition, provides a brief explanation of each academic vocabulary word, followed by a prompt that motivates students to practice using the term.

- Academic vocabulary is taken from words appearing in the unit.
- Students work with a partner to read the explanations of academic vocabulary words used in the unit.
- Each explanation is accompanied by an activity or question that prompts students to demonstrate their understanding of the new word.

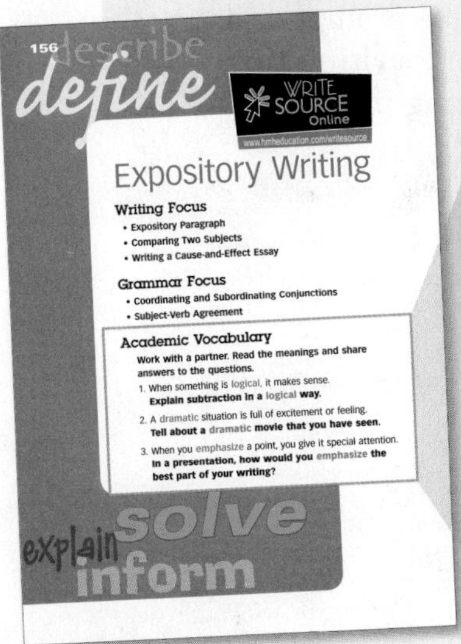

Academic Vocabulary

Work with a partner. Read the meanings and share answers to the questions.

1. When something is logical, it makes sense.
   Explain subtraction in a logical way.
2. A dramatic situation is full of excitement or feeling.
   Tell about a dramatic movie that you have seen.
3. When you emphasize a point, you give it special attention.
   In a presentation, how would you emphasize the best part of your writing?

How is test preparation covered?

Each core forms of writing unit in the Student Edition prepares students for responding to testing prompts. **If students complete their work in each of the core units, they will have learned the skills necessary for success on any type of writing assessment.** Here are some of the main features in the Student Edition that address testing.

Core Writing Units

The *Write Source* program teaches descriptive, narrative, expository, and persuasive writing, and literary response—the main forms of writing included on writing assessments.

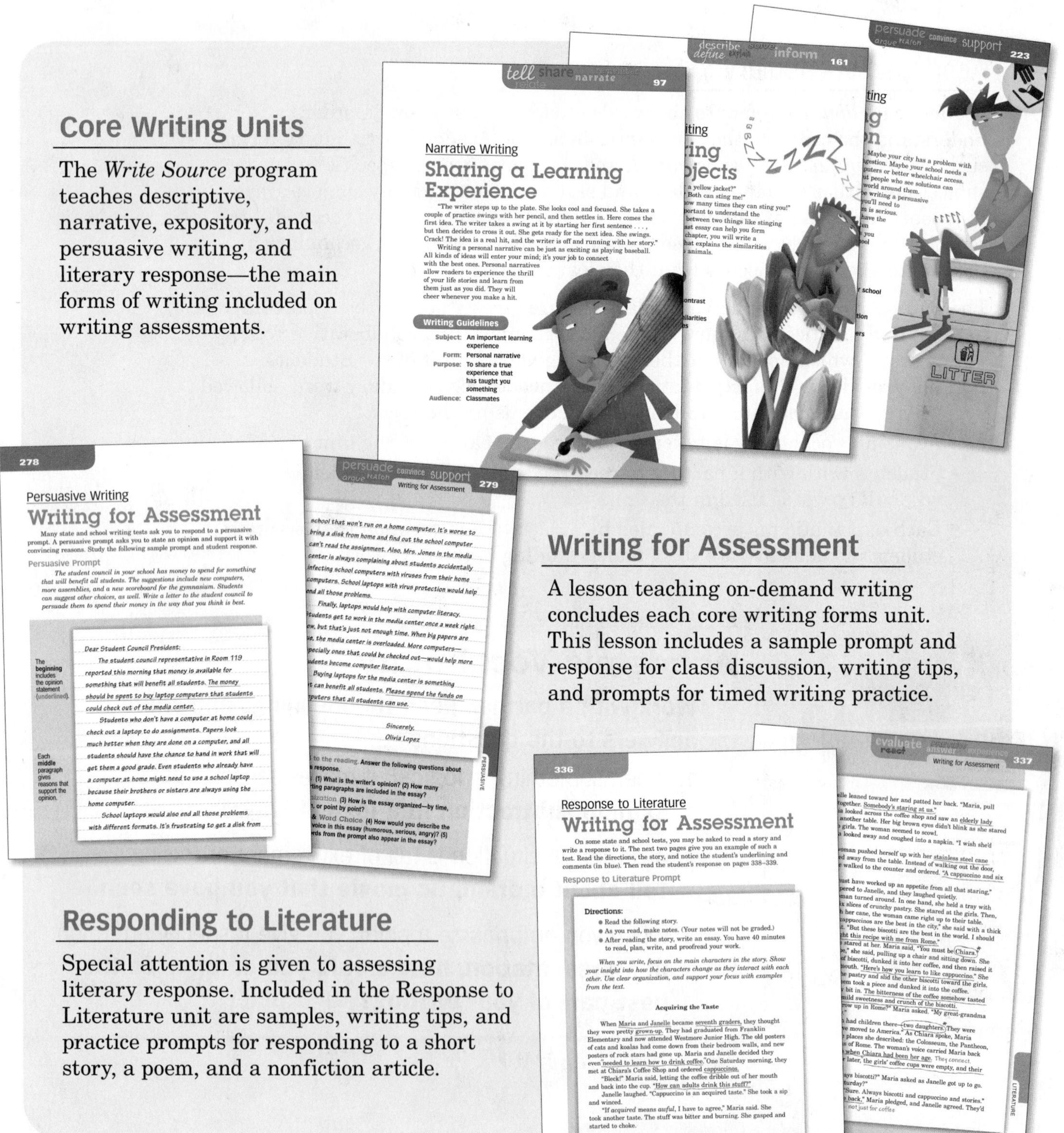

Writing for Assessment

A lesson teaching on-demand writing concludes each core writing forms unit. This lesson includes a sample prompt and response for class discussion, writing tips, and prompts for timed writing practice.

Responding to Literature

Special attention is given to assessing literary response. Included in the Response to Literature unit are samples, writing tips, and practice prompts for responding to a short story, a poem, and a nonfiction article.

Taking Classroom Tests

The chapter on test-taking includes a section entitled "Taking Essay Tests" that helps students analyze the key words in essay questions.

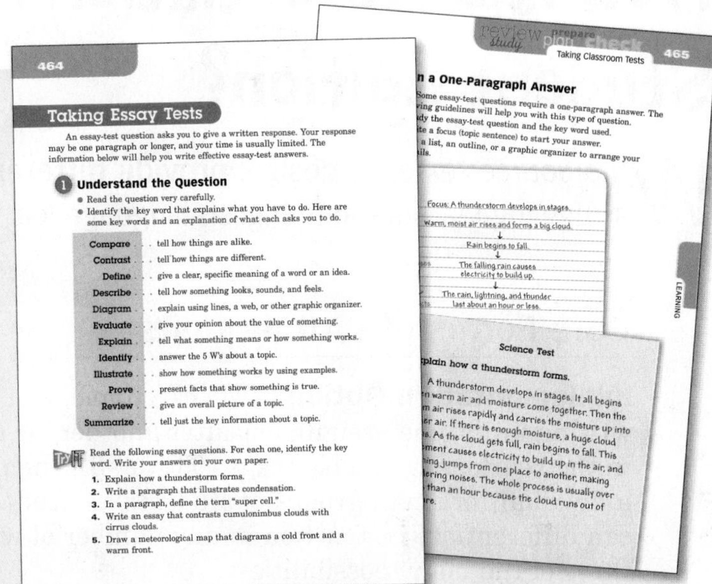

464

Taking Essay Tests

An essay-test question asks you to give a written response. Your response may be one paragraph or longer, and your time is usually limited. The information below will help you write effective essay-test answers.

1 Understand the Question

- Read the question very carefully.
- Identify the key word that explains what you have to do. Here are some key words and an explanation of what each asks you to do.

Compare	tell how things are alike.
Contrast	tell how things are different.
Define	give a clear, specific meaning of a word or an idea.
Describe	tell how something looks, sounds, and feels.
Diagram	explain using lines, a web, or other graphic organizer.
Evaluate	give your opinion about the value of something.
Explain	tell what something means or how something works.
Identify	answer the 5 W's about a topic.
Illustrate	show how something works by using examples.
Prove	present facts that show something is true.
Review	give an overall picture of a topic.
Summarize	tell just the key information about a topic.

Try It Read the following essay questions. For each one, identify the key word. Write your answers on your own paper.

1. Explain how a thunderstorm forms.
2. Write a paragraph that illustrates condensation.
3. In a paragraph, define the term "super cell."
4. Write an essay that contrasts cumulonimbus clouds with cirrus clouds.
5. Draw a meteorological map that diagrams a cold front and a warm front.

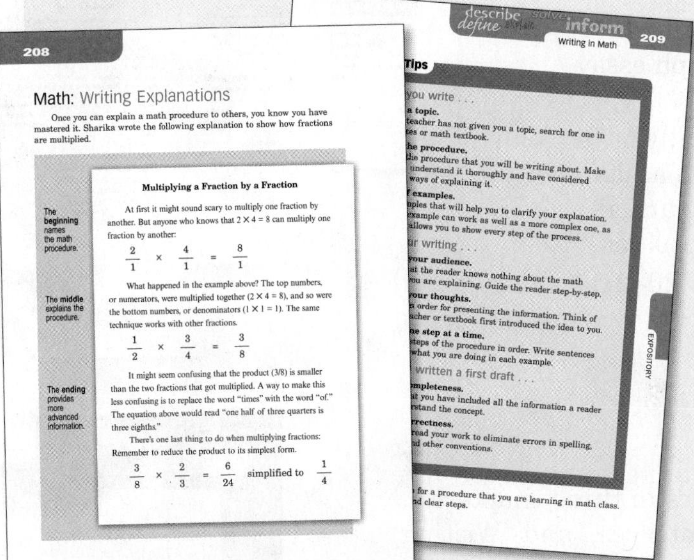

208

Math: Writing Explanations

Once you can explain a math procedure to others, you know you have mastered it. Sharika wrote the following explanation to show how fractions are multiplied.

Multiplying a Fraction by a Fraction

The **beginning** names the math procedure.

At first it might sound scary to multiply one fraction by another. But anyone who knows that $2 \times 4 = 8$ can multiply one fraction by another:

$$\frac{2}{1} \times \frac{4}{1} = \frac{8}{1}$$

The **middle** explains the procedure.

What happened in the example above? The top numbers, or numerators, were multiplied together ($2 \times 4 = 8$), and so were the bottom numbers, or denominators ($1 \times 1 = 1$). The same technique works with other fractions.

$$\frac{1}{2} \times \frac{3}{4} = \frac{3}{8}$$

The **ending** provides more advanced information.

It might seem confusing that the product (3/8) is smaller than the two fractions that got multiplied. A way to make this less confusing is to replace the word "times" with the word "of." The equation above would read "one half of three quarters is three eighths."

There's one last thing to do when multiplying fractions: Remember to reduce the product to its simplest form.

$$\frac{3}{8} \times \frac{2}{3} = \frac{6}{24} \text{ simplified to } \frac{1}{4}$$

Writing Across the Curriculum

The writing-across-the-curriculum assignments at the end of the core writing units help students prepare for on-demand writing in content-based tests.

Test Prep for Grammar Skills

Tests at the end of each section in the "Proofreader's Guide" follow a standardized test format. Familiarity with this formatting will help students do their best on tests of writing ability.

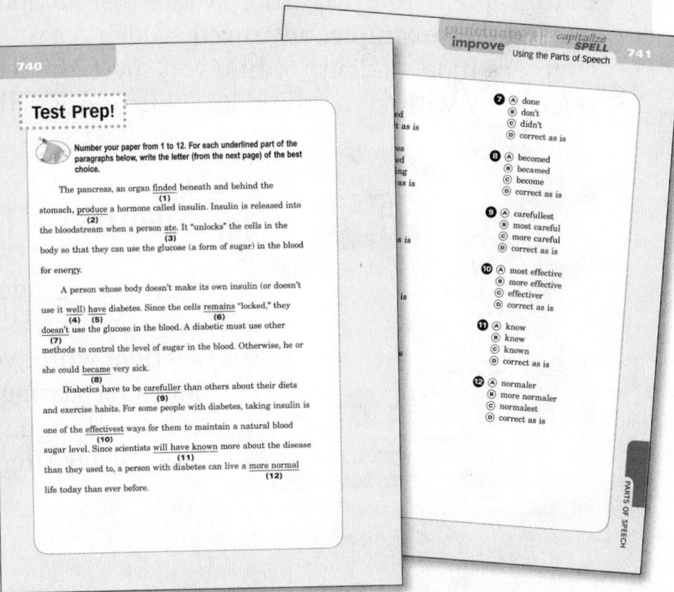

740

Test Prep!

Number your paper from 1 to 12. For each underlined part of the paragraphs below, write the letter (from the next page) of the best choice.

The pancreas, an organ finded (1) beneath and behind the stomach, produce (2) a hormone called insulin. Insulin is released into the bloodstream when a person ate (3). It "unlocks" the cells in the body so that they can use the glucose (a form of sugar) in the blood for energy.

A person whose body doesn't make its own insulin (or doesn't use it well (4)) have (5) diabetes. Since the cells remains (6) "locked," they doesn't (7) use the glucose in the blood. A diabetic must use other methods to control the level of sugar in the blood. Otherwise, he or she could became (8) very sick.

Diabetics have to be carefuller (9) than others about their diets and exercise habits. For some people with diabetes, taking insulin is one of the effectivest (10) ways for them to maintain a natural blood sugar level. Since scientists will have known (11) more about the disease than they used to, a person with diabetes can live a more normal (12) life today than ever before.

741

7. Ⓐ done Ⓑ don't Ⓒ didn't Ⓓ correct as is
8. Ⓐ becomed Ⓑ becamed Ⓒ become Ⓓ correct as is
9. Ⓐ carefullest Ⓑ most careful Ⓒ more careful Ⓓ correct as is
10. Ⓐ most effective Ⓑ more effective Ⓒ effectiver Ⓓ correct as is
11. Ⓐ know Ⓑ knew Ⓒ known Ⓓ correct as is
12. Ⓐ normaler Ⓑ more normaler Ⓒ normalest Ⓓ correct as is

How is differentiation handled in the Student Edition?

Write Source texts, by design, **provide differentiation** in writing instruction—from struggling learners and English-language learners to advanced, independent students.

Core Forms of Writing Units

261

Persuasive Writing

Creating an Editorial

Every major newspaper has an "Op/Ed" page, which is short for "Opinion/Editorial." An editorial is a short essay that gives a writer's opinion about a timely event or issue. Many times during the history of our country, editorials have paved the way for great changes.

In this chapter, you will be writing an editorial of your own. Perhaps your school is having a crisis over the food choices in the vending machines. Or maybe some sports teams are arguing over who gets to use the gymnasium after school. In an editorial, you can give your opinion about the events happening around you.

Writing Guidelines

Subject: A school issue
Form: Editorial
Purpose: To persuade the reader
Audience: Classmates

Implementation Options: You can implement the forms of writing units, one assignment after another, as delineated in the yearlong timetable (pages TE-32–35), helping individuals or small groups of students as needed. Or you can differentiate instruction in any number of ways. Here are three of the many possibilities:

- Have **struggling learners** focus on the single-paragraph writing assignment in each unit while other students complete the multiparagraph essay assignment.
- Have **advanced learners** work individually or in small groups on the multiparagraph composition assignment in each unit, while you guide struggling learners step by step through the development of the composition.
- Conduct a **writing workshop** (pages TE-20–21), asking students to develop one or more assignments in a unit at their own pace.

Basic Grammar and Writing

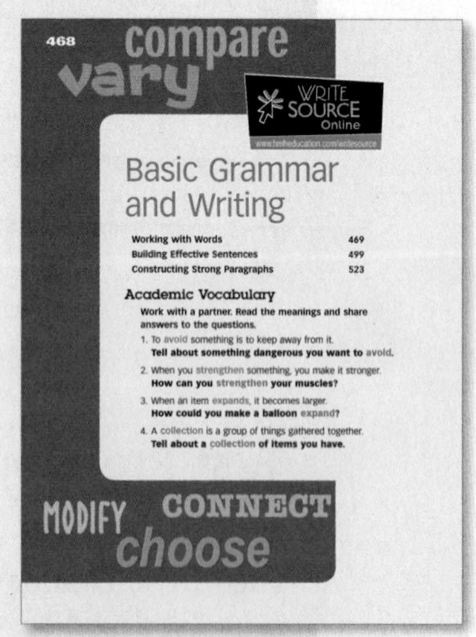
468

Basic Grammar and Writing

Working with Words	469
Building Effective Sentences	499
Constructing Strong Paragraphs	523

Academic Vocabulary

Work with a partner. Read the meanings and share answers to the questions.

1. To avoid something is to keep away from it. **Tell about something dangerous you want to avoid.**
2. When you strengthen something, you make it stronger. **How can you strengthen your muscles?**
3. When an item expands, it becomes larger. **How could you make a balloon expand?**
4. A collection is a group of things gathered together. **Tell about a collection of items you have.**

"Basic Grammar and Writing" covers the basics in three chapters: "Working with Words," "Building Effective Sentences," and "Writing Paragraphs." You can differentiate instruction with these chapters as needed. For example, advanced students can complete the work in these chapters independently while you cover the lessons more carefully and selectively with struggling students and English language learners.

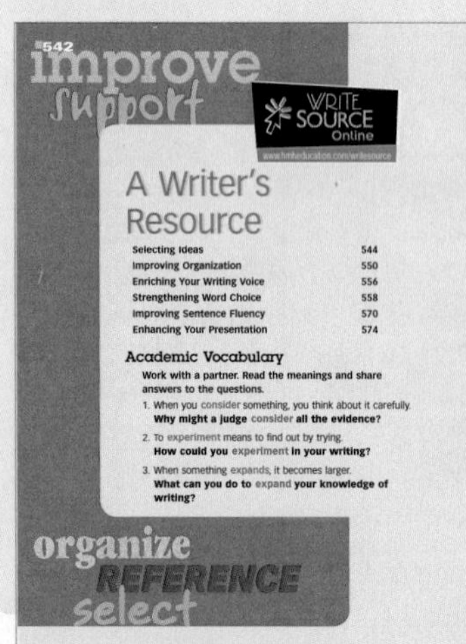
542

A Writer's Resource

Selecting Ideas	544
Improving Organization	550
Enriching Your Writing Voice	556
Strengthening Word Choice	558
Improving Sentence Fluency	570
Enhancing Your Presentation	574

Academic Vocabulary

Work with a partner. Read the meanings and share answers to the questions.

1. When you consider something, you think about it carefully. **Why might a judge consider all the evidence?**
2. To experiment means to find out by trying. **How could you experiment in your writing?**
3. When something expands, it becomes larger. **What can you do to expand your knowledge of writing?**

A Writer's Resource

Advanced students can find their own answers to writing questions in this section, while you can find minilesson ideas for struggling learners and English language learners with specific writing needs.

How is differentiation handled in the TE?

The Teacher's Edition provides point-of-use differentiation for struggling learners, English language learners, and advanced learners.

Struggling Learners

The Struggling Learners notes allow you to customize lessons to meet the needs of students who may have difficulty completing the work. These notes provide alternative approaches, extra practice, or additional insights.

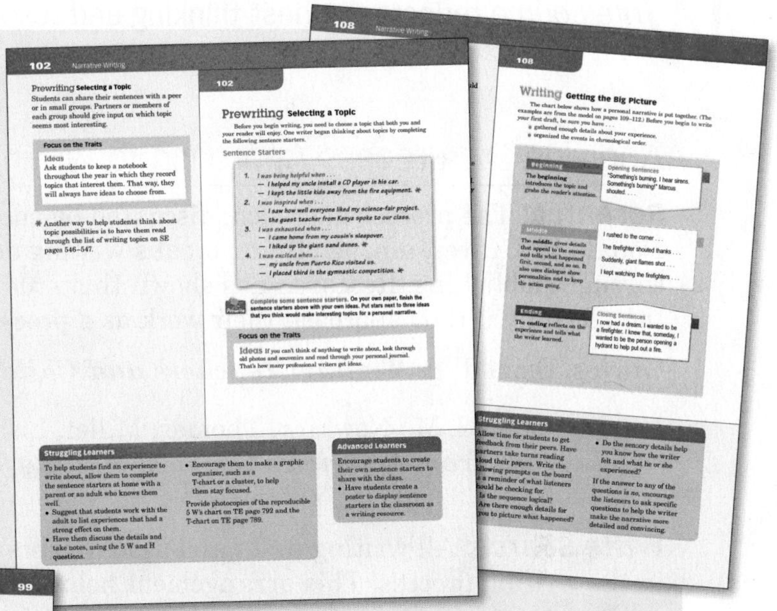

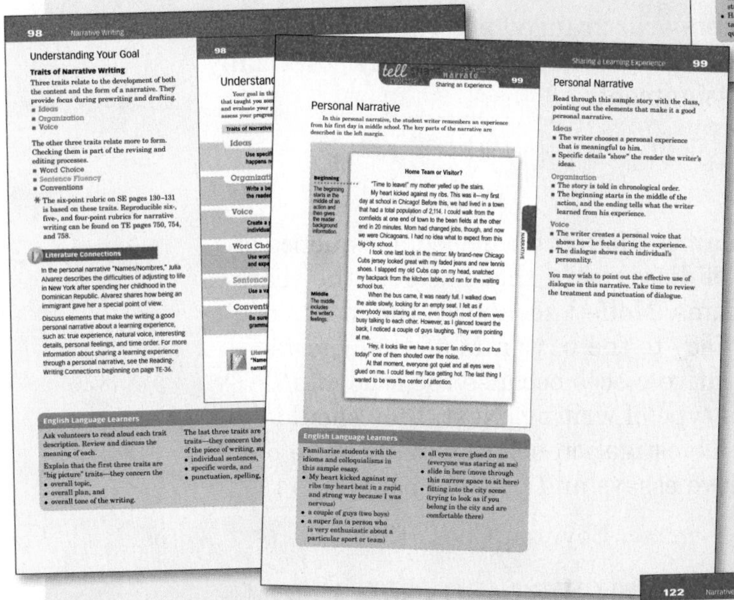

English Language Learners

The English-Language Learners notes help you to guide students with limited language skills through the lessons. These notes provide extra practice, alternative approaches, connections to first languages, glossaries of new terms, demonstration ideas, and more.

Advanced Learners

The Advanced Learners notes help you enhance the lessons for students who need to be challenged. Some of the notes extend the lessons.

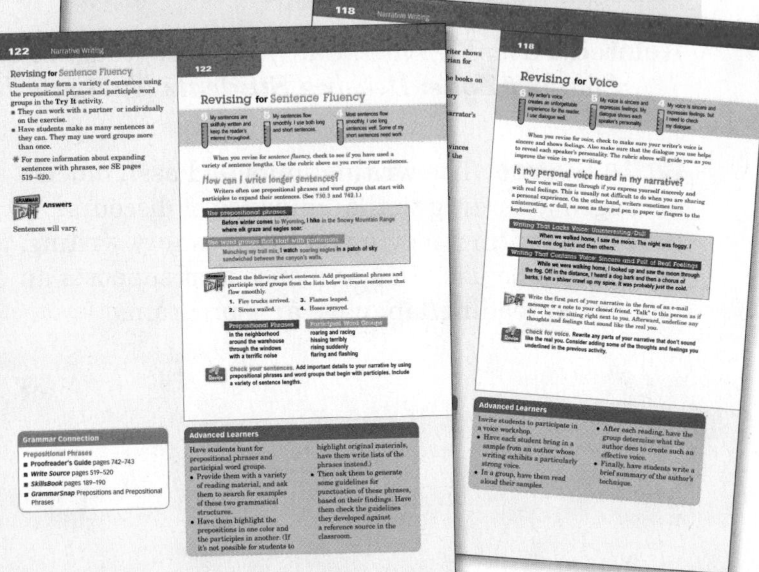

What research supports the *Write Source* program?

Write Source reflects the best thinking and research on writing instruction.

Applying the Process Approach to Writing

Research: The process approach, discussed by educators Donald M. Murray and Donald H. Graves, among others, breaks writing down into a series of steps—prewriting through publishing. Research has shown that students write more effectively and thoughtfully if they approach their work as a process rather than as an end product.

Graves, Donald. H. ***Writing: Teachers and Children at Work.*** Heinemann, 2003.

Murray, Donald. M.; Newkirk, Thomas; Miller, Lisa C. ***The Essential Don Murray: Lessons from America's Greatest Writing Teacher.*** Boynton/Cook Heinemann, 2009.

Write Source: All writing units and assignments are arranged according to the steps in the writing process. This arrangement helps students manage their work, especially in the case of longer essay or research report assignments.

Sequencing Assignments

Research: Writing instructor and researcher James Moffett developed a sequence of writing assignments—known as the "universe of discourse"—that has over the years served countless English/language arts classrooms. Moffett sequences the modes of writing according to their connection or immediacy to the writer. Moffett suggests that students first develop descriptive and narrative pieces because the students have an immediate, personal connection to this type of writing. Next, they should develop informational pieces that require some investigation before moving on to more challenging, reflective writing, such as persuasive essays and position papers.

Moffett, James. ***Teaching the Universe of Discourse.*** Boynton/Cook, 1987.

Related Title: Fleischer, Cathy; Andrew-Vaughn, Sarah. ***Writing Outside Your Comfort Zone: Helping Students Navigate Unfamiliar Genres.*** Heinemann, 2009.

Write Source: The writing units and assignments in the *Write Source* texts are arranged according to the "universe of discourse," starting with descriptive and narrative writing, moving on to expository writing, and so on. These assignments are designed to be used in a sequence that supports an existing writing curriculum or integrated reading/language arts program.

Implementing a Writing Workshop

Research: Countless respected writing instructors and researchers have advocated the importance of establishing a community of writers in the classroom. Teachers can establish such a community by implementing a writing workshop. In a writing workshop, students are immersed in all aspects of writing, including sharing their work with their peers.

Atwell, Nancie. ***In the Middle: New Understandings About Writing, Reading, and Learning.*** Heinemann, 1998.

Write Source: The instruction in *Write Source* is clearly presented so that most students can work independently on their writing in a workshop. In addition, the core forms of writing units contain innumerable opportunities for workshop minilessons.

Producing Writing with Detail

Research: Rebekah Caplan learned through her teaching experience that students don't automatically know how to add details to their personal, informational, and persuasive writing. She discovered with her students that adding detail to writing is a skill that must be practiced regularly. To address this problem, Caplan came up with the "show-me" sentence strategy, in which students begin with a basic idea—"My locker is messy"—and create a brief paragraph that shows rather than tells the idea.

Caplan, Rebekah. ***Writers in Training: A Guide to Developing a Composition Program.*** Dale Seymour Publications, 1984.

Related Title: Bernabi, Gretchen S.; Hover, Jayne; Candler, Cynthia. ***Crunchtime: Lessons to Help Students Blow the Roof Off Writing Tests—and Become Better Writers in the Process.*** Heinemann, 2009.

Write Source: *Daily Language Workouts* contains a series of show-me sentences that teachers can implement as a regular classroom warm-up.

Meeting Students' Diverse Needs

Research: Many students in today's classrooms struggle with writing. For struggling students, following the writing process is not enough. According to the research done by James L. Collins, struggling students need specific strategies and aids to help them become better writers. Collins found that these students benefit from skills instruction integrated into the process of writing, color coding and signposts in the presentation of instructional material, the use of graphic organizers, instructions presented in discreet chunks of copy, and so on.

Collins, James L. ***Strategies for Struggling Writers.*** Guilford Press, 1998.

Related Title: Cruz, M. Colleen; Calkins, Lucy. ***A Quick Guide to Reaching Struggling Writers, K–5.*** FirstHand/Heinemann, 2008.

Write Source: The core writing forms units contain all the key features from Collins' work. As a result, the units are well suited to struggling learners and English language learners.

Yearlong Timetable

This suggested yearlong timetable presents one possible sequence of writing and language skills units based on a five-days-per-week writing class. A logical sequence of units and lessons is built into the timetable. This logical sequence, progressing from personal to more challenging forms, can also support an existing writing curriculum or integrated reading/language arts program.

First Quarter

Week	Writing Lessons	*Write Source*	Grammar and Writing Skills
1	Getting Started (activities, TE pages 794–797*) **Understanding the Writing Process**	1–3 5–10	**Skills Assessments:** Using the Right Word Test Prep 688–689
			Punctuation Test Prep 616–617
2	**One Writer's Process** Prewriting, Writing, Revising	11–28	**Skills Assessment:** Editing for Mechanics Test Prep 628–629
3	**Journals and Learning Logs** Writing to Learn Activities	431–438 439–440	**Skills Assessment:** Sentences Test Prep 696–697
	Understanding the Traits of Writing **Writing a Descriptive Paragraph**	33–44 71–74	Adjectives, prepositional phrases
4	**Using a Rubric** **Peer Responding**	45–56 29–32	**Skills Assessment:** Spelling Test 644
5	**Listening and Speaking** **Publishing Your Writing** **Creating Your Portfolio**	417–422 57–64 65–69	**Skills Assessment:** Parts of Speech Test Prep 740–741 and 749
6	**Writing a Descriptive Essay: Describing a Place** **Peer Responding**	75–82 29–32	Specific nouns, compound adjectives, sentence combining (key words and phrases)
7	**Descriptive Essay: Describing a Place** ***(cont'd)*** Practical Writing: Classified Ad *(opt.)*	82 90–91	Spelling, capitalization
8	**Constructing Strong Paragraphs**	523–539	Punctuation, capitalization and abbreviations, plurals, numbers
9	**Writing a Narrative Paragraph: A Great Moment** Portfolio Review	93–96	Verbs, conjunctions, commas (compound sentences and introductory clauses and phrases)

*All remaining page numbers in the timetable refer to the Student Edition.

Second Quarter

Week	Writing Lessons	*Write Source*	Grammar and Writing Skills
1	**Writing a Narrative Essay: Sharing an Experience** (Model, Prewriting, Writing)	97–112	Punctuating dialogue
2	**Narrative Essay** *(cont'd)* (Revising, Editing)	113–128	Transitive and intransitive verbs, verbals (participles), prepositional phrases, interjections, punctuating dialogue, commas (equal adjectives)
3	**Peer Responding**	29–32	
	Narrative Essay *(cont'd)* (Publishing)	129	
	Assessing, Reflecting	130–134	
	Writing an Expository Paragraph: Compare Two Things	157–160	Complete sentences (subjects, predicates), using the right word
4	**Writing an Expository Essay: Comparison-Contrast** (Model, Prewriting, Writing)	161–176	Transitions
5	**Expository Essay** *(cont'd)* (Revising, Editing)	177–192	Specific nouns, appositives, nonrestrictive phrases and clauses, coordinating and subordinating conjunctions, unity, comparative and superlative adjectives and adverbs, commas (explanatory phrases and clauses), subject-verb agreement
6	**Peer Responding**	29–32	
	Expository Essay *(cont'd)* (Publishing, Assessing, Reflecting)	193–198	
	Response Paragraph (Model)	283–286	Punctuating and capitalizing titles
7	**Response to Literature: Writing a Book Review** (Model, Prewriting, Writing)	287–300	Quotations
8	**Book Review** *(cont'd)* (Revising, Editing)	301–316	Run-on sentences, nouns and verbs, combining sentences (appositives), verbs (active vs. passive and tense shifts), subject-verb agreement
	Peer Responding	29–32	
	Book Review *(cont'd)* (Publishing)	317	
	Assessing, Reflecting	318–322	
9	Portfolio Review	65–69	

Third Quarter

Week	Writing Lessons	*Write Source*	Grammar and Writing Skills
1	**Writing Stories** (Prewriting, Writing)	343–348	
2	**Writing Stories** *(cont'd)* (Revising, Editing, Publishing)	348–349	Punctuating dialogue, verbs, sentence combining (compound subjects and predicates), rambling sentences, sentence problems, commas in a series
3	**Writing a Phase Autobiography** (Model, Prewriting, Writing)	135–140	
	(Revising, Editing, Publishing)	141–142	Sentence combining, nouns, end punctuation, using the right word
4	**Persuasive Paragraph: Problem-Solution**	219–222	Apostrophes, using the right word
5	**Persuasive Writing—Problem-Solution Essay** (Model, Prewriting, Writing)	223–238	
6	**Problem-Solution Essay** *(cont'd)* (Writing, Revising, Editing)	239–254	Compound and complex sentences, semicolons and colons, adverbs, spelling, tenses, pronouns and pronoun-antecedent agreement
	Peer Responding	29–32	
	(Publishing)	255	
	Assessing, Reflecting	256–260	
	Writing for Assessment	214–216	
7	**Writing a Poetry Review** (Model, Prewriting, Writing)	323–327	
	(Revising, Editing)	328	Complex sentences (relative pronouns), using the right word
	(Publishing)	328	
8	**Writing a Cause-Effect Essay** (Model, Prewriting, Writing)	199–204	
	(Writing, Revising, Editing)	204	Complete sentences, comma splices and run-ons, double negatives
9	Making Oral Presentations Portfolio Review	423–430	

Fourth Quarter

Week	Writing Lessons	*Write Source*	Grammar and Writing Skills
1	**Writing Poems: Free Verse Poem** (Model, Prewriting, Writing, Revising, Editing)	353–357	Parts of speech (review), apostrophes, hyphens, spelling
	Parts of Speech Poem and Other Forms (concrete, acrostic, 5 W's)	358–359	
2	**Research Writing Skills**	363–376	
	Taking Notes	441–448	
	Summary Paragraph—(Model)	377–378	
3	**Summary Paragraph** *(cont'd.)* (Prewriting, Writing, Revising, Editing)	379–380	Indefinite pronouns, complex sentences, sentence problem (review), subject-verb agreement, using the right word
4	**Research Report—Inspiring Person** (Prewriting)	381–391	
5	**Research Report** *(cont'd.)* (Prewriting, Writing)	392–402	
6	**Research Report** *(cont'd.)* (Revising)	405–406	Sentence variety and ellipses, sentence expanding, pronouns, wordiness
	(Editing, Publishing)	407–410	Punctuating a works-cited page, comma rules (review), sentence problems (review), misplaced modifiers, pronoun-antecedent agreement, parts of speech (review)
7	**Multimedia Presentations**	411–415	
8	**Writing an Editorial** (Model, Prewriting, Writing, Revising, Editing, Publishing)	261–266	Sentence combining, using the right word
9	**Freestyle Writing Project** (Choice) **Journal and Portfolio Review** **Final Reflection Essay**		

Reading-Writing Connection

The literary works listed on pages TE-36 through TE-43 provide high-interest **mentor texts** that you can use to inspire your students as you teach the different forms of writing. Use these texts to accentuate **writer's craft**:

- Read **strong beginnings** or **strong endings** to inspire students as they create their own beginnings and endings.
- Read paragraphs that **develop ideas** or demonstrate **strong organization**.
- Read from two different examples to **contrast voice**.
- Read from different authors to examine their **sentence structure**.

Narrative Books for Grades 6–8

Kensuke's Kingdom
Michael Morpurgo, Stuart Paterson, 2006

Hatchet
Gary Paulsen, 1999

Flight to Freedom
Ana Veciana-Suarez, 2002

Finding My Hat
John Son, 2003

Hattie Big Sky
Kirby Larson, 2006

Cuba 15
Nancy Osa, 2003

On the Wings of Heroes
Richard Peck, 2007

Yellow Star
Jennifer Roy, 2006

Warriors Don't Cry
Melba Pattillo Beals, 1995

Kira-Kira
Cynthia Kadohata, 2006

Journey
Patricia Maclachlan, 1993

As Long As There Are Mountains
Natalie Kinsey-Warnock, 2001

Criss Cross
Lynne Rae Perkins, 2005

Lincoln: A Photobiography
Russell Freedman, 1987

The Voice That Challenged a Nation: Marian Anderson and the Struggle for Equal Rights
Russell Freedman, 2004

Eleanor Roosevelt: A Life of Discovery
Russell Freedman, 1997

The Life and Death of Crazy Horse
Russell Freedman, Amos Bad Heart Bull, 1996

No Pretty Pictures: A Child of War
Anita Lobel, 2000

Chinese Cinderella: The True Story of an Unwanted Daughter
Adeline Yen Mah, 2001

Sir Walter Ralegh and the Quest for El Dorado
Marc Aronson, 2000

Spellbinder: The Life of Harry Houdini
Tom Lalicki, 2000

The Greatest: Muhammad Ali
Walter Dean Myers, 2001

The Circuit: Stories from the Life of a Migrant Child
Francisco Jiménez, 1997

Knots in My Yo-yo String: The Autobiography of a Kid
Jerry Spinelli, 1999

Gandhi, Great Soul
John B. Severance, 1997

Helen Keller: Rebellious Spirit
Laurie Lawlor, 2001

Holes
Louis Sachar, 1998

Bridge to Terabithia
Katherine Paterson, 1977

Number the Stars
Lois Lowry, 1989

Roll of Thunder, Hear My Cry
Mildred D. Taylor, 1976

Maniac Magee
Jerry Spinelli, 1990

Where the Red Fern Grows
Wilson Rawls, 1961

Dragonwings
Laurence Yep, 1975

Grab Hands and Run
Frances Temple, 1993

The Young Landlords
Walter Dean Myers, 1979

The Witch of Blackbird Pond
Elizabeth George Speare, 1971

Nothing but the Truth
Avi, 1991

Year of Impossible Goodbyes
Sook Nyul Choi, 1991

Hoops
Walter Dean Myers, 1981

Journey of the Sparrows
Fran Leeper Buss, 1991

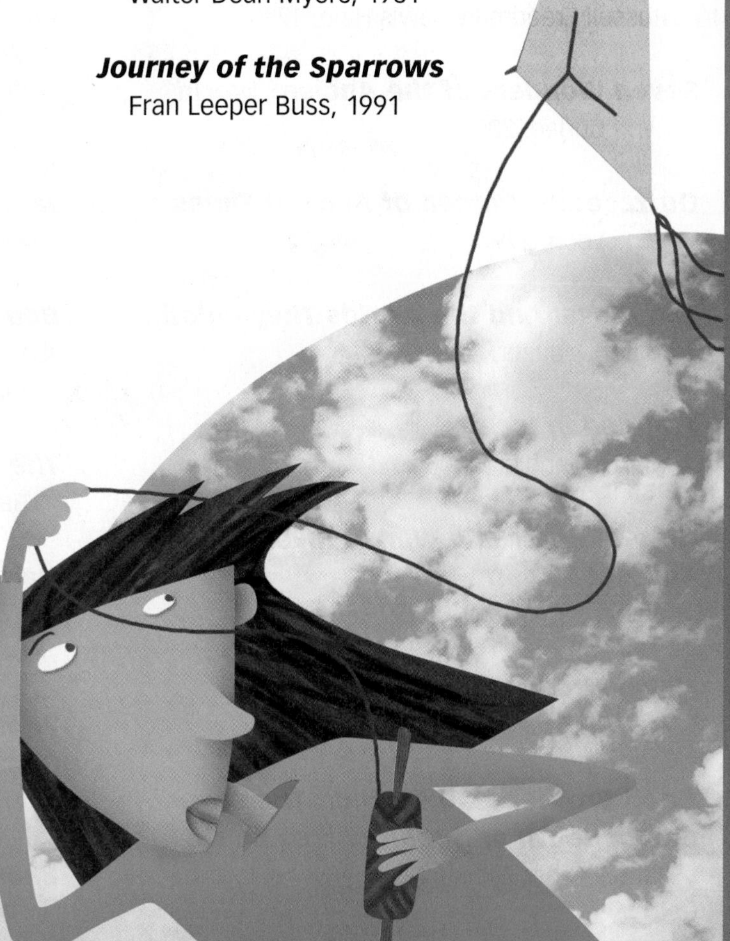

Expository Books for Grades 6–8

Harriet Tubman, Secret Agent: How Daring Slaves and Free Blacks Spied for the Union During the Civil War
Thomas B. Allen, 2006

An American Plague: The True and Terrifying Story of the Yellow Fever Epidemic of 1793 (Newbery Honor Book)
Jim Murphy, 2003

Black Potatoes: The Story of the Great Irish Famine, 1845–1850
Susan Campbell Bartoletti, 2005

Across America on an Emigrant Train
Jim Murphy, 1994

Kids at Work: Lewis Hine and the Crusade Against Child Labor
Russell Freedman, Lewis Hine, 1995

Seven Wonders of the Ancient World
Lynn Curlee, 2002

Outrageous Women of Ancient Times
Vicki León, 1997

Ten Kings: And the Worlds They Ruled
Milton Meltzer, 2002

Trapped in Ice!
Martin Sandler, 2006

How to Enter and Win an Invention Contest
Edwin J. C. Sobey, 1999

Navajo Code Talkers
Nathan Aaseng, 1992

Good Brother, Bad Brother: The Story of Edwin Booth and John Wilkes Booth
James Cross Giblin, 2005

We Were There, Too! Young People in U.S. History
Phillip Hoose, 2001

Nature's Fury: Eyewitness Reports of Natural Disasters
Carole G. Vogel, 2000

Turn It Loose: The Scientist in Absolutely Everybody
Diane Swanson, Warren Clark, 2004

Digging for Bird Dinosaurs: An Expedition to Madagascar
Nic Bishop, 2002

How to Survive in Antarctica
Lucy Jane Bledsoe, 2006

Frederick Douglass: For the Great Family of Man
Peter Burchard, 2003

Remembering Manzanar: Life in a Japanese Relocation Camp
Michael L. Cooper, 2002

Bodies from the Ash: Life and Death in Ancient Pompeii
James M. Deem, 2005

The Middle Ages: An Illustrated History
Barbara A. Hanawalt, 1999

Harlem Stomp! A Cultural History of the Harlem Renaissance
Laban Carrick Hill, 2004

Photo Odyssey: Solomon Carvalho's Remarkable Western Adventure 1853–54
Arlene B. Hirschfelder, 2000

Charro: The Mexican Cowboy
George Ancona, 1999

Rats! The Good, the Bad, and the Ugly
Richard Conniff, 2002

Into the Volcano: A Volcano Researcher at Work
Donna Donovan-O'Meara, 2007

Made You Look: How Advertising Works and Why You Should Know
Shari Graydon, Warren Clark, 2003

Friendly Foes: A Look at Political Parties
Elaine Landau, 2003

The Buffalo and the Indians: A Shared Destiny
Dorothy Hinshaw Patent, William Munoz, 2006

How to Build Your Own Prize-Winning Robot
Edwin J. C. Sobey, 2002

Dragonart: How to Draw Fantastic Dragons and Fantasy Creatures
J. "NeonDragon" Peffer, Jessica Peffer, 2005

How to Drive an Indy Race Car
David Rubel, Gregory Truett Smith, James Westwater, Edward Keating, 1992

How Nature Works
Reader's Digest Editors, 1991

Bravo! Brava! A Night at the Opera: Behind the Scenes with Composers, Cast, and Crew
Anne Siberell, Frederica von Stade, 2001

Lacrosse: The National Game of the Iroquois
Diane Hoyt-Goldsmith, 1998

Dia's Story Cloth: The Hmong People's Journey of Freedom
Dia Cha, 1998

Extraordinary People with Disabilities
Deborah Kent, Kathryn A. Quinlan, 1997

Black Holes & Supernovae (Secrets of Space)
David E. Newton, 1997

So, You Wanna Be a Rock Star? How to Create Music, Get Gigs, and Maybe Even Make It Big!
Stephen Anderson, 1999

Phineas Gage: A Gruesome but True Story About Brain Science
John Fleischman, 2004

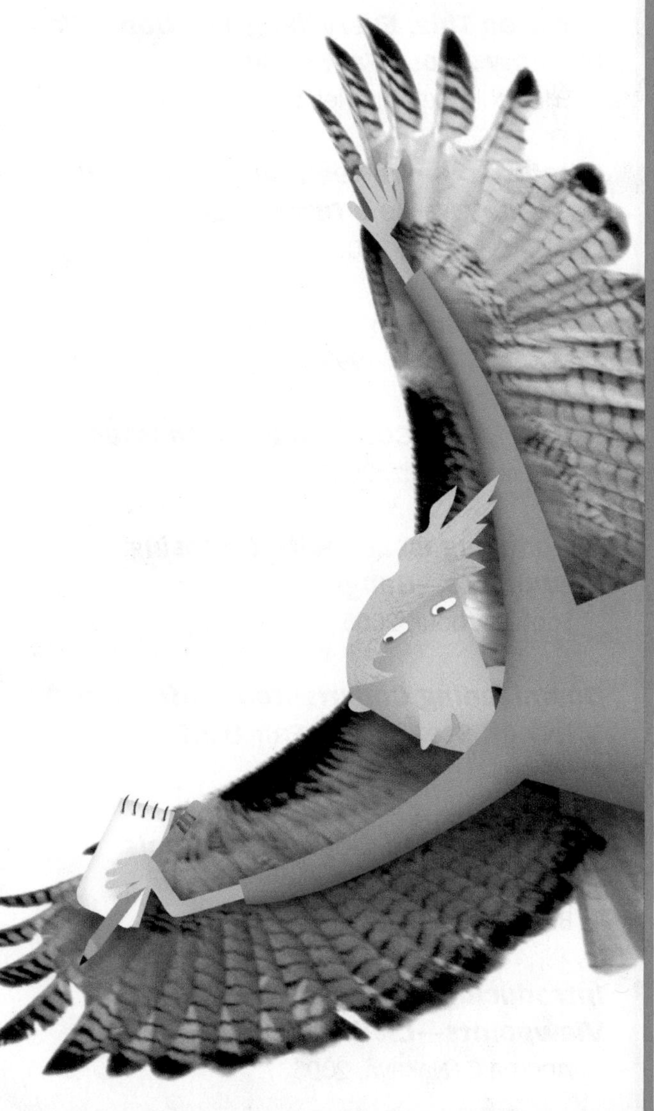

Persuasive Books for Grades 6–8

Free the Children: A Young Man Fights Against Child Labor and Proves That Children Can Change the World
Craig Kielburger, Kevin Major, 1999

We Need to Go to School: Voices from the Rugmark Children
Tanya Roberts-Davis, 2003

It's Our World, Too!
Phillip Hoose, 2002

A Kid's Guide to Giving
Freddi Zeiler, 2006

Chew on This: Everything You Don't Want to Know About Fast Food
Eric Schlosser, Charles Wilson, 2006

Catch the Spirit: Teen Volunteers Tell How They Made a Difference
Susan K. Perry, 2006

Animal Rights—Yes or No?
Marna A. Owen, 1993

School Dress Codes: A Pro/Con Issue
Barbara C. Cruz, 2001

Introducing Issues with Opposing Viewpoints—Gangs
Scott Barbour, 2005

Downloading Copyrighted Stuff From The Internet: Stealing Or Fair Use?
Sherri Mabry Gordon, 2005

Separate Sexes, Separate Schools: A Pro/Con Issue
Barbara C. Cruz, 2000

Introducing Issues with Opposing Viewpoints—Civil Liberties
Andrea C. Nakaya, 2005

Speak Out! Debate and Public Speaking in the Middle Grades
John Meany, 2005

Advertising: Information or Manipulation?
Nancy Day, 1999

Introducing Issues with Opposing Viewpoints—Advertising
Eleanor Stanford, 2006

Introducing Issues with Opposing Viewpoints—UFOs
Jamuna Carroll, 2006

Causes of Crime: Distinguishing Between Fact and Opinion
Stacey L. Tipp, 1991

Taking Action: How to Get Your City to Build a Public Skate Park
Justin Hocking, 2005

Stand Up for Your Rights
Paul Atgwa, 2000

Why It's Great to Be a Girl: 50 Awesome Reasons Why We Rule!
Jacqueline Shannon, 2007

Volunteering to Help in Your Neighborhood
Claudia Isler, 2000

Made You Look: How Advertising Works and Why You Should Know
Shari Graydon, Warren Clark, 2003

Take Action! A Guide to Active Citizenship
Marc Kielburger, 2002

Books About Responding to Literature for Grades 6–8

Dear Author: Students Write About the Books That Changed Their Lives
Weekly Reader's Read Magazine, 1995

The Bookmark Book
Carolyn S. Brodie, Debra Goodrich, Paula K. Montgomery, 1996

What a Novel Idea! Projects and Activities for Young Adult Literature
Katherine Wiesolek Kuta, 1997

Literature Circle Guide: Holes
Tonya Ward Singer, 2002

Literature Circle Guide: Maniac Magee
Perdita Finn, 2001

Literature Circle Guide: Roll of Thunder, Hear My Cry
Rebecca Callan, 2003

10 Ready-to-Go Book Report Projects
Rebekah Elmore, 1999

Wham! Its a Poetry Jam: Discovering Performance Poetry
Sara Holbrook, 2002

Gifted Books, Gifted Readers: Literature Activities to Excite Young Minds
Nancy J. Polette, 2000

Exploring Diversity: Literature Themes and Activities for Grades 4–8
Jean E. Brown, Elaine C. Stephens, 1996

Plays of America from American Folklore for Young Actors: Grade Level 7–12
L. E. McCullough, 1996

The Young Actor's Book of Improvisation: Dramatic Situations from Shakespeare to Spielberg
Sandra Caruso, Susan Kosoff, 1998

Teaching Literary Elements: Easy Strategies and Activities to Help Kids Explore and Enrich Their Experiences with Literature (Grades 4–8)
Tara McCarthy, 1999

Big Talk: Poems for Four Voices
Paul Fleischman, 2000

Newbery Authors of the Eastern Seaboard: Integrating Social Studies and Literature, Grades 5–8
Joanne Kelly, Charles Kelly, 1994

50 Fun-Filled Crosswords & Word Searches Based on Favorite Books (Grades 4–8)
Steve Herrmann, 1999

The American Hero in Children's Literature: A Standards-Based Approach
Carol M. Butzow, John W. Butzow, 2005

Reading Response Trifolds for 40 Favorite Novels
Jennifer Cerra-Johansson, 2004

Teaching Writing with Picture Books as Models (Grades 4–8)
Rosanne Jurstedt, 2000

Meet the Authors (Grades 5–8)
Deborah Kovacs, 1999

The Song Shoots Out of My Mouth: A Celebration of Music
Jaime Adoff, Martin French, 2002

The Place My Words Are Looking For: What Poets Say About and Through Their Work
Paul B. Janeczko, 1990

Children of Promise: African-American Literature and Art for Young People
Charles Sullivan, 2002

Books About Creative Writing for Grades 6–8

Live Writing: Breathing Life into Your Words
Ralph Fletcher, 1999

Poems from Homeroom: A Writer's Place to Start
Kathi Appelt, 2002

Swimming Upstream: Middle School Poems
Kristine O'Connell George, 2002

Seeing the Blue Between: Advice and Inspiration for Young Poets
Paul B. Janeczko, 2006

Neighborhood Odes
Gary Soto, 2005

The Invisible Ladder: An Anthology of Contemporary American Poems for Young Readers
Liz Rosenberg, 1996

I Never Said I Wasn't Difficult: Poems
Sara Holbrook, 1997

Who Do You Think You Are? Stories of Friends and Enemies
Hazel Rochman, 1997

13: Thirteen Stories That Capture the Agony and Ecstasy of Being Thirteen
James Howe, 2003

Shelf Life: Stories by the Book
Gary Paulsen, 2003

Little Worlds: A Collection of Short Stories for the Middle School
Peter Guthrie, 1985

A Kick in the Head: An Everyday Guide to Poetic Forms
Paul B. Janeczko, 2005

Technically, It's Not My Fault: Concrete Poems
John Grandits, 2004

Notebook Know-How: Strategies for the Writer's Notebook
Aimee Buckner, 2005

America Street: A Multicultural Anthology of Stories
Anne Mazer, 1993

Cricket Never Does: A Collection of Haiku and Tanka
Myra Cohn Livingston, Kees De Kiefte, 1997

What's Your Story? A Young Person's Guide to Writing Fiction
Marion Dane Bauer, 1992

Our Stories: A Fiction Workshop for Young Authors
Marion Dane Bauer, 1996

Writing Magic, Creating Stories That Fly
Gail Carson Levine, 2006

Yoga for the Brain: Daily Writing Stretches that Keep Minds Flexible and Strong
Dawn DiPrince, Cheryl Miller Thurston, 2006

Unjournaling: Daily Writing Exercises that Are NOT Personal, NOT Introspective, NOT Boring!
Dawn DiPrince, 2006

Jump Write In!: Creative Writing Exercises for Diverse Classrooms, Grades 6–12
WritersCorps, 2005

Setting the Stage for Creative Writing: Plot Scaffolds for Beginning and Intermediate Writers
Shannon O'Day, 2006

350 Fabulous Writing Prompts (Grades 4–8)
Jacqueline Sweeney, Stephanie Peterson, 1999

Reference Books for Grades 6–8

The American Heritage Student Dictionary
Houghton Mifflin, 1994

The American Heritage Student Thesaurus
Paul Hellweg, 2006

The American Heritage® Student Science Dictionary
Editors of the American Heritage Dictionaries, 2002

The Kingfisher Student Atlas
Philip Wilkinson, 2003

The Usborne Internet-Linked Encyclopedia of World History
Jane Bingham, 2001

The Kingfisher History Encyclopedia
Editors of Kingfisher, 2004

The World Almanac for Kids 2007
Editors of World Almanac, 2006

Webster's New Explorer Dictionary of Synonyms & Antonyms
Merriam-Webster, 2003

The Oxford Children's Book of Famous People
Oxford University Press, 1995

The Biographical Dictionary of African Americans
Rachel Kranz, Philip J. Koslow, 1999

Biographical Dictionary of Modern World Leaders: 1992 to the Present
John C. Fredriksen, 2003

Encyclopedia of Native America
Trudy Griffin-Pierce, 1995

New York (Eyewitness Travel Guides)
DK Publishing, 2006 (series)

National Parks Travel Journal (Travel Journal Guides)
AAA, 2003 (series)

Natural Disasters: Atlas in the Round
Clare Oliver, 2001

Hurricanes, Tsunamis, and Other Natural Disasters (Kingfisher Knowledge)
Andrew Langley, 2006

1000 Years of Famous People
Clive Gifford, 2002

The New York Public Library Kid's Guide to Research
Deborah Heiligman, 1998

The New York Public Library Student's Desk Reference
New York Public Library Staff, 1995

The New York Public Library Amazing Hispanic American History: A Book of Answers for Kids
New York Public Library, George Ochoa, 1998

The Facts on File Dictionary of Proverbs
Martin H. Manser, 2007

Kid's Visual Reference of the United States
Blackbirch Press, 2002

Art: An A-Z Guide
Shirley Greenway, 2000

Music: An A-Z Guide
Nicola Barber, 2002

Libraries and Reference Materials (Straight to the Source)
John Hamilton, 2004

Scope and Sequence

Skills taught and/or reviewed in the *Write Source* program, grades K–8, are featured in the following scope and sequence chart.

FORMS OF WRITING

Grades	K	1	2	3	4	5	6	7	8
Narrative Writing									
sentences	■	■							
paragraph	■	■	■	■	■	■	■	■	■
narrative prompts		■	■	■	■	■	■	■	■
narrative essay			■	■	■	■	■	■	■
phase autobiography								■	■
Expository Writing									
sentences	■	■							
paragraph		■	■	■	■	■	■	■	■
expository prompts		■	■	■	■	■	■	■	■
expository essay			■	■	■	■	■	■	■
classification essay							■		■
cause-and-effect essay								■	
comparison-contrast essay								■	■
Persuasive Writing									
sentences		■							
paragraph		■	■	■	■	■	■	■	■
persuasive prompts			■	■	■	■	■	■	■
persuasive letter			■	■	■	■	■	■	■
persuasive essay				■	■	■	■	■	■
editorial								■	■
problem-solution essay								■	■
personal commentary									■
position essay									■
Response to Literature									
sentences		■							
paragraph		■	■	■	■	■	■	■	■
response prompts		■	■	■	■	■	■	■	■
book review		■	■	■	■	■	■	■	■
journal response					■	■	■	■	■
response to literature							■	■	■
letter to an author									■
theme analysis									■

Grades	K	1	2	3	4	5	6	7	8
Descriptive Writing									
sentences	■	■							
paragraph		■	■	■	■	■	■	■	■
descriptive essay			■	■	■	■	■	■	■
descriptive prompts				■	■	■			
Creative Writing									
poetry		■	■	■	■	■	■	■	■
story	■	■	■	■	■	■	■	■	■
play			■	■	■	■			
Research Writing									
research report		■	■	■	■	■	■	■	■
multimedia presentation			■	■	■	■	■	■	■
summary paragraph				■	■	■	■	■	■
Research Skills									
interview an expert		■	■	■	■	■	■	■	■
online research/using the Internet		■	■	■	■	■	■	■	■
understanding the parts of a book		■	■	■	■	■	■	■	■
using a dictionary, a thesaurus, or an encyclopedia		■	■	■	■	■	■	■	■
using diagrams, charts, graphs, and maps		■	■	■	■	■	■	■	■
using reference sources		■	■	■	■	■	■	■	■
using the library		■	■	■	■	■	■	■	■
note taking/summarizing		■	■	■	■	■	■	■	■
using a card catalog			■	■	■	■	■	■	■
using periodicals or magazines			■	■	■	■	■	■	■
using time lines			■	■	■	■	■	■	■
asking questions				■	■	■	■	■	■
bibliography (works cited)				■	■	■	■	■	■
The Tools of Learning									
improving viewing skills		■	■	■	■	■			
interviewing skills		■	■	■	■	■	■	■	
giving speeches		■	■	■	■	■	■	■	■
journal writing	■	■	■	■	■	■	■	■	■
learning logs		■	■	■	■	■	■	■	■
listening in class	■	■	■	■	■	■	■	■	■
taking classroom tests		■	■	■	■	■	■	■	■
note taking				■	■	■	■	■	■
completing writing assignments							■	■	■

THE WRITING PROCESS

Grades	K	1	2	3	4	5	6	7	8
Prewriting									
Selecting a Topic									
draw pictures		■	■						
make lists	■	■	■	■	■	■	■	■	■
sentence starters		■	■	■	■	■	■	■	■
chart			■	■	■	■	■	■	■
cluster			■	■	■	■	■	■	■
brainstorm					■	■	■	■	■
character chart					■	■		■	■
freewrite					■	■	■	■	■
Gathering Details									
drawing	■	■							
story map		■	■	■					
cluster	■	■	■	■	■	■	■	■	■
answer questions		■	■	■	■	■	■	■	■
details chart/sheet		■	■	■	■	■	■	■	■
gathering grid		■	■	■	■	■	■	■	■
list details/reasons		■	■	■	■	■	■	■	■
sensory chart	■	■	■	■	■	■	■	■	■
selecting main reasons			■	■	■	■	■	■	■
five W's			■	■	■	■	■	■	■
time line	■			■	■	■	■	■	■
table diagram					■	■	■	■	■
opinion statement							■	■	■
counter an objection								■	■
Organizing Details									
time order		■	■	■	■	■	■	■	■
Venn diagram			■	■	■	■	■	■	■
plot chart				■	■	■	■	■	■
time line				■	■	■	■	■	■
note cards				■	■	■	■	■	■
outline ideas				■	■	■	■	■	■
order of importance					■	■	■	■	■
order of location					■	■	■	■	■
Writing									
topic sentence	■	■	■	■	■	■	■	■	■
opinion statement		■	■	■	■	■	■	■	■
facts, examples	■	■	■	■	■	■	■	■	■
supporting details/reasons		■	■	■	■	■	■	■	■
interesting facts/details			■	■	■	■	■	■	■

Grades	K	1	2	3	4	5	6	7	8
make comparisons			■	■	■	■	■	■	■
dialogue			■	■	■	■	■	■	■
transitions			■	■	■	■	■	■	■
call to action			■	■	■	■	■	■	■
closing sentences			■	■	■	■	■	■	■
final comment/interesting thought			■	■	■	■	■	■	■
focus or thesis statement				■	■	■	■	■	■
action words				■	■	■	■	■	■
direct quotations				■	■	■	■	■	■
sensory details				■	■	■	■	■	■
high point of story				■	■	■	■	■	■
explain theme				■	■	■	■	■	■
reflect on a change, a feeling, an experience, a person				■	■	■	■	■	■
restate opinion/thesis					■	■	■	■	■
summarize					■	■	■	■	■
personal details						■	■	■	■
propose a solution							■	■	■
summarize a problem								■	■
share a new insight								■	■
counter an objection						■	■	■	■
emphasize a key idea								■	■
point-by-point discussion									■
Revising									
Ideas									
sensory details	■	■	■	■	■	■	■	■	■
topic sentence			■	■	■	■	■	■	■
supporting details			■	■	■	■	■	■	■
dialogue				■	■	■	■	■	■
unnecessary details				■	■	■	■	■	■
focus statement					■	■	■	■	■
Organization									
order of ideas/details	■	■	■	■	■	■	■	■	■
transition words		■	■	■	■	■	■	■	■
order of importance			■		■	■	■	■	■
overall organization			■	■	■	■	■	■	■
order of location			■	■	■	■	■	■	■
logical order			■	■	■	■	■	■	■
clear beginning			■	■	■	■	■	■	■
time order			■	■	■	■	■	■	■

Grades	K	1	2	3	4	5	6	7	8
Voice									
natural		■	■	■	■	■	■	■	■
convincing				■	■	■	■	■	■
interested				■	■	■	■	■	■
dialogue					■	■	■	■	■
fits audience/purpose					■	■	■	■	■
formal/informal					■	■	■	■	■
knowledgeable					■	■	■	■	■
Word Choice									
sensory words/details	■	■	■	■	■	■	■	■	■
specific nouns			■	■	■	■	■	■	■
action verbs				■	■	■	■	■	■
connotation					■	■	■	■	■
modifiers					■	■	■	■	■
onomatopoeia						■	■	■	■
descriptive words						■	■	■	■
vivid verbs						■	■	■	■
connotation								■	■
Sentence Fluency									
complete sentences		■	■	■	■	■	■	■	■
variety of lengths			■	■	■	■	■	■	■
kinds of sentences			■	■	■	■	■	■	■
combining sentences				■	■	■	■	■	■
compound sentences				■	■	■	■	■	■
complex sentences					■	■	■	■	■
expanded sentences					■	■	■	■	■
variety of beginnings					■	■	■	■	■
types of sentences					■	■	■	■	■
Editing									
capitalization	■	■	■	■	■	■	■	■	■
grammar/punctuation/spelling	■	■	■	■	■	■	■	■	■
proper nouns	■		■	■	■	■	■	■	■
proper adjectives				■	■	■	■	■	■
Publishing									
publish in a variety of ways	■	■	■	■	■	■	■	■	■
review own work to monitor growth		■	■	■	■	■	■	■	■
self- and peer-assessing writing		■	■	■	■	■	■	■	■
use portfolios to save writing		■	■	■	■	■	■	■	■
use published pieces as models for writing		■	■	■	■	■	■	■	■

WRITING ACROSS THE CURRICULUM

Grades	K	1	2	3	4	5	6	7	8
Narrative Writing									
reading		■							
music		■	■						
social studies			■			■	■	■	■
practical				■			■	■	■
science				■	■		■	■	■
Expository Writing									
social studies		■		■		■	■	■	■
math		■			■	■	■	■	■
reading *		■	■	■	■	■	■	■	■
science			■		■		■	■	■
practical			■	■	■	■	■	■	■
Persuasive Writing									
health		■							
science			■	■	■	■	■	■	■
social studies			■			■	■	■	■
practical				■	■	■	■	■	■
math					■		■	■	■
Descriptive Writing									
math		■	■				■	■	■
science		■	■		■	■	■	■	■
practical			■				■	■	■
social studies					■	■	■	■	■

* The models included in the "Response to Literature" section demonstrate expository writing within the reading curriculum.

GRAMMAR

	K	1	2	3	4	5	6	7	8
Understanding Sentences									
word order		■	■	■					
declarative		■	■	■	■	■	■	■	■
exclamatory		■	■	■	■	■	■	■	■
interrogative		■	■	■	■	■	■	■	■
complete sentences and fragments		■	■	■	■	■	■	■	■
simple subjects		■	■	■	■	■	■	■	■
simple predicates		■	■	■	■	■	■	■	■
correcting run-on sentences		■	■	■	■	■	■	■	■
compound			■	■	■	■	■	■	■
imperative			■	■	■	■	■	■	■
complete predicates				■	■	■	■	■	■

Understanding Sentences (Continued)	K	1	2	3	4	5	6	7	8
complete subjects				■	■	■	■	■	■
compound predicates				■	■	■	■	■	■
compound subjects				■	■	■	■	■	■
prepositional phrases				■	■	■	■	■	■
appositive phrases					■	■	■	■	■
clauses, dependent and independent					■	■	■	■	■
complex					■	■	■	■	■
modifiers					■	■	■	■	■
noun phrases					■	■	■	■	■
verb phrases					■	■	■	■	■
Using the Parts of Speech									
Nouns									
singular and plural		■	■	■	■	■	■	■	■
common/proper		■	■	■	■	■	■	■	■
possessive			■	■	■	■	■	■	■
singular/plural possessive			■	■	■	■	■	■	■
specific				■	■	■	■	■	■
abstract/concrete					■	■	■	■	■
appositives					■	■	■	■	■
collective/compound					■	■	■	■	■
object					■	■	■	■	■
predicate					■	■	■	■	■
subject					■	■	■	■	■
gender					■	■	■	■	■
Verbs									
contractions with *not*		■	■	■	■	■	■	■	■
action	■	■	■	■	■	■	■	■	■
linking		■	■	■	■	■	■	■	■
past tense		■	■	■	■	■	■	■	■
present tense		■	■	■	■	■	■	■	■
subject-verb agreement		■	■	■	■	■	■	■	■
future tense			■	■	■	■	■	■	■
helping			■	■	■	■	■	■	■
singular/plural			■	■	■	■	■	■	■
irregular				■	■	■	■	■	■
simple tense				■	■	■	■	■	■
active/passive voice					■	■	■	■	■
direct objects					■	■	■	■	■
indirect objects					■	■	■	■	■
perfect tense					■	■	■	■	■

Grades	K	1	2	3	4	5	6	7	8
transitive/intransitive					■	■	■	■	■
participles						■	■	■	■
continuous tense							■	■	■
gerunds							■	■	■
infinitives							■	■	■
Pronouns									
personal		■	■	■	■	■	■	■	■
antecedents		■	■	■	■	■	■	■	■
singular and plural		■	■	■	■	■	■	■	■
possessive		■	■	■	■	■	■	■	■
subject and object			■	■	■	■	■	■	■
demonstrative/interrogative					■	■	■	■	■
gender					■	■	■	■	■
indefinite					■	■	■	■	■
intensive and reflexive					■	■	■	■	■
relative					■	■	■	■	■
Adjectives									
adjectives	■	■	■	■	■	■	■	■	■
comparative/superlative		■	■	■	■	■	■	■	■
articles			■	■	■	■	■	■	■
compound				■	■	■	■	■	■
positive				■	■	■	■	■	■
proper				■	■	■	■	■	■
demonstrative					■	■	■	■	■
equal					■	■	■	■	■
indefinite					■	■	■	■	■
predicate					■	■	■	■	■
Interjections									
interjections		■	■	■	■	■	■	■	■
Adverbs									
of manner			■	■	■	■	■	■	■
of place	■		■	■	■	■	■	■	■
of time			■	■	■	■	■	■	■
that modify verbs			■	■	■	■	■	■	■
of degree					■	■	■	■	■
that modify adjectives and adverbs					■	■	■	■	■
comparative/superlative					■	■	■	■	■
comparing with adverbs					■	■	■	■	■
irregular forms					■	■	■	■	■
positive					■	■	■	■	■

Grades	K	1	2	3	4	5	6	7	8
Conjunctions									
coordinating			■	■	■	■	■	■	■
correlative					■	■	■	■	■
subordinating					■	■	■	■	■
Prepositions									
prepositions	■		■	■	■	■	■	■	■
prepositional phrases				■	■	■	■	■	■
Mechanics									
Capitalization									
pronoun "I"		■	■	■	■	■	■	■	■
days, months, holidays		■	■	■	■	■	■	■	■
first words	■	■	■	■	■	■	■	■	■
names of people	■	■	■	■	■	■	■	■	■
proper nouns		■	■	■	■	■	■	■	■
titles used with names		■	■	■	■	■	■	■	■
titles		■	■	■	■	■	■	■	■
beginning of a quotation		■	■	■	■	■	■	■	■
geographic names			■	■	■	■	■	■	■
abbreviations			■	■	■	■	■	■	■
proper adjectives				■	■	■	■	■	■
words used as names				■	■	■	■	■	■
names of historical events					■	■	■	■	■
names of religions, nationalities					■	■	■	■	■
organizations					■	■	■	■	■
particular sections of the country					■	■	■	■	■
trade names/official names					■	■	■	■	■
letters to indicate form or direction							■	■	■
specific course names							■	■	■
Plurals									
irregular nouns		■	■	■	■	■	■	■	■
most nouns		■	■	■	■	■	■	■	■
nouns ending with *sh*, *ch*, *x*, *s*, and *z*			■	■	■	■	■	■	■
nouns ending in *y*			■	■	■	■	■	■	■
adding an *'s*					■	■	■	■	■
compound nouns					■	■	■	■	■
nouns ending with *f* or *fe*					■	■	■	■	■
nouns ending with *ful*					■	■	■	■	■
nouns ending with *o*					■	■	■	■	■

Grades	K	1	2	3	4	5	6	7	8
Abbreviations									
days and months			■	■	■	■	■	■	■
state postal abbreviations				■	■	■	■	■	■
titles of people		■	■	■	■	■	■	■	■
addresses			■	■	■	■	■	■	■
acronyms				■	■	■	■	■	■
initialisms				■	■	■	■	■	■
Numbers									
numbers 1 to 9				■	■	■	■	■	■
numbers only				■	■	■	■	■	■
sentence beginnings				■	■	■	■	■	■
very large numbers				■	■	■	■	■	■
numbers in compound modifiers							■	■	■
time and money							■	■	■
Punctuation									
Periods									
after an initial/an abbreviation		■	■	■	■	■	■	■	■
at the end of a sentence	■	■	■	■	■	■	■	■	■
as a decimal point				■	■	■	■	■	■
after an indirect question							■	■	■
Question Marks									
after questions	■	■	■	■	■	■	■	■	■
after tag questions					■	■	■	■	■
to show doubt					■	■	■	■	■
Exclamation Points									
for words, phrases, and sentences	■	■	■	■	■	■	■	■	■
for interjections		■	■	■	■	■	■	■	■
Commas									
in a series		■	■	■	■	■	■	■	■
in dates		■	■	■	■	■	■	■	■
in friendly letters		■	■	■	■	■	■	■	■
after introductory words		■	■	■	■	■	■	■	■
with interjections		■	■	■	■	■	■	■	■
in a compound sentence			■	■	■	■	■	■	■
in addresses			■	■	■	■	■	■	■
to set off dialogue			■	■	■	■	■	■	■
in direct address			■	■	■	■	■	■	■
in numbers				■	■	■	■	■	■
to separate equal adjectives				■	■	■	■	■	■

Commas (Continued)	K	1	2	3	4	5	6	7	8
to set off appositives					■	■	■	■	■
to set off interrupters					■	■	■	■	■
to set off phrases					■	■	■	■	■
to set off titles of people							■	■	■
Apostrophes									
in contractions		■	■	■	■	■	■	■	■
to form plural possessive nouns			■	■	■	■	■	■	■
to form singular possessive nouns			■	■	■	■	■	■	■
to form some plurals					■	■	■	■	■
to replace omitted numbers/letters					■	■	■	■	■
with indefinite pronouns					■	■	■	■	■
to show shared possession					■	■	■	■	■
in possessives w/ compound nouns							■	■	■
to express time or amount							■	■	■
Underlining and Italics									
for titles		■	■	■	■	■	■	■	■
for special words					■	■	■	■	■
for scientific and foreign words							■	■	■
Quotation Marks									
for direct quotations			■	■	■	■	■	■	■
for titles			■	■	■	■	■	■	■
for special words					■	■	■	■	■
for quotations within a quotation							■	■	■
Colons									
between hour and minutes				■	■	■	■	■	■
in business letter				■	■	■	■	■	■
to introduce a list of items				■	■	■	■	■	■
for emphasis							■	■	■
to introduce sentences							■	■	■
Hyphens									
in word division				■	■	■	■	■	■
in compound words					■	■	■	■	■
in fractions					■	■	■	■	■
to create new words					■	■	■	■	■
to join letters and words					■	■	■	■	■
to avoid confusion or awkward spelling							■	■	■
to make adjectives							■	■	■

Grades	K	1	2	3	4	5	6	7	8
Parentheses									
to add information				■	■	■	■	■	■
Dashes									
for emphasis					■	■	■	■	■
to show a sentence break					■	■	■	■	■
to show interrupted speech					■	■	■	■	■
Ellipses									
to show a pause					■	■	■	■	■
to show omitted words					■	■	■	■	■
Semicolons									
in a compound sentence					■	■	■	■	■
to separate groups (that have commas) in a series						■	■	■	■ ■
with conjunctive adverbs							■	■	■
Usage									
Spelling									
high-frequency words		■	■						
consonant endings				■	■	■	■	■	■
i before *e*				■	■	■	■	■	■
silent *e*				■	■	■	■	■	■
words ending in *y*				■	■	■	■	■	■
Using the Right Word		■	■	■	■	■	■	■	■
Penmanship									
word space, letter space		■	■						
write legibly		■	■	■	■	■	■	■	■
margins/spaces				■	■	■	■	■	■

Meeting the Common Core State Standards

The following correlation clearly shows how the *Write Source* program helps you meet grade-specific **Common Core State Standards for English Language Arts,** along with their companion **College and Career Readiness (CCR)** standards. Students are expected to meet grade-specific standards by the end of the school year, thereby working steadily toward meeting the more general expectations described by the CCR standards.

Pages referenced appear in the Teacher's Edition as well as the Student Edition.

Writing Standards

Text Types and Purposes

College and Career Readiness Standard 1. Write arguments to support claims in an analysis of substantive topics or texts, using valid reasoning and relevant and sufficient evidence.

Grade 7 Standard 1. Write arguments to support claims with clear reasons and relevant evidence.

a. Introduce claim(s), acknowledge alternate or opposing claims, and organize the reasons and evidence logically.	**Student Edition pages:** 220–222, 224, 228–230, 232, 234–237, 242–243, 264–266, 268–269, 270–271, 272–273, 274–275, 276–278, 334–335 **Net-text:** Persuasive Writing
b. Support claim(s) with logical reasoning and relevant evidence, using accurate, credible sources and demonstrating an understanding of the topic or text.	**Student Edition pages:** 220–222, 225–226, 229–232, 235, 236–237, 240–241, 244–245, 262–263, 266, 268–269, 270–271, 272–273, 274–275, 276–277, 278–280, 334–335 **Net-text:** Persuasive Writing
c. Use words, phrases, and clauses to create cohesion and clarify the relationships among claim(s), reasons, and evidence.	**Student Edition pages:** 232, 234, 236–237, 238, 244–245, 246–247, 248–249, 264–265 **Net-text:** Persuasive Writing
d. Establish and maintain a formal style.	**Student Edition pages:** 220, 225–226, 231, 235–238, 244–245, 246–247, 248–249, 262–266, 268–269, 270–271, 272–273, 274–275, 276–278 **Net-text:** Persuasive Writing
e. Provide a concluding statement or section that follows from and supports the argument presented.	**Student Edition pages:** 220, 222, 226, 234, 237, 238, 243, 263, 268, 270, 272, 274, 276, 279 **Net-text:** Persuasive Writing

Text Types and Purposes (continued)

College and Career Readiness Standard 2. Write informative/explanatory texts to examine and convey complex ideas and information clearly and accurately through the effective selection, organization, and analysis of content.

Grade 7 Standard 2. Write informative/explanatory texts to examine a topic and convey ideas, concepts, and information through the selection, organization, and analysis of relevant content.

a. Introduce a topic clearly, previewing what is to follow; organize ideas, concepts, and information, using strategies such as definition, classification, comparison/contrast, and cause/effect; include formatting (e.g., headings), graphics (e.g., charts, tables), and multimedia when useful to aiding comprehension.	**Student Edition pages:** 60–64, 72, 74, 76–77, 80–82, 84–85, 86–87, 88–89, 90–91, 158, 160, 162, 163–164, 168–170, 172–175, 180–181, 196–197, 200–201, 202–203, 204, 206–207, 208–209, 210–211, 212–213, 214–216, 284–286, 289–290, 292–293, 296–297, 298–299, 302–303, 324–328, 332–333, 336–341, 378–380, 382–386, 388–395, 398–402, 412–415, 435–440, 466–467 **Net-text:** Descriptive Writing, Expository Writing, Response to Literature, Research Writing
b. Develop the topic with relevant facts, definitions, concrete details, quotations, or other information and examples.	**Student Edition pages:** 72–74, 76–79, 81, 84–85, 86–87, 88–89, 90–91,158–160, 162, 163–164, 167–168, 174–175, 178–179, 180–181, 196–197, 200–201, 203–204, 206–207, 208–209, 210–211, 212–213, 214–216, 284–286, 289–290, 292–294, 296–297, 298–299, 303, 325, 327–328, 332–333, 336–341, 390–391, 395, 398–402, 406, 435–440, 466–467 **Net-text:** Descriptive Writing, Expository Writing, Response to Literature, Research Writing
c. Use appropriate transitions to create cohesion and clarify the relationships among ideas and concepts.	**Student Edition pages:** 39, 74, 116–117, 174, 204, 249, 298, 304, 426, 525, 528, 534, 539, 561, 572–573 **Net-text:** Descriptive Writing, Narrative Writing, Expository Writing, Persuasive Writing, Response to Literature
d. Use precise language and domain-specific vocabulary to inform about or explain the topic.	**Student Edition pages:** 73–74, 82, 85, 86–87, 88–89, 90–91, 160, 162, 164, 174–175, 184–185, 200–201, 204, 206–207, 208–209, 210–211, 212–213, 214–215, 400–401, 406 **Net-text:** Descriptive Writing, Expository Writing, Research Writing

Text Types and Purposes (continued)

e. Establish and maintain a formal style.	**Student Edition pages:** 72, 76–77, 80–83, 84–85, 86–87, 88–89, 90–91, 158, 163–164, 182–183, 200–201, 206–207, 208–209, 210–211, 212–213, 214–215, 378–380, 382–386, 398–402 **Net-text:** Descriptive Writing, Expository Writing, Research Writing
f. Provide a concluding statement or section that follows from and supports the information or explanation presented.	**Student Edition pages:** 72, 77, 82, 84, 87, 88, 158, 164, 175, 176, 201, 204, 206, 208, 210, 212, 215, 216, 284, 286, 339 **Net-text:** Descriptive Writing, Expository Writing, Response to Literature
College and Career Readiness Standard 3. Write narratives to develop real or imagined experiences or events using effective technique, well-chosen details, and well-structured event sequences.	
Grade 7 Standard 3. Write narratives to develop real or imagined experiences or events using effective technique, relevant descriptive details, and well-structured event sequences.	
a. Engage and orient the reader by establishing a context and point of view and introducing a narrator and/or characters; organize an event sequence that unfolds naturally and logically.	**Student Edition pages:** 95–96, 98–100, 102–104, 108–111, 116–117, 136–137, 144–145, 146–147, 148–149, 150–151, 152–154, 330–331, 344–349, 354–357, 358, 359, 432–433 **Net-text:** Narrative Writing, Creative Writing
b. Use narrative techniques, such as dialogue, pacing, and description, to develop experiences, events, and/or characters.	**Student Edition pages:** 96, 104–106, 108–111, 119, 141, 144–145, 146–147, 148–149, 150–151, 152–154, 330–331, 344–345, 348, 350–352, 354, 356, 358–359, 360–361, 432–433 **Net-text:** Narrative Writing, Creative Writing
c. Use a variety of transition words, phrases, and clauses to convey sequence and signal shifts from one time frame or setting to another.	**Student Edition pages:** 104, 110–111, 122–123, 152–154 **Net-text:** Narrative Writing
d. Use precise words and phrases, relevant descriptive details, and sensory language to capture the action and convey experiences and events.	**Student Edition pages:** 96, 98, 100, 105, 110–111, 114–115, 120–121, 123, 140–141, 144–145, 148–149, 150–151, 152–154, 330–331, 346–347, 355 **Net-text:** Narrative Writing, Creative Writing
e. Provide a conclusion that follows from and reflects on the narrated experiences or events.	**Student Edition pages:** 96, 98, 100, 103, 108, 112, 137, 153, 144, 148, 150, 153, 330, 345 **Net-text:** Narrative Writing, Creative Writing

Production and Distribution of Writing

College and Career Readiness Standard 4. Produce clear and coherent writing in which the development, organization, and style are appropriate to task, purpose, and audience.

Grade 7 Standard 4. Produce clear and coherent writing in which the development, organization, and style are appropriate to task, purpose, and audience.	**Student Edition pages:** 72–74, 76–82, 84–85, 86–87, 88–89, 90–91, 94–96, 98–112, 114–115, 116–117, 136–142, 144–145, 146–147, 148–149, 150–151, 152–154, 158–160, 162–176, 178–179, 180–181, 200–204, 206–207, 208–209, 210–211, 212–213, 214–216, 220–221, 225–238, 240–241, 242–243, 262–266, 268–269, 270–271, 272–273, 274–275, 278–280, 284–286, 289–316, 324–325, 330–331, 332–333, 334–335, 336–341, 344–349, 354–357, 358, 359, 382–408, 432–433, 434, 435–438, 439–440, 452–458 **Interactive Whiteboard Lessons:** Descriptive Writing, Narrative Writing, Expository Writing, Persuasive Writing, Response to Literature, Creative Writing, Research Writing **Net-text:** Descriptive Writing, Narrative Writing, Expository Writing, Persuasive Writing, Response to Literature, Creative Writing, Research Writing

College and Career Readiness Standard 5. Develop and strengthen writing as needed by planning, revising, editing, rewriting, or trying a new approach.

Grade 7 Standard 5. With some guidance and support from peers and adults, develop and strengthen writing as needed by planning, revising, editing, rewriting, or trying a new approach, focusing on how well purpose and audience have been addressed.	**Student Edition pages:** 6–10, 12–13, 14–15, 16–23, 12–13, 14–15, 16–23, 29–32, 33–44, 46–53, 54–55, 73–74, 78–79, 81–82, 95–96, 101–107, 113–124, 125–128, 130–131, 132–134, 138, 141, 142, 159–160, 165–170, 177–188, 189–192, 194–195, 196–198, 202–204, 221–222, 227–232, 239–250, 251–254, 256–257, 258–260, 264, 266, 268–277, 285–286, 291–294, 301–312, 313–316, 318–319, 320–322, 328, 346–348, 349, 357, 379–380, 401–402, 403–404, 412–413 **Interactive Whiteboard Lessons:** Descriptive Writing, Narrative Writing, Expository Writing, Persuasive Writing, Response to Literature, Creative Writing, Research Writing **Net-text:** Descriptive Writing, Narrative Writing, Expository Writing, Persuasive Writing, Response to Literature, Creative Writing, Research Writing

Production and Distribution of Writing (continued)

College and Career Readiness Standard 6. Use technology, including the Internet, to produce and publish writing and to interact and collaborate with others.	
Grade 7 Standard 6. Use technology, including the Internet, to produce and publish writing and link to and cite sources as well as to interact and collaborate with others, including linking to and citing sources.	**Student Edition pages:** 60–64, 193, 212–213, 255, 266, 317, 349, 357, 409, 412–415, 435 **Interactive Whiteboard Lessons:** Descriptive Writing, Narrative Writing, Expository Writing, Persuasive Writing, Response to Literature, Creative Writing, Research Writing **Net-text:** Descriptive Writing, Narrative Writing, Expository Writing, Persuasive Writing, Response to Literature, Creative Writing, Research Writing

Research to Build and Present Knowledge

College and Career Readiness Standard 7. Conduct short as well as more sustained research projects based on focused questions, demonstrating understanding of the subject under investigation.	
Grade 7 Standard 7. Conduct short research projects to answer a question, drawing on several sources and generating additional related, focused questions for further research and investigation.	**Student Edition pages:** 85, 89, 149, 167, 178, 211, 271, 331, 388–393 **Net-text:** Expository Writing, Research Writing
College and Career Readiness Standard 8. Gather relevant information from multiple print and digital sources, assess the credibility and accuracy of each source, and integrate the information while avoiding plagiarism.	
Grade 7 Standard 8. Gather relevant information from multiple print and digital sources, using search terms effectively; assess the credibility and accuracy of each source; and quote or paraphrase the data and conclusions of others while avoiding plagiarism and following a standard format for citation.	**Student Edition pages:** 364–376, 391–393, 397, 401, 403–404 **Net-text:** Research Writing

Research to Build and Present Knowledge (continued)

College and Career Readiness Standard 9. Draw evidence from literary or informational texts to support analysis, reflection, and research.

Grade 7 Standard 9. Draw evidence from literary or informational texts to support analysis, reflection, and research.

a. Apply grade 7 Reading standards to literature (e.g., "Compare and contrast a fictional portrayal of a time, place, or character and a historical account of the same period as a means of understanding how authors of fiction use or alter history").	**Student Edition pages:** 76–77, 148–149, 284–286, 289–290, 292–316, 324–328, 334–335, 336–341 **Net-text:** Descriptive Writing, Response to Literature
b. Apply grade 7 Reading standards to literary nonfiction (e.g. "Trace and evaluate the argument and specific claims in a text, assessing whether the reasoning is sound and the evidence is relevant and sufficient to support the claims").	**Student Edition pages:** 84–85, 86–87, 88–89, 98–100, 136–137, 200–201, 214–215, 320, 438, 446–448, 452–458 **Net-text:** Narrative Writing, Expository Writing

Range of Writing

College and Career Readiness Standard 10. Write routinely over extended time frames (time for research, reflection, and revision) and shorter time frames (a single sitting or a day or two) for a range of tasks, purposes, and audiences.

Grade 7 Standard 10. Write routinely over extended time frames (time for research, reflection, and revision) and shorter time frames (a single sitting or a day or two) for a range of discipline-specific tasks, purposes, and audiences.	**Student Edition pages:** 2, 3, 6, 7, 9, 40, 42, 47, 49, 51, 52, 55, 67, 73–82, 85, 89, 101–128, 136–142, 145, 147, 149, 151, 154, 158, 159–160, 164, 165–188, 200–204, 206–207, 208–209, 210–211, 212–213, 214–216, 220, 221–222, 224–254, 262–266, 268–269, 270–271, 272–273, 274–275, 278–280, 284–286, 288–316, 324–328, 330–331, 332–333, 334–335, 344–349, 352, 354–357, 358, 359, 361, 378–380, 382–386, 388–395, 398–402, 412–415, 453–457, 465, 466–467, 473, 476, 479, 481, 482, 483, 485, 489, 492, 494, 496, 500, 502, 503, 504, 505, 506, 507, 508, 509, 510, 511, 512, 513, 514, 515, 516, 517, 518, 520, 522, 512, 526, 527, 528, 529, 537, 581, 584, 589, 591, 595, 597, 599, 601, 603, 605, 609, 611, 615, 619, 621, 623, 625, 631 **Interactive Whiteboard Lessons:** Descriptive Writing, Narrative Writing, Expository Writing, Persuasive Writing, Response to Literature, Creative Writing, Research Writing **Net-text:** Descriptive Writing, Narrative Writing, Expository Writing, Persuasive Writing, Response to Literature, Creative Writing, Research Writing

Language Standards

Conventions of Standard English

College and Career Readiness Standard 1. Demonstrate command of the conventions of standard English grammar and usage when writing or speaking.	
Grade 7 Standard 1. Demonstrate command of the conventions of standard English grammar and usage when writing or speaking.	
a. Explain the function of phrases and clauses in general and their function in specific sentences.	**Student Edition pages:** 122, 123, 185, 191, 310, 495, 512, 515–517, 519, 520, 698, 700
b. Choose among simple, compound, complex, and compound-complex sentences to signal differing relationships among ideas.	**Student Edition pages:** 248, 249, 252, 515, 516, 517
c. Place phrases and clauses within a sentence, recognizing and correcting misplaced and dangling modifiers.	**GrammarSnap:** Adjectival Phrases; Adjectival Clauses; Adverbial Clauses; Misplaced and Dangling Modifiers
College and Career Readiness Standard 2. Demonstrate command of the conventions of standard English capitalization, punctuation, and spelling when writing.	
Grade 7 Standard 2. Demonstrate command of the conventions of standard English capitalization, punctuation, and spelling when writing.	
a. Use a comma to separate coordinate adjectives (e.g., *It was a fascinating, enjoyable movie* but not *He wore an old[,] green shirt*).	**GrammarSnap:** Commas to Separate Equal Adjectives
b. Spell correctly.	**Student Edition pages:** 9, 22, 74, 85, 89, 91, 96, 126, 128, 142, 149, 160, 190, 192, 204, 207, 209, 216, 222, 254, 266, 273, 280, 286, 316, 328, 349, 357, 374–375, 380, 404, 413, 492, 632–633, 642–651 **Net-text:** Descriptive Writing, Narrative Writing, Expository Writing, Persuasive Writing, Response to Literature, Creative Writing, Research Writing

Knowledge of Language

College and Career Readiness Standard 3. Apply knowledge of language to understand how language functions in different contexts, to make effective choices for meaning or style, and to comprehend more fully when reading or listening.

Grade 7 Standard 3. Use knowledge of language and its conventions when writing, speaking, reading, or listening.

a. Choose language that expresses ideas precisely and concisely, recognizing and eliminating wordiness and redundancy.	**Student Edition pages:** 74, 78–79, 80, 82, 85, 121, 184, 269, 273, 493 **Net-text:** Descriptive Writing, Narrative Writing, Expository Writing

Getting-Started Activities

The *Write Source* student edition is full of helpful resources that students can access throughout the year while they are developing their writing skills.

Getting started activities are provided as copy masters on TE pages 794–796. (See the answer keys on TE page 797.) These activities will

- help students discover the kinds of information available in different sections of the book,
- teach students how to access that information, and
- familiarize students with the layout of the book.

The more familiar students are with the text, the more proficient they will be in using it as a resource.

Scavenger Hunts

Students enjoy using scavenger hunts to become familiar with a book. The scavenger hunts we provide can be done in small groups or as a class. They are designed for oral answers, but you may want to photocopy the pages for students to write on. You may also vary the procedure by first having students take turns finding the items and then, on the next scavenger hunt, challenging students to "race" for the answers.

794

Scavenger Hunt 1: Find the Fours

Directions Find the following "fours" in your book by turning to the pages listed in parentheses.

1. **Four** reasons to write (page 2)
2. **Four** on a rubric means ______ (page 46)
3. **Four** ways to publish in school (page 58)
4. **Four** sentence starters that can help you select a topic (page 102)
5. **Four** tips to remember as you write middle paragraphs (page 110)
6. **Four** types of fuzzy thinking to avoid (page 231)
7. **Four** questions that an adverb can answer (page 490)
8. **Four** parts of a plot line (page 347 or 351)
9. **Four** good listening habits (page 418)
10. **Four** ways to improve sentence style (page 511)

After your students have completed each scavenger hunt, you can challenge them to create their own versions. For example, small groups can work together to create "Find the Fours" or "Search for Sixes" scavenger hunts and then exchange their "hunts" with other groups.

Other Activities

- **Problem Resolution** Give students the following assignment: Across the top of a sheet of paper, write down three things you find difficult about school (e.g., taking notes, taking tests, writing essays, spelling, using commas). Then explore your book to find chapters, sections, examples, and so on, that might help you with your problem area. Under each problem, write the titles or headings and the page numbers where you can find help. Keep this sheet to use throughout the year.
- **Help Wanted** A variation on the above activity is to have students write down all the subject areas they study and list under each heading the parts of the book that might help them in that subject.
- **Thought-Trap Poem** Have students write a thought-trap poem: After reviewing the book, close it. The first line of your poem will be the title of the book. Then list thoughts and feelings about the book, line by line. When you have listed everything you want to say, "trap" your thoughts by repeating the title.
- **Poster** Have pairs of students create poster-size advertisements for the book. Each ad should have a headline, list important features (what is in the book) and benefits (whom it can help and how), show an example of illustrations (made by tracing or copying), and urge readers of the ad to get their books now!
- **Pen Pal Letter** Have students imagine that they are each going to send a copy of *Write Source* to a pen pal in another state. Have each student write a letter to send along with it to tell the pen pal about the book.

Special Challenge: Develop questions that teams of students try to answer using the book. Pattern this activity after a popular game show.

HOUGHTON MIFFLIN HARCOURT

WRITE SOURCE

Authors
Dave Kemper, Patrick Sebranek, and Verne Meyer

Illustrator
Chris Krenzke

GREAT SOURCE®

HOUGHTON MIFFLIN HARCOURT

Welcome to the Wraparound Teacher's Edition!

Writing is a journey to unexplored realms, and *Write Source* can be your guide.

The Teacher's Edition will guide you on this journey as well. In the following pages, you'll find not only lesson objectives and instructions, but also these special features at point of use:

- Writing Traits Tips
- Teaching Tips
- Integrated Grammar, Literature, Writing Craft, and Technology
- Assessment Options and Test Prep
- Notes for Students of English as a Second Language
- Accommodations and Modifications for Struggling Students
- Enrichments for Advanced Students

Welcome to your writing adventure! Welcome to *Write Source*.

Thanks to the Teachers!

This program would not have been possible without the input of many teachers and administrators from across the nation. As we originally developed this K–12 series, we surveyed hundreds of teaching professionals, and as we revised this series, we have implemented the feedback of even more. Our grateful thanks goes out to each of you. We couldn't have done it without you!

Reviewers

Ilene R. Abrams
Cobb County School District
Marietta, GA

Dawn Calhoun Bray
Houston County School System
Warner Robins, Georgia

Doreen A. Caswell
Mary G. Montgomery
Semmes, Alabama

Tricia Dugger
St. Lucie County Schools District
Ft. Pierce, FL

Vallie J. Ericson
Sheboygan Area School District
Sheboygan, Wisconsin

Paula Denise Findley
Arkansas River Educational Cooperative
White Hall, Arkansas

Mary M. Fisher
Arlington Public Schools
Arlington, MA

Michelle Harden-Brown
Savannah-Chatham Southwest Middle
Savannah, Georgia

Kevin F. Harrington
Baldwin Middle School
Baldwin, New York

Beverly Canzater Jacobs
Solon City Schools
Solon, Ohio

Alissa Lowman
Hillside Middle School
Northville, Michigan

Elizabeth F. Manning
A.E. Phillips Laboratory School
Ruston, Louisiana

Rhea Mayerchak
Omin Middle School
Boca Raton, Florida

Steve Mellen
Prince George's County Public Schools
Temple Hills, Maryland

Diana L. Mooney
Lake Denoon Middle School
Muskego, Wisconsin

Ellen Nielsen
Clovis Unified School District
Clovis, California

Geraldine Ortego
Lafayette Parish District Office
Lafayette, Louisiana

Deborah Richmond
Ferry Pass Middle School
Pensacola, FL

Addie Rae Tobey
Shaker Heights Middle School
Shaker Heights, Ohio

Jodi Turchin
Silver Lakes Middle School Board of Broward County
North Lauderdale, FL

Bridget Wetton
Alpine Union School District
San Diego, California

Susan Wilson
South Orange/Maplewood School District
South Orange, New Jersey

Robert Wright
Sebastian River Middle
Sebastian River, FL

Peggy Zehnder
Bellingham School District
Bellingham, Washington

Printed in the U.S.A.

ISBN 978-0-547-48503-4

1 2 3 4 5 6 7 8 9 10 0914 19 18 17 16 15 14 13 12 11 10

4500000000 A B C D E F G

Quick Guide

The *Write Source* Voice

For over 30 years, our student books have spoken directly to students. We see ourselves as writers speaking to other writers.

As a result, the *Write Source* voice is always encouraging, like an older classmate who genuinely wants a younger one to succeed. We believe that every student can learn to write and that every writer can improve. Throughout this book, your students will hear a voice that says, "You can do it!"

In the same way, the material in the wraparound text speaks directly to you. After all, we are simply teachers speaking to other teachers, and so we use the same encouraging voice.

Whether you're a seasoned writing teacher or a fresh new face, we are certain that these materials in your hands can make a big difference for your students. We hope you agree!

CONSTRUCTING STRONG PARAGRAPHS

Creating Paragraphs

Every core unit begins with a paragraph assignment in the major form: descriptive, narrative, expository, persuasive, and response to literature. This chapter provides further support, guidelines, models, and practice for students who are still working to perfect paragraph building skills. The chapter also helps students develop a paragraph into a full essay.

Creating Resourceful Writers

This section equips students with specific, traits-based strategies that they will use over and over during the writing process. Each new concept is introduced by a question that most seventh-grade writers have asked at one time or another—followed by an answer to the question and a specific strategy for implementing the answer.

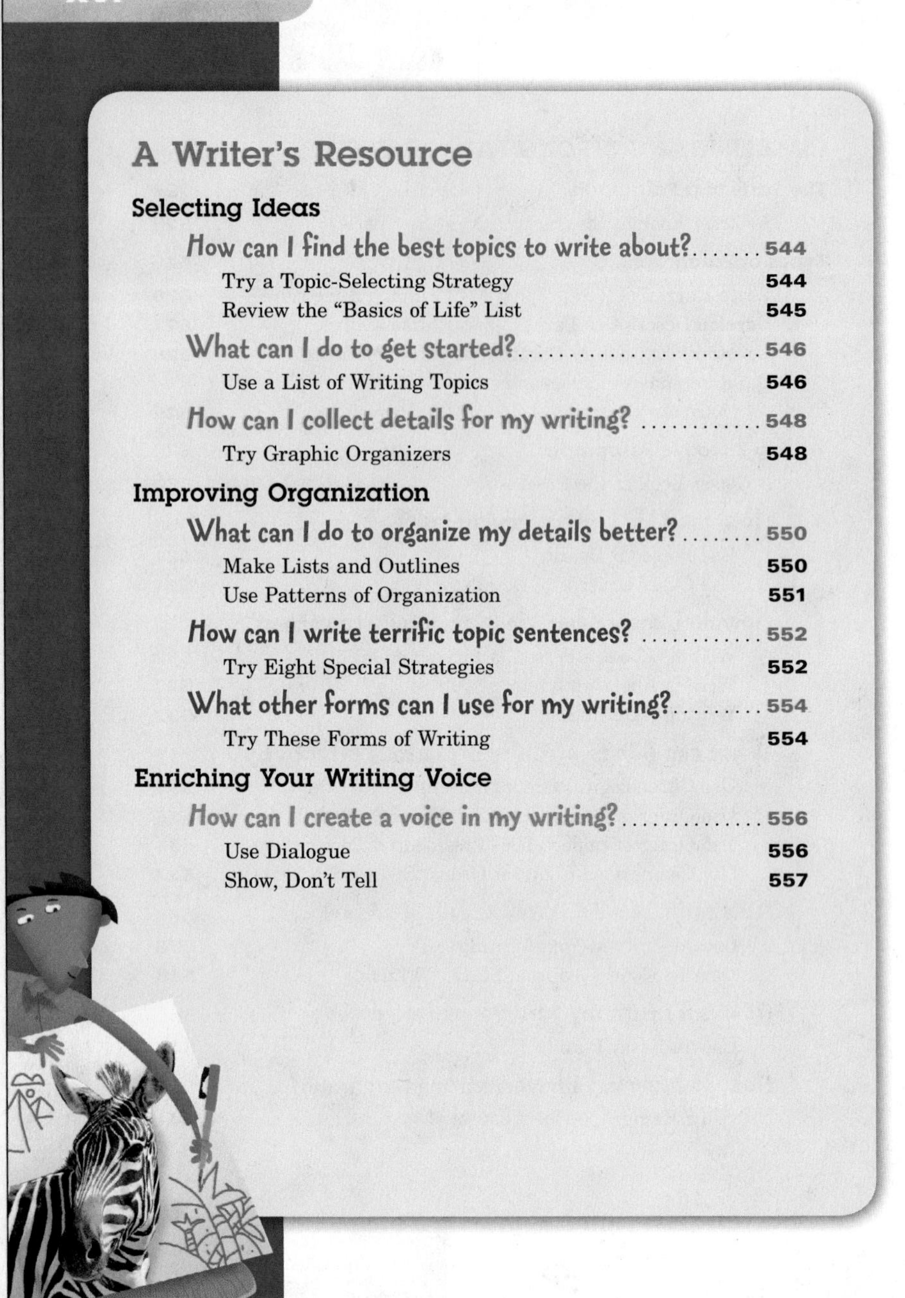
xvi

A Writer's Resource

Using the +1 Trait: Presentation

Sometimes the traits are referred to as the six traits +1 because presentation is so crucial to the success of any form of writing. Each of the core units includes a page that focuses on presentation and publishing. This section also provides support for effectively presenting ideas on the page.

Perfecting Conventions

The "Proofreader's Guide" includes the rules of punctuation, mechanics, usage, sentence creation, and parts of speech. The rules are accompanied by engaging example text and activities to test knowledge.

Also, as the "Test Prep!" box indicates, the major sections end with test-prep pages to help students study for grammar tests.

Cross-references in this Teacher's Edition connect to other resources, such as *SkillsBook* activities.

Proofreader's Guide

Test Prep!

The "Proofreader's Guide" includes test-prep pages to help you study for tests on punctuation, mechanics, usage, sentences, and the parts of speech.

Why Write?

When Walter was a toddler, his mother passed away. His father was too poor to raise him, so he ended up as a foster child. He also suffered from a speech impairment. Walter didn't have much going for him, did he?

Of course, he hated to speak in front of the class in school. Then in fifth grade, Walter was asked to read something he had written for a speech assignment. His own writing contained words that he was able to pronounce. Afterward, he felt much better about himself and continued to write stories and poems. So began the incredible writing life of Walter Dean Myers, the award-winning author of *Hoops* and *Fast Sam, Cool Clyde, and Stuff.*

We now know how important writing has been to Walter Dean Myers. Read on to find out how writing can be important to you.

What's Ahead

- **Reasons to Write**
- **Starting Points for Writing**

KEEP

WRITE

Why Write?

Discuss the story about Walter Dean Myers in the introduction. Talk with students about their experiences with writing. Point out that we all have the need and desire to show how we feel and what we know. Once we learn how to put words together skillfully, we can express just about anything with our writing.

Writing can be a joyful experience. Writers discover things about themselves through the writing process. Playfulness, humor, intelligence, and introspection—all of these can be expressed through writing.

Throughout the year, encourage students to reach beyond their limits to create writing that is individual, meaningful, and thoughtful.

Advanced Learners

Encourage students to research their favorite authors to find out how they got started in their writing careers. Allow time for oral sharing so that the stories may serve to motivate and inspire the entire class.

Reasons to Write

Investigate reasons to write with the following questions:

- Have you written for all of these reasons?
- Which of these reasons to write are the easiest to carry out? The hardest?
- Which of the reasons is the most important to you? The least important?
- In which classes would writing to learn be most helpful to you? Why?

Invite students to suggest additional reasons to write:

- Promote ideas, programs, or products in the arena of business.
- Publish information as a record of facts, statistics, and so on for future reference.

Reasons to Write

Why should you write? Actually, there are many good reasons to write, and four of the most important are listed below. If you write for one or more of these reasons, you can expect good things to happen.

Writing for All the Right Reasons

You can write about your experiences by keeping a personal journal. Just set aside 10 or 15 minutes every day and write about the people, places, and events in your life. (See pages 431–434 for more information.)

Writing in a personal journal helps you make sense of everything that is happening in your world. It also helps you gain confidence in your ability to write.

To Learn

Writing about new or complex ideas presented in your classes will help you to understand the ideas better. It's best to do this kind of writing in a special notebook or learning log. Think of the writing that you do in a learning log as an ongoing conversation about the subjects you are studying. (See pages 435–438 for more information.)

To Show Your Understanding

You are assigned paragraphs, essays, and reports to see how well you are learning. You are also asked to answer prompts on assessment tests. These types of assignments require that you (1) understand your subjects, and (2) use your best writing skills.

To Share Ideas

Writing narratives, stories, and poems allows you to use your imagination and creativity. These forms of writing are meant to be shared.

Write to learn. Write nonstop for 5 to 8 minutes about one of your classes. Discuss any new concepts you may be covering in that class. Decide how this new information relates to what you already know. Try to sort out any ideas that confuse you.

English Language Learners

Limited language skills may make the **Write to learn** activity challenging. De-emphasize the time limit and encourage students to write freely for as long as they can.

Starting Points for Writing

Every day you do things that you feel good about. You hear things that make you angry. You become curious about how something works. These common, everyday thoughts and happenings make excellent starting points for writing. The list of prompts below will also help you get started on your own writing.

Writing Prompts

Best and Worst, First and Last
My worst day
My craziest experience
The hardest thing I've ever done
My best moment
My greatest creation

Inside Education
My best class ever
Dear Blackboard,
A good assembly
I memorized every word.
A classmate I admire

Where? What? Why?
Where do I draw the line?
What should everyone know?
What should I do next?
Why are people always in such a rush?

It could only happen to me!
It sounds crazy, but . . .
Putting my foot in my mouth
Guess what I just heard?
Creepy, crawly things
Whatever happened to my . . .
I got so mad when . . .

As My World Turns
My secret snacks
A day in the life of my pet
When I played the rebel
When I'm in charge
Last time I went shopping, I . . .

Find a topic. On a piece of paper titled "Writing Prompts," list the five headings shown above—"Best and Worst, First and Last," "Inside Education," and so on. Leave space between each heading, and write one or two new prompts under each. Add others to the list throughout the school year. Use these prompts as starting points for your personal writing.

English Language Learners

The sample prompts contain some idioms. Pair English language learners with "brainstorming partners"—cooperative, language-proficient students—who will help them with the idioms and brainstorm appropriate prompts.

- putting my foot in my mouth (saying something at the wrong time; saying something embarrassing)
- draw the line (stop something from continuing; make one's position clear)
- played the rebel (did not conform to the expected)
- when I'm in charge (if I made all the decisions; used to introduce a wished-for situation)

Starting Points for Writing

Have students list the writing prompt headings and sample topics in a spiral notebook and add more of them throughout the year. The notebook can also be used for other writing tasks, such as prewriting assignments, first drafts, and rubric assessments. This will help students keep track of these important items. When students want to review them at a later date, they'll know exactly where to go.

The Writing Process Overview

Common Core Standards Focus

Writing 5: With some guidance and support from peers and adults, develop and strengthen writing as needed by planning, revising, editing, rewriting, or trying a new approach, focusing on how well purpose and audience have been addressed.

Writing 6: Use technology, including the Internet, to produce and publish writing and link to and cite sources as well as to interact and collaborate with others, including linking to and citing sources.

Language 1: Demonstrate command of the conventions of standard English grammar and usage when writing or speaking.

Language 2: Demonstrate command of the conventions of standard English capitalization, punctuation, and spelling when writing.

Writing Process

- **Prewriting** Explore topics, gather details, and plan the organization.
- **Writing** Using the prewriting plan, complete a first draft.
- **Revising** Based on the six traits of effective writing, revise drafts by adding, deleting, and rearranging text.
- **Editing** Check revised writing for correctness, prepare a final copy, and proofread the final copy for errors.
- **Publishing** Share work with others.

Focus on the Traits

- **Ideas** Establishing a clear focus and collecting specific details
- **Organization** Forming a clear beginning, middle, and ending
- **Voice** Developing a special way of saying things that fits the audience
- **Word Choice** Using specific nouns and verbs to deliver a clear message
- **Sentence Fluency** Writing sentences that create a smooth flow
- **Conventions** Checking for errors in punctuation, capitalization, spelling, and grammar

Technology Connections

Write Source Online
www.hmheducation.com/writesource

- ***Net-text***
- ***Bookshelf***
- ***GrammarSnap***
- ***Portfolio***
- ***Essay Scoring***
- ***Writing Network features***
- ***File Cabinet***

 ***Interactive Whiteboard Lessons***

Suggested Writing Process Unit (Four Weeks)

Week	Day	Writing and Skills Instruction	Student Edition: Writing Process Unit	Student Edition: Resource Units*	SkillsBook	Daily Language Workouts
Week 1	1–2	**Getting Started** (activities, TE pages 794–797)	1–3	652–687 and Test Prep, 688–689	Assessment —Using the Right Word, 66	4–5, 78
Week 1	3–5	**Understanding the Writing Process**	5–10	579–615 (+), and Test Prep, 616–617	Assessment Punctuation, 27–28, 47–48	
Week 2	6–7	**One Writer's Process,** (Goals)	11–12			6–7, 79
Week 2		(Prewriting, Writing)	13–15			
Week 2	8–9	(Revising, Editing, Publishing)	16–26	618–627 and Test Prep, 628–629, 630–641	Assessment —Mechanics, 57–58	
Week 2	10	(Assessing) (Reflecting)	27–28			
Week 3	11	**Keeping Journals and Learning Logs**	431–438			8–9, 80
Week 3	12	Writing-to-Learn Activities	439–440			
Week 3	13–15	**Understanding the Traits of Writing** (Ideas)	33–37			
Week 3		(Organization, Voice)	38–40			
Week 3		(Word Choice, Sentence Fluency, Conventions)	41–44	690–695 and Test Prep, 696–697, 698–701	Assessment —Grammar 135–136	
Week 4	16	**Using a Rubric**	45–51			10–11, 81
Week 4		Assessing	52–56	642–651 and Spelling 643–644		
Week 4	17	**Peer Responding**	29–32			
Week 4	18	**Listening and Speaking**	417–422			
Week 4	19	**Publishing Your Writing**	57–64			
Week 4	20	**Creating a Portfolio**	65–69	702–748 and Test Prep, 740–741		

* These units are also located in the back of the Teacher's Edition. Resource Units include "Basic Grammar and Writing," "A Writer's Resource," and "Proofreader's Guide."

(+) This activity is located in a different section of the *Write Source Student Edition.* If students have already completed this activity, you may wish to review it at this time.

Teacher's Notes for the Writing Process

This overview for the writing process includes some specific teaching suggestions for the unit.

Writing Focus

Understanding the Writing Process (pages 5–10)

As computer processors become faster, students grow increasingly impatient with delays. Not surprisingly, they become impatient with their writing. Yet, they must learn patience if their writing is to improve. This chapter focuses on a methodical approach to writing to help students learn how to express themselves better.

Understanding the Traits of Writing (pages 33–44)

Emphasize the traits of good writing. Students need a standard to combat numerous examples of bad writing available in some newspapers, magazines, and books. Students who give careful attention to these traits will improve their writing.

Academic Vocabulary

Read aloud the academic terms, as well as the descriptions and questions. Model for students how to read one question and answer it. Have partners monitor their understanding and seek clarification of the terms by working through the meanings and questions together.

Minilessons

School Zone, Drive Slowly! — Understanding the Writing Process

- In 15 seconds, **CHOOSE** a topic to write about. Then in two minutes, **WRITE** a five-sentence paragraph on your topic. **DISCUSS** your paragraph with a classmate. What was the biggest problem during this exercise?

Taking It to Heart — One Writer's Process

- **READ** Kaylie's first draft about judo (pages 14–15 in your textbook). **REVIEW** her reflections and revision (pages 16–17). **APPLY** her reflections to one of your own essays. **MAKE** notes about your essay as she did. Then **REVISE** your essay accordingly.

Response — Peer Responding

- **READ** about peer responding on SE pages 30–31. **LIST** five things you would want a responder to tell you about your writing.

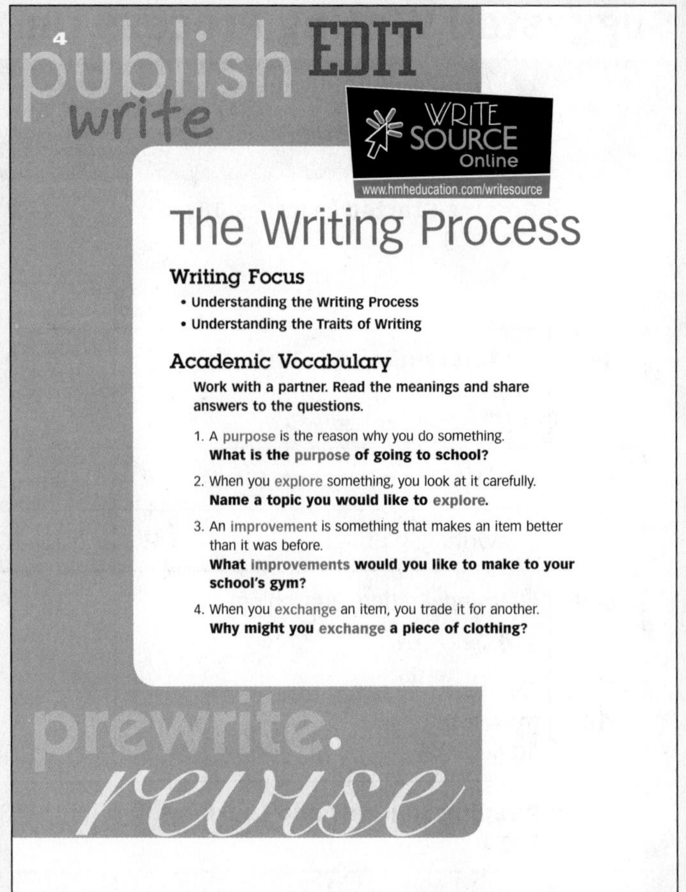

4

publish EDIT write

WRITE SOURCE Online

www.hmheducation.com/writesource

The Writing Process

Writing Focus

- Understanding the Writing Process
- Understanding the Traits of Writing

Academic Vocabulary

Work with a partner. Read the meanings and share answers to the questions.

1. A purpose is the reason why you do something. **What is the purpose of going to school?**
2. When you explore something, you look at it carefully. **Name a topic you would like to explore.**
3. An improvement is something that makes an item better than it was before. **What improvements would you like to make to your school's gym?**
4. When you exchange an item, you trade it for another. **Why might you exchange a piece of clothing?**

prewrite. revise

Goals — Publishing Your Writing

- **WRITE** one long-term writing goal. (I plan to be a screenplay writer for TV.) **WRITE** two short-term writing goals. (All the paragraphs in my essay will be tied to any topic.)

5

Understanding the Writing Process

Take your time. These three words may be the best advice you will ever receive when it comes to writing. No one can write well by trying to do everything at once. As author Lloyd Alexander says, "Unless you're a genius, I don't see how you could get everything right the first time."

To do your best work, you need to take your writing through a series of steps—the writing process. The steps are *prewriting, writing the first draft, revising, editing,* and *publishing.* As you complete each step, your writing will get closer and closer to a finished product that will please both you and your readers.

This chapter will help you learn more about the writing process and build some valuable writing habits.

What's Ahead

- **Building Good Writing Habits**
- **The Writing Process**
- **The Process in Action**
- **Getting the Big Picture**

Understanding the Writing Process

Objectives

- build good writing habits
- understand the five steps of the writing process

Share these insights into the writing process with students.

- Writing is a process that takes time and effort.
- Most successful writers don't get it right the first time. They rewrite, move sections around, and delete passages that don't work.
- J. K. Rowling, author of the popular Harry Potter series, decided to use a chapter that she originally wrote for the first book in the series, *The Sorcerer's Stone,* as the first chapter in a later book.

Building Good Writing Habits

Lead a discussion about the forms of writing that students most enjoy—stories, essays, letters, poems, or e-mail messages. Ask:

- What kind of writing do you do most often?
- Do you think that "practice makes perfect" when it comes to writing?

* Additional information about forms of writing is on SE pages 554–555.

As students begin their nonstop writing, or **freewriting** (*see below*), emphasize that they shouldn't be overly concerned about spelling or style. They should just get their ideas down on paper.

Building Good Writing Habits

Someone once said that writing is too much fun to be left to professional writers. This is very true, especially when you make writing an important part of your life. If you're ready to get into writing, follow the tips below.

Write as well as you can each time you write.

You will feel good about your writing if it is the result of your best efforts.

> Quality is its own reward.
> —William Zinsser

Try different forms of writing.

Stories, letters, e-mail messages, essays, poems—they all have something to teach you about writing.

> I wrote my first poems and short stories perched on a fire escape high above the backyards.
> —Sharon Bell Mathis

Become a student of writing.

Learn as much as you can about writing, including the traits of effective writing. (See pages 33–44.)

> Good writing is about making good choices when it comes to picking the tools you plan to work with.
> —Stephen King

Write about a quotation. Write nonstop for 5 to 8 minutes about one of the quotations above. Consider what it means to you.

Teaching Tip: Freewriting

One way to help students feel more comfortable with writing is by providing them with opportunities to freewrite. When students freewrite, they put their ideas down on paper without worrying too much about the rules of writing. Punctuation, spelling, and other mechanics are secondary to the ideas students are trying to express. Freewriting is a helpful tool to use whenever you want your students to explore a topic in preparation for a longer piece of writing. It is also a good tool for introducing students with limited English to the writing process, since they do not need to pay as much attention to the conventions.

Struggling Learners

To further explore the various writing forms, have students retrieve reading materials such as textbooks, library books, newsletters, magazines, assignment logs, and memos from their desks and backpacks.

* In pairs, students then can classify the various texts using the definition chart on SE pages 554–555.

The Writing Process

The best writers use the writing process to help them complete their work. The steps in the process are described below.

PROCESS

The Steps in the Writing Process

Prewriting

At the start of an assignment, a writer explores possible topics before selecting one to write about. Then the writer collects details about the topic and plans how to use them.

Writing

During this step, the writer completes the first draft using the prewriting plan as a guide. This draft is a writer's *first* chance to get everything down on paper.

Revising

After reviewing the first draft, the writer changes any ideas that are not clear or complete. A wise writer will ask at least one other person to review the draft, as well.

Editing

A writer then checks his or her revised writing for correctness before preparing a neat final copy. The writer proofreads the final copy for errors before sharing or publishing it.

Publishing

This is the final step in the writing process. Publishing is to a writer what an exhibit is to an artist—an opportunity to share his or her work with others.

Analyze your process. On your own paper, explain the parts of the writing process that you find are (1) the easiest, and (2) the hardest to complete. Share your analysis with your classmates.

The Writing Process

The Steps in the Writing Process

After students share the steps that are the easiest and the hardest for them, put their results in a chart on the board. Discuss the results with the class and see if any patterns emerge. For example, if you find that most students say editing is the hardest part, ask the students why this step seems most difficult. Their responses will help you to know where extra instruction is needed for student writing projects.

English Language Learners

To further explore the various writing forms, have students retrieve reading materials such as textbooks, library books, newsletters, magazines, assignment logs, and memos from their desks and backpacks.

* In pairs, students then can classify the various texts using the definition chart on SE pages 554–555.

The Process in Action

Prewriting **Selecting a Topic**

Discuss various ways to choose a writing topic. You might suggest the following:

- Browse in the school library.
- Do an Internet search.
- Look through classroom books and materials.
- Talk with teachers, classmates, or family members.

Prewriting **Gathering Details**

Gathering details is a key part of the prewriting process. Since students' writing will be based on specific information, they must make sure they spend enough time learning about their topic before they begin writing. The details they include in their writing will provide the support to show that the topic is truly interesting and worth writing about.

Writing **Developing the First Draft**

Emphasize that the first draft serves as a starting point. Some students tend to be perfectionists. It's important to stress that writing is a gradual process and that students will refine their writing each step of the way.

The Process in Action

This page and the next show you the writing process in action. Use this information as a general guide for each of your writing assignments. The graphic below reminds you that, during an assignment, you can move back and forth between the steps in the writing process.

Prewriting Selecting a Topic

- Search for possible writing topics that meet the requirements of the assignment.
- Select a specific topic that really interests you.

Gathering Details

- Learn as much as you can about the topic before you start writing.
- Consider what to emphasize in the writing—either an interesting part of the topic or your personal feelings about it. This will be the focus, or thesis, of your writing.
- Decide which details you want to include in your writing. Also decide on the best way to organize the details.

Writing Developing the First Draft

- When you write your first draft, concentrate on getting your ideas on paper. Don't try to produce a perfect piece of writing.
- Use the details you collected and your prewriting plan as general guides, but feel free to add new ideas as you go along.
- Make sure your writing has a beginning, a middle, and an ending.

Write on every other line and on only one side of the paper when using pen and paper. Double-space on a computer. This will give you room for revising, the next step in the process.

English Language Learners

Reassure them that each step in the writing process will be explained in the pages that follow. Then help them grasp the main ideas related to each step by calling on classmate volunteers to paraphrase each step.

Struggling Learners

Since generating topics can be a source of frustration, give students a head start by having them write one topic on a slip of paper (for example, pets, wishes, jobs, sports, injuries, vacations, embarrassing moments). Collect the topics, read each one aloud, and give students one minute to jot down any ideas or experiences that come to mind.

Revising Improving Your Writing

- Review your first draft after setting it aside for a while.
- Use these questions as a general revising guide:
  - **Do I sound interested in my topic?**
  - **Do I say enough about my topic?**
  - **Are the ideas clear and in the right order?**
  - **Does the beginning draw the reader into the writing?**
  - **Does the closing remind the reader about the importance of the topic?**
  - **Are the nouns specific and the verbs strong?**
  - **Are the modifiers (adjectives and adverbs) clear and well chosen?**
  - **Are the sentences varied? Do they read smoothly?**
- Try to have at least one other person review your work.
- Make as many changes as necessary to improve your first draft.

Editing Checking for Conventions

- Edit for correctness by checking for punctuation, capitalization, spelling, and grammar errors. Also ask someone else to check your writing for errors.
- Then prepare a neat final copy of your writing. Proofread this copy for errors before sharing it.

Publishing Sharing Your Writing

- Share your finished work with your classmates, teacher, friends, and family members.
- Consider including the writing in your portfolio.
- Think about submitting your writing to your school newspaper or some other publication. (See pages 57–64 for ideas.)

Consider the process. **Each step in the writing process is important. However, some experts say that prewriting and revising are especially important steps. In a brief paragraph, explain the importance of either prewriting or revising.**

Advanced Learners

Have students brainstorm and make a classroom chart of sentence starters they could use when helping one another revise their writing, such as

- I like the way you . . .
- Can you explain how . . .
- I can picture in my mind . . .
- Right here you could . . .

Revising Improving Your Writing

Remind students that authors usually revise their work several times before it is published. Revising is the time to make large-scale changes such as adding sentences, deleting material, or moving text. The goal is to make writing clear and appealing for readers.

Editing Checking for Conventions

Encourage students to use the dictionary to check their spelling. The Proofreader's Guide, SE pages 579–749, offers useful information on punctuation, mechanics, spelling, and grammar. Suggest that students use the Editing and Proofreading Marks on the inside back cover of the student edition. For a copy master, see TE page 788.

Publishing Sharing Your Writing

Throughout the year, encourage all students to share their writing. Invite interested students to read their work aloud. For those students less eager to read aloud, create a reading box into which students can place their writing. Provide quiet time during the week when students can read each other's writing.

Checking Kaylie's Editing for Conventions

Before writing a final copy, Kaylie checked her essay for conventions—spelling, punctuation, capitalization, and grammar. (See inside the back cover of this book for a list of the common editing and proofreading marks.)

Corrections are made to spelling.

Grammar errors are corrected.

Punctuation errors are fixed.

Teenagers have different ways to stay in shape. Some teens like to skate board or bike, while others like to play basketball or soccer. Still others enjoy working out or jogging. Then there are those who stay fit by practicing judo. Judo is a fun sport, a ~~fitnes~~ fitness program, and a way of life all rolled into one. Students involved in judo keep their bodies in top shape.

Most people have ~~herd~~ heard of judo, but they don't know much about it. Judo became a sport in the early 1880s. At that time, a man named professor Jigoro Kano created the sport. Professor Kano based judo on an ~~anscient~~ ancient combative activity called jujitsu. He called his new sport the "gentle way" because it focused on fitness, self-discipline, and character development. Neither punching nor kicking is used in judo.

Judo equipment is very simple. Each student ~~wares~~ wears a white, long-sleeved uniform called a "gi." This uniform is tied with a belt that shows the student's rank. Junior students begin with a white belt and . . .

Review Kaylie's editing for conventions in the paragraphs above. Did you find some of the same errors when you edited her earlier draft on page 21?

Checking Kaylie's Editing for Conventions

Using the inside back cover of the student edition, show students how to apply proofreader's marks to their writing. Make up a writing sample containing a variety of errors related to punctuation, spelling, and grammar. Hand out the writing sample and go over it with your students. Use an overhead projector to demonstrate how to use proofreader's marks.

Answers

Answers will vary.

Advanced Learners

Explain that words that sound the same but have different spellings and meanings are called *homophones*. Have students locate the homophones in Kaylie's editing (*heard/herd* and *wears/wares*), and then brainstorm and list other examples, such as *size/sighs, not/knot,* or *write/right.* Discuss how homophones can cause confusion.

Publishing Sharing Your Writing

Make (or have students make) a classroom poster listing the Tips for Handwritten Copies (using handwriting) and Tips for Computer Copies (using a large font on the computer). Mount exemplary student models on each poster. Encourage students to refer to the appropriate poster whenever they prepare to publish their writing.

Publishing Sharing Your Writing

Kaylie used the tips below to help her write the final copy of her story. (See pages 25–26.)

Focus on Presentation

Tips for Handwritten Copies

- Use blue or black ink and write neatly.
- Write your name following your teacher's instructions.
- Skip a line and center your title; skip another line and start your writing.
- Indent every paragraph and leave a one-inch margin on all four sides.
- Write your last name and page number on every page after page 1.

Kaylie Brandt

The Gentle Way

Teenagers have different ways to stay in shape. Some teens like to skateboard or bike, while others like to play basketball or soccer. Still others enjoy working out or jogging. Then there are those who stay fit by practicing judo. Judo is a fun sport, a fitness program, and a way of life all rolled into one. Students involved in judo keep their bodies in top shape.

Most people have heard of judo, but they don't know much about it. Judo became a sport in the early 1880s. At that time, a man named Professor Jigoro Kano created the sport. Professor Kano based judo on an ancient combative activity called jujitsu. He called his new sport the "gentle way" because it focused on fitness, self-discipline, and character development. Neither punching nor kicking is used in judo.

Judo equipment is very simple. Each student wears a white, long-sleeved uniform called a "gi." This uniform is tied with a belt that shows the student's rank. Junior students begin with a white belt and then move up to yellow, orange, and green belts. After that, a student moves up to blue, brown, and black belts. These belts help partners know each other's level so they can train and compete safely. Training is done on mats, often in a special school called a "dojo."

The three basic judo techniques include throws, grapples, and break-falls. Throws are ways to take an opponent down. They are made with specific hand, foot, and hip movements.

Brandt 2

Brandt 2

Kaylie Brandt

The Gentle Way

Teenagers have different ways to stay in shape. Some teens like to skateboard or bike, while others like to play basketball or soccer. Still others enjoy working out or jogging. Then there are those who stay fit by practicing judo. Judo is a fun sport, a fitness program, and a way of life all rolled into one. Students involved in judo keep their bodies in top shape.

Most people have heard of judo, but they don't know much about it. Judo became a sport in the early 1880s. At that time, a man named Professor Jigoro Kano created the sport. Professor Kano based judo on an ancient combative activity called jujitsu. He called his new sport the "gentle way" because it focused on fitness, self-discipline, and character development. Neither punching nor kicking is used in judo.

Judo equipment is very simple. Each student wears a white, long-sleeved uniform called a "gi." This uniform is tied with a belt that shows the student's rank. Junior students begin with a white belt and then move up to yellow, orange, and green belts. After that, a student moves up to blue, brown, and black belts. These belts help partners know each other's level so they can train and compete safely. Training is done on mats, often in a special school called a "dojo."

Tips for Computer Copies

- Use an easy-to-read font and a 12-point type size.
- Double-space and leave a one-inch margin around each page.

Kaylie's Final Copy

Kaylie was proud of her final essay. It introduced the reader to her favorite physical activity.

Kaylie Brandt

The Gentle Way

Teenagers have different ways to stay in shape. Some teens like to skateboard or bike, while others like to play basketball or soccer. Still others enjoy working out or jogging. Then there are those who stay fit by practicing judo. Judo is a fun sport, a fitness program, and a way of life all rolled into one. Students involved in judo keep their bodies in top shape.

Most people have heard of judo, but they don't know much about it. Judo became a sport in the early 1880s. At that time, a man named Professor Jigoro Kano created the sport. Professor Kano based judo on an ancient combative activity called jujitsu. He called his new sport the "gentle way" because it focused on fitness, self-discipline, and character development. Neither punching nor kicking is used in judo.

Judo equipment is very simple. Each student wears a white, long-sleeved uniform called a "gi." This uniform is tied with a belt that shows the student's rank. Junior students begin with a white belt and then move up to yellow, orange, and green belts. After that, a student moves up to blue, brown, and black belts. These belts help partners know each other's level so they can train and compete safely. Training is done on mats, often in a special school called a "dojo."

Kaylie's Final Copy

Tell students to read Kaylie's final essay to themselves. Then have a volunteer read it aloud to the class. Tell students to turn to SE page 12. Ask:

- Do you think Kaylie did a good job of meeting the goals of expository writing? Why?
- For which goals did the writing seem especially strong?

Discuss Kaylie's final essay with each of the writing goals in mind. Consider dividing the class into six small groups. Have each group focus on one of the trait goals. Afterward, ask a volunteer from each group to share how successfully Kaylie's final essay addressed that group's trait goal.

Kaylie's Final Copy (cont'd)

Invite students to share one thing they learned about the writing process by observing how Kaylie developed her essay from start to finish. Then have them share one thing they learned about judo by reading Kaylie's essay. What part(s) of the writing process helped Kaylie convey that information?

26

Brandt 2

The three basic judo techniques include throws, grapples, and break-falls. Throws are ways to take an opponent down. They are made with specific hand, foot, and hip movements. Grapples allow a student to control an opponent. A main objective in a judo match is to hold an opponent on his back, much like in wrestling. Break-fall techniques help students avoid injury when they are being thrown to the mat. These techniques are practiced over and over again during training sessions.

Judo offers a wide range of physical benefits. Generally, it helps students lose weight if they are heavy and gain solid muscle if they are really skinny. Judo also makes students stronger because most of the training involves reacting to physical resistance. Specifically, judo helps develop flexibility. During training, students are constantly bending and twisting. In addition, it improves students' reflexes because they learn how to act as quickly as possible to their opponents' moves.

As judo students train, they become more self-confident and disciplined. In this way, judo promotes physical and mental fitness. The overall goal is to master the basic techniques, not to show up opponents in competitions. Students of all ability levels can feel safe because judo is so structured. The instructors are highly trained and approach judo with respect and confidence. As students advance with their training, they often come to see judo as an honorable and gentle way of life.

Assessing the Final Copy

Kaylie's teacher used a rubric like the one that appears on pages 194–195 to assess Kaylie's final copy. A 6 is the very best score that a writer can receive for each trait. The teacher also included comments under each trait.

4 Ideas

Your essay introduces an activity you love. I still want to know more about the physical part of judo.

5 Organization

Your writing has a clear beginning, middle, and ending.

4 Voice

I wanted to hear more about your experiences as a student of judo.

4 Word Choice

You explain new terms, but your nouns and verbs could be more specific.

4 Sentence Fluency

Your sentences are easy to follow. You could have varied some of your sentence beginnings.

6 Conventions

Your essay is free of careless errors.

Review the assessment. Do you agree with the comments and scores made by Kaylie's teacher? Why or why not? Explain your feelings in a brief paragraph.

Assessing the Final Copy

Compare the scores given by Kaylie's teacher with the evaluation your class gave the essay based on the goals on SE page 12. Then tell students to refer back to Kaylie's first draft on SE pages 14–15. Ask them to think about the scores she would have received if she had handed in her first draft. Discuss how much her writing changed and improved from the first draft to the final copy.

Review the assessment.

Answers will vary.

Reflecting on Your Writing

As students read Kaylie's reflection sheet, point out her honesty. Tell students that it is important for them to try to look clearly at their writing. Encourage students to keep their reflections in their notebooks and review them periodically to assess their accomplishments and areas in which they still need to improve.

Reflecting on Your Writing

After the whole process was finished, Kaylie filled out a reflection sheet. This helped her think about the assignment and plan for future essays.

Kaylie Brandt

My Expository Essay

1. *The best part of my essay is . . .*
   that I have introduced my classmates to a new physical activity. They now know some basic information about judo.
2. *The part that still needs work is . . .*
   my voice. I should've sounded more interested in my topic. Still, I came a long way!
3. *The main thing I learned about writing an expository essay is . . .*
   it must contain information that truly interests readers.
4. *In one of my next essays, I would like to . . .*
   write more about actual judo competitions.
5. *Here is one question I still have about writing an expository essay:*
   How important is it to add my personal thoughts and feelings?

Struggling Learners

Discuss the term *reflection* as it is used here, helping students come up with synonyms such as *thinking back, studying,* or *analyzing.* Compare this process to looking at one's reflection in a mirror, a process that can affirm (My hair looks great today) or lead to change (This shirt doesn't match these pants).

Peer Responding

In 1609, Galileo started experimenting with lenses and tubes. He was trying to create an instrument that would magnify things that were very small or very far away. He and others eventually devised microscopes and telescopes. With these two tools, people suddenly could see their world in a whole new way.

Sometimes a classmate can act as a microscope or telescope for your writing. Through another person's eyes, you can see things in your writing that you never knew were there. A peer response can point out not only what could be improved but also what is already working well!

What's Ahead

- Peer-Responding Guidelines
- Sample Peer Response Sheet

Peer Responding

Objectives

- to understand the guidelines for peer responding
- to practice responding to a peer's writing

Stress to students that peer responding is an important part of the writing process. If students listen closely during a peer-responding session, both the writer and the responders can gain valuable information. The writer, of course, gathers helpful suggestions about his or her piece of writing. The responders gather tips that they can apply to their own writing. It's a "win-win" situation for everyone.

Peer-Responding Guidelines

Try to keep peer-responding groups small—three or four students per group.

The Author's Role

If some students are intimidated by the idea of sharing their writing with their peers, remind them that a peer-responding session is designed to be helpful. The purpose of the session is to gain insights into the development of a piece of writing. Help students to see peer-responding sessions as another useful tool to use when writing.

Peer-Responding Guidelines

At first, you may work with only one person: a teacher or a classmate. This person does not expect your writing to be perfect. He or she knows that you are still working on your paper.

Later, you may have a chance to work with a small group. After a while, you will find that responding to someone's writing is much easier than you thought it would be.

The Author's Role

Select a piece of writing to share and make a copy of it for each group member.

Guidelines	Sample Responses
• **Introduce your piece of writing.** But don't say too much about it.	*This paper is about Wilma Mankiller. I got interested in her from a TV show.*
• **Read your writing out loud.** Or ask group members to read it silently.	*Ms. Mankiller was the first woman chief of the Cherokee Nation. . . .*
• **Invite your group members to comment.** Listen carefully.	*Okay, everyone, now it's your turn to talk. I'm listening.*
• **Take notes** so you will remember what was said.	*Did I make it clear that she had a muscle disease?*
• **Answer all questions** the best you can. Be open and polite.	*Yes, she did have a kidney transplant.*
• **Ask for help from your group** with any writing problems you are having.	*What do you think of my title? Does the ending seem right?*

English Language Learners

Giving and receiving criticism regarding writing skills will be difficult for these students. One-on-one conferences with the teacher can provide a supportive environment for evaluating a written piece. If you assign group work, be sure to pair students with cooperative partners or put them in very supportive small groups.

The Responder's Role

Responders should show an interest in the author's writing and treat it with respect.

Guidelines	Sample Responses
Listen carefully. Take notes so that you can make helpful comments.	*Notes: Why did Ms. Mankiller want to be chief?*
Look for what is good about the writing. Give some positive comments. Be sincere.	*Your explanation of her childhood is very clear.*
Tell what you think could be improved. Be polite when you make suggestions.	*Could you add more details about her actual time as chief?*
Ask questions if you need more information.	*What does she do now?*
Make other suggestions. Help the writer improve her or his work.	*Could you include a picture of Ms. Mankiller?*

Helpful Comments

In all your comments, be as specific as you can be. This will help the writer make the best changes.

Instead of . . .	Try something like . . .
Your writing is boring.	Most of your sentences begin with "There" or "It."
I can't understand one part.	The part about her schooling isn't very clear.
What about the final quotation?	Perhaps you should check the wording of the final quotation.

Try It In a class discussion, share your experiences with peer responding. When have you done it? Was it helpful? What would you do differently next time?

Advanced Learners

Invite students who enjoy performing to prepare, practice, and act out a peer-responding session for the class. The skits could depict effective author/responder roles.

The Responder's Role

Emphasize that responders should begin their comments with something positive. Remind them to give concrete suggestions rather than simply say that they like or don't like a certain part of the writing.

Helpful Comments

Sometimes it helps to narrow the focus of a peer-responding session. Tell students to focus only on one or two goals during a session. For example, they can focus on ideas and organization for one session and voice for another session.

Answers

Answers will vary.

Sample Peer Response Sheet

Peer response sheets are helpful because students can keep them and refer to them as they begin to revise. Point out that the sample peer response sheet contains specific comments. For example, the responder suggests that the writer add to her ending, *and* she makes a specific suggestion about what might be added.

Many students are reluctant to criticize their classmates' work. Consider the following strategies the first time you work with peer response sheets:

- Model the process with the students. Then let them reciprocate by modeling a peer response with something that you have written.
- Allow each student to have peer response sessions with at least three classmates. Encourage students to give detailed feedback while being tactful. Always have them begin by saying what they like about the writing.

Sample Peer Response Sheet

Your teacher may want you and a classmate to react to each other's first draft by completing a response sheet like the one below. (Sample comments are included.)

Peer Response Sheet

Writer: *Keisha* Responder: *Angie*

Title: *"My Own Room"*

What I liked about your writing:

** In the opening, background details about sharing a room with your sister are great.*

** Your writing voice shows that you love your new room.*

** The comparison you make in the first paragraph helps me picture your closet.*

Changes I would suggest:

** In the second paragraph, check your description of what is on your walls. Are the details organized by location?*

** You could add to the ending. Could you share a final feeling about your room?*

Practice. Exchange a recent first draft with a classmate.

1. Read the draft once to get an overall feel for it.
2. Then read the paper again, paying careful attention to its strengths and weaknesses.
3. Fill out a response sheet like the one above.

Understanding the Traits of Writing

When a dedicated hairstylist gives a haircut, she has two people to please—the customer, so the person comes back for more haircuts, and herself, because this is her chosen profession.

This holds true for professional writers, too. First, they want to please the readers so that they become loyal fans; and second, they want to please themselves because their writing reflects directly on their own thoughts and feelings.

Good writers know that they must pay careful attention to the *ideas, organization, voice, word choice, sentence fluency,* and *conventions* in everything they write. You should do the same in each of your writing assignments. This chapter discusses the six traits found in all good writing. Once you understand them, you will know how to make your own essays and stories the best they can be.

What's Ahead

- **Introducing the Traits**
- **Understanding Ideas**
- **Understanding Organization**
- **Understanding Voice**
- **Understanding Word Choice**
- **Understanding Sentence Fluency**
- **Understanding Conventions**

Understanding the Traits of Writing

Objectives

- understand each of the six traits of effective writing
- apply the concepts of the traits to writing

The more you discuss the traits, the better your students will understand them. Mention individual traits in some way every day, both when you're discussing literature and when your students are working on writing assignments.

Introducing the Traits

During the school year, create trait centers around the classroom. At each of the six centers, place a box filled with examples of good writing in which you have highlighted that particular trait. Place relevant resources at the centers. For example, put a dictionary and a thesaurus at the Word Choice center, and place a copy of the SE text tabbed at the Proofreader's Guide. Encourage students to use the index to find answers to their convention questions at the Conventions center. At the Ideas center, provide newspapers, magazines, postcards, and other interesting printed materials. Encourage students to visit the trait centers often.

* The six-point rubric that appears in each of the core units on SE pages 130–131, 194–195, 256–257, and 318–319 is based on these traits. For reproducible rubrics in six-, five-, and four-point scales, see TE pages 750–761.

Introducing the Traits

Writing is made up of six main traits, or qualities. Each of these traits is important for every essay, story, or report that you develop. This page explains how the traits work in the best writing.

Ideas

Effective writing has a clear message, purpose, or focus. The writing contains plenty of specific ideas and details.

Organization

Strong writing has a clear beginning, middle, and ending. The overall writing is well organized and easy to follow.

Voice

The best writing reveals the writer's voice—or special way of saying things. The voice also fits the audience and purpose.

Word Choice

Good writing contains strong words, including specific nouns and verbs. Strong words help deliver a clear message.

Sentence Fluency

Effective writing flows smoothly from one sentence to the next. Sentences vary in length and begin in a variety of ways.

Conventions

Good writing is carefully edited to make sure it is easy to understand. The writing follows the rules for punctuation, grammar, and spelling.

One additional trait to consider is the presentation of your writing. Good writing looks neat and follows guidelines for margins, spacing, indenting, and so on. The way the writing looks on the page attracts the reader and makes him or her *want* to read on.

Struggling Learners

To emphasize the importance of the traits in writing, compare them to requirements for math homework. For example, students cannot simply write the answers on a sheet of paper. They must show their work, show the steps in order, and add labels and explanations to get their ideas across effectively.

Understanding Ideas

Ideas are the beginning and the end of good writing. That is why the best writers are constantly thinking of good ideas for their stories and essays. Author Jane Yolen knows the importance of good ideas: "I keep an idea file. I always scribble down ideas when I get them."

What types of ideas will you find in good writing?

The best writing (1) starts with a **well-chosen topic**—one that interests you (the writer) and works well for the assignment, (2) continues with **main points** that support the topic, and (3) ends with **important details** that explain the main points.

What makes a writing topic good?

Good writing topics are neither too general nor too specific. They cover just the right amount of information for the assignment.

Sample Assignment: Share an unforgettable experience—a specific event that has meant a lot to you.

	Possible Topics
● ***Too Broad***	Being a baseball fan
● ***Too Narrow***	Buying a pack of baseball cards
● ***Just Right***	Visiting the Mets' training camp

How should I write about a topic?

Effective writing has focus. In other words, the story or essay pays special attention to a certain part of a topic or to a specific feeling you have about the topic. Notice how the following statement puts a topic into clear focus.

Focus Statement:
During my visit to the Mets' training camp (topic), *I was able to get autographs from my two favorite players* (a certain part).

Identify a specific topic and write an effective focus statement based on the following assignment: Recall an unforgettable experience—a specific event that has meant a lot to you.

Understanding Ideas

Brainstorm with students to list sources for ideas. Suggest the following:

- personal journal
- family scrapbook
- school library
- Internet
- classroom resources
- talking to friends or family

Before students begin writing their focus statements for the **Try It** activity, have them share their topics. Help students shape their topics if they seem too specific or too broad.

Answers

Answers will vary.

English Language Learners

Use the following ideas to help students understand focus statements:

- A focus statement tells *why* a writer has chosen a particular topic. It makes the writer's main idea clear to the reader.
- In the example, the writer thought about the topic (visiting the Mets' training camp) and then asked, "Why was it special?" or "What do I feel is most important about this topic?" Answering that question led the writer to complete the focus statement.
- Students can practice writing focus statements using simple sentence starters, such as *Dogs make great pets because . . .* or *The best part of my vacation was . . . .* Tell them to keep such focus statements in mind as they do the **Try It** activity.

Struggling Learners

If students have difficulty generating ideas for an unforgettable experience, prompt them with questions, such as

- Have you seen a surprising sight while on a trip?
- Have you met someone who made a big impression on you?
- Have you received an unexpected gift?

Tell students that using all three kinds of details makes writing more interesting. To help students appreciate this point, have them complete this activity:

- Students write a paragraph about the most recent holiday they celebrated.
- They try to include at least two sensory details, two reflective details, and two memory details.
- Pairs of students exchange papers. Partners identify the different types of details in each other's paragraphs.

 **Answers**

Answers will vary.

How many main points do I need to support my topic and focus?

In most cases, you should have at least two or three main points to help support your writing idea. However, don't try to cover too much territory. If you do, your writing may become hard to follow. Each main point should be covered in a separate paragraph.

> **Focus Statement:** *During my visit to the Mets' training camp, I was able to get autographs from my two favorite players.*

Main supporting points:

- Waiting in the parking lot for players to arrive
- Getting an autograph from one of my favorite players
- Getting an autograph from another favorite player

Where do I find the best details?

Make sure to use a variety of details to develop or explain each main point. Many of these details will come from your personal thoughts; others will come from talking to other people or reading about the topic in books and articles. Here are the three main types of personal details.

Personal Details

Sensory details come from the writer's senses.

I saw my favorite player get out of his van.

Reflective details come from the writer's thoughts and feelings.

I was so excited that I thought I would drop my cards.

Memory details come from the writer's experience and knowledge.

He made the all-star team last year.

 Review one of your personal narratives or essays. On a piece of paper, list at least one sensory, one reflective, and one memory detail that you used.

English Language Learners

Before students work on the **Try It** activity, provide additional examples of sensory details (the spicy smell of pizza, the soft fur of a puppy), reflective details (thrilled to meet my favorite singer, proud to win the race), and memory details (my soccer team's first game, the day my baby sister was born).

Advanced Learners

Have students brainstorm and display a list of similes, metaphors, and analogies that create powerful details.

How can I gather more details?

Sometimes you may need a jump start to find additional details for your writing. Here are some different ways to find the information you may need.

Ask questions: You can list questions that come to mind and then find answers to them. You can ask the 5 W's—*who? what? when? where?* and *why?*—about your topic. Add *how?* for even better coverage. (See "Analyze" below for more structured questions.)

Analyze: Think about your topic very carefully by answering two or more of the following questions.

- What parts does my topic have? *(Break it down.)*
- What do I see, hear, or feel when I think about it? *(Describe it.)*
- What is it similar to? What is it different from? *(Compare it.)*
- What are its strengths and weaknesses? *(Evaluate it.)*
- What can I do with it? How can I use it? *(Apply it.)*

Freewrite: Write freely about your topic from a number of different angles. Doing this can often help you uncover new ideas to use in your writing.

Try to write nonstop for at least 5 to 8 minutes to keep your mind open to all kinds of ideas. (See page 439 for more information.)

Select one of the topics below. Then, on your own paper, answer three of the questions from "Analyze" above. What new thing did you learn about the topic?

Possible topics: earning extra money, getting in shape, a locker room, a junk drawer, a personal injury

How can I hold my reader's interest?

The best writing has something to say. It contains a lot of specific details that grab the reader's attention.

Passage with Few Details

The leadership council raised a lot of money and then gave some of that money to a local mission.

Same Passage with Specific Details

The McKinley Leadership Council raised $3,000 for local charities and then gave $400 to the Lake Street Mission to help feed homeless people.

PROCESS

Students can refer to this page whenever they are feeling "stuck." Answering these questions should help them move forward. Students might write down the questions listed here in their writing notebooks. That way, they can find them whenever they need help gathering details.

Answers

Answers will vary.

Understanding Organization

Point out that in the graphic organizer, the beginning and ending both point toward the middle because it is the "meat" of the essay. Discuss how this basic form of organization works in various forms of writing.

- **In narrative writing,** a personal reminiscence or biographical story (just as in a fictional narrative), there is a beginning, a middle, and an ending (like a plot line).
- **Expository, informational writing,** whether a how-to or a major research report, begins by introducing the topic. The middle supports the topic with facts, examples, statistics, and so on. This type of writing also needs an ending to bring all the information together in a conclusion or to make a final point.
- **In persuasive writing,** the beginning introduces the cause, position, or purpose. The middle seeks to prove the point being promoted, and the ending calls for agreement or action.
- **In analytical writing,** the beginning sets out what will be explored. The middle methodically breaks things down point by point, and the ending draws everything together to share an insight or a conclusion.

Understanding Organization

Strong writing is well organized from start to finish. Writer Stephen Tchudi (pronounced "Judy") calls organizing a paper the "framing" process: "Just as a carpenter puts up a frame of a house before tacking on the outside walls, a writer needs to build a frame for a paper."

How should I organize my writing assignments?

Each of your essays should have a meaningful beginning, middle, and ending. The graphic that follows shows the basic shape of effective writing.

Beginning

Start with interesting information and state the focus (underlined).

Last year, my grandpa gave me the best present ever. He took me to three baseball training camps. . . . <u>During my visit to the Mets' camp, I was able to get autographs from my two favorite players.</u>

Middle

Present the main supporting points and details.

We arrived at the Mets' camp early and waited in the parking lot. . . .

All of a sudden, a black custom van parked in the area reserved for the players. . . .

Later a red sports car pulled into the lot. . . .

Ending

Review the essay and offer a final thought.

Was I ever lucky! I got autographs from my two favorite Mets. . . .

I guess you could say on that day the ball really bounced my way.

How can transitions help me organize my writing?

Linking words and phrases (transitions) can help you organize the details in your narratives, descriptions, and essays. (Also see pages 572–573.)

Descriptions: You can use the following transitions, which show location, to arrange details in your descriptions.

above	across	below	in the front	on the right	near	in the back

In the front of the snack shop, you will find a small counter on the right surrounded by rows and rows of candy bars. Across from the counter, bags of chips, pretzels, and popcorn are neatly stacked. In the back of the shop, a cooler contains sports drinks, bottled water, and sodas. . . .

Personal narratives: You can use the following transitions, which show time, to arrange details in your narratives. These types of transitions also work well for "how-to" or process essays.

after	before	during	first	second	today	next	then

Next I got Sammy Sosa's autograph. He is my favorite player. I was speechless. Then I watched for other players to arrive just for the fun of it. . . .

Comparison-contrast essays: You can use the following transitions to organize comparisons.

(when comparing)	like	also	both	in the same way	similarly
(when contrasting)	but	still	yet	on the other hand	unlike

Both red blood cells and white blood cells play important roles. Red blood cells transport oxygen throughout your body, and white blood cells protect your body against infection. Unlike red blood cells, most white blood cells live only a few days.

Persuasive essays: You can use the following transitions to organize the details in your persuasive essays.

first of all	in addition	equally as important	most importantly

First of all, carrying out the death penalty is a very slow process. . . . In addition, capital punishment is very expensive. . . . Most importantly, many people believe that capital punishment is morally wrong. . . .

Try It Review a narrative, a description, or an essay that you have written. Underline any transitions that you find. Do they organize your writing, making it easier to follow? Could you add any more transitions?

PROCESS

Transitions play a key role in the writing process. Transitions express relationships between ideas, between sentences, and between paragraphs. They are critical to the development of a logical, well-organized piece of writing and to the smooth flow of ideas.

The examples of transitions on this page focus on connecting ideas and sentences. For a clear demonstration of transitions used to connect paragraphs, have students turn to SE page 81 and look briefly at the middle paragraphs of a descriptive essay.

Tell students that they can refer to this page and to the pages at the back of the book (SE pages 572–573) whenever they are working on their transitions. Students may also want to keep a list in their writing notebooks.

Try It Answers

Answers will vary.

Understanding Voice

Voice is probably the hardest trait for students to grasp because it is the most abstract. One way to make the trait of voice clearer is by telling students to think about their audience. Once students focus on an audience, they can begin to tailor their ways of expressing themselves to those specific readers.

When students are writing for a general audience or their classmates, remind them to concentrate on making their writing personal by writing as honestly and sincerely as they can.

Answers

Answers will vary, but there should be noticeable differences between the note to the teacher and the note to a friend.

40

Understanding Voice

Writer Donald Murray says that voice is the "person in the writing." When the writer's voice or personality is strong, the reader stays interested. Something about the writer's way of using words attracts the reader.

How can I write with voice?

If the real you shines through in your writing, it will have voice. To have voice, you must be honest and sincere in what you write.

This passage lacks voice because you can't hear the writer.

Coach Brown requires us to complete pull-ups in a very specific way. He doesn't allow any unnecessary movements. He positions himself close to the bar with a yardstick in hand. As soon as there is any movement . . .

This passage has voice because you can hear the writer.

For Coach Brown, there is only one way to complete a pull-up—his way. For one thing, he doesn't allow any kicking, wriggling, or squirming. He stands right next to the bar and taps us on the stomach if . . .

How important is audience when it comes to voice?

Your audience is very important because it impacts the tone of your voice. For example, in a letter to the school board, you would try to sound formal and respectful. In a personal narrative shared with classmates, you would try to sound more casual and relaxed.

Audience Adults (school administrators, businesspeople, city officials)
Voice Serious, formal, respectful, and thoughtful
Art classes greatly benefit all students. . . .

Audience Peers (classmates, friends, and students in other schools)
Voice Engaging, usually informal, casual, and relaxed
Art classes give kids a chance to be creative. . . .

Write a brief note to a teacher explaining something that you really like about the class. Then write another note, this time to a friend in the class, about the same topic. The tone of each note should be different.

English Language Learners

Relate a writer's use of voice to the more familiar meaning of *voice*—the sound of someone speaking. Point out that speakers use different tones of voice (happy, scared, proud) to express different feelings. They also use different words for different audiences. For example, have students imagine that a young boy was frightened because he got lost in the woods.

- What words would he use to relate this experience to his grandmother?
- What different words might he use to relate the experience to his best friend?

Have students keep these points in mind as they work on the **Try It** activity.

Struggling Learners

Bring in a variety of periodicals from the school library. Have each student select one article and read the first paragraph aloud to the group. Together, categorize the voice used by the author. Discuss how the nature of the topic or the style of the magazine determines the voice.

Understanding Word Choice

Author Gloria D. Miklowitz says, "Write visually, write clearly, and make every word count." If you follow her advice, you will create a lot of specific images (word pictures), making your writing very enjoyable to read. *Remember:* Your writing is only as good as the words that you use.

PROCESS

What should I know about descriptive words?

The best writing contains specific adjectives and adverbs. For example, you may tell readers that Beau is a farm dog, but telling them that he is a *bossy* farm dog says so much more. On the other hand, remember to use descriptive words selectively. Writing sounds unnatural if it contains too many of them.

A Sentence Containing Too Many Adjectives

Josie served delicious, spicy, homemade beef tamales.

A Sentence Containing the Right Number of Adjectives

Josie served delicious beef tamales.

Avoid overusing the following adjectives: *cool, big, pretty, small, fun, bad, nice,* and *good*. They are used so much that they carry little meaning.

Use adverbs when they are needed to describe the action in a sentence. For example, the adverb *barely* makes the action clearer in the following sentence: "We barely squeezed through the subway door before it shut."

How do words affect the feeling of my writing?

The words that you use directly affect the **connotation**, or feeling, of your writing. Let's say that you are describing a scary dream. You wouldn't use the word "dream" or "fantasy" because neither one has the right feeling. The word "nightmare," however, does have the right feeling. Check a thesaurus if you have trouble finding a word with both the right meaning and the right feeling.

Look through a classroom thesaurus. On your own paper, write one entry that interests you. Under that word, list three or four synonyms. Share your findings with a classmate. Try to explain the connotation, or feeling, of each synonym.

Teaching Tip: Connotations

A word's *connotation* is the general feeling that a word suggests. Write the words *stubborn* and *persistent* on the board. Tell students that both words are used to describe someone who doesn't give up. However, *stubborn* has a negative connotation and implies that someone is unreasonable.

English Language Learners

Point out that just as there are different shades of colors, there are also shades of meaning in words with similar meanings. Share the following pairs of words as examples:

- big, enormous (a big book, an enormous elephant)
- crying, whining (a crying baby, a whining goalie)
- loud, deafening (loud music, deafening blast)

Understanding Word Choice

Ask students to highlight words like *cool, big, pretty, small, fun, bad, nice, very,* and *good* in something they have written. Discuss why these overused words become meaningless. Then have them replace words with more specific synonyms.

Incorporate vocabulary-building techniques into your teaching by asking students to keep a running list of new words from their reading. Encourage them to use the new words in their writing.

✱ Additional information on vocabulary-building techniques is on SE pages 562–563.

English is a complex language with many words that express the same thing. However, each word has different shades of meaning. Students will gain insights into the richness of the English language as they learn about **connotations** *(see below)*.

 **Answers**

Answers will vary.

Understanding Sentence Fluency

Write the following pairs of sentences on the board. Tell students to combine each pair of sentences.

- Seventh graders eat lunch at noon. Sixth graders eat lunch at one o'clock.
- Some people do instant messaging all day. I prefer to talk to my friends on the phone.
- I exercise every day. I don't want to get out of shape.

Review with students some of the conjunctions that they use to combine sentences: *and, but, because, since, or, when, for, until, although,* and *as.*

Review the different ways of expanding sentences that are shown in the student edition. Ask:

- What kind of information is added to these sentences? (information that answers the questions *when? how? what?*)
- What other kinds of information could you add to expand sentences? (information that would answer the questions *who? why?*)

* Additional information about writing more effective sentences is on SE pages 570–571.

Understanding Sentence Fluency

Writing that succeeds shares the main message in an effective way. That is why good writers pay careful attention to each sentence they write. As author Cynthia Ozick states, "I never go to the next sentence until the previous one is perfect."

What does it mean to write fluent sentences?

Sentences are fluent when they all work together to make your writing enjoyable to read. When checking for sentence fluency, you should be able to say these things about your writing :

- Every sentence in my paper is important.
- Someone else could read my paper aloud and like the sound of it.
- Short, choppy sentences have been combined. (See pages **512–514**.)
- My sentence beginnings and lengths are varied. (See pages **511** and **522**.)
- Transition words and phrases—*first, for example*—connect the ideas.

How can I improve my sentence style?

The information above identifies two key things that you can do to improve your sentence style: (1) Combine short, choppy sentences, and (2) vary your sentence beginnings and lengths. You can also improve your sentence style by expanding your simple sentences in a number of ways. (See pages **512–517**.)

You can expand simple sentences before the subject and verb.

Simple sentence: **Todd completed his assignment.**
Expanded sentence: Before first hour, **Todd completed his assignment.**

You can expand simple sentences after the subject and verb.

Simple sentence: **Tisha spoke.**
Expanded sentence: **Tisha spoke** confidently during the meeting.

You can expand a simple sentence from within.

Simple sentence: **Coach Brown explained the play.**
Expanded sentence: **Coach Brown** carefully **explained the** new running **play** at the start of practice.

On your own paper, expand each of the sentences below in at least two different ways.

Erin talked to her friend. Richard studied.

What sentence structures should I avoid?

Avoid writing too many sentences that begin with "There is" and "There are" or that contain "be" verbs *(is, are, was, were)*. You should also avoid rambling sentences that contain too many *and*'s.

Sentences Beginning with "There is" and "There are"

There is a funny-looking cat sitting on our front porch.
There are three annoying crows cawing in our backyard.

Sentences Improved by Deleting "There is" and "There are"

A funny-looking cat is sitting on our front porch.
Three annoying crows are cawing in our backyard.

Sentences Containing "Be" Verbs *(is, are, was, were)*

Rosa is a persuasive speaker in debates.
Ellis and Roy are creative painters.

Sentences Improved by Making Another Word in Each Sentence into a Verb

Rosa speaks persuasively in debates.
Ellis and Roy paint creatively.

Rambling Sentences Containing too Many "And's"

After the *Titanic* sank, the International Ice Patrol was formed and its job was to report icebergs and the United States gave this vital job to the U.S. Coast Guard.

A Rambling Sentence Improved by Deleting an "And" and Making Two Sentences

After the *Titanic* sank, the International Ice Patrol was formed, and its job was to report icebergs. The United States gave this vital job to the U.S. Coast Guard.

Try It On your own paper, write three sentences that begin with "There is" or "There are." Exchange papers with a classmate and rewrite each other's sentences, deleting "There is" and "There are."

PROCESS

Rambling sentences often mirror the way students speak—a nonstop pouring out of thoughts. Explain that the word *and* connects closely related subjects or ideas and should not be used to connect just any ideas.

In the improved rambling sentence example, point out that both parts of the first sentence concern the International Ice Patrol. The *and* connects two closely related thoughts having to do with the formation and responsibility of the International Ice Patrol. In the second sentence, although the topic is still the same, the subject shifts away from the International Ice Patrol to the United States and the U.S. Coast Guard.

Answers

Answers will vary.

Advanced Learners

Explain that writers who submit their work to magazines and newspapers are often given specific word counts for their stories and articles. Some contests also limit the number of words a contestant can use. Discuss how the hints on this page could help writers stay within their limits by writing more economically, yet effectively.

Understanding Conventions

Students will use a checklist similar to this one during the editing stage in each of the core writing units (narrative, expository, persuasive, response to literature). At that time, you may choose to have students focus on only one or two of the conventions that are particularly troublesome.

Take the time now to have students familiarize themselves with the Proofreader's Guide in the back of the pupil edition. Ask them to find the rules in the Proofreader's Guide that correspond to each checklist item.

1. 579.1, 580.1, 580.4
2. 590.2
3. 582.1
4. 604.4, 606.1
5. 624.1
6. 618.1, 618.2
7. and 8. pages 642–651
9. pages 722, 724
10. 728.1
11. pages 652–689

Understanding Conventions

Good writing follows the conventions, or basic rules, of the language. These rules cover punctuation, capitalization, grammar, and spelling. When you follow these rules, the reader will find your writing much easier to understand and enjoy.

How can I make sure my writing follows the rules?

A checklist like the one below can guide you as you look over your writing for errors. When you are not sure about a certain rule, refer to the "Proofreader's Guide" (pages 578–749).

Conventions

PUNCTUATION

_____ **1.** Do I use end punctuation after all my sentences?
_____ **2.** Do I use commas correctly in compound sentences?
_____ **3.** Do I use commas correctly in a series?
_____ **4.** Do I use apostrophes correctly to show possession (*that girl's purse* and *those girls' purses*)?

CAPITALIZATION

_____ **5.** Do I start every sentence with a capital letter?
_____ **6.** Do I capitalize the proper names of people and places?

SPELLING

_____ **7.** Have I checked my spelling using a spell-checker?
_____ **8.** Have I also checked the spelling by myself?

GRAMMAR

_____ **9.** Do I use correct forms of verbs (*had gone,* not *had went*)?
_____ **10.** Do my subjects and verbs agree in number (*the boy eats* and *the boys eat*)?
_____ **11.** Do I use the right word (*to, too,* or *two*)?

Have at least one other person check your writing for conventions. Professional writers have trained editors to help them with this step in the process. You should ask your classmates, teachers, and family members for help.

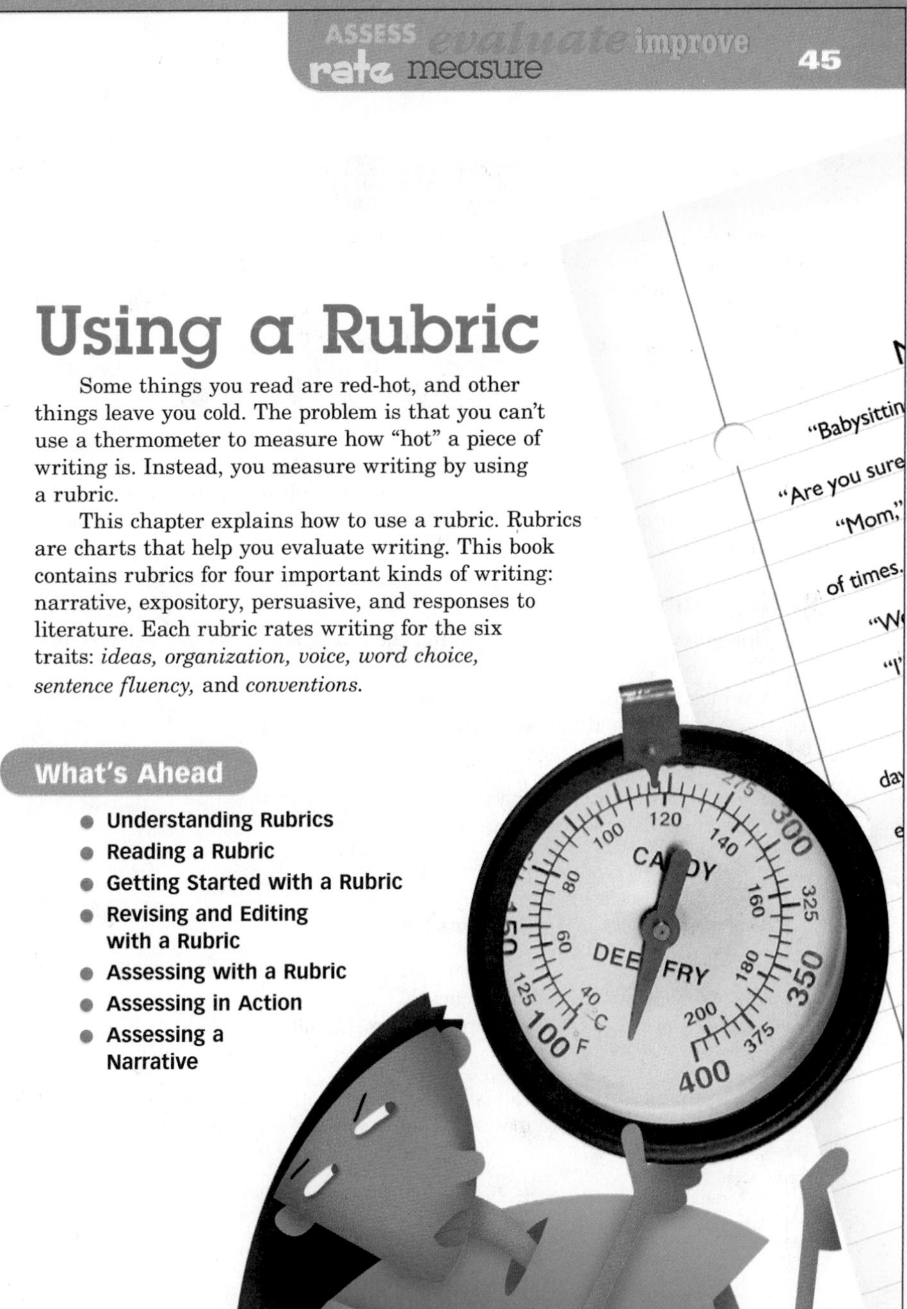

Using a Rubric

Some things you read are red-hot, and other things leave you cold. The problem is that you can't use a thermometer to measure how "hot" a piece of writing is. Instead, you measure writing by using a rubric.

This chapter explains how to use a rubric. Rubrics are charts that help you evaluate writing. This book contains rubrics for four important kinds of writing: narrative, expository, persuasive, and responses to literature. Each rubric rates writing for the six traits: *ideas, organization, voice, word choice, sentence fluency,* and *conventions.*

What's Ahead

Using a Rubric

Objectives

- understand how to read a rubric
- learn how to revise and edit with a rubric
- learn how to assess with a rubric

This lesson explains the different uses of rubrics in this book:

- to set writing goals
- to revise and edit a piece of writing
- to assess a piece of writing

Ask:

- Have you used rubrics before?
- How did you use them?
- Were the rubrics helpful?

Copy Masters

Assessment Sheet (TE pp. 52, 56)

Understanding Rubrics

Explain that a rubric score is not a grade. It is intended to be a tool to help students improve their writing.

The rubric reinforces the importance of each of the traits by scoring each one separately. This scoring system is immensely helpful to students. For example, if a student consistently gets high scores for Ideas but lower scores for Organization, the student gets a clear message that she or he needs to spend more time on the second trait.

Understanding Rubrics

Once you understand how to use these rubrics, you will find it easy to assess your writing. And more importantly, you will understand what you need to do to improve as a writer.

Your essays, reports, and stories can be rated for each of the main traits of writing—*ideas, organization, voice, word choice, sentence fluency,* and *conventions.* For example, in one of your essays, the ideas may be "strong" and the organization may be "good." That would give you a 5 for ideas and a 4 for organization.

Rating Guide

This guide will help you understand the rating scale.

A **6** means that the writing is truly amazing. It goes way beyond the requirements for a certain trait.

A **5** means that the writing is very strong. It clearly meets the main requirements for a trait.

A **4** means that the writing is good. It meets most of the requirements for a trait.

A **3** means that the writing is okay. It needs work to meet the main requirements for a trait.

A **2** means that the writing is poor. It needs a lot of work to meet the requirements for a trait.

A **1** means that the writing is incomplete. It is not yet ready to assess for a trait.

English Language Learners

Stress the positive aspects of using a rubric:

- It can show you how to make your writing better.
- It can show how many new skills you are mastering.
- It can give you a personal goal (changing a 3 to a 4).

Reading a Rubric

For the rubrics in this book, each trait has its own color bar (green for *ideas*, pink for *organization*, and so on). There is a description for each rating to help you evaluate for a particular trait.

Rubric for Narrative Writing

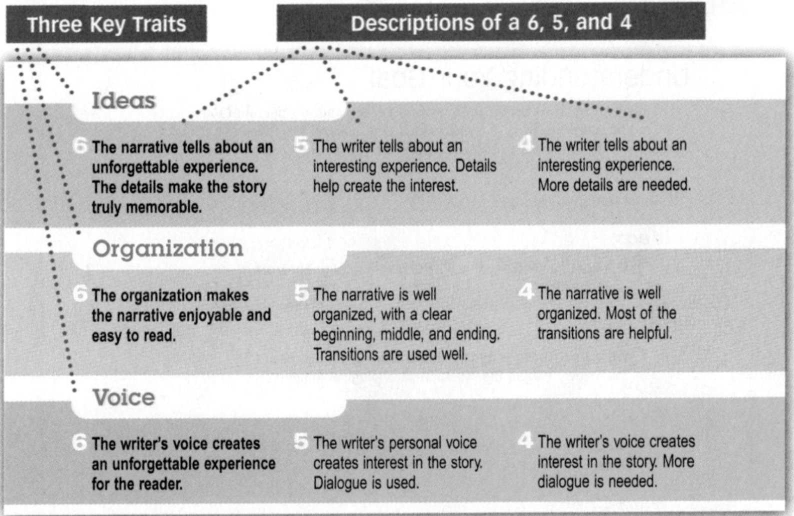

Guiding Your Writing

Learning how to use a rubric helps you . . .

- think like a writer—understanding your goal,
- make meaningful changes in your writing—using the traits of writing, and
- assess your final copies—rating their strengths and weaknesses.

Reflect on your work with rubrics. On your own paper, explain your experience with rubrics. When have you used them? How well did they work for you? What have they taught you about writing? If you've never used a rubric, explain how you have generally evaluated your writing. Share your thoughts with your class.

PROCESS

Reading a Rubric

Guiding Your Writing

Encourage students to refer to the rubrics often to guide them as they write. Take a close look at the Rubric for Narrative Writing. Have volunteers read aloud the descriptions listed under each category. Point out the subtle differences between the descriptions for a score of 6 and a score of 5. Then point out the differences between the descriptions for a score of 5 and a score of 4.

If you wish, have students turn briefly to the complete Rubric for Narrative Writing on SE pages 130–131. Help students see that there is always something missing or lacking in the description for a score of 4 and lower.

* Reproducible six-, five-, and four-point rubrics for narrative writing are available on TE pages 750, 754, and 758.

Getting Started with a Rubric

Tell students that this page is a "pre-rubric" page, which explains the goals of writing in terms of the six traits of effective writing. Students will refer to this rubric as a planning guide for the writing unit. Using the narrative unit on SE pages 92–155, show students how the rubric is embedded in the following pages:

- traits of narrative writing (SE page 98)
- revising and editing for the traits (SE pages 114–127)
- assessing narrative writing (SE pages 130–131)

For every writing assignment, students will find it helpful to study the rubric for their overall planning and then use the different parts of the rubric at the appropriate stages of the writing process.

Getting Started with a Rubric

At the beginning of each main writing unit, you will see a page like the one below. This page, which is arranged according to the traits of writing, explains the main requirements for developing the writing in the unit.

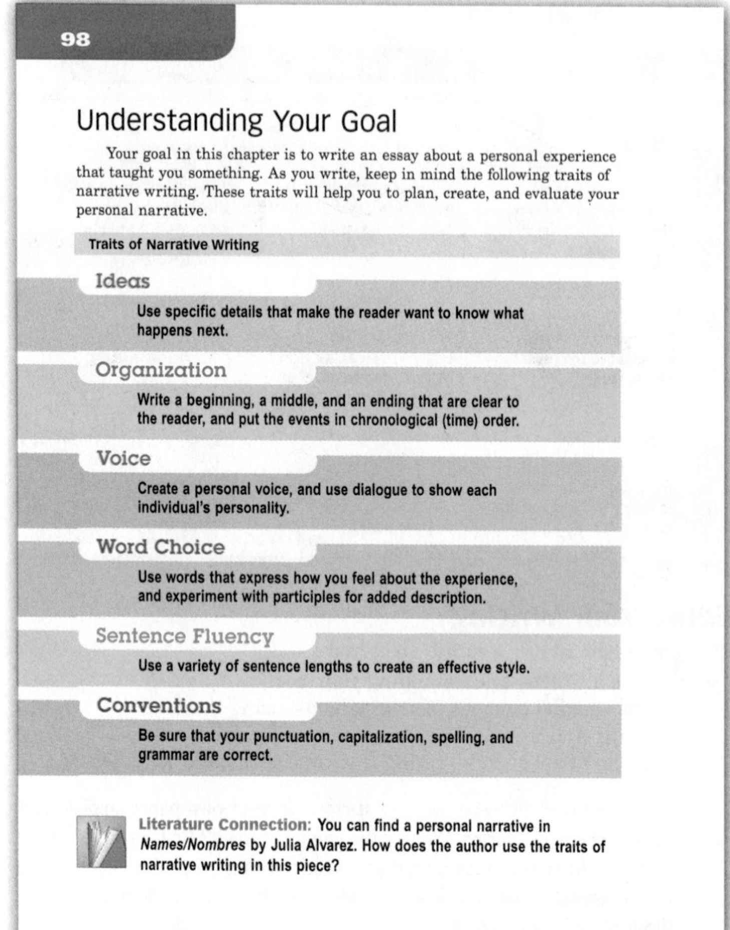

98

Understanding Your Goal

Your goal in this chapter is to write an essay about a personal experience that taught you something. As you write, keep in mind the following traits of narrative writing. These traits will help you to plan, create, and evaluate your personal narrative.

Traits of Narrative Writing

Ideas

Use specific details that make the reader want to know what happens next.

Organization

Write a beginning, a middle, and an ending that are clear to the reader, and put the events in chronological (time) order.

Voice

Create a personal voice, and use dialogue to show each individual's personality.

Word Choice

Use words that express how you feel about the experience, and experiment with participles for added description.

Sentence Fluency

Use a variety of sentence lengths to create an effective style.

Conventions

Be sure that your punctuation, capitalization, spelling, and grammar are correct.

Literature Connection: You can find a personal narrative in *Names/Nombres* by Julia Alvarez. How does the author use the traits of narrative writing in this piece?

Struggling Learners

Have students read aloud the characteristics of a "6" rating for *Ideas* using the rubrics on SE pages 130, 194, 256, and 318 to demonstrate how the criteria change depending on the type of writing required. This will help them understand how the purpose and form of writing relates to ideas.

A Closer Look at Understanding Your Goal

To use the "Understanding Your Goal" rubric at the beginning of each writing unit, follow these steps.

1. **Review the entire chart** to get the big picture about the form of writing.
2. **Focus your attention** on *ideas, organization,* and *voice* at the beginning of a writing project because these traits are so important. (See the chart below.)
3. **Read the requirements** under each of these three traits. When you consider *ideas*, for example, try to do these things:
   - Include all of the important details.
   - Make the reader want to know what happened next.
4. **Make sure to talk to your teacher** if you have any questions about the requirements for the assignment.

A Special Note About the Traits

At each step in the writing process, certain traits are more important than others. Keep this point in mind as you use a rubric.

During **Prewriting** and **Writing**, focus on the *ideas, organization,* and *voice* in your writing.

During **Revising**, focus on *ideas, organization, voice, word choice,* and *sentence fluency.* (For some assignments, your teacher may ask you to concentrate most of your attention on one or two of these traits.)

During **Editing** and proofreading, focus on *conventions.*

When **Assessing** a final copy, consider all six traits. (For some assignments, your teacher may ask you to assess a piece of writing for just a few of the traits.)

Write a paragraph. Review the traits rubric on page 48. Then write a short paragraph sharing a learning experience, keeping these traits in mind.

A Closer Look at Understanding Your Goal

Students should be encouraged to return to the goal page periodically during each unit. It will help them monitor their attention to the traits throughout the writing process.

A Special Note About the Traits

Ask:
Why do you think different traits are emphasized at different stages of the writing process? (There are different tasks to accomplish at each stage of the writing process. Certain tasks match different traits; for example, choosing a topic and gathering details deal with ideas.)

Writing a paragraph is a good way to focus on the traits of writing in a condensed form. Because a paragraph is short, students should find that they can concentrate on the traits without being overwhelmed by the length of the writing.

Revising and Editing with a Rubric

Encourage students to refer to the rubric strips often when they write. Tell them that they can refer to the strips to assess their progress as their writing takes shape. In this way, students can improve their writing and gain a clearer idea of how their work compares to the standards in the rubric.

Answers

Answers will vary.

Revising and Editing with a Rubric

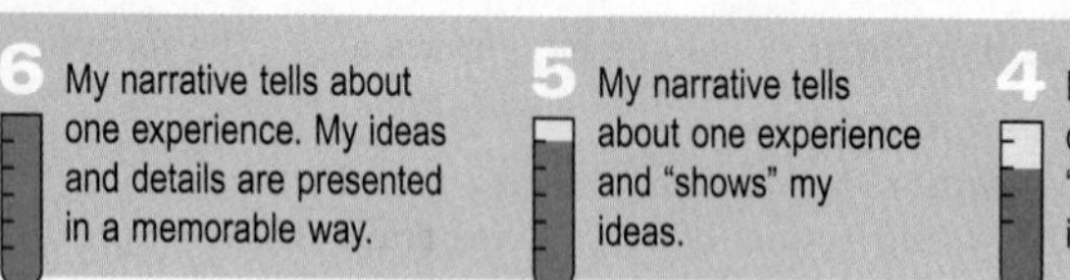

In each main writing unit, you will find a strip at the top of the pages dealing with revising and editing. Each strip covers one of the traits of writing and will help you improve your first drafts. The strip at the top of these two pages focuses on *ideas* for narrative writing.

How can I use each strip to evaluate my first draft?

To use the strip, start by reading the number 5 description. Number 5 in the strip above says that your first draft should tell about one experience and "show" your ideas. Decide if your writing should get a 5 for ideas. If not, check the description for 6 or 4 and so on. Remember that a 5 means that the writing is *strong* for that trait.

Sometimes it's hard to know for sure if a first draft deserves a 6, 5, or another number for a trait. Just come as close as you can to choosing the appropriate number, and revise your writing as needed.

Review the sample paragraph below. Then rate the paragraph for ideas and explain your rating. (See pages 46–47 for help with rating a paper.)

I'll never forget the first time I saw our school library. Our librarian met us at the entrance, and she told us to enter the library as quietly as possible. As soon as she said this, Jerry Howell collided with Yvonne Davis, who yelled, "You klutz!" The librarian said, "Shhhh!"

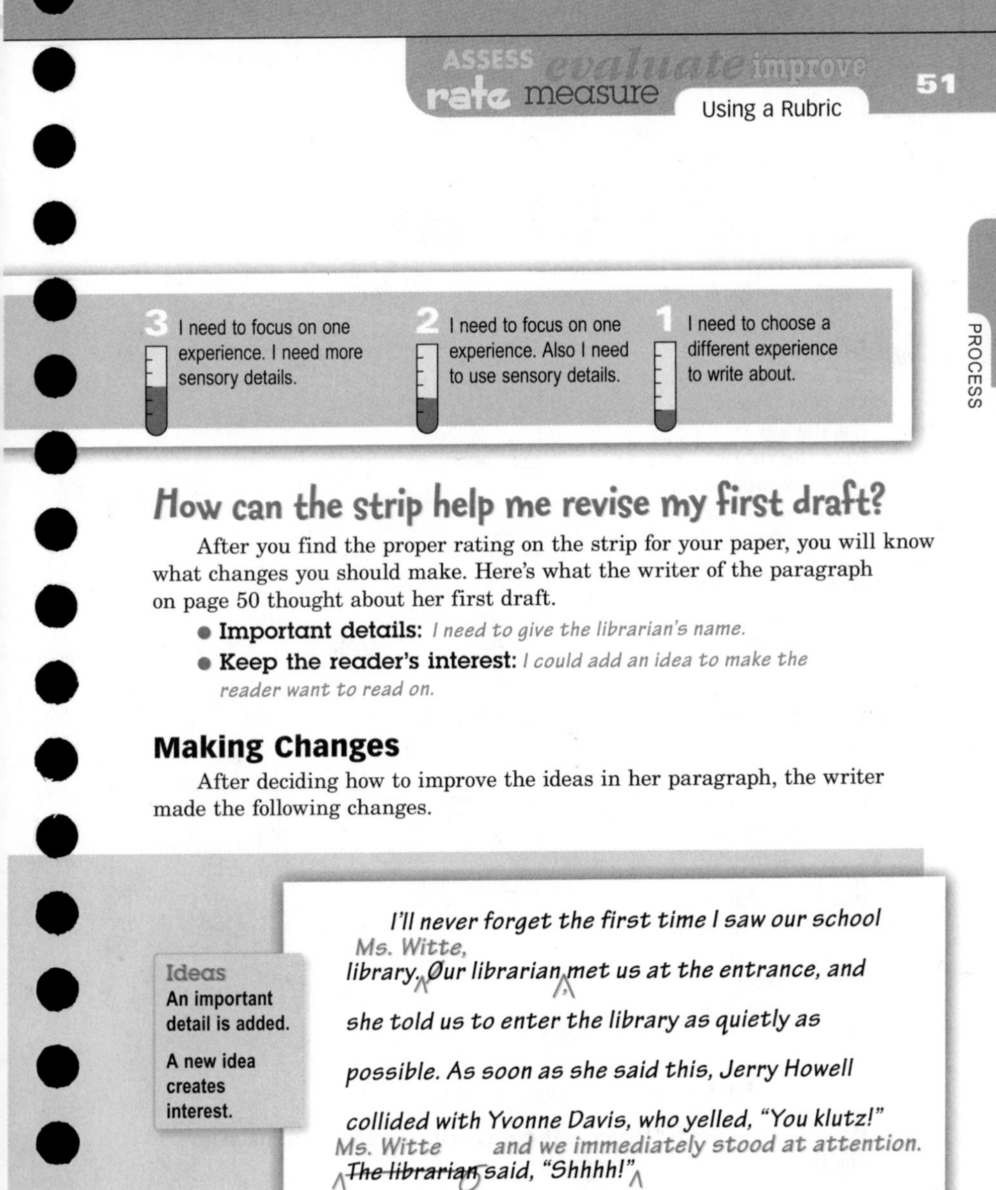

3	2	1
I need to focus on one experience. I need more sensory details.	I need to focus on one experience. Also I need to use sensory details.	I need to choose a different experience to write about.

PROCESS

How can the strip help me revise my first draft?

After you find the proper rating on the strip for your paper, you will know what changes you should make. Here's what the writer of the paragraph on page 50 thought about her first draft.

- **Important details:** *I need to give the librarian's name.*
- **Keep the reader's interest:** *I could add an idea to make the reader want to read on.*

Making Changes

After deciding how to improve the ideas in her paragraph, the writer made the following changes.

Ideas
An important detail is added.
A new idea creates interest.

I'll never forget the first time I saw our school library. ~~Our~~ librarian, Ms. Witte, met us at the entrance, and she told us to enter the library as quietly as possible. As soon as she said this, Jerry Howell collided with Yvonne Davis, who yelled, "You klutz!" ~~The librarian~~ Ms. Witte said, "Shhhh!" and we immediately stood at attention.

Revise **Revise your paragraph.** Review and revise the paragraph you wrote on page 49. Use the strip on these two pages as a guide.

Making Changes

As students make changes to the paragraphs they wrote for SE page 49, walk around the classroom to make sure that students are finding ways to improve their writing. If they have difficulty finding places to revise, make suggestions on how they can sharpen their writing.

Assessing with a Rubric

Have students use an assessment sheet like the one shown here for all of their writing assignments (TE page 787). Use the assessment sheet in conjunction with the reflection sheet (on SE page 28) for a thorough self-review process. Encourage students to refer to these assessment sheets throughout the year to gauge their progress in specific areas of the writing process.

Assessing with a Rubric

Follow the three steps below when you use a rubric—like the one on page 53—to assess a piece of writing.

1. **Create an assessment sheet.** On your own paper, list the key traits from the rubric (*ideas, organization,* and so on). Draw a line before each trait for your score and skip two or three lines between each trait for comments.

2. **Read the final copy.** Get an overall feeling for the writing to help you evaluate it.

3. **Assess the writing using the rubric.** To get started, read the descriptions for *ideas*, starting with the 5 rating. Decide which rating best fits the writing and put that number on your assessment sheet.

4. **Provide comments.** Under each trait, write one thing you liked and one thing that could be improved.

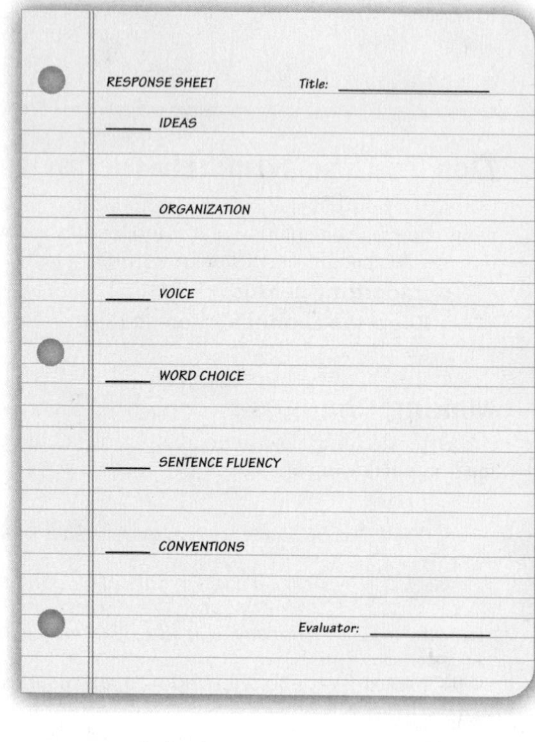

Assess your experience paragraph. Create an assessment sheet like the one above. Then evaluate your paragraph using the narrative rubric on pages 130–131. For each trait, try to write down something you did well and then something you'd like to improve. (See the sample on page 55.)

Struggling Learners

Begin by pairing students who are intimidated by rubrics with supportive partners. After they review the writing, have them discuss possible ratings and the reasons behind them. The writer will be more confident in assigning a number to each trait and adding helpful comments.

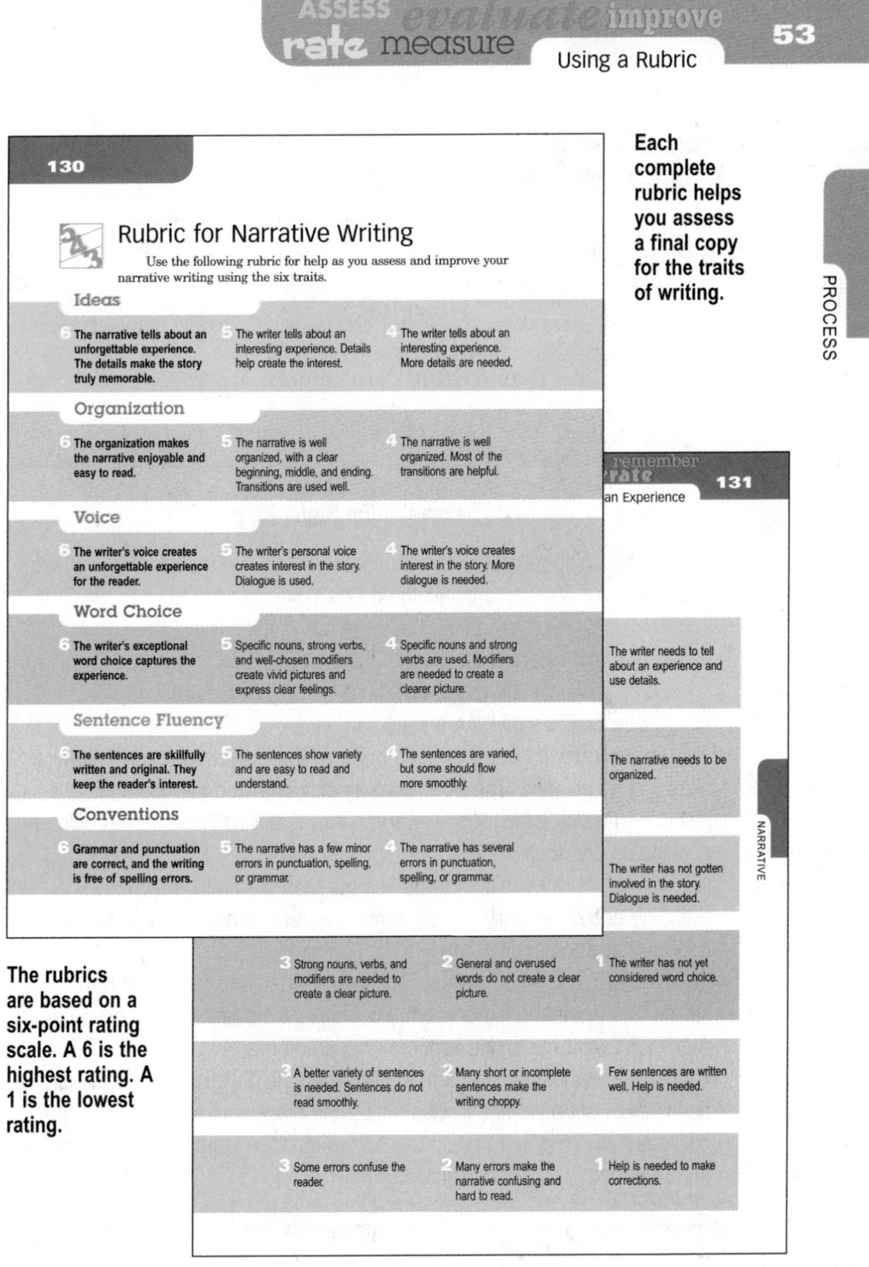

130

Rubric for Narrative Writing

Use the following rubric for help as you assess and improve your narrative writing using the six traits.

	6	5	4
Ideas	**The narrative tells about an unforgettable experience. The details make the story truly memorable.**	The writer tells about an interesting experience. Details help create the interest.	The writer tells about an interesting experience. More details are needed.
Organization	**The organization makes the narrative enjoyable and easy to read.**	The narrative is well organized, with a clear beginning, middle, and ending. Transitions are used well.	The narrative is well organized. Most of the transitions are helpful.
Voice	**The writer's voice creates an unforgettable experience for the reader.**	The writer's personal voice creates interest in the story. Dialogue is used.	The writer's voice creates interest in the story. More dialogue is needed.
Word Choice	**The writer's exceptional word choice captures the experience.**	Specific nouns, strong verbs, and well-chosen modifiers create vivid pictures and express clear feelings.	Specific nouns and strong verbs are used. Modifiers are needed to create a clearer picture.
Sentence Fluency	**The sentences are skillfully written and original. They keep the reader's interest.**	The sentences show variety and are easy to read and understand.	The sentences are varied, but some should flow more smoothly.
Conventions	**Grammar and punctuation are correct, and the writing is free of spelling errors.**	The narrative has a few minor errors in punctuation, spelling, or grammar.	The narrative has several errors in punctuation, spelling, or grammar.

remember rate ... an Experience 131

	3	2	1
Ideas			The writer needs to tell about an experience and use details.
Organization			The narrative needs to be organized.
Voice			The writer has not gotten involved in the story. Dialogue is needed.
Word Choice	Strong nouns, verbs, and modifiers are needed to create a clear picture.	General and overused words do not create a clear picture.	The writer has not yet considered word choice.
Sentence Fluency	A better variety of sentences is needed. Sentences do not read smoothly.	Many short or incomplete sentences make the writing choppy.	Few sentences are written well. Help is needed.
Conventions	Some errors confuse the reader.	Many errors make the narrative confusing and hard to read.	Help is needed to make corrections.

PROCESS

NARRATIVE

Each complete rubric helps you assess a final copy for the traits of writing.

The rubrics are based on a six-point rating scale. A 6 is the highest rating. A 1 is the lowest rating.

Tell students to turn to the rubric for narrative writing on SE pages 130–131. Guide the class through a close examination of this rubric. Emphasize that, in many cases, there are subtle differences between two scores. Students should begin to understand that small changes add up to big improvements in their writing.

✱ The complete six-point rubric for narrative writing is found on SE pages 130–131. Reproducible six-, five-, and four-point rubrics for narrative writing are available on TE pages 750, 754, and 758.

Assessing in Action

Have students read "Moms Can Be Right" to themselves. Pass out stacks of sticky notes, and tell students to place the sticky notes on the page wherever the writing contains problems or errors. Suggest that students read the passage twice. Afterward, ask them whether they noticed more problems during their second reading. Discuss why you might see more errors the second time around.

Assessing in Action

On this page and on page 55, you can see how one student used a rubric to assess her writing.

Narrative Writing

In the following narrative, the writer shares a memorable baby-sitting experience. As you read the narrative, pay special attention to its strong points and weak points. **(The writing does contain errors.)**

Moms Can Be Right

"Baby-sitting is alot harder then it looks," my mom said. "Are you sure you want your first job to be for three kids?"

"Mom," I said, "I'll be fine. I've gone baby-sitting with Ellie a bunch of times. She and I have taken care of there kids before."

"Well, I really think you should have some jobs with one child."

"I'll be fine," I said. "You'll see."

I don't know if I could of been more wrong! I showed up on Friday night just as planned. The boys were already changed into there pjs and I just had to watch them. Mrs. Taylor ran thru the list of things they could and couldn't do and then headed for an office party.

The first twenty minutes was fine but then the show they were watching ended. So they got out some toys and started playing. Alex was good and wanted to sit on my lap, so I let him.

Then Robbie was in tears. Robbie screamed and yelled but Max just smiled and run into another room. I couldn't get up fast enough because Alex didn't want me to. He kept crawling up on me.

I had only just gotten them to bed when the Taylor's walked back in. I hadn't even got a chance to clean up. Their place was a total mess. They didn't say anything, but I could tell they weren't too happy. They paid me and I felt bad for not listening to my mom.

Sample Assessment

To complete the response to "Moms Can Be Right," the student writer used the rubric for narrative writing on pages 130–131. Beneath each trait, she identified one strength (*1.*) and one weakness (*2.*) in her writing.

RESPONSE SHEET *Title: Moms Can Be Right*

4 IDEAS
1. *The details in the first part are effective.*
2. *More specific details would help the rest of the essay.*

3 ORGANIZATION
1. *The narrative starts right in the middle of the action.*
2. *Transitions besides "then" should be used.*

3 VOICE
1. *The writer's voice can sometimes be heard.*
2. *Dialogue is needed in the second part of the narrative.*

3 WORD CHOICE
1. *The words are easy to follow.*
2. *Some words could be more specific ("good," "bad").*

4 SENTENCE FLUENCY
1. *The sentences in the first part read smoothly.*
2. *Sentence combining could help the last paragraph.*

4 CONVENTIONS
1. *The dialogue is punctuated correctly.*
2. *There are spelling and grammar errors.*

Evaluator: Maria Peña

Review the assessment. On your own paper, explain why you agree with the response above (or why you don't). Consider each trait carefully.

PROCESS

After students write their own thoughts about the response sheet scores for the **Review the assessment** activity, discuss each rubric trait and its score. Ask students to explain why they agree or disagree with the scores given for each of the traits. Have them use specific details to support their responses.

English Language Learners

Have students work with language-proficient partners or supportive small groups as they review the model assessment. Have them discuss why the writer gave herself each assessment rating. Be sure to stress that she looked at her writing on her own, and her goal was to find places in her writing that were good and others that she might improve.

Assessing a Narrative

The more students work with the rubrics, the more comfortable they will be with using them. Pass out sticky notes and a blank assessment sheet (TE page 787) for students to use as they read. After they fill out their assessment sheets, review their ratings trait by trait. Evaluate the comments made after each rubric point. How could students make their comments more helpful or specific?

Assessing a Narrative

As you read through the essay below, pay attention to the strengths and weaknesses in the writing. Then follow the directions at the bottom of the page. **(This writing does contain errors.)**

Cookies, Anyone?

Chocolate chip muffins, carmel rolls, peanut butter cookies, fudge brownies. Do these things make your mouth water? Baking these snacks and deserts is my specialty.

It started one year when my mom and I walked through Ryan's Discount Store. It was the start of summer vacation and I was looking for something to keep me busy. I saw a beautiful chrome Home-Bake oven.

I said, "Mom, look at this oven. It would be so much fun!"

She replied, "Well, your birthday is coming up. We'll see what we can do."

Luckily, I did get the oven and started baking right away. After a few weeks of making prepackaged cookies and cakes in my Home-Bake, my Mom bought me a new cookbook. Now I could make more complicated breakfasts, dinners, and snacks.

I remember the first time I made dinner for my family. Using my new cookbook, I made Tacos. I read the recipe over at least five times before begining. My family was so impressed.

Although I like making dinners for my family my favorite thing to do is baking. I started with easy recipes that didn't have alot of ingredients. I practiced making things like cookies and brownies. Now I like to make things that take longer like candy and layer cakes.

The thing I like best about baking is sharing it. Sometimes I bake cookies for older people in church. I love to see their smiles when I share my baking with them, I've learned that the best thing about having a talent is sharing it with others.

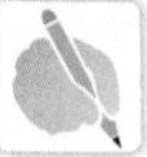

Use a narrative rubric. Assess the narrative essay you have just read using the rubric on pages 130–131 as a guide. Before you get started, create an assessment sheet like the one on page 55 in this chapter. ***Remember:*** **Leave room after each trait for comments.**

Publishing Your Writing

Publishing refers to the different ways that you can present your finished writing. Sharing a story in class is one form of publishing. Posting a poem on your own Web site is another form. In one way, publishing is the most important step in the writing process because it helps you take pride in your work. It is also one of the best ways to connect in a meaningful way with others.

Your writing is ready for publication when it reflects your true thoughts and feelings from start to finish. Your writing must also be as close to error-free as you can make it.

This chapter will help you get your writing ready to publish and give you a variety of publishing ideas. (Also see "Creating a Portfolio" on pages 65–69.)

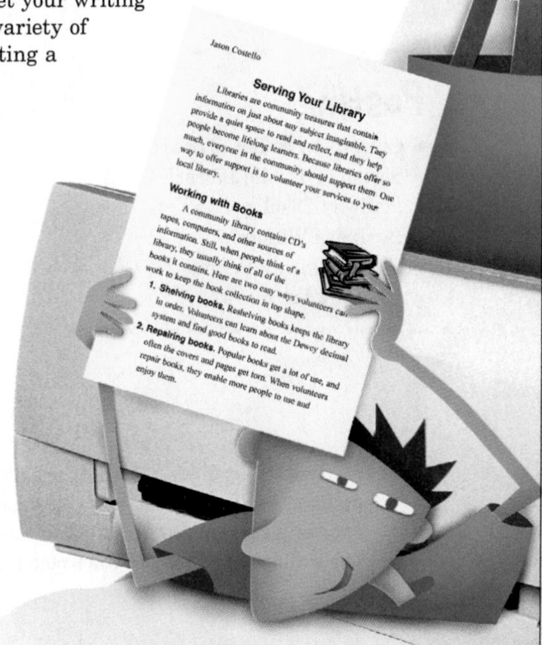

What's Ahead

Publishing Your Writing

Objectives

- understand the purpose of publishing
- learn about specific guidelines for publishing
- create a design for an essay or report
- learn about making Web sites and online publishing

It is important for students to perceive publishing as an enriching and important step in the writing process. When students know that their writing will be published, they put more effort into their work and take ownership of it. The more publishing choices you provide, the greater the enjoyment and stimulation for your students.

Suggest that students make a book out of their favorite stories. Or have students collaborate on a classroom newspaper, write letters to their elected officials, manage a class Web site, or make posters about a current issue in your school or community. There is no limit to the number of publishing ideas that your students can experience. The objective is to engage your students in publishing activities that show off their hard work.

Sharing Your Writing

Brainstorm for more publishing ideas. Then tell students to make a list of four or five forms of publishing that they will attempt during the school year. Be sure to allow time in your schedule for students to fulfill their publishing goals. When students work on a writing assignment that they are especially proud of, encourage them to select a publishing format that will present their work in the best light.

As students plan their writing for publication, discuss the importance of following the required formatting guidelines. Consider sharing sample guidelines for submissions to a few magazines or writing contests.

* Additional information about format and guidelines is on SE pages 576–577.

Sharing Your Writing

Some publishing ideas are easy to carry out, like sharing your writing with your classmates. Other publishing ideas take more time and effort, like entering a writing contest. Try a number of these publishing ideas during the school year. All of them will help you grow as a writer.

Performing

- Sharing with Classmates
- Reading to Various Audiences
- Preparing a Multimedia Presentation
- Videotaping for Special Audiences
- Performing Onstage

In School

- School Newspapers
- School Literary Magazines
- Classroom Collections
- Writing Portfolios

Self-Publishing

- Family Newsletters
- Greeting Cards
- Bound Writings
- Online Publications

Posting

- Classroom Bulletin Boards
- School or Public Libraries
- Hallway Display Cases
- Business Windows
- Clinic Waiting Rooms
- Literary/Art Fairs

Sending It Out

- Local Newspapers
- Area Historical Society
- Young Writers' Conferences
- Magazines and Contests
- Various Web Sites

Plan your publishing. Identify one piece of writing that you would like to perform. Explain why and how you would perform this writing. Then identify another piece that you would like to send out. Explain why you would send this writing out and where you would send it.

Preparing to Publish

Your writing is ready to publish when it is clear, complete, and correct. Getting your writing to this point requires careful revising and editing. Follow the tips below to help you prepare your writing for publication.

Publishing Tips

- **Ask for advice during the writing process.**
  Be sure your writing answers any questions your readers may have about your topic.
- **Check the ideas, organization, voice, word choice, and sentence fluency in your writing.**
  Every part of your writing should be clear and complete.
- **Work with your writing.**
  Continue working until you feel good about your writing from beginning to end.
- **Check your writing for conventions.**
  In addition, ask at least one classmate to check your work for this trait. Another person can catch errors that you miss.
- **Prepare a neat finished piece.**
  Use a pen (blue or black ink) and one side of the paper if you are writing by hand. If you are writing with a computer, use a font that is easy to read. Double-space your writing.
- **Know your options.**
  Explore different ways to publish your writing. (See page 58.) As you become more confident in your writing ability, you will become more interested in publishing your writing.
- **Follow all publication guidelines.**
  Just as your teacher wants assignments presented in a certain way, so do the newspapers, magazines, or Web sites that review the writing you submit.

Save all drafts for each writing project. This will help you keep track of the changes you have made. If you are preparing a portfolio, you may be required to include early drafts as well as finished pieces.

Preparing to Publish

Publishing Tips

Emphasize the importance of getting input from peers. Tell students that everyone benefits from having someone else read and critique their work. After working on a piece of writing for a while, most writers will miss a few things that need to be changed or corrected.

Designing Your Writing

Bring in a variety of magazine and newspaper articles for students to study. Point out the design features that make the articles interesting, such as effective typestyles, graphics, and **sidebars** *(see below)*. One way to give students practice using graphics in their writing is by giving them just the text of an article from a newspaper or magazine. Leave out all the graphic devices, and tell students to design graphics to go with the text. Then compare their work with the original.

* Additional information about graphics is on SE pages 574–575.

Designing Your Writing

Whenever you write, always focus on the content or information first. Then think about how you want your paper to look. For handwritten papers, write neatly in blue or black ink on clean paper. When using a computer, follow the guidelines below.

Typography

- Use an easy-to-read font. Generally, a serif font is best for the body, and a sans serif style is used for contrast in headings.

  The letters of serif fonts have "tails"—as in this sentence.

  The letters of sans serif styles are plain—as in this sentence.
- Use a title and headings. Headings break writing into smaller parts, making the writing easier to follow.

Spacing and Margins

- Use one-inch margins on all sides of your paper.
- Indent the first line of every paragraph.
- Use one space after every period and comma.
- Avoid awkward breaks between pages. Don't leave a heading or the first line of a paragraph at the bottom of a page or a column. Never split a hyphenated word between pages or columns.

Graphic Devices

- If possible, use bulleted lists in your writing. Often, a series of items works best as a bulleted list (like the ones on this page).
- Include graphics where appropriate. A table, a chart, or an illustration can help make a point clearer. But keep each graphic small enough so that it doesn't dominate the page. A larger graphic can be displayed by itself on a separate page.

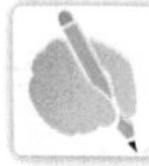

Share effective design. Find an article in a magazine or newspaper that contains many design features. Share the article with the class and identify the features. Do all of the features work effectively?

Teaching Tip: Sidebars

Most students are aware of sidebars in magazine or newspaper articles, but they may not know what they are called. Students who are interested in writing for the school newspaper will benefit from learning more about sidebars, and other students may want to use them to make their published pieces more interesting.

Tell students that a sidebar serves as an addition to the main content of an article, providing a brief look at a related topic or idea. The text of a sidebar is usually just three or four paragraphs in length. Occasionally, a sidebar may be a simple chart or graph. Sidebars are set off from the rest of the page in a visually appealing way.

Struggling Learners

Students with more limited computer experience can work with peers who know how to format bullets, insert clip art, and so on. A student of any academic skill level might be a computer graphics expert. Look for opportunities for everyone to share his or her design expertise.

Computer Design in Action

The following two pages show a well-designed student essay. The side notes explain all of the design features.

The title is 18-point type.

The main text is 12-point type and double-spaced throughout.

Headings are 14-point type.

A graphic is inserted for visual interest.

Numbered lists identify options.

Jason Costello

Serving Your Library

Libraries are community treasures that contain information on just about any subject imaginable. They provide a quiet space to read and reflect, and they help people become lifelong learners. Because libraries offer so much, everyone in the community should support them. One way to offer support is to volunteer your services to your local library.

Working with Books

A community library contains CD's, tapes, computers, and other sources of information. Still, when people think of a library, they usually think of all of the books it contains. Here are two easy ways volunteers can work to keep the book collection in top shape.

1. **Shelving books.** Reshelving books keeps the library in order. Volunteers can learn about the Dewey decimal system and find good books to read.
2. **Repairing books.** Popular books get a lot of use, and often the covers and pages get torn. When volunteers repair books, they enable more people to use and enjoy them.

Computer Design in Action

Point out how the design makes the text more readable. The boldface headings serve to identify the text that follows and to break the text into smaller portions.

Tell students that their design should match the tone of their content. For example, if they're designing a serious essay, they shouldn't add funny clip art. They should strive to make the design and the content complementary.

When students finish designing their writing, give the class time to share their completed work. Discuss how the process went and whether students think that their writing benefits from the design treatment they chose.

The writer's last name and the page number appear on every page starting with page 2.

Costello 2

Working with People

Another way to help out at the library is to work with others. Volunteers can use their people skills in one of the following ways:

- **Reading out loud.** Most libraries have children's story hours and need extra people to read to children. This is a good choice for people who like entertaining others.
- **Being read to.** Sometimes children have trouble reading, and it may be helpful for them to read out loud to another person. Volunteers can be good listeners and help struggling readers improve.
- **Matching people with materials.** Another volunteer job is helping people locate books or other library resources.

A bulleted list helps organize the essay.

Finding Your Place

Stop in and have a talk with your local librarian after deciding which services you can offer. See how you can volunteer to make your library the best it can be for everyone in your community.

Margins are at least one inch all around.

Design a page. **Create an effective design for an essay or a report you've already written. Share your design with a classmate to get some feedback: Does your design make the writing clear and easy to follow? Does your design distract the reader in any way?**

Making Your Own Web Site

You can make your own Web site if your family has an Internet account. Ask your provider how to get started. If you are using a school account, ask your teacher for help. Then start designing your site. Use the questions and answers below as a starting point.

How do I plan my site?

Think about the purpose of your Web site and how many pages you need. Will one page be enough space, or will you require several pages? Check out other sites for ideas. Then make sketches to plan your pages.

How do I make the pages?

Start each page as a text file by using your computer. Many new word processing programs let you save a file as a Web page. If yours doesn't, you will have to add HTML (Hypertext Markup Language) codes to format the text and make links to graphics and other pages. You can find instructions for HTML on the Net or at the library.

How do I know whether my pages work?

You should always test your pages. Using your browser, open your first page. Then follow the links to make sure they work correctly and that all the pages look right.

How do I get my pages on the Net?

You must upload your finished pages to the Internet. (Ask your Internet provider how to do this.) After the upload, visit your site to make sure it still works. Also, check it from other computers if possible.

How do I let people know about my site?

Once your site is up, e-mail your friends and tell them to visit it!

Try It Visit a number of different sites for ideas. On your own paper, answer these questions about each one: What is especially good about this site? What could be better? Also talk about these sites with your classmates and friends. When designing your own pages, refer to your research for ideas.

Making Your Own Web Site

Students can create Web pages without publishing them. That way you and the class can review the content and give some feedback to the creator. If possible, set up a class Web site that is accessible only to other students in your school. Your class can post news about the latest field trip or class project. Or have your students make a classroom newsletter or a showcase of exemplary writing that you post on your Web site for the rest of the school to read and enjoy.

Answers

Answers will vary.

Publishing Online

Provide careful guidance as students explore online publishing opportunities. Stress the importance of thoroughly checking out a site before submitting any information.

Encourage students to search for appropriate sites. Help them generate a shared list of approved Web sites to use when publishing their writing.

Publishing Online

The Internet offers many publishing opportunities, including online magazines and writing contests. The information below will help you submit your writing on the Net. (At home, always get a parent's approval first. In school, follow all guidelines for computer use.)

How should I get started?

Check with your teacher to see if your school has its own Web site where you can post your work. Also ask your teacher about other Web sites. There are a number of online magazines that accept student writing. Visit some of these magazines to learn about the types of writing they usually publish.

How do I search for possible sites?

Use a search engine to find places to publish. Some search engines offer their own student links.

How do I submit my work?

Before you do anything, make sure that you understand the publishing guidelines for each site. Be sure to share this information with your teacher and your parents. Then follow these steps:

- **Send your writing in the correct form.**
  Some sites have online forms. Others will ask you to send your writing by mail or e-mail. Always explain why you are sending your writing.
- **Give the publisher information for contacting you.**
  However, don't give your home address or any other personal information unless your parents approve.
- **Be patient.**
  A site should contact you within a week to confirm that your work has arrived. However, it may be several weeks before you hear whether your writing will be used or not.

Search for Web sites. Use the guidelines above to search the Internet for sites that publish student work. Create a list of sites to share with the class. When you complete writing assignments, consider submitting your work for publication using on the Web sites from your class list.

Creating a Portfolio

Would it be fair if people judged your overall writing ability by looking at the very first thing that you wrote in the fall? Not at all. It would be like meeting someone for the first time as you shuffled down to breakfast, still half asleep. Obviously, you would not make your best impression at such a moment.

Your writing skills can be judged best by looking at a collection of your writing developed throughout a grading period. This type of collection is often called a *writing portfolio*, and it gives a clear, complete picture of you as a writer.

This chapter will help you develop a writing portfolio. It includes information about the types and parts of portfolios, plus planning ideas.

What's Ahead

- **Types of Portfolios**
- **Parts of a Portfolio**
- **Planning Ideas**
- **Sample Portfolio Reflections**

Creating a Portfolio

Objectives

- understand types of portfolios
- understand parts of a portfolio
- learn how to create a portfolio

A writing portfolio contains a well-chosen sampling of a student's work. With a portfolio, the student, the teacher, and the student's parents can easily see a student's progress over the course of a grading period.

Ask students whether they have created writing portfolios in the past. Discuss how they used the portfolio and whether it was a useful tool for their writing.

Types of Portfolios

Discuss the different types of portfolios:

- Which type of portfolio would you find most fun to develop?
- Which type of portfolio would be the most helpful and meaningful to you?
- Which type of portfolio do you think your family would appreciate most?

Types of Portfolios

There are four basic types of portfolios you should know about: a showcase portfolio, a growth portfolio, a personal portfolio, and an electronic portfolio.

Showcase Portfolio

A showcase portfolio presents the best writing you have done in school. A showcase is the most common type of portfolio and is usually put together for evaluation at the end of a grading period.

Growth Portfolio

A growth portfolio shows your progress as a writer. It contains many writing assignments and shows how your writing skills are developing:

- writing beginnings and endings,
- writing with voice,
- using specific details, and
- using transitions.

Personal Portfolio

A personal portfolio contains writing you want to keep and share with others. Many professional people—including writers, artists, and musicians—keep personal portfolios. You can arrange this type of portfolio according to different types of writing, different themes, and so on.

Electronic Portfolio

An electronic portfolio is any type of portfolio (showcase, growth, or personal) available on a CD or a Web site. Besides your writing, you can include graphics, video, and sound with this type of portfolio. This makes your writing available to friends and family members no matter where they are!

Rate your growth. On your own paper, list two or three skills that show how your overall writing ability is developing. Also list one or two skills that you need to work on. Make sure to review several pieces of writing before you make your choices.

English Language Learners

Help students select pieces of writing for their showcase or growth portfolios. As you compare pieces, emphasize how their language and writing skills have improved, and focus on specific strong points in the examples of "best" writing in their showcase portfolios.

Advanced Learners

Have students interview adults in various career fields about the use of professional portfolios.

- What kind of portfolios are used? (individual, company, subject-specific, survey, and so on)
- How are portfolios used? (job applications, job evaluations, proposals, and so on)
- What is included in portfolios? (an overview showing different styles, different approaches to the same subject, and so on)

Parts of a Portfolio

A showcase portfolio is one of the most common types of portfolios used in schools. It may contain the parts listed below, but always check with your teacher to be sure.

- A **table of contents** lists the writing samples you have included in your portfolio.
- A **brief essay** or **letter** introduces your portfolio—telling how you put it together, how you feel about it, and what it means to you.
- A **collection of writing samples** presents your best work. Your teacher may require that you include all of your planning, drafting, and revising for one or more of your writings.
- A **cover sheet for each sample** explains why you selected it.
- **Evaluations**, **reflections**, or **checklists** identify the basic skills you have mastered, as well as those skills that you still need to work on.

Gathering Tips

- **Keep track of all your work.** Include prewriting notes, first drafts, and revisions for each writing assignment. Then, when you put together a portfolio, you will have everything that you need.
- **Store all of your writing in a pocket folder or computer file.** This will help you keep track of your writing as you build your portfolio.
- **Set a schedule for working on your portfolio.** You can't put together a good portfolio by waiting until the last minute.
- **Take pride in your work.** Make sure that your portfolio shows you at your best.

Write a cover sheet. Think of the best piece of writing you've done this year. Why is it your best piece? What parts are especially good? How did other people react to the writing? Then write a sample cover sheet for this writing, explaining why you would include it in your portfolio.

Parts of a Portfolio

It is important for students to know which parts of a portfolio are most important to you. Make your expectations clear from the start of the school year. Check their portfolios from time to time to make sure that they are including the parts you requested.

Gathering Tips

Students need to keep their day-to-day writing folder organized so that when it comes time to pull materials for their portfolio, they will be able to find the material they need. A few organizing tips follow:

- Date each piece by hand or with a date stamp.
- Clip related materials together.
- Separate different assignments with colored paper.

English Language Learners

At first, students may benefit from oral, rather than written, reflections on their work. Have them work with trusted partners. Direct both partners to select one piece of writing from their showcase portfolios and explain to their partners why they feel that it is among their best pieces of work. Have them base their cover sheets on the thoughts they expressed during the discussion. After the activity, ask them questions such as the following:

How did following the writing process help you make this piece of writing one of your best?

Encourage them to remember and build on this success.

Planning Ideas

Emphasize to students the importance of saving all their writing, especially early works that may show weaknesses. Their portfolios are intended to show their progress, not just the highlights.

Planning Ideas

The following tips will help you choose your best pieces of writing to include in your portfolio.

1 Be patient.

Don't make quick decisions about which pieces of writing to include in your portfolio. Just keep gathering everything—including all of your drafts—until you are ready to review all of your writing assignments.

2 Make good decisions.

When it's time to choose writing for your portfolio, review each piece. Remember the feelings that you had during each assignment. Which piece makes you feel the best? Which one did your readers like the best? Which one taught you the most?

3 Reflect on your choices.

Read the sample reflections on page 69. Then answer these questions about your writing:

- Why did I choose this piece?
- Why did I write this piece? (What was my purpose?)
- How did I write it? (What was my process?)
- What does it show about my writing ability?
- How did my peers react to this writing?
- What would I do differently next time?
- What have I learned since writing it?

4 Set future writing goals.

After putting your portfolio together, set some goals for the future. Here are some goals that other students have set:

I will write about topics that really interest me.
I will spend more time on my beginnings and endings.
I will make sure that my sentences read smoothly.
I will support my main points with convincing details.

Plan a portfolio cover. On a piece of plain paper, design a cover for a portfolio folder. Include your name and an interesting title. Add sketches or photos related to your writing, your classes, your favorite hobby, and so on.

Sample Portfolio Reflections

When you take time to reflect on your writing assignments, think about the process that you used to develop each one. Also think about what you might do differently next time. The following samples will help you with your own reflections.

Student Reflections

If I had to write another comparison essay, I would think more carefully about my topics. To make effective comparisons, there must be a number of meaningful similarities and differences to write about. I would also do a lot more research before I started my writing. When my classmates rated my essay, I could tell that they had a lot of questions about the information I included. Next time, I will seek their advice much earlier in the writing process.

—Anna Hernandez

My persuasive essay on proposing a solution turned out really well. This happened because I felt so strongly about my topic. I really do think that students would become better writers if we had a writing lab open before and after school. I learned from this essay that the words and ideas come easy if I have strong feelings about a topic. I also learned that these strong feelings helped make my writing voice sound really convincing. —Roy Baker

Professional Reflections

I wrote *Mad Merlin* by combining legends of Camelot with histories and myths. As I look back at the novel, though, I see it is mostly about my own life. Good fiction is that way—creative in the details, but otherwise full of truth.

—J. Robert King

With each book I write, I become more and more convinced that the books have a life of their own, quite apart from me. —Madeleine L'Engle

Sample Portfolio Reflections

Student Reflections

As students choose materials for their portfolios, they may find themselves reflecting on writing that they did earlier in the school term. This delay before reflecting can be helpful because it allows for students to gain added perspective. They will not be so close to the writing, and they can evaluate it more dispassionately.

Professional Reflections

Point out that professional writers make new discoveries about their work when they take a look back. These two quotations show how writers become so absorbed in the writing process that they themselves don't always see the patterns they have created. They need time and distance to look back and see the shape and life that they have given to their writing.

Advanced Learners

Invite students to copy all of the professional author quotes from this unit onto index cards and create an inspirational bulletin board for the classroom. Encourage all class members to add new professional writers' reflections that they find in published articles or on book jackets throughout the year.

Descriptive Writing Overview

Common Core Standards Focus

Writing 4: Produce clear and coherent writing in which the development, organization, and style are appropriate to task, purpose, and audience.

Language 3a: Choose language that expresses ideas precisely and concisely, recognizing and eliminating wordiness and redundancy.

Writing Forms

- Descriptive Paragraph
- Describing a Place

Focus on the Traits

- **Ideas** Using specific, sensory details
- **Organization** Creating a logical description based on order of location
- **Voice** Revealing the writer's personality through personal details
- **Word Choice** Choosing words with the right connotation
- **Sentence Fluency** Writing a variety of sentence types to improve sentence flow
- **Conventions** Checking for errors in punctuation, capitalization, spelling, and grammar

Literature Connections

- ***"Fish Cheeks"*** by Amy Tan

Technology Connections

Write Source Online
www.hmheducation.com/writesource

- ***Net-text***
- ***Bookshelf***
- ***GrammarSnap***
- ***Portfolio***
- ***Writing Network features***
- ***File Cabinet***

Interactive Whiteboard Lessons

Suggested Descriptive Writing Unit (Three Weeks)

Week	Day	Writing and Skills Instruction	*Student Edition*		*SkillsBook*	*Daily Language Workouts*	*Write Source Online*
			Descriptive Writing Unit	Resource Units*			
Week 1	1–4	**Descriptive Paragraph: A Place**	71–74			12–13, 82	*Interactive Whiteboard Lessons*
		Skills Activities: • Adjectives		488, 732–733	175–176		*GrammarSnap*
		• Prepositional Phrases		495, 700–701, 742 (+)			
	5	**Descriptive Essay: A Place** (Model) Literature Connections "Fish Cheeks"	75–77				
Week 2	6	(Prewriting)	78–79			14–15, 83	*Net-text*
	7–8	(Writing)	80–82				*Net-text*
	9–10	(Revising)	82				*Net-text*
		Skills Activities: • Specific Nouns		470–471, 702–703	143–144		*GrammarSnap*
		• Compound Adjectives		488, 732 (+)	177–178		*GrammarSnap*
		• Sentence Variety		513, 582–583	7–8, 113–114, 115–116		
Week 3	11–12	(Editing)	82			16–17, 84	*Net-text*
		Skills Activities: • Spelling		642–643	59–60		
		• Capitalization		624–625	49–50		
	13	Writing Across the Curriculum	83–89				
	14–15	**Practical Writing** (Classified Ad)	90–91				
		Skills Activities: • Adjectives		489, 732 (+), 734–735 (indefinite, predicate)	179–180		

* These units are also located in the back of the Teacher's Edition. Resource Units include "Basic Grammar and Writing," "A Writer's Resource," and "Proofreader's Guide."
(+) This activity is located in a different section of the *Write Source Student Edition.* If students have already completed this activity, you may wish to review it at this time.

Teacher's Notes for Descriptive Writing

This overview for descriptive writing includes some specific teaching suggestions for this unit.

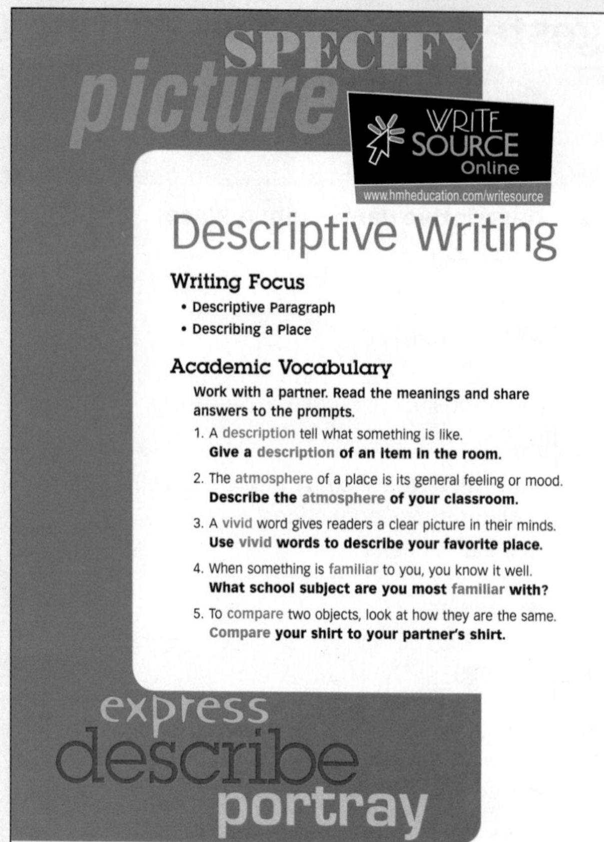

Writing Focus

Descriptive Paragraph (pages 71–74)

When students write a descriptive paragraph, they need to keep focused so that the words are clear and sentences don't wander. After a reader is finished with such a paragraph, she or he will know what the writer saw.

Describing a Place (pages 75–91)

Good authors create interesting characters with believable dialogue. These writers also go out of their way to describe the place of action so that the reader can imagine a newly painted room, a dirty horse stall, or a rugged mountain. These descriptions add depth to the story line. The story's characters cease to be words on a page and come alive in the world the writer has created. Students would do well to study the place descriptions found in classic and contemporary novels.

Academic Vocabulary

Read aloud the academic terms, as well as the descriptions and questions. Model for students how to read one question and answer it. Have partners monitor their understanding and seek clarification of the terms by working through the meanings and questions together.

Minilessons

The Picture — Descriptive Paragraph

- **THINK** about how the five senses can be used to describe a place. Which senses should be emphasized? **IMAGINE** the restaurant "World's Juiciest Burgers." In a 5-senses chart, **LIST** details that you would include to let your reader know what the restaurant is like.

Bird's-Eye View — Describing a Place

- **READ** the description on page 81 in your textbook. **DRAW** a map of the yard showing where things are located according to the writer. **COMPARE** your map with a partner's.

Descriptive Writing

Descriptive Paragraph

All kids have a favorite place where they like to spend time, either alone or with their friends. It could be a room at home, a particular spot in the park, or maybe a neighborhood restaurant with the "World's Juiciest Burgers."

In this chapter, you will write a paragraph to describe a favorite place. You will need to use plenty of sensory details to re-create this place. Your goal is to help readers see the sights, smell the aromas, feel the atmosphere, and hear the sounds as if the readers were right there with you.

Writing Guidelines

Subject: A favorite place
Purpose: To describe one of your favorite places
Form: Descriptive paragraph
Audience: Classmates

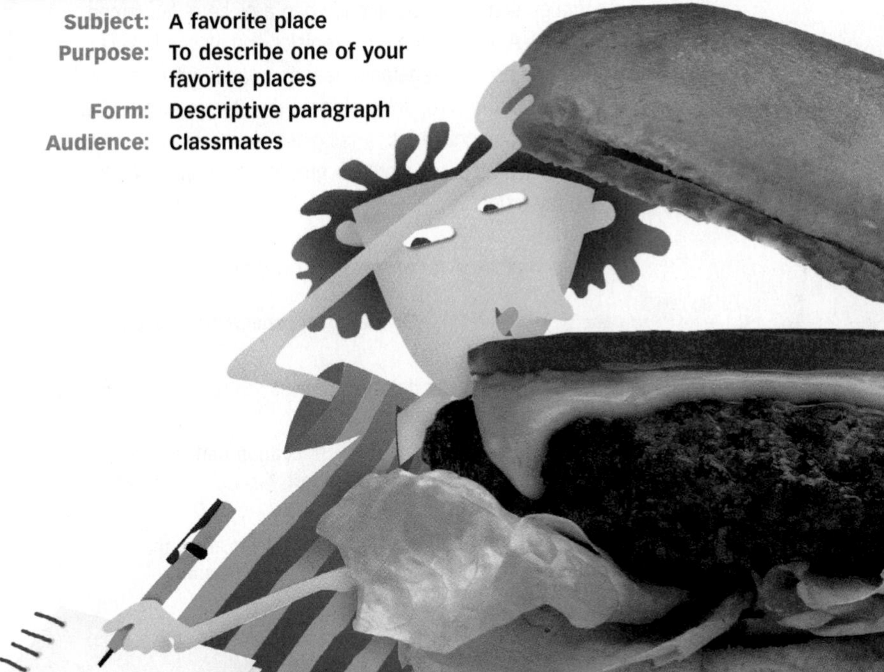

Copy Masters

Sensory Chart (TE p. 73)

Descriptive Paragraph

Objectives

- understand the content and structure of a descriptive paragraph
- choose a topic (a favorite place) to write about
- plan, draft, revise, and edit a descriptive paragraph

A **descriptive paragraph** uses sensory details to help the reader clearly imagine a person, a place, a thing, or an idea. An effective paragraph contains three main parts:

- a topic sentence
- the body
- a closing sentence

* Additional information about developing a descriptive paragraph is on SE page 527.

Select from a short story or novel a paragraph that describes a place.

- Ask students to sketch what they see in their mind as you read aloud the paragraph.
- Invite students to share their drawings and identify details from the passage that helped them develop a mental image of the place.

Technology Connections

Use this unit's Interactive Whiteboard Lesson to introduce descriptive writing.

 ***Interactive Whiteboard Lessons***

Descriptive Paragraph

Discuss how the writer's use of direction words (for example, *Above him on the wall, next to the counter, on the cash register,* and *at the cold, shiny chrome counter*) helps the reader to picture where things are in the deli.

Respond to the reading.

Review the questions orally with students.

Answers

Ideas 1. Possible choices:
- Bob is wiping the counter
- giant pictures on the wall
- pie in the round display case
- sign on cash register
- cold, shiny chrome counter
- Bob pours a thick smoothie
- fresh strawberry on top

Organization 2. far to near

Voice & Word Choice 3. Possible choices:
- familiar sights and smells
- As usual
- He greets all his regular customers this way

Descriptive Paragraph

In a descriptive paragraph, you use details to paint a vivid picture of one person, place, thing, or event. You start with a **topic sentence** that tells what the paragraph is about. Then, in the **body** of the paragraph, you add the specific details. The **closing sentence** brings the description to an end.

Bob's Deli

Topic Sentence — When I walk through the door at Bob's Deli, familiar sights and smells greet me. **Body** — As usual, Bob is wiping the counter, even though it's spotless. "Hey, you," he says. He greets all his regular customers this way. Above him on the wall, giant pictures of sandwiches and salads make me even hungrier than I already am. At least six kinds of pie fill a round display case that stands next to the counter. It looks as though someone has already had a piece of the lemon meringue. A sign on the cash register announces today's special—a bowl of vegetable beef soup and half a sandwich. I sit down at the cold, shiny chrome counter and watch Bob pour a thick smoothie into a tall glass. **Closing Sentence** — As he plops a fresh strawberry on top, my stomach growls, and I am ready to place my order.

Respond to the reading. On your own paper, answer each of the following questions.

- ☐ **Ideas** (1) What details did the writer use to "paint" a picture? Name three of them.
- ☐ **Organization** (2) Which order of location pattern did the writer use (left to right, right to left, top to bottom, far to near)?
- ☐ **Voice & Word Choice** (3) What phrases show that the writer really likes Bob's Deli? List two of them.

Grammar Connection

Prepositional Phrases
- **Proofreader's Guide** pages 700–701, 742 (+)
- ***Write Source*** page 495
- ***GrammarSnap*** Prepositions and Prepositional Phrases

English Language Learners

Read the paragraph aloud and have students try to sketch what the writer describes. Then reread the paragraph. As you read about each part of the scene, have students point to it in their drawings. Encourage them to write the words that show spatial relations—*above, next to, on, at*—in the appropriate places on their drawings.

Advanced Learners

Provide several magazines such as *National Geographic* and *Smithsonian* that feature rich, descriptive paragraphs. Have students locate and list in a learning log or journal especially effective adjectives and adverbs. Encourage students to periodically add to their lists. These lists will model for students how professional writers describe people, places, and things.

Prewriting Selecting a Topic

To get started, think about places you could write about. Clustering is one way to begin. The writer of the paragraph on page 72 used a cluster like the one below to remember some favorite places.

Cluster

Prewrite

Select a topic. Create your own cluster to identify possible places to write about in your paragraph. Then "star" one place you'd like to describe.

Gathering Details

Collect plenty of sensory details about your topic, even though you might not use all of them in your paragraph. Choose details that will help you create a clear, vivid description.

Prewrite

Collect your details. Use the following questions to help you remember important details.

- What are the main sights and sounds?
- Are there any parts in this place that stand out?
- What colors are important?
- What smells and tastes do you connect with this place?
- What feelings do you have about it?
- What happens in this place?

DESCRIPTIVE

Prewriting Selecting a Topic

To help students generate ideas for their clusters, ask them to think about these questions:

- Where do you and your family like to go for vacation?
- Where do you go when you want to think or be alone?
- Where do you like to eat? listen to music? walk? get together with friends? read? play sports?

* See SE page 544 for more about using clustering.

Students can look through family photo albums, souvenirs, scrapbooks, and **personal journals** *(see below)* for more ideas.

Prewriting Gathering Details

Have students use the questions to determine if they know the place they've chosen well enough to describe it in detail.

Encourage students to jot down as many details about their topic as they can to answer the questions. They can refer to these details when they write their paragraph.

Teaching Tip: Personal Journals

Personal journals provide students with opportunities to write about a variety of topics. Students can describe people, places, things, and ideas while details are fresh in their minds. As a result, such writing can provide a rich source of material for writing ideas. (See SE pages 432–434 for more on keeping journals.)

English Language Learners

Suggest that students think about their favorite places in the school or classroom. If they write about a place that is familiar to you, it will be easier to coach them effectively by asking guiding questions.

Struggling Learners

To better focus students' attention on sensory details, advise them to close their eyes to imagine a favorite place. Then have them record their details on the reproducible sensory chart (TE page 793). Demonstrate chart usage by asking students to suggest more details for the chart on SE page 347 as you categorize the details on the board.

Writing Creating Your First Draft

Remind students that order of location tells where one thing is in relation to something else. Hold **writing conferences** *(see below)* to provide additional guidance.

Students often rely on stock phrases to conclude a piece of writing. Tell students to avoid a closing sentence that begins with

- That's why I like ______
- These are the reasons that ______

Revising Improving Your Writing

Have students ask themselves the revising questions and have a partner read the draft and offer suggestions for revising based on the questions.

Editing Checking for Conventions

After students have edited their paragraph, invite them to share their paragraph with the class.

Writing Creating Your First Draft

The goal of a first draft is to get all of your ideas and details down on paper. Remember that everything does not have to be perfect in a first draft. You can make as many changes as you want later on.

- Start your paragraph with a topic sentence that identifies a favorite place and interests your reader.
- Think about how you want to organize your sentences. Order of location (top to bottom, left to right, near to far) works well for many descriptions. See page 551 for information about other patterns.
- Choose transitions from the list below to help you show location. See pages 572–573 for more transitions.

  above, below, beside to the left, to the right on top of, next to
- End with a sentence that brings your description to a close. See the closing sentence in the model on page 72.

Write your first draft. Use the guidelines above when you write. Be sure to add specific details that appeal to your reader's senses

Revising Improving Your Writing

When you revise, focus first on the ideas and organization in your writing. You may move, delete, or change parts of your writing as necessary.

Revise your paragraph. Use the following questions as a guide.

1. Does my topic sentence identify the place I'm describing?
2. Have I included enough sensory details?
3. Have I put the details in the best order?
4. Do I use specific nouns, verbs, and adjectives?
5. Do I use complete sentences that read smoothly?

Editing Checking for Conventions

Carefully edit your revised paragraph for punctuation, capitalization, spelling, and grammar.

Edit and proofread your work. Use the conventions checklist on page 128 as you edit. Then write a neat final copy.

Grammar Connection

Adjectives

- **Proofreader's Guide** pages 732–733
- ***Write Source*** page 488
- ***SkillsBook*** pages 175–176
- ***GrammarSnap*** Adjectives and Adverbs

Teaching Tip: Writing Conferences

Brief, one-on-one discussions can help students focus their ideas and gain confidence.

To help students organize their ideas according to location, suggest that they

- draw a sketch of the place they plan to describe
- use the drawing to describe orally where things are in relationship to one another
- write transition words, such as the ones listed above, on their drawing as they describe it.

Descriptive Writing

Describing a Place

"Ah, my room. . . . Let me show you around. Do you see how I display all my stylish clothes across the floor? Do you hear the gentle snoring of my dog Urfie as he warms the foot of my bed? Do you detect that strange odor coming from the closet? Ah hah! That must be my gym shoes."

When you describe a familiar place, you take your reader on a tour using your best words. Your goal is to let the reader see the things around you, hear what is happening, and maybe even smell the gym shoes!

Writing Guidelines

Subject: A place you know well
Form: Descriptive essay
Purpose: To describe a familiar place
Audience: Classmates

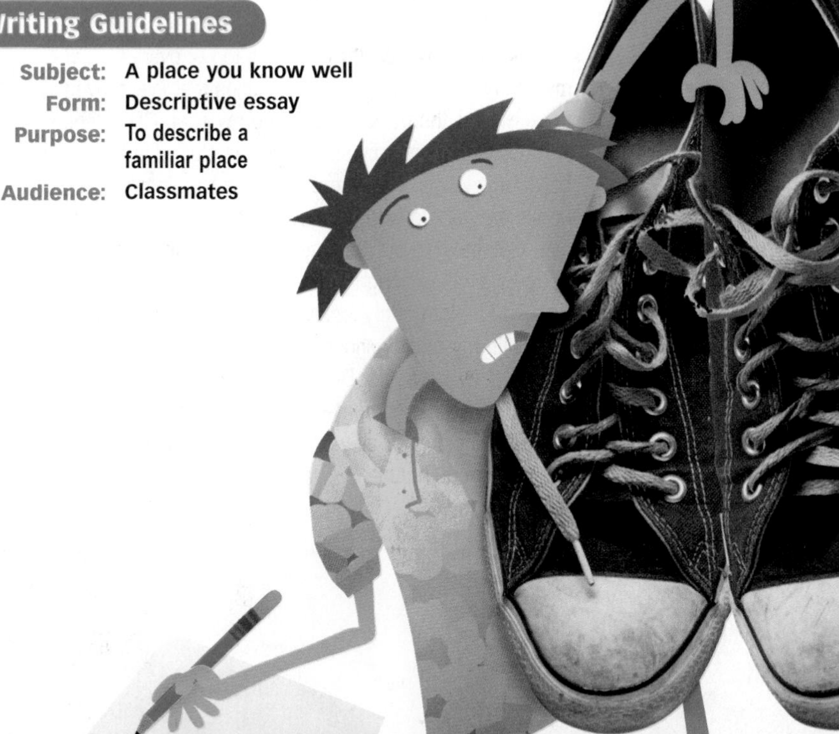

Describing a Place

Objectives

- understand what a descriptive essay is
- understand the content and form of a descriptive essay
- plan, draft, revise, edit, and publish a descriptive essay

A **descriptive essay** is a piece of writing that

- describes in great detail a certain person, place, thing, or idea;
- uses sensory details to create a clear mental image of a certain person, place, thing, or idea.

Ask students to read the introduction to this section silently. Then invite a volunteer to conduct an oral tour of the classroom, using a tone and style similar to the casual tone and style used in the first paragraph. Encourage the volunteer to be creative.

Advanced Learners

Point out that this section's introductory paragraph includes details involving the senses. Ask students to identify the senses mentioned (sight, hearing, and smell).

- Challenge students to identify two more senses and embellish the paragraph by incorporating details that involve these additional senses.
- Encourage students to rewrite the paragraph including sentences about the additional senses.
- Invite students to share their paragraph with the class.

Copy Masters

Sensory Chart (TE pp. 77, 78)

T-chart (TE p. 78)

Descriptive Essay

Read through this sample essay with the class, pointing out the elements that make it a good descriptive essay.

Ideas

- The writer captures the reader's interest by calling his school locker his home away from home.
- A variety of sensory details creates a strong image of the locker.

Organization

- The locker is described in order of location.

Voice

- Personal details about the items inside the locker reveal the writer's personality.

Descriptive Essay

In the sample essay that follows, the writer describes his locker. As you read the description, look at the notes in the left margin. They explain the important parts of the essay.

Beginning
The beginning shows why this place is special.

Middle
The middle paragraphs describe the locker from top to bottom.

My Home Away from Home

Blue metal lockers line the hallways in our school. Each locker is identical except for the brass number attached to the door. Locker number 379 is mine. This locker is my home away from home for the year.

When I click open my locker, the smell of peanut butter escapes from a brown paper lunch bag on the top shelf. Under the bag, the sleeve of my old olive green sweatshirt dangles off the shelf. On top of everything is my favorite blue cap. Some magazines that I've shoved up there, way in the back, almost hide my dead CD player.

All winter long, my ski jacket was stuffed in the middle part of my locker. Now the only things hanging on the hooks are my red warm-up jacket and my bag full of dirty gym clothes. Phew. That smell mixed with the peanut butter is almost enough to make me gag.

The bottom of my locker is like a mini dump site. It is filled with my muddy shoes, broken pencils, and a pile of sticky candy wrappers. Buried underneath all of that are dozens of old assignments and, probably, some things I've been looking for all year. I'll know for sure when I dig everything out in June.

Middle
Special attention is given to the locker door.

Some of my most important stuff is attached to the inside of my locker door. Near the top, I've taped two pictures of my favorite rock group. Around the edges, I've jammed in a bunch of notes from my friends. Below the notes, a collection of fridge magnets from my favorite pizza places hold up a huge photo of me with the 10-pound bass I landed last summer.

Ending
The ending gives more insight into the writer's personality.

On the last day of school, I'll take down the pictures and throw out the candy wrappers and trash. I'll stuff all the important things into my backpack and grab those smelly gym clothes. When I close my locker for the last time and head for home, it will feel as if I've just completed another chapter in my life.

DESCRIPTIVE

Respond to the reading. **Answer the following questions about the essay.**

- ☐ **Ideas & Organization (1) Which details rely on a sense other than sight? (2) How is the essay organized?**
- ☐ **Voice & Word Choice (3) Which details reveal the most about the writer's personality?**

Literature Connections: For an example of descriptive language, read author Amy Tan's description of prawns and her mother's cooking in "Fish Cheeks."

Suggest that a volunteer read this descriptive essay aloud. This may serve to inspire students as they prepare to write their own descriptive essay.

Respond to the reading.

Answers

Ideas & Organization 1. Possible choices:

- sound: click
- smell: peanut butter, smelly gym clothes
- touch: sticky candy wrappers

2. order of location

- top to bottom inside the locker
- top to bottom on the inside of the locker door

Voice & Word Choice 3. Possible choices: Details that describe photos, notes from friends, favorite old clothes, and the comparison of cleaning his locker to ending a chapter in his life make the writer seem sentimental and philosophical.

If you wish, ask students to write descriptions of their lockers modelled after the sample essay.

Literature Connections

In the personal essay "Fish Cheeks," author Amy Tan describes her mother's cooking and an important lesson her mother teaches her. Discuss ways she keeps her essay interesting, including: natural voice, focus on one event, vivid description, specific details, and humor.

For more information about personal essays, see the Reading-Writing Connections beginning on page TE-36.

English Language Learners

After students have completed the **Respond to the reading** activity, give them practice with gathering sensory details

- Give each student a copy of the reproducible sensory chart (TE page 793).
- Encourage students to use the sample essay as a guide to think about what's in their own locker and to list these details under the appropriate heading on the chart.
- Invite students to share their charts with each other.

Prewriting Selecting a Topic

Suggest that students look at the clusters they created on SE page 73 for ideas for their topic charts.

Prewriting Gathering Details

Have students review the questions to help them determine two things about the topic they've chosen:

- Can they generate enough sensory details to write an essay about that particular place?
- Is the place they have chosen too big or too small to describe in an essay?

Remind students that their goal is to make readers understand why this place is special and important. Every detail should help them achieve this goal.

* See Writing About a Place on SE page 532 for more tips on using details effectively.

Technology Connections

Students can use the added features of the Net-text as they explore this stage of the writing process.

Write Source Online ***Net-text***

Prewriting Selecting a Topic

The topic for your essay should be a place that is very familiar to you. Make sure that you choose a place that isn't too big or too small. Think of places that you can describe in a few paragraphs with many interesting details. A topic chart like the one below can help you organize your thoughts.

Topic Chart

Places	Specific Topics
Home	*– my bedroom* *– our backyard* *– the kitchen*
School	*– (my locker)* *– the music room* *– the office*
Other	*– Gus's Pizza* *– my grandma's kitchen* *– the city beach*

Create a topic chart. Make a chart like the one above, using *Home, School,* and *Other.* Think of two or three specific topics for each category. Circle the one specific topic that you would like to write about.

Gathering Details

One way to gather details is to make a list of sensory details. Sensory details help the reader see, feel, smell, taste, and hear what is being described.

Collect details. Gather sensory details for your description by answering the following questions.

1. What do you see when you look around your place? (Think about colors, shapes, and sizes.)
2. What sounds do you hear?
3. What smells do you notice?
4. What textures can you touch?
5. What tastes or feelings come to mind?

English Language Learners

Encourage students to go to the place they've chosen to write about, if possible, to gather details. Have students use sketches, words, or phrases to create a web or to fill in a copy of the reproducible sensory chart (TE page 793) while they are in their chosen place.

Struggling Learners

Before having students gather sensory details, play a short descriptive segment of an audio book that is of interest to your students. This lets students "hear" how descriptive language allows the reader to picture a scene without actually seeing it.

Have students use the reproducible sensory chart (TE page 793) to gather their details.

- Suggest that students add *Colors* and *Shapes* in the *Sights* column, leaving space for writing.
- Students can then use their completed charts to write sentences for their essay.

Organizing Your Details

You can use order of location (spatial order) to arrange the details in a description. For example, you may decide to organize the details from top to bottom or from left to right or farthest to nearest. The writer of the essay on pages 76–77 organized the details from top to bottom on a list.

Organizing List

1. *Open the locker door.*
2. *Describe what's on the top shelf.*
3. *Tell what's hanging in the middle part.*
4. *Draw a mental picture of what's on the bottom.*
5. *Describe the inside of the locker door.*
6. *Share the details of the last day of school.*

DESCRIPTIVE

Organize your details. Decide which order works best for your description (top to bottom, left to right, far to near). Then write an organizing list like the one above for your essay.

Using Similes and Metaphors

Similes and metaphors can make descriptive writing clearer and more creative. They can help readers see the description in their minds. The writer of the essay on pages 76–77 uses a metaphor in the opening paragraph and a simile in the third middle paragraph.

- A **simile** compares two different things using *like* or *as*.
  The bottom of my locker is like a mini dump site.
- A **metaphor** compares two different things without using *like* or *as*.
  This locker is my home away from home for the year.

Write a simile and a metaphor to compare your place with other things. If you like how your comparisons turn out, include them in your essay.

Prewriting Organizing Your Details

Before students create their list, suggest that they

- spend time at the place (if possible) jotting notes and making sketches about where things are in relation to one another,
- bring photographs of the place to class to use as a reference when creating the organizing list.

* For more about using order of location to organize details, see SE page 535.

After reading aloud the information about similes and metaphors, have the class create a new simile and metaphor, using the model examples as starters.

- My locker is like ____
- This locker is ______.

Answers

Answers will vary. Ask students to share their similes and metaphors in small groups to get feedback.

English Language Learners

Have students use their graphic organizer, photograph, or sketch they have made of the place they are describing to list a few things in the place. Then, next to each thing, have them identify something that the item is like. For example:

- soft chair in media center—hug
- sound of students talking about their books—bees buzzing

Demonstrate how to turn these comparisons into similes and metaphors.

- The chair felt like a hug.
- The students were busy bees buzzing around the library.

Encourage students to incorporate some of the similes and metaphors they create with you into their writing.

Writing Starting Your Descriptive Essay

Point out to students that they are about to begin a first draft. Emphasize that

- they shouldn't worry about writing perfectly now, because they will revise and edit later;
- they should write on every other line, or double-space if typing, to leave room for revisions.

Writing Using Words with Feeling

To help students understand connotation, read aloud the set of words below. Explain that each word has a different meaning, or connotation. Ask students to describe the different feeling each word evokes.

- noise, racket, melody, hum

Make sure students have access to a thesaurus or synonym finder so they can look for words with just the right feeling for their essay.

If students can't decide how to start their essay, tell them to experiment with both styles of beginning paragraphs.

Technology Connections

Students can use the added features of the Net-text as they explore this stage of the writing process.

***Write Source Online* Net-text**

Writing Starting Your Descriptive Essay

The beginning paragraph should get your reader's attention and identify your topic—a familiar place. Here are two ways to get started.

Beginning Paragraph

- **Put yourself in the description.** You can do this by serving as the narrator. This means that you will use "I" and describe the place through your eyes.

The writer tells how she feels.

When I stand on our back step and look out, I see more than just a backyard. I see my family's "summer home," a small, relaxing plot of land protected by a redwood fence.

- **Begin with background information.** This information will help your reader better understand or appreciate your topic.

The writer shows why this place is special.

When my mom's job forced us to move into the city, she decided to create a quiet place for us to relax. That's just what she did in our backyard. With a lot of work, we now have a peaceful "getaway" to enjoy.

Using Words with Feeling

Don't settle for just any word to capture the description of the place you are describing. Use words that have the right meaning and the right feeling, or connotation. (*Connotation* means "the feeling that a word suggests.")

The writer of each of the beginning paragraphs above uses words like "summer home," "relaxing," "quiet," and "peaceful" because they all have the right feeling—the backyard is a place to unwind and enjoy yourself.

Write your beginning paragraph. Write a beginning that catches your reader's interest and focuses on your topic. Make sure to use words with the right feeling. If you don't like how your first opening turns out, try again.

English Language Learners

Ask students how *noise, racket, melody,* and *hum* are alike. Point out that although they all describe sounds, they have different connotations. Ask students to name things each word could describe (noise—train; racket—barking dogs; melody—music; hum—fan).

Struggling Learners

Caution students that if they write in the first person, they should avoid using the word *I* to begin their descriptive essay.

As a group, practice rewording *I* sentences.

- Example: I like attending school football games.
- Revision: On Friday nights, I like attending school football games.

Developing the Middle Part

In the middle paragraphs of the essay, describe your familiar place. Use your organizing list from page 79 as a guide for your writing.

Middle Paragraphs

In the middle paragraphs, the writer first describes the three sides of the backyard before focusing on the lawn in the center.

Each middle paragraph focuses on a different part of the yard.

The underlined phrases show the organization of the essay.

Along the fence at the left side of the yard are my mom's famous red rosebushes. They explode with color all summer long. A flat stone walkway running in front of the bushes makes it easy to admire and smell the flowers. These stones are smooth and warm against my bare feet.

Against the back fence is a small white shed. The shed holds my mom's garden tools and an old push mower. It also holds our bicycles and a lot of sports equipment, including my favorite basketballs. On rainy days, I like to stand in the shed and hear the raindrops hitting the metal roof.

My mother's vegetable garden runs next to the fence on the right side of the yard. Mom always plants beans in that space. As the bean plants grow, she carefully ties them to stakes to keep them from falling over. In the front of this garden is a row of golden yellow marigolds. Their distinct smell is supposed to keep the rabbits away from the beans.

At the heart of our yard, is the lawn itself. A crab apple tree towers over the back of the yard and provides plenty of shade. In front of the tree is a wooden lawn swing that gets plenty of use, especially in the evening. To the right of the swing is a yellow plastic sandbox where my little brother and sister play for hours at a time.

Write your middle paragraphs. Use sensory details in your paragraphs to help the reader imagine how your place looks, feels, sounds, and smells.

Writing Developing the Middle Part

Before having students write their middle paragraphs, discuss the sample.

- Have students pay particular attention to how the writer uses transition words and phrases—*along, against, next to, the heart of*—to guide the reader and show where objects are located in the yard and in relation to each other.
- Then ask students to point out details in the sample that create the strongest images in their mind and best capture the writer's feelings about the topic.

As they write their middle paragraphs, remind students to review

- their prewriting notes,
- their organizing list,
- and the similes and metaphors they created.

✱ For more about finding and using interesting details, see SE page 531.

English Language Learners

Help students write "skeleton" sentences that will serve as topic sentences and establish the organizational structure of their essay. For example:

The first thing I see in the school library corner is ______.

While I look for a book, I hear _______.

Once I settle in a chair with a book, I feel ______.

Struggling Learners

Have students use their organizing list from SE page 79 to create a visual organizer.

- Write on the board headings for the listed locations—*top shelf, middle, bottom, locker door.*
- Have students refer to the sample essay on SE pages 76–77 and list descriptive objects under each heading.
- Instruct students to use index cards, writing one heading on each card, to imitate this process for their own familiar place.
- Then have them write complete sentences from the descriptive phrases.

Writing Ending Your Essay

Help students understand the effect of a strong ending by discussing the sample. Ask the following questions:

- What ideas and images does the writer use to end the essay?
- Do you think the ending works? Why or why not?
- How does the ending make you feel about the writer?
- What thoughts linger in your mind after reading the ending?

Revising and Editing

Suggest that students work in groups of five to revise their essays.

- Students pass their papers around, and each member of the group can revise for one of the five traits (ideas, organization, voice, word choice, and sentence fluency).
- Students can each use a different colored pencil to write suggestions for revisions based on the question given for their particular trait.

Technology Connections

Have students use the Writing Network features of the Net-text to comment on each other's drafts.

***Write Source Online* Net-text**

Writing Ending Your Essay

The ending paragraph should clearly signal that your description is complete. In the last sentence or two, leave your reader with a final idea or image—something that will keep her or him thinking about your topic.

Ending Paragraph

The writer makes a final comment about the topic.

Beyond my yard lies a busy city. On hot summer nights, when we relax in the yard, I can hear the rush of freeway traffic and the call of far-off train whistles. I'm sure that someday I'll join the traffic or follow the train whistles, but for now, I'm happy right here.

Write your ending paragraph. Use interesting details that will keep this place in your reader's memory for some time.

Revising and Editing

You can improve your first draft by adding, deleting, or changing some details. Keep these questions in mind when you revise.

Revise your first draft. Revise your first draft using the questions below as a guide.

- ☐ **Ideas** Have I included enough sensory details about the place?
- ☐ **Organization** Do I use order of location to organize the details?
- ☐ **Voice** Do I sound like I really care about the subject and the reader?
- ☐ **Word Choice** Do I use descriptive words from start to finish?
- ☐ **Sentence Fluency** Do my sentences flow smoothly? Do I vary sentence lengths and beginnings?

Edit your description. Once you have completed your revising, use the checklist on page 128 to correct any errors in your essay. Then write a neat final copy to share.

Grammar Connection

Specific Nouns

- **Proofreader's Guide** pages 702–703
- ***Write Source*** pages 470–471
- ***SkillsBook*** pages 143–144
- ***GrammarSnap*** Nouns Overview

Compound Adjectives

- **Proofreader's Guide** pages 732 (+)
- ***Write Source*** page 488
- ***SkillsBook*** pages 177–178
- ***GrammarSnap*** Adjectives and Adverbs

Sentence Variety (combining with key words and phrases)

- **Proofreader's Guide** pages 582–583 (commas in a series)
- ***Write Source*** page 513
- ***SkillsBook*** pages 7–8, 113–114, 115–116
- ***GrammarSnap*** Simple, Compound, and Complex Sentences

English Language Learners

As part of the group revision process, assign students with limited language ability the trait of Organization. Students can make a quick sketch to show order of location. Model this, using the sample middle paragraphs on SE page 81.

Descriptive Writing

Across the Curriculum

Wouldn't it be great if you could teach a parrot to recite the Gettysburg Address? Wouldn't it be even greater if you could teach your parrot not to recite the speech all day and all night? Finally, wouldn't it be the greatest if you could write an ad that describes your parrot so well that a kind and caring bird lover comes to buy him? Descriptive writing can be useful.

Sometimes, descriptive writing can also be useful in completing class assignments. For example, in social studies, you could describe a famous person or place. In math, you could describe a geometric object, or in science, you could describe the result of a lab experiment.

What's Ahead

- **Social Studies:** Describing a Famous Place
- **Math:** Writing a Geometric Riddle
- **Science:** Writing a Lab Report
- **Practical Writing:** Writing a Classified Ad

Copy Masters

Venn Diagram (TE p. 84)

5 W's Chart (TE pp. 85, 86, 87)

Across the Curriculum

Objective

- apply what students have learned about descriptive writing to other curriculum areas

The lessons on the following pages provide samples of descriptive writing students might do in different content areas. The particular form used in each content area may also be used in a different content area (for example, students could write a riddle just as well in science as in math).

Assigning these forms of writing will depend on

- the skill level of your students,
- the subject matter they are studying at any particular time, and
- the writing goals of your school, district, or state.

Social Studies: Describing a Famous Place

Use the notes in the margin to discuss the organization of the essay.

Ask a volunteer to read the descriptive essay aloud. Discuss how the sample essay compares with the descriptive essay that students wrote earlier in the unit. Provide each student with a copy of the reproducible Venn diagram (TE page 791), or draw a Venn diagram on the board and ask students to help you fill it in.

Similar:
- Both essays describe a place.
- Both essays use order of location to organize ideas.
- Both essays use interesting and specific details.

Different:
- The sample essay relies on concrete details; the student's essay relies on sensory details.
- The sample essay doesn't contain details that reveal the writer's personality or feelings; the student's essay does.
- The sample essay has a factual tone; the student's essay has an emotional tone.

Social Studies: Describing a Famous Place

Use descriptive writing when you need to explain the features of a famous place. Think about a modern or an ancient structure that you have read about or visited. The writer below chose to write about the ancient Roman Colosseum.

The Roman Colosseum

The **beginning** shares important background information.

A modern football stadium is about the same size as the Roman Colosseum was. Between 50,000 and 75,000 spectators attended events there for hundreds of years after it was completed in 80 C.E.

Without using modern machinery, the Romans built the huge Colosseum on the site of a marsh. They drained water and then cut an oval donut shape into the clay base. On top of the base, they poured layers of cement, more than 36 feet thick. Next, they built supporting brick walls, about 9 feet wide, around both the inner and outer walls of the foundation.

The **middle** describes the place from the bottom to the top.

Just below ground level, the Romans built a maze of tunnels, rooms, and passages on top of the concrete base. This area held equipment, scenery, and even wild animals. Huge hoists lifted both gladiators and animals to the ground level.

At ground level, sand covered the wooden floor of the arena. Nets attached to tall poles protected the audience from the wild beasts.

Above the arena, spectators sat and viewed the events of the day. Just like today, there were sections of preferred seating. The outer walls of the Colosseum stood four stories high and enclosed the seating area. Each of the first three stories had 80 identical arches, and each arch held a statue. Forty rectangular windows circled the fourth story.

The **ending** gives the reader something to think about.

When people visit the Colosseum today, they will see the ruins, but they can still imagine sitting among the ancient Romans in this famous place.

Writing Tips

Before you write . . .

- **Choose a famous place that interests you.** Select a place related to a subject you are studying in social studies class.
- **Do your research.** Learn about your place. Look at pictures of it and read about its history and culture.
- **Take notes.** Collect important details that will help create a clear description in the reader's mind.

Cluster

During your writing . . .

- **Write a clear beginning, middle, and ending.** Begin with a fact or a comparison. Then, describe the place using precise words. End with a final thought that inspires your reader to find out even more about your famous place.
- **Organize your thoughts.** Describe your place in order of location, from top to bottom, from left to right, or from near to far.
- **Use an engaging voice.** Your writing should give the impression that you know a lot about the place and are interested in it.

After you've written a first draft . . .

- **Check for completeness.** Make sure that you have included enough information so that the reader can imagine your place in his or her mind.
- **Check for correctness.** Proofread your essay to make sure there are no mistakes in punctuation, capitalization, spelling, or grammar.

Choose a famous place that interests you and learn more about it. Then write a clear, complete description to share with your classmates.

Writing Tips

Coordinate with social studies teachers to compile a list of places that students have been studying that might be suitable for them to describe.

- Provide students with a copy of this list.
- Allow time for students to research their topic.
- Stress that although they will need background information for their essay, they should focus on facts and details that describe their topic.

Invite students to give their finished essays as oral presentations.

 **Answers**

Answers will vary.

English Language Learners

Adapt the assignment by asking students to select a photograph of a famous place from a textbook.

- Tell them to focus on material they have already studied.
- As students read the text, the photograph will support comprehension as they take notes.
- Then have students write a description based on the picture and their notes.

Advanced Learners

Invite student pairs to visit a local site of interest (e.g., a battlefield, a house from the 1700s). Encourage them to gather details about it on a copy of the reproducible 5 W's chart (TE page 792). Challenge partners to create a tourist brochure (either by hand or on the computer) describing the site's historical significance and points of interest.

Math:
Writing a Geometric Riddle

Read aloud the riddle with students.

- Ask how many of them solved the riddle before looking at the answer.
- Ask what descriptive details in the riddle helped them know the right answer. (Possible responses: Ancient wonder, giant square, four triangle faces, polyhedron, oasis)

Provide additional examples of riddles to help students get the idea of how to use descriptive details creatively.

- Consult with math teachers who may be able to provide riddles that use geometric terms.
- Have students solve the riddles and identify the descriptive details that helped them get the right answer.

Math: Writing a Geometric Riddle

Descriptive writing can be used to write about objects. Below, a student writes a riddle for math class using geometrical terms.

The writer uses personification to describe the object.

The writer rhymes the second and fourth lines.

An Ancient Wonder

I stand upon a giant square
And have four triangle faces.
My polyhedron family
Lives near a large oasis.
What am I?

Answer: An Egyptian pyramid

More About Riddles

Riddles are rewarding mental exercises. They encourage you to use your imagination and build new language skills. Riddles are also creative forms of descriptive writing. The simplest form of riddle, the "What Am I?" riddle, has been around for a long time. Court jesters used this type of riddle to entertain kings and queens for centuries.

Struggling Learners

This activity is extremely challenging. Students will benefit from a step-by-step demonstration of the process of geometric riddle writing.

Use the 5 W's chart (TE page 792). Using the bicycle as an example, have students provide details. Possible responses:

- Who: people of all ages, racers
- What: circular wheels, rectangular pedals, triangular frame, oval chain
- When: 1800s to the present
- Where: worldwide usage
- Why: sport, transportation

Possible sample riddle:
Without my two circular wheels
Set in a triangular frame,
The Tour de France race
Could not have gained its fame.
What am I?

Writing Tips

Before you write . . .

- **Think about different geometric shapes and figures.** There are many to choose from such as the triangle, rectangle, square, parallelogram, pentagon, cube, sphere, and arc.
- **Look at the world around you.** Choose an object to describe that contains specific geometric shapes and figures. The object is the answer to your riddle.
- **Study your object.** Find out as much as you can about the object. Reading about it and answering the 5 W's are two ways to gather information for your description.
- **Jot down details.** Write down specific words and phrases to describe your object. Be sure to include some geometric terms.

During your writing . . .

- **Be creative.** Think of different ways to write your riddle. Here are a few suggestions.

  Use metaphors. Compare the appearance of the object to something else.

  Use personification. Describe the object as if it were a living thing.

  Create a surprise ending. Let the ending take a funny or unexpected twist.

  Make it rhyme. Try to make your riddle rhyme. It's a great exercise for your mind.

After you've written a first draft . . .

- **Check for completeness.** Have you used the best words to describe your object? Have you included enough information for readers to answer the riddle?
- **Check for correctness.** Are the words spelled correctly? Do you use the correct words *(angle, angel; right, write)*?

Try It Write a geometrical "What Am I?" riddle of your own following the tips above. Share your riddle with your classmates.

Writing Tips

Have students work in small groups to try to come up with at least one familiar object for each of the geometric shapes and figures listed (triangle, rectangle, square, parallelogram, pentagon, cube, sphere, and arc).

- Suggest that they look in their social studies and science textbooks for ideas, as well as in magazines like *National Geographic* and *Smithsonian* (for example, a tree trunk, a Native American tepee, the dome and column on Jefferson's Monticello, the American flag, and so on).
- After students have a list of objects, partners can work together to write a riddle for an object on their list.
- Invite students to share their finished riddle orally.

Provide each student with a copy of the reproducible 5 W's chart (TE page 792) to use for gathering information.

Answers

Answers will vary.

English Language Learners

Have students begin by writing simple riddles about individual geometric shapes rather than about complex structures that incorporate multiple shapes. Tell them that riddles don't have to rhyme. For example:

- I have four sides. Each of my sides is the same length. What am I? (a square)
- I have a wide, round top. I have a pointed bottom. You can put ice cream in me. What am I? (a cone)

Science:
Writing a Lab Report

Discuss the format of the sample lab report with students. Help them make the connection between writing a good science lab report and good descriptive writing.

- Have them point out details in the report that help them see and understand the different stages of the experiment.
- Then ask students why it's important for them to be able to write good descriptions for their lab reports. (Possible responses: so their teacher can see that they did the experiment correctly and can understand the results; so that other readers can picture the experiment and the results)

Invite volunteers to share actual lab reports they have written for science class. Have the writers and their classmates suggest places where more description could have improved the lab report.

Science: Writing a Lab Report

In science class, you may be asked to write a lab report. The student report below describes which variables (variety of conditions) make mold grow fastest on bread.

In the **beginning** the purpose is stated, variables are listed, and a hypothesis is given.

A Moldy Problem

PURPOSE: Find out what conditions will make mold grow fastest on bread.

VARIABLES: Temperature and moisture

HYPOTHESIS: Mold will grow fastest on bread that is kept warm and moist.

The **middle** clearly describes the experiment and what the writer observed.

EXPERIMENT: Three slices of freshly baked white bread were put into sandwich bags and labeled A, B, and C. A small amount (2 T.) of water was placed in Bag A, and the bag was placed inside a warm, dark cabinet. Bags B and C got no water. Bag B was placed in the refrigerator and Bag C was placed inside a cool, dark cabinet. The bags were checked daily for one week, and any changes were observed.

OBSERVATIONS: Nothing happened until the fifth day. The bread in the refrigerator appeared fresh. The bread in the cool, dark cabinet had no mold. The moist bread in the warm cabinet was starting to grow spots of greenish-gray mold on the crust.

The **ending** reports the writer's conclusion.

CONCLUSION: The hypothesis that mold will grow fastest on bread that is kept warm and moist was correct. It was expected that the mold would appear sooner than it did.

Writing Tips

Before you write . . .

- **Choose a topic that interests you.**
  Select a science topic related to a subject you are studying in school.
- **Research your topic and plan your experiment.**
  Read about your topic and jot down important details. Then decide what your experiment will be.

During your writing . . .

- **State the purpose, the variables, and your hypothesis.**
  Write a statement that describes what you want to do. Tell which variables you will test. Then write a hypothesis telling what you think you will find out from your experiment.
- **Organize your details.**
  Use time order to describe the procedure you followed (what happened first, second, next, and so on).
- **Use strong, colorful words.**
  A good description contains strong verbs, and specific nouns, adjectives, and adverbs.
- **Clearly state your observations and conclusion.**
  Describe what happened during your experiment. Your conclusion should tell whether or not your hypothesis was correct.

Time line

Subject:
① ② ③ ④ ⑤

After you've written a first draft . . .

- **Check for completeness.**
  Be sure that you have clearly stated the purpose, variables, hypothesis, and conclusion. Check your experiment and observation. Be sure you include all the important details.
- **Check for correctness.**
  Proofread your report for punctuation, capitalization, spelling, and grammar.

Try It Select and perform a science experiment. Then describe it in a lab report using the tips above as a guide.

Writing Tips

Before assigning the **Try It** activity,

- consult with students' science teachers;
- coordinate this assignment with an actual lab experiment that students are conducting in science class;
- obtain copies of the standard form for science lab reports, if students are required to use one, and have them use it for this assignment;
- take time to review the writing tips.

Answers

Answers will vary.

English Language Learners

Conduct a simple experiment such as dropping vinegar on a piece of chalk. Students will smell the vinegar, see bubbles forming, and possibly hear fizzing.

- Encourage students to use drawings and captions to describe the reaction.
- Ask if anyone can explain what happened (chalk is made from a type of rock that dissolves when it is combined with an acid, such as vinegar).
- Guide students in using their drawings and captions to complete the **Try It** activity.

Struggling Learners

For the **Try It** activity, perform a simple science experiment as a class. (Possible topics: static electricity, mixing colors) Provide a standard form for taking notes and highlight lab report components as they are addressed during the experiment. Then have students expand their notations into complete sentences for their final copy.

Practical Writing:
Creating a Classified Ad

Discuss the sample ads with students. Ask students to

- point out the descriptive details in the ads,
- tell why the descriptive details in the real ads are important, and
- tell how the descriptive details in the just-for-fun ads create humor.

To give students practice writing ads before assigning the **Try It** activity, encourage them to take turns re-creating the sample ads by adding and replacing the original details with new details.

Practical Writing:
Creating a Classified Ad

In everyday life, you will find descriptive writing used in many ways. Classified newspaper ads usually contain lots of descriptive writing. Students created the ads below.

Specific details, such as color, size, location, and price, are listed.

Real Ads

FOUND: Small black and white cat. Red collar with silver bell and pearls. Found near 5th and Walnut. Call Julie, 555-4321, after 3:00 p.m.

FOR SALE: Radio-controlled boat. Bright yellow racer. Dual, rechargeable, nickel-cadmium battery. Like new. $10. Call Colin at 555-1234.

Contact information, names, and phone numbers are included.

Just-for-Fun Ads

LOST: Blue denim backpack. Tuna sandwich, dirty gym clothes, and math book inside. Need by 3rd period tomorrow. Reward. Call Jake, 555-4231.

FOR SALE: Parrot named Lincoln. Recites Gettysburg Address. $20, cage included. Call 555-1342 and ask to talk to Lincoln.

Writing Tips

Before you write . . .

- **Do some research.**
  Look at classified ads in your local newspaper. Find some ads with clear descriptions to use as models.
- **Select a topic for your ad.**
  Choose an animal or an item that can be lost, found, or for sale.
- **Gather specific details.**
  List important features to describe your item.
- **Jot down contact information.**
  Think about how and when you would like the reader to contact you.

During your writing . . .

- **Organize your thoughts.**
  Name the animal or item that is lost, found, or for sale. Clearly describe it. End by telling the reader how to contact you.
- **Use colorful words.**
  A good description contains strong verbs, and specific nouns, adjectives, and adverbs.
- **Be brief.**
  Most newspapers charge by the word for classified ads. The more words you use, the more your ad will cost. So make every word count.

After you've written a first draft . . .

- **Check for completeness.**
  Do you name the item? Have you included enough details to make your description clear? Is your contact information complete? Is your ad interesting to read?
- **Check for correctness.**
  Make sure you've asked only necessary questions and have worded them in the best way.

Try It Create a classified ad. It can be real or imagined (see the examples on the facing page). Use the tips above as a guide.

Writing Tips

Provide students with the classified section of local newspapers to find models for their ads.

If time allows, have students talk to students in other classes to find out about animals or items that are for sale, lost, or have been found. Students can take careful notes about each animal or item and then write real classified ads for the **Try It** activity.

Try It Answers

Answers will vary.

After students have completed their ads, have them display the ads on a poster or a bulletin board.

- Students can try to make their display resemble the classified section of a newspaper.
- If students have written real ads, suggest that they post them in prominent places in the school (if permitted). This shows students how good descriptive writing can be useful in real life and provide a public service.

Advanced Learners

Have students study the layout of a classified ad page from a newspaper or magazine. Challenge them to work together to create an entire page of classified ads.

- The group can write all of the ads as a group or ask classmates to contribute some ads.
- Direct students to determine the size of the ads and then type or write out the ads.
- Have students lay out the ads (cut and paste) using the newspaper or magazine page as a model.
- If possible, photocopy the page of ads and distribute it to the class.

Grammar Connection

Adjectives

- **Proofreader's Guide** pages 732 (+), 734–735 (Indefinite, predicate)
- ***Write Source*** page 489
- ***SkillsBook*** pages 179–180
- ***GrammarSnap*** Adjectives and Adverbs

Narrative Writing Overview

Common Core Standards Focus

Writing 3: Write narratives to develop real or imagined experiences or events using effective technique, relevant descriptive details, and well-structured event sequences.

Language 2a: Use a comma to separate coordinate adjectives (e.g., It was a fascinating, enjoyable movie but not He wore an old[,] green shirt).

Writing Forms

- Narrative Paragraph
- Sharing a Learning Experience
- Writing a Phase Autobiography

Focus on the Traits

- **Ideas** Using specific details
- **Organization** Arranging main events in chronological order
- **Voice** Including the use of dialogue to express each character's personality
- **Word Choice** Expressing how the writer feels, using participles, adjectives, and adverbs to make stronger nouns and more active verbs
- **Sentence Fluency** Combining sentences to vary sentence length and sentence form and thus improve the flow and smoothness of the narratives
- **Conventions** Checking for errors in punctuation, capitalization, spelling, and grammar

 **Literature Connections**

- ***Names/Nombres*** by Julia Alvarez
- ***It's Not About the Bike*** by Lance Armstrong

 **Technology Connections**

Write Source Online
www.hmheducation.com/writesource

- ***Net-text***
- ***Bookshelf***
- ***GrammarSnap***
- ***Portfolio***
- ***Writing Network features***
- ***File Cabinet***

 ***Interactive Whiteboard Lessons***

Suggested Narrative Writing Unit (Five Weeks)

	Day	Writing and Skills Instruction	Student Edition: Narrative Writing Unit	Student Edition: Resource Units*	SkillsBook	Daily Language Workouts	Write Source Online
Week 1	1–4	**Narrative Paragraph: A Great Moment** (Model)	93–96			18–19, 85	*Interactive Whiteboard Lessons*
		Skills Activities: • Verbs		480, 482, 718–719	163–164		*GrammarSnap*
		• Conjunctions		496, 744–745	197–198		*GrammarSnap*
		• Commas (in compound sentences and introductory clauses and phrases)		516, 590–591	23–24		
	5	**Sharing a Learning Experience** Literature Connections *Names/Nombres*	97–100				
	opt.	*Speeches*	428–429				

* These units are also located in the back of the Teacher's Edition. Resource Units include "Basic Grammar and Writing," "A Writer's Resource," and "Proofreader's Guide."
(+) This activity is located in a different section of the *Write Source Student Edition.* If students have already completed this activity, you may wish to review it at this time.

Week	Day	Writing and Skills Instruction	Student Edition: Narrative Writing Unit	Student Edition: Resource Units*	SkillsBook	Daily Language Workouts	Write Source Online
Week 2	6–7	(Prewriting)	101–106			20–21, 86	*Net-text*
		Skills Activities: • Punctuating Dialogue		588–589 (+), 598–599, 600–601	31–32		*GrammarSnap*
	8–10	(Writing)	107–112				*Net-text*
Week 3	11–14	(Revising)	113–124			22–23, 87	*Net-text*
		Skills Activities: • Connotation (transitive and intransitive verbs)		728–729	171–172		
		• Verbals (participles)		485, 520, 730–731	173–174		
		• Prepositional Phrases		519, 742–743	189–190		
		• Interjections		588–589, 746–747	19–20, 193–194		
		• Dashes		612–613	43, 44		
		Peer Responding (Model)	29–32				
	15–16	(Editing and Publishing)	125–129				*Portfolio, Net-text*
		Skills Activities: • Punctuating Dialogue		588 (+), 598 (+), 600 (+)			*GrammarSnap*
		• Commas (equal adjectives)		586–587	13–14		
Week 4	17	(Assessing) (Reflecting)	130–133, 134			24–25, 88	
	18	Writing Across the Curriculum	143–149				*Net-text*
		Skills Activities: • Pronoun (person, number)		479, 712–713	155–156		
	19–20	Narrative Writing for Assessment	152–154				
Week 5	21–25	**Phase Autobiography** (Model) Literature Connections *It's Not About the Bike*	135–137			26–27, 89	
		(Prewriting)	138–139				*Net-text*
		(Writing and Revising)	140–141	485, 520, 730–731	173–174		*Net-text*
		Skills Activities: • Sentence Combining		496 (+), 516–517 (+), 698 (+), 746 (+)	121–122		*GrammarSnap*
		• Nouns		470 (+), 471 (+), 704–705	145–146		
		(Editing and Publishing)	142				*Net-text*
		Skills Activities: • End Punctuation		518, 579–581	3–4		*GrammarSnap*
		• Using the Right Word		652–655	61–62		

* These units are also located in the back of the Teacher's Edition. Resource Units include "Basic Grammar and Writing," "A Writer's Resource," and "Proofreader's Guide."
(+) This activity is located in a different section of the *Write Source Student Edition.* If students have already completed this activity, you may wish to review it at this time.

Teacher's Notes for Narrative Writing

This overview for narrative writing includes some specific teaching suggestions for the unit.

Writing Focus

Narrative Paragraph (pages 93–96)

Let students know that a good story doesn't have to be about some amazing event or heroic act. Even a trip to a local store can make for an interesting narrative. It's a matter of really telling the story. The chapter uses a student-faculty basketball game to show how it's done.

Sharing a Learning Experience (pages 97–134)

Formal education provides excellent opportunities for learning. Still, everyday experiences can teach us a great deal. Point out that students learn more than they realize through their experiences. For example, even a small sliver can be painful, and a kind word can calm a frightened child.

Writing a Phase Autobiography (pages 135–142)

Since a phase can be a rite of passage or a time of adjustment to changing circumstances, some students will have much to write about while others may struggle. Help them think about a time in their lives when life changed. Suggest that they focus on a time period of several months rather than a few hours or days.

Grammar Focus

For support with this unit's grammar topics, consult the resource units (Basic Grammar and Writing, A Writer's Resource, and Proofreader's Guide.

Academic Vocabulary

Read aloud the academic terms, as well as the descriptions and questions. Model for students how to read one question and answer it. Have partners monitor their understanding and seek clarification of the terms by working through the meanings and questions together.

Minilessons

Details, Details — Writing a Narrative Paragraph

- **THINK** of a great moment in your life. **LIST** a detail for each of your five senses that relates to your experience. Then **TELL** a partner about your moment. Try to **INCLUDE** all the details from your list.

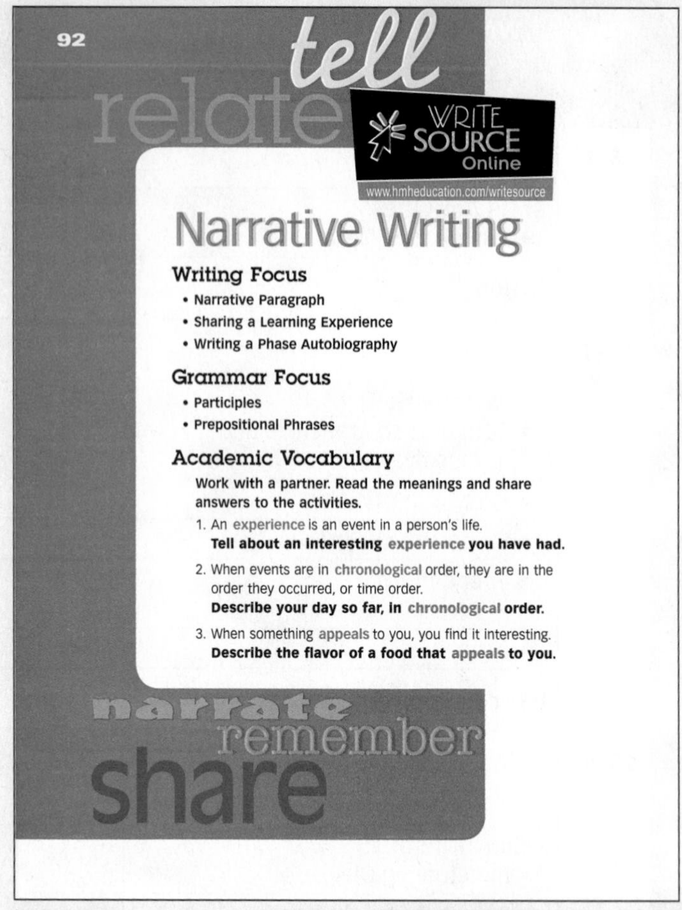

Embarrassed — Sharing a Learning Experience

- **THINK** of a time when you were embarrassed. How did you feel? Did someone come to your rescue? **SHARE** your experience with a partner. **WRITE** a sentence telling what you learned.

What's in a Name? — Writing a Phase Autobiography

- **READ** "Selecting a Topic" on SE page 138. **WRITE** the letters of your name down the left side of a piece of paper. Then **LIST** a topic about your experiences suggested by each letter.

No Electronics — Writing for Assessment

- **LIST** the electronic devices you use. How important are they? Which ones would you be willing to give up and why? **WRITE** an impromptu paragraph that tells what you would do if you could no longer use these items.

Narrative Writing

Narrative Paragraph

Think of a time when something really exciting happened to you. Maybe you won a basketball game, or caught a big fish, or got an "A on a tough test. Now imagine telling a friend all about it. That's what a "narrative" is—a story about something that has happened. We all tell such stories at one time or another.

In this chapter, you will write a paragraph that tells about a great moment in your life. Once you are finished, you and your classmates can share these personal stories with each other.

Writing Guidelines

Subject: A great moment
Form: Narrative paragraph
Purpose: To entertain
Audience: Classmates

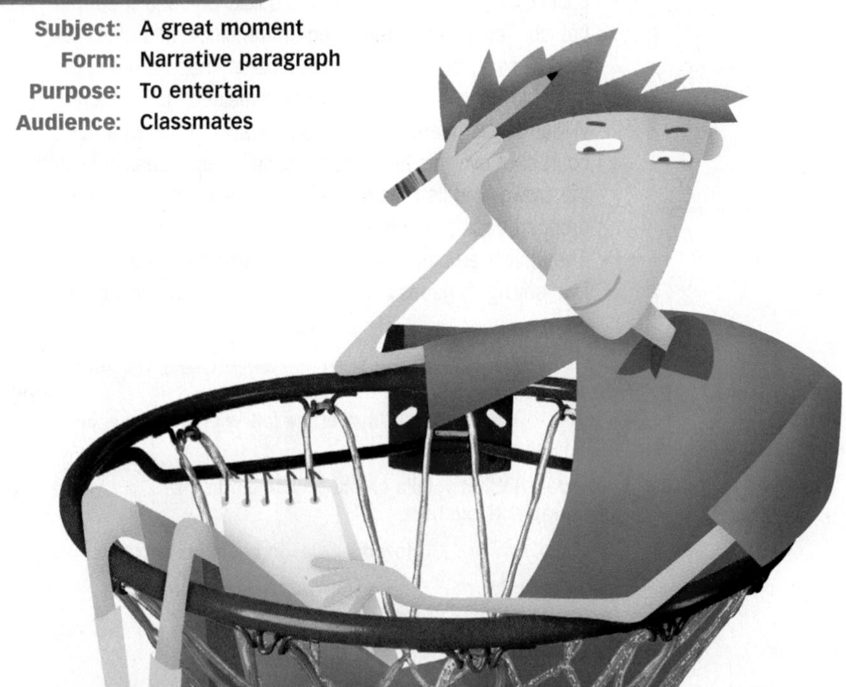

Copy Masters

Time Line (TE p. 95)

Narrative Paragraph

Objectives

- understand the content and structure of a narrative paragraph
- choose a topic (an exciting moment) to write about
- plan, draft, revise, and edit a narrative paragraph

A **narrative paragraph** tells a story. Many narrative paragraphs share an important experience with the reader. Paragraphs usually have a topic sentence, the body, and a closing sentence.

* Additional information about paragraphs is on SE pages 524–525.

Writer's Craft

Quick stories: Ask students to think about commercials that tell a story. Have students recount some of their favorites. Point out that the writer of the commercial had to tell a complete story in 30 seconds. The writer, in effect, created a narrative paragraph.

Encourage students to think of their narrative paragraphs as quick commercials that capture an experience they had.

Technology Connections

Use this unit's Interactive Whiteboard Lesson to introduce narrative writing.

 ***Interactive Whiteboard Lessons***

Narrative Paragraph

Before doing the page, ask:

- What stories have you read or seen that describe an exciting experience? (adventure books, true-life magazines, action movies, and so on)
- What made them exciting? (personal challenge, race against time, confronting an adversary, and so on)

✱ For more information about writing a narrative paragraph, see SE page 526.

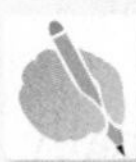

Respond to the reading.

Answers

Ideas **1.** Possible choices: the score (42 to 40); the remaining time (one minute, ten seconds, two seconds, buzz); specific verbs (dodged, swatted, roared, bounced, snatched, knocked, hurled, sailed, dropped, flipped, erupted); other descriptive words and phrases (quick, desperation, beautiful, held its breath, silent swish, high five)

Organization **2.** He begins with a topic sentence that identifies the experience.

Voice & Word Choice **3.** Possible choices: dodge, swatted, roared, bounced, snatched, knocked, hurled, sailed, dropped, flipped.

Narrative Paragraph

By remembering the great experiences in your life and telling stories about them, you can relive those times over and over. In the following narrative paragraph, Devon opens with a **topic sentence** that identifies the experience. Next, the **body** of his paragraph recalls the events. Finally, the **closing sentence** tells how the experience ended.

Getting Game

Topic Sentence

The teachers were winning the annual student-faculty basketball game 42 to 40. One minute remained, and Coach Williams had the ball. He tried to dodge around me at midcourt, but I reached in and swatted the ball away from him. The crowd roared as the ball bounced toward our basket, but Mrs. Jenkins was too quick. She snatched the ball up. Ten seconds remained on the clock. Mrs. Jenkins tried to pass, but one of my teammates knocked the ball right into my hands. Two seconds remained, and Coach Williams was guarding me. In desperation, I hurled a half-court shot over his head. The ball sailed up—beautiful—and the crowd held its breath. BUZZ! With a silent swish, the shot dropped through the hoop. Our score flipped to 43. The stands erupted, and Coach Williams gave me a high five, saying, "I guess I've found next year's shooting guard."

Body

Closing Sentence

Respond to the reading. Answer the following questions on your own paper.

- ☐ Ideas **(1) What details create excitement in the paragraph? Name two.**
- ☐ Organization **(2) How does Devon begin his narrative?**
- ☐ Voice & Word Choice **(3) What verbs re-create the action? List three or four.**

English Language Learners

If students are unfamiliar with basketball, the **Respond to the reading** questions may be difficult for them. Pair them with a partner and have them work together to discuss possible responses.

When assigning partners, peer conferences, or discussion groups, be aware of the needs and feelings of students who may be hesitant when asked to share their ideas in extended oral discussions or in written work. Pair or group them with cooperative, considerate students who are proficient in English.

Prewriting Selecting a Topic

How do you choose a great moment to write about? Devon used a listing strategy to help him think about exciting moments he had experienced. Part of his list follows.

Topics List

Rode the "Plunge"
Got a first at the solo and ensemble contest
Fed a sea lion
Scored the winning shot in basketball
Did my first gainer dive

List your ideas. On your own paper, write a list of exciting experiences or great moments you have had. Choose one experience to write about.

Gathering Details

To collect details for his narrative paragraph, Devon decided to make a time line. Not every detail ended up in the final draft, but the time line did give Devon a good plan for starting to write.

Time Line

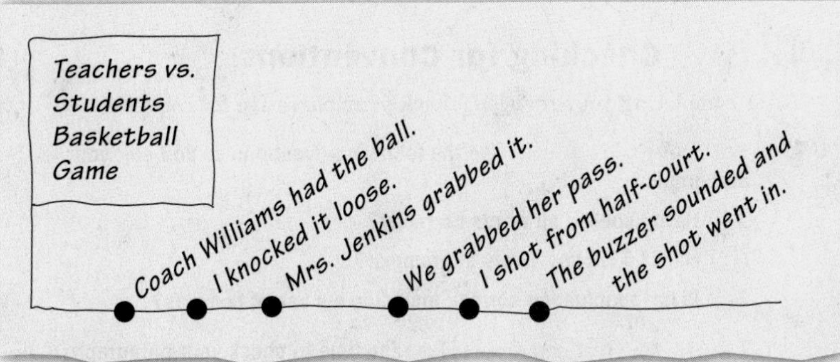

List your details. Make a time line of details for the event you will write about. Make sure to list them in the correct order.

English Language Learners

Remind students that they needn't worry about form or conventions when they freewrite. They should simply keep their pen moving and write the first things that come to mind. If they struggle to remember a word, encourage them to write around it or just move on without it.

Prewriting Selecting a Topic

To get started on selecting a topic:

- Brainstorm with students about exciting events in their lives.
- Begin a class list, and then give students a few minutes to make their own lists.
- Have students share their ideas with a partner or as a class.

Prewriting Gathering Details

Have students choose two events from their list (above) and do a 5-minute freewrite for each one.

- Ask them to consider both freewrites and decide which one is more interesting to them.
- Have students organize the details from their freewrite using an organizing list or a time line. Provide photocopies of the reproducible time line on TE page 790.

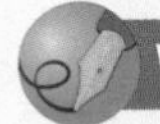

Writer's Craft

Reflective details: An exciting experience is most naturally depicted in time order—first one thing happens, then something else happens, then a third thing happens. However, to re-create a more thoughtful experience, writers often move back and forward in time. They include not only the sensory details and actions of the moment, but also the memories (which extend backward in time) and hopes (which extend forward).

Writing Creating Your First Draft

As students write, they should refer to their list or time line. Remind them to include strong action verbs and specific nouns so that readers feel as though they are part of the experience.

Revising Improving Your Paragraph

Have students hold **peer conferences** *(see below)* to help with revisions. Have them exchange the draft with a partner. Explain that they should get and give input on these elements:

- places to use stronger verbs and more specific nouns
- unnecessary details to delete

* For more information about using powerful verbs effectively, see SE page 482.

Editing Checking for Conventions

Encourage students to focus on one area (spelling, grammar, punctuation) each time they read their paragraph.

Writing Creating Your First Draft

A narrative paragraph has a topic sentence, a body, and a closing sentence. Each part serves a different purpose.

- The topic sentence introduces the narrative.
- The body uses details to describe what happened.
- The closing sentence wraps up the narrative.

Write your first draft. Review your time line and then write your narrative paragraph. Include details to make your readers feel that they are experiencing the event for themselves.

Revising Improving Your Paragraph

In a piece of writing as short as a narrative paragraph, it's important for every sentence to work well. Keep these tips in mind as you revise.

- **Revise with a reader's eye.** Pretend you are reading the paragraph for the first time. What parts work well? What parts still need work?
- **Keep the action moving.** Use strong action verbs and specific nouns to hold the reader's interest. Cut any unnecessary details.
- **Build to a climax.** Have the events in your paragraph lead up to a moment of crisis. Then resolve the crisis at the end.

Revise your paragraph. Revise with a focus on ideas, organization, voice, word choice, and sentence fluency. Make sure your narrative grabs the reader's interest and holds it to the end.

Editing Checking for Conventions

After completing your revision, check your narrative for conventions.

Edit your paragraph. Use the following questions as you edit your paragraph.

1. **Have I spelled all words correctly?**
2. **Have I fixed any errors in grammar?**
3. **Is my punctuation correct, including my use of commas?**

Proofread your narrative. Take the time to check your paragraph carefully for any errors. Then make a clean final copy to share with your classmates.

Grammar Connection

Verbs

- **Proofreader's Guide** pages 718–719
- ***Write Source*** pages 480, 482
- ***SkillsBook*** pages 163–164
- ***GrammarSnap*** Transitive and Intransitive Verbs

Conjunctions

- **Proofreader's Guide** pages 744–745
- ***Write Source*** page 496
- ***SkillsBook*** pages 197–198
- ***GrammarSnap*** Coordinating Conjunctions

Commas

- **Proofreader's Guide** pages 590–591
- ***Write Source*** page 516
- ***SkillsBook*** pages 23–24

Teaching Tip: Peer Conferences

Peer conferences allow students to help each other with their writing. Assign students to small groups and have them exchange papers. Group struggling learners and English language learners with considerate, cooperative students who have a good command of both the language and the writing skills.

tell share remember narrate relate 97

Narrative Writing

Sharing a Learning Experience

"The writer steps up to the plate. She looks cool and focused. She takes a couple of practice swings with her pencil, and then settles in. Here comes the first idea. The writer takes a swing at it by starting her first sentence . . . , but then decides to cross it out. She gets ready for the next idea. She swings. Crack! The idea is a real hit, and the writer is off and running with her story."

Writing a personal narrative can be just as exciting as playing baseball. All kinds of ideas will enter your mind; it's your job to connect with the best ones. Personal narratives allow readers to experience the thrill of your life stories and learn from them just as you did. They will cheer whenever you make a hit.

Writing Guidelines

Subject: An important learning experience
Form: Personal narrative
Purpose: To share a true experience that has taught you something
Audience: Classmates

Struggling Learners

To generate ideas, students may think about characters from stories, books, or movies who learn a lesson from an experience. Focus on

- the name of the character,
- brief background or setting,
- a description of the experience, and
- the lesson that the character learned.

Copy Masters

Rubrics (TE p. 98)

T-chart (TE pp. 97, 101, 102, 112)

5 W's Chart (TE pp. 101, 102, 103)

Sensory Chart (TE pp. 105, 114, 115)

Time Line (TE p. 116)

Proofreading Marks (TE p. 117)

Assessment Sheet (TE p. 133)

Sharing a Learning Experience

Objectives

- understand what a personal narrative is
- understand the content and form of a personal narrative
- plan, draft, revise, edit, and publish a personal narrative

A **personal narrative** is a story about yourself. It tells about

- what you did,
- what happened to you, and
- what you learned from the experience.

Some students may not recognize they have learned from an experience. Use a photocopy of the reproducible T-chart on TE page 789 to create a chart with the headings *When I . . .* and *I learned . . . .* List the following events in the first column. Make photocopies and tell students to fill in the second column for one or more of the entries.

When I . . .

- took care of my younger brother (sister, cousin, neighbor)
- went to camp
- helped my best friend (grandmother, parents, next-door neighbor)

Understanding Your Goal

Traits of Narrative Writing

Three traits relate to the development of both the content and the form of a narrative. They provide focus during prewriting and drafting.

- Ideas
- Organization
- Voice

The other three traits relate more to form. Checking them is part of the revising and editing processes.

- Word Choice
- Sentence Fluency
- Conventions

* The six-point rubric on SE pages 130–131 is based on these traits. Reproducible six-, five-, and four-point rubrics for narrative writing can be found on TE pages 750, 754, and 758.

Literature Connections

In the personal narrative "Names/Nombres," Julia Alvarez describes the difficulties of adjusting to life in New York after spending her childhood in the Dominican Republic. Alvarez shares how being an immigrant gave her a special point of view.

Discuss elements that make the writing a good personal narrative about a learning experience, such as: true experience, natural voice, interesting details, personal feelings, and time order. For more information about sharing a learning experience through a personal narrative, see the Reading-Writing Connections beginning on page TE-36.

Understanding Your Goal

Your goal in this chapter is to write an essay about a personal experience that taught you something. The following traits will help you to plan, create, and evaluate your personal narrative. Use the rubric on pages 130–131 to assess your progress.

Traits of Narrative Writing

Ideas

Use specific details that make the reader want to know what happens next.

Organization

Write a beginning, a middle, and an ending that are clear to the reader, and put the events in chronological (time) order.

Voice

Create a personal voice, and use dialogue to show each individual's personality.

Word Choice

Use words that express how you feel about the experience, and experiment with participles for added description.

Sentence Fluency

Use a variety of sentence lengths to create an effective style.

Conventions

Be sure that your punctuation, capitalization, spelling, and grammar are correct.

Literature Connections: You can find a personal narrative in "Names/Nombres" by Julia Alvarez. How does the author use the traits of narrative writing in this piece?

English Language Learners

Ask volunteers to read aloud each trait description. Review and discuss the meaning of each.

Explain that the first three traits are "big picture" traits—they concern the

- overall topic,
- overall plan, and
- overall tone of the writing.

The last three traits are "detail" traits—they concern the finer aspects of the piece of writing, such as

- individual sentences,
- specific words, and
- punctuation, spelling, and so on.

Struggling Learners

Create a word wall that focuses on words for feelings.

- Start with basic words such as *happy, sad,* or *mad.*
- Have students brainstorm synonyms that are more vivid and interesting.
- Encourage students to use resources, including the thesaurus and dictionary.

Personal Narrative

In this personal narrative, the student writer remembers an experience from his first day in middle school. The key parts of the narrative are described in the left margin.

Beginning
The beginning starts in the middle of an action and then gives the reader background information.

Middle
The middle includes the writer's feelings.

Home Team or Visitor?

"Time to leave!" my mother yelled up the stairs.

My heart kicked against my ribs. This was it—my first day at school in Chicago! Before this, we had lived in a town that had a total population of 2,114. I could walk from the cornfields at one end of town to the bean fields at the other end in 20 minutes. Mom had changed jobs, though, and now we were Chicagoans. I had no idea what to expect from this big-city school.

I took one last look in the mirror. My brand-new Chicago Cubs jersey looked great with my faded jeans and new tennis shoes. I slapped my old Cubs cap on my head, snatched my backpack from the kitchen table, and ran for the waiting school bus.

When the bus came, it was nearly full. I walked down the aisle slowly, looking for an empty seat. I felt as if everybody was staring at me, even though most of them were busy talking to each other. However, as I glanced toward the back, I noticed a couple of guys laughing. They were pointing at me.

"Hey, it looks like we have a super fan riding on our bus today!" one of them shouted over the noise.

At that moment, everyone got quiet and all eyes were glued on me. I could feel my face getting hot. The last thing I wanted to be was the center of attention.

Personal Narrative

Read through this sample story with the class, pointing out the elements that make it a good personal narrative.

Ideas
- The writer chooses a personal experience that is meaningful to him.
- Specific details "show" the reader the writer's ideas.

Organization
- The story is told in chronological order.
- The beginning starts in the middle of the action, and the ending tells what the writer learned from his experience.

Voice
- The writer creates a personal voice that shows how he feels during the experience.
- The dialogue shows each individual's personality.

You may wish to point out the effective use of dialogue in this narrative. Take time to review the treatment and punctuation of dialogue.

English Language Learners

Familiarize students with the idioms and colloquialisms in this sample essay.

- My heart kicked against my ribs (my heart beat in a rapid and strong way because I was nervous)
- a couple of guys (two boys)
- a super fan (a person who is very enthusiastic about a particular sport or team)
- all eyes were glued on me (everyone was staring at me)
- slide in here (move through this narrow space to sit here)
- fitting into the city scene (trying to look as if you belong in the city and are comfortable there)

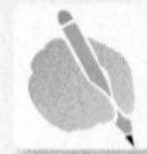

Respond to the reading.

Answers

Ideas **1.** his first day in a new school in Chicago

Organization **2.** in time (chronological) order (with some necessary background information in the opening paragraph)

3. Possible answers:

- tells what the writer learned from the experience (that it is best to be yourself)
- explains a good outcome of the experience (meeting his great friend Al)

Voice & Word Choice **4.** Possible choices:

- heart kicked against my ribs
- no idea what to expect
- one last look
- everybody was staring at me
- all eyes were glued on me
- face getting hot
- sigh of relief

Writer's Craft

Mentor text: Many students in today's highly transient society have experienced being the new kid in town, like the boy in "Home Team or Visitor?" Direct such students to *Finding My Hat* by John Son. He writes with warmth and humor about the universal experience of trying to fit in, and his narrative could be a comfort for students facing the same challenge.

Middle
The middle includes dialogue that connects the action and gives information.

Suddenly, this big kid stood up and said, "Slide in here." I was glad to get out of the aisle, away from all those eyes. I slid in next to the window and breathed a sigh of relief. The big kid sat down beside me, and the bus started moving.

"I'm Al," he said, shaking my hand. "Don't let those two bother you. You'll soon find out that they're some of the biggest baseball fans in our school."

"I'm Lewis," I said.

Al grinned and said, "You know, you do kind of look like a tourist."

We both laughed, and suddenly I felt a lot better. Right then I decided that the next day I'd wear the same kind of clothes I had worn at my old school. I wouldn't worry about fitting into the city scene.

Ending
The ending tells what the writer learned from his experience.

I thought I needed to impress everyone, but I learned that it's always best to just be myself. I also realized that every day is full of surprises. How could I know that in the middle of an embarrassing moment, I'd meet someone like Al, who would become a great friend?

Respond to the reading. What makes "Home Team or Visitor?" a well-written narrative? To find out, answer the following questions.

- ☐ **Ideas (1) What specific experience does the writer choose to share with the reader?**
- ☐ **Organization (2) How does the writer organize the narrative? (3) What is the purpose of the ending part?**
- ☐ **Voice & Word Choice (4) What words and phrases show how the writer feels about this experience?**

English Language Learners

Explain the side note on SE page 100 that says: *The middle includes dialogue that connects the action and gives information.*

The dialogue helps move the story forward, for example, when Al offers a seat to Lewis. The dialogue gives information when Al introduces himself.

Struggling Learners

Point out that the author communicated the feeling of nervousness without ever using the word *nervous.* Review the word choices Lewis made (see answer to **Respond to reading** item 4).

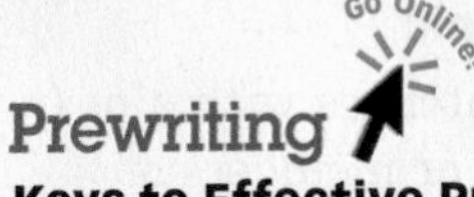

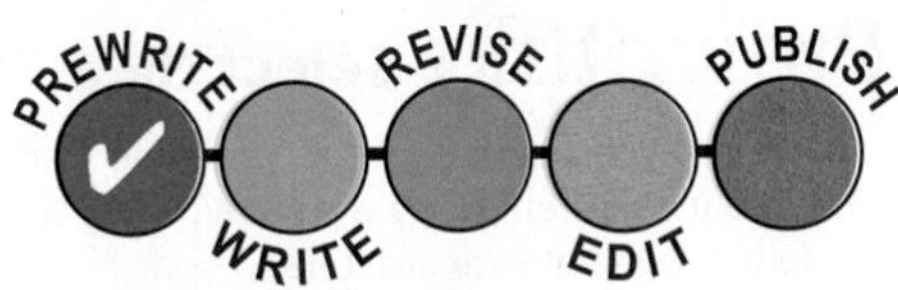

Prewriting

Choosing a topic that interests you can make all the difference in your personal narrative. Along with choosing an interesting topic, you will also gather and organize details in this prewriting section.

Keys to Effective Prewriting

1. Select an experience that you remember well.
2. Think about the lesson you learned from the experience.
3. Write freely about your experience and then check to see how many of the 5 W and H questions you can answer.
4. Use a list or graphic organizer to put the events in time order.
5. Gather details about sights, sounds, smells, and other sensory details related to your experience.
6. Consider how you can use dialogue in your narrative.

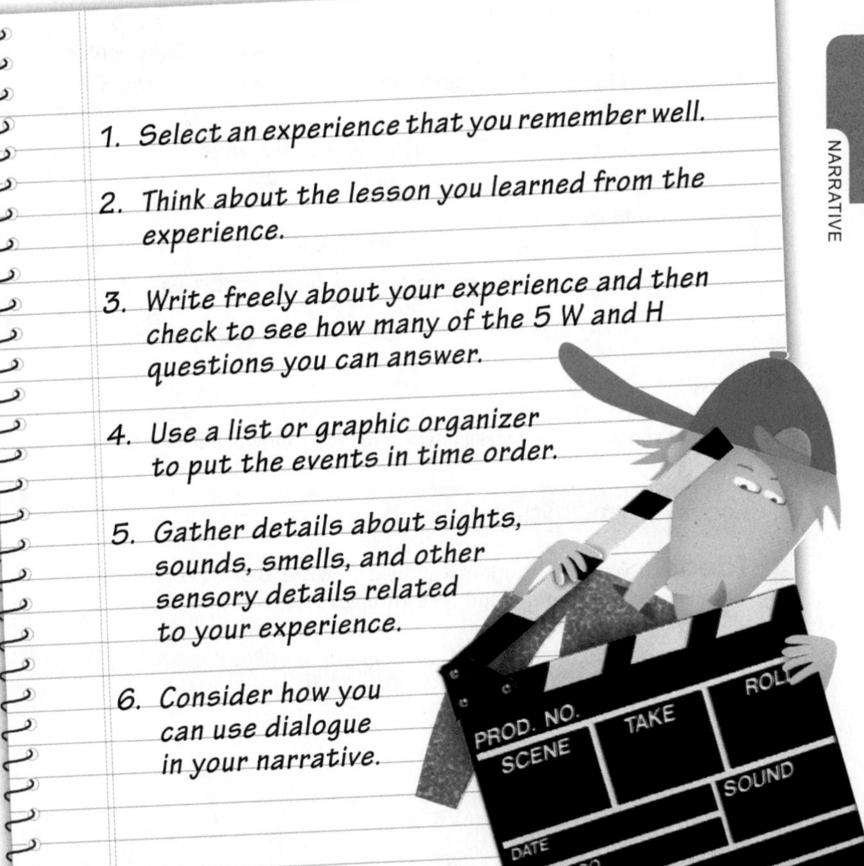

NARRATIVE

Prewriting

Go Online!

Keys to Effective Prewriting

Remind students that the prewriting stage is when they get ready to write.

Keys to Effective Prewriting explains the process students will be guided through on SE pages 102–106.

- Students can revisit the T-chart they created at the beginning of the section (TE page 97). Have them add at least three more experiences now that they've read the example.
- Ask them to freewrite about one of their experiences for 5 to 10 minutes. Have students underline the phrases in their freewrites that answer the **5 W and H questions** *(see below).*

Technology Connections

Students can use the added features of the Net-text as they explore this stage of the writing process.

Write Source Online **Net-text**

Teaching Tip: 5 W and H Questions

If students need a refresher on the 5 W and H questions, remind them that they are questions that begin with *who, what, when, where, why,* or *how.*

Point out that reporters use the 5 W and H questions when gathering information for articles. Have students brainstorm a list of events that have occurred in school recently.

- Divide the class into groups of three, with one reporter and two witnesses per group. Then assign three events to each group.
- Have reporters interview their witnesses about one event and gather the answers to the 5 W and H questions (provide photocopies of the reproducible chart on TE page 792). Reporters should write the answers in the form of a narrative paragraph.
- Have each student take a turn being the reporter, so that all three events are "covered."

Prewriting Selecting a Topic

Students can share their sentences with a peer or in small groups. Partners or members of each group should give input on which topic seems most interesting.

Focus on the Traits

Ideas
Ask students to keep a notebook throughout the year in which they record topics that interest them. That way, they will always have ideas to choose from.

* Another way to help students think about topic possibilities is to have them read through the list of writing topics on SE pages 546–547.

Prewriting Selecting a Topic

Before you begin writing, you need to choose a topic that both you and your reader will enjoy. One writer began thinking about topics by completing the following sentence starters.

Sentence Starters

1. *I was being helpful when . . .*
   — *I helped my uncle install a CD player in his car.*
   — *I kept the little kids away from the fire equipment.* *
2. *I was inspired when . . .*
   — *I saw how well everyone liked my science-fair project.*
   — *the guest teacher from Kenya spoke to our class.*
3. *I was exhausted when . . .*
   — *I came home from my cousin's sleepover.*
   — *I hiked up the giant sand dunes.* *
4. *I was excited when . . .*
   — *my uncle from Puerto Rico visited us.*
   — *I placed third in the gymnastic competition.* *

Complete some sentence starters. On your own paper, finish the sentence starters above with your own ideas. Put stars next to three ideas that you think would make interesting topics for a personal narrative.

Focus on the Traits

Ideas If you can't think of anything to write about, look through old photos and souvenirs and read through your personal journal. That's how many professional writers get ideas.

Struggling Learners

To help students find an experience to write about, allow them to complete the sentence starters at home with a parent or an adult who knows them well.

- Suggest that students work with the adult to list experiences that had a strong effect on them.
- Have them discuss the details and take notes, using the 5 W and H questions.
- Encourage them to make a graphic organizer, such as a T-chart or a cluster, to help them stay focused.

Provide photocopies of the reproducible 5 W's chart on TE page 792 and the T-chart on TE page 789.

Advanced Learners

Encourage students to create their own sentence starters to share with the class.

- Have students create a poster to display sentence starters in the classroom as a writing resource.

Focusing on Your Topic

You've identified some possible experiences to write about. Now you need to think about what you have learned from each of them. Below, the writer used a chart to list three interesting experiences and the lessons learned.

Focus Chart

My Experiences		Lessons I Learned
Climbing the sand dunes	→	I shouldn't hike alone.
(Watching the warehouse burn)	→	I want to be a firefighter.
Placing in a competition	→	The more I practice, the better I perform.

Focus on a topic. Using your three starred ideas from the activity on page 102, make a chart like the one above. Then circle the experience you could write about in your narrative.

Remembering the Details

Isabella used two gathering techniques. First, she wrote freely, and then she answered the 5 W and H questions.

Freewriting

My brother was shouting. I heard sirens. Fire trucks flew past. I ran down to the corner. Smoke was coming out of the warehouse's windows. One firefighter asked me to help her. I did. I kept watching her. I'd like to be a firefighter.

Who was in the experience?—my brother, the firefighter, me
What happened?—a warehouse caught on fire
When did it happen?—last summer
Where did it happen?—in my neighborhood
Why did I get interested?—a firefighter asked for help
How did I change?—now want to be a firefighter

Remember your details. Write nonstop about your topic for 5 minutes. Also answer the 5 W and H questions about your topic.

NARRATIVE

Struggling Learners

If students are reluctant to describe or retell an experience that is painful or embarrassing, explain that even simple, daily experiences can yield an important lesson that can affect a person in a positive way.

Prewriting Focusing on Your Topic

Discuss what kinds of lessons students can learn from their experiences. For example, they can learn

- how to do something new,
- new information,
- more about their own or others' personalities or choices, or
- a lesson about what not to do.

Thinking about different kinds of learning will help students broaden the range of experiences they can use as topics.

Prewriting Remembering the Details

Another way to remember details is to think about the experience chronologically.

- As students recall what happened first, next, and so on, they may jog their memories about specifics that they can use in their writing.
- Remind them to think about the 5 W and H questions (provide photocopies of the reproducible chart on TE page 792) while going through the remembering process.

Prewriting Putting Events in Order

Explain that when writing in **chronological order** *(see below)*, students should use transition words to make the sentences and paragraphs flow smoothly.

- Brainstorm transition words with the class. Create a list on the board, beginning with these words: *first, second, next, then, finally.*
- Create a sample paragraph about going to the school library or going shopping, using these and other transition words.

✱ For more practice in using chronological order, see SE page 534.

Focus on the Traits

Organization

Have students identify which items in their Quick List will be at the beginning (B), middle (M), and end (E). If the organization is tight enough, they might choose to write the middle before the beginning or the beginning and end before the middle if that will help their thoughts flow more easily.

Prewriting Putting Events in Order

Once you've gathered your details, it's time to put the main events in order. Most narratives are organized in chronological (time) order. That means the events, or scenes, appear in the order in which they happened. Isabella used a quick list to get her events in order.

Quick List

Watching the Fire

1. *My brother started shouting.*
2. *The sirens got louder.*
3. *Fire trucks flew past our apartment.*
4. *I ran down to the corner.*
5. *The warehouse was burning.*
6. *A woman firefighter asked me for my help.*
7. *I kept the little kids away.*
8. *I watched how she handled the equipment.*

Lesson Learned: I'd like to be a firefighter someday.

Make your quick list like the one above. Look back at your details to get started. List the main scenes of your experience. Then add the lesson you learned. You may find that you need to add more information.

Focus on the Traits

Organization As you begin your first draft, keep in mind that the beginning, the middle, and the ending are equally important. Carefully develop each part so that when the parts are put together, they form an inspiring narrative.

Teaching Tip: Chronological Order

Give students some practice with arranging events in chronological (time) order and with using transition words. Stage a brief skit at the start of class.

- Ask volunteers to describe what happened at the beginning of class today.
- Write three or four sentences that describe the beginning of class on chart paper. Leave space between each sentence.
- Cut the sentences into individual strips and hand each strip to a student.
- Have students arrange themselves in the order that the events took place, holding the sentences so that the class can read them.
- Then ask for suggested transition words to make the sentences flow smoothly.

Gathering Sensory Details

Sensory details help the reader see, hear, smell, taste, and feel what is being described. The chart below shows some of the sensory details Isabella remembered.

Sensory Detail Chart

I saw...	I heard . . .	I smelled . . .	I felt . . .
racing fire trucks	screaming sirens	smoke	the spray of water
shooting flames	firefighters shouting orders	burning tires	waves of heat
dark smoke	shattering windows	chemical fumes	
heavy hoses	noisy kids	exhaust fumes	
leaning ladders			

NARRATIVE

Create a sensory detail chart. Make a chart of sensory details for your experience. Then write down words or phrases that describe the events in your quick list on page 104.

Focus on the Traits

Voice It's important to use your writer's voice to show feelings. For example, the phrases *bolted out the front door* and *heart pumping fast* show excitement and fear.

Prewriting Gathering Sensory Details

Provide copies of the reproducible sensory chart on TE page 793. Students can warm up by working with a partner to create and fill in a sensory detail chart about a familiar place (a restaurant, a park, and so on). Remind them to focus on each sense.

Students can also organize sensory details using a cluster for each sense.

* For more practice with sensory details, see SE page 488.

Focus on the Traits

Voice
Ask partners to write two or three sentences about their setting that incorporate sensory details and also show their feelings.

English Language Learners

If students have difficulty with the concept of voice, point out that when we speak, we use different tones of voice to show different feelings. Call on volunteers to model this with short sentences. (I'm scared. I'm really proud. I'm thrilled.)

Then point out that because readers cannot hear writers' tones of voice, writers must choose their words carefully so that readers can understand their feelings. In other words, word choice is to writers as pitch and tone are to speakers. Use examples to show how a writer might express the feelings that were spoken in the earlier sentences. (It was a spooky, dark night. I did better on the test than I expected!)

Review SE page 40 with students, if time allows.

Struggling Learners

Have students spend time each day focusing on just one sense. Ask them to record what they find. For example, on the day they focus on smell, they might note how peculiar their basement smells or what the grass smells like when they play soccer. Have them keep a sensory journal and remind them about this exercise when their writing lacks sensory details.

Prewriting Adding Dialogue

For more practice with comparing third-person description and dialogue, do the following activity:

- Have two students spend a minute or so talking with each other in simple sentences. Suggest some topics of interest, such as a school event.
- Write some of their exact words on the board without any punctuation.
- Have the class first describe (in writing) what they said.
- Then have them write exactly what was said with correct punctuation. They can use the second and third columns (*Without Dialogue and With Dialogue*) of the chart as a model.

* For more information about how to punctuate dialogue correctly, see SE pages 556, 588, 598, 600, 624.

Prewriting Adding Dialogue

There are many different reasons to use dialogue, or conversation, in your narrative. You can use it to show a speaker's personality, to keep the action moving, or to add information. The chart below shows different ways the writer can express the same idea. The dialogue examples are taken from the model on pages 99–100.

Use dialogue to . . .	Without Dialogue	With Dialogue
Show a speaker's personality	One of the kids started shouting that I looked like a super fan.	"Hey, it looks like we have a super fan riding on our bus today!" one of them shouted over the noise.
Keep the action moving	Suddenly this big kid stood up and told me to slide in next to him. I was glad to get away from all of those eyes.	Suddenly, this big kid stood up and said, "Slide in here." I was glad to get out of the aisle, away from all those eyes.
Add information	The big kid told me his name and not to be bothered by the other kids. I told him my name, too.	"I'm Al," he said, shaking my hand. "Don't let those two bother you. . . ." "I'm Lewis," I said.

Plan some dialogue for your narrative. Plan to use dialogue in at least three places in your essay—one time for each of the ways listed above. (See pages 126 and 556 for more about punctuating dialogue.)

Grammar Connection

Punctuating Dialogue

- **Proofreader's Guide** pages 588–589, 598–599, 600–601
- ***SkillsBook*** pages 31–32
- ***GrammarSnap*** Punctuating Dialogue

English Language Learners

Limited language skills may make writing natural-sounding dialogue challenging.

- Point out that many authors have taught themselves to be excellent listeners. For example, when authors are listening to the radio or watching television, or when they are in a public place such as a checkout line at a store, they listen to conversations very carefully. This helps them to train their "writing ears" so that they can write dialogue that sounds natural and reveals the personalities of the speakers.
- Encourage students to listen to conversations among their friends and family and to jot down notes so that they can work on training their "writer's ears."

Go Online!

Writing

After you have finished gathering and organizing your ideas, you are ready to begin writing the first draft of your narrative. Write as if you were telling a friend about your experience.

Keys to Effective Writing

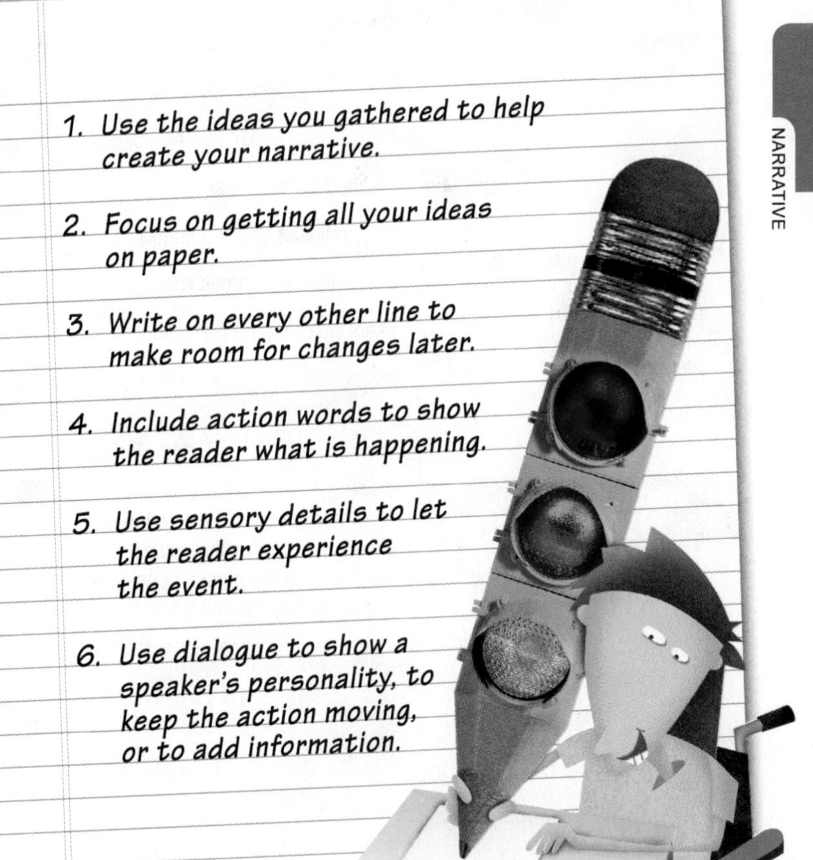

NARRATIVE

Go Online!

Writing

Keys to Effective Writing

Remind students that the writing stage is when they get to write, or draft, their ideas on paper.

Keys to Effective Writing explains the process students will be guided through on SE pages 108–112.

Suggest that students refer to these strategies as they write their drafts.

- Remind them that they should focus on the goals for ideas, organization, voice, and word choice at this stage of the writing process.
- Have them reread the descriptions of these traits on SE page 98.

Technology Connections

Students can use the added features of the Net-text as they explore this stage of the writing process.

Write Source Online **Net-text**

Test Prep!

The best way to write a first draft is to write freely, getting ideas down on paper. By encouraging your students to write freely, you can help them develop fluency and prepare for on-demand writing situations.

Often in an on-demand situation, students have a short amount of time for their writing—perhaps 45 minutes, five of which should be spent in planning, and five in editing. If you challenge students to write their first drafts in a similar amount of time (such as one class period), you can help them write freely and prepare to respond to narrative prompts.

Writing Getting the Big Picture

The following activity can help students organize their narratives:

- Divide your papers into thirds, as you would fold a business letter.
- Label the three areas *Beginning, Middle,* and *Ending.*
- Write the events of your experience in each area.

Remind students that as they review their details, they should begin thinking about an attention-grabbing beginning that starts in the middle of the action and an ending that helps the reader understand what the writer learned. Encourage students to share their stories orally before they begin writing *(see below).*

Writing Getting the Big Picture

The chart below shows how a personal narrative is put together. (The examples are from the model on pages 109–112.) Before you begin to write your first draft, be sure you have . . .

- gathered enough details about your experience.
- organized the events in chronological order.

Beginning

The **beginning** introduces the topic and grabs the reader's attention.

Opening Sentences
"Something's burning. I hear sirens. Something's burning!" Marcus shouted. . . .

Middle

The **middle** gives details that appeal to the senses and tells what happened first, second, and so on. It also uses dialogue show personalities and to keep the action going.

I rushed to the corner . . .

The firefighter shouted thanks . . .

Suddenly, giant flames shot . . .

I kept watching the firefighters . . .

Ending

The **ending** reflects on the experience and tells what the writer learned.

Closing Sentences
I now had a dream. I wanted to be a firefighter. I knew that, someday, I wanted to be the person opening a hydrant to help put out a fire.

English Language Learners

Remind students that their writing should sound as if they're telling the story to a friend. Have partners trade the papers they made above. Then have them take turns retelling their story. The listening partner should take notes on details and word choices that are not on their partner's paper. Remind students not to speak too fast.

Struggling Learners

Allow time for students to get feedback from their peers. Have partners take turns reading aloud their papers. Write the following prompts on the board as a reminder of what listeners should be checking for.

- Is the sequence logical?
- Are there enough details for you to picture what happened?
- Do the sensory details help you know how the writer felt and what he or she experienced?

If the answer to any of the questions is *no,* encourage the listeners to ask specific questions to help the writer make the narrative more detailed and convincing.

Starting Your Personal Narrative

Now that you have a plan, you can begin writing about your experience. Your first paragraph should get your reader's attention and introduce your topic. Write freely, using words that sound as if you were talking to a friend. You can begin your narrative in several different ways.

Beginning
Middle
Ending

- **Start with interesting details.**

  It's common to hear sirens wailing through the city. In fact, I usually don't pay attention to them. Then one day the sirens came screaming right past my apartment and stopped at the corner.

- **Use sensory details to grab the reader's attention.**

  When was the last time you were at the scene of a fire? Every time I think about the warehouse fire, I remember the thick smoke reaching into the air and the stench of burning tires.

- **Begin with a person speaking.**

  "Something's burning. I hear sirens. Something's burning!" Marcus shouted.

Beginning Paragraph

The writer grabs the reader's attention with dialogue.

The writer introduces her experience.

"Something's burning. I hear sirens. Something's burning!" Marcus shouted. I usually don't pay too much attention to my little brother. However, as the wailing sirens got louder, I thought maybe this time he was right. Just then, two fire trucks flew past our apartment building. I bolted out the front door and immediately felt my heart pumping fast. The trucks had stopped at the end of our block.

Write a beginning. On your own paper, write the beginning for your narrative. Try using one of the three suggestions above.

NARRATIVE

Writing Starting Your Personal Narrative

Direct students to write different **beginnings** *(see below)* for their narrative.

- If possible, they should try one of each kind described on the page.
- Then ask them to share the beginnings with a partner or in a small group and get feedback on which is the most effective in getting the reader's attention.

Literature Connections

Mentor texts: Professional writers strive to capture their readers' attention from the very first sentence. Here are some examples from modern classics:

"My sister, Lynn, taught me my first word: kira-kira."

—Cynthia Kadohata, *Kira-Kira*

"Home base . . . was a branchy box elder tree in front of the Hiser's house out by the curb."

—Richard Peck, *On the Wings of Heroes*

"*Ba-room, ba-room, ba-room, baripity, baripity, baripity, baripity*—Good."

—Katherine Patterson, *Bridge to Terabithia*

Teaching Tip: Beginnings

Expose students to as many good beginnings as possible.

- Read a few examples from books or magazine articles, and discuss as a class why the beginnings are effective.
- Have students explore material in the classroom library looking for good beginnings. Allow them to share their findings with the class. Ask them to identify which of the three kinds of beginning each example represents.
- Invite students to share beginnings of books they'll never forget. Encourage them to explain what it was about each beginning that grabbed their attention.

Writing Developing the Middle Part

Remind students that in a first draft, they don't need to worry about conventions (spelling, punctuation, and grammar).

- Direct their attention first to ideas and organization and then to choosing words (strong action words, specific nouns, sensory details, and dialogue) to make the experience come alive for the reader.
- Encourage students to try to punctuate dialogue in their draft. Remind them to indent paragraphs to indicate a change in speakers.

Writing Developing the Middle Part

You have your reader's attention. Now you need to keep it by adding just the right details. Remember that even though you may be interested in every little thing that happened, your reader may not be. Stay focused and include only those details that make your experience come alive. Here are a few things to remember as you write your middle paragraphs.

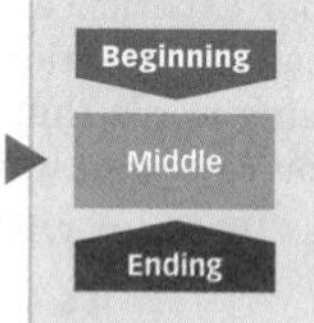

- **Put your events in the order in which they happened.**
- **Appeal to your reader's senses.**
- **Create a clear picture with action words.**
- **Use dialogue to show a speaker's personality, to keep the action moving, or to add information.**

Middle Paragraphs

I rushed to the corner and saw the firefighters charging toward the abandoned warehouse across the street. A firefighter in a bulky coat, a yellow helmet, and big boots was attaching a huge snakelike hose to the hydrant. "Do me a favor," she said. "Stand back and keep those kids away from my rig." I could see a group of neighborhood kids, including my brother, running up to the fire truck.

"Marcus, Paulo, Maria!" I shouted. "You and your friends come here and stay away from that truck!"

The firefighter shouted thanks as she ran toward the burning, smoking warehouse. Then more sirens screamed to the scene. Suddenly,

Dialogue moves the action along.

Sensory details let the reader "see" and "hear" the experience.

English Language Learners

Demonstrate some of the different ways that people speak. Tell students to pay attention to how you say a sentence because it can reveal your attitude and feelings. After each sentence, ask students to tell you how you said the sentence.

- Come over here. (whisper)
- Come over here. (laugh)
- Come over here! (shout)
- Come over here. (groan)

Encourage students to take over the modeling activity while you make a list of verbs. Copy the list for students to keep as a reference.

Struggling Learners

Help students build a strong verb vocabulary by playing a game of *Verb Charades*. Give them time to think of action verbs they can act out. Then have them take turns acting out the action while classmates suggest multiple verbs. Encourage them to use descriptive verbs. For example, rather than *run*, try *race* or *dash*.

Sensory details capture the excitement.

Dialogue adds information.

Dialogue shows personality.

giant flames shot into the sky, and a dark tower of smoke swirled into the air like a tornado. Above the shouts of firefighters, an explosion rocked the ground, and windows shattered. I watched my firefighter friend handle the hose as the powerful spray of water poured down on the blaze. "Some of those firemen aren't men," Marcus said, tugging on my shirt.

"You're right, Marcus, but they are all working together to put out the fire." I kept watching the firefighters wrestling with the huge hoses, smashing holes in the smoking roof, and climbing the leaning ladders.

"Bet you couldn't do that," Marcus said.

"Bet I could!" I answered.

NARRATIVE

Write your middle paragraphs. As you begin to write your middle paragraphs, be sure you look at all of the details you collected on pages 103–105. Also keep the following tips in mind.

Drafting Tips

- **Remember that your purpose** is to tell your classmates about an experience that taught you something.
- **Write freely.** Don't worry about getting everything just right. Just relax and let your ideas flow.
- **Add any new ideas** you remember as you write your first draft.

Struggling Learners

Concern over conventions and word choice can slow down students. Provide some strategies for students that will help them stay in a writing rhythm. For example:

- Advise students not to stop writing to use a dictionary to check spelling. Tell them to say the word out loud, slowly, and try to use the right letters to record the sounds they hear. They should circle the word as one to check later.
- Although students should be using strong action words, if nothing pops into their minds while writing, have them circle any current word they would like to replace. They can try to think of a substitute later and/or use a thesaurus.

The following activity can be used throughout the writing process:

- Form student groups of three for peer conferences. Ask students to remember the members of their group, or post lists in the classroom. Students will rejoin these groups as they progress through the steps of the writing process.
- Give each member a different colored pen or pencil (red for action words, blue for sensory details, and green for dialogue).
- Have members circle or underline each example of their element that they find and make a brief note in the margin about how the example is used (for example, sensory detail grabs the reader's attention).
- Then have them pass the paper to the next member in the group so that each member reads all three papers.
- When the writer gets her or his paper back, it will be clear how frequently action words, sensory details, and dialogue appear in the draft. This, along with the readers' notes, will provide feedback on where the writer can make the narrative stronger.

Writing Ending Your Personal Narrative

Students need to understand that their ending paragraph must serve two purposes. It must conclude the narrative and explain what was learned.

Before students begin writing, provide them with a photocopy of the reproducible T-chart on TE page 789.

- In one column, have them record the events of their ending.
- In the other column, have them write what they learned.
- Have students use ideas from both columns to compose the ending.

Writer's Craft

Beginnings and endings: An old rule of stand-up comedians is to start with the second best joke and end with the best one. The reason for this rule is that the final joke is the one that will linger in the minds of listeners.

In the same way, a narrative needs to start strong and finish even stronger. To do so, writers use a number of strategies:

- Provide a strong final image
- Include a powerful quotation
- Show the importance of the experience
- Connect the events to life in general

Encourage students to experiment with their endings to leave a strong impression.

Writing Ending Your Personal Narrative

There are two important things to remember as you get ready to write your ending: (1) reflect on the experience, and (2) share what you learned from it. *Note:* The writer of this model used dialogue to add a final detail.

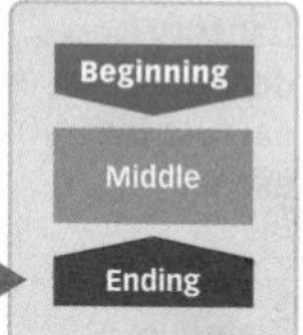

Ending Paragraph

By early evening the firefighters had gone, but the people were still standing around on the sidewalk talking about the fire. I heard a man say, "Some squirrels chewed on electrical wires." Maybe tomorrow things would get back to normal, but I would never be the same. I now had a dream. I wanted to be a firefighter. I knew that, someday, I wanted to be the person opening a hydrant to help put out a fire.

The writer tells the reader what she learned from her experience.

Write your ending. In a final paragraph, tell the reader what you learned from your experience. Remember to keep it simple but interesting.

Form a complete first draft. Put together a complete copy of your first draft. Then you will be ready to revise your writing.

Drafting Tips

- **If you are having trouble writing your ending, wait awhile.** Then read through the narrative aloud. Think about all the ways this experience is important and how it has changed you.

Revising

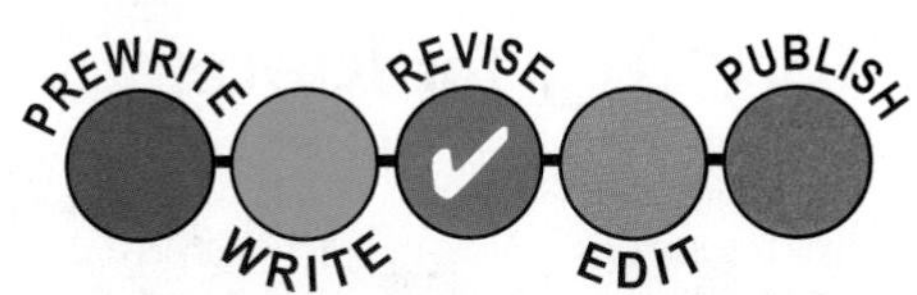

As you revise, you get the chance to take your essay to the next level. You've already written about the major ideas. Now it's time to add, delete, or move certain parts in order to make your narrative even better.

Keys to Effective Revising

1. Put your narrative aside for a while. Then, when you're ready to revise, you'll have a fresh outlook about it.
2. Read your narrative out loud. Be sure your writing voice sounds like you.
3. Check your beginning, middle, and ending. Make sure each part works well.
4. Mark any parts that seem confusing.
5. Make sure your words capture your experience.
6. Use the editing and proofreading marks inside the back cover of this book.

NARRATIVE

Go Online!

Revising

Keys to Effective Revising

Remind students that revising is the stage during which they make large-scale changes such as adding sentences, paragraphs, or dialogue. It is the time to delete ideas or details that do not fit the narrative. It's also the point at which writers experiment with moving blocks of text. They may decide to start in the middle of the action instead of at the original chronological beginning of their story.

Keys to Effective Revising explains the process students will be guided through on SE pages 114–124.

- Students should review the goals on SE page 98 and keep them in mind as they revise their drafts.
- If students are familiar with the revising process and you feel they can work independently, direct them to review the checklist on SE page 124. Be sure they understand the goal of each question in the checklist before they begin revising their writing.

Peer Responding

A constructive peer response helps a writer zero in on the specific revision strategies that will make the biggest difference in their work. Instruct students first to indicate what they like about the writing, and then to give suggestions for improvement. (See "Peer Responding" on pages 29–32.)

Technology Connections

Have students use the Writing Network features of the Net-text to comment on each other's drafts.

Write Source Online ***Net-text***

Revising for Ideas

The rubric strips that run across all of the revising pages (SE pages 114–123) are provided to help students focus their revising and are related to the full rubric on SE pages 130–131.

The two specific revising questions for each trait represent just a sampling of all the possible approaches to revising for each trait.

 **Answers**

1. H (and F)
2. S
3. F
4. S
5. F
6. S
7. F
8. SM

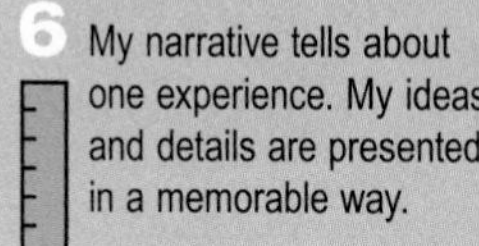

Revising for Ideas

6 My narrative tells about one experience. My ideas and details are presented in a memorable way.	**5** My narrative tells about one experience and "shows" my ideas.	**4** My narrative tells about one experience. I need to "show" more of my ideas instead of "tell" about them.

When you revise for *ideas,* be sure you have focused on one experience. Check to see that you use a variety of sensory details to "show" your ideas. The rubric above will guide you as you improve your ideas.

Have I used a variety of sensory details?

You have used a variety of sensory details if you have appealed to most of the reader's senses.

 In the paragraph below, some of the sensory details have been underlined. Identify each numbered detail, using "S" for See, "H" for Hear, "F" for Feel, or "SM" for Smell.

With a groan, I pulled on my heavy backpack (F) and headed off barefoot up the giant sand hills (S) at Sleeping Bear Dunes. At first, I thought this hike would be easy. Then, about halfway up, I began huffing and puffing (1) like an old steam engine (2). My feet sank deep into the cold (3) white sand (4). Although my leg muscles were burning, (5) I kept trudging up and up. Once at the top, I saw the icy-blue lake (6) and enjoyed the cool breeze (7) blowing a fresh scent (8) my way.

 **Check your sensory details.** Read through your first draft. Underline and label each sensory detail, using the following labels: "S"—See, "H"—Hear, "SM"—Smell, "T"—Taste, and "F"—Feel. Have you included a variety of sensory details? Have you used sensory details in your beginning, middle, and ending?

English Language Learners

Have students work with cooperative, language-proficient partners during revision. If they have difficulty expressing sensory details, encourage them to shut their eyes and imagine themselves back in the experience. Then have partners prompt them by asking questions such as

- What do you see?
- What sounds do you hear?

Have partners jot down notes on a photocopy of the reproducible sensory chart on TE page 793. Then have partners use the notes to suggest how students might convey various sensory details with vivid verbs and specific nouns.

3 I need to focus on one experience. I need more sensory details.

2 I need to focus on one experience. Also I need to use sensory details.

1 I need to choose a different experience to write about.

Do I "show" instead of "tell"?

If you have created a detailed picture of your experience by using vivid descriptions in your writing, then you have *shown* your ideas.

Telling: **I saw damage from the tornado.**

Showing: **The tornado ruined our street. The winds roared out of the southwest about 3:00 p.m. and hit us hard. Along our street, all the houses are now missing either a roof or a front porch. A huge oak tree smashed down on four parked cars. Broken glass, tree limbs, and dangling electrical wires made moving on our street impossible. No one was seriously injured, although two people were taken to the clinic for cuts.**

Try It Use one of the following sentences for a topic sentence. Write a paragraph full of details that *show* rather than *tell*.

1. Yesterday's class was a blast.
2. My mother works very hard.

Revise **Review your details.** Make sure your details "show" your ideas. Use action verbs and concrete nouns.

Ideas
Sensory details are checked for vivid pictures that "show" the experience.

(SM—Smell) Something's burning. (H—Hear) I hear sirens. Something's burning!" (H—Hear) Marcus shouted. I usually don't pay too much attention to my little brother. However, as the (H—Hear) wailing sirens got louder, I thought maybe this time he was right. Just then, (S—See) two fire trucks flew past our apartment building. I bolted out the . . .

To begin the revising process, divide the class into groups of three. If possible, have students re-form the same groups they worked in for their peer conferences on TE page 111. It would be helpful if the same students worked together on the same pieces throughout the writing process.

- As one student reads, the others listen for **sensory details** *(see below)* that use strong action verbs and concrete nouns. They should use the rubric strip as a guide.
- Listeners point out strengths in the writing and make specific suggestions for how to show more details.

* For more information about how writers can show instead of tell to make their writing more effective, see SE page 557.

Try It Answers

Answers will vary, but paragraphs should include details that show, rather than tell, about the topic.

Teaching Tip: Sensory Details

If students have difficulty focusing on sensory details, have them brainstorm words to describe a familiar place that offers many sensory details. Some choices are the school cafeteria, a movie theater, an amusement park or fairground, or a nearby city.

- As a class, fill in the reproducible sensory chart on TE page 793 with details about that place.
- Then provide each student with a copy of the sensory chart to use for their own essay. Have students complete the copy master before they proceed with their writing.

Revising for Organization

Use the peer conference groups formed on TE pages 111 and 115.

- Ask the groups to examine the rubric strip on these pages. Remind students that the object of peer conferencing is to help each other improve their writing.
- Have students in each group exchange their drafts. Ask each member to try to identify what type of organization the author used.
- Instruct them to develop a time line of the events in the narrative. Provide photocopies of the reproducible time line on TE page 790.
- When they have completed the time line, have them go back and comment on each entry, focusing specifically on organization. For example, a student might note that the beginning grabs readers' attention or that the order of events in the middle is unclear.

After the time lines are complete, have students give the time line they made to the writer. Allow time for students to discuss what they found. These time lines will help each writer see how a reader understands the essay and will assist the writer with any organizational revisions.

Revising for Organization

6	5	4
My organization makes my narrative enjoyable and easy to read.	My events are in time order, and I use transitions well. I have a clear beginning, middle, and ending.	My events are in time order. Most of my transitions are helpful. I have a beginning, a middle, and an ending.

Your narrative needs to have a strong beginning, middle, and ending. As you revise for *organization,* use the rubric strip above to guide you.

Did I choose the best way to begin my narrative?

You can check how well your beginning works by answering the following questions. (See page 109 for ideas.)

1. What method do I use to grab the reader's attention?
2. As I read over my narrative again, can I see that a different beginning would work better? (If you answered "yes" to the second question, try another beginning.)

Reread your opening. Make any necessary changes to improve your beginning.

How do I know if the middle is well organized?

Your middle is well organized if you put your events in the order in which they happened. It's also important that your middle be organized in such a way that your reader can move through it easily. Transition words can help tie ideas, sentences, and paragraphs together. The transitions below tie things together by time and work well in narratives.

before	while	immediately	soon	then
during	suddenly	next	later	after
finally	when	afterward	until	as soon as

Review for time order. Check the middle paragraphs of your narrative to make sure your events are in chronological order. Rearrange the events if necessary. Also check to see how well you have used transitions to help the reader move easily through your narrative. (See pages 572–573 for more transitions.)

Struggling Learners

Students may need help filling in the time line. Using a volunteer's narrative, do a think-aloud to model the thinking process needed to make a time line of an essay. Focus on main-idea sentences and transition words that indicate time order for each paragraph.

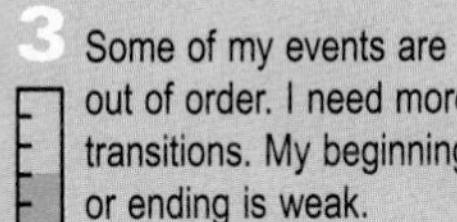

3 Some of my events are out of order. I need more transitions. My beginning or ending is weak.

2 I need to use time order and transitions in order to create a clear beginning, middle, and ending.

1 My narrative is confusing. I need to learn about time order.

Does my ending work well?

You will know whether your ending is successful after you answer the following questions.

1. Does my narrative end soon after the most important or intense moment?
2. Does my whole narrative lead up to the lesson I learned?
3. Will the reader be left with unanswered questions? (If you answered "yes," make changes to bring the reader to a satisfying ending.)

Check your ending. Use the questions listed above to see if you have written a winning ending.

NARRATIVE

Organization
Transitions are added to move the events along.

The firefighter shouted thanks as she ran toward the burning, smoking warehouse. ^Then More sirens screamed to the scene. ^Suddenly, Giant flames shot into the sky, and a dark tower of smoke swirled into the air like a tornado. Above the shouts of firefighters, an explosion rocked the ground, and windows shattered. I watched my firefighter . . .

If students need a refresher, review the use of proofreading marks as shown at the bottom of the page and on the inside back cover of the student edition. For a copy master, see TE page 788. Guide students to see how proofreading marks are shortcuts that help them make changes to improve their writing.

English Language Learners

To review the "show, don't tell" concept, make sure students understand that throughout the middle of their essays, they need to use strong sensory details to *show* readers exactly what happened. Now, in the ending, they need to *tell* the readers what the experience taught them, or why it was special.

Struggling Learners

If students have trouble incorporating transition words in their essays, have them work with a partner to find where transition words could be added to help the flow of the story. The list of words on SE page 116 focuses on time order.

* Refer students to SE pages 572–573 for other options.

Revising for Voice

Use picture books to model how a writer shows voice. Consult with your school librarian for suggested titles.

- List the main events from one of the books on the board.
- Then read aloud a portion of the story concerning a main event.
- Ask students to point out how the narrator's voice brings the event to life.

Explain that when sharing a personal experience, a writer's voice is what convinces the reader that the events are true and the writer really experienced them.

Answers

Answers will vary but should sound like the writer.

Revising for Voice

6	5	4
My writer's voice creates an unforgettable experience for the reader. I use dialogue well.	My voice is sincere and expresses feelings. My dialogue shows each speaker's personality.	My voice is sincere and expresses feelings, but I need to check my dialogue.

When you revise for *voice,* check to make sure your writer's voice is sincere and shows feelings. Also make sure that the dialogue you use helps to reveal each speaker's personality. The rubric above will guide you as you improve the voice in your writing.

Is my personal voice heard in my narrative?

Your voice will come through if you express yourself sincerely and with real feelings. This is usually not difficult to do when you are sharing a personal experience. On the other hand, writers sometimes turn uninteresting, or dull, as soon as they put pen to paper (or fingers to the keyboard).

Writing That Lacks Voice: Uninteresting/Dull

When we walked home, I saw the moon. The night was foggy. I heard one dog bark and then others.

Writing That Contains Voice: Sincere and Full of Real Feelings

While we were walking home, I looked up and saw the moon through the fog. Off in the distance, I heard a dog bark and then a chorus of barks. I felt a shiver crawl up my spine. It was probably just the cold.

Write the first part of your narrative in the form of an e-mail message or a note to your closest friend. "Talk" to this person as if she or he were sitting right next to you. Afterward, underline any thoughts and feelings that sound like the real you.

Check for voice. Rewrite any parts of your narrative that don't sound like the real you. Consider adding some of the thoughts and feelings you underlined in the previous activity.

English Language Learners

Reading aloud their drafts will help students "hear" their voice and identify passages that seem uninteresting, too formal, unclear, or in need of vivid new words.

Advanced Learners

Invite students to participate in a voice workshop.

- Have each student bring in a sample from an author whose writing exhibits a particularly strong voice.
- In a group, have them read aloud their samples.
- After each reading, have the group determine what the author does to create such an effective voice.
- Finally, have students write a brief summary of the author's technique.

3 My voice is sometimes dull. I need to improve the dialogue I've used.

2 My voice sounds uninteresting and dull. I need to add dialogue.

1 I need to understand how to write my story.

Does my dialogue show each speaker's personality?

Your dialogue shows each speaker's personality if it sounds natural and expresses true thoughts and feelings. Dialogue that works well helps the reader get to know each speaker. (See page 556.)

Sample Dialogue: Shows Each Speaker's Personality

"Well, don't just stand there. Grab a shovel. We've got a garden to plant," Mrs. Walters, our next-door neighbor, bellowed at me.

"Me? Garden? I don't think so," I replied.

"Here. Put on these gloves. We don't want to hurt those tender hands of yours," she said.

"Come on, Mrs. Walters. I don't do gardens," I pleaded.

"Nonsense. Your mother said that you needed a project, so let's get to work," she barked.

NARRATIVE

Check the dialogue in your narrative. Do I include enough dialogue? Does it sound realistic and show each speaker's personality? If you can't answer "yes" to these questions, then revise the dialogue in your narrative.

Voice
Dialogue helps reveal the personality of the writer and of Marcus.

I kept watching the firefighters wrestling with the huge hoses, smashing holes in the smoking roof, and climbing the leaning ladders.

"Bet you couldn't do that," Marcus said.

"Bet I could!" I answered.

Have two students read aloud the sample dialogue. As a class, list words and phrases from the passage that help them get to know each speaker. Possible choices:

Mrs. Walters:
- Well, don't just stand there.
- Grab a shovel.
- We've got a garden to plant.
- bellowed
- those tender hands of yours
- Nonsense.
- get to work
- barked

Writer:
- Me? I don't think so.
- Come on
- I don't do gardens.
- pleaded

Clues come through actual dialogue and the speaker tags that tell *how* each person spoke.
- Have students list three or four adjectives to describe Mrs. Walters and the writer.
- Invite students to share their adjectives with the class and explain why they chose them.

English Language Learners

This sample dialogue provides an opportunity for students to explore the use of vivid verbs to describe the tone of voice of a speaker.
- Read aloud, or have a volunteer read aloud, the line Mrs. Walters "bellowed," showing students exactly what a bellow is (a loud but low, gruff voice).
- Then repeat with the line that Mrs. Walters "barked."
- Then challenge classmates to say certain sentences in voices that could be described as grumbling, mumbling, chattering, growling, giggling, and lecturing.
- Encourage students to replace the dull verb *said* with more vivid substitutes whenever they write speaker tags.

Struggling Learners

Tell students that when someone says, "You have an attitude," it's usually not a compliment. When writing a narrative, though, it is important to show a character's personality and attitude. Both should be evident in characters' dialogue and also in the speaker tags. Invite students to check their dialogue for the right "attitude."

Revising for Word Choice

Using a variety of words makes writing richer and more appealing, and encourages writers to find words that are exactly right for each sentence.

Give students practice in varying their words in this activity called "Once Is Enough."

- Students circle each verb, adverb, and adjective in their narrative. Each can be used only once.
- Students replace any words that are repeated. They can work with a partner or in their peer conference groups.
- They can **use a thesaurus** *(see below)* to find other words.
- Ban overused words, such as *said, nice, interesting, went, fun, good,* and *pretty.*

Answers

Example 1. nervousness: stomach flips, heart throbs, knees tremble, deep breath, plaster on a smile, shaky step

Example 2. enthusiasm: show the world, every move locked, ready, bolts of energy

Example 3. determination: march to coach, have to do, place in top three, camping at the gym

120

Revising for Word Choice

6 My exceptional word choice captures the experience.	**5** I use specific words that add feeling. I use participles to improve my writing.	**4** Most of my words add the feeling I want to create. I experiment with participles.

When you revise for *word choice,* check that you've used words that express specific feelings. Also check to see whether you have used participles correctly.

Have I used words that express the right feeling?

You know you have chosen words with the right feeling if the words express your *attitude* about your topic. The examples below demonstrate how certain words show different feelings.

Read the examples and decide which one expresses *determination*, which one *nervousness*, and which one *enthusiasm*. What specific words help to express each feeling? Write your answers on your own paper.

Example 1

The applause signals that I'm next. My stomach begins doing flips. Heart throbbing and knees trembling, I make my way up what seems like a dozen steps. Reaching the mat, I take a deep breath, plaster on the expected smile, and take the first shaky step into my routine.

Example 2

In a few minutes, I'll show the world my routine. With every move locked in my brain, I glance in the mirror. My hair, makeup, and costume are ready and so am I! Bolts of energy travel from my toes to my fingertips as the announcer calls my name.

Example 3

After the competition, I march over to my coach and ask, "What do I have to do to place in the top three?" He instantly sits me down and finds his calendar. From now on, I'll be camping out at the gym.

Revise for word choice. Think about the feeling you want to express. List words that fit that feeling. Have you used them in your narrative? Make changes to express the correct feeling in your writing.

Grammar Connection

Transitive and Intransitive Verbs

- **Proofreader's Guide** pages 728–729
- ***SkillsBook*** pages 171–172
- ***GrammarSnap*** Transitive and Intransitive Verbs

Interjections

- **Proofreader's Guide** pages 588–589, 746–747
- ***SkillsBook*** pages 19–20, 193–194

Dashes

- **Proofreader's Guide** pages 612–613
- ***SkillsBook*** pages 43, 44

Teaching Tip: Using a Thesaurus

If students need a refresher in using a thesaurus, explain that there are generally two kinds:

- dictionary style, in which the words are organized alphabetically;
- indexed style, in which you look up the word in question in the index and then follow the references you find there.

3 I need to add more words that express specific feelings. I also need to use participles.

2 I keep using the same words again and again. I need to use words that express specific feelings.

1 I need help choosing words that express the feelings in my narrative.

How can participles improve my writing?

Participles are powerful adjectives that help writers strengthen their writing. They are formed by adding *ing* and *ed* to verbs. Compare the following sentences. (See page 485 and 730.3.)

Without a Participle

Leaves decay and fill the forest with a rich smell. (verb)

With a Participle

The rich smell of decaying leaves fills the forest. (*ing* participle)

NARRATIVE

Change the verbs in parentheses into participles by adding *ing* or *ed*. For each item, write the participle along with the noun it modifies. Then write a sentence using the new word group.

1. (close) door
2. (crackle) campfire
3. (laugh) children
4. (whine) puppies
5. (surprise) faces
6. (annoy) sounds

Expand your choice of words. Look through your narrative. Are there any nouns that could be modified with a participle?

Word Choice
Participles replace wordy phrases and modify nouns.

I kept watching the firefighters wrestling with the huge hoses, smashing holes in the ~~roof that had smoke coming out of it~~ smoking roof, and climbing the ~~ladders that were leaning against the warehouse~~ leaning ladders.

To give students practice using participles, have them work in pairs to think of some unusual verbs and use them as participles in sentences.

Model with these examples:

- crack; The children hid the *cracked* vase from their mother.
- threaten; The *threatening* clouds dampened Taniko's spirits.
- snooze; Jack's *snoozing* bulldog snored loudly.

Have each pair share their favorite with the class.

Answers

Sentences will vary but should include the following participial phrases:

1. closing (or closed) door
2. crackling campfire
3. laughing children
4. whining puppies
5. surprised faces
6. annoying sounds

Struggling Learners

Assist students with finding nouns in their stories that could be modified with a participle.

- Direct students' attention to the Word Choice sample at the bottom of the page.
- Point out that the participles came from the phrases that modified the nouns.
- Explain that the participles answer the questions *What kind of roof? What kind of ladders?*
- Assist students with finding similar phrases in their own writing, by asking *what kind of* questions about the nouns they modify, and by changing words in their sentences into participles.

Grammar Connection

Verbals

- **Proofreader's Guide** pages 730–731
- ***Write Source*** pages 485, 520
- ***SkillsBook*** pages 173–174

Revising for Sentence Fluency

Students may form a variety of sentences using the prepositional phrases and participle word groups in the **Try It** activity.

- They can work with a partner or individually on the exercise.
- Have students make as many sentences as they can. They may use word groups more than once.

* For more information about expanding sentences with phrases, see SE pages 519–520.

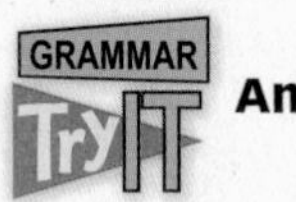

Answers

Sentences will vary.

Revising for Sentence Fluency

6 My sentences are skillfully written and keep the reader's interest throughout.	**5** My sentences flow smoothly. I use both long and short sentences.	**4** Most sentences flow smoothly. I use long sentences well. Some of my short sentences need work.

When you revise for *sentence fluency,* check to see if you have used a variety of sentence lengths. Use the rubric above as you revise your sentences.

How can I write longer sentences?

Writers often use prepositional phrases and word groups that start with participles to expand their sentences. (See **730.3** and **742.1**.)

Use prepositional phrases.

Before winter comes to Wyoming, I hike in the Snowy Mountain Range where elk graze and eagles soar.

Use word groups that start with participles.

Munching my trail mix, I watch soaring eagles in a patch of sky sandwiched between the canyon's walls.

Read the following short sentences. Add prepositional phrases and participle word groups from the lists below to create sentences that flow smoothly.

1. Fire trucks arrived.
2. Sirens wailed.
3. Flames leaped.
4. Hoses sprayed.

Prepositional Phrases	Participial Word Groups
in the neighborhood	roaring and racing
around the warehouse	hissing terribly
through the windows	rising suddenly
with a terrific noise	flaring and flashing

Check your sentences. Add important details to your narrative by using prepositional phrases and word groups that begin with participles. Include a variety of sentence lengths.

Grammar Connection

Prepositional Phrases

- **Proofreader's Guide** pages 742–743
- ***Write Source*** pages 519–520
- ***SkillsBook*** pages 189–190
- ***GrammarSnap*** Prepositions and Prepositional Phrases

Advanced Learners

Have students hunt for prepositional phrases and participial word groups.

- Provide them with a variety of reading material, and ask them to search for examples of these two grammatical structures.
- Have them highlight the prepositions in one color and the participles in another. (If it's not possible for students to highlight original materials, have them write lists of the phrases instead.)
- Then ask them to generate some guidelines for punctuation of these phrases, based on their findings. Have them check the guidelines they developed against a reference source in the classroom.

3 Most of my sentences flow smoothly. I need to use a few long sentences.

2 My sentences are all the same length. I need to expand or shorten some.

1 Most of my sentences need to be rewritten.

How can I use short sentences effectively?

You can sometimes use short sentences to draw attention to important points in your writing. Notice how the writer of the paragraph below uses two short sentences.

My great-grandmother's school had a fascinating name connected to a mystery. Long before the school was built, maybe even before Grandma was born, Native Americans had discovered a strange pit on the land. The pit was full of broken bones. Maybe an ancient hunter had dug the pit to trap animals, which would fall into it and break their bones when they hit bottom. Maybe the pit had been a dump where a long-ago tribe threw its garbage. The mystery of the pit was never solved, but it did provide a name for Grandma's school. The name was Broken Bone.

Review your narrative. Find a place where you can use a short sentence to stress an important idea. Reread that part of the essay to see if your special sentence is effective.

Sentence Fluency
A prepositional phrase adds a detail, and a short sentence stresses an important idea.

By early evening
^The firefighters had gone, but the people were still standing around on the sidewalk talking about the fire. I heard a man say, "Some squirrels chewed on electrical wires." Maybe tomorrow things would get back to normal, but I would never be the same.^ I wanted to be a firefighter. I . . .
I now had a dream.

Have students rejoin their peer conference groups and study the rubric strip. The groups should focus on sentence fluency.

- Do the narratives use long sentences that flow smoothly?
- Do the narratives have short sentences that stress an important idea?

Struggling Learners

After working to expand short sentences with phrases and word groups, students may find it confusing now to be told to find a place where they can use a short sentence.

- Make sure they understand why sentences like the ones in the **Try It** activity on SE page 122 should be expanded (too many short sentences don't flow smoothly).
- Then direct attention to the Sentence Fluency sample at the bottom of this page.
- Read aloud the next-to-last sentence, but add . . . *because I had a dream.* Point out that adding the idea as a clause (instead of as a separate sentence) makes the sentence very long.
- Then read the two separate sentences aloud, as they are written in the sample. Make sure students understand how the short sentence *I now had a dream* stresses an important idea and how it has more impact as a short sentence.
- Explain that the goal is to have a variety of sentence lengths, as shown here in the sample.

Revising Using a Checklist

Advise students to use the checklist as a tool to help them improve their writing.

- They should reflect on each question and do some revisions in any area in which they answer *no.*
- For more feedback, each student should have a member of his or her peer conference group complete this checklist after reading the writer's revised work. They should discuss any areas that the reviewer does not check off.

Revising Using a Checklist

Check your revising. On a piece of paper, write the numbers 1 to 12. If you can answer "yes" to a question, put a check mark after that number. If not, continue to work with that part of your essay.

Ideas

_____ **1.** Do I focus on one experience?
_____ **2.** Do I include a variety of sensory details?
_____ **3.** Do I "show" my readers my ideas?

Organization

_____ **4.** Are my beginning, middle, and ending effective?
_____ **5.** Are the events arranged in chronological order?
_____ **6.** Do the transitions work well?

Voice

_____ **7.** Have I created a personal voice?
_____ **8.** Does the dialogue show each speaker's personality?

Word Choice

_____ **9.** Have I chosen words that express the right feeling?
_____ **10.** Have I used any participles?

Sentence Fluency

_____ **11.** Have I used a variety of sentence lengths?
_____ **12.** Have I used a short sentence or two to stress a point?

Make a clean copy. When you've finished revising your essay, make a clean copy before you begin to edit.

English Language Learners

Have students work with trusted partners to complete the checklist. Encourage them to read aloud their essays, pausing at the end of each paragraph to discuss each question on the checklist. Direct their partners to point out strong passages and offer helpful suggestions for places that could be strengthened.

Struggling Learners

Encourage students who are having difficulty with the items on the checklist to communicate with you in writing. They should try to determine where their confusion is. For example, they could be having trouble with terms (*sensory, chronological,* and so on) or with a concept (transitions that work well). Identifying the problem is the first step toward solving it. Then you can work with them one on one to try to find a solution.

Have students and their partners focus on one or two traits at a time. It may take several days to read a revised draft for all of the traits.

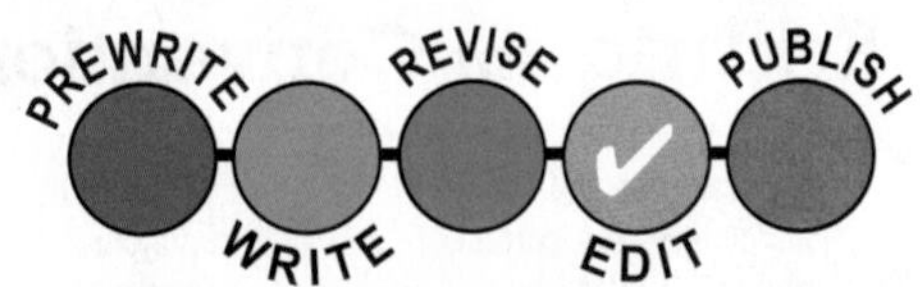

Editing

After you've finished revising your narrative, it's time to edit it for your use of conventions: punctuation, capitalization, spelling, and grammar.

Keys to Effective Editing

1. Use a dictionary, a thesaurus, and the "Proofreader's Guide" in the back of this book.
2. Check for any words or phrases that may be confusing to the reader.
3. Check your writing for correct punctuation, capitalization, spelling, and grammar.
4. If you use a computer, edit on a printed computer copy and then enter your changes on the computer.
5. Use the editing and proofreading marks inside the back cover of this book.

NARRATIVE

Editing

Keys to Effective Editing

Keys to Effective Editing explains the process students will be guided through on SE pages 126–128.

Share these hints with students:

- Always make editing marks in a color other than blue or black. This makes them easier to see.
- Remind students that while the spell-check and grammar-check features on their word-processing software are useful tools, they are not always correct or thorough. They cannot replace careful editing by the writer and her or his peers.

It is helpful to have several people provide feedback in the editing stage of writing. Have each student edit his or her own piece. Then have students ask two other people to look at the piece: a trusted peer and perhaps a parent or an older sibling. After others have read the essay for editing corrections, schedule a student-teacher **writing conference** *(see below).*

Technology Connections

Students can use the added features of the Net-text as they explore this stage of the writing process.

***Write Source Online* Net-text**

Teaching Tip: Writing Conference

Writing conferences can be short, one-on-one conversations that occur as you circulate around the classroom, or they can be more lengthy, formal conversations that you and a student schedule at a critical stage in the process. Your students' needs will dictate the approach you take at any one time.

Struggling Learners

Students should look over their work several times, focusing on one convention each time. They can circle places where they think their work needs correction. They should go back to these areas to fix them once they have read through the entire narrative. Also, reading their essay backward will help students find errors in spelling.

Editing for Conventions

Review punctuating dialogue by writing the following on the board:

- Dad requested, "Please mow the lawn before you go to Matt's house."

Review the punctuation with the class. Then move the speaker tag:

- "Please mow the lawn before you go to Matt's house," Dad requested.

Point out punctuation changes. Now place the speaker tag in the middle of the quotation:

- "Please mow the lawn," Dad requested, "before you go to Matt's house."

Discuss the differences in the punctuation marks in this version. Ask students to move the speaker tag in each of the sample sentences and adjust the punctuation.

Answers

1. "Dad called," my sister said, "to let you know that he'll pick you up after practice."
2. "Owen is coming with us," said Antonio. "Do you want to come along?"
3. "Mom will be home any minute," Marcus said. "We better clean up the kitchen."

Editing for Conventions

6 My grammar and punctuation are correct, and the copy is free of spelling errors.	**5** I have a few minor errors in punctuation, spelling, or grammar.	**4** I have some errors in punctuation, spelling, or grammar.

When you edit for *conventions*, you fix any errors in spelling, grammar, capitalization, and punctuation. The rubric above will help you edit for conventions.

Did I punctuate my dialogue correctly?

You will know your dialogue is punctuated correctly if you remember to follow the rules. (See page 556, and pay special attention to the examples below.)

When a speaker is identified in the middle of a quotation . . .

"**Did I tell you**," **asked Luis**, "**that I rented the DVD you like?**"

- Quotation marks set off the first part of the quotation. The words identifying the speaker follow a comma and quotation marks.
- The words that interrupt the quotation (sometimes called a *dialogue tag*) are followed by a comma.
- Quotation marks set off the last part of the quotation.

When both parts of the quotation are complete sentences . . .

"**Tell me what you think**," **said Eric**. "**That movie is full of action**."

- Quotation marks are placed before and after each quotation.
- A period follows the words that identify the speaker.

GRAMMAR Try It Rewrite the following sentences using the correct punctuation.

1. Dad called my sister said to let you know that he'll pick you up after practice.
2. Owen is coming with us said Antonio Do you want to come along?
3. Mom will be home any minute Marcus said We better clean up the kitchen.

Edit your dialogue. Review the dialogue in your narrative and fix any punctuation errors that you find.

Grammar Connection

Punctuating Dialogue

- **Proofreader's Guide** pages 588 (+), 598 (+), 600 (+)
- ***GrammarSnap*** Punctuating Dialogue

Struggling Learners

Explain that varying speaker tag placement will prevent repetition and make students' writing more interesting.

- Encourage them to check the dialogue in their essays to see if they can make improvements.
- Remind them, while they are looking, to consider substitutes for *said*.
- Remind students that the character's personality should be obvious not only from what is said but also from the way she or he speaks.

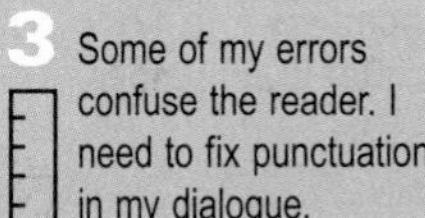

3 Some of my errors confuse the reader. I need to fix punctuation in my dialogue.

2 I need to correct many errors that make my narrative and dialogue hard to read.

1 I need help making corrections, especially with my dialogue.

Have I punctuated equal adjectives correctly?

Commas are used to separate equal adjectives. How can you tell if the adjectives are equal? Try two tests: (1) put the word *and* between the adjectives, or (2) reverse the adjectives' order. Then read the sentence. If the meaning of the sentence remains clear, the adjectives are equal. (See 586.2.)

Equal Adjectives Separated with a Comma

The loud, squealing tires warned the pedestrians of a speeding car.
(*loud* and *squealing*) or (*squealing, loud*)

Unequal Adjectives Without a Comma

Many curious spectators gathered to watch the firefighters.
(*Many* and *curious* do not modify spectators equally. They cannot be interchanged.)

NARRATIVE

Check your adjectives. Find a place where you have equal adjectives and make sure they are punctuated correctly.

Conventions
Quotation marks are added to the dialogue.

A comma separates equal adjectives.

"Marcus, Paulo, Maria!" I shouted. "You and your friends come here and stay away from that truck!"

The firefighter shouted thanks as she ran toward the burning, smoking warehouse. Then more sirens screamed to the scene. Suddenly, giant . . .

Remind students that adjectives add sensory details and make writing more effective. However, students should be careful to choose only those adjectives that provide a clear picture and add to the narrative. Just as they should not overload french fries with salt, they should not overload their writing with a series of adjectives for each noun.

Struggling Learners

Before they edit their essays for equal adjectives, invite students to act out a skit for clarification.

- Make up word cards for each word in the sentence *He was a short grouchy man.*
- Give each actor a word card. Give one student a word card for *and.*
- Have students arrange themselves so that the words they hold form a sentence.
- When it's not clear which adjective should come first, have students switch places. Then have them try to insert *and*. If there is no change in meaning, the adjectives are equally important and a comma is needed.

To check for equal adjectives in their drafts, suggest that students highlight the adjectives. Then have them find any that are side by side.

Grammar Connection

Equal Adjectives

- **Proofreader's Guide** pages 586–587
- ***SkillsBook*** pages 13–14
- ***GrammarSnap*** Commas to Separate Equal Adjectives

Editing Using a Checklist

Give students a few moments to look over the Proofreader's Guide (SE pages 578–749 in the back of the student edition. Throughout the year, they can refer to the instruction, rules, and examples to clarify any checklist items or to resolve questions about their own writing.

Encourage students to customize the editing checklist by adding questions that address the types of errors they often make.

- These questions will serve as reminders for them to check on specific items within a category that they find difficult.
- As students improve their writing skills, they can eliminate these additional questions from their checklists and see the progress they've made.

Creating a Title

Students can work in pairs to brainstorm creative ideas for titles. Then they can work together to choose the title that is most effective.

Editing Using a Checklist

Check your editing. On a piece of paper, write the numbers 1 to 12. If you can answer "yes" to a question, put a check mark after that number. If not, continue to edit for that convention.

Conventions

PUNCTUATION

_____ **1.** Do I use end punctuation after all my sentences?
_____ **2.** Do I use commas after introductory word groups and transitions?
_____ **3.** Do I use commas between equal adjectives?
_____ **4.** Do I punctuate dialogue correctly?
_____ **5.** Do I use apostrophes to show possession *(a boy's bike)*?

CAPITALIZATION

_____ **6.** Do I start all my sentences with capital letters?
_____ **7.** Do I capitalize all proper nouns?

SPELLING

_____ **8.** Have I spelled all my words correctly?
_____ **9.** Have I double-checked the words my spell-checker may have missed?

GRAMMAR

_____ **10.** Do I use correct forms of verbs *(had gone*, not *had went)*?
_____ **11.** Do my subjects and verbs agree in number? (She and I *were* going, not She and I *was* going.)
_____ **12.** Do I use the right words *(to, too, two)*?

Creating a Title

- Use strong, colorful words: **The Perfect Mask**
- Give the words rhythm: **Sirens, Firefighters, and a Dream**
- Be imaginative: **Home Team or Visitor?**

English Language Learners

Have students work with the same partners they had during the revision stage.

- Have the partner read aloud the essay and pause after reading each sentence to check for any errors in conventions.
- Encourage writers to note in their learning logs any conventions that seem particularly troublesome. Point out that when they edit future writing assignments, they should pay special attention to these points.

In addition, you can schedule an editing conference with each student. For each error found, write the Proofreader's Guide topic number in the margin on the same line.

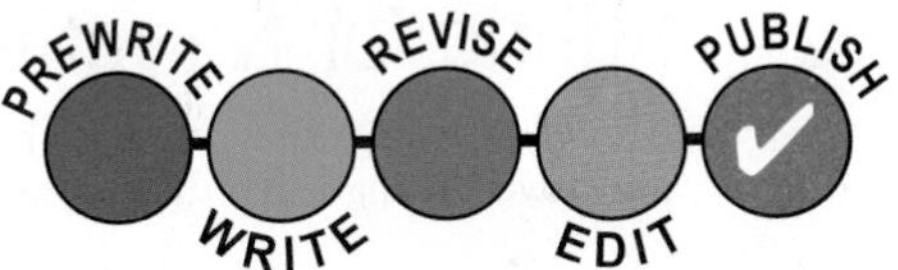

Publishing

Sharing Your Narrative

After you have worked so hard to improve your narrative, make a neat, final copy to share. You may also decide to present your story in the form of an illustrated book, a script, or a reading. (See the suggestions below.)

Make a final copy. Follow your teacher's instructions or use the guidelines below to format your story. (If you are using a computer, see page 60.) Create a clean copy of your narrative and carefully proofread it.

Focus on Presentation

- Use blue or black ink and write neatly.
- Write your name in the upper left corner of page 1.
- Skip a line and center your title; skip another line and start your writing.
- Double-space your essay.
- Indent every paragraph and leave a one-inch margin on all four sides.
- Write your last name and the page number in the upper right corner of every page after the first one.

Write a Script

Turn your narrative into a play. Write a script for the events in your narrative. Assign parts. Practice and perform your play for another class.

Read to an Adult

Share your narrative with an adult. Have the adult tell you what he or she liked best.

Create an Illustrated Book

Make a neat copy of your essay, including illustrations of the main events. Add a cover and share your book with younger students.

NARRATIVE

Publishing

Sharing Your Narrative

In addition to the suggestions listed on the student text page, students can share their work by passing it around a table.

- Have small groups sit in circles or around large tables.
- Each student should pass his or her writing to the left.
- All students should read the paper they are holding and make notes as they read.
- When everyone is done, students should repeat the step until all students have read all papers.
- Then they can discuss each narrative and what they enjoyed most about it.

Another way to share is to have students read aloud their own writing. See "Making Oral Presentations" on SE pages 423–430. The writer knows best how the narrative should sound, and everyone should hear the author's voice. Encourage students to practice reading aloud their work to friends or family members before presenting it to the class.

Technology Connections

Remind students that they can use the Writing Network features of the Portfolio to share their work with peers.

***Write Source Online* Portfolio**

***Write Source Online* Net-text**

Struggling Learners

Explain and model these strategies for fluency that will help students prepare for their oral presentation:

- Pay attention to punctuation—it will help with phrasing.
- Read with expression so the audience will get a feeling from your tone of voice as well as your writing.
- Read aloud at a pace that allows the listeners to hear every word.
- Project your voice.
- Practice reading your piece until you can do it smoothly.

Rubric for Narrative Writing

Remind students that a rubric is a chart that helps them evaluate their writing. The rubrics in this book are based on a six-point scale, in which a score of 6 indicates an amazing piece of writing and a score of 1 means the writing is incomplete and not ready to be assessed. There is a rubric for each of the basic traits of writing—ideas, organization, voice, word choice, sentence fluency, and conventions.

Point out that rubrics are helpful tools while writing, as well. They can tell writers what elements to include in their writing and how to effectively present those elements.

* Reproducible six-, five-, and four-point rubrics for narrative writing can be found on TE pages 750, 754, and 758.

Rubric for Narrative Writing

Use the following rubric for help as you assess and improve your narrative writing using the six traits.

Ideas

6	5	4
The narrative tells about an unforgettable experience. The details make the story truly memorable.	The writer tells about an interesting experience. Details help create the interest.	The writer tells about an interesting experience. More details are needed.

Organization

6	5	4
The organization makes the narrative enjoyable and easy to read.	The narrative is well organized, with a clear beginning, middle, and ending. Transitions are used well.	The narrative is well organized. Most of the transitions are helpful.

Voice

6	5	4
The writer's voice creates an unforgettable experience for the reader.	The writer's personal voice creates interest in the story. Dialogue is used.	The writer's voice creates interest in the story. More dialogue is needed.

Word Choice

6	5	4
The writer's exceptional word choice captures the experience.	Specific nouns, strong verbs, and well-chosen modifiers create vivid pictures and express clear feelings.	Specific nouns and strong verbs are used. Modifiers are needed to create a clearer picture.

Sentence Fluency

6	5	4
The sentences are skillfully written and original. They keep the reader's interest.	The sentences show variety and are easy to read and understand.	The sentences are varied, but some should flow more smoothly.

Conventions

6	5	4
Grammar and punctuation are correct, and the writing is free of spelling errors.	The narrative has a few minor errors in punctuation, spelling, or grammar.	The narrative has several errors in punctuation, spelling, or grammar.

English Language Learners

Students may be discouraged by the complexity of the rubric, as well as the possibility that their early writing samples may have lower scores than they would like.

- Stress that the rubric is to be used by each writer on her or his own work, not as a judgment tool by others.
- Also stress that the goal of the rubric is to help a writer improve his or her skills.
- Help students use this rubric to score their essays.
- Point out how each improvement they made during revising and editing improves their score. This helps students see progress.

3 The writer needs to focus on one experience. Some details do not relate to the story.	**2** The writer needs to focus on one experience. Details are needed.	**1** The writer needs to tell about an experience and use details.
3 The order of events needs to be corrected. More transitions need to be used. One part of the narrative is weak.	**2** The beginning, middle, and ending all run together. The order is unclear.	**1** The narrative needs to be organized.
3 A voice can usually be heard. More dialogue is needed.	**2** The voice is weak. Dialogue is needed.	**1** The writer has not gotten involved in the story. Dialogue is needed.
3 Strong nouns, verbs, and modifiers are needed to create a clear picture.	**2** General and overused words do not create a clear picture.	**1** The writer has not yet considered word choice.
3 A better variety of sentences is needed. Sentences do not read smoothly.	**2** Many short or incomplete sentences make the writing choppy.	**1** Few sentences are written well. Help is needed.
3 Some errors confuse the reader.	**2** Many errors make the narrative confusing and hard to read.	**1** Help is needed to make corrections.

Evaluating a Narrative

Ask students if they agree with the sample self-assessment on SE page 133. If they agree with the criticisms, ask them to suggest improvements based on the comments in the self-assessment. If they disagree with any comment, ask them to explain why.

Possible suggestions:

Ideas: more sensory details—The strong smell of wet paper and glue made my nose wrinkle.

Organization: weak ending—My mask didn't win a prize because I let my ego get in the way.

Voice: add some dialogue—"You should add some color," Mr. Cardinelli told me. "I want to use only black and white," I replied.

Word Choice: used "beautiful" too often—change *beautiful eyes and a beautiful nose and mouth* to *large, oval eyes, a straight nose, and a delicate mouth*

Sentence Fluency: confusing sentences—My art teacher, Mr. Cardinelli, talked about color, style, and texture. I was good at art, so I didn't listen much to him. I was . . .

Conventions: words spelled incorrectly—*paper mashay* should be *papier mâché, medeavil* should be *medieval*

Evaluating a Narrative

As you read the narrative below, focus on the writer's strengths and weaknesses. **(The essay contains some errors.)** Then read the student self-evaluation on page 133.

The Perfect Mask

The slippery wet paper mashay felt good in my hands. I put the first strips over the form of a mask that I made in art class. It was the start of the project that I planned to enter in the school art fair. The art fair was a big deal at our school, so I wanted to make sure my project would win.

I didn't listen much to my art teacher, Mr. Cardinelli. He talked about color, style, texture, and stuff like that. I was good at art. I was probably one of the best students in my class. So, I just did my own thing.

I wanted my mask to look like a beautiful medeavil woman. I gave her beautiful eyes and a beautiful nose and mouth. Mr. Cardinelli said that I didn't have to do her so perfect. I also gave her thick, black curls and a beautiful, white headdress. Mr. Cardinelli said I should use more colors, but I wanted to use only black and white.

The day of the art fair came and all the masks were hung on a wall in the gym. I noticed that mine looked different from all the others. Above the masks there was a huge sign that said, USING COLOR IN ABSTRACT ART. I realized then that I had missed the whole point of the assignment.

My mask didn't win a prize. On that day, I learned that listening to the teacher's instructions might be a good idea.

English Language Learners

Before students suggest improvements, explain the meanings of the following idioms:

- a big deal (something that is very important)
- and stuff like that (and similar features)
- did my own thing (did what I wanted to do)
- missed the whole point (didn't understand the main idea)

Student Self-Assessment

The assessment below shows how the writer of "The Perfect Mask" rated her essay. She used the rubric and number scales on pages 130–131 to rate each trait. Then she made two comments for each trait. The first one showed something she liked in her essay. The second comment pointed out something that she felt could be done better.

4 Ideas

1. *I wrote about one main experience.*
2. *I could have added more sensory details.*

3 Organization

1. *I did a good job organizing things by time.*
2. *My ending is weak.*

4 Voice

1. *I like the way my voice sounds.*
2. *I could have used some dialogue between Mr. C and me.*

2 Word Choice

1. *I like the description in my first sentence.*
2. *I used the word "beautiful" too many times.*

4 Sentence Fluency

1. *I used a variety of sentences.*
2. *A couple of my sentences are confusing.*

5 Conventions

1. *I punctuated my sentences correctly.*
2. *I wasn't sure how to spell two words.*

Use the rubric. Assess your narrative using the rubric shown on pages 130–131.

1. On your own paper, list the six traits. Leave space after each trait to write one strength and one weakness.
2. Then choose a number (from 1 to 6) that shows how well each trait was used.

NARRATIVE

To give students additional practice with evaluating a narrative essay, use a reproducible assessment sheet (TE page 787) and one or both of the **benchmark papers** listed in the Benchmark Papers box below. For your benefit, a completed assessment sheet is provided for each benchmark paper.

Test Prep

Performing a self-assessment gives students a dry run for learning the type of criteria that professional scorers will use in evaluating their on-demand writing. The six traits of writing used in this self-assessment correlate strongly with the criteria used on most writing assessments.

Benchmark Papers

Lost Trust (strong)

- Copy Master TE pp. 763–765

My Summer in Michigan (fair)

- Copy Master TE pp. 766–768

Reflecting on Your Writing

Emphasize that writers need to think about their work after they complete a final copy. Analyzing their writing strengths and weaknesses will help them improve their future work.

- Ask students to consider where they should focus their efforts during their next writing assignment.
- Ask students to keep their reflection with their narrative so they can refer to it the next time they write.

Literature Connections

Reflection: Reflection helps students internalize what they have learned and carry it forward to their next writing projects. All professional writers reflect on their work and, as you will see in the following quotations, some love reflection and some hate it.

"I am very foolish over my own book. I have a copy which I constantly read and find very illuminating. Swift confesses to something of the sort with his own compositions."

—J. B. Yeats writing to his son, W. B. Yeats

"If there is a special Hell for writers it would be in the forced contemplation of their own works, with all the misconceptions, the omissions, the failures that any finished work of art implies."

—John Dos Passos

Reflecting on Your Writing

You've worked hard to write a narrative that your classmates will enjoy. Now take some time to think about your writing. Finish each sentence starter below on your own paper. Thinking about your writing will help you see how you are growing as a writer.

My Narrative

1. *The best part of my narrative is . . .*
2. *The part that still needs work is . . .*
3. *The main thing I learned about writing a personal narrative is . . .*
4. *In my next narrative, I would like to . . .*
5. *Here is one question I still have about writing a narrative:*

Narrative Writing

Phase Autobiography

The *Saturn V* rocket that carried the first astronauts to the moon used three stages. The first stage was basically an engine with a big fuel tank of hydrogen and oxygen. Its job was to push the rocket past the atmosphere. The second stage propelled the rocket into space, toward the moon. The third stage of the rocket included the space capsule and the landing module. Each stage had its own purpose.

Our lives also have stages, or phases. Each phase serves a different purpose. In a phase autobiography, you tell about a stage or phase in your own life and what effect it has had on you. Your goal is to entertain your readers while showing them a little bit about who you are.

Writing Guidelines

Subject: A time of personal change
Form: Phase autobiography
Purpose: To tell about a phase in your life
Audience: Classmates

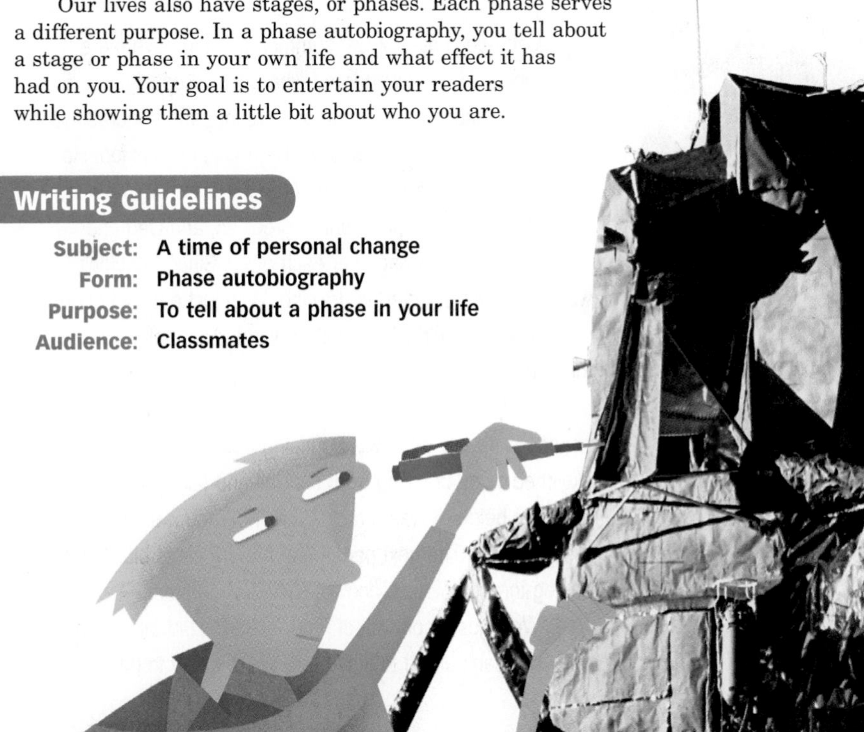

Copy Masters

Time line (TE p. 139)

5 W's chart (TE p. 139)

Phase Autobiography

Objectives

- understand the content and structure of a phase autobiography
- use narrative writing skills to create a phase autobiography
- plan, draft, revise, edit, and share a phase autobiography

A **phase autobiography** tells about a stage in your own life and what effect it has had on you.

Ask students the difference between a biography and an autobiography. (A biography tells about the life of a person other than the writer; an autobiography is an account of a person's life told by that person.)

If possible, consult the school librarian for examples of autobiographies. Read a short excerpt from one or more of the samples. Point out that an autobiography often has a foreword that was written by another person. Read an excerpt from one or more forewords as an example of biographical writing.

Phase Autobiography

Before reading the model, review what students have learned about the content and form of a narrative. Have them reread the rubric on SE pages 130–131.

To familiarize students with possible subjects for a phase autobiography, try the following:

- Ask students to list some stages in their own lives. Emphasize that they should think about how events over a period of time affected them, rather than recalling a single moment or event.
- Brainstorm some life transitions they have experienced. Possible choices are the following:
  - ☐ the birth of a sibling
  - ☐ a move to a new school or town
  - ☐ beginning a hobby or sport

Phase Autobiography

We all go through phases or stages. Sometimes those stages are school related, like graduating from elementary school and beginning middle school. Other stages are more personal, like moving to a new town, learning to play chess, or making a new friend. A phase autobiography tells how events over a period of time affect a person. In the following sample, Andy tells about a summer he spent drawing.

Beginning
The beginning introduces the stage.

Middle
The middle provides details about the stage.

Rocket to Mars

At the beginning of last summer, my dad gave me a sketchbook. At first I wondered what I would do with it. I wasn't planning to be an artist or anything, and I figured I'd catch up on a few TV shows. Then Dad lost his job. He was home all day every day, and the TV was his. We were living in a cramped apartment in Brooklyn, and Dad and I were always stumbling over each other. Since I couldn't watch my shows, I started drawing. With just a pencil and my sketchbook, I could be in another world. And that world was full of rockets.

The first drawing in my sketchbook showed a needle-tipped rocket just as it was bounding from the launchpad. I sketched in ice cracking from the hull and falling toward the firestorm below. It was a rocket caught in the moment of breaking free. The next pages had more rockets blasting off, ripping through clouds, and reaching for the stars.

"We're just about out of money, Son," Dad told me one day. "We can't afford to stay here. We're going to have to move."

Struggling Learners

Before reading the model, ask students if they have heard of the term *setting the stage.* In theater, it means setting up the scenery and getting the props in place to get ready for the play.

- Help students see the analogy between setting the stage in theater and writing the first paragraph of a phase autobiography.
- Ask students what needs to be done in the first paragraph of a phase autobiography to set the stage.
- Then direct students to "Rocket to Mars" so they can examine how Andy set his stage.

tell share remember narrate relate

Phase Autobiography 137

Middle
A series of events occur during this stage.

Suddenly, I couldn't draw rockets. Each time I tried, the hull would shift this way or that. Nothing was sleek anymore, but clunky and bent. My rockets evolved into space stations—pages and pages of space stations. They just floated there above the earth. I'd put little windows in them, and inside you could see me sitting at a table, drawing pictures, or Dad tending pots with space plants in them.

"Son, I got a new job!" Dad told me near the end of summer. "We don't have to move after all!"

Dad started his new job, and I had the TV back. The funny thing was, I didn't care about watching TV so much anymore. I was too busy drawing. My space stations got land put under them, and they became Mars bases. And I drew my dad and me standing outside, waving, next to a field of space plants.

Ending
The ending shows how the person changed.

Now I'm taking art classes in school, learning to draw people. One of these days, maybe I'll be an artist for NASA.

NARRATIVE

Respond to the reading. Answer the following questions.

- ☐ **Ideas** (1) What details does Andy provide about his art and his home during this phase?
- ☐ **Organization** (2) What problem is identified in the beginning? (3) How is this problem resolved in the end?
- ☐ **Voice & Word Choice** (4) What words and phrases give you clues about Andy's personality? Name two.

Literature Connections: You can find another example of a phase autobiography in *It's Not About the Bike* by Lance Armstrong.

Respond to the reading.

Answers

Ideas 1. There are three stages:

- When he and his dad are in a cramped apartment together, he draws rockets.
- When it looks as though they have to move, he draws space stations.
- When they don't have to move, he draws Mars bases.

Organization 2. His dad loses his job and takes over the TV.

3. His dad gets a new job, but Andy is not interested in TV anymore.

Voice & Word Choice 4. Possible choices:

- be in another world
- full of rockets
- bounding from the launchpad
- breaking free
- blasting off
- ripping through clouds
- reaching for the stars
- too busy drawing
- artist for NASA

Literature Connections

In his phase autobiography *It's Not About the Bike,* Lance Armstrong describes an important transition in his life from champion cyclist to cancer patient. Armstrong tells about his love for his sport and about a special relationship he forms with his nurse, LaTrice, on his road to recovery.

Discuss the elements that make the story a good phase autobiography. For more information about phase autobiographies, see the Reading-Writing Connections beginning on page TE-36.

Advanced Learners

In "Rocket to Mars," the writer uses symbols to represent his feelings. Rockets symbolize a wish to escape, space stations symbolize a feeling of uncertainty about what will happen, and the new Mars base symbolizes a new life. Symbolism allows writers to represent abstract ideas with concrete images—to show instead of tell. Here is a situation without symbolism:

Jerry wanted Charise to take him back, but she wasn't interested.

Now, here is the same situation with symbolism.

Jerry held the bouquet out to Charise, but she slammed the door, chopping the flowers in half.

In this situation, the bouquet symbolizes Jerry's hope for reconciliation, and the slammed door chopping off the flowers symbolizes Charise's rejection.

Prewriting Selecting a Topic

Guide students through the events on the life map.

- Ask them to figure out how many years there are between events.
- Note that there are two events listed for age 12.
- Discuss which events could be the topic of a phase autobiography. These should last over a period of time. Point out that only Andy would know which events had an important effect on him.

Encourage students to be creative and have fun as they create their own life map.

Technology Connections

Students can use the added features of the Net-text as they explore this stage of the writing process.

 ***Write Source Online* Net-text**

Prewriting Selecting a Topic

You've been through many stages in your life, but which one should you write about? A life map can help you decide on a topic.

A life map begins at your birth and continues to the present. The pictures represent important events in your life, and the numbers or dates indicate your age or the year for each event. Andy made the following life map.

Life Map

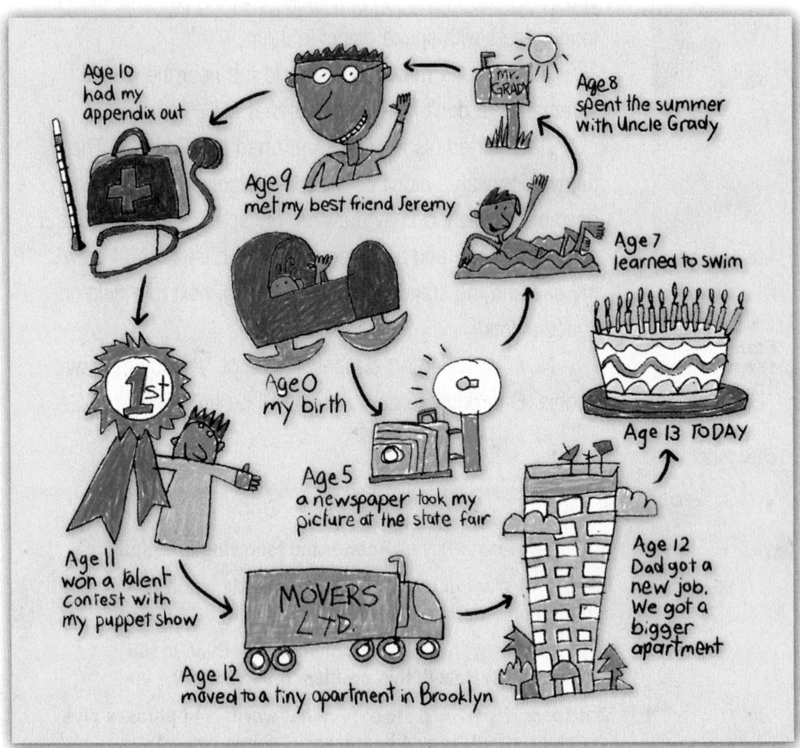

Prewrite **Make a life map.** Draw your own life map. Then review it, looking for a stage to write about. The stage must include a number of events over a period of time. For example, Andy could have written about learning to swim or spending the summer with his uncle. Select a stage to write about.

Struggling Learners

Students may need extra thinking time before making their life maps.

- Have small groups brainstorm events in their lives. Listening to others' ideas can serve as a catalyst.
- Have students record important events on index cards and put the cards in order before starting their life maps.

Grouping Details

To write your phase autobiography, you'll need to list events in time order. A time line can help you gather and organize these details. Remember that you can't include everything that happened, so you must focus on the most important events.

Write the first event at the top of the time line and list other events in order below it. Andy made the following time line to gather details for his phase autobiography.

Time Line

1	Dad gave me a sketchbook.
2	Dad lost his job.
3	I started drawing rockets.
4	Dad said we'd have to move.
5	My rockets became space stations.
6	Dad got a better job.
7	My space stations became Mars bases.
8	I started taking drawing classes.

Make a time line. Put together a time line showing the story details of the stage you've chosen. Start with the first detail at the top and then list the rest in the order they happened.

Another good way to gather details for a narrative is to make a 5 W's chart. Label the columns *Who? What? When? Where?* and *Why?* Then fill in the table with answers to those questions. (See page 549.)

NARRATIVE

Prewriting Gathering Details

Provide photocopies of the reproducible time line on TE page 790. Once students have created a time line for their topic, ask them to make a 5 W's chart (provide photocopies of the reproducible chart on TE page 792). Note that much of the same information will overlap between the time line and the 5 W's chart, but it may be grouped in different ways.

Work with the class to model the answers for the sample narrative.

- *Who?* the writer
- *What?* He drew rockets, then space stations, then Mars bases; finally, he took art classes.
- *When?* during the summer
- *Where?* in his small apartment
- *Why?* at first, because his dad was out of work and was watching TV, so he needed something else to do; later, because he really liked it

Struggling Learners

If students struggle with the related terms and concepts in this section, the following overview may be beneficial:

- A **personal narrative** focuses on one event, and the outcome is change.
- A **phase autobiography** focuses on a stage (or phase) of life, which is made up of several events, and the outcome is also change.
- To choose a stage (or phase) of life to write about, make a life map that shows all the big events in your life. Choose a phase that includes a number of events that together represent a stage of your life.
- To make a time line of the stage, include every small but important event you experienced that led to the change.

Writing Creating Your First Draft

Have students write three beginnings and share them with a partner or in a small group. Based on other students' reactions, the writer will be able to choose the best starting sentence.

Remind students that they should use their graphic organizers (time lines and/or 5 W's charts) as a guide as they write their beginning, middle, and ending. They should feel free to add, change, or leave out details or events in order to build the story and keep the reader interested.

Technology Connections

Students can use the added features of the Net-text as they explore this stage of the writing process.

Write Source Online Net-text

Writing Creating Your First Draft

With your time line in mind, begin writing your phase autobiography. Use the tips below to guide your writing.

Beginning

Draw the reader in and introduce the stage you are describing.

- **Start with the first event.** Tell what began this stage in your life. Andy, for example, started by saying that his dad gave him a sketchbook.
- **Start in the middle of the action.** Begin with action or dialogue to draw the reader in quickly. Imagine, for instance, the effect of Andy starting with the quotation, "What am I going to do with a sketchbook?"
- **Start with an interesting fact.** Find a fact that the reader might want to know: Did you know that NASA uses artists to paint scenes from other worlds?

Middle

Let your story unfold and bring it to a high point.

- **Be selective.** Include events that keep the story moving along. Leave out unneeded details.
- **Use sensory details.** Use sights, sounds, and other sensory details so that the reader feels involved in the story.
- **Use action and dialogue.** Show, don't tell. Let your reader see things happening and hear what is said. Don't just tell about what happened.
- **Build to a high point.** Increase the action to a point of excitement or tension. Make your reader want to keep reading to find out what happens next.

Ending

Describe how the stage ends. Consider using one of the following approaches for your ending.

- **Reveal why the stage was important.** Make sure your reader understands the significance of this stage.
- **Tell how the experience changed you.** Tell what you learned from the stage or how you are different because of it.

Write your first draft. Review your time line and then write your phase autobiography. Include details that make the story clear and interesting.

English Language Learners

Explain that the idiom *draw the reader in* means "get the reader's attention," and that *let your story unfold and bring it to a high point* means "develop your story, writing the events in time order, and build up to the event that is the most exciting."

✱ Draw a rising action/falling action plot diagram on the board (see SE page 351) and use it to diagram the events (rising action, climax, and falling action) of either a simple, familiar story or the student model on SE pages 136–137.

Struggling Learners

Before completing the writing stage, students may need feedback from you. Ask them to submit their concerns in writing so that you can respond. Tell them to be specific, using the examples listed above; for example, "I want help on the middle" is too vague. More specific is, "I don't think my writing reaches a high point, but I can't figure out how to do that."

Revising Improving Your Writing

Revise your first draft with the following traits in mind.

- ☐ **Ideas** Have you focused on the key or most important details?
- ☐ **Organization** Are your ideas in the best order?
- ☐ **Voice** Does your personality show in the way you tell the story? Does the dialogue in your story sound natural?
- ☐ **Word Choice** Have you used strong nouns and verbs?
- ☐ **Sentence Fluency** Does your story carry the reader along smoothly from sentence to sentence? Are your sentences varied?

Voice
More natural wording is used.

Ideas
An unnecessary detail is cut.

Sentence Fluency
Sentences are changed for variety.

Word Choice
A more colorful adjective is used.

Organization
A sentence is moved for better order.

At the beginning of last summer, ~~When the hot season arrived,~~ my dad gave me a sketchbook. At first I wondered what I would do with it. ~~Who gives a kid a sketchbook?~~ I wasn't planning to be an artist or anything*, and I figured* I'd catch up on a few TV shows. Then Dad lost his job. He was home all day every day, and the TV was his. We were living in a *cramped* ~~small~~ apartment in Brooklyn, and Dad and I were always stumbling over each other. With just a pencil and my sketchbook, I could be in another world. And that world was full of rockets. Since I couldn't watch my shows, I started drawing.

NARRATIVE

Revise to improve your first draft. Revise your phase autobiography. Make sure your writing grabs the reader's interest and holds it to the end.

Grammar Connection

Sentence Combining

- **Proofreader's Guide** pages 698 (+), 746 (+)
- ***Write Source*** pages 496 (+), 516–517 (+)
- ***SkillsBook*** pages 121–122
- ***GrammarSnap*** Simple, Compound, Complex, and Compound-Complex Sentences

Nouns

- **Proofreader's Guide** pages 704–705
- ***Write Source*** pages 470 (+), 471 (+)
- ***SkillsBook*** pages 145–146
- ***GrammarSnap*** Nouns Overview

Revising Improving Your Writing

After reviewing and discussing the page, have students work together to revise their work.

- Put students into groups of five. Each member of the group is responsible for one of the listed traits. (Conventions are addressed during editing.)
- Students create a suggestion sheet that lists the five traits, separated by several lines.
- Each writer should attach this sheet to her or his own draft and pass it to the left. Reviewers for each trait read the writer's draft and write one to three suggestions per trait on the attached sheet.
- Remind students to be specific. For example, if they suggest that there should be more sentence variety, they should indicate which sentences they think should be changed or combined.

* For more information on improving sentence style, see SE pages 511–514.

Technology Connections

Have students use the Writing Network features of the Net-text to comment on each other's drafts.

Write Source Online ***Net-text***

Editing Checking Your Work

Review the use of proofreading marks as shown on the inside back cover of the student edition.

After students have edited their own work, they can check each other's work:

- Arrange students in groups of four. Assign each person in the group a type of convention (punctuation, capitalization, spelling, grammar).
- Have them use a different colored pencil to code the edits (for example, red is for punctuation, green is for capitalization, and so on).
- Each student should edit a paper for a specific item and then pass it to the next student.
- When each student has seen all four papers, return the papers to the authors.

* For practice in making sure that subjects and verbs agree, see SE page 508.

Publishing Sharing Your Writing

Put final copies of class writing in a binder to share in the class or display in the school library.

If time allows, arrange a class reading or presentation to which parents are invited.

Technology Connections

Students can use the added features of the Net-text as they explore this stage of the writing process.

Write Source Online ***Net-text***

Editing Checking Your Work

While a phase autobiography is not as formal as a report, it should still be free of errors in punctuation, capitalization, spelling, and grammar.

Conventions

Once your autobiography sounds the way you want it to, check your punctuation, capitalization, spelling, and grammar. Use the following checklist.

PUNCTUATION

_____ **1.** Do I use end punctuation after all my sentences?
_____ **2.** Do I use commas correctly?
_____ **3.** Do I use apostrophes to show possession *(a boy's bike)*?

CAPITALIZATION

_____ **4.** Do I start all my sentences with capital letters?
_____ **5.** Do I capitalize all proper nouns?

SPELLING

_____ **6.** Have I spelled all my words correctly?

GRAMMAR

_____ **7.** Do I use correct forms of verbs (*had gone,* not *had went*)?
_____ **8.** Do my subjects and verbs agree in number? (She and I *were* going, not She and I *was* going.)
_____ **9.** Do I use the right words *(to, too, two)*?

Edit your autobiography. Make sure your words are lively and that your sentences flow smoothly. Also carefully proofread your final copy.

Publishing Sharing Your Writing

A phase autobiography shouldn't be allowed to gather dust. It should be shared! This type of writing is perfect for sending to family and friends by mail or e-mail. It also makes an interesting addition to a family Web site. Magazines that accept student writing are also good places for a phase autobiography. Finally, this sort of writing should definitely be kept in a journal or portfolio to be read again in later years.

Share your phase autobiography. Find one way to share your phase autobiography with relatives or friends. **(See page 129.)**

Grammar Connection

End Punctuation

- **Proofreader's Guide** pages 579–581
- ***Write Source*** page 518
- ***SkillsBook*** pages 3–4
- ***GrammarSnap*** Punctuating Dialogue

Using the Right Word

- **Proofreader's Guide** pages 652–655
- ***SkillsBook*** pages 61–62

Advanced Learners

Ask students to search for an autobiography by a person with whom they have something in common. For example, if a student's narrative is about overcoming an obstacle in sports, he or she may choose Lance Armstrong's autobiography.

- After students read the autobiography, have them write a paragraph or two about the similarities and differences between their narrative and the one they chose to read.
- They should include this comparison when they publish their writing, either by incorporating it into their own draft or by including it as a foreword or an afterword.

Narrative Writing

Across the Curriculum

What is a kite? Paper, wood, string . . . but when you put those pieces together in the right way, the kite suddenly soars to the skies.

What is a narrative? People, events, places . . . but when you carefully build a narrative, it can soar to the sky. Sometimes a narrative soars so far and so fast, it carries you away with it.

For example, in social studies, a firsthand observation report can carry you away to another culture. In math, learning-log entries can help you explore new concepts. In science, a story script can explain a topic you are studying. And in any class, incident reports give you the opportunity to record events you have personally observed. The following chapter will lead you through these kinds of narrative writing and also prepare you for a narrative writing test.

What's Ahead

- **Social Studies:** Writing About a Cultural Experience
- **Math:** Writing a Learning-Log Entry
- **Science:** Writing a TV Script
- **Practical Writing:** Creating an Incident Report

Copy Masters

Sensory Chart (TE p. 145)

5 W's Chart (TE pp. 145, 151)

Across the Curriculum

Objectives

- apply what students have learned about narrative writing to other curriculum areas
- practice writing for assessment

The lessons on the following pages provide samples of response writing students might do in different content areas. The particular form used in each content area may also be used in a different content area (for example, students can write a TV script for social studies just as well as for science).

Assigning these forms of writing will depend on

- the skill level of your students,
- the subject matter they are studying in different content areas, and
- the writing goals of your school, district, or state.

Social Studies: Writing About a Cultural Experience

Model writing about **cultural experiences** *(see below)* with the class. Base the narrative on a familiar event, such as a Fourth of July parade or picnic. Get input from the students. This will provide an example for students who have limited experience with other cultures.

Social Studies: Writing About a Cultural Experience

You don't have to travel to another country to have a cultural experience. Restaurants, festivals, and exhibits can give you interesting information about other cultures. The following narrative, written for a social studies class, tells about an ethnic meal.

An Indian Meal

The **beginning** introduces the experience.

My grandma came from India, so to celebrate her 60th birthday, my family went to an Indian restaurant. Grandma wanted me to try the foods she had eaten as a young woman. It turned out to be a very interesting experience.

The **middle** provides details.

As we walked into the restaurant, we were greeted by a hostess in a silk sari decorated with gold. She seated us. Then Grandma ordered samosas for each of us. The samosas were crispy, fried pastry pockets stuffed with mashed potatoes, peas, and other spicy vegetables or ground lamb. My samosa was very hot, but very good!

Then the waitress brought out several more dishes. A big silver bowl held mounds of steaming white rice. Two small baskets had large slices of nan bread. In the middle of the table, a round pot held spicy chicken curry. Grandma showed me how to tear off some bread and use it to scoop up my curry. The curry was unbelievably hot! Soon I was using the nan bread between dishes just to cool off my mouth!

The **ending** reflects on the experience.

Grandma ordered dessert, which included kheer—a rice pudding with almonds, pistachios, cardamom, and saffron. It was better than ice cream. Sitting there, eating my kheer, I could just imagine when Grandma was my age, eating the same food in India.

Teaching Tip: Cultural Experiences

Explain that a cultural experience includes any activity that gives us some understanding of the customs of a particular country or group of people.

- Invite students who originated from other countries to share some personal experiences from their homeland.
- Invite all students to share where their parents, grandparents, or other relatives originated, and any customs or traditions they observe. Suggest that students do some research by speaking with the older members of their families.
- Create a bulletin-board display of the various cultures represented in the room, and include in the display any pictures or writing that the students offer.

English Language Learners

This activity provides an excellent opportunity for students from other cultures to lead the class in a discussion regarding interesting cultural experiences. If time permits, encourage these students' family members to visit the class with photographs, items, and stories related to favorite holidays or customs.

Writing Tips

Before you write . . .

- **Select a topic.**
  Write about the specific experience your teacher assigns or choose an experience that relates to what you are studying in social studies.
- **Take notes about what you experience.**
  Record specific details. Use all your senses: sight, hearing, smell, taste, and touch.

Sensory Chart

Subject:				
Sights	Sounds	Smells	Tastes	Feelings

During your writing . . .

- **Set the scene.**
  Describe where and when you had the experience.
- **Include specific details.**
  Use concrete nouns and vivid verbs.
- **Explain new terms.**
  Give the reader any background information that is needed to understand the experience.

After you've written a first draft . . .

- **Revise your first draft.**
  Make sure that your narrative is complete, easy to follow, and interesting.
- **Check for accuracy.**
  Double-check your facts and details.
- **Edit for correctness.**
  Check for spelling, punctuation, and grammar errors.

Think about cultural events that happen where you live: parades, festivals, holiday services, concerts, and so forth. Choose one event you would feel comfortable attending, and write an eyewitness account of your experience.

Writing Tips

As a warm-up, ask students to do a 5- to 10-minute freewrite about a cultural experience related to their family's background or to a topic about another culture they have recently studied. Remind them to include

- explanatory information,
- sensory details, and
- answers to the 5 W and H questions.

Prepare students for the **Try It** activity.

- Encourage them to act as a reporter for the event.
- Provide photocopies of the reproducible sensory chart on TE page 793 and the 5 W's chart on TE page 792 for students to use during note taking.

Answers

Answers will vary but should include specific sensory details that show, rather than tell, about the event.

Struggling Learners

Some students may be more productive using a cluster than doing a freewrite as a warm-up activity. Suggest that they approach the cluster in a series of rounds. For each round, they will go back to the cluster and fill in more information.

- Round 1: Choose an event for the center of the cluster.
- Round 2: Answer the 5 W and H questions (provide photocopies of the reproducible chart on TE page 792). Add this information to the cluster.
- Round 3: List sensory details for each answer to the 5 W and H questions (provide photocopies of the reproducible sensory chart on TE page 793). Add this information to the cluster.

Math:
Writing a Learning-Log Entry

Give students practice using the information they would put in a learning log in a variety of formats.

- They can turn this learning-log entry into a letter to a parent or a friend about the class.
- They can write a how-to pamphlet that incorporates the math and personal information.
- They can create an outline for teaching the concept to younger students.

If appropriate, explore the prefixes, suffixes, or math-related words.

Math: Writing a Learning-Log Entry

When you write in a learning log, you make a personal connection to the things you are learning in class. In his math class, Ethan wrote a learning-log entry based on his experience of building kites. (Also see page **437**.)

The **beginning** tells what is being studied.

Friday, September 24:

Today in math class we learned about angles. Angles are created when two lines extend from a point. Three types of angles are vertical, complementary, and supplementary.

The **middle** contains explanations and examples.

- *— Vertical angles are opposite each other. They share one point called a vertex.*
- *— Complementary angles add up to 90°.*
- *— Supplementary angles add up to 180°.*

Angles can be found in places besides math books. For example, last summer when my brother and I made kites, the kites had all sorts of angles created by the wood frame.

The **ending** relates the information to the student's experience.

Now, by learning to recognize and measure different angles, the next kites I build will be even better!

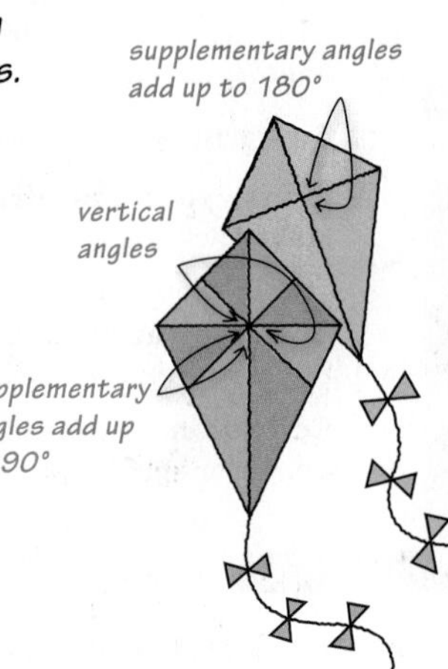

Writing Tips

Before you write . . .

- **Format your learning log.**
  Set up your learning log so that you like the way it looks. Also, make sure to follow your teacher's guidelines.
- **Pay attention in class.**
  Take notes to make sure you understand the material your teacher presents.

During your writing . . .

- **Record the date.**
  Write the date of each learning-log entry.
- **Write down what you are learning.**
  Record the most important facts.
- **Reflect on the information.**
  Relate what you are learning to your own experiences.
- **Include sketches.**
  Make sketches in your learning log if your teacher shows you a picture of something interesting. Also copy and label any important diagrams that help explain a concept.

After you've written a first draft . . .

- **Reread your work.**
  Read your learning-log entries to review the material and decide if you need to add any details.
- **Use your learning log.**
  Return to your learning log whenever you are asked to write a paper for that class. It will be full of excellent topics for writing assignments.

Write a learning-log entry about something you recently learned in math class. Record the facts and include sketches or equations to explain concepts. (See page **437** for another math learning log.)

Writing Tips

Since students will refer back to these log entries and may share them with others, it would be beneficial to incorporate graphic organizers, charts, diagrams, or illustrations to make the information clear. Neatness and logical formatting are also helpful.

Answers

Answers will vary but should include labeled diagrams or sketches and should relate to personal experiences, if appropriate.

English Language Learners

To stimulate thought and build confidence in students' language skills, suggest some simple examples for them to explain through words and pictures. For example, have them use words and pictures to explain the difference between a triangle and a square, or the difference between the fractions $\frac{1}{2}$ and $\frac{2}{1}$.

Struggling Learners

Encourage students to write more than a retelling of the latest math lesson. Explain they also need to show that they can apply the new information to their own experiences.

- Direct their attention to Ethan's entry as an example, and remind them that making a personal connection is one of the best ways to remember what they've learned.
- Using a recent math lesson, do a Think-Aloud to demonstrate the steps you would go through to show you've learned a new math concept. Include an example of a personal connection, inviting them to participate in the process.

Science: Writing a TV Script

Consult with your students' science teachers to coordinate this assignment with the current curriculum.

- Allow students to work in pairs to create the script.
- Students should focus on both the scientific content and the storytelling aspects of their scripts.
- If possible, involve their science teachers to ensure students present the concepts accurately.

Science: Writing a TV Script

When you write a factual TV script, you are telling a story to make an idea clearer. This type of narrative writing is helpful for learning a scientific concept. In the sample below, a student used a classroom experience to help explain the different types of clouds.

The **beginning** sets the scene.

Characters: *Student, Tai; Teacher, Mr. Hynek*
Setting: *School courtyard*

Tai: Why are these clouds all feathery, Mr. Hynek? Shouldn't clouds be fluffy?

Mr. Hynek: Clouds have many different shapes. Remember the clouds yesterday?

Tai: They looked like a gray blanket. What were they?

The **middle** uses dialogue to explain the scientific ideas.

Mr. Hynek: They were stratus clouds, Tai. Since stratus clouds are low to the ground, they make everything look gray. Fog is a type of stratus cloud at ground level. Stratus clouds bring rain or drizzle.

Tai: They did yesterday! Which clouds are fluffy?

Mr. Hynek: Those are cumulus clouds. When they are small and fluffy, cumulus clouds usually mean fair weather. If they grow really tall, they can become thunderheads and bring rain or storms.

Tai: Today I see feathery clouds reaching across the sky. The sun is shining, and the sky is bright blue. It looks like good weather for today.

Mr. Hynek: Right, Tai. Cirrus clouds tend to be high in the sky. Sometimes the ends of cirrus clouds curl in thin streamers. Cirrus clouds usually mean fair weather.

The **ending** closes the scene.

Tai: Now when I look at the clouds, I see a lot more than just fluff!

Advanced Learners

Have students generate some script guidelines (such as beginning with the speaker's name, how to handle stage directions, and so on). They can research the conventions of script writing by looking in a style manual or by examining some plays from the classroom library. Create a copy master of their guidelines for other students to use as a reference.

Writing Tips

Before you write . . .

- **Select an interesting science topic.**
  Review the chapters you have recently studied in your science book. Select a topic that interests you and isn't too complicated.
- **Get your science facts correct.**
  Check into the facts behind your topic.
- **Imagine ways to dramatize the topic.**
  Think in terms of storytelling—characters, settings, actions, and dialogue.

During your writing . . .

- **Let the story tell itself.**
  Experiment with your script and have fun as you write.
- **Be clear and direct.**
  Explain the idea or concept as simply and clearly as possible.
- **Keep it conversational.**
  Write natural-sounding dialogue.

After you've written a first draft . . .

- **Revise your first draft.**
  Make sure that your script is conversational, easy to follow, and interesting.
- **Check for accuracy.**
  Double-check your facts and details.
- **Edit for correctness.**
  Check for punctuation, capitalization, spelling, and grammar errors.

Try It Search for a science topic that you would like to write a TV script about. Invent characters, situations, and dialogue that could help you explain the topic. Then write your script.

Writing Tips

Once students have revised and edited their scripts, they should practice reading aloud the parts or cast other students in their skit. After rehearsing, students can act out the plays for the class.

Answers

Answers will vary but should center around and explain a simple science concept.

Struggling Learners

If time permits, collect several short scripts to share with students for analysis. Help them see how the format facilitates the reading of the script.

Have students brainstorm ideas for the **Try It** activity.

- Include character names and a setting for each idea.
- List each idea and its details on chart paper. Post the lists in the classroom, and encourage students to refer to the charts as they write their script.
- Have students select one idea to develop into a script, either on their own or in a small group.

Advanced Learners

For students who enjoy a challenge, suggest adding humor to their script.

- Remind them of the character Amelia Bedelia (created by Peggy Parish), who interpreted everything literally.
- Encourage students to add their own witty twists, as long as the facts remain clear to the audience.

Practical Writing: Creating an Incident Report

Point out that police often write incident reports at the scenes of accidents. One problem with collecting information from eyewitnesses, however, is that different people often see and remember different things when events happen quickly.

Try this demonstration.

- Place 10 to 15 everyday objects (pen, ruler, key, earring, dime, and so on) on a tray and cover the tray with a cloth napkin.
- Ask a student to come up and stand by the covered tray. Uncover the tray for a period of five seconds, keeping the contents hidden from the rest of the class, and then cover it again.
- Ask the student to write down everything that is on the tray.
- Repeat this several times with different students. Compare the students' lists for accuracy and completeness.

Change the items on the tray. Then vary the time that the tray is uncovered and see how this affects the outcome.

Practical Writing: Creating an Incident Report

When you see an accident, you may be asked to write up an incident report telling just what you observed. It's important that you include everything you saw in a clear way. The following incident report was written by the student set director of a middle school play.

INCIDENT REPORT

The **beginning** names the student and gives the date.

Ronnette Williams
May 13, 2010

An accident happened today at 4:15 p.m. on the auditorium stage. I was there as student set director, and so were Ms. Davis and the following students: Randy Dover, Danielle Walters, Maylie Royce, and Sumey Lee.

The **middle** answers each of the 5 W's: *who, what, where, when, and why.*

Here's what happened. We were moving the flats for *Phantom of the Country Opera* when one tipped over and fell on Randy Dover. Ms. Davis saw the flat fall, shouted a warning, and tried to catch it herself. The flat hit Randy's shoulder and knocked him down. Ms. Davis pulled the flat off Randy, and he scrambled out.

The **ending** tells the outcome of the incident.

Randy said he wasn't hurt, but Ms. Davis found a small scrape on his shoulder. She sent him to Nurse Hollenkomf. Randy was checked by the nurse, who treated his scrape and released him. Ms. Davis asked me to write up a report of what I saw. She also asked Randy to write a report.

English Language Learners

To provide practice in using language to recall events and details in the correct order and with accuracy, have students work with language-proficient partners to write incident reports on familiar tales, such as "Goldilocks and the Three Bears" or "The Three Little Pigs." Provide picture books for them to refer to for accurate details.

Writing Tips

Before you write . . .

- **Follow a proper format.** Ask your teacher or school administrator if there is an incident report form you should fill out. Otherwise, base your report on the sample on page 150.
- **Review the facts.** Jot down notes to yourself that answer the 5 W's: *who, what, when, where,* and *why.*

5 W's Chart

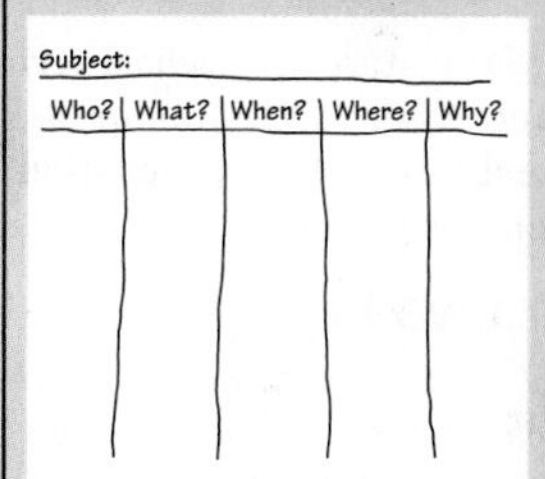

During your writing . . .

- **Be objective.** Report what happened. Avoid blaming anyone or adding your own opinion.
- **Be honest.** Record what you witnessed. Don't tell half-truths or change events slightly to produce a certain outcome..
- **Be complete.** Provide all the information that teachers, advisors, or administrators would need.

After you've written a first draft . . .

- **Review your statements.** Make sure that your sentences are clear and complete. Check to see that you have answered all the 5 W's.
- **Check your accuracy.** Double-check dates, times, facts, and details.
- **Edit for correctness.** Check punctuation, capitalization, spelling, and grammar.

NARRATIVE

Using the report on page 150 as a guide, write an incident report as if you had witnessed the following accident.

Who: Todd MacFarland
What: Hit his thumb with a hammer
When: At 4:30 p.m. on May 14, 2010
Where: In the wings of the auditorium stage
Why: Working on the set for *Phantom of the Country Opera*
Follow-up: Nurse Hollenkomf checked to make sure the thumb wasn't broken, and she washed and bandaged it, and sent Todd home for the night.

Writing Tips

Have students work with a partner to practice writing an incident report using the writing tips.

- Direct partners to discuss accidents they have witnessed and choose one to report. The partner who witnessed the accident can relate the details while the other partner takes notes.
- Provide photocopies of the 5 W's chart on TE page 792 for note taking.
- Encourage both partners to refer to the writing tips as one partner relates the accident details and the other takes notes.
- Then have partners work together to write the incident report.

 **Answers**

Answers will vary but should include all the details provided and be clear and accurate.

Advanced Learners

Have students choose an article from the newspaper and bring it in for you to review for appropriateness.

- Then have students write an incident report.
- Challenge them to memorize their reports and either present them to the class as a broadcast or videotape them for later viewing.
- Encourage students to watch televised news reports by various reporters to get hints on format, use of one's voice, and appropriate expressions.

Grammar Connection

Pronouns (person, number)

- **Proofreader's Guide** pages 712–713
- ***Write Source*** page 479
- ***SkillsBook*** pages 155–156
- ***GrammarSnap*** Pronoun-Antecedent Agreement

Writing for Assessment

If your students must take school, district, or state assessments this year, focus on the writing form on which they will be tested.

Review the main traits of a narrative. Ask students to look for these traits as they read the model:

- an experience described through details
- has a beginning, a middle, and an end
- told in time order
- uses natural language and dialogue to express the writer's feelings and personality

Narrative Writing

Writing for Assessment

Many state and school writing tests ask you to respond to a narrative prompt. A narrative prompt asks you to recall a personal experience or respond to a "what if" question. Study the following sample prompt and student response.

Narrative Prompt

Suppose that you lived in a world where there were no televisions, computers, or video games. Tell a story about what you and your friends did one Saturday.

The **beginning** states the focus of the narrative (underlined).

Last Saturday was the first nice spring day this year. My friends and I spent the whole day together. We hadn't made any special plans, but we still had a fun-filled day.

I woke up just before 8:00 that morning because there was a scraping noise outside my bedroom window. Looking out, I saw my friend Cal digging a hole near our back fence. My other friend Rob was standing there watching, and his little sister Marcie, who follows Rob everywhere, was holding a can.

"What do you think you're doing?" I yelled from my window.

Each **middle** paragraph tells a main part of the story.

"Digging worms," said Cal. "Find your fishing stuff and get down here!"

By 8:30 we were on our way to the lake. The sun was already warming us up, and soon it was too hot for jackets, so we tied them around our waists. When we got to the lake, we settled down on a pier, tossed our lines in the water, and watched the sun's reflection dance on the

English Language Learners

Work with students to analyze the writing prompt.

- Ask a volunteer to rephrase the prompt in her or his own words.
- Then repeat with other, similar prompts, such as *Recall an event that taught you a lesson. Tell what happened and what you learned.*
- Stress that rephrasing the prompt in their own words is a good strategy that will help them focus on what they should write.

waves. Soon the fish started nibbling the worms off our hooks. That annoyed Rob because he is afraid of worms, and every time Marcie had to bait his hook for him, Cal and I laughed. By lunchtime we had a stringer full of bluegills and rock bass.

Specific details are used throughout the narrative.

When we got home, Mom made lunch for us, and for the first time this year, it was warm enough to eat outside at the picnic table. After lunch, we played cards for a while. We had to play war because Marcie doesn't know any other games, but it was fun to play it again because you can yell and act up like a little kid.

Pretty soon five or six other kids showed up looking for something to do. We decided to play baseball in the lot near the cemetery. A great thing happened during that game. I became the first one in the neighborhood to hit a home run over the cemetery fence. I came close a couple of times last year, so this was a turning point in my career. We'll play ball after supper every night this summer.

The **ending** paragraph reflects on the experience.

All in all, it was a great day. It's amazing that all a guy like me needs to have fun is a can of worms, a deck of cards, a baseball, and a few friends.

NARRATIVE

Respond to the reading. Answer the following questions about the sample response.

- ☐ **Ideas (1) What is the focus of the writer's response? (2) What are some of the key details in the writing?**
- ☐ **Organization (3) How is the response organized?**
- ☐ **Voice & Word Choice (4) Do the writer's feelings come through in his word choice? Give examples.**

Respond to the reading.

Answers

Ideas 1. his unplanned but fun-filled Saturday
2. Possible choices:

- the friends, including Rob's little sister, Marcie
- the warmth of the day so they can fish and eat outdoors
- details surrounding the worms—the sound of digging them wakes him, Marcie baits Rob's hooks, fish nibble them
- playing war
- playing baseball and hitting a home run over the fence

Organization 3. in time order

Voice & Word Choice 4. Yes; possible choices:

- first nice spring day
- fun-filled day
- follows Rob everywhere
- sun . . . warming us up
- watched the sun's reflection dance on the waves
- laughed
- had a stringer full
- first time this year
- fun to play
- yell and act up like a little kid
- great thing happened
- first one . . . to hit a home run over the cemetery fence
- turning point
- great day
- amazing
- have fun

Advanced Learners

Direct students' attention to the last paragraph. Invite them to offer their opinions of the first sentence. Challenge them to write an alternate closing paragraph. Encourage them to share their versions with the class.

Writing Tips

Point out that students must approach writing-on-demand assignments differently from open-ended writing assignments and that timed writing creates pressures for everyone.

Narrative Prompts

To teach students who must take timed assessments how to approach their writing, allow them the same amount of time to write their response essay as they will be allotted on school, district, or state assessments. Break down each part of the process into clear chunks of time. For example, you might give students

- 10 minutes for reading, note taking, and planning,
- 25 minutes for writing,
- 10 minutes for editing and proofreading.

Tell students when time is up for each section. Start the assignment at the top of the hour or at the half-hour to make it easier for students to keep track of the time.

154

Writing Tips

Use the following tips as a guide when responding to a narrative writing prompt.

Before you write . . .

- **Understand the prompt.** Remember that an narrative prompt asks you to tell a story.
- **Plan your time wisely.** Spend several minutes planning before you start writing. Use a time line to help you put your ideas in order.

Time line

Subject:
① ② ③ ④ ⑤

During your writing . . .

- **Decide on a focus for your narrative.** Use key words from the prompt as you write your focus statement.
- **Be selective.** Tell only the main events in your narrative.
- **End in a meaningful way.** Reflect on the importance of the narrative.

After you've written a first draft . . .

- **Check for completeness and correctness.** Present events in order. Delete any unneeded details and neatly correct any errors.

Narrative Prompts

- Make up a story in which you accidentally broke something that belonged to someone else. What did you do as a result?
- Think of something important that happened in your life. It doesn't have to be earthshaking, but it should be something that has meaning for you. Tell the story of what happened and why it has made a difference to you.

Plan and write a response. Respond to one of the prompts listed above. Complete your writing within the time limit your teacher sets. Afterward, list one part of your response that you like and one part that could be better.

Narrative Writing in Review

Purpose: In narrative writing, you tell a story about something that has happened.

Topics: Narrate . . . an experience that taught you something,
a time of personal change, or
a memorable event.

Prewriting

Select a topic from your own life. Look through old photos or your journal for ideas. Also, use sentence starters to get you thinking about possible topics. (See page 102.)

Remember the details by writing freely and answering the 5 W's. (See page 103.)

Organize details about the people involved and the order of events. List sensory details to use in the narrative. Add dialogue to show the speaker's personality or to keep the action moving. (See page 104–106.)

Writing

In the beginning, grab the reader's attention by using interesting details or dialogue. (See page 109.)

In the middle, tell the events of the story in time order. Use sensory details, dialogue, and action words to create a clear picture for the reader. (See pages 110–111.)

In the ending, tell why the experience was important and how it taught you something. (See page 112.)

Revising

Review the ideas, organization, and voice first. Then check **word choice** and **sentence fluency**. Use "showing" instead of "telling" in your narrative. (See pages 114–124.)

Editing

Check your writing for conventions. Review punctuation of dialogue, and ask a friend to check the writing, too. (See pages 126–128.)

Make a final copy and proofread it for errors before sharing it with other people. (See page 129.)

Assessing

Use the narrative rubric to assess your finished writing. (See pages 130–131.)

Narrative Writing in Review

Refer students to this page whenever they begin a narrative paragraph or essay. Allow them to refer to this review while they are doing a sample assessment so that they can focus on the writing. As they become more familiar with the writing form during the year, they will need to refer to the list less frequently.

Expository Writing Overview

Common Core Standards Focus

Writing 2: Write informative/explanatory texts to examine a topic and convey ideas, concepts, and information through the selection, organization, and analysis of relevant content.

Language 2: Demonstrate command of the conventions of standard English capitalization, punctuation, and spelling when writing.

Language 3a: Choose language that expresses ideas precisely and concisely, recognizing and eliminating wordiness and redundancy.

Writing Forms

- Expository Paragraph
- Comparing Two Subjects
- Writing a Cause-and-Effect Essay

Focus on the Traits

- **Ideas** Using details to compare and contrast two subjects
- **Organization** Providing point-by-point comparison
- **Voice** Writing with an original and enthusiastic voice
- **Word Choice** Choosing precise language and including informative definitions that fit the audience
- **Sentence Fluency** Using coordinating and subordinating conjunctions to improve sentence flow
- **Conventions** Checking for errors in punctuation, capitalization, spelling, and grammar

Literature Connections

- **"Borders of Baseball: U.S. and Cuban Play"** from *The World Almanac*
- **"Like Black Smoke: The Black Death's Journey"** by Diana Childress

Technology Connections

Write Source Online
www.hmheducation.com/writesource

- ***Net-text***
- ***Bookshelf***
- ***GrammarSnap***
- ***Portfolio***
- ***Writing Network features***
- ***File Cabinet***

Interactive Whiteboard Lessons

Suggested Expository Writing Unit (Five Weeks)

	Day	Writing and Skills Instruction	Student Edition: Expository Writing Unit	Student Edition: Resource Units*	SkillsBook	Daily Language Workouts	Write Source Online
Week 1	1–4	**Expository Paragraph: Compare Two Things**	157–160	537 (order)		28–29, 90	*Interactive Whiteboard Lessons*
		Skills Activities: • Complete Sentences		500–501, 690–691, 692–693	69–70, 73–74		
		• Using the Right Word		660–667	63		
	opt.	*Speeches*	428–429				
	5	**Expository Essay: Comparison-Contrast** (Model) Literature Connections "Borders of Baseball: U.S. and Cuban Play"	161–164				

* These units are also located in the back of the Teacher's Edition. Resource Units include "Basic Grammar and Writing," "A Writer's Resource," and "Proofreader's Guide."
(+) This activity is located in a different section of the *Write Source Student Edition.* If students have already completed this activity, you may wish to review it at this time.

Week	Day	Writing and Skills Instruction	Student Edition: Expository Writing Unit	Student Edition: Resource Units*	SkillsBook	Daily Language Workouts	Write Source Online
Week 2	6–7	(Prewriting)	165–170			30–31, 91	*Net-text*
	8–10	(Writing)	171–176		89		*Net-text*
Week 3	11–13	(Revising)	177–188			32–33, 92	*Net-text*
		Skills Activities: • Specific Nouns and Appositives		471 (+), 702 (+), 586–587 (appositives)	147–148		*GrammarSnap*
		• Nonrestrictive Phrases and Clauses		517, 584–585	15–16		
		• Coordinating and Subordinating Conjunctions		496 (+), 497, 498, 744 (+), 746–747 (conjunctions)	195–196		
		• Unity		538, 539			
	14–15	(Editing and Publishing)	189–193				*Net-text, Portfolio*
		Skills Activities: • Commas (explanatory phrases and clauses)		584 (+), 588 (+)	17–18		
		• Comparative and Superlative Adjectives and Adverbs		487, 491, 734 (+), 738–739	181–182, 185–186		*GrammarSnap*
		• Subject-Verb Agreement		508–509	105–106		
		• Tenses (irregular verbs)		480–481, 720–723	172–174		
Week 4	16–17	(Assessing) (Reflecting)	194–197, 198			34–35, 93	
	18	Writing Across the Curriculum	205–211				
	opt.	*Speeches*	428–429				
	opt.	*Practical Writing: E-Mail Request*	212–213	518 (+)	119–120		
	19–20	Expository Writing for Assessment	214–216				
Week 5	21–25	**Cause-Effect Essay:** (Model) Literature Connections "Like Black Smoke: The Black Death's Journey"	199–201			36–37, 94	
		(Prewriting)	202–203				*Net-text*
		(Writing)	204				*Net-text*
		(Revising)	204				*Net-text*
		Skills Activities: • Complete Sentences		502–503, 690 (+), 692 (+)	92		
		• Comma Splices and Run-Ons		506	93–94		
		(Editing)	204				*Net-text*
		Skills Activities: • Double Negatives		510	101–102		

* These units are also located in the back of the Teacher's Edition. Resource Units include "Basic Grammar and Writing," "A Writer's Resource," and "Proofreader's Guide."
(+) This activity is located in a different section of the *Write Source Student Edition.* If students have already completed this activity, you may wish to review it at this time.

Teacher's Notes for Expository Writing

This overview for expository writing includes some specific teaching suggestions for this unit.

Writing Focus

Expository Paragraph (pages 157–160)

A comparison-contrast paragraph is a good way to explain two different, yet similar items (for example: car models, food types, plant varieties). Showing students how to do this well will help them in their future work. A student model will lead through the planning and writing process.

Comparing Two Subjects (pages 161–198)

Because teachers often ask students to write in depth when comparing and contrasting two subjects, students need to master the comparison-contrast essay. To write a thorough comparison-contrast essay, students will have to carefully study the two subjects they have chosen. In the process, your students will discover that this kind of essay allows them to write about very similar or very different topics.

Writing a Cause-and-Effect Essay (pages 199–204)

The second multiparagraph form in this unit is the cause-and-effect essay. Like any two-part essay, this form can be challenging to organize. The chapter models effective organization for a topic that has one cause and many effects, and it guides students in selecting a similar type of topic. Cause-and-effect essays require students to deepen their thinking by exploring the connections between actions and reactions.

Grammar Focus

For support with this unit's grammar topics, consult the resource units (Basic Grammar and Writing, A Writer's Resource, and Proofreader's Guide).

Academic Vocabulary

Read aloud the academic terms, as well as the descriptions and questions. Model for students how to read one question and answer it. Have partners monitor their understanding and seek clarification of the terms by working through the meanings and questions together.

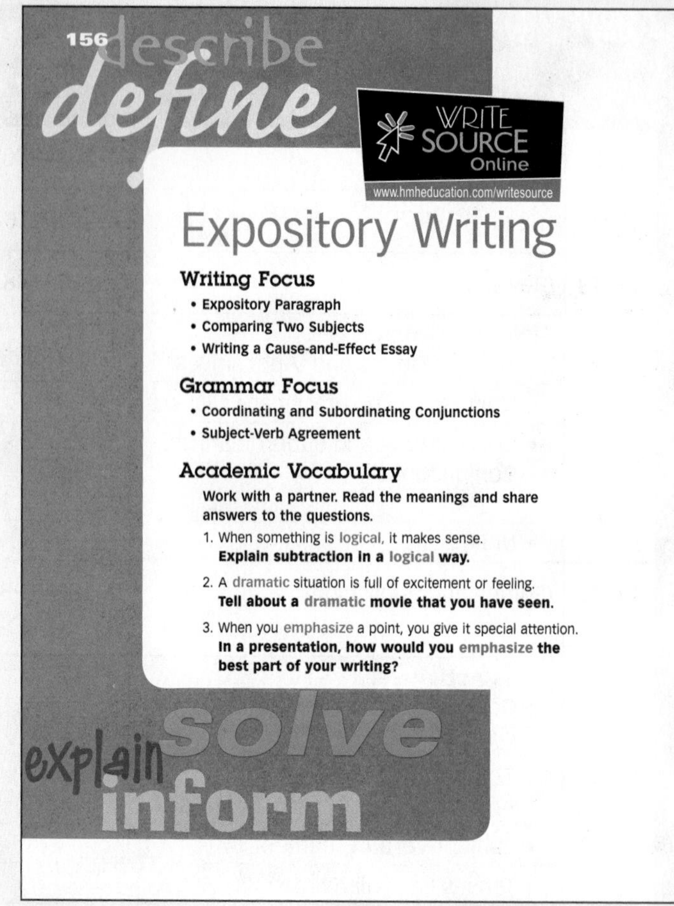
156 describe define

WRITE SOURCE Online
www.hmheducation.com/writesource

Expository Writing

Writing Focus
- Expository Paragraph
- Comparing Two Subjects
- Writing a Cause-and-Effect Essay

Grammar Focus
- Coordinating and Subordinating Conjunctions
- Subject-Verb Agreement

Academic Vocabulary

Work with a partner. Read the meanings and share answers to the questions.

1. When something is logical, it makes sense. **Explain subtraction in a logical way.**
2. A dramatic situation is full of excitement or feeling. **Tell about a dramatic movie that you have seen.**
3. When you emphasize a point, you give it special attention. **In a presentation, how would you emphasize the best part of your writing?**

Minilessons

Expository Topic — Expository Topic

- **LIST** two items that you could compare and contrast. For ideas, think about things you have heard in the news and things that have happened in school. **WRITE** a couple sentences explaining why you chose the topics you did.

Charting Your Course — Comparing Two Subjects

- **REVIEW** the Venn diagram on page 549 of your textbook. **RESPOND** to the following prompt: Pick one of the categories listed below, and then choose two items from that category that you would recommend to friends. (books, magazines, movies, CD's, video games)
- **DRAW** a Venn diagram listing the similarities and differences between your two choices.

Cause and Effect — Writing a Cause-and-Effect Essay

- Think of an accident you or someone you know has had. **LIST** as many possible causes as you can for this event. **LIST** as many effects as you can. **CHOOSE** what you believe is the major cause and what is the major effect.

157

Expository Writing

Expository Paragraph

What's the difference between a school bus driver and a cold? One knows the stops, and the other stops the nose!

All kidding aside, when you explain the similarities and differences between two things, you are comparing and contrasting them. Doing this helps you to understand each thing better. In an expository paragraph (a paragraph that *explains*), you can compare and contrast all sorts of things: soul music and R & B, science fiction and fantasy, or even tacos and pizza.

In this chapter you will write a comparison-contrast paragraph about two similar things. Maybe next time someone says, "What's the difference between . . . ?," you'll already know the answer!

Writing Guidelines

Subject: Two things to compare and contrast
Form: Expository paragraph
Purpose: To share knowledge
Audience: Classmates

Expository Paragraph

Objectives

- understand the content and structure of an expository paragraph
- choose a topic (compare and contrast two similar things) to write about
- plan, draft, revise, and edit an expository paragraph

An **expository paragraph** explains something to readers. It can explain one of the following:

- how to do or make something
- how things are similar or different
- the causes of something
- the kinds of something
- the definition of something

Paragraphs have a topic sentence, the body, and a closing sentence.

* For more information about how to construct expository paragraphs, see SE page 528.

Technology Connections

Use this unit's Interactive Whiteboard Lesson to introduce expository writing.

 ***Interactive Whiteboard Lessons***

English Language Learners

If students need additional support in order to understand the concept of expository writing, show them examples from texts such as the following:

- a textbook
- a newspaper account of an event
- a nonfiction book about a subject of interest
- a how-to book

Try to provide examples that

- show how to do or make something,
- compare and contrast two similar things,
- demonstrate cause and effect,
- identify the kinds of something.

Have students read the examples to familiarize themselves with the genre.

Copy Masters

Venn Diagram (TE p. 160)

T-chart (TE p. 160)

Expository Paragraph

Help students focus on major aspects of two things when comparing and contrasting. They should think about how the two topics are similar and different in

- appearance
- materials, equipment, or ingredients
- rules or methods
- behaviors

Point out that the details (ways to eat, ingredients, preparation) discussed in the sample **comparison-contrast paragraph** *(see below)* help readers understand the similarities and differences between tacos and pizza.

Respond to the reading.

Answers

Ideas 1. comparing and contrasting tacos and pizza

Organization 2. compares tacos and pizza together (point by point)

Voice & Word Choice 3. informal: totally, a lot in common, American favorite, basically, loaded, fixings, right along, go fast

Expository Paragraph

The simplest form of expository writing is the expository paragraph. It usually starts with a **topic sentence**, which lets the reader know what the paragraph will be about. The **body** sentences give details that *support* the topic sentence, and the **closing sentence** ends the explanation. The paragraph below compares and contrasts a student's two favorite foods.

What'll It Be: Tacos or Pizza?

Topic Sentence: Tacos and pizza might seem totally different, but they actually have a lot in common.

Body: Even though tacos come from Mexico, and pizza comes from Italy, each food is an American favorite. Both are foods with a solid base you can pick up and eat. Tacos have a tortilla shell made from ground corn or flour. Pizzas are cooked on a crust that is basically a flat loaf of bread. Both foods are loaded with toppings. One way they are different is that taco fixings get cooked separately and then put together, but pizza ingredients get baked right along with the crust. Ingredients for both tacos and pizza include meats, cheeses, sauces, and vegetables.

Closing Sentence: These foods have one more thing in common: They go fast when served!

Respond to the reading. On your own paper, answer each of the following questions.

- ☐ **Ideas** (1) What is the topic of the paragraph?
- ☐ **Organization** (2) Does the essay focus on one food at a time (subject by subject) or compare tacos and pizza together (point by point)?
- ☐ **Voice & Word Choice** (3) Is the voice of this paragraph formal or informal? Which words make it that way?

Teaching Tip: Comparison-Contrast Paragraph

Provide practice with writing a comparison-contrast paragraph. As a class, write a paragraph that compares apples and oranges.

- As a class, complete a Venn diagram showing features of each type of fruit.
- Use the diagram to compose a topic sentence.
- Add details (similarities: both are fruits, similar in size, sweet, seeds, grow on trees; differences: color, texture, skin versus rind, thin skin, thick rind, grow in temperate climate, grow in tropics).
- End the paragraph with a good closing sentence.
- Write the completed paragraph on chart paper and display it.

Prewriting Selecting a Topic

Selecting a topic for a comparison-contrast paragraph is easy. Start by listing things that interest you. Then, for each item on your list, write down at least one other thing you could compare it to.

The writer of the paragraph on page 158 created the following list of topics. Afterward he crossed out ideas that were too similar or too different.

Topics List

Topics to Compare

~~Cars~~	~~Boats~~
Skateboards	Scooters
~~Mountains~~	~~Clouds~~
Baseball	Softball
Tacos	Pizza

Make a list and select a topic. Using the list above as a guide, jot down a few topics or items that interest you. For each, write at least one thing that might make an interesting comparison and contrast. Choose two items with enough similarities and differences to write a comparison-contrast paragraph.

Writing a Topic Sentence

Once you have two things to compare, it's time to write a topic sentence that introduces your comparison-contrast paragraph.

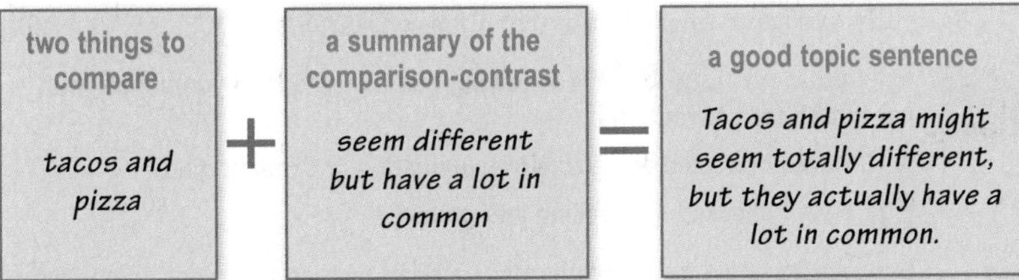

two things to compare		a summary of the comparison-contrast		a good topic sentence
tacos and pizza	+	*seem different but have a lot in common*	=	*Tacos and pizza might seem totally different, but they actually have a lot in common.*

Write your topic sentence. Use the basic formula above to write a topic sentence for your paragraph. You may need to try a few different versions to make sure this sentence says what you want it to say. (See page 553.)

EXPOSITORY

Advanced Learners

Have students imagine they are advertising executives who have been hired by the United States government to promote tourism. Challenge them to choose two geographical regions of interest (such as New England and the Florida Everglades) and create a promotional brochure that includes a comparison-contrast paragraph.

The paragraph should include

- a topic sentence that introduces the two places, and
- details that attract visitors and compare and contrast the regions for seasonal interest (for example, visit New England in the summer and visit Florida in the winter).

Students can include graphics, such as photographs and maps.

Prewriting Selecting a Topic

Suggest some general categories that students can explore for topic ideas, such as sports, pets, nearby towns or cities, vacations, or relatives. To help students come up with associated things within the categories to compare and contrast, play a word association game:

- Choose a category.
- One student says a word related to the category; another student says an associated word that comes to mind. (For example, in the category pets, someone says dogs, and another says cats, fish, or horses.)
- Write the pairs of words on the board.
- Decide which pairs share similarities and differences that would make a good comparison-contrast paragraph.

✱ For more topic ideas, see the "Basics of Life" list on SE page 545.

Prewriting Writing a Topic Sentence

✱ To learn additional strategies for writing a good topic sentence, see SE pages 552–553.

177
Comparing Two Subjects

Revising

Now that you have all your ideas on paper, it's time to begin revising. You might add or remove details, shift sentences around, and refine your writing to make it clear and smooth.

Keys to Effective Revising

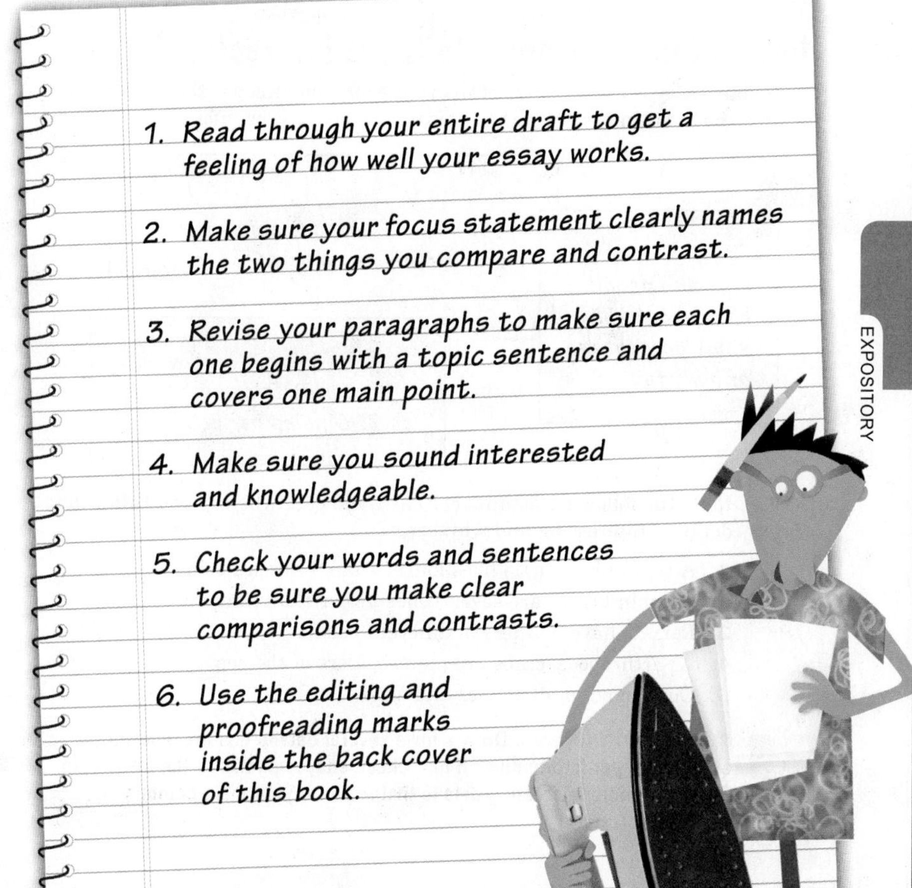

1. Read through your entire draft to get a feeling of how well your essay works.
2. Make sure your focus statement clearly names the two things you compare and contrast.
3. Revise your paragraphs to make sure each one begins with a topic sentence and covers one main point.
4. Make sure you sound interested and knowledgeable.
5. Check your words and sentences to be sure you make clear comparisons and contrasts.
6. Use the editing and proofreading marks inside the back cover of this book.

EXPOSITORY

Revising

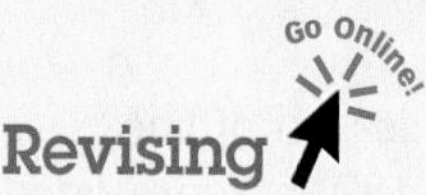

Keys to Effective Revising

Remind students that revising is the stage during which they look at their writing to be sure that the ideas and details are interesting, complete, well organized, and clear.

Keys to Effective Revising explains the process students will be guided through on SE pages 178–188.

- Students should review the goals on SE page 162 and keep them in mind as they revise.
- Remind students that they shouldn't look for everything at once. They should follow the Keys to Effective Revising list one item at a time.
- Point out that the following pages will guide students through the revising process step by step.

Peer Response

Ask your students to trade papers with peers and read and constructively respond to each other's work. A peer response helps students know which of the following revision strategies they really need.

Writing Workshop

Students can also self-assess their work for ideas, organization, voice, word choice, and sentence fluency. Suggest that they use the rubric strips atop each of the following page spreads.

Technology Connections

Have students use the Writing Network features of the Net-text to comment on each other's drafts.

***Write Source Online* Net-text**

Revising for Ideas

The rubric strips that run across all of the revising pages (SE pages 178–187) are provided to help students focus their revising and are related to the full rubric on SE pages 194–195.

To encourage students' creativity, have a contest to find the most interesting fact.

- Have students read aloud their favorite facts from their essay and cite the source to validate accuracy.
- Ask the class to decide which fact is the most interesting (or choose the best in several categories—strange, amazing, surprising, and so on).
- Students can also write their facts on poster boards around the room. Label these by category: Strange, Amazing, and so on. Invite the class to cast votes for the winners.

Answers

Answers may vary, but many students will find items 1, 2, and 4 new and interesting, while items 3 and 5 are less interesting because the information is familiar.

Revising for Ideas

6	5	4
I make my topic fascinating, and my essay contains many interesting details.	My topic is interesting, and I balance comparison and contrast details.	My topic is clear and balanced, but I could use a few more interesting details.

To revise your comparison-contrast essay for *ideas*, check to see if you have included interesting details. Also make sure you have a balance of similarities and differences. The rubric strip above and the following questions and answers can help you.

How do I know if my details are interesting?

If your essay contains only details that everybody knows, the reader will be bored. Look for information that amazes, entertains, or informs.

Amazing
Cows have four stomachs, one of which can hold up to 40 gallons.

Entertaining
Pigs and people have about the same percentage of body fat.

Informative
A peregrine falcon can dive at 200 miles per hour.

Read the following details. For each, indicate whether you think the detail is interesting and why.

1. A typical box turtle lives longer than a human being.
2. Dolphin brains are seven times larger than human brains.
3. Parrots have feathers of different colors.
4. As arthropods, crabs are giant spiders of the sea.
5. Dogs come in all shapes and sizes.

Review your details. Do you have several details that are amazing, entertaining, or informative? If not, check encyclopedias or the Internet to find a few more interesting details that relate to your main points.

Struggling Learners

Students may need help in determining which details are interesting to their readers.

- Have students exchange essays with a partner.
- Each student should highlight details that are amazing, entertaining, or informative in their partner's essay.
- Students with fewer than three highlighted details should research their topics further to find additional details to interest their readers.

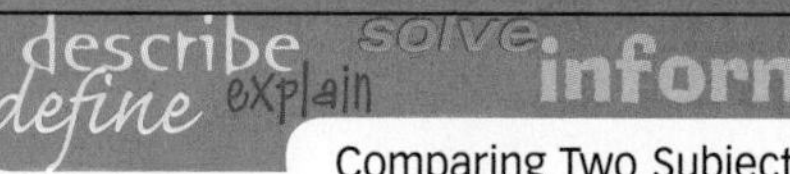

Comparing Two Subjects 179

3 My topic isn't clear, and some details are boring. I need to balance my comparisons and contrasts.

2 I need many more interesting details and must balance them.

1 I need a new topic and help figuring out how to gather interesting details.

Do I have a balance of similarities and differences?

The quickest way to tell if you have balanced similarities and differences is to look for comparison and contrast words in your essay (see page 174). Do you use about the same number of comparison words *(similar, like, also)* and contrast words *(instead, even so, but)*?

Read the following paragraph. On your own paper, list comparison words used in the paragraph. Then read the paragraph again and list contrast words. Is the paragraph balanced?

Jellyfish and octopi have similar body structures, but they also have many differences. Both have a large head or dome with tentacles around a central mouth. Even so, a jellyfish does not have a true brain, whereas an octopus has a large brain. Octopi have big, sensitive eyes, but jellyfish have no eyes. Instead, their head is light-sensitive, and that helps to guide them through the water. Each creature uses tentacles to bring food to its mouth. Also, octopi and jellyfish are similar because they lack bones.

Check for comparisons and contrasts. Review your first middle paragraph for comparison words. Then check for contrast words. Do you have about the same number of each? If not, revise your essay to balance the number of similarities and differences.

Ideas
An interesting detail helps balance comparisons and contrasts.

They have similar shapes, with long bodies, dorsal fins on their backs, pectoral fins on their bellies, and tails. ^The shark's tail is vertical, but the dolphin's tail is horizontal. On the whole, white sharks are bigger than dolphins. . . .

EXPOSITORY

Use highlighters or colored pencils to identify words that signal a comparison or a contrast. Have students examine those signal words for both balance and variety. Encourage students to avoid repeating the same signal words.

Answers

- Comparison words—similar, also, both, each, also, similar
- Contrast words—differences, even so, whereas, but, instead
- The paragraph is balanced.

English Language Learners

Another way for students to determine whether their essay is balanced is to have them put an *S* above any sentence that tells about a similarity and a *D* above any that tells about a difference. If students have many more of one type of detail, they need to revise their essay to achieve more balance.

Revising for Organization

As students "hopscotch" their own draft for organization, have them make sure they have included the correct details for both animals. If students find they are missing details about one point for a certain animal, have them refer back to their gathering grid or do some additional research.

Writer's Craft

Organization: Organization is one of the most challenging aspects of any two-part essay. For a comparison-contrast essay, the problem is that there are two subjects, and they have similarities and differences.

Your students have learned **point-by-point** organization, which addresses a certain point for both subjects before moving to the next point.

Another approach is **subject-by-subject** organization, in which one subject is treated fully, and then the other is treated. This structure is simpler, but it leaves the reader to mentally compare and contrast all the points.

A third approach is **similarities-and-differences** organization, in which all the similarities between the subjects are discussed, and then all the differences.

Revising for Organization

6 I use clear point-by-point organization that helps my reader understand and appreciate my essay.

5 I use clear point-by-point organization in my details, and my paragraphs have unity.

4 Each paragraph is about one main point, though a few of my details aren't in the best order.

When you revise your essay for *organization*, make sure that you have covered your details point by point. Also make sure your paragraphs have unity. The rubric strip above can guide your revision.

Did I organize my details point by point?

One way to check your essay for point-by-point organization is to make a "hopscotch chart" for each middle paragraph. A chart like this can help you see if you covered each detail for both subjects. If you write about the body shape of the shark, you should also write about the body shape of the dolphin. (The hopscotch chart to the right was created by Luc to check the details in his first middle paragraph on page 174.)

Body shape	
Shark	Dolphin
Body size	
Shark	Dolphin
Body color	
Shark	Dolphin
Body texture	
Shark	Dolphin

Create your own hopscotch chart. In the body of your paper, choose one of your middle paragraph and graph the details in it using a hopscotch chart.

1. **Write the first type of detail (for example, "Body shape") in a single box.**
2. **Draw double boxes below.**
3. **If you covered that detail for an animal, write its name in one of the double boxes.**
4. **Don't "hop" to the next single box until you have covered the detail for both animals.**
5. **Repeat the process for each detail in the paragraph.**

Revise your details. If you forgot to cover one type of detail for a specific animal, revise your essay to include the detail.

English Language Learners

Explain the word *hopscotch* is the name of a game that uses a grid like the graphic shown. The game has many variations in cultures around the world. The word *hopscotch* may help students remember this helpful comparison-contrast graphic organizer.

3 Some details are in the wrong paragraphs or in the wrong order.

2 The reader may be confused about my main points and the order of the details.

1 I need help understanding point-by-point organization and unity.

How can I check my paragraphs for unity?

You'll know that your paragraphs have unity if each one deals with one main point, a point that is stated in the topic sentence. Every sentence in the paragraph should support the topic sentence. (Also see page 538.)

Read the following paragraph. Pay special attention to the main point stated in the topic sentence. Then indicate which details should be removed because they do not support the topic sentence.

Both lions and tigers are carnivores that hunt for their meat, though they go about it in different ways. Among lions, the lionesses are the best hunters. They stalk and bring down prey and then drag it back to the pride. Male lions are the ones with manes. Tigers, on the other hand, are solitary, so both males and females must know how to hunt. Tigers live in India, but lions live in Africa. Although lions and tigers have been known to attack humans, both great cats prefer hunting and eating wild game.

Check the unity of your paragraphs. Read through each paragraph, checking to see whether all the details support the main point in the topic sentence. Remove any details that do not.

Organization
A new detail corrects the point-by-point organization, and an unrelated detail is deleted.

Dolphins are picky eaters, unlike ... *which*
Then dolphins swallow the food whole. Sharks also eat marine mammals like seals and otters. ~~White sharks have many teeth.~~ In fact, white sharks will eat just about anything, including license plates, . . .

EXPOSITORY

Have students review their paragraphs for unity using highlighters or colored pencils.

- Highlight the topic sentence in the first paragraph.
- Use the same colored highlighter to highlight sentences anywhere in the essay that relate to that topic sentence.
- Repeat the process, using a different colored highlighter for the topic sentence and related sentences of each paragraph.
- If any sentence does not support its topic sentence, revise by using the 3 *R's* strategy: rewrite, relocate, or remove.

If students need a refresher on how to mark their drafts, review the use of proofreading marks as shown at the bottom of the page and on the inside back cover of the text.

Answers

Details to remove: Male lions are the ones with manes. Tigers live in India, but lions live in Africa.

Struggling Learners

After students have highlighted each topic sentence and supporting sentence in a different color, have them number each supporting sentence. Numbering the detail sentences helps students check the organization of their paragraphs. As students read their sentences in the numbered order, they may decide to reorder some details.

Revising for Voice

Overusing words and sentence patterns is a common problem. Students need to have a strategy for avoiding this, especially in writing assignments where signal and transition words appear frequently.

- Have students examine their drafts for sentence patterns.
- Have students work with a partner to code their drafts according to the patterns shown here.
- After coding, students will be able to check for variety of patterns in their work and revise to avoid sounding predictable.

Answers

Answers will vary, but paragraphs should include several of the comparison and contrast patterns shown on this page.

Writer's Craft

Varying patterns: Often a first draft will sound like the sample paragraph above—filled with facts but devoid of flow. The writing sounds choppy and almost singsong. Since the human mind is a pattern-finding organ, when a pattern is too predictable, the reader sees only the pattern and not the ideas contained in the pattern.

Encourage students to try some of the other patterns to create a pleasing flow and rhythm.

182

Revising for Voice

6 My voice is original, and I sound eager to share my knowledge with the reader.

5 My voice is original, and I show interest in informing the reader.

4 My voice is original, but in places I could sound more interested.

When you check your essay for *voice*, you want to make sure your writing sounds original and enthusiastic. The rubric strip above can guide your revision.

Is my voice original, or is it too predictable?

Your voice sounds predictable if you repeat the same sentence pattern over and over. Read the following paragraph. Notice how predictable the writing becomes.

> Both butterflies and moths come from larvae. Both insects go through metamorphosis. Butterflies create a chrysalis. Moths create a cocoon. Both insects turn into pupae. Butterflies come out with colorful wings. Moths come out with pale wings. Both insects let their wings dry. Butterflies fly off during the day. Moths fly off during the night. Butterflies drink nectar from flowers. Moths eat leaves from trees.

The reason this voice sounds so predictable is that the writer uses just one pattern for his comparisons: "Both A and B do the same thing." He also uses just one pattern for his contrasts: "A does one thing. B does a different thing." Here are some other patterns that the writer should try.

Comparison	Contrast
A and B are similar in that . . . A does one thing, and B also . . .	Even though A does one thing, B . . . A and B are completely different because . . .
B is like A because both . . . Just as A does one thing, B also . . .	Unlike A, B . . . On the one hand, A . . . On the other hand, B . . .

Rewrite the predictable paragraph above. Use some of the comparison and contrast patterns shown above to make the voice sound original.

Revise

Revise for voice. **Review your essay and look for places where your voice sounds too predictable. Try some of the patterns from above to make your voice sound more original.**

English Language Learners

It may be easier for students to locate repeated patterns or words if they hear their writing read aloud. Have them work with a partner. As the partner reads aloud the essay, the student should stop the reader whenever a repetitive or predictable word is heard and underline or highlight it.

describe solve define explain inform 183
Comparing Two Subjects

3 Sometimes my voice sounds predictable. I need to show more interest.

2 I sound predictable. I need to show interest.

1 I need help understanding what voice is.

Does my voice sound enthusiastic?

Your voice is enthusiastic if it sounds like you want to share information with the reader. When your teacher is enthusiastic about a subject, she or he will use verbal cues to show that enthusiasm: "Here's the really amazing part," "Look how easy this is," "Can you believe that?" In your writing, you can also use cues like these to show your enthusiasm.

Read the following enthusiastic paragraph. Find verbal cues that show the writer is eager to share information with the reader.

> Of course, black bears have black fur, and polar bears have white fur, but let's look a little deeper. Under a black bear's fur is light gray skin, but under a polar bear's fur is black skin. Why would that be? It's an incredible adaptation. A polar bear's fur is translucent, like fiber optics. The hairs actually carry sunlight down to the black skin, which absorbs it, warming up the bear. So when it comes to black bears and polar bears, their color isn't as black-and-white as it might seem.

Revise **Add cues to show enthusiasm. Review your essay. Are there places where you list facts without showing any real interest in them? If so, add a verbal cue (words or phrases) to show enthusiasm. Don't overdo it, however.**

EXPOSITORY

Voice
Changes make the voice less predictable and more enthusiastic.

White sharks tend to cruise the oceans alone, but dolphins swim in pods, or schools, of between 10 and 500 creatures. Amazingly, Dolphins have been seen in groups of more than 2,000! In their pods, dolphins make clicks and . . .

Caution students against using too many verbal cues to show their enthusiasm. Point out that one of the most effective ways to incorporate enthusiasm and interest is to find and include unusual and fascinating facts and statistics.

Look at the fact that has been added to the essay in the box at the bottom of the page. Then discuss the unusual information in the paragraph about black bears and polar bears. Challenge students to uncover remarkable data about their topic that will help convey genuine interest.

Try It Answers

Possible answers: look a little deeper, Why would that be?, incredible adaptation, hairs actually carry sunlight, isn't as black-and-white as it might seem

English Language Learners

Model how to revise a detail sentence using verbal cues.

- Choose a sentence from a paragraph in the student edition, for example, on page 179, and write it on the board.

  Octopi have big, sensitive eyes, but jellyfish have no eyes.
- Point out that the fact that jellyfish have no eyes is pretty amazing.
- Encourage students to choose verbal cues from the class list (see Advanced Learners box) to rewrite the sentence in several ways.

  (Possible ways: . . . but incredibly, jellyfish have no eyes. . . . jellyfish have no eyes. That's amazing.)

Advanced Learners

Before assigning the **Revise** activity, ask students to help you compile a list of additional verbal cues that show enthusiasm. Post the list for class reference. (Possible responses: interestingly, incredibly, surprisingly, how amazing that, how remarkable that, an astounding fact, an unforgettable, an impressive, phenomenal, extraordinary)

Revising for Word Choice

Students should find and replace general nouns with more specific and precise terms.

- Have students circle any general nouns in their drafts.
- Using more precise terms will avoid repetition and make writing more accurate and informative.

Answers

1. cub
2. pride
3. dens
4. mane
5. coats, fur
6. claws
7. carnivores
8. omnivores
9. endangered
10. preserves

Revising for Word Choice

6	5	4
Precise and accurate words and definitions make my essay informative and enjoyable to read.	Precise words and definitions help make my essay clear.	Most of my words are specific enough, though maybe I need to define some.

To revise your essay for *word choice*, make sure you have used precise and accurate terms to describe your animals. Also, if you use a term that might be unfamiliar to your reader, always provide a definition. The rubric strip above can help you revise for word choice.

Do I use terms that are precise and accurate?

There are precise terms to describe every animal. For example, ducks have *bills* instead of *beaks*, and chickens have *beaks* instead of *bills*. You might write about a *flock* of geese or sheep, but you wouldn't write about a *herd* of geese. In your essay, you use terms that fit the animals you are describing.

Read the following sentences. From the terms in parentheses, choose the one that is precise and accurate.

1. The young of both a lion and a bear is called a *(foal, cub)*.
2. A lion lives in a *(clan, pride)*.
3. Bears tend to be solitary, and they live in *(dens, burrows)*.
4. The male lion has a *(beard, mane)*.
5. Lions and bears both have thick *(coats, coverings)* of *(hair, fur)*.
6. Each of these large beasts has long *(nails, claws)*.
7. Since lions eat only meat, they are strict *(carnivores, scavengers)*.
8. Because bears eat berries, roots, insects, and meat, they are considered to be *(vegetarians, omnivores)*.
9. Due to overhunting, both animals have become *(extinct, endangered)*.
10. Now many lions and bears are protected and live on wildlife *(farms, preserves)*.

Revise for precise words. Read your essay, looking for words that aren't precise or accurate for the animal you are describing. Underline and then replace them with more precise words. You may need to check your science book, an encyclopedia, or a Web site to find the right words to use.

3 In places, I might have used words that are unclear or too general.

2 Many of my words are too general, and some are incorrect.

1 I need help finding precise words and definitions for my essay.

When should I explain words?

Sometimes when you use a precise word for an animal, your reader might not be familiar with the meaning of the word. For words like this, you need to add a definition or an explanation. Your explanation should make the word clear without disrupting the flow of the essay. See the sample definition below.

A male orangutan makes a long call, which is the sound that marks his territory.

Try It For each sentence that follows, choose an ending that explains the word without interrupting the flow.

1. An orangutan gets around by brachiating,
   - **a.** a word that means moving around.
   - **b.** using its arms to swing from branch to branch.
2. A chimpanzee gets around by knuckle-walking,
   - **a.** using its fists and feet to amble across the ground.
   - **b.** which means that it gets its hands dirty.
3. Both animals are frugivores,
   - **a.** or "fruit eaters."
   - **b.** which comes from the Latin word for "fruit" *(fructus)* and the Latin word for "eating" *(vore)*, much like carnivore comes from "meat" *(carne)* and "eat" *(vore)*.

Add definitions. Check your essay for difficult words. Add explanations that make the meaning clear without interrupting the flow of the essay.

EXPOSITORY

Word Choice
An explanation is added.

In their pods, dolphins make clicks and squeals for communication and echolocation, which is using sound to locate objects. Sharks don't . . .

Make sure students understand that including a definition in the text helps the reader to better understand the topic. Caution, however, that overuse of this strategy will make it less effective.

- Advise students to include definitions only when words are special terms that are integral to the topic or when words will not be familiar to readers.
- Also point out that foreign words should be underlined and explained in context, by providing a definition.

Answers

1. b
2. a
3. a

English Language Learners

For students who do not have a wide vocabulary, many common words may seem unfamiliar. For additional input about which words need to be defined, have students work on adding definitions with a partner. Partners can offer their opinions about which words are likely to be well known to a general audience.

Grammar Connection

Specific Nouns and Appositives

- **Proofreader's Guide** pages 702 (+), 586–587 (appositives)
- ***Write Source*** page 471 (+)
- ***SkillsBook*** pages 147–148
- ***GrammarSnap*** Appositives

Nonrestrictive Phrases and Clauses

- **Proofreader's Guide** pages 584–585
- ***Write Source*** page 517
- ***SkillsBook*** pages 15–16
- ***GrammarSnap*** Commas to Set Off Explanatory Phrases or Clauses

Revising for Sentence Fluency

Help students distinguish sentences with compound subjects and predicates from compound sentences. All use coordinating conjunctions to connect or contrast equal ideas. Write on the board:

1. Julia **shopped** at the pet store, but Jack **went** to the shoe store.
2. Sandy and Rebecca **went** to the shoe store.
3. Julia **ate** at the restaurant and **shopped** at the shoe store.

Discuss the three sentences.

- Sentence 1 is a compound sentence; there is a subject and verb on both sides of the conjunction; a comma separates the two parts.
- Sentence 2 has a compound subject; the conjunction connects two or more subject nouns; the subjects share the predicate(s); no comma needed.
- Sentence 3 has a compound predicate; a conjunction connects two or more verbs; the predicate verbs share the same subject(s); no comma is needed.

* For more information about how conjunctions can connect words, groups of words, and sentences, see SE pages 496–498.

Answers

1.–2. and; words; compared
3.–4. but; clauses; contrasted

Revising for Sentence Fluency

6	5	4
My sentences are polished, and my ideas are clearly connected.	My sentences flow well, and I use coordinating and subordinating conjunctions.	Most sentences flow well, and I use a few conjunctions, but I might need more.

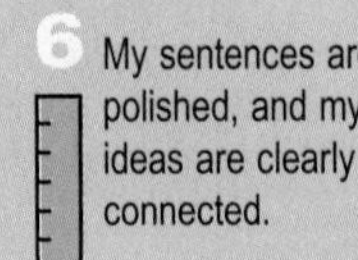

When you revise your essay for *sentence fluency*, you need to consider using conjunctions. Conjunctions are the workhorses of comparison-contrast writing because they help you connect similarities and differences. The rubric strip above and the questions below can guide your revision.

How can coordinating conjunctions help me compare and contrast?

Coordinating conjunctions can help you compare and contrast equal ideas smoothly and clearly.

Comparison and, so **Contrast** but, yet, or

Fish and sea mammals need oxygen to breathe.
(This sentence uses *and* to compare two nouns.)
Fish get oxygen from water, but sea mammals breathe air.
(This sentence uses *but* to contrast two clauses.)
Sea mammals are at home in the water or on land.
(This sentence uses *or* to contrast two phrases.)

Read each sentence below and find any coordinating conjunctions. List what kind of equal ideas are being joined—words, phrases, or clauses. Finally, tell whether the two ideas are being compared or contrasted.

1. Seals and sea otters are marine mammals.
2. Both animals are playful and sleek.
3. Seals hunt fish, but otters dive for oysters on the seafloor.
4. Both animals enjoy sunbathing, but seals do so in huge groups.

Review your use of coordinating conjunctions. Read your essay. Find one place where you use a coordinating conjunction to compare equal ideas. Find another where you use a coordinating conjunction to contrast equal ideas. Look for other places where coordinating conjunctions could help you compare and contrast.

Grammar Connection

Coordinating and Subordinating Conjunctions

- **Proofreader's Guide** pages 744 (+), 746–747 (conjunctions)
- ***Write Source*** pages 496 (+), 497, 498
- ***SkillsBook*** pages 195–196
- ***GrammarSnap*** Coordinating Conjunctions, Subordinating Conjunctions

describe solve define explain inform 187
Comparing Two Subjects

3 My sentences are a little choppy in spots, and I need to use subordinating conjunctions.

2 My sentences do not read smoothly. I need to use conjunctions.

1 I need help understanding sentence fluency and conjunctions.

How can subordinating conjunctions help me compare and contrast?

Subordinating conjunctions connect unequal ideas. These conjunctions are especially useful for creating strong contrasts. (Also see pages **744** and **746**.)

Strong Contrasts

although, even though, where, though, even so, however, because

In the paragraph below, find subordinating conjunctions that create strong contrasts. For each, indicate what is being contrasted.

Although seals are clever hunters, otters have developed an ingenious technique for opening oysters. Otters float on their backs and balance stones on their bellies. Even though this may look silly, the technique allows otters to crack oysters open by hitting them on the stones. Though seals are known for performing tricks, this oyster trick is one they'll never master because they have no hands.

Check your use of subordinating conjunctions. Read your essay and look for a sentence where you used a subordinating conjunction to create a strong contrast. If you don't find one, create a strong contrast by combining two short sentences using a subordinating conjunction.

Sentence Fluency

Adding conjunctions improves sentence fluency.

Most dolphins are no more than 8 feet long, but White sharks often grow to be 16 feet! Though Sharks and dolphins have similar coloring, with gray backs and white bellies, Their skin feels completely different . . .

EXPOSITORY

A writer can use subordinating conjunctions to vary sentence patterns, add details and supporting information, combine ideas, and emphasize contrasts. Remind students that a variety of sentence beginnings and patterns makes writing more interesting.

Analyze the **Try It** paragraph with students.

- In the first sentence, the reader learns that seals are clever hunters, but otters are ingenious.
- In the third sentence, the dependent clause says the technique may appear silly, but the independent clause shows that it is, in fact, very effective.
- Finally, the last sentence completes the contrast by pointing out why the seal cannot master this technique.

Answers

- although; seals and otters
- even though; the technique of otters floating on their backs with stones on their bellies looking silly but being effective
- though; seals do tricks but not the otters' oyster technique

English Language Learners

Write models of sentences that have subordinating conjunctions on chart paper. Ask volunteers to add examples from their papers. Display the sentences as students do the **Revise** activity. They may use the model sentences as patterns for creating additional sentences that use subordinating conjunctions.

Revising Using a Checklist

Ask students to respond to the checklist questions by

- noting specific examples in their draft that reflect each question rather than by simply checking off the boxes.
- exchanging their drafts with a partner, then reading their partner's draft and completing the checklist.

Schedule **peer conferences** *(see below)* to discuss any areas that the classmate does not check off.

Revising Using a Checklist

Check your revising. On a piece of paper, write the numbers 1 to 12. If you can answer "yes" to a question, put a check mark after that number. If not, continue to work with that part of your essay.

Ideas

_____ **1.** Do I have a clear and focused topic?
_____ **2.** Have I included plenty of interesting details for both subjects?
_____ **3.** Do I have enough comparisons and contrasts?

Organization

_____ **4.** Have I written an effective beginning?
_____ **5.** Have I used point-by-point organization?
_____ **6.** Do my body paragraphs have unity?

Voice

_____ **7.** Does my voice sound original?
_____ **8.** Does my voice sound enthusiastic?

Word Choice

_____ **9.** Do I use precise and accurate words?
_____ **10.** Do I define difficult words

Sentence Fluency

_____ **11.** Do I use coordinating conjunctions to compare and contrast?
_____ **12.** Do I use subordinating conjunctions to create strong contrasts?

Make a clean copy. When you've finished revising, make a clean copy of your essay before you edit. This makes checking for conventions easier.

Teaching Tip: Peer Conferences

Students can benefit from giving and receiving one-on-one feedback with peers. They learn to treat their role as reviewer seriously and to respect the work of their classmates.

- First, have students review and revise their own work, using the checklist.
- Then assign partners, or allow students to select a partner.
- To prepare students for their task, reread the list of goals on SE page 162 with them.
- Next, discuss the scoring rubric on SE pages 194–195.
- Direct students to take turns reading aloud their draft to their partner (reviewer), who should respond to the questions on the checklist.
- Finally, have partners hold a peer conference to go over the checklists and discuss any items on which they don't agree or that are not checked off.

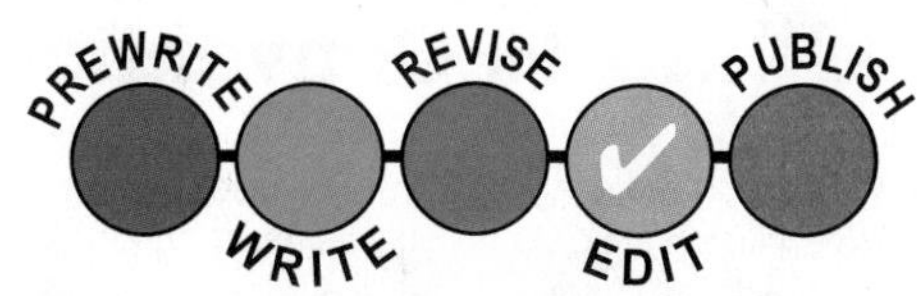

Editing

After you are done revising, your essay is ready for editing. As you edit, focus on conventions: punctuation, capitalization, spelling, and grammar.

Keys to Effective Editing

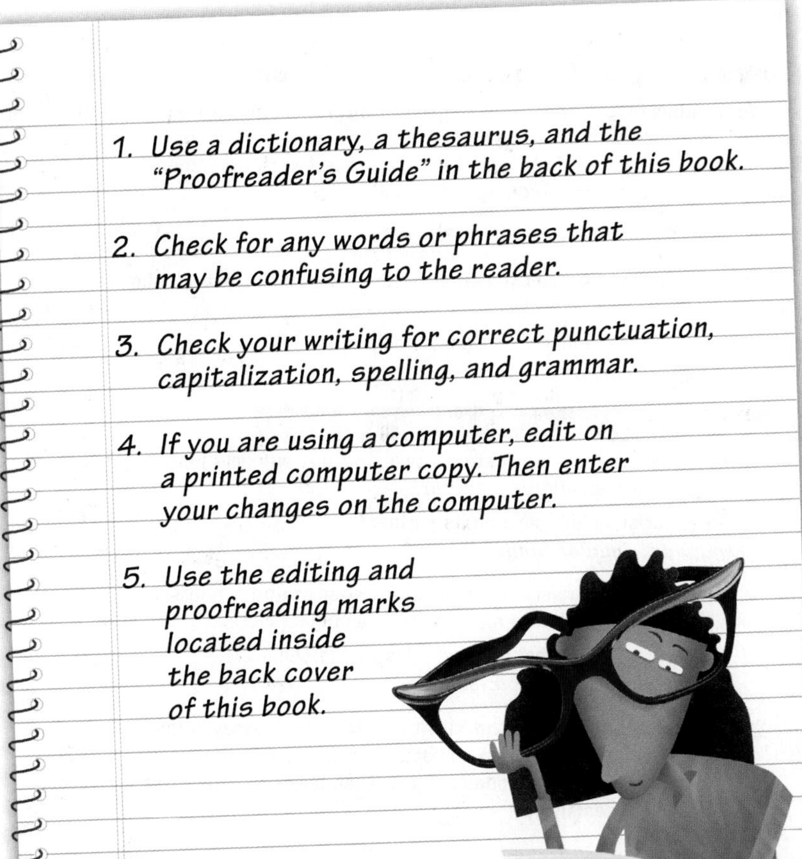

EXPOSITORY

Editing

Keys to Effective Editing

Keys to Effective Editing explains the process students will be guided through on SE pages 190–192.

It is helpful to have several people provide feedback in the editing stage of writing. Each student should edit his or her own piece first and use the editing and proofreading marks on the inside back cover of the student edition. (For a copy master, see TE page 788.) Then have students seek feedback from at least one reviewer:

- ask a trusted peer to check for spelling errors
- allow a parent or an older sibling to look over the piece for correct punctuation
- schedule a student-teacher editing conference

Students can ask each reviewer to mark her or his editing suggestions with a different colored pencil.

Technology Connections

Students can use the added features of the Net-text as they explore this stage of the writing process.

Write Source Online ***Net-text***

Resources stocks Fox Lake with walleye. Other new types of animals have shown up, too. Canada geese stop at Fox Lake when they migrate. Cranes have moved in on the south side of the lake, and a family of otters lives among the cattails.

Specific details make each effect clear.

Every season in Lower Forks feels different because of the dam. Before, when the snow melted, the river was fast and deep. It often flooded. As summer came on, the river calmed down to run only about a foot deep. Now, spring rarely brings any flooding. After a long dry summer, the river bed below the dam is sometimes only inches deep. Every winter, Fox Lake freezes over, which the river seldom did.

Ending

The ending reflects thoughtfully on the cause and its effects.

After the 2001 flood, it was obvious that Lower Forks needed help. A dam on the Fox River got rid of the flooding, created Fox Lake, and made a new wetland habitat. Lower Forks used to be just a river town, but now it is also a lake town, and that fact affects everyone.

Respond to the reading. On your own paper, write answers to the following questions about the sample essay.

- ☐ **Ideas** (1) What is the cause explained in the essay? (2) What are several of the effects?
- ☐ **Organization** (3) How did the writer organize the effects?
- ☐ **Voice & Word Choice** (4) What words and phrases show the writer's knowledge of this topic?

Literature Connections: You can find another example of a cause-and-effect essay in "Like Black Smoke: The Black Death's Journey" by Diana Childress.

Respond to the reading.

Answers

Ideas 1. a big flood in 2001

2. Possible answers: changed the landscape by creating a lake and wetlands; people use motor and fishing boats instead of canoes; people catch walleye instead of catfish; there are new animals (Canada geese, cranes, otters); the lake freezes each winter; there is no more flooding

Organization 3. Each middle paragraph explains a main effect.

Voice & Word Choice 4. Possible answers: this town, landscape, cattails, wetland, portage, Department of Natural Resources, migrate, habitat, affects everyone

Literature Connections

In the cause-and-effect essay "Like Black Smoke: The Black Death's Journey," Diana Childress describes the causes and devastating effects of the Black Death. She explains what caused the disease to spread, as well as the ways the disease affected people and regions.

Discuss how the essay is organized and the elements that make it a good example of a cause-and-effect essay.

Mentor texts: Check out these books that outline causes and effects:

An American Plague: The True and Terrifying Story of the Yellow Fever Epidemic of 1793 by Jim Murphy

Black Potatoes: The Story of the Great Irish Famine, 1845–1850 by Susan Campbell Bartoletti

Kids at Work: Lewis Hine and the Crusade Against Child Labor by Russell Freedman and Lewis Hine

Nature's Fury: Eyewitness Reports of Natural Disasters by Carole G. Vogel

For more information about cause-and-effect writing, see the Reading-Writing Connections beginning on page TE-36.

Prewriting Selecting a Topic

If students have not had experience with freewriting, they may have been conditioned to think through their ideas before they begin to write them down. Help students write freely about a topic.

- Model the process by thinking aloud and using an overhead projector to record your thoughts. Use a topic, such as the weather and how a forecast will affect your plans for an outdoor activity. Ask students to add their own thoughts.
- Then ask students to do a 3-minute freewrite about a change in their community or school. Remind them to write without pausing or thinking about the quality of writing. They will learn freewriting can lead to a solid idea.

Prewriting Gathering Details

As an alternative strategy, students can gather details using a cluster. Label the central circle with the cause and surround the circle with possible effects.

Technology Connections

Students can use the added features of the Net-text as they explore this stage of the writing process.

Write Source Online **Net-text**

Prewriting Selecting a Topic

Whether you live in a quiet town like Lower Forks or in a bustling city like Los Angeles, one change can cause many other changes. For this assignment, you'll need to find a change in your school or community that has had many effects. Rosalva used freewriting to think about changes around her.

Freewriting

Well, here goes. Changes. I don't know any changes off the top of my head. Dad said there was going to be a superstore built in Kingston, only I guess that's in the future, so I don't know yet what will happen from that. I wish I could just get out of here and go down to the lake. Hey, that's something. I remember when they built the dam, and how everything changed after that. . . .

Select your topic. Freewrite about changes in your school or community. Concentrate on changes that you know a lot about. Keep writing until you find a change that has had many effects.

Gathering Details

Once you have selected a change (cause), it's time to think about the effects it has had. One easy way to think about effects is to use a cause-effect chart. Rosalva used the following chart to gather details about her topic.

Cause-Effect Chart

Cause: *Lower Forks Dam*

Effect: *wetlands*, *lake*, *dead trees*, *cranes*, *no canoeing*, *houses gone*, *otters*, *catfish gone*, *no spring floods*

Gather details. Create your own cause-effect chart using the sample above as a guide. Write your cause at the top. Then write all the effects you can think of below it. Draw arrows to connect the cause to the effects.

English Language Learners

Point out how in the sample freewrite it sounds as if the writer is talking to herself. Emphasize that in freewriting, students should get down ideas any way they can. Invite students to use quick sketches along with words, phrases, and sentences in their freewriting.

Struggling Learners

Before assigning the prewrite activity:

- Discuss recent changes in the school, community, or region.
- Preview and provide articles from class, school, or local newspapers.
- Have students work in pairs to find ideas on which to base their freewriting.

Grouping Details

Next you need to organize the details you have gathered. Rosalva reviewed her cause-effect chart and noticed that the effects fell into three categories. She also added details as she worked.

Grouping Chart

The landscape	*People and animals*	*How the seasons feel*
lake	*otters*	*no spring floods*
wetlands	*catfish gone*	*frozen lake in winter*
dead trees	*cranes*	*water low in summer*
homes gone	*no canoeing*	

Group your details. Review your cause-effect chart. Notice how some details are related. Group your effects into two, three, or four different categories.

Creating an Organized List

In your cause-and-effect essay, each part has a different job. The opening paragraph introduces the cause. Each middle paragraph tells about one of the effects. The closing paragraph reflects on both the cause and effects. Rosalva used the following directions to create an organized list of ideas for her essay.

Directions / Organized List

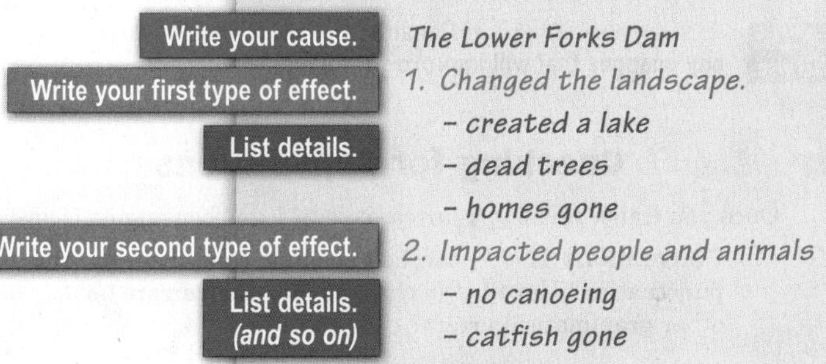

Create an organized list. Use the directions above to make your own organized list of ideas. Include details from your cause-effect chart.

EXPOSITORY

Prewriting Grouping Details

Explain that each category in the grouping chart will become a paragraph. Be sure students understand that each detail must be related to the category in order to provide paragraph unity.

✱ For more information about making sure that all details fit into a unified paragraph, see SE page 538.

Prewriting Creating an Organized List

Suggest that students arrange the categories in the list in order of importance. Or, when applicable, encourage them to put the categories in the correct sequence (such as a cause that has a chain of effects).

Struggling Learners

Provide an outline template of the organized list where students may input their information. Use a box format, with key word or phrase prompts (for example, *Cause, First type of effect,* and so on), to make it easier for students to transfer the information from their cause-and-effect chart.

Writing Creating Your First Draft

* To review the characteristics of a paragraph and an essay, and to plan an essay, see Use an Essay Plan on SE page 540.

Revising Improving Your Writing

Students should refer to the Rubric for Expository Writing on SE pages 194–195 as they revise their drafts.

Editing Checking for Conventions

Have students edit their own work using the conventions checklist on SE page 192.

Once students have edited their own work, have them exchange papers with at least one peer. Another student can often find errors in conventions that the writer has missed.

This assignment could be submitted for publication to a school or community newspaper as an article or a letter to the editor.

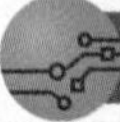

Technology Connections

Have students use the Writing Network features of the Net-text to comment on each other's drafts.

Write Source Online ***Net-text***

Writing Creating Your First Draft

Look over your organized list and these tips before you write your essay.

- **BEGINNING** Capture your reader's interest. Then write a focus statement that names the cause and lists or summarizes its effects.
- **MIDDLE** Create a separate paragraph for each effect. Begin each paragraph with a topic sentence and support it with details.
- **ENDING** Write an ending that thoughtfully sums up your essay.

Write your first draft. Follow the tips above to create the first draft of your cause-and-effect essay.

Revising Improving Your Writing

Think about how you used the following traits in your first draft before you revise your essay.

- ☐ **Ideas** Do I clearly name the cause? Do I include enough details for each effect? Are all my details related to the effects?
- ☐ **Organization** Does my beginning contain a clear focus statement? Does each middle paragraph begin with a strong topic sentence? Does my ending reflect on the cause and its effects? Do I use transitions to connect my thoughts?
- ☐ **Voice** Do I show knowledge and interest in the topic?
- ☐ **Word Choice** Do I use specific nouns and action verbs?
- ☐ **Sentence Fluency** Are my sentences smooth and easy to read?

Revise your writing. Consider the questions above as you revise. Make any changes that will improve your essay.

Editing Checking for Conventions

Once you finish revising your essay, edit it by focusing on *conventions*.

- ☐ **Conventions** Have I checked spelling, capitalization, and punctuation? Have I also checked for usage errors (*to, too, two*) and other grammatical errors?

Edit your work. Edit your essay using the questions above. Have a trusted classmate edit your essay as well. Then make a final copy and proofread it.

Grammar Connection

Complete Sentences

- ***Proofreader's Guide*** pages 690 (+), 692 (+)
- ***Write Source*** pages 502–503
- ***SkillsBook*** page 92
- ***GrammarSnap*** Complete Sentences and Sentence Fragments

Comma Splices and Run-Ons

- ***Write Source*** page 506
- ***SkillsBook*** pages 93–94
- ***GrammarSnap*** Punctuating Compound Sentences

Double Negatives

- ***Write Source*** page 510
- ***SkillsBook*** pages 101–102

Struggling Learners

For students who need help beginning their cause-and-effect essay in a way that captures the reader's interest, suggest these two strategies:

- Begin with a fact (as the sample on SE page 200 does).
- Begin with a question (Have you ever been caught in a flood?).

Expository Writing

Across the Curriculum

Because expository writing shares information, you will use it throughout your school day, in just about every class.

This chapter gives you several examples of expository writing for different classes—an informative letter written for social studies, directions for a math procedure, a definition of a scientific process, and an e-mail that requests information. Finally, you will practice responding to an expository prompt.

Whatever the class, sharing your knowledge with a reader is often the key to communication and learning.

What's Ahead

- **Social Studies**: Writing a Friendly Letter
- **Math**: Writing Explanations
- **Science**: Writing an Extended Definition
- **Practical Writing**: Writing an E-Mail Request

Across the Curriculum

Objectives

- apply what students have learned about expository writing to curriculum areas
- practice writing for assessment

The lessons on the following pages provide samples of expository writing that students might do in different subject areas. The particular form used in each content area may also be used in a different content area (for example, students could write an extended definition just as well in social studies as in science).

Assigning these forms of writing will depend on

- the skill level of your students,
- the subject matter they are studying in different content areas, and
- the writing goals of your school, district, or state.

Social Studies:
Writing a Friendly Letter

Emphasize that students must focus on the sharing of information and inclusion of details, rather than on personal information about themselves. Point out how the author of the sample provides a number of facts through personal anecdotes that will be interesting to the recipient. The tone of the letter is informal and friendly.

Literature Connections

Mentor text: For a fascinating book of friendly letters written to a student, see *Letters to a Young Poet* by Rainer Maria Rilke. From 1903 to 1908, the great German poet kept up a correspondence with a young, would-be poet. The letters speak about poetry and also about how to remain a sensitive and observant soul in a harsh world.

Social Studies:
Writing a Friendly Letter

Even though e-mail is fast and convenient, a friendly letter is still a wonderful way to send information to someone. The following letter was written by a student who was getting to know a pen pal from a different country.

The letter follows the friendly letter format.

100 Crabtree Way
Naples, FL 34100
January 12, 2009

Dear Soon-Li,

The **beginning** gives a greeting.

Thanks for the pictures and your letter about Seoul! I really like the photo of all the ships going in and out of the port. I can't even imagine what it would be like to be in a city with 9 million people!

I'd like to tell you about Naples, Florida, where I live. Naples is a lot smaller than Seoul. Our population is only about 24,000, though more people live here in the winter. Naples is farther south than most American cities, and it is beautiful. All along the west side run smooth, sandy beaches and the blue waters of the Gulf of Mexico. Often I can see dolphins from the beaches. The marinas hold thousands of boats, including some big yachts.

The **body** includes the writer's thoughts and ideas.

Naples is near the Everglades, a huge swamp with alligators, wild birds, and even deer and bears. Some alligators get to be six or eight feet long! My dad and I like to rent a canoe and spend hours paddling through the mangrove swamps. They are like a big green maze with twisty water paths. The roots of the trees stick up out of the water, which is really clear and warm.

The **closing** is polite and friendly.

Next time you write, could you tell me more about Korea? I hope that someday you can come and see my city, and that I can come and see yours!

Your friend,

Sam Johnson

English Language Learners

To make the sample letter more meaningful, help students locate Naples, Florida, and Seoul, South Korea, on a map. Help students identify specific facts the writer shares with his pen pal.

Writing Tips

Use the following tips as a guide when you are asked to write an informative letter.

Before you write . . .

- **Choose a focus.**
If you are writing to introduce yourself, you should share whatever information is appropriate. Be friendly and complete. If you are responding to a letter, review it. Try to answer whatever questions the writer may have asked.
- **Organize your thoughts.**
Decide which details will be most interesting to your reader and plan your letter around those details.

During your writing . . .

- **Be specific.**
Use clear details so that your reader will understand the information you are sharing.
- **Be enthusiastic.**
Let your interest show in your voice and word choice.

After you've written a first draft . . .

- **Check for completeness.**
Make sure you have provided whatever information your reader needs to understand your letter.
- **Check for correctness.**
Read your letter, looking for errors. If possible, have someone else read it as well. Make sure your writing is free of errors in punctuation, capitalization, spelling, and grammar. Write or print a clean final copy.

Imagine that Soon-Li is your pen pal. Write an unsent letter to her describing the place where you live. Try to explain what makes where you live different from other places.

Writing Tips

Review the friendly letter format:

- The writer's address is in the heading (right of center).
- The salutation is followed by a comma.
- The parts are the beginning, the body, the informal closing, and the signature (aligned with address and date).
- Each new paragraph is indented.

If students need help getting started, brainstorm details about the community that might interest students elsewhere.

To make the assignment more interesting, try to arrange a pen-pal relationship with students from another school or region.

Answers

Answers will vary but should include specific details about the place the student lives, as well as how it resembles or differs from other places.

English Language Learners

As a prewriting activity, encourage students to find photographs or create drawings of community features that they would like to describe to Soon-Li. Tell students to look at the pictures often as they write.

Advanced Learners

To extend this activity, have the class create a time capsule.

- Have students write a letter to themselves describing their day, telling future goals, and expressing feelings about their school, community, or country.
- Collect the letters (sealed in self-addressed, stamped envelopes) and store them in a shoebox that is taped shut and labeled with a date five years in the future.
- Explain that you will open the time capsule on the specified date and send the letters, which will become part of the students' personal histories.

Math: Writing Explanations

Tell students that they should consider their audience in deciding on the voice they should use.

- The tone of the sample is informal ("At first it might sound scary, . . . But anyone who knows that . . . ").
- Model a solution and explanation to this operation with more formal language.

Emphasize that students must break down the procedure into steps, as though they are teaching someone who does not know how to do the calculation.

Literature Connections

Mentor text: For hundreds of math explanations, you need turn no further than your math book. Whenever a new concept is introduced, the page explains the concept and provides examples. With your students, review a page from your math book, discussing how the different parts of the explanation work. Then challenge students to come up with their own math explanations.

Math: Writing Explanations

Once you can explain a math procedure to others, you know you have mastered it. Sharika wrote the following explanation to show how fractions are multiplied.

Multiplying a Fraction by a Fraction

The **beginning** names the math procedure.

At first it might sound scary to multiply one fraction by another. But anyone who knows that 2 X 4 = 8 can multiply one fraction by another:

$$\frac{2}{1} \times \frac{4}{1} = \frac{8}{1}$$

The **middle** explains the procedure.

What happened in the example above? The top numbers, or numerators, were multiplied together (2 X 4 = 8), and so were the bottom numbers, or denominators (1 X 1 = 1). The same technique works with other fractions.

$$\frac{1}{2} \times \frac{3}{4} = \frac{3}{8}$$

The **ending** provides more advanced information.

It might seem confusing that the product (3/8) is smaller than the two fractions that got multiplied. A way to make this less confusing is to replace the word "times" with the word "of." The equation above would read "one half of three quarters is three eighths."

There's one last thing to do when multiplying fractions: Remember to reduce the product to its simplest form.

$$\frac{3}{8} \times \frac{2}{3} = \frac{6}{24} \text{ simplified to } \frac{1}{4}$$

Writing Tips

Before you write . . .

- **Select a topic.**
  If your teacher has not given you a topic, search for one in your notes or math textbook.
- **Study the procedure.**
  Review the procedure that you will be writing about. Make sure you understand it thoroughly and have considered different ways of explaining it.
- **Think of examples.**
  Pick examples that will help you to clarify your explanation. A simple example can work as well as a more complex one, as long as it allows you to show every step of the process.

During your writing . . .

- **Think of your audience.**
  Imagine that the reader knows nothing about the math procedure you are explaining. Guide the reader step-by-step.
- **Organize your thoughts.**
  Decide on an order for presenting the information. Think of how your teacher or textbook first introduced the idea to you.
- **Focus on one step at a time.**
  Present the steps of the procedure in order. Write sentences that explain what you are doing in each example.

After you've written a first draft . . .

- **Check for completeness.**
  Make sure that you have included all the information a reader needs to understand the concept.
- **Check for correctness.**
  Edit and proofread your work to eliminate errors in spelling, punctuation, and other conventions.

Try It Write directions for a procedure that you are learning in math class. Use examples and clear steps.

English Language Learners

Help students choose a simple math procedure to explain.

- Have them write for younger students.
- If possible, ask elementary school students to test the explanations for effectiveness.
- Ask younger students to respond to the explanations with comments and questions about the procedure.

Advanced Learners

Invite students to ask math teachers if they would like to have a written explanation for a particular procedure.

Have students write an explanation for their favorite computation. Then have students give the completed explanation to the math teacher to use for class instruction.

Writing Tips

Students may want to go into more detail about the final procedure described at the end of the explanation on SE page 208. In this case, they could explain exactly how to reduce the product to its simplest form (by dividing the numerator and the denominator by the largest common factor, 6).

Once students have written their explanations, have them

- trade papers with a partner,
- try to follow the instructions without relying on any prior knowledge, and
- revise their work based on their partner's experience.

Answers

Answers will vary but should include examples that clarify the explanation of the math procedure.

Science:
Writing an Extended Definition

Ask students to explain natural processes they have studied.

- Students may use a step-by-step explanation of the process.
- They may incorporate the use of comparison-contrast or cause-and-effect techniques as they elaborate on the definition.
- They should use and define precise terms.
- They should use signal words and transitions as they compare and contrast examples or show cause-and-effect relationships.

Science: Writing an Extended Definition

A definition of a science term or process can be complicated. An essay that defines a term and includes examples, explanations, and many details is called an *extended definition*. The following student essay is an extended definition of a natural process.

What Is Metamorphosis?

The **beginning** provides a basic definition of the term.

Some animals grow by changing from one form to another. This process is called metamorphosis. A creature that goes through metamorphosis has one form as an infant and a completely different one as an adult. Differences can include shape, size, diet, and even habitat. Animals such as amphibians, crustaceans, and insects go through metamorphosis.

The **middle** provides examples and supporting details.

One example of metamorphosis occurs in frogs. They begin life as tadpoles, which are small, legless animals with long tails. Tadpoles live completely in the water, like fish. As tadpoles mature into frogs, they grow legs and gradually lose their tails. Frogs cannot live underwater. Instead, they must breathe air.

Butterflies also go through an amazing metamorphosis. They start out in a larva stage, in which they are caterpillars with many short legs. In the pupa stage, caterpillars wrap themselves in a chrysalis (a cocoon) and become dormant, which is like a very deep sleep. While dormant, they do not eat or move around, but they do change. When the butterfly finally breaks out of its chrysalis, it has wings, a different body, and six long legs.

The **ending** gives the reader something to think about.

People grow up, but they don't go through metamorphosis. As a result, they won't roll out of bed one morning and discover they have grown wings!

Writing Tips

Before you write . . .

- **Choose a topic.**
  The glossary at the back of a science book would be a good starting point.
- **Do your research.**
  Make sure you thoroughly understand the term or process that you are going to define. Consult several sources if you have questions about a topic.

Cluster

Details
Details
Term
Details
Details

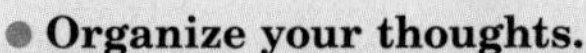

- **Organize your thoughts.**
  Write a statement that defines the term. Then plan how you will extend that definition with facts and examples.

During your writing . . .

- **Define your term.**
  Place your basic definition in the first paragraph.
- **Extend the definition.**
  Provide the reader with facts and examples that help explain the scientific term.
- **Use a comparison or a contrast.**
  Compare examples that fit the definition with those that don't. Note how the student writer compares the growth of animals that undergo metamorphosis with that of humans, who don't.

After you've written a first draft . . .

- **Get feedback.**
  Ask a classmate or family member to read your definition. Listen for any questions you could clear up or answer in a revision.
- **Proofread carefully.**
  Go over your essay to make sure that there are no mistakes in punctuation, capitalization, spelling, or grammar.

Write an extended definition about a scientific term related to nature or the environment.

Writing Tips

This sample uses a more formal tone than the one used in the extended math explanation on SE pages 208–209. This kind of voice and language would also be appropriate in an extended explanation.

Try It Answers

Answers will vary but should include examples, explanations, and many details to explain the scientific term.

English Language Learners

Assist students in using sequential drawings or a sequence chain to outline their ideas before writing.

Struggling Learners

For students who have difficulty deciding what scientific term to define and explain in detail, provide more specific direction by suggesting possible topics. Ask science teachers for topics students have been studying. (Possible topics: chlorophyll, evaporation, camouflage, digestion, migration)

Practical Writing:
Writing an E-Mail Request

Many students are familiar with writing and sending e-mail messages. However, writing an e-mail request requires a more formal voice and format than sending a casual e-mail note to a friend.

Some similar formatting and conventions apply for an e-mail request for information as would be appropriate for a business letter. Examine the sample and point out the following similarities:

- A colon follows the salutation.
- The message is concise.
- The paragraphs are not indented, and a line is skipped after each one.
- The closing is polite.

Note the differences:

- The heading includes the recipient's e-mail address and a subject line.
- The closing includes the student's e-mail address.
- The tone or voice of the message is slightly less formal than a business letter might be (huge, amazing, use of exclamation point).

Practical Writing:
Writing an E-Mail Request

E-mail allows quick communication between people across town—or across the world. The following e-mail message was sent by a student to request information from a businessperson she had met on a field trip.

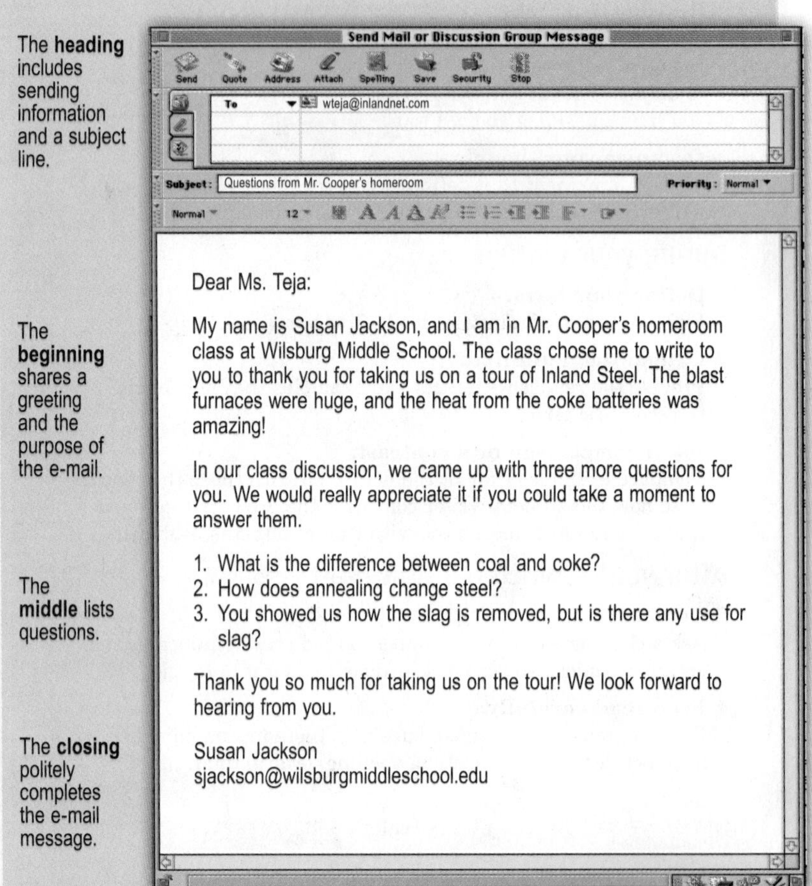

Dear Ms. Teja:

My name is Susan Jackson, and I am in Mr. Cooper's homeroom class at Wilsburg Middle School. The class chose me to write to you to thank you for taking us on a tour of Inland Steel. The blast furnaces were huge, and the heat from the coke batteries was amazing!

In our class discussion, we came up with three more questions for you. We would really appreciate it if you could take a moment to answer them.

1. What is the difference between coal and coke?
2. How does annealing change steel?
3. You showed us how the slag is removed, but is there any use for slag?

Thank you so much for taking us on the tour! We look forward to hearing from you.

Susan Jackson
sjackson@wilsburgmiddleschool.edu

Grammar Connection

E-Mail Request

- ***Write Source*** page 518 (+)
- ***SkillsBook*** page 119–120

Advanced Learners

When questions arise in class, solicit volunteers for a "fact-finding force." Assign these students to research the topic. (Example: It has been said that the Great Wall of China is the only man-made structure that can be seen from outer space. Is this fact or fiction?) The fact-finding force would decide to whom an e-mail request for information should be sent (in this case, NASA) and compose a polite request for information.

Writing Tips

Before you write . . .

- **Know your goal.**
  Think about what information you need. Then write a few questions for the person.
- **Think about your reader.**
  Ask a reasonable number of questions that can be easily answered.

During your writing . . .

- **Fill in the heading.**
  Complete the e-mail's heading. Then type in a subject line that tells your reader the topic at a glance.
- **Greet your reader and state your purpose.**
  Identify yourself, be polite, and make sure your reason for writing is clear.
- **Give important facts.**
  Provide any details that the reader needs to understand your request.

After you've written a first draft . . .

- **Check your facts.**
  Double-check the information you include in your e-mail.
- **Tune up your questions.**
  Make sure you've asked only necessary questions and have worded them in the best way.
- **Proofread carefully.**
  Review your e-mail to make sure that there are no mistakes in punctuation, capitalization, spelling, or grammar.

Remember a field trip you really enjoyed. Think of three questions you would like to ask about the place that you visited. Write an e-mail to a person who works at the location and politely ask your questions. You may decide if you want to send the e-mail.

Writing Tips

Remind students to use the spell-check feature to check their e-mail message for spelling errors. Emphasize that they should not use instant-messaging shorthand in their e-mail requests (for example, *LOL* for "laugh out loud," *ttyl* for "talk to you later," and so on) because the audience for this type of message requires a formal tone.

Answers

Answers will vary. Remind students this is a practice exercise and that the e-mail should not be sent, unless you have approved sending it.

Writing for Assessment

If your students must take school, district, or state assessments this year, focus on the writing form they will be tested on.

Review the main traits of an expository essay. Ask students to look for these traits as they read the model:

- shows comparison-contrast or cause and effect through details
- has a clear beginning, middle, and ending
- uses precise terms and defines them when appropriate

Expository Writing

Writing for Assessment

Many state and school writing tests ask you to respond to an expository prompt. An expository prompt will ask you to explain something or to share information. Study the sample prompt and the student response below.

Expository Prompt

No two people are exactly alike. Think of two people you know well. How are they similar, and how are they different? In an essay, compare and contrast two friends or two relatives. Include details about their appearance and personality as well as why each person is important to you.

The **beginning** introduces the focus of the writing (underlined).

We all need friends in our lives. I have two wonderful long-distance friends, Jayni and Berto. Jayni lives in Chicago in my grandmother's apartment building. Whenever I visit my grandmother, Jayni and I have a lot of fun together. I met Berto in chess camp, and I see him every summer. Although these friends are very different, they are equally important to me.

The **middle** paragraphs each explain a different part of the focus.

Jayni and Berto are the same age, but there are a lot of differences in their appearances. Of course, the main difference is that Jayni is a girl and Berto is a boy. Jayni has very dark skin and black, curly hair. Her eyes are light amber, almost golden. Berto has much lighter skin, but his eyes are so dark they are almost black. His hair is smooth and dark brown with red highlights. Jayni is as tiny as a little elf. She moves quickly and always seems to be running. Berto, on the other hand, is as tall and solid as a tree. He always takes his time, even when he should be in a hurry.

Each of my friends has a unique personality. Jayni is more serious and worries too much about everything from schoolwork to her basketball team. If she gets a poor mark, she panics. If she doesn't start or get to play a lot, she practices harder. Berto also gets good grades, but he never seems too concerned about his schoolwork. He could probably do even better if he'd just work a little harder. When he plays soccer, Berto doesn't seem to mind if he's not the star player. He has just as good a time sitting on the bench, cheering for the others.

Each of my long-distance friends is important to me, but for different reasons. When I'm feeling down about something, or when I have a problem, I know I can always count on both of them, but in different ways. Jayni is the one I e-mail for serious advice and help. But I know Berto can make me laugh, and his calm voice on the phone always helps me feel better.

The **ending** reinforces the focus.

I am lucky to have these great friends. I have other friends in school and in the neighborhood, but Jayni and Berto are special. I seem to have a connection with each of them that keeps our friendship close across the miles. They fill different spaces in my life, and each of them offers a special bond that isn't affected by distance.

Respond to the reading. Answer the following questions to see how these traits were used in the sample response.

- ☐ **Ideas (1) What is the focus of the writer's comparison and contrast? (2) What key words in the prompt also appear in the essay?**
- ☐ **Organization (3) How is the response organized—subject by subject or point by point?**
- ☐ **Voice & Word Choice (4) What words show the writer's feelings about these two friends?**

Use the rubric on SE pages 194–195 as a guide while you assess this sample with students.

Respond to the reading.

Answers

Ideas 1. two special long-distance friends **2.** friends, different, important, appearance, personality

Organization 3. point by point

Voice & Word Choice 4. Possible answers: wonderful, important to me, tiny as a little elf, tall and solid as a tree, unique, count on both, lucky, special, connection with each, keeps our friendship close, fill different spaces, special bond

Writing Tips

Point out that students must approach writing-on-demand assignments differently from open-ended writing assignments and that timed writing creates pressures for everyone.

Expository Prompts

To teach students who must take timed assessments how to approach their writing, allow them the same amount of time to write their expository essay as they will be allotted on school, district, or state assessments. Break down each part of the process into clear chunks of time. For example, you might give students

- 10 minutes for reading, note taking, and planning,
- 20 minutes for writing,
- 10 minutes for editing and proofreading.

Tell students when time is up for each section. Start the assignment at the top of the hour or at the half-hour to make it easier for students to keep track of the **time** *(see below)*.

216

Writing Tips

Use the following tips as a guide when responding to an expository writing prompt.

Before you write . . .

- **Understand the prompt.**
  Remember that an expository prompt asks you to explain.
- **Plan your time wisely.**
  Spend several minutes planning before starting to write. Use a graphic organizer (Venn diagram) to help you organize your ideas.

Venn Diagram

During your writing . . .

- **Decide on a focus for your essay.**
  Keep your main idea or purpose in mind as you write.
- **Be selective.**
  Use examples and explanations that directly support your focus.
- **End in a meaningful way.**
  Remind the reader about the importance of the topic.

After you've written a first draft . . .

- **Check for completeness and correctness.**
  Present your details in a logical order and correct errors in capitalization, punctuation, spelling, and grammar.

Expository Prompts

- Few students enjoy doing homework, even though they know that it's important. Explain why homework is an important part of learning.
- Write an essay about something you learned recently that made you think. Explain what you learned and why it was important to you.

Plan and write a response. Respond to one of the prompts above. Complete your writing within the period of time your teacher gives you. Afterward, list one part that you like and one part that could have been better.

Teaching Tip: Timed Writing

Different students will approach timed writing differently. Encourage students to customize their process to suit their needs. Ask them:

- How did you begin? (an outline, a chart, a freewrite)
- How effective do you think your approach was?
- What would you do differently next time?

English Language Learners

Introduce a Question-Answer-Details chart as a prewriting tool.

- Under *Question,* they rephrase the prompt as a question. (Why is homework important?)
- Under *Answer,* they write their main idea. (Homework helps students learn better.)

Expository Writing in Review

Purpose: In expository writing, you *explain something* to readers.

Topics: Explain . . . how to do or make something,
how things are similar or different,
the causes of something,
the kinds of something, or
the definition of something.

Prewriting

Select a topic that you know something about, or one that you want to learn about. (See page 166.)

Gather the important details and organize them according to time order, point-by-point, or in order of importance. (See pages 167–168 and 170.)

Write a focus statement, telling exactly what idea you plan to cover. (See page 169.)

Writing

In the beginning, introduce your topic, say something interesting about it, and state your focus. (See page 173.)

In the middle, use clear topic sentences and specific details to support the focus. (See pages 174–175.)

In the ending, summarize your writing and make a final comment about the topic. (See page 176.)

Revising

Review the ideas, organization, and voice first. Then review for **word choice** and **sentence fluency.** Make sure that you use terms that are clear and accurate. (See pages 178–188.)

Editing

Check your writing for conventions. Also have a trusted classmate edit your writing. (See pages 190–192.)

Make a final copy and proofread it for errors before sharing it. (See page 193.)

Assessing

Use the expository rubric to assess your finished writing. (See pages 194–195.)

Expository Writing in Review

Refer students to this page whenever they begin an expository paragraph or essay. They can also review the information here when they have specific questions about any aspect of the expository writing process. As students become more familiar with this writing form, they will need to look at the checklist less frequently.

Point out that expository writing is the form of writing most relied on in academics.

Persuasive Writing Overview

Common Core Standards Focus

Writing 1: Write arguments to support claims with clear reasons and relevant evidence.

Language 1b: Choose among simple, compound, complex, and compound-complex sentences to signal differing relationships among ideas.

Writing Forms

- Persuasive Paragraph
- Proposing a Solution
- Creating an Editorial

Focus on the Traits

- **Ideas** Using clear reasoning that informs and convinces
- **Organization** Forming a logical, smooth flow of ideas with a clear call to action
- **Voice** Developing a natural, positive, and convincing voice
- **Word Choice** Using persuasive vocabulary that fits the audience and does not include inflammatory words
- **Sentence Fluency** Including a variety of sentence types that flow easily
- **Conventions** Checking for errors in punctuation, capitalization, spelling, and grammar

Literature Connections

- **"Homeless"** by Anna Quindlen
- **"Do Professional Athletes Get Paid Too Much?"** by Justin Hjelm

Technology Connections

Write Source Online
www.hmheducation.com/writesource

- ***Net-text***
- ***Bookshelf***
- ***GrammarSnap***
- ***Portfolio***
- ***Writing Network features***
- ***File Cabinet***

Interactive Whiteboard Lessons

Suggested Persuasive Writing Unit (Five Weeks)

Week	Day	Writing and Skills Instruction	*Student Edition* Persuasive Writing Unit	*Student Edition* Resource Units*	*SkillsBook*	*Daily Language Workouts*	*Write Source Online*
Week 1	1–5	**Persuasive Paragraph: Problem/Solution**	219–222			38–39, 95	*Interactive Whiteboard Lessons*
		Skills Activities: • Apostrophes		604–605, 606–607	37		
		• Using the Right Word		668–676	64		
	opt.	*Speeches*	428–429				
Week 2	6	**Persuasive Essay: Problem/Solution** (Model) Literature Connections "Homeless"	223–226			40–41, 96	
	7–8	(Prewriting)	227–232				*Net-text*
	9–10	(Writing)	233–238				*Net-text*

* These units are also located in the back of the Teacher's Edition. Resource Units include "Basic Grammar and Writing," "A Writer's Resource," and "Proofreader's Guide."
(+) This activity is located in a different section of the *Write Source Student Edition.* If students have already completed this activity, you may wish to review it at this time.

Week	Day	Writing and Skills Instruction	Student Edition: Persuasive Writing Unit	Student Edition: Resource Units*	SkillsBook	Daily Language Workouts	Write Source Online
Week 3	11–13	(Revising)	239–250			42–43, 97	*Net-text*
		Skills Activities: • Compound and Complex Sentences		516 (+), 517 (+), 590 (+), 698–699,	121–122, 123–124		
		• Semicolons and Colons		594–595, 596–597	29–30		*GrammarSnap*
		• Adverbs		490, 492–493, 736–737	183–184		
	14–15	(Editing and Publishing)	251–254, 255				*Net-text, Portfolio*
		Skills Activities: • Spelling		642 (+), 644			
		• Tenses		481 (helping), 720–721, 724–725	166–167, 169–170		*GrammarSnap*
		• Pronouns and Pronoun-Antecedent Agreement		712 (+), 714–715	157–158, 159–160		
Week 4	16–17	(Assessing) (Reflecting)	256–259, 260			44–45, 98	
	opt.	*Speeches*	428–429				
	18	Writing Across the Curriculum	267–273				
	opt.	*Practical Writing: Business Letter*	274–277				
		Skills Activities: • Commas (Dates, Addresses)		582 (+)	11–12		
		• Capitalization		618–619, 626–627	51–52, 53–54		
	19–20	Persuasive Writing for Assessment	278–280				
Week 5	21–25	**Editorial** (Model) Literature Connections "Do Professional Athletes Get Paid Too Much?"	261–263			46–47, 99	
		(Prewriting)	264				*Net-text*
		(Writing)	265				*Net-text*
		(Revising)	266				*Net-text*
		Skills Activities: • Sentence Combining		498 (+), 515 (+), 516 (+), 517 (+), 698 (+)	75–76, 127–128		*GrammarSnap*
		(Editing)	266				*Net-text*
		Skills Activities: • Using the Right Word		678–683	65		
		• End Punctuation			5–6		

* These units are also located in the back of the Teacher's Edition. Resource Units include "Basic Grammar and Writing," "A Writer's Resource," and "Proofreader's Guide."
(+) This activity is located in a different section of the *Write Source Student Edition.* If students have already completed this activity, you may wish to review it at this time.

Teacher's Notes for Persuasive Writing

This overview for persuasive writing includes some specific teaching suggestions for the unit.

Writing Focus

Persuasive Paragraph (pages 219–222)

Persuasive arguments are necessary when a choice must be made. Most of the time several options are available, but only one can be followed. Students should understand that persuasion is a fine art requiring practice. A successful persuasive essay doesn't just list good reasons for or against some action. Instead, a well-crafted persuasive essay presents the argument in a way that leads a reader to support the writer's ideas.

Proposing a Solution (pages 223–260)

Students think of and read about solutions to problems every day. Anyone can make a wild suggestion; the challenge is proposing a solution that will solve the problem, and not result in more trouble. For example, if everyone carpooled there would be far fewer cars on the road. However, not everyone can carpool for a number of legitimate reasons. Good ideas can help solve serious problems, but the ideas need to be presented well. This chapter is designed to help students learn to consider a problem, propose a solution, and argue for its adoption.

Creating an Editorial (pages 261–266)

Although your students will be asked to write an editorial in this chapter's work, many of them may never write another editorial. However, understanding how editorials work will give your students a critical eye when reading the Op/Ed page.

Grammar Focus

For support with this unit's grammar topics, consult the resource units (Basic Grammar and Writing, A Writer's Resource, and Proofreader's Guide).

Academic Vocabulary

Read aloud the academic terms, as well as the descriptions and questions. Model for students how to read one question and answer it. Have partners monitor their understanding and seek clarification of the terms by working through the meanings and questions together.

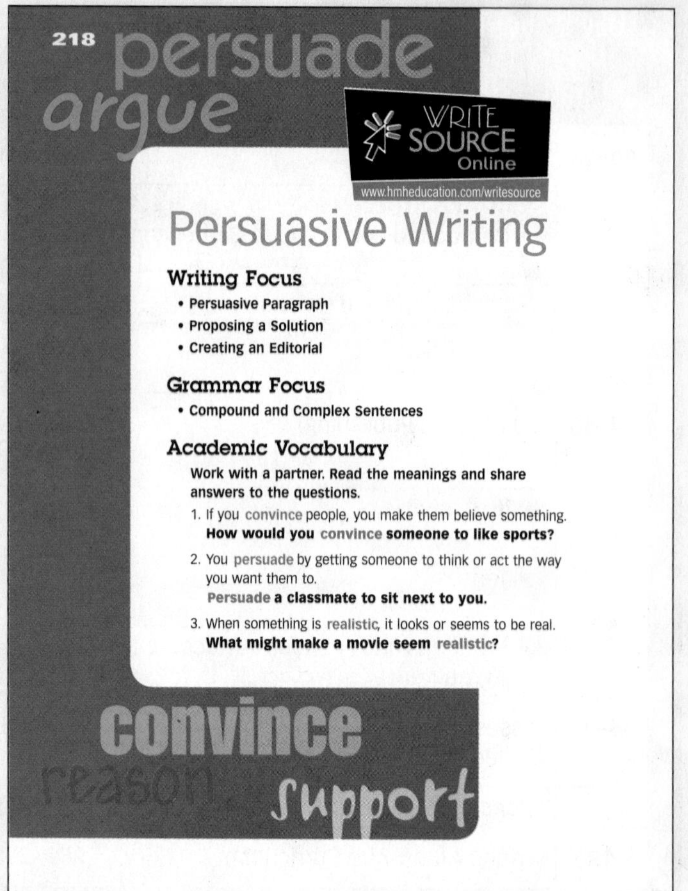
218 persuade argue

Persuasive Writing

Writing Focus
- Persuasive Paragraph
- Proposing a Solution
- Creating an Editorial

Grammar Focus
- Compound and Complex Sentences

Academic Vocabulary

Work with a partner. Read the meanings and share answers to the questions.

1. If you convince people, you make them believe something. **How would you convince someone to like sports?**
2. You persuade by getting someone to think or act the way you want them to. **Persuade a classmate to sit next to you.**
3. When something is realistic, it looks or seems to be real. **What might make a movie seem realistic?**

convince reason support

Minilessons

Time Is Money — Persuasive Paragraph

- **READ** the paragraph on SE page 220. Do you agree with the writer's argument? Why or why not? **JOT** down a list of alternative ways to deal with boredom. **DISCUSS** your thoughts about her argument and your alternatives with a classmate.

Keep on Schooling? — Proposing a Solution

- **STUDY** the following question: What can be done during the summer to keep students from losing what they have learned so that fall classes don't have to spend so much time reviewing the previous year's lessons?
- **WRITE** your opinion statement (your proposal) and then support it with three important points. Also **LIST** at least one important point against your proposal. **SHARE** your ideas with a classmate.

I Think . . . — Creating an Editorial

- **FIND** an editorial in the local or school newspaper. **CHOOSE** an editorial with which you agree. Why do you agree with the editorial? Write a paragraph to persuade your class to accept the editorial's position.

219

Persuasive Writing

Persuasive Paragraph

Are you too busy for breakfast? Try Go-Go-Cereal! Are you sick of unwanted e-mail? Try Mail Hound 3000! Need money? Send for *100 Ways to Get Rich.* Often, commercials try to persuade viewers by presenting a problem and proposing a solution. In 30 seconds, commercials like this can convince some viewers to buy a product or service.

Do you have the power to persuade someone in 30 seconds or less? In this chapter, you will write a persuasive paragraph. First, you'll briefly present a problem that you know about from personal experience. Then you will propose a solution to the problem. Think of your paragraph as a 30-second commercial and see if you can convince your reader to "buy into" your solution.

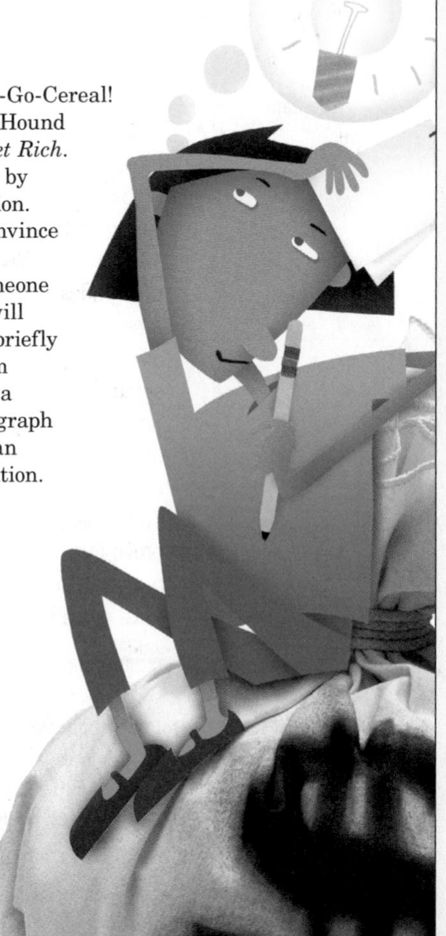

Writing Guidelines

Subject: A problem and a convincing solution
Form: Persuasive paragraph
Purpose: To propose a solution
Audience: Classmates, teachers, or parents

Persuasive Paragraph

Objectives

- learn the content and structure of a persuasive paragraph
- choose a topic (a problem) and propose a solution
- plan, draft, revise, and edit a persuasive paragraph

A **persuasive essay** presents a problem and convinces the reader to agree with the offered solution.

To familiarize students with a persuasive paragraph, ask them to respond in a **freewrite** *(see below)* to the following prompt: *Write about a time you tried to persuade your parents to do something. Include the arguments you used. Were you able to convince them?*

- Share the freewrites in groups.
- Compile a class list of topics.
- Discuss which arguments were effective and why. (Good solutions require thinking logically about the problem.)

* For more information and another example of a persuasive paragraph, see SE page 529.

Technology Connections

Use this unit's Interactive Whiteboard Lesson to introduce persuasive writing.

 ***Interactive Whiteboard Lessons***

Teaching Tip: Freewriting

Explain that when they freewrite, students should write without stopping to organize thoughts, correct errors, or consider content.

Encourage students to

- get thoughts on paper without considering form and style,
- keep their pen moving, and
- look at freewriting as thinking with a pen in their hand.

English Language Learners

Clarify the meaning of persuasion before introducing the unit.

- Present a synonym for *persuade*, such as *convince.*
- Do a role-play to illustrate the concept. For example, ask a student to try to persuade you to give a pen to him or her. Resist at first, and then let the student convince you.

Persuasive Paragraph

Review the parts of a paragraph.

- Hold up a closed lunch bag with a drawing of a light bulb on the front of the bag. The bag represents a paragraph. The topic sentence expresses the main idea (light bulb) and gets the reader to "open the bag."
- Have three 3 × 5 index cards inside the bag, with the words *interesting detail* on each. As you take out the cards, explain that the body of a paragraph is made up of several details. Put the cards back in the bag.
- A paragraph ends with a closing sentence that leaves the reader thinking. Show students a drawing on the back of the bag of a person with a thinking cloud above her or his head.

Respond to the reading.

Answers

Ideas 1. She is broke and wants to get a job on Saturdays.

Organization 2. In the fifth sentence, she first mentions changing the family rule.

Voice & Word Choice 3. make the . . . honor roll; job . . . would not stop them from . . . homework; prove that he or she is responsible; turn . . . extra time into . . . extra money

Persuasive Paragraph

A persuasive paragraph starts with a **topic sentence** that presents the problem. The **body** sentences explain the problem and convince the reader to agree with a proposed solution. The **closing sentence** sums up the solution. The persuasive paragraph below was written by Sarah, a student who wanted to convince her parents to change a family rule.

Topic Sentence

Body

Closing Sentence

Time Is Money

Some teenagers have a problem: They're bored and broke. They have too much time and too little money. The problem often stems from a family rule that forbids teenage siblings from working until they reach a certain age, usually 16 or older. Instead, they are supposed to focus on homework and grades. The fact that the teenagers remain bored and broke won't change until this type of rule is changed. Why alter it? Many teenagers make the A-B honor roll each semester and do their homework every night. A part-time job on the weekends would not stop them from completing their homework. Often, such a rule was made because an older sibling had grade problems once he or she started working. To be fair, however, each individual should have a chance to prove that he or she is responsible. All teenagers want to do is turn their extra time into a little extra money and feel that they have some control over their lives.

Respond to the reading. On your own paper, answer each of the following questions.

- ☐ **Ideas** (1) What problem does the writer present, and what solution does she propose?
- ☐ **Organization** (2) Where does the writer switch from talking about the problem to talking about the solution?
- ☐ **Voice & Word Choice** (3) What words or phrases show that the writer truly believes in the solution?

English Language Learners

Be sure students understand that the word *broke* in the persuasive paragraph on this page means "without money."

Struggling Learners

- ✱ Refer students to SE page 529 for an example of writing a personal opinion.
- Read through the paragraph with students.
- Have them list three strong details that support the writer's opinion in the body of the paragraph.

Prewriting Selecting a Topic

Your first step in writing a persuasive paragraph is to choose a problem to write about. For a paragraph, it's best to focus on a problem that you believe you can actually solve. Sarah used a cluster to think about possible topics.

Topics Cluster

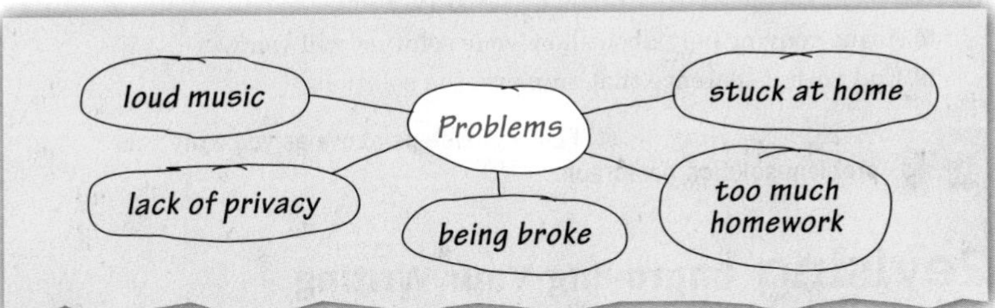

Create a cluster. Use the sample above as a guide to create your own cluster about problems you believe you can solve. Choose one problem to write about in a paragraph.

Defining the Problem and Solution

Once you have selected a problem, present it in a topic sentence. Beneath it, write a few sentences about possible solutions, just as Sarah did below.

Problem-Solution Chart

Topic Sentence: *Some teenagers have a big problem: They're bored and broke.*

Solution 1: *Parents should raise the allowance.*

Solution 2: *Teenagers should find free things to do.*

Solution 3: *Parents should change the family rule about getting a job.* *

Create a problem-solution chart. Write a sentence that names the problem you will be writing about. Then write three or four sentences that propose solutions. Put a star next to the best solution for your paragraph.

PERSUASIVE

Prewriting Selecting a Topic

Divide the class into three groups. Give each group a different focus for brainstorming:

- family
- school
- friends

Have each group brainstorm problems in the area they have been assigned. Have students use a cluster for their problems.

* For more ways to generate lists of topics, look at the "Basics of Life" List on SE page 545.

Prewriting

Defining the Problem and Solution

Ask students to work independently to create the problem-solution chart for their topic.

- Have students share their charts in their group.
- Ask students to assist one another in starring the best solution to their problem.

Writing Creating the First Draft

Before they write a first draft, have students list three main points that support their starred solution.

Demonstrate with another lunch bag and a problem generated by the student groups on TE page 221:

- Write the problem as a topic sentence on the front of the bag.
- Place three index cards inside that explain the starred solution.
- On the back of the bag, write a closing sentence about the problem that leaves the reader thinking.

Revising Improving Your Writing

Have students exchange their revised paragraphs with a partner for more revising suggestions.

Editing Checking for Conventions

Suggest that students focus first on reading for correct punctuation and then on reading for spelling and grammar errors. Refer students to the Proofreader's Guide in the back of their book to resolve questions as they edit their writing.

Writing Creating the First Draft

Once you have written a sentence about the problem and a sentence about the solution, you are ready to write your first draft. Follow these guidelines.

- Start with your topic sentence, which tells about the problem.
- Provide details that convince the reader the problem needs to be solved.
- Write a sentence that introduces the solution.
- Argue convincingly about how your solution will work.
- End with a sentence that sums up the solution.

Write your first draft. Follow the steps above as you write your problem-solution paragraph.

Revising Improving Your Writing

Read over your first draft. Consider how well you have handled the *ideas, organization, voice, word choice,* and *sentence fluency* in your paragraph.

Revise your paragraph. Review and improve your paragraph as needed. Think about the following questions as you work on your writing.

1. Do I clearly present a problem and propose a solution?
2. Do I move logically from the problem to the solution?
3. Do I use a convincing, positive voice?
4. Do I use words that sound natural and sincere?
5. Have I written complete sentences that flow smoothly?

Editing Checking for Conventions

When you edit your paragraph, pay special attention to conventions.

Edit your paragraph. Use the following questions to guide your editing.

1. Do I use correct end punctuation throughout my paragraph?
2. Have I checked for mistakes in spelling and grammar?

Proofread your paragraph. Before sharing your paragraph, make a final copy and proofread it one more time for errors.

Grammar Connection

Apostrophes

- **Proofreader's Guide** pages 604–605, 606–607
- ***SkillsBook*** page 37

Using the Right Word

- **Proofreader's Guide** pages 668–676
- ***SkillsBook*** page 64

English Language Learners

If students need help with organizing their paragraphs, provide a frame that they can use:

A problem I have is ___. The best way to solve the problem is ___. This solution will work because ___. (Summary sentence) ___.

Struggling Learners

Have a writing conference with each student.

- Discuss each of the five revision questions.
- Ask them to show you how they answered the questions by citing specific lines from their first draft and pointing out changes that they made in the paragraph.

Persuasive Writing

Proposing a Solution

It's easy to see problems. Maybe your city has a problem with litter or noise pollution or congestion. Maybe your school needs a new gymnasium or more computers or better wheelchair access. Everyone can see problems, but people who see solutions can make a real difference in the world around them.

In this chapter, you will be writing a persuasive problem-solution essay. First, you'll need to convince the reader the problem is serious. Then you must show that you have the best solution. With a well-written problem-solution essay, perhaps you can solve a problem in your school or community.

Writing Guidelines

Subject: A problem in your school or community
Form: Persuasive essay
Purpose: To propose a solution
Audience: Classmates and community members

Proposing a Solution

Objectives

- understand the purpose, content, and form of a persuasive problem-solution essay
- plan, draft, revise, edit, and publish a persuasive problem-solution essay

A **persuasive essay** presents a problem, convinces the reader that there is a need to fix the problem, and then offers a solution as the best way to accomplish that.

Writer's Craft

Reader's needs: Persuasion is not a matter of forcing the reader to act or think in a certain way. It's a matter of appealing to the reader's needs and desires. In that way, the problem-solution format gets at the heart of persuasion. It focuses on a problem the reader has and a way to solve the problem.

Note how this approach is common in commercials. At the beginning of a commercial, the people are shown frustrated, bewildered, or in trouble—they have a problem. Then the product or service comes along, and the people end the commercial with big grins on their faces.

Advanced Learners

Ask students to research various environmental problems and some potential solutions.

- Ask students to collaborate and present their findings on poster board or chart paper, using a gathering chart similar to the one on SE page 229.
- Have them post their problem-solution possibilities as well.

Copy Masters

T-chart (TE p. 229)

5 W's Chart (TE pp. 230, 240)

Understanding Your Goal

Traits of Problem-Solution Writing

Three traits relate to the development of the content and the form. They provide a focus during prewriting and writing.

- Ideas
- Organization
- Voice

The other three traits relate more to form. Checking them is part of the revising and editing processes.

- Word Choice
- Sentence Fluency
- Conventions

* The six-point rubric on SE pages 256–257 is based on these traits. Reproducible six-, five-, and four-point rubrics for persuasive writing can be found on TE pages 752, 756, and 760.

Test Prep!

You'll note that this goals rubric focuses on the same six traits as the assessment rubric on pages 256–257. By incorporating the traits throughout the process, *Write Source* prepares your students for final assessment. The program also helps them prepare for on-demand writing tests, which tend to use rubrics that correlate strongly to the traits of writing.

Literature Connections

In the problem-solution essay "Homeless," Anna Quindlen describes an interaction she had with a homeless woman in a bus terminal. She uses that experience as a launching board and explores the problem of homelessness. Quindlen offers ways the reader can start addressing the problem in a positive way.

Discuss elements that make the piece a good problem-solution essay. For additional persuasive models, see the Reading-Writing Connections beginning on page TE-36.

Understanding Your Goal

Your goal in this chapter is to write a well-organized persuasive essay that proposes a solution to a problem. The traits listed in the chart below will help you plan and write your essay.

Traits of Problem-Solution Writing

Ideas

Convince the reader about a problem and propose your solution.

Organization

Develop an essay with a clear opinion statement and well-organized paragraphs.

Voice

Sound confident and convincing about the problem and your solution.

Word Choice

Use persuasive words that are appropriate for your audience.

Sentence Fluency

Use simple, compound, and complex sentences to create an essay that flows smoothly.

Conventions

Check your writing for errors in punctuation, capitalization, spelling, and grammar.

Literature Connections: For another example of problem-solution writing, read "Homeless" by Anna Quindlen.

Problem-Solution Essay

A problem-solution essay is usually organized in two parts: (1) the writer convinces the reader that there is a problem, and (2) the writer persuades the reader to help with the solution. In the following essay, a student writes about a pollution problem at a local beach.

Beginning
The beginning introduces the problem and gives an opinion statement (underlined).

Middle
The first middle paragraph convinces the reader the problem is serious.

The second middle paragraph proposes a solution.

Waterfront Rescue

If people visited City Beach last summer, they probably noticed the mess. Litter was scattered across the picnic area, and cans and bottles were all over the beach. The condition of City Beach has become a big community problem, and it won't be solved until everyone gets involved.

Mr. Sean Johnson of the city's maintenance department said the city can pay for just eight hours of work at the beach every week. This means that a worker comes to the park only one day each week. He or she empties the trash barrels but doesn't have time to gather all the trash left on the ground. When people leave their trash under the picnic tables or on the beach, it never gets picked up. Other people see how messy the area is, and they leave litter behind, too.

The big problem at City Beach needs a big solution. Students from Lakeview School could be part of that solution. They could form a committee to keep the beach cleaner next summer. They might even start a tradition, and the students from Lakeview could do this every year.

First, the committee would need to organize volunteers to spend Saturday morning at the beach just before it opens

PERSUASIVE

Problem-Solution Essay

Read through this sample essay with the class, pointing out the elements that make it a good example of persuasive writing.

Ideas
- The writer identifies the problem and presents details to persuade the reader of the serious nature of the problem.
- The writer offers a solution.

Organization
- The writer presents a clear opinion statement about the problem and how to fix it.
- The actions needed to solve the problem are conveyed in well-organized paragraphs.
- The writer answers an objection and sends a call to action in the ending.

Voice & Word Choice
- The writer presents the problem and solution in a confident and convincing tone.
- The writer uses persuasive words and phrases.

Sentence Fluency
The writer varies sentence patterns.

Conventions
The grammar, punctuation, and spelling are correct.

Respond to the reading.

Answers

Ideas 1. Possible choices:
- cans and bottles litter the beach
- city can only pay for a worker to empty the trash barrels
- trash never gets picked up

2. Possible choices:
- form a committee and start a tradition
- kids could wear protective gloves
- recycle bottles and cans
- add more barrels and signs
- remind people that there is a fine for littering

Organization 3. Paragraphs 1 and 2
4. Paragraphs 3 through 5

Voice & Word Choice 5. Possible choices:
- mess
- scattered
- all over
- big community problem
- make it their job
- first ones to enjoy

The other middle paragraphs persuade the reader to help solve the problem.

for the summer. Kids could wear protective gloves as they go around the park and pick up litter. They could put bottles and cans in recycling bins. Hot dogs, soda, and ice cream could be served to everyone who helps.

After the beach is cleaned up, the committee should add more garbage barrels and some "no littering" signs. Local organizations and businesses could sponsor the barrels. The signs could be bright and colorful, but they should also remind people that there is a fine for littering in the park.

Ending

The ending answers a possible objection and calls the reader to action.

Some people might say it's not the job of Lakeview students to clean the beach, but if they make it their job, they can be the first ones to enjoy a clean beach. Also, once people see that the park is being cleaned, they may volunteer to help, too. Lakeview students should take charge of cleaning City Beach and make it attractive once again!

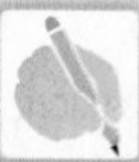

Respond to the reading. Answer the following questions about the sample essay.

- ☐ **Ideas** (1) What details convince the reader to take the problem seriously? (2) What details persuade the reader to help solve the problem?
- ☐ **Organization** (3) Which paragraphs deal with the problem? (4) Which paragraphs deal with the solution?
- ☐ **Voice & Word Choice** (5) What words or phrases make the voice of the writer persuasive?

Teaching Tip: Problem-Solution Questions

Help students identify the question that each paragraph answers. Write the questions in the form of a chart.

Paragraph 1: What is the problem?

Paragraph 2: Why is it important?

Paragraph 3: What is a solution? Why will it work?

Paragraph 4: How can the reader help?

Paragraph 5: Why might someone think the solution will not work? What does the writer want the reader to do?

Use these questions to guide students' prewriting activities.

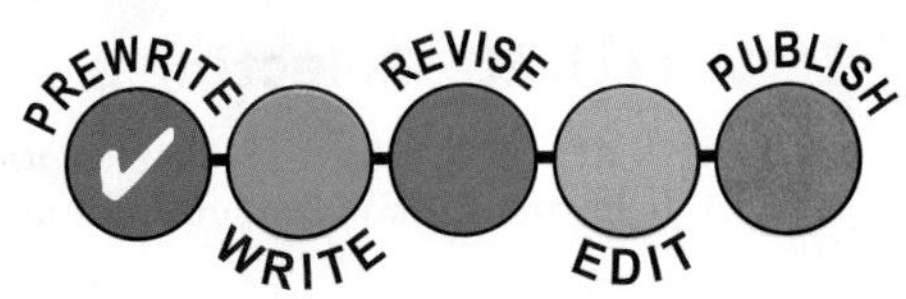

Prewriting

Before you begin to write, you'll need to select a topic, gather details, and organize your ideas. This process is called prewriting.

Keys to Effective Prewriting

1. Select a problem that you care about and that fits the assignment.
2. List possible solutions and choose one.
3. Gather details about the problem and the solution.
4. Write a clear opinion statement to guide you.
5. Create a list or an outline as a planning guide.

PERSUASIVE

Prewriting

Keys to Effective Prewriting

Remind students of the purpose of the prewriting stage in the writing process. (It's when the writer gets ready to write.)

Keys to Effective Prewriting explains the process students will be guided through on SE pages 228–232.

Use this brainstorming activity to generate topic ideas. Present these focus areas:

- neighborhood issues
- local issues (city or town)
- state issues
- national issues
- world issues

Form groups of five students according to their interests and abilities so that they will feel successful as they brainstorm. Have each group choose a different focus area.

To help students think of topics, introduce some issues. Invite students to look for ideas in newspapers and magazines that you make available. Each group should create a cluster of problems around its focus.

Technology Connections

Students can use the added features of the Net-text as they explore this stage of the writing process.

Write Source Online **Net-text**

Prewriting Selecting a Problem

Help students focus on a topic they care about. Make sure their topic generates some logical and creative solutions.

Focus on the Traits

Ideas
The strongest essays will be ones in which students have chosen a problem that concerns them.

* Refer students to the Problem-Solution Writing Prompts on SE page 546 and the Persuasive Sample Topics on SE page 547.

Prewriting Selecting a Problem

The first step in writing a problem-solution essay is to select a problem. A cluster can help you think of the problems all around you.

Topics Cluster

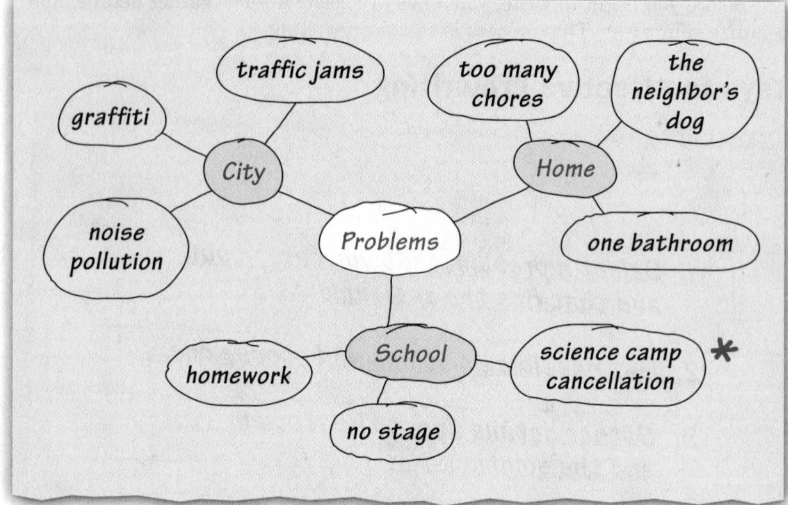

Prewrite **Create a cluster.** Use the cluster above as a guide for creating your own topics cluster. Then use the questions below to help choose the best topic.

1. Which problem do I know a lot about?
2. Which problem could I help solve?

Focus on the Traits

Ideas The best writing always begins with strong ideas. In this case, the main idea of your essay is a problem that you can help solve. After you select your topic, you'll gather more details about the problem so that you can propose a realistic solution.

English Language Learners

Help students identify topics that satisfy the assignment.

- Orally list topics.
- Have students determine whether a topic fulfills the directions (example: not enough gym equipment in school).
- When students disagree, ask them to explain their thinking.

Struggling Learners

To modify the prewriting activity for students with spatial organization difficulties, have them replace the extended cluster format with a linear graphic organizer such as a multi-tiered table graph (resembling a family tree). This format requires students to focus on one problem and move from general to specific.

Advanced Learners

Invite students to find and add topics to the gathering chart they began on TE page 223.

- Ask students to scan newspaper headlines for local, national, and world issues.
- Tell students to take notes based on television, radio, or Internet news reports.

Gathering Details About the Problem

Your reader will have two questions about the problem: (1) why does this problem exist, and (2) why should the problem be solved? A chart like the one below can help you gather persuasive details such as facts, examples, and quotations.

Gathering Chart

Problem: The school board might cancel science camp.

Why does the problem exist?	*Why should the problem be solved?*
Science camp costs $30 per student. *This year science camp would cost $3,000.* *The school budget has been cut.* *The economy has been bad.* *Everybody goes or nobody goes.*	*Without science camp, we wouldn't get to do our outdoor projects.* *-mini-steam engines* *-solar panels* *Nature is the place to learn about nature.* *-rock and plant identification* *-birds, animals, insects* *Sixth graders want us to save the camp, too.*

Gather answers. Make your own chart like the one above. In one column, list reasons for the problem. In the other, list reasons why the problem should be solved.

Focus on the Traits

Organization A problem-solution essay has two parts. The first part will convince the reader that a problem exists. The second part will propose a solution that the reader can help with. By organizing your details carefully, you can make your essay both clear and persuasive.

PERSUASIVE

Prewriting

Gathering Details About the Problem

Provide photocopies of the reproducible T-chart on TE page 789 for students to use for their gathering charts.

Have each group (formed for the lesson on TE page 227) gather details about a selected topic from their group cluster using a gathering chart. Students will be more prepared to complete their own chart after this experience. Some can use the group's chart as a basis for their problem-solution essay.

Focus on the Traits

Organization

Have students refer to their gathering chart.

- Discuss which order they think would be most persuasive (working from weakest to strongest tends to be most convincing).
- Ask students to number the two lists in their chart in the order in which they will present the items.

English Language Learners

Tell students they don't need to write in complete sentences when they are filling in their charts. Words and phrases are acceptable as long as they communicate the ideas clearly.

Struggling Learners

Students can simplify the chart.

- Label one column "Reasons for the Problem."
- Label the other column "Possible Solutions."
- Have students discuss their charts with a partner to see if their reasons and solutions are convincing.

Advanced Learners

Assist students in getting information about their problem so that they can identify realistic solutions.

- Have them ask others about the problem.
- Help them arrange to invite a guest speaker with knowledge about the problem.

Prewriting Proposing a Solution

Have the groups that were formed for gathering details about the problem (TE page 229) reconvene to address the sentence starter. Each group should work together to create a list of possible solutions.

Then students can work individually on a topic of their choice, or they can use solutions from the list that the group developed.

Prewriting

Gathering Details About the Solution

Provide photocopies of the reproducible 5 W's chart on TE page 792.

Students can organize their details point by point or by order of importance—from most to least important, or from least to most important.

Prewriting Proposing a Solution

A problem can have many possible solutions. Use a sentence starter like the one below and make a list of as many solutions as you can think of.

Sentence Starter

Science camp will be canceled unless . . .
the economy gets better.
the school board cuts something else.
parents volunteer to run science camp at the school.
students figure out how to raise $3,000 per year. *
a miracle happens.

Write down solutions. Use a sentence starter that states your problem and ends with a word such as "unless" or "until." Write as many solutions as you can. Which solution could you and your reader help bring about? Put a star next to the best solution.

Gathering Details About the Solution

Now that you have chosen a solution, you need to figure out just how it would work. To persuade your reader to join in the solution, you need to answer every question the reader might have. The 5 W's and H can help.

5 W's and H Chart

Who?	*Principal Jeffries, the student council, and all Wadsworth Middle School students*
What?	*Raise $3,000 per year to fill a "science camp fund"*
Where?	*In the school district*
When?	*Right away*
Why?	*So that science camp won't be canceled*
How?	*By holding fund-raisers like talent auctions and bake sales*

Collect your details. Think about your solution. Then answer the 5 W's and H about it.

Struggling Learners

Help students figure out how to organize the details.

- Ask students to think about what needs to be done first, next, and so on.
- For solutions that have no particular order and appear to be equally valid, tell students to try reading the points in different orders until they find the most logical presentation.

Avoiding Fuzzy Thinking

The details you have gathered will help you convince the reader that the problem needs to be solved and that your solution will work. However, when you present these details, you need to avoid errors in logic, or "fuzzy thinking."

Avoid jumping to conclusions.
The only reason that the school board would cut science camp is that they never experienced it themselves.
There could be many reasons the school board would cut science camp, not just this one.

Avoid bandwagoning.
Everybody thinks cutting science camp is a bad decision.
Many people thinking something is bad doesn't necessarily make it bad.

Avoid misleading comparisons.
Cutting science camp is like cutting down a tree.
Though both situations include "cutting," the similarities end there.

Avoid appealing only to emotion.
If science camp gets cut, the whole school will be in mourning.
Giving details about the negative effects is more convincing than talking about how sad everyone would be.

Read the following statements. For each one, indicate what type of "fuzzy thinking" it shows.

1. Cutting science camp is like stealing from the seventh-grade class.
2. Everybody thinks science camp should be saved.
3. If Principal Jeffries wants the whole school to be completely depressed, he can go ahead and cancel science camp.
4. Without science camp, science grades will drop.

Focus on the Traits

Voice A persuasive voice needs to be logical and confident. By avoiding "fuzzy thinking," you can keep the reader on your side.

English Language Learners

Since this use of the word *fuzzy* will probably be unfamiliar to students, spend a few moments clarifying the meaning.

- Help students understand that in this context, *fuzzy* means unclear, unconvincing, and not sensible.

Prewriting Avoiding Fuzzy Thinking

Use the following activity to help students understand how to avoid fuzzy thinking, or errors in logic.

- Have students fold a sheet of paper into fourths. They should label the paper *Fuzzy Thinking,* and record one type in each of the four corners: jumping to conclusions, bandwagoning, misleading comparisons, and appealing only to emotion.
- Instruct them to look through newspapers and magazines to find an example of each type. If examples can't be found, have students work in pairs to create examples.

 **Answers**

1. misleading comparison
2. bandwagoning
3. appealing only to emotion
4. jumping to conclusions

Focus on the Traits

Voice
Remind students that their goal is to sound confident and convincing about the problem and their proposed solution.

Prewriting Organizing Your Essay

Discuss what the numbered sections of the organized list have in common (each lists facts and details).

- Point out that every paragraph needs a topic sentence related to the essay topic (the problem and the solution).
- Each paragraph also needs facts and details that support its topic sentence.

Tell students to consider the arguments against their opinion. They should

- try to anticipate objections a reader might raise to their essay position,
- address these concerns, and
- incorporate information that refutes these arguments.

Prewriting Planning Your Essay

An opinion statement names the problem and proposes a solution.

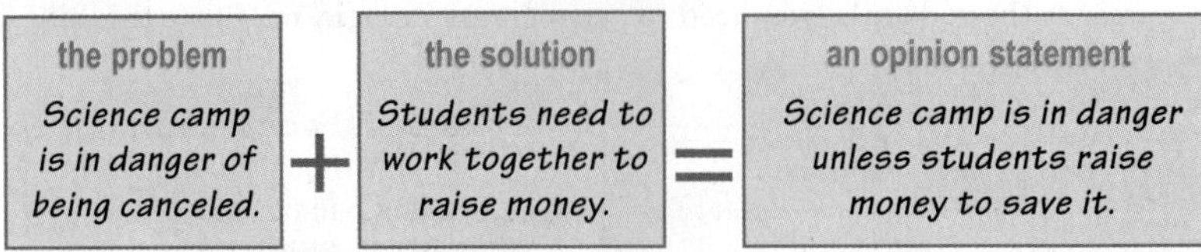

Write your opinion statement. Use the formula above to write your opinion statement. Name the problem and propose your solution.

Organizing Your Essay

The directions below can help you create an organized list for your essay.

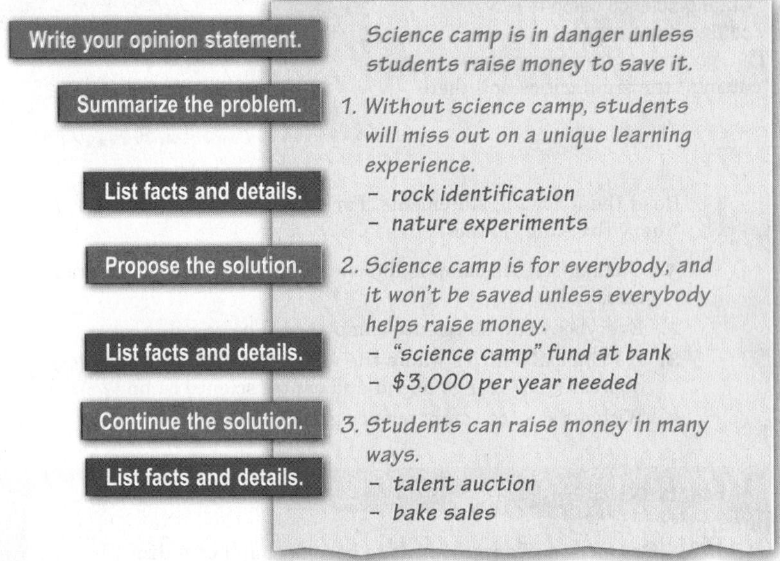

Make an organized list. To create your list, follow the "Directions" above. You will use this list as a guide when you write.

Struggling Learners

Remind students to refer to their earlier planning and prewriting to create their organized list. They should refer to the Gathering Chart on SE page 229 for information about the problem, and to the Sentence Starter and 5 W's and H Chart on SE page 230 for information about the solution. With this material at hand, you can then help students get started on their lists, starting with the opinion statement.

233
Proposing a Solution

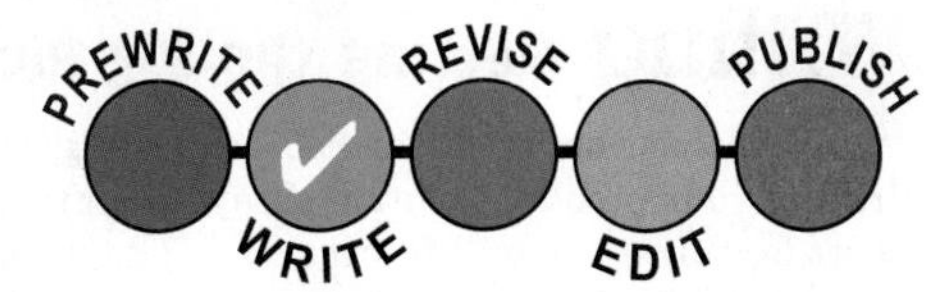

Writing

Once you finish creating a plan for your problem-solution essay, you are ready to put your ideas on paper.

Keys to Effective Writing

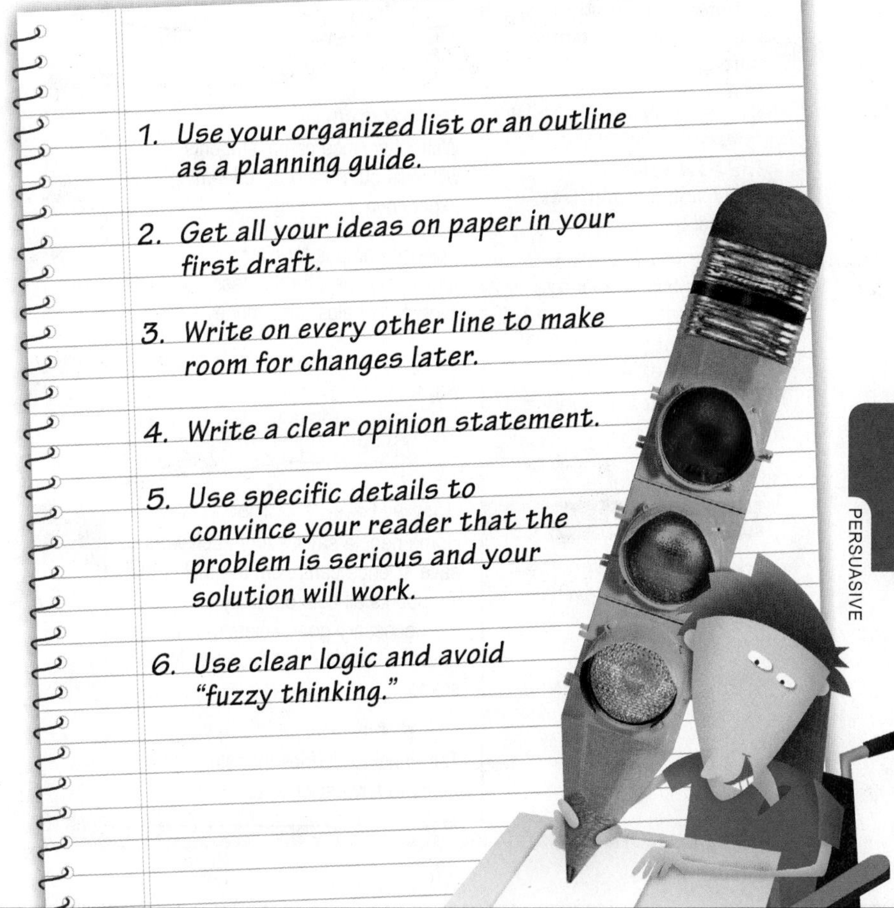

PERSUASIVE

Writing

Keys to Effective Writing

Remind students that the writing stage is when they get to develop their ideas on paper.

Keys to Effective Writing explains the process students will be guided through on SE pages 234–238.

Review the goals that students should keep in mind as they begin to write their problem-solving essay.

- Turn back to SE page 224 and read the goals together.
- Remind students that they should focus on the goals for the first three traits—ideas, organization, and voice—as they write a first draft. The other traits are more strongly emphasized in later steps in the writing process.

Writing Workshop

This section includes three activities to help scaffold students through the drafting stage: "Starting Your Essay," "Developing the Middle Part," and "Ending Your Essay." These three activities can also function as minilessons for small-group or whole-class instruction. Each activity introduces a key skill, models specific strategies, and encourages your students to try the skill.

Technology Connections

Students can use the added features of the Net-text as they explore this stage of the writing process.

Write Source Online ***Net-text***

Writing Getting the Big Picture

After reading the page, ask students to focus on why each part of the essay is important to the whole writing piece.

- Ask students to "remove" or cover the beginning and discuss why it is needed to introduce the essay.
- Take turns "removing" each part, discussing why it is important to the whole essay.

Writing Getting the Big Picture

Now that you have finished prewriting, you are ready to create a first draft of your problem-solution essay. The graphic that follows shows how the parts of your essay will fit together. (The examples are from the student essay on pages 235–238.)

Beginning

The **beginning** introduces the problem and provides the opinion statement.

Opening Sentences

Science camp is in danger unless students raise money to save it.

Middle

The **first middle** paragraph summarizes the problem.

The **second middle** paragraph proposes a solution.

Other middle paragraphs contain details about the solution.

Topic Sentences

Without science camp, students will miss out on a unique learning experience.

Science camp is for everybody, and it won't be saved unless everybody helps raise money for it.

Students can raise money in many ways.

Ending

The **ending** answers an objection and gives a call to action.

Answer to an Objection

Some people say it's too much work to save science camp, but the fact is that if students all help out, they can reach the necessary goal. Science camp is a terrific tradition that deserves to be saved.

Call to Action

Tell Principal Jeffries that students are ready to save science camp.

Struggling Learners

As an alternative to the organized list, students may use the questions they generated in the **Teaching Tip** activity on TE page 226 to structure their first draft.

Explain that they should

- base the beginning of their essay on information related to the questions for paragraphs 1 and 2,
- base the middle on the questions for paragraphs 3 and 4, and
- base the ending on the questions for paragraph 5.

Starting Your Essay

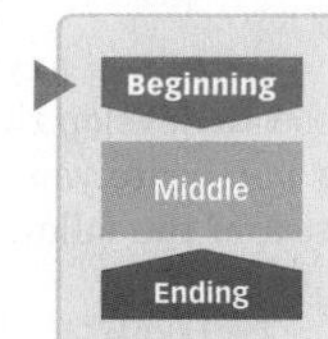

It's time to create your first draft. In the first paragraph of your persuasive essay, you will introduce the problem and provide your opinion statement. Before you do that, though, you need to get the reader's attention. Here are some strategies.

- **Ask a question:** What makes Wadsworth Middle School really special?
- **Quote someone:** "Nature is the best laboratory for learning about nature."
- **Share an experience:** When Lee Baker saw a sandhill crane at science camp, he knew he wanted to go into wildlife management.
- **Give background information:** The state cut money to schools this year, which means that Wadsworth Middle School might have to cancel science camp.

Beginning Paragraph

The following essay captures the reader's attention by beginning with a quotation. The writer introduces the problem and gives an opinion statement.

A quotation gets the reader's attention.

The problem is introduced.

The opinion statement is given (underlined).

"Nature is the best laboratory for learning about nature." Ms. Jacobson says this whenever she talks about science camp. For 10 years, every seventh grader at Wadsworth Middle School has attended the three-day camp in May. Sixth graders spend a whole year looking forward to "their turn," and eighth graders wish they could go again. Now science camp might be canceled because of budget cuts. Science camp is in danger unless students raise money to save it.

PERSUASIVE

Write an opening. **Write the beginning paragraph of your problem-solution essay. Use one of the four strategies above to get your reader's attention. Then introduce the problem and write your opinion statement.**

Struggling Learners

Help students begin their essays with an effective lead.

- They may want to quote one of their sources. (Remind them to request permission if necessary.)
- Remind students to punctuate quotations correctly.

* To review how to set off a speaker's exact words, refer students to SE page 598.

Writing Starting Your Essay

Use the following activity to provide practice in writing effective leads.

- Fold a piece of paper into fourths and label each with one of the four ways to start an opening paragraph:
  - □ Ask a question.
  - □ Quote someone.
  - □ Share an experience.
  - □ Give background information.
- Compose four different leads and write them on the paper.
- Get an opinion from another student to determine which lead is the most effective for the essay.
- Save these papers for another activity in the revising section, in which students learn four additional strategies.

Writing Developing the Middle Part

Examine the structure of the middle part of a problem-solution essay.

- Have students write the numbers 1 through 3 down the left side of a sheet of paper, leaving eight lines between each number.
- Write one topic sentence from the sample next to each number.
- Work with a partner to list the facts and examples in each paragraph that support the topic sentence.
- Have the class compare lists.

Writing Developing the Middle Part

After you have written your opening paragraph, you need to develop the middle part, or the body, of your essay. As you write your middle paragraphs, use your organized list and the following tips.

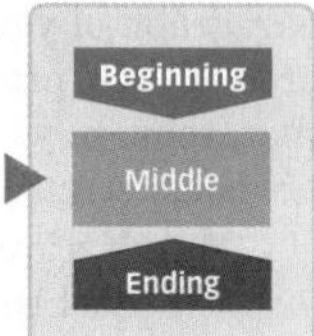

1. The **first middle paragraph** summarizes the problem.

2. The **second middle paragraph** proposes a solution.

3. The **other middle paragraphs** contain details that convince the reader your solution will work.

Middle Paragraphs

Without science camp, students will miss out on a unique learning experience. In science class, students learn to identify rocks by picking them up out of a box. At science camp, they learn to identify rocks by finding them in cliff sides or riverbeds. Science camp also lets students experiment with different forms of energy. For example, students get to build miniature steam engines that are powered by campfires. They also make solar panels that heat camp water. These experiences would be tough to create in a classroom. Science camp helps students understand nature while it teaches them to work with each other.

The topic sentence summarizes the problem.

The body convinces the reader with details.

The closing sentence tells why the problem needs a solution.

Struggling Learners

Before students write their middle paragraphs, refer them to the organized list on SE page 232. Demonstrate how the color-coded information was used in the essay on SE pages 236–237. Then ask students to explain how they will incorporate information from their own organized lists into their essays.

Topic Sentence	Science camp is for everybody, and it won't be saved unless everybody helps raise money for it.
The second middle paragraph introduces a solution.	To get started, Principal Jeffries and the student council could set up a "science camp fund" at a local bank. One student and an adult could be responsible for keeping the account. Every year, science camp costs $3,000. That sounds expensive, but if every student at Wadsworth
Closing Sentence	raises just $10, the fund would be filled.
Topic Sentence	Students can raise money in many ways.
This middle paragraph offers details about the solution.	For example, they could hold a talent auction. By raking lawns, cleaning gutters, baby-sitting, or using other talents, students can meet the goal. They could also arrange a rummage sale, or they could hold a bake sale. Students could even ask local businesses to sponsor them.
Closing Sentence	If Wadsworth students all work together, they can easily raise the money.

Write your middle paragraphs. Create middle paragraphs for your problem-solution essay. Follow the guidelines on page 236.

PERSUASIVE

Drafting Tips

- **Follow the plan** in your organized list.
- **Use facts, examples, and quotations** to convince the reader to take the problem seriously and help solve it.
- **Avoid "fuzzy thinking."**
- **Use a convincing voice.**

Some students find it helpful to organize and write their **topic sentences** *(see below)* for the three middle paragraphs in advance. Then they can add details and elaboration as their final step to complete the body of the essay. Other students find this approach too restricting and prefer to compose each paragraph in order.

Writing Drafting Tips

* Discuss how students can make their voice convincing using the following guidelines:
- Choose positive words, such as *students will* or *we can,* to describe actions.
- Use transition words to clarify your points. See SE page 573.
- Use an upbeat, firm, and confident tone.
- Use stronger, more confident words than *we might* or *maybe we could* when making suggestions.

Teaching Tip: Topic Sentences

A topic sentence states the main idea of a paragraph.

- The topic sentence is usually the first sentence in the paragraph; all the information in the paragraph relates to or supports that sentence.
- If some details do not relate to the topic sentence, then either the information needs to be removed or the topic sentence needs to be revised.
- Students should be able to identify the topic sentence in every paragraph in an essay.
- If students were to develop their topic sentences in order, in paragraph form, the paragraphs should form a clear essay.

* See SE pages 552–553 for pointers on writing good topic sentences.

Struggling Learners

Remind students to add details for each topic sentence, using a logical organization.

Writing Ending Your Essay

Students often have trouble writing effective endings. Provide this structure to give students who are not intuitive writers a clear and simple way to construct an effective ending:

- First, answer an objection.
- Then create a call to action.

Writing Ending Your Essay

Answering an Objection

In the ending, or conclusion, you should try to answer a main objection your reader might have. Use the formula below as a basic guide to answer an objection.

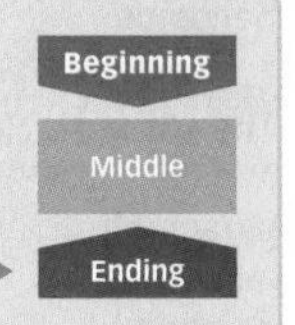

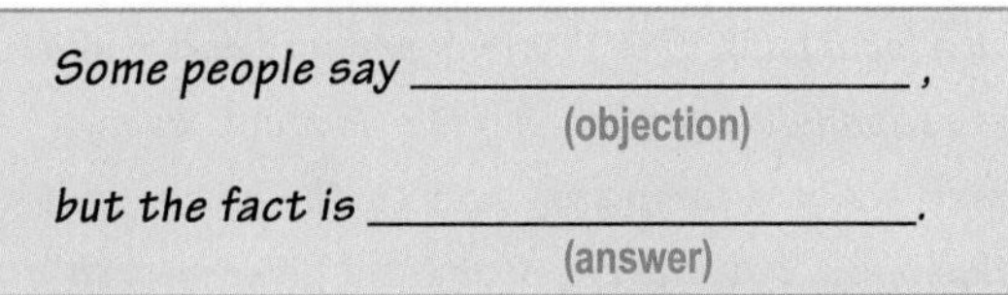

Creating a Call to Action

A call to action is a command that tells the reader specifically how to help solve the problem. See the examples that follow.

- **Tell Principal Jeffries that students are ready to save science camp.**
- **Sign Ms. Jacobson's petition to save science camp.**
- **Support the science camp at the student council meeting Monday.**

Ending Paragraph

An objection is answered.

A call to action asks the reader to help.

Some people say it's too much work to save science camp, but the fact is that if students all help out, they can reach the necessary goal. Science camp is a terrific tradition that deserves to be saved. Tell Principal Jeffries that students are ready to save science camp.

Write your ending. Write the final paragraph of your essay. First answer any objection your reader might have. Then summarize the problem and solution and call your reader to action.

Form a complete first draft. Write a complete copy of your essay. Skip every other line if you write by hand, or double-space if you use a computer.

Struggling Learners

Some students may need help in answering objections before attempting to write this part of their essay. Working with each student individually,

- summarize the problem and solution presented in the body,
- suggest a possible objection to the solution,
- encourage the student to answer your objection, and
- help each student write the answer as part of the ending to his or her essay.

Advanced Learners

Before assigning the writing activity, do the following:

- Have students compile a list of alternatives to the first words in the sample above. (Possible responses: *It could be argued, Those who disagree propose, Opponents may feel*)
- Copy and distribute the list to encourage a variety of starting points.

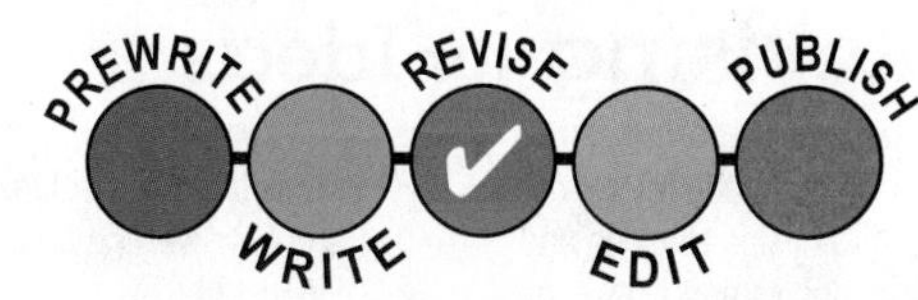

Revising

When you revise, you add or remove details, shift parts of the essay, and work on creating a more persuasive voice. You also check your word choice and refine your sentences.

Keys to Effective Revising

1. *Read through your entire draft to get a feeling of how well your essay works.*
2. *Make sure your opinion statement names the problem and proposes a solution.*
3. *Check your paragraphs to make sure they follow your writing plan.*
4. *Revise your voice if it does not sound convincing.*
5. *Make sure your words and sentences are strong and clear.*
6. *Use the editing and proofreading marks inside the back cover of this book.*

PERSUASIVE

Revising

Keys to Effective Revising

Keys to Effective Revising explains the process students will be guided through on SE pages 240–250.

Review the goals on SE page 224 that students should keep in mind as they revise their problem-solving essays. Remind students that using a revising checklist helps them to read their essay critically and to improve their writing.

Peer Responding

Have your students read and respond to each other's writing. Doing so helps students see the strengths and weaknesses in their work, and it helps them pinpoint specific ways to revise.

Writing Workshop

Instead of asking students to work through all the revising activities on the following pages, use the activities as minilessons. If a group of students is having difficulty with ideas, present the ideas pages to them. If a different group is struggling with voice, use the voice material. This section is intended to give students just the support they need—but no more.

Technology Connections

Have students use the Writing Network features of the Net-text to comment on each other's drafts.

***Write Source Online* Net-text**

Struggling Learners

During the revising process, students should evaluate their first draft for each trait individually—ideas, organization, voice, word choice, sentence fluency, and conventions. Although a rubric strip for each trait appears at the top of the two-page spread where it is discussed, some students may need prompting to use the rubric.

Revising for Ideas

The rubric strips that run across all of the revising pages (SE pages 240–249) are provided to help students focus on different traits in their revisions and are related to the full rubric on SE pages 256–257.

Writer's Craft

The anatomy of the question: There are two ways to form a question. You can begin the question with one of the 5 W's and H: *who, what, when, where, why,* and *how.* You can also begin a question with one of the helping verbs: *is, am, are, was, were, can, could, will, would, shall, should, may, might, must, has, have, had, do, does,* or *did.* Think of it this way: the 5 W's and H ask questions about people, places, things, and ideas (nouns). The helping verbs ask questions about actions or states of being (verbs).

In this way, the English language equips writers and readers to ask questions about any piece of information they don't have.

Revising for Ideas

6 I persuade my reader by using reasons and details and answering all the objections.

5 My details are persuasive, and I answer the reader's biggest objection.

4 My details are persuasive, but I do not answer an objection.

When you revise a problem-solution essay for *ideas*, you should check to make sure you have included enough persuasive details and have answered an objection. The rubric strip above can guide you.

How can I use details to persuade?

You can use details to convince your reader that the problem is serious and that your solution will work. During prewriting, you gathered details to answer the reader's questions about the problem and your solution. Now you will check to make sure these details appear in your essay.

Reviewing Details About the Problem

The details in your beginning paragraph and your first middle paragraph should provide clear answers to the following questions.

- Why does this problem exist?
- Why should the problem be solved?

Reviewing Details About the Solution

The details in your other middle paragraphs should provide clear answers to the following questions.

1. **Who** should help solve this problem?
2. **What** should they do to solve the problem?
3. **When** should they begin?
4. **Where** should they work?
5. **Why** should they help out?
6. **How** should they get involved?

Review your details. Read your first draft. Answer each of the questions above using details from your essay. If your essay is missing any important details, revise your writing to include them.

Struggling Learners

As an alternative to the revising activity, you could simply ask students to label with the 5 W's and H the part of their first draft that discusses the solution. If students end up with only a few labels, then they should consider adding more detail.

Answers

1. does not respond in a satisfying way
2. does not mention a concern
3. does not mention a concern

3 I need more details about the problem or solution, and I should answer an objection.	2 My essay lacks persuasive details and doesn't answer an objection.	1 I need to learn how to use details to persuade.

Have I answered a main objection?

You have answered an objection if you have mentioned a concern that a reader might have and then answered the concern in a satisfying way.

Reader's Concern

Some people say we don't need intramural sports,

Satisfying Answer

but intramural teams help students keep physically fit.

Read the following answers to objections. Indicate what is wrong with each: either the answer does not mention a concern, or the answer does not respond to the concern in a satisfying way.

1. Some people may think the crossing at Kane Street and Harper Avenue is safe, but those people are wrong.
2. The fact is that busywork wastes everybody's time.
3. Although most students like our school mascot, I don't.

Revise your writing. **Check to see that you have effectively answered an objection. Revise as needed.**

Ideas
An answer to an objection is improved.

Some people say it's too much work to save science camp, but the fact is that ~~those people have no idea what they're talking about~~ if students all help out, they can reach the necessary goal easily. Science. . .

PERSUASIVE

English Language Learners

Help students evaluate their answering of the objection. Label for them the two parts of their answer—the *reader's concern* and the *satisfying answer.* If a student's sentence is missing either part, or the answer doesn't read smoothly, suggest possible improvements.

Advanced Learners

Have students find an opinion piece in a newspaper (editorial, letter, column) that answers at least one objection. Ask for volunteers to share their articles with the class. Instruct students to pay special attention to the wording of the counterargument. Then ask them to revisit their own answer to an objection to see if it is stated in the best way.

Revising for Organization

Ask students to find the paper with the sample leads they completed for TE page 235. In that section, they folded a paper into fourths and labeled each fourth with one way to begin an opening paragraph.

Direct students to turn the page over and add the four additional ways of starting essays:

- Sum up the problem.
- Make a shocking statement.
- Begin with "if."
- Describe a dramatic scene.

As students practice each strategy, they can determine the most effective lead and become more comfortable with using the different options.

Revising for Organization

6	5	4
My organization follows a well-developed plan, grabs the reader's attention, and has a clear call to action.	My beginning gets the reader's attention, and my ending has a call to action.	My beginning gets the reader's attention, but the call to action needs some work.

When you revise for *organization*, you check your essay to see that you have followed your organized list. Then you make sure that your beginning captures your reader's attention and that your ending gives a clear call to action. The rubric strip above can help.

Does my beginning capture my reader's attention?

Your first sentence is the most important one for capturing your reader's attention. To make sure you have the best first sentence, try several versions. On page 235, you were given four strategies: ask a question, quote someone, share an experience, or give background information. Here are four additional strategies for getting your reader's attention.

- **Sum up the problem.**
  The bill for science camp is $3,000 per year.
- **Make a shocking statement.**
  The seventh graders could lose the best part of the school year.
- **Begin with "if."**
  If we don't act, science camp might be canceled.
- **Describe a dramatic scene.**
  All the cabins stand empty, and all the campfires have burned out.

Revise

Try different beginnings. Review the strategies above and those on page 235. Then follow these instructions.

1. Choose two strategies you have not yet tried.
2. Write two new versions of your beginning sentence.
3. Share all three beginnings with a classmate and ask which beginning does the best job of capturing his or her attention.
4. Choose the best beginning.

Struggling Learners

When students work from an organized list, they often end up with a string of ideas that are not connected smoothly. Review the transitions on SE page 39 with students. Then have them look for transitions between sentences and between paragraphs that they could use in their essays.

3 I should improve both my beginning and my call to action.

2 The beginning, middle, and ending all run together and don't work well.

1 I need help organizing my essay.

Does my ending contain a clear call to action?

A clear call to action lets the reader know just what she or he should do to help with the solution. Your call to action needs to be

- specific,
- realistic, and
- stated as a polite command.

Read the following unclear calls to action. On your own paper, indicate what the problem is with each call to action: not specific, not realistic, or not stated as a command. (There may be more than one problem.)

1. It would be nice if students donated money to the drama club.
2. Do everything you can to make our streets safe!
3. As a student of Lincoln Middle School, demand your rights to approve the school budget!
4. Clean up the planet!
5. It's time for all good students to help out with recycling.

Revise **Check your call to action. Make sure that your call to action is specific, realistic, and stated as a polite command.**

Organization An unclear call to action is improved.

Science camp is a terrific tradition that deserves to be saved. ~~*Somebody ought to do something about this problem.*~~ Tell Principal Jeffries that students are ready to save science camp.

PERSUASIVE

Encourage students to consider whether they would be willing to respond to their own call to action (or if they are already planning to do so). Point out that if the call to action is not something they are actually willing to do, then others may not be willing to do it either. Suggest that students rethink the call to action if they themselves would not be willing or motivated to respond to it.

Answers

1. not stated as a command
2. not specific
3. not realistic
4. not specific, not realistic
5. not stated as a command, not specific

Struggling Learners

Help auditory learners decide whether or not the endings in the **Try It** activity are stated as polite commands.

- Read each sentence aloud, using appropriate intonation.
- Ask students to consider whether or not each call to action is specific and realistic, by identifying words and phrases that support their claims.
- Possible word choices: *would be nice if* (a suggestion, not a command): *everything you can* (not specific): *demand* (unrealistic); *clean up* (not specific and unrealistic); *help out* (not specific); and *it's time for* (not a command).

Revising for Voice

To emphasize the effectiveness of concise phrases over wordy ones, have students complete the following **role-playing** activity *(see below)*.

- Set up a scene where a parent is asking a child to turn down the volume of a music player.
- One student acts out the scene as the parent and complains a lot before getting to the point. (Example: "It's noisy in here. Why can't I concentrate? Don't you have homework to do? Peace and quiet would be a nice change.")
- A second student acts out the same scene, speaking directly but politely. (Example: "Please turn down that music so that I can do my work.")
- Discuss which approach is more likely to achieve immediate results.
- Ask students to come up with and role-play other scenes that demonstrate rambling versus concise language.

Answers

Possible answers:

1. A new policy for adjusting the thermostat would make all rooms more comfortable.
2. An enforced speed limit on the road with the bike route would protect cyclists.

Revising for Voice

6	5	4
My voice is confident and persuasive and convinces my readers.	My voice is confident and persuasive throughout the essay.	My voice is confident, but I need to include more suggestions to be persuasive.

To revise for *voice*, check your writing to make sure it sounds confident and persuasive. The rubric strip above can help you.

How can my voice sound more confident?

One way to sound more confident is to make your point in the fewest words possible. Confident writing says a lot with a few words, and it is convincing. Writing that is not confident uses many words that say very little.

Not Confident

It might be a useful solution to the problem of too many cars in front of the school if the school could have a different place marked out for people to come to drop off or pick up students.

Confident

New parking rules could solve the traffic jams before and after school.

Read the following sentences that lack a confident voice. Rewrite each in as few words as you can.

1. The problem that there are some rooms that are warm and stuffy could be helped if there were some sort of policy about adjusting the thermostat.
2. If people would slow down when they are driving along the road with the bike route, then maybe it wouldn't be quite so tough for cyclists to use the route to get places.

Revise for voice. Read your essay and look for places where you could say the same thing using fewer words. Revise your writing to make it sound more confident.

Teaching Tip: Role-Playing

If students are unfamiliar with role-playing, explain that it means to act something out. When they role-play, they imagine they are someone else. The purposes of role-playing include

- to practice something,
- to demonstrate something,
- to learn about something from someone else's perspective.

3 At times my voice sounds confident, but it never is persuasive.

2 I need to sound confident and persuasive throughout.

1 I need to understand how to create a confident and persuasive voice.

How can my voice sound more persuasive?

One way to make your voice sound more persuasive is to include a few suggestions. These are two types of suggestions: mild and strong.

- **Suggestions:** A mild suggestion uses a verb such as *may, could, would;* a strong suggestion uses a verb such as *should, ought,* or *must.*

Read the following statements. Turn each one into a mild or strong suggestion using one of the verbs listed above.

1. It is up to students to help with recycling day.
2. It is important that classmates know that teasing isn't allowed.
3. Students don't report accidents to teachers.
4. Seventh graders help sixth graders learn new skills.
5. It is a good idea for students to walk home in pairs instead of alone.

Add suggestions or commands. Check your essay. If the voice needs to be more persuasive in parts, add suggestions.

PERSUASIVE

Voice
A statement is turned into a suggestion, and an important point is said in fewer words.

One student and an adult ~~are~~ could be responsible for keeping the account. ~~Taken on a yearly basis, the general expenses for science camp are round about in the range of $3,000 for the whole group of seventh graders who go.~~ Every year, science camp costs $3,000. That sounds expensive . . .

The **Try It** activity tells students to rewrite the statements as either mild or strong calls to action. For a more complete exploration, have students rewrite these sentences in both styles.

Fold a piece of notebook paper in half to form two columns. Label one side *Mild Suggestions* and the other side *Strong Suggestions.* Have students rewrite each of the five statements in the text as both mild and strong calls to action.

Try It Answers

Possible answers:

1. Students should help with recycling day.
2. Classmates must know that teasing isn't allowed.
3. Students ought to report accidents to teachers.
4. Seventh graders could help sixth graders learn new skills.
5. Students could walk home in pairs instead of alone.

English Language Learners

Conduct a writing conference with any student who is struggling to incorporate an effective voice.

- Review **Understanding Voice** on SE page 40.
- Read aloud portions of the student's essay that are not persuasive.
- Discuss the information in question with the student.
- Jot down his or her words and phrases from your conversation and explain how they could be used to make the student's writing more persuasive.
- Give the student your notes and encourage him or her to use what you've written for the revision.
- Then read aloud the revisions so the student can hear the improvement.

Revising for Word Choice

Sometimes a writer who feels strongly about an issue does not realize that she or he has used inflammatory words to argue a point. Have students exchange their work with at least one other student. A fresh eye may pick up on words that are inappropriate.

Answers

Possible choices:
line 1: must be crazy (insult)
line 3: disintegrate (exaggeration)
line 4: fat-cat (name-calling)
lines 6–7: must not believe in education (insult, exaggeration)
line 7: dislike kids (insult, exaggeration)
line 8: rattling their skulls (exaggeration)
line 9: doomed (exaggeration)

Revising for Word Choice

- **6** My words are engaging and positive, and they fit my audience and purpose.
- **5** I have avoided inflammatory words and am not too formal or too casual.
- **4** I use no inflammatory words, but some words might be too formal or casual.

When you check your essay for *word choice*, make sure you have avoided inflammatory words. Also make sure that you have used words that fit your audience and purpose. Use the rubric strip above to guide you.

What are inflammatory words and phrases?

Inflammatory words and phrases will upset or anger the reader. If you anger a reader, you'll have a hard time getting him or her to help with your solution. Inflammatory language includes insults, name-calling, and unrealistic exaggerations. If you feel a word or phrase in some way may upset the reader, make sure to change it.

Read the following two paragraphs. Find at least five examples of inflammatory language and tell why each might upset the reader.

The town council must be crazy to suggest that the new bypass be placed right next to the school. Truck traffic on the road will rumble past until the school walls disintegrate. The only reason this bypass route is suggested is to protect the fat-cat property owners on the other side of the town.

People who would vote for the bypass must not believe in education, or maybe they just dislike kids. How can students learn anything with all that truck traffic rattling their skulls? We need to speak up, or the school is doomed.

Check for inflammatory words. Read over your essay, imagining that you are a typical reader. Check each word (and phrase) to make sure you haven't said anything to insult your reader. Remove inflammatory words.

English Language Learners

Students need to understand the challenging vocabulary and figurative language in the writing sample before attempting the **Try It** activity. Be sure students comprehend the following words and phrases:

- rumble past (drive by, making a loud noise)
- disintegrate (break apart)
- fat-cat (very rich)
- rattling their skulls (making so much noise that their heads are shaken)
- doomed (destined to come to an unhappy end)

3 I have some inflammatory words and struggle with words that are too formal or casual.

2 I can't avoid inflammatory words and slang because of my strong feelings.

1 I need to learn about word choice for persuasive writing.

Do my words fit my audience and purpose?

To be persuasive, the words you choose should not be too formal or too casual. Words that are too formal sound stiff and unnatural. On the other hand, words that are too casual aren't very convincing. The following examples show how appropriate word choice makes writing more persuasive.

Too Formal

The student council should address this concern with the utmost speed.

Too Casual

The student council should hash out this deal A.S.A.P.

Just Right

The student council should discuss this problem right away.

Check for appropriate word choice. Read through your essay. Look for words that are too formal or too casual. Replace them with words that fit your audience and purpose.

Word Choice
Casual word choice is corrected, and an inflammatory word is removed.

Without science camp, students will miss out on a ~~totally awesome~~ unique learning experience. In science class, students learn to identify rocks by picking them up out of a ~~stupid~~ box. At science camp, they learn to identify rocks by finding them in cliff . . .

PERSUASIVE

Display a few problem-solution essays on an overhead for discussion. (Try to use essays from past years.) As you read each essay aloud, instruct students to listen for words that might be too causal or too formal for the intended **audience** *(see below)*. Have students suggest replacement words as needed.

Teaching Tip: Audience

Some students may need help with the concept of audience. Review SE page 40. Have students role-play to practice appropriate language for different audiences.

Example: Set up a scene in which a teenager describes a difficult test he or she took. Have the student describe the test to a friend, then to a parent or a teacher, and finally to a young sibling.

- Remind students to use the appropriate degree of formality or informality in word choice.
- Have the class discuss how the description was adapted for each audience.

Revising for Sentence Fluency

Use this mnemonic device to help students memorize seven common coordinating conjunctions:

ON San **F**rancisco **BAY**
(ONSFBAY: *or, nor, so, for, but, and, yet*)

Answers

1. The sports teams need new equipment, and the band needs new sheet music.
2. Archery is offered in the summer recreation program, yet it is not offered in regular gym class.
3. The history class is planning a field trip to the museum next week, but they might go to a historical site instead.

Revising for Sentence Fluency

6	5	4
My sentences flow smoothly, and people will enjoy reading them.	I use compound sentences for equal ideas and complex sentences for unequal ideas.	I use a variety of sentences, but I need some complex sentences.

When you revise for *sentence fluency*, make sure you have used a variety of sentences—simple, compound, and complex. Use the rubric strip above.

Do I use compound sentences well?

Compound sentences can add variety and balance to your writing. When you have two ideas that are equally important, you can express them best in a compound sentence. A compound sentence consists of two simple sentences that are usually joined by a comma and a coordinating conjunction such as *and, but, or, nor, so, for,* or *yet.* (See page 516.)

Two Equal Ideas

The school will pay half the cost of the spring production.
The drama club will need to raise money to pay for the rest.

One Compound Sentence

The school will pay half the cost of the spring production, but the drama club will need to raise money to pay for the rest.

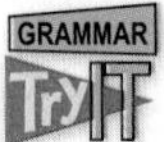

Combine each of the following pairs of simple sentences into one compound sentence. Use a different conjunction in each sentence.

1. The sports teams need new equipment. The band needs new sheet music.
2. Archery is offered in the summer recreation program. It is not offered in regular gym class.
3. The history class is planning a field trip to the museum next week. They might go to a historical site instead.

Check your use of compound sentences. Read your essay and look for compound sentences. If you do not use many, look for short sentences that express equal ideas. Join them with a comma and a coordinating conjunction to form a compound sentence.

Grammar Connection

Compound and Complex Sentences

- **Proofreader's Guide** pages 590 (+), 698–699
- ***Write Source*** pages 516 (+), 517 (+)
- ***SkillsBook*** pages 121–122, 123–124
- ***GrammarSnap*** Simple, Compound, Complex, and Compound-Complex Sentences

Struggling Learners

Give students additional practice in using coordinating conjunctions correctly. Discuss how each conjunction affects a sentence. For example, *but* changes the direction of the sentence; *or* signals another choice or alternative; *and* offers an addition. Caution students to avoid beginning a sentence with a coordinating conjunction.

persuade convince support argue reason 249 Proposing a Solution

3	In some places, I use too many simple sentences. I need to combine some of them.
2	My writing has too many simple sentences. I need to combine many of them.
1	Most of my sentences need to be rewritten.

Do I use complex sentences well?

Complex sentences help to show the different kinds of connections between the ideas in your writing. Special transitions called *subordinating conjunctions* can be used to create these connections. (See page 517.)

Time		Cause-Effect		Comparison-Contrast	
after	until	because	so that	although	though
before	when	in order that	that	as though	where
till	while	provided that	unless	even though	whereas

For each complex sentence, tell what connection the subordinating conjunction makes: *time, cause-effect, comparison-contrast.*

1. Because the school building is old, some restrooms aren't accessible.
2. The student body must vote before the PTO can decide.
3. Though testing is important, learning is even more important.
4. When the annex is finished, everyone will have computer access.
5. Unless we act now, the marching band will be cut.

Create connections between ideas. Read your essay and look for complex sentences. If you do not use many, look for places where they could be used.

Sentence Fluency Simple sentences are combined into a complex and a compound sentence.

Science camp helps students understand nature. It teaches them to work with each other. [edit: "while" inserted; "It" changed to "it"]

Science camp is for everybody. It won't be saved unless everybody helps raise money for it. [edit: "and" inserted; "It" changed to "it"]

PERSUASIVE

Use the following ideas to practice writing complex sentences.

- Students choose three subordinating conjunctions from the *time* category and use them in sentences. They should first use the subordinating conjunction to begin the sentence and then rearrange their sentence so the conjunction is in the middle of the sentence.
- Repeat this with the cause-effect conjunctions and the comparison-contrast conjunctions. Example: *After I finish my homework, I will eat dinner. I will eat dinner after I finish my homework.* Make sure students recognize which version needs a comma.

* For more practice in developing complex sentences, see SE page 517.

Answers

1. cause-effect
2. time
3. comparison-contrast
4. time
5. cause-effect

English Language Learners

Help students build their vocabulary of subordinating conjunctions.

* Use the examples and the list of conjunctions on SE page 553 to demonstrate this skill.

Create your own "Why-What" and "Yes, But" sentences with original ideas generated by students.

Revising Using a Checklist

After students have used the checklist for their own work, have them work in pairs and read each other's essays.

- Ask each student to complete a Peer Response Sheet such as the one shown on SE page 32. They should use the checklist to help them focus their responses.
- Then have partners discuss the comments and recommended changes.

Revising Using a Checklist

Check your revising. On a piece of paper, write the numbers 1 to 12. If you can answer "yes" to a question, put a check mark after that number. If not, continue to work with that part of your essay.

Ideas

_____ **1.** Do I focus on a clear problem and solution?
_____ **2.** Have I included persuasive details about the problem and the solution?
_____ **3.** Have I answered a reader's possible objection?

Organization

_____ **4.** Have I followed my organized list or outline?
_____ **5.** Does my beginning capture my reader's attention?
_____ **6.** Does my ending include a clear call to action?

Voice

_____ **7.** Does my voice sound confident?
_____ **8.** Does my voice sound persuasive?

Word Choice

_____ **9.** Have I avoided inflammatory words?
_____ **10.** Have I chosen words that are not too formal or too casual?

Sentence Fluency

_____ **11.** Do I use compound sentences well?
_____ **12.** Do I use complex sentences well?

Make a clean copy. When you've finished revising, make a clean copy before you edit. This makes checking for conventions easier.

Grammar Connection

Semicolons and Colons

- **Proofreader's Guide** pages 594–595, 596–597
- ***SkillsBook*** pages 29–30
- ***GrammarSnap*** Semicolons and Colons

Adverbs

- **Proofreader's Guide** pages 736–737
- ***Write Source*** pages 490, 492–493
- ***SkillsBook*** pages 183–184
- ***GrammarSnap*** Adjectives and Adverbs

Editing

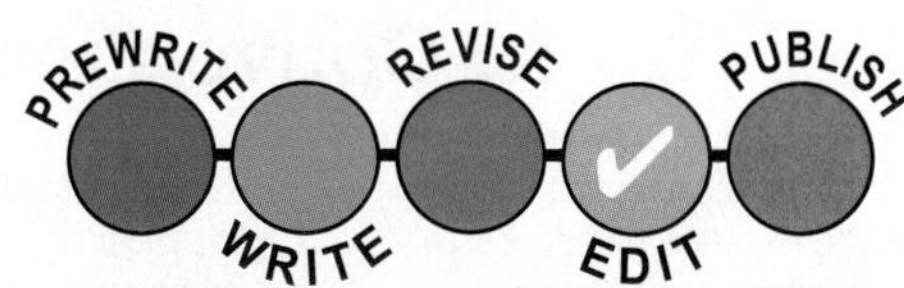

Once you are finished revising, you need to edit for punctuation, spelling, capitalization, and grammar. These rules are called *conventions*.

Keys to Effective Editing

1. *Use a dictionary, a thesaurus, and the "Proofreader's Guide" in the back of this book.*
2. *Check for any words or phrases that may be confusing to the reader.*
3. *Check your writing for correct punctuation, capitalization, spelling, and grammar.*
4. *If you are using a computer, edit on a printed computer copy. Then enter your changes on the computer.*
5. *Use the editing and proofreading marks inside the back cover of this book.*

PERSUASIVE

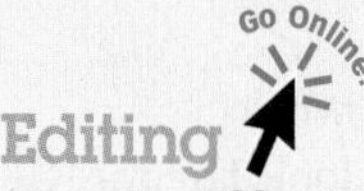

Editing

Keys to Effective Editing

The Keys to Effective Editing explains the process students will be guided through on SE pages 252–254.

- If students are overwhelmed by the editing tasks, one solution is to organize them in editing groups. Assign each member of the group a different editing task, such as checking for correct punctuation or checking for correct spelling.
- Have each student begin by checking her or his own work for that type of error and then pass the essay to the student on the left. Continue the "round robin" editing until every student in the group has checked each paper.
- Make sure that students take turns being responsible for a different task during different "round robin" sessions.

Technology Connections

Students can use the added features of the Net-text as they explore this stage of the writing process.

***Write Source Online* Net-text**

English Language Learners

Ask students to focus their attention on the third key to effective editing—conventions.

- Provide specific examples of the types of errors they will be most likely to find. Base your examples on your observations of student papers during the stages of drafting and revising.
- Tell students to look for each kind of error, one at a time.

Editing for Conventions

If students are editing their own work independently, suggest that they look through their essays several times, focusing on one type of error (punctuation, capitalization, spelling, grammar) at a time.

Remind students that compound sentences are made up of two independent clauses and that a comma must be used before the conjunction that separates the two clauses.

* Refer students to SE page 590 for more examples of using a comma in a compound sentence.

Answers

1. Everybody has homework, but some of us also play sports after school.
2. Homework requires concentration, and noise breaks concentration.
3. Study hall has become a problem, so we need a solution.

Editing for Conventions

6	5	4
My grammar and punctuation are correct, and the essay is free of spelling errors.	I have a few minor errors in punctuation, spelling, or grammar.	I need to correct some errors in punctuation, spelling, and grammar.

When you edit for *conventions*, you need to pay attention to spelling, punctuation, capitalization, and grammar. These two pages will help you check your compound and complex sentences for correct punctuation. The rubric strip above can also guide your editing.

Do I correctly punctuate compound sentences?

A correctly punctuated compound sentence will have a comma before the coordinating conjunction *(and, but, or, nor, for, so, yet).* When you created the three compound sentences on page 248, you may have accidentally left out the comma or the conjunction. (See page 516.)

Missing Comma

The school will pay for half the cost of the spring production but the drama club will need to raise money to pay for the rest.

Missing Conjunction (Comma Splice)

The school will pay for half the cost of the spring production, the drama club will need to raise money to pay for the rest.

Missing Comma and Conjunction (Run-On)

The school will pay for half the cost of the spring production the drama club will need to raise money to pay for the rest.

Rewrite the following compound sentences to correct the error.

1. Everybody has homework some of us also play sports after school.
2. Homework requires concentration and noise breaks concentration.
3. Study hall has become a problem, we need a solution.

Check errors in compound sentences. Check the compound sentences in your essay. Make sure each has a comma and a coordinating conjunction. Fix any errors you find.

persuade convince support argue reason 253 Proposing a Solution

3 I need to correct errors that may confuse the reader.
2 I need to correct many errors that make my essay difficult to read.
1 I need help making corrections.

Do I correctly punctuate complex sentences?

Punctuating complex sentences can be a little tricky. If the dependent clause comes first in the sentence, a comma follows it. If the dependent clause comes at the end of the sentence, a comma is usually not needed.

After the school board meets, *(dependent clause)*
students will find out about the new school schedule. *(independent clause)*

We will have to elect a new student council president *(independent clause)*
before the school year ends. *(dependent clause)*

GRAMMAR Try It Rewrite each of the following sentences to correct the error.

1. When students don't respect the rules study hall becomes gab hall.
2. Often students can't finish their work, because study hall is too loud.
3. Until we fix this problem nobody will be able to work.

Edit **Check for errors in complex sentences.** **Check your complex sentences to make sure that you have correctly punctuated them.**

Conventions
A comma splice is fixed, and a punctuation error is corrected in a complex sentence.

They could also arrange a rummage sale, or they could hold a bake sale. Students could even ask local businesses to sponsor them. If Wadsworth students all work together, they can easily raise the money.

PERSUASIVE

To make sure students understand dependent and independent clauses, have them use their own words to write a rule that explains the difference.

Since writing complex sentences may be relatively new to some students, ask them to pay particular attention as they edit for these sentences. Check students' work individually to be sure they understand how to write and punctuate complex sentences.

GRAMMAR Try It **Answers**

1. When students don't respect the rules, study hall becomes gab hall.
2. Often students can't finish their work because study hall is too loud.
3. Until we fix this problem, nobody will be able to work.

Struggling Learners

Some students may need practice in punctuating their compound and complex sentences.

- On chart paper, display several sentences without punctuation.
- Give each student a sticky note with an oversized comma on it.
- Have each student try to punctuate one sentence. Discuss each response.

Advanced Learners

Ask students to write a series of compound and complex sentences with correct punctuation.

- Have them transpose the sentences onto chart paper, leaving out all punctuation.
- Use the sentences on the chart paper for the Struggling Learners activity on this page or for a full-class activity.

Editing Using a Checklist

Be sure students have been through all stages of the editing process before they apply the checklist to their essays.

Give students a few moments to look over the Proofreader's Guide in the back of their book. Throughout the year they can refer to the instruction, rules, and examples to clarify any checklist items or to resolve questions about their own writing.

Creating a Title

Many authors create titles after they have finished a piece of writing. Adding an effective title takes practice.

Encourage students who added a title early on to consider that they may need to refine it as they adjust the essay.

Hold a title-writing workshop.

- Students suggest topics.
- The class brainstorms several title choices.
- Volunteers read their work aloud. The class brainstorms titles for these essays.
- Students examine titles from published articles about problems and proposed solutions, in order to get some ideas for their own titles.

Editing Using a Checklist

Check your editing. On a piece of paper, write the numbers 1 to 12. If you can answer "yes" to a question, put a check mark after that number. If not, continue to edit for that convention.

Conventions

PUNCTUATION

_____ **1.** Do I use end punctuation after all my sentences?
_____ **2.** Do I use commas before coordinating conjunctions in compound sentences?
_____ **3.** Do I use a comma after a dependent clause at the beginning of a complex sentence?
_____ **4.** Do I use quotation marks around any direct quotations?

CAPITALIZATION

_____ **5.** Do I start all my sentences with capital letters?
_____ **6.** Do I capitalize all proper nouns and proper adjectives?

SPELLING

_____ **7.** Have I spelled all words correctly?
_____ **8.** Have I double-checked the words my spell-checker may have missed?

GRAMMAR

_____ **9.** Do I form comparative and superlative forms correctly?
_____ **10.** Do I use correct forms of verbs *(had gone,* not *had went)*?
_____ **11.** Do my subjects and verbs agree in number? (Jack and Jill *are* going, not Jack and Jill *is* going)?
_____ **12.** Do I use the right words *(to, too, two)*?

Creating a Title

- Restate the call to action: **Stop the Bulldozers!**
- Write a slogan: **Science Camp for All**
- Be creative: **A Band on the Run**

Grammar Connection

Spelling

- **Proofreader's Guide** pages 642 (+), 644

Tenses

- **Proofreader's Guide** pages 720–721, 724–725
- ***Write Source*** page 481 (helping)
- ***SkillsBook*** pages 165–166, 169–170
- ***GrammarSnap*** Verb Tense Consistency

Pronouns and Pronoun-Antecedent Agreement

- **Proofreader's Guide** pages 712 (+), 714–715
- ***SkillsBook*** pages 157–158, 159–160
- ***GrammarSnap*** Pronoun-Antecedent Agreement

255
Proposing a Solution

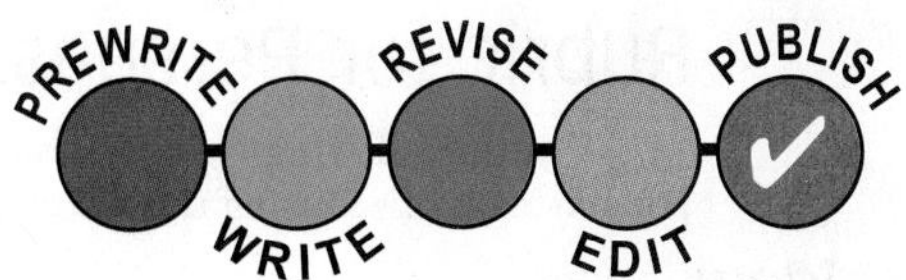

Publishing

Sharing Your Essay

After all your work to write, revise, and edit your problem-solution essay, you'll want to make a neat final copy to share. You may also want to propose your solution to a group, submit it to a newsletter, or advertise it with a poster.

Make a final copy. Follow your teacher's instructions or use the guidelines below to format your essay. (If you are using a computer, see page 60.) Create a clean final copy of your essay and carefully proofread it.

Focus on Presentation

- Use blue or black ink and write neatly.
- Write your name in the upper left corner of page 1.
- Skip a line and center your title; skip another line and start your writing.
- Indent every paragraph and leave a one-inch margin on all four sides.
- Write your last name and the page number in the upper right corner of every page after the first one.

Make an Oral Presentation

Decide what group could help with your solution—your class, the student council, a student club, the PTA or PTO, or some other group. Arrange to present your paper orally at the group's next meeting.

Submit to a School Newspaper or Web Site

Prepare your problem-solution essay for the school newspaper or Web site. Format your paper according to the submission guidelines and send it in.

Create a Poster

Develop a poster based on your essay. Decide what pictures, slogans, and details to include. Create your poster and put it up where it can make a difference.

PERSUASIVE

Publishing

Sharing Your Essay

Organize a way for students to share their work. Have students do one or more of the following:

- Put together one issue of a class newspaper and make it available to all classes.
- **Design a Web site** *(see below)* where the essay topics are discussed.
- Invite interested people to the class to hear presentations about the issues discussed in the essays.
- Create a school display of posters and charts related to the problems and solutions discussed in the essays.

Technology Connections

Remind students that they can use the Writing Network features of the Portfolio to share their work with peers.

Write Source Online **Portfolio**

Write Source Online **Net-text**

Teaching Tip: Designing Web Sites

Designing Web sites may seem like a daunting task, but don't let that stop you from encouraging students to give it a try.

- Investigate whether your Internet service provider (ISP) allows you to have a free Web site.
- Follow any directions offered by the ISP.
- Examine information available online and in books that explains how to go about designing a Web site.

* For more information about publishing online, see SE page 64.

Rubric for Persuasive Writing

Review the six traits of effective writing as reflected in the rubric. Discuss which trait descriptions deal most specifically with persuasive writing (ideas, organization, voice, word choice). Point out that the descriptions about sentence fluency and conventions apply across all forms of writing.

* Reproducible six-, five-, and four-point rubrics for persuasive writing can be found on pages 752, 756, and 760.

Rubric for Persuasive Writing

Use the following rubric as you assess and improve your persuasive writing using the six traits.

Ideas

6	5	4
The clear reasoning informs and convinces the reader.	The essay has a clear opinion statement. Persuasive details support the writer's opinion.	The opinion statement is clear, and most details support the writer's opinion.

Organization

6	5	4
The organization presents a smooth flow of ideas from beginning to end.	The beginning contains the opinion statement. The middle provides clear support. The ending reinforces the writer's opinion.	The beginning contains the opinion statement. The middle provides support. The ending needs work.

Voice

6	5	4
The writer's voice is confident, positive, and completely convincing.	The writer's voice is confident and helps persuade the reader.	The writer's voice is confident. It needs to persuade the reader.

Word Choice

6	5	4
Precise words create a clear message to engage and persuade the audience.	Precise words create a clear message and fit the purpose.	Accurate words create a message. More persuasive words are needed.

Sentence Fluency

6	5	4
The sentences flow smoothly, and people will enjoy reading the variety of sentences.	Variety is seen in both the types of sentences and their beginnings.	Varied sentence beginnings are used. Sentence variety would make the essay more interesting to read.

Conventions

6	5	4
The grammar and punctuation are correct, and all the words are spelled correctly.	Grammar and punctuation errors are few. The reader is not distracted by the errors.	Grammar and punctuation errors are seen in a few sentences. They distract the reader in those areas.

Struggling Learners

Simplify the rubric on SE pages 256–257 for students who may find it overwhelming. Replace the complete sentence descriptions of each rating strip with bulleted key words and phrases.

persuade convince support argue reason 257 Proposing a Solution

3 The opinion statement is clear. More persuasive details are needed.	2 The opinion statement is unclear. Persuasive details are needed.	1 An opinion statement, reasons, and details are needed.
3 The beginning has an opinion statement. The middle and ending need more work.	2 The beginning, middle, and ending run together.	1 The organization is unclear. The reader is easily lost.
3 The writer's voice needs to be more confident and persuade the reader.	2 The writer's voice rambles on without any confidence.	1 The writer's voice can't be heard.
3 More precise and accurate words are needed to create a clear message.	2 The words do not create a clear message.	1 Word choice has not been considered.
3 Varied sentence beginnings are needed. Sentence variety would make the essay more interesting.	2 Most of the sentences begin the same way. Most sentences are simple. Compound and complex sentences are needed.	1 Sentence fluency has not been established. Ideas do not flow smoothly.
3 There are a number of errors that may confuse the reader.	2 Frequent errors make the essay difficult to read.	1 Nearly every sentence contains errors.

Test Prep!

The six traits of writing were first identified in the 1960s by Paul Diederich and a group of 50 professionals who reviewed student papers and brainstormed the qualities that made writing strong. In 1983, a group of educators in Beaverton, Oregon, learned of Diederich's work and replicated it, settling on a similar set of six traits. A separate team in Missoula, Montana, simultaneously ran a study that identified the same basic group of traits.

Thereafter, Northwest Regional Educational Labs (NREL) in Portland and later Great Source in Boston (through Vicki Spandel, who had been a part of the NREL team) did much to teach the world about traits-based instruction.

Put simply, the six traits provide a universal set of criteria for strong writing. They correlate very well to the rubrics used in most state testing. Using the traits throughout the writing process, therefore, prepares students for any writing test they will face.

Evaluating a Persuasive Essay

Ask students if they agree with the sample self-assessment on SE page 259. Then ask them to suggest improvements for "The Right Kind of B-Ball" based on the comments in the self-assessment.

Ideas: more reasons that donkey basketball is a problem—donkey hooves will damage the basketball court, donkeys could bring in a lot of dirt, donkeys could become frightened and bolt into the crowd

Organization: call to action—urge other school members to write to the student council

Voice: more serious tone—stupid, How about, blast, completely cool, tons of cash

Word Choice: more precise and less colloquial language—get money, get the school together, Course, Maybe a rider . . .,

Sentence Fluency: more sentence variety—compound sentences in the second and fourth paragraphs

Conventions: grammar—any more different, affect, splitted, even rougher to try; capitalization—student council, car washes, students

Evaluating a Persuasive Essay

As you read the problem-solution essay that follows, focus on the writer's strengths and weaknesses. Then read the student self-assessment on the next page. **(The student essay below contains some errors.)**

The Right Kind of B-Ball

Every Student Council needs money, and Ellingstad Middle school isn't any more different than others. In the past, student council fund raisers have included Candygrams and Car Washes. These fun activities not only get money but also get the school together. This year's activity, though, is turning into a big stupid problem. Some students may think donkey basketball is a funny sport, but others are worried about the affect on the donkeys.

In donkey basketball, a student team takes on a faculty team both sides have to ride donkeys as they play the game. Course, donkeys are stubborn. Maybe a rider is trying to move down court, the donkey might not want to go. What next? People start shouting at the donkeys, and sometimes they're even rougher to try to make the donkey move. That's when the game stops being funny and starts being a problem. Many Students at Ellingstad say so. Fifty of them signed a petition.

The student Council needs a fund raiser that will get money and be also a blast. The kids that have signed the petition have a solution. Instead of donkey basketball, how about wheelchair basketball?

The Voree Volcanoes are a wheelchair basketball team that have won regional championships. They offer a fund raiser. They play against students and even loan them wheelchairs to use the Volcanoes even spot the student team 50 points! The money would get splitted between the student council and the Volcanoes. This game would be completely cool, would make tons of cash, and would help a great team.

The student council of Ellingstad Middle School may need money, but they also need a fund raiser everybody likes. Donkey basketball is a problem, but wheelchair basketball can be the solution!

English Language Learners

Help students with any terminology they may not know:

- B-Ball (basketball)
- fund raisers (events to earn money for a particular cause)
- Candygrams (candy that is sent to someone along with a message, as you might send a greeting card)
- court (here, *court* refers to the floor on which the game is played)
- blast (here, a colloquial word for a fun time)
- petition (a document that requests a particular action and is signed by people who are in support of the action)
- spot (to give the other team unearned points before the game has begun)

Student Self-Assessment

The assessment that follows includes the student's comments about his essay on page 258. In each first comment, the student mentions something positive from the essay. In each second comment, the student points out an area for possible improvement. (The writer used the rubric and number scale on pages 256–257 to complete this assessment.)

5 Ideas

1. *I included strong details about the problem and solution.*
2. *Some readers won't agree about donkey basketball.*

4 Organization

1. *I followed my plan for organization.*
2. *I forgot to include a call to action.*

3 Voice

1. *I tried to sound confident and persuasive.*
2. *I don't sound serious enough in places.*

3 Word Choice

1. *I cut out most inflammatory words—though "stupid" is still there.*
2. *In some places, my words seem weak.*

3 Sentence Fluency

1. *I used all kinds of sentences.*
2. *Some places don't flow well.*

3 Conventions

1. *I gave myself a 3 because I tried to fix convention problems.*
2. *I bet there are still some problems.*

PERSUASIVE

Use the rubric. Assess your essay using the rubric on pages 256–257.

1. On your own paper, list the six traits. Leave room after each trait to write at least one strength and one weakness.
2. Then choose a number (from 1 to 6) that shows how well you think you used each trait.

To give students additional practice with evaluating a persuasive essay, use a reproducible assessment sheet (TE page 787) and one or both of the **benchmark papers** listed in the Benchmark Papers box below. For your benefit, a completed assessment sheet is provided for each benchmark paper.

Struggling Learners

Help students focus on the self-assessment process.

- Ask them to examine their writing for positive points and areas of improvement for the first three traits (ideas, organization, and voice) in one class period.
- Have them go through their work in a second class period to look for strengths and weaknesses for the remaining three traits (word choice, sentence fluency, and conventions).

Benchmark Papers

Support Our Animal Shelter (strong)

- TE pp. 775–777

Baby-Sitting Isn't for the Untrained (fair)

- TE pp. 778–780

Reflecting on Your Writing

Emphasize that writers need to think about their work even after they complete a final copy. This will help them improve their future work.

Have students date and save their reflections. Each time they add a new one, they should reread earlier reflections to see how they are progressing as writers. Encourage students to notice how their writing skills have improved over time.

Reflecting on Your Writing

Take some time to reflect on the problem-solution essay you have just completed. On your own paper, finish each starter sentence below. Your thoughts will help you prepare for your next writing assignment.

My Problem-Solution Essay

1. *The best part of my essay is . . .*
2. *The part that still needs work is . . .*
3. *The prewriting activity that worked best for me was . . .*
4. *The main thing I learned about writing a persuasive essay is . . .*
5. *In my next problem-solution essay, I would like to . . .*
6. *Here is one question I still have about writing a problem-solution essay:*

Persuasive Writing

Creating an Editorial

Every major newspaper has an "Op/Ed" page, which is short for "Opinion/Editorial." An editorial is a short essay that gives a writer's opinion about a timely event or issue. Many times during the history of our country, editorials have paved the way for great changes.

In this chapter, you will be writing an editorial of your own. Perhaps your school is having a crisis over the food choices in the vending machines. Or maybe some sports teams are arguing over who gets to use the gymnasium after school. In an editorial, you can give your opinion about the events happening around you.

Writing Guidelines

Subject: A school issue
Form: Editorial
Purpose: To persuade the reader
Audience: Classmates

English Language Learners

Help students to summarize ideas in an editorial. Ask them these questions:

- What is the topic of the editorial?
- What opinions does the writer express about the topic?
- What changes does the writer call for?

Creating an Editorial

Objectives

- recognize the structure of an editorial
- use what was learned from the persuasive problem-solution essay to write an editorial
- plan, draft, revise, edit, and share an editorial

Provide students with copies of the local newspaper for the current day. Divide students into groups of three. Ask them to find the Op/Ed page, which is usually opposite the Editorial page. If the newspaper has a table of contents, students may use it to locate the Editorial and Op/Ed pages.

Ask each group to choose an editorial or Op/Ed piece that interests them. Have each group take turns summarizing the piece for the class and explaining why they chose it.

Editorial

Ask students to compare the Op/Ed piece "Let the Kids Choose" to Op/Ed pieces they found for TE page 261. They should look for differences in length, level of formality, and topic.

Students should find the topic of the editorial relevant. Discuss some additional questions about it. For example:

- Do vending machine prices differ from school to school? Why?
- Who decides what is put in the vending machines?
- Should your school install vending machines (if it does not have any)? Explain your answer.
- Does your school limit when the vending machines can be on?

Invite students to do a 5- to 10-minute freewrite about the vending-machine issues in their school.

Editorial

An editorial expresses an opinion about a timely event. The editorial that follows was written by Hassan and published in his local newspaper.

Beginning
The issue is introduced, and the opinion statement is given (underlined).

Let the Kids Choose

A group of parents has asked the school board to remove the vending machines from Lincoln Middle School. They say that the soda and junk foods in the machines are creating bad eating habits among students. These parents are probably right, but removing vending machines won't solve the problem. <u>Lincoln Middle School should keep its vending machines so that students have more food choices, not fewer.</u>

Middle
The middle paragraphs support the writer's opinion.

A healthy diet is based on wise food choices. Removing the vending machines only removes the decisions students have to make about the foods they eat. The problem isn't the machines but what's in them. Machines that now hold only soda could just as easily hold juice, milk, and bottled water. Machines full of candy, cookies, and donuts could hold fruit snacks, nuts, and low-salt pretzels.

That doesn't mean that all the chips, cookies, donuts, and soda should be removed from the machines. If only healthy snacks are provided, students still won't learn anything about making smart choices. Instead, the vending machines should offer wholesome foods and other foods

English Language Learners

Some students need a more concrete way to organize their thoughts. Help them create and fill in a three-column organizer concerning school vending machines.

- Have them label the three columns *Plus, Minus,* and *Interesting*.
- Under *Plus*, they write words or phrases about benefits of the machines.
- Under *Minus*, they write notes related to the problems.
- Under *Interesting*, they write other relevant thoughts about school vending machines that do not fit in the other columns.

Struggling Learners

Introduce "Let the Kids Choose" as an example of an editorial essay.

- Read it aloud while students follow along in their books.
- As students read it a second time on their own, have them focus on the ideas, organization, and word choice.

side by side. Then students will have to learn how to choose for themselves.

Ending
The opinion is summed up in a thoughtful way.

Healthy eating habits begin with wise food choices. Removing the vending machines won't help students learn anything about healthy food choices, but stocking those machines with a mix of foods will.

Bridgewood Gazette

OPINION/EDITORIAL

City Voices: Let the Kids Choose

A group of parents has asked the school board to remove the vending machines from Lincoln Middle School. They say that the soda and junk foods in the machines are creating bad eating habits among students. These parents are probably right, but removing vending machines won't solve the problem. Lincoln Middle School should keep its vending machines so that students have more food choices, not fewer.

A healthy diet is based on wise food choices. Removing the vending machines only removes the decisions students have to make about the foods they eat. The problem isn't the machines but what's in them. Machines that now hold only soda could just as easily hold juice, milk, and bottled water. Machines full of candy, cookies, and donuts could hold fruit snacks, nuts, and low-salt pretzels.

That doesn't mean that all the chips, cookies, donuts, and soda should be removed from the machines. If only healthy snacks are provided, students still won't learn anything about making smart choices. Instead, the vending machines should offer wholesome foods and other foods side by side. Then students will have to learn how to choose for themselves.

Healthy eating habits begin with wise food choices. Removing the vending machines won't help students learn anything about healthy food choices, but stocking those machines with a mix of foods will.

Respond to the reading. Answer the following questions.

- ☐ **Ideas** (1) What is Hassan's opinion? (2) What details offer the strongest support? Name two.
- ☐ **Voice & Word Choice** (3) How would you describe the writer's voice? (4) What words make it sound that way?

Literature Connections: For another example of persuasive writing, read the editorial "Do Professional Athletes Get Paid Too Much?" by Justin Hjelm.

PERSUASIVE

Respond to the reading.

Answers

Answers will vary. Possible answers:

Ideas 1. Keep the vending machines so students can learn how to make good choices.
2. Replace some of what is in the machines with healthier foods; let students learn to make healthy choices by allowing them to have a choice.

Voice & Word Choice 3. confident and convincing
4. Possible choices:
- removing vending machines won't solve the problem
- The problem isn't the machines but what's in them.
- smart choices
- learn how to choose
- Healthy eating habits begin with wise food choices.

Literature Connections

In the editorial "Do Professional Athletes Get Paid Too Much?" Justin Hjelm argues that professional athletes make far too much money. Hjelm anticipates objections to his claim and provides several answers to those objections in order to support his opinion.

Discuss the organization and strengths of the editorial, and encourage students to point out details that make Hjelm's argument persuasive. For additional persuasive models, see the Reading-Writing Connections beginning on page TE-36.

Advanced Learners

Students may want to invite an editor from the local newspaper to visit your class. Students can write questions to ask him or her about some of the editorials that address issues in your community.

Prewriting Selecting a Topic

Students can also brainstorm topics by thinking about their daily schedule. As they list their classes and interactions of the day, they should write down any problems or annoyances that occur regularly. For example, they might note the traffic in the hallway that makes it difficult to get to class on time or the lines in the cafeteria that leave little time to eat.

* Refer students to SE page 546 for some editorial writing prompts.

Prewriting Supporting Your Opinion

If students cannot think of at least three supporting reasons for their opinion, they should

- ask other students who share their opinion, or
- consider choosing another topic.

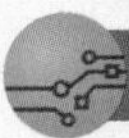

Technology Connections

Students can use the added features of the Net-text as they explore this stage of the writing process.

Write Source Online ***Net-text***

Prewriting Selecting a Topic

An editorial gives an opinion about a current event or issue, so the best way to find a topic for an editorial is to focus on things happening around you. When Hassan received his assignment to write an editorial, he used sentence starters to make a list of all the current events he could think of.

Sentence Starters

At Lincoln Middle School,

the biggest problem is . . . the gym locker rooms are gross.
. . . that some homework is busywork.
the worst change is . . . removing the vending machines.
the one change I would make is . . . adding a study hall.
. . . starting school later!

Use sentence starters. Use the sentence starters above to think about issues or problems in your school. Finish each sentence with your opinion. Review your opinions and choose the one issue that will make the best editorial.

Supporting Your Opinion

Now that you have selected an opinion, it's time to come up with reasons to support it. Hassan used a table diagram. The "tabletop" gives his opinion, and the "table legs" are reasons that support it.

Table Diagram

Opinion	*Lincoln Middle School should keep its vending machines.*		
Support	*students need the chance to choose good foods*	*the problem isn't the machines, but the junk food*	*machines should have all kinds of food in them*

Create a table diagram. Use the sample above as a guide to create your own table diagram. Write your opinion in the top box and your supporting reasons underneath. Come up with at least three reasons.

Struggling Learners

If any students have difficulty completing the writing assignment independently, lead them through the writing process in a small group. Their final product will be a group-authored editorial.

- Choose a topic that is relevant for students. It should be an issue related to the community or the school, such as building a sports facility or cutting funds for a favorite program.
- Choosing a topic students feel strongly about will help them write in a persuasive voice.
- Plan to send the finished piece to the local newspaper. This will motivate students to do their best work. The group writing experience will build confidence and skills.

Refining Your Opinion Statement

Now that you have selected an opinion and come up with reasons to support it, you are ready to write your opinion statement. An effective opinion statement gives your opinion and sums up the reasons for it.

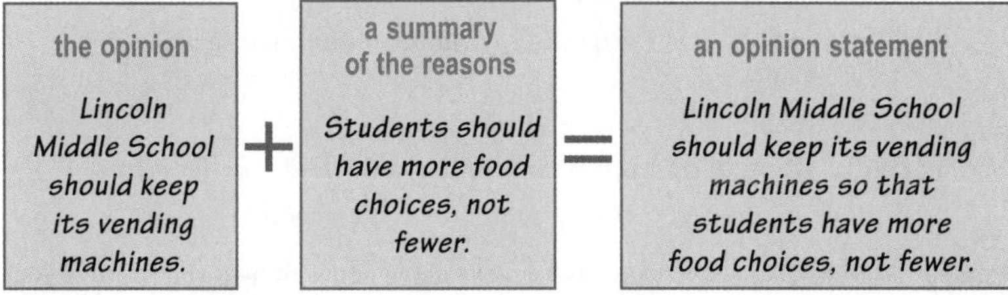

Write an opinion statement. Create an opinion statement that combines your opinion with your reasons. Use the formula above as a guide.

Writing Creating Your First Draft

As you write your editorial, make sure each part does its job.

- **Beginning paragraph:** Introduce your topic and give your opinion statement.
- **Middle paragraphs:** Present your reasons in a logical order or in order of importance. (See page 551 for help.)
- **Closing paragraph:** Reflect on your opinion and reasons and give your reader something to think about.

Write your first draft. Let your table diagram list and the tips above guide you as you write your editorial.

tip Always think about your audience. In order to convince a reader to agree with you, avoid offending her or him. Therefore, don't blame or sharply criticize anyone in your editorial. Also avoid inflammatory words that are likely to make people angry. (See page 246.)

PERSUASIVE

Prewriting Refining Your Opinion Statement

Have students write the two parts of their opinion statement (opinion and summary of reasons) as simple sentences and then combine them into a compound or complex sentence. Suggest that students refer back to SE pages 248–249 for tips on combining sentences.

Writing Creating Your First Draft

Remind students that putting ideas in a logical order means organizing information in a way that makes sense. Most often, the writing begins with the main idea and is followed by details. At times, the details may lead to the main idea.

Arranging information in order of importance means the details are presented either from most to least important, or from least to most important.

* For an example of a paragraph that is organized using order of importance, see SE page 536.

Students can use the added features of the Net-text as they explore this stage of the writing process.

Write Source Online ***Net-text***

Revising Improving Your Writing

Students should review the rubric for persuasive writing on SE pages 256–257 before they revise their drafts.

* For a review of the difference between general and specific nouns, see SE page 471.

Publishing Sharing Your Editorial

To better understand how different audiences affect what issues are addressed in publications, students should

- examine editorials in local newspapers and school publications,
- listen to radio or television editorials, and
- read online newspaper editorials from other areas.

Ask students to identify the intended audience for each editorial.

Technology Connections

Have students use the Writing Network features of the Net-text to comment on each other's drafts.

Write Source Online ***Net-text***

Revising Improving Your Writing

Revise your first draft by focusing on the following traits of writing.

- ☐ **Ideas** Do I clearly state my opinion? Do I provide supporting reasons? Do I include details for each reason?
- ☐ **Organization** Do I organize my sentences and paragraphs in the best order?
- ☐ **Voice** Is my voice polite and convincing?
- ☐ **Word Choice** Do I use strong action verbs and specific nouns?
- ☐ **Sentence Fluency** Do my sentences read smoothly?

Revise your editorial. Use the questions above to help you improve your writing.

Editing Checking for Conventions

Once you finish revising your editorial, polish it by focusing on *conventions.*

- ☐ **Conventions** Have I checked for errors in punctuation, capitalization, spelling, and grammar?

Edit your editorial. Check the conventions in your writing. Make a clean final draft and proofread it for any remaining errors.

Publishing Sharing Your Editorial

Because editorials share opinions about timely events or issues, this type of writing is made for publication. To find the right place to publish your editorial, ask yourself the following questions.

- Who is my audience? (Classmates? Parents? People in the community? People who belong to a specific organization?)
- What publication do these people read? (A local newspaper? A school paper or Web site? A PTO or PTA newsletter?)
- How can I submit my editorial to this publication? (What are the guidelines? How should I send in my writing?)

Publish your editorial. Use the questions above to help you find the right place to send your editorial for publication. Prepare your work according to the submission guidelines and send it in.

Grammar Connection

Sentence Combining

- ***Proofreader's Guide*** page 698 (+)
- ***Write Source*** pages 498 (+), 515 (+), 516 (+), 517 (+)
- ***SkillsBook*** pages 75–76, 127–128
- ***GrammarSnap*** Simple, Compound, and Complex Sentences

Using the Right Word

- ***Proofreader's Guide*** pages 678–683
- ***SkillsBook*** page 65

End Punctuation

- ***SkillsBook*** pages 5–6

English Language Learners

Note that the word *edit* is the root of the words *editorial* and *editor.*

- Ask students to look up each of these words in the dictionary and record the definitions.
- Discuss the skills students are learning to use in their editing.

Talk about what an editor does (find the right words, craft careful sentences, and check copy for correctness).

Advanced Learners

If students have trouble getting their editorials published, have advanced learners develop and edit a publication that includes the editorials written by the class.

Persuasive Writing

Across the Curriculum

Some people think it's tough to be persuasive, but guinea pigs disagree. They use one sound to persuade their owners to feed them: "Reeeeeeeet!" They use another sound to persuade their owners to pet them: "Puuuuurrrrrr!" Imagine that! With two simple sounds, a guinea pig can persuade people to do just what it wants. You can be just as persuasive as a guinea pig—both in and out of school—by using convincing words and ideas.

In this chapter, you will see how persuasive writing is used in many settings. For example, in social studies, you may write a campaign speech. In math, you may compile data into a persuasive graph. For science, you may write a proposal for a science-fair project. And beyond the classroom, you may write a persuasive letter to convince someone to take action. Finally, you'll even learn how to be persuasive on a writing test.

What's Ahead

- **Social Studies:** Writing a Campaign Speech
- **Math:** Creating a Graph
- **Science:** Writing a Proposal
- **Practical Writing:** Drafting a Business Letter

Across the Curriculum

Objectives

- apply what students have learned about persuasive writing to other curriculum areas
- practice writing for assessment

The lessons on the following pages provide samples of persuasive writing students might do in different content areas. The particular form used in one content area may also be used in another content area (for example, students can create a graph just as well in social studies or science as in math).

Assigning these forms of writing will depend on

- the skill level of your students,
- the subject matter they are studying at a particular time, and
- the writing goals of your school, district, or state.

Social Studies:
Writing a Campaign Speech

Discuss whether students have heard campaign speeches by candidates during elections for national, state, or local office. Examine the model campaign speech with them.

- Ask students to explain why this speech can be considered a persuasive form of writing. (The writer tries to persuade listeners to vote for him.)
- Discuss how this speech differs from the persuasive writing that students have done so far. (Instead of discussing a problem or an opinion, the writer discusses his qualifications as a candidate.)

Social Studies: Writing a Campaign Speech

In a democracy, leaders are chosen by a vote, and candidates give speeches to persuade people to vote for them. The following speech was written by a middle school student running for student council president.

Elect Suzie Ruiz!

The **beginning** grabs the listeners' attention and presents the main issue.

Have you, or any of your friends, had to serve a detention at Garfield Middle School this year? Do you know someone who had to eat lunch in the office? Many students have felt the effects of the new policies here at Garfield. Even though the ideas behind these rules are good, we want to make sure the new policies are fair to everyone. If you elect me president of the student council, I will work with Principal MacKekkin and the school board to change the way these policies are applied.

The **middle** provides reasons for the main issue.

I'm calling for a student court in which peers can advise the principal about a student who may have broken a rule. The student court can make sure all students receive reasonable punishments. It also can take the burden off Principal MacKekkin and the teachers of always being "the bad guys."

This paragraph lists the qualifications of the candidate.

My opponents promise that they will make life here at Garfield better, but they are not offering any real suggestions about how they will do it. I am. In addition to my idea of a student court, I have plans for new fund-raisers and other activities. I am well qualified to represent students from across the student body. I play clarinet in band, write for the school paper, and run track. I'm a good student and a good listener.

The **ending** calls for listeners to vote.

So, if you want someone who will fight for student rights, elect Suzie Ruiz. Thank you for your time and for your votes!

English Language Learners

Be sure students understand the meanings of the following words and phrases as they are used in the speech:

- serve a detention (stay after school for disobeying a rule)
- ideas behind (reasons)
- applied (used)
- take the burden off (share the responsibility)

Advanced Learners

To provide more examples of campaign speeches for the entire class, ask students to conduct research on campaign speeches of past presidential candidates. Discuss whether the candidate's ideas, voice, and word choice were effective in getting the candidate elected.

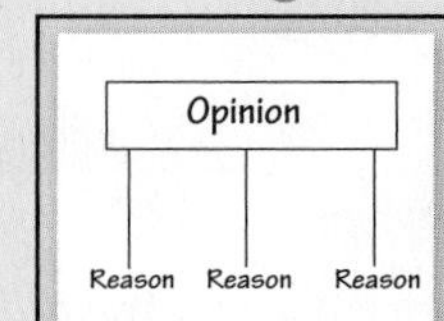

Writing Tips

Before you write . . .

Table Diagram

- **Decide on a main issue for your campaign speech.**
  Choose one main reason for your campaign. Make sure it is something students care about and can easily remember.
- **Organize your speech.**
  Think of an opening statement that will grab the listeners' attention. Plan the other points you will make and write down your qualifications.

During your writing . . .

- **Use details and examples.**
  Be specific about what you have to offer to voters and make your main reason a strong one.
- **Be concise.**
  Don't let your speech run on for very long. Make each sentence count and make sure each paragraph follows logically.
- **Be dramatic.**
  Show that you feel strongly about representing your listeners.

After you've written a first draft . . .

- **Review your beginning and ending.**
  Make sure you get the listeners' attention and leave them with a memorable call for votes.
- **Read the speech aloud and check its length.**
  Smooth out any places where you trip over the words. Time your performance to make sure it fits within the time allowed. If possible, tape your speech, or read it to a friend. Ask for comments. (See pages 423–430.)

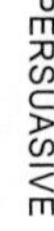

Imagine that you are running for student council. Write a short speech to convince your classmates to elect you.

Writing Tips

Emphasize the need for candidates to consider the audience for their campaign speeches. If candidates want to earn votes, they need to know what the audience wants and find ways to convince the audience that they can provide those things.

Try It Answers

Answers will vary, but students should include a main issue, have a good beginning and ending, use details, and be concise.

English Language Learners

To help students come up with a topic, have them brainstorm as a class:

- Identify a few issues pertinent to your school.
- Write these issues on the board.
- Invite students to express their views about each issue before they begin writing.
- Record the ideas that students express; write key words and phrases under each issue listed on the board.
- Suggest that students pick one issue as the writing idea for their campaign speech.

Advanced Learners

Ask students to deliver part (or all) of a presidential campaign speech they discovered in their research for the **Advanced Learners** activity on TE page 268. If possible, have them find speeches of rival candidates, and ask two volunteers to deliver them. Discuss what issues were important at the time of the campaign.

Math: Creating a Graph

Ask students to find examples of graphs in newspapers, brochures, and magazines. Discuss the ways in which **graphs** can be **misleading** *(see below).*

Math: Creating a Graph

Statistics can be very persuasive, especially when they appear in a graph. The following report was written by a student who wanted to show the health risks of smoking.

The **beginning** introduces the topic.

The **middle** introduces the graph and provides statistics.

The **ending** gives the source of the information.

Up in Smoke

What is in the cigarette smoke that makes it so harmful? Most people know that it contains two deadly substances: nicotine and tar. People may not also know that the cigarette smoke contains poison gases like carbon monoxide, ammonia, formaldehyde, and hydrogen cyanide.

As the chart below shows, cigarette smoke kills both smokers and nonsmokers. Between 2000 and 2006, the number of Americans who died from secondhand smoke was more than a hundred thousand. Among smokers, there were nearly half a million deaths per year. The message is clear: smoking kills smokers and nonsmokers alike.

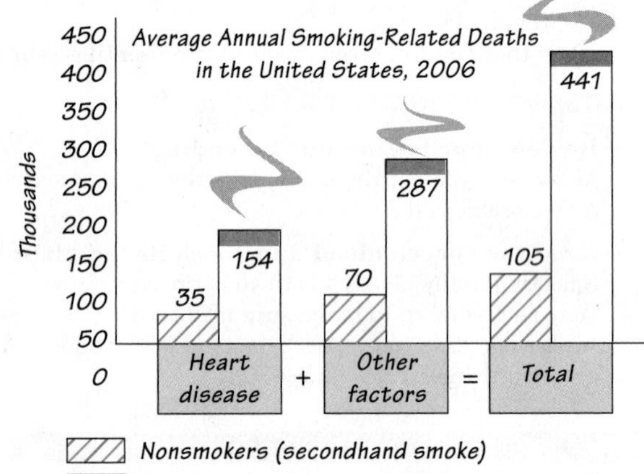

Source: American Heart Association

Teaching Tip: Misleading Graphs

Students may not understand how data can be misleading. Explain that when a person makes a graph, she or he has to decide what interval of numbers to use. By making the increments too small or too large, the person can make the graph appear convincing when the figures really aren't. Draw an example on the board to illustrate the point (for example, an increase in class size from 25 to 30 would look very different if the vertical axis were in increments of 1 instead of in increments of 10).

Another way graphs can be misleading is if they represent data collected from a small, biased sample. Help students create accurate graphs in their work.

Struggling Learners

As students examine examples of graphs, have them use a table diagram to identify the main idea and two or three supporting details communicated by each graph.

Writing Tips

Before you write . . .

- **Decide what you are trying to prove.**
  State your opinion in a simple sentence, such as "Smoking kills smokers and nonsmokers alike." Keep your focus in mind as you create your graph.
- **Research thoroughly.**
  Look at several well-respected sources. Find statistics that help you prove your opinion.
- **Plan your graph.**
  Decide how to make the information most persuasive. Consider different kinds of graphs, such as pie, line, or bar graphs. (See page 575.)

During your writing . . .

- **Record the date.**
  Write the date of each learning-log entry.
- **Quickly introduce your topic.**
  Give background information. Then write a few sentences that will help the reader understand what your graph shows.
- **Use colors and strong images.**
  Dress up your graph, but make sure that the reader will have no difficulty understanding what you are trying to show.
- **Cite your sources.**
  List where you got the statistics for your graph.

After you've written a first draft . . .

- **Check your math.**
  Return to your sources to make sure your dates and numbers are correct.
- **Create a final version of your graph..**
  Make sure your graph is correct and clean. Proofread it a final time.

Think of a health or fitness issue. Write an opinion that you think you can prove with a graph. Then research the topic to find the numbers you want. Finally, create a persuasive graph.

Writing Tips

Remind students who use the Internet as a source for information that **Web sites** *(see below)* that end in *.edu, .org,* or *.gov* usually have more dependable data.

Give students guidance in choosing reasonable topics that can be illustrated by graphs.

 **Answers**

Answers will vary, but students should introduce the topic and the graph, do careful research, and have a source for their information.

Teaching Tip: Web Sites

Monitor students' Web use to insure they are using their time wisely.

- Model how to choose effective keywords for searches.
- Remind them that information on the Internet isn't always accurate.
- Discuss how to recognize dependable sites.
- Urge them to use at least two reliable sources.

Struggling Learners

Have students collect data in their own classroom. For example, they might

- survey students about the kinds of homework they find most useful,
- create a graph to show the results, and
- write a paragraph to persuade you to focus on those types of assignments.

Advanced Learners

For the **Try It** activity, encourage students to select a health or fitness issue that has affected a family member or friend (such as a friend with exercise-induced asthma). Challenge them to represent their statistics on several types of graphs (such as pie, bar, and line graphs) and to star the most persuasive format.

Science: Writing a Proposal

Consult with the science teacher about the timing of this section. Many middle schools require students to complete a science-fair project. Students will be more motivated to do this assignment if they are actually submitting a proposal for a real project.

If necessary, alter the assignment by asking students to write a proposal to a teacher of their choice that describes a long-term project they are willing to undertake.

Suggest that students choose a topic they know something about. For example, they might explore a project related to

- skateboarding
- swimming
- climbing
- food preparation
- baby-sitting
- caring for a pet

Science: Writing a Proposal

A well-written proposal can give you an advantage. In the proposal below, a student outlines a science-fair project and asks his teacher for approval.

Traction and Four-Wheel Drive

The **beginning** describes the project.

Description: I'd like to test how well a motorized model truck climbs surfaces made of different materials and at different angles. I will create graphs to show how far and how fast the truck climbs in each situation.

The **middle** tells about the materials, the schedule, and the procedure.

Materials: I will use a radio-controlled four-wheel drive model truck, a plank, a protractor, a stopwatch, graph paper, and colored pencils. The different surface materials will include the following: water, aluminum foil, sandpaper, and loose sand.

Schedule: By March 2, I will have the materials collected and put together. By March 9, I will have run all my tests for different materials at different angles. By March 16, my display will be ready for the science fair.

Procedure:

- For each surface, the plank will be pitched at 10°, 20°, 30°, 40°, and 50°.
- First, I will test the plain wooden ramp at each pitch.
- Then I will repeat the experiment with the plank wet, with the plank coated with aluminum foil, coated with sandpaper, and finally coated with loose sand.
- I will create graphs displaying how far and how fast the truck climbed in each situation.

The **ending** focuses on the expected results.

Conclusion: I believe this experiment will show different levels of traction. Please let me know if this proposal is accepted. Any suggestions are welcome.

Advanced Learners

When appropriate, encourage students to cite research and include drawings or diagrams to enhance their proposals.

Writing Tips

Before you write . . .

- **Select a topic.** Find a science topic that interests you.
- **Plan your project.** Think of how to demonstrate or test your topic. What materials will you need?
- **Organize the proposal.** Follow the proposal format your teacher gives you or use the sample on page 272 as a guide. A graphic organizer such as a time line could help you plan your writing.

Time Line

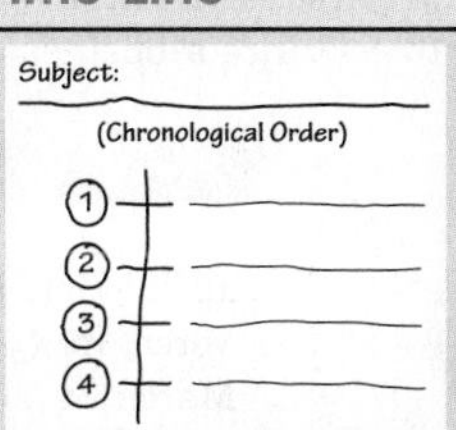

During your writing . . .

- **Be complete.** Give a quick overview of the project. Then list materials, provide a schedule, and talk about the procedure you will follow.
- **Be concise.** Get right to the point. Include only necessary information and important details.

After you've written a first draft . . .

- **Check for completeness.** Review your proposal as if you were the teacher and knew nothing about your idea. List any questions you might have. Then revise the proposal so that it answers those questions.
- **Edit your proposal.** Check your punctuation, capitalization, spelling, and grammar. Proofread your final copy.

PERSUASIVE

Try It Imagine a science-fair project you would be interested in doing. Using the tips above, write a proposal for it.

English Language Learners

Provide books that describe simple science experiments.

- Have students select an experiment and write a proposal that tells what they plan to do and why they would like to do it.
- Ask each student to use a storyboard format (see SE page 414) with captioned illustrations to show the steps of the experiment.

Writing Tips

Note that students may need to do some research on a project in order to write a proposal that includes a list of specific materials, a reasonable time frame, and a clear procedure. Help them focus their research efforts. Suggest that for their topic, some students may wish to replicate an experiment.

Answers

Answers will vary, but students should explain how they will demonstrate the topic and provide a materials list, a schedule, and a summary of the procedure.

Practical Writing:
Drafting a Business Letter

Have students send their letters to a community member. Discuss how this builds a good partnership between the school and the community.

Have students share any responses they receive.

- This will motivate students and reward their efforts.
- Post each response in the classroom with a copy of the student's persuasive letter.

Point out that an effective business letter is an example of persuasive writing at its best.

- The letter persuades the recipient to take action.
- It includes descriptive and expository details to convince the reader.

Practical Writing:
Drafting a Business Letter

In real-world situations, one of the best ways to get something done is to write a persuasive letter. The letter below was written by a student who wanted to convince a business owner to buy some guinea pigs from her.

The letter follows the correct format. (See pages 276–277.)

1212 Maple Park
Voree, IN 46300
March 24, 2011

Bruce Reynolds, Owner
Pet Project Pet Store
341 Jones Street
Voree, IN 46300

Dear Mr. Reynolds:

The **beginning** introduces the issue and asks a question.

Last year I bought two long-haired guinea pigs from your store, and this year we have five guinea pigs. Are you interested in buying the three babies? They are all female and six weeks old, and I have included pictures of them. We would like to sell them back to you if you are interested.

The **body** of the letter uses details to persuade the reader.

Our veterinarian checked the three babies, and they are in fine health. We also had the veterinarian neuter the father so that we won't have more guinea pigs to care for.

The **closing** includes a polite call to action.

Please let me know if you are interested in buying our guinea pigs. You may call me at 555-9770 after 3:30 p.m. Otherwise, I will create fliers to sell them myself. Thanks for your time.

Sincerely,

Jessica Botticini

Jessica Botticini

Grammar Connection

Commas (Dates, Addresses)

- **Proofreader's Guide** pages 582 (+)
- ***SkillsBook*** pages 11–12

Writing Tips

Use the following tips as a guide when you are asked to write a persuasive letter.

Before you write . . .

- **Select a topic.**
  Think of something you would like another person to do—send you information, join a club, or come to your school.
- **Gather information.**
  Collect all the details your reader will need to know in order to be persuaded.

During your writing . . .

- **Get right to the point.**
  Identify yourself and tell the person why you are writing. Give only important details.
- **Be businesslike.**
  Write in a clear, business-like voice. Be reasonable in any requests you make.
- **Provide an easy response.**
  Make sure there is an easy way that your reader can agree to help. For example, you could enclose a response postcard with your name and address filled in and postage paid.

After you've written a first draft . . .

- **Check for completeness.**
  Make sure you have given the reader all the information he or she needs.
- **Check for correctness.**
  Double-check names and addresses and all facts. Proofread your letter for errors in punctuation, capitalization, spelling, and grammar.

PERSUASIVE

Try It Think of a problem in your school or community. Come up with a solution and decide on a person who could help get the job done. Write a persuasive business letter to that person. (You may send the letter, or you may simply treat it as a school assignment.)

Advanced Learners

Discuss local charities and their missions (examples: homeless shelter—house, feed, and clothe homeless people; literacy program—teach people to read; animal rescue league—shelter and find homes for stray animals).

Ask students to

- choose one charity to assist (consult the school's principal or parent-teacher organization);
- brainstorm ways to help (raising money, gathering supplies, providing volunteers);
- create a list of local and regional businesses that could donate money, items, or services;
- work with a partner to write a persuasive business letter to one company; and
- as a follow-up, write thank-you notes to contributors.

Writing Tips

A quick way for students to find effective topics is to revisit the problem-solution essay (SE pages 223–260) or editorial (SE pages 261–266) that they wrote. Writing to a local community member who is in some way connected to the issue they chose will make the letter more meaningful.

Answers

Answers will vary but should include the correct format and a request and details that will help persuade the person to agree.

Parts of a Business Letter

Do not assume that students know how to address envelopes. This skill needs explicit, direct instruction. Share these steps with students:

- Print or write the address neatly in the center of the envelope. Include the name, street address, city and state, and Zip Code.
- Print or write the complete return address neatly in the upper-left corner of the envelope.
- Place the stamp in the upper-right corner of the envelope.

Model how to fold a business letter in thirds so that when the reader opens it, he or she sees the greeting of the letter first.

Distribute samples of business envelopes so that students can place their folded letters in them.

276

Parts of a Business Letter

1. The **heading** includes your address and the date. Write the heading at least one inch from the top of the page at the left-hand margin.
2. The **inside address** includes the name and address of the person or organization you are writing to.
   - If the person has a title, be sure to include it. (If the title is short, write it on the same line as the name. If the title is long, write it on the next line.)
   - If you are writing to an organization or a business—but not to a specific person—begin the inside address with the name of the organization or business.
3. The **salutation** is the greeting. Always put a colon after the salutation.
   - If you know the person's name, use it in your greeting.
     Dear Mr. Christopher:
   - If you don't know the name of the person who will read your letter, use a salutation like one of these:
     Dear Store Owner:
     Dear Sir or Madam:
     Dear Madison Soccer Club:
4. The **body** is the main part of the letter. Do not indent the paragraphs in your letter; instead, skip a line after each one.
5. The **closing** comes after the body. Use **Yours truly** or **Sincerely** to close a business letter. Capitalize only the first word of the closing and put a comma after the closing.
6. The **signature** ends the letter. If you are using a computer, leave four spaces after the closing; then type your name. Write your signature in the space between the closing and the typed name.

See page 577 for more about writing letters as well as a set of guidelines for addressing envelopes properly.

Grammar Connection

Capitalization

- **Proofreader's Guide** pages 618–619, 626–627
- ***SkillsBook*** pages 51–52, 53–54

English Language Learners

Make overhead transparencies of the letter on SE page 274 or other examples of business letters. Use the transparencies to point out the parts as you introduce the information on this page.

Advanced Learners

Discuss how the U.S. Postal Service has standardized the addressing of envelopes. Ask students to think about why the guidelines advocate using all capital letters and no punctuation.

* Refer students to SE page 577 for samples of letter and envelope formats.

Business-Letter Format

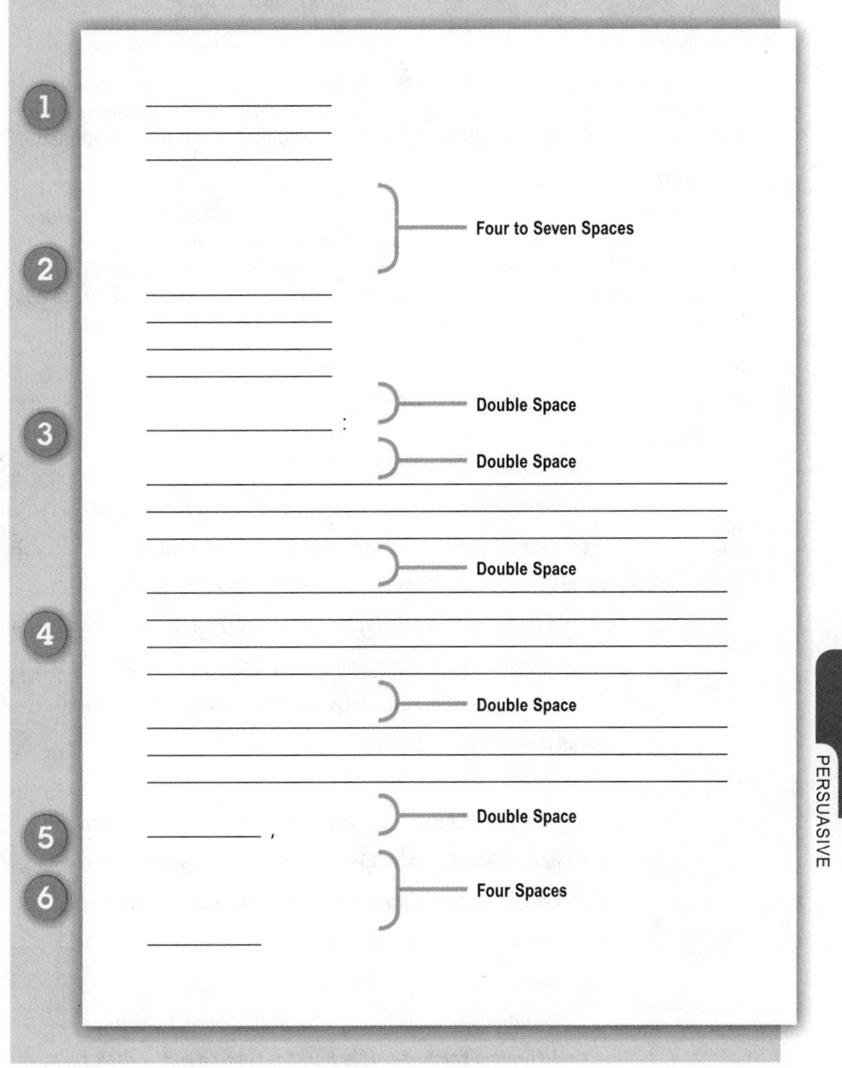

Business-Letter Format

This is a good opportunity to use technology, since many software products offer business-letter templates.

Students often have difficulty lining up their margins correctly when writing on lined notebook paper. If they are writing by hand, have students lightly rule lines on writing paper as guides for left and right margins. Similarly, if they are writing on unlined paper, suggest that they place the paper on top of a piece of lined paper. If necessary, they can darken the lines with a pen so that they show through to the writing paper.

Writing for Assessment

If your students must take school, district, or state assessments this year, focus on the writing form on which they will be tested.

Review the main traits of this kind of persuasive writing (listed below) before working through the model and before doing the activity that follows:

- a clearly stated opinion
- reasons to support the opinion
- logical organization that flows
- convincing language
- call to action

Consider having students respond to the prompt on SE page 278. They will find writing their own version of the sample answer an easier task than writing to an entirely new prompt. This will help prepare them to respond to the prompts on SE page 280 entirely on their own.

Persuasive Writing

Writing for Assessment

Many state and school writing tests ask you to respond to a persuasive prompt. A persuasive prompt asks you to state an opinion and support it with convincing reasons. Study the following sample prompt and student response.

Persuasive Prompt

The student council in your school has money to spend for something that will benefit all students. The suggestions include new computers, more assemblies, and a new scoreboard for the gymnasium. Students can suggest other choices, as well. Write a letter to the student council to persuade them to spend their money in the way that you think is best.

The **beginning** includes the opinion statement (**underlined**).

Each **middle** paragraph gives reasons that support the opinion.

Dear Student Council President:

The student council representative in Room 119 reported this morning that money is available for something that will benefit all students. The money should be spent to buy laptop computers that students could check out of the media center.

Students who don't have a computer at home could check out a laptop to do assignments. Papers look much better when they are done on a computer, and all students should have the chance to hand in work that will get them a good grade. Even students who already have a computer at home might need to use a school laptop because their brothers or sisters are always using the home computer.

School laptops would also end all those problems with different formats. It's frustrating to get a disk from

persuade convince support argue reason
Writing for Assessment 279

school that won't run on a home computer. It's worse to bring a disk from home and find out the school computer can't read the assignment. Also, Mrs. Jones in the media center is always complaining about students accidentally infecting school computers with viruses from their home computers. School laptops with virus protection would help end all those problems.

Finally, laptops would help with computer literacy. Students get to work in the media center once a week right now, but that's just not enough time. When big papers are due, the media center is overloaded. More computers—especially ones that could be checked out—would help more students become computer literate.

The **ending** closes the essay with a call to action (**underlined**).

Buying laptops for the media center is something that can benefit all students. Please spend the funds on computers that all students can use.

Sincerely,
Olivia Lopez

PERSUASIVE

Respond to the reading. Answer the following questions about the sample response.

- ☐ **Ideas** (1) What is the writer's opinion? (2) How many supporting paragraphs are included in the essay?
- ☐ **Organization** (3) How is the essay organized—by time, location, or point by point?
- ☐ **Voice & Word Choice** (4) How would you describe the writer's voice in this essay (humorous, serious, angry)? (5) What words from the prompt also appear in the essay?

Respond to the reading.

Answers

Ideas 1. The money should be used to buy laptop computers.
2. three

Organization 3. point by point

Voice & Word Choice 4. serious
5. student council, computers, money . . . for something that will benefit all students, spend

Writing Tips

Point out that students must approach writing-on-demand assignments differently from open-ended writing assignments.

Persuasive Prompts

Allow students the same amount of time to write their response essay as they will be allotted on school, district, or state assessments. Break down each part of the process into clear chunks of time. For example, you might give students

- 10 minutes for reading, note taking, and planning,
- 25 minutes for writing,
- 10 minutes for editing and proofreading.

Tell students when time is up for each section. Start the assignment at the top of the hour or at the half-hour to make it easier for students to keep track of the time.

Writing Tips

Before you write . . .

- **Understand the prompt.** Remember that a persuasive prompt asks you to state and support an opinion.
- **Plan your time.** Spend a few minutes planning before you start to write. Use a graphic organizer (table diagram) as a guide.

Table Diagram

Opinion

Reason Reason Reason

During your writing . . .

- **Form an opinion statement.** Think of an opinion that you can clearly support.
- **Build your argument.** Think of reasons that support your opinion.
- **End effectively.** Tell readers what you would like to see done.

After you've written a first draft . . .

- **Check for clear ideas.** Rewrite any ideas that sound confusing.
- **Check for conventions.** Correct errors in punctuation, spelling, capitalization, and grammar.

Persuasive Prompts

- Your parents are thinking about forbidding you to watch television during the school week. How do you feel about that? Write a letter to your parents expressing your opinion.
- What would the ideal lunch menu for the day look like? The food should be both good tasting and good for you. Write an essay to convince your school principal to adopt your menu.

Plan and write a response. Respond to one of the prompts above. Complete your writing within the period of time your teacher gives you. Then, list one part that you like and one part that could have been better.

Struggling Learners

Tell students to turn each statement under the bullets in "During your writing. . ." into a question:

- What is your opinion?
- What reasons support it?
- What would you like to see done?

Ask students to list words and phrases under each question. They can turn these notes into sentences to use in their response.

Persuasive Writing in Review

Purpose: In persuasive writing, you work to *convince* people to think the way you do about something.

Topics: Persuade readers . . . to agree with your opinion,
to take an action,
to support a cause, or
to solve a problem.

Prewriting

Select a topic that you care about, one that you can present confidently and that is appropriate for your audience. (See page 228.)

Gather details about your topic. (See page 229.)

Organize your ideas in a list or an outline. Put your opinion statement at the top, followed by topic sentences and supporting details. (See page 232.)

Writing

In the beginning, give background information and clearly state your opinion. (See page 235.)

In the middle, write a paragraph for each main point. Use supporting facts and examples to persuade your reader. (See pages 236–237.)

In the ending, answer an objection, restate your opinion, and make a call to action. (See page 238.)

Revising

Review the ideas, organization, and voice first. Next, check for **word choice** and **sentence fluency.** Avoid inflammatory words. Use a confident, persuasive voice and a variety of sentences. (See pages 240–250.)

Editing

Check your writing for conventions. Ask a friend to edit the writing, too. (See pages 252–254.)

Make a final copy and proofread it for errors before sharing it with your audience. (See page 255.)

Assessing

Use the persuasive rubric as a guide to assess your finished writing. (See pages 256–257.)

Persuasive Writing in Review

Advise students to use this page as a reference when they begin persuasive writing for any class. As they become more familiar with the writing form, they will need to refer to the list less frequently.

Response to Literature Overview

Common Core Standards Focus

Writing 9: Draw evidence from literary or informational texts to support analysis, reflection, and research.

Language 2: Demonstrate command of the conventions of standard English capitalization, punctuation, and spelling when writing.

Writing Forms

- Response Paragraph
- Interpreting a Story
- Poetry Review

Focus on the Traits

- **Ideas** Developing a clear focus statement that shows a specific insight into a character and states the theme
- **Organization** Creating flow from idea to idea with transitions
- **Voice** Using an interested voice that matches the feeling of the story
- **Word Choice** Choosing clear, concise words and words with the right connotations
- **Sentence Fluency** Achieving clarity, flow, and smoothness by combining short, choppy sentences and by fixing run-on sentences
- **Conventions** Checking for errors in punctuation, capitalization, spelling, and grammar

Literature Connections

- **"Serf on the Run"** by Rebecca Barnhouse
- **"Three Essays on *Barrio Boy*"** (a selection from Holt McDougal *Elements of Literature*)

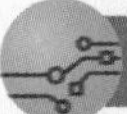

Technology Connections

Write Source Online
www.hmheducation.com/writesource

- ***Net-text***
- ***Bookshelf***
- ***GrammarSnap***
- ***Portfolio***
- ***Writing Network features***
- ***File Cabinet***

Interactive Whiteboard Lessons

Suggested Response to Literature Unit (Four Weeks)

Week	Day	Writing and Skills Instruction	Student Edition: Respose to Literature Unit	Student Edition: Resource Units*	SkillsBook	Daily Language Workouts	Write Source Online
Week 1	1–3	**Response Paragraph: Character** (Model)	283–286			48–49, 99	*Interactive Whiteboard Lessons*
		Skills Activities: • Punctuating Titles		600 (+), 602–603	33–34		
	opt.	*Speeches*	428–429				
	4–5	**Book Review: An Interpretation** Literature Connections "Serf on the Run"	287–290				
		(Prewriting)	291–294				*Net-text*

* These units are also located in the back of the Teacher's Edition. Resource Units include "Basic Grammar and Writing," "A Writer's Resource," and "Proofreader's Guide."
(+) This activity is located in a different section of the *Write Source Student Edition.* If students have already completed this activity, you may wish to review it at this time.

Week	Day	Writing and Skills Instruction	Student Edition: Respose to Literature Unit	Student Edition: Resource Units*	SkillsBook	Daily Language Workouts	Write Source Online
Week 2	6	(Writing)	295–300			50–51, 100	*Net-text*
	7–8	(Revising)	301–312				*Net-text*
		Skills Activities: • Word Choice		472–473, 482 (+)	141–142		
		• Run-On Sentences		506 (+)	95–95		
		• Combining Sentences (appositives)		512	133–134		
		• Verbs (active vs. passive)		482 (+), 726–727			
	9–10	(Editing)	313–316				*Net-text*
		Skills Activities: • Verb Tenses (shifts in tense)		483, 724 (+)			
		• Punctuating Appositives		512 (+), 588 (+)	21–22		
		• Irregular Verbs		481 (+) (irregular), 722–723	167–168		
		• Subject-Verb Agreement		508 (+), 509 (+), 694–695	107–108		
Week 3	11	(Assessing) (Publishing) (Reflecting)	318–321, 317, 322			52–53, 101	*Portfolio, Net-text*
	opt.	*Speeches*	428–429				
	12	Response Writing for Assessment	336–341				
	13	**Poetry Review** (Model) Literature Connections "Three Essays on *Barrio Boy*"	323–325				
	14	(Prewriting)	326				*Net-text*
	15	(Writing)	327				*Net-text*
Week 4	16-19	(Revising)	328			54–55, 102	*Net-text*
		Skills Activities: • Complex Sentences (with relative pronouns)		514, 706 (+)	129–130		*GrammarSnap*
		(Editing, Publishing)	328				*Net-text*
		Skills Activities: • Using the Right Word		658–659			
		• Subject-Verb Agreement		508 (+), 509 (+)	109		*GrammarSnap*
	20	Writing Across the Curriculum	329–333				

* These units are also located in the back of the Teacher's Edition. Resource Units include "Basic Grammar and Writing," "A Writer's Resource," and "Proofreader's Guide."
(+) This activity is located in a different section of the *Write Source Student Edition.* If students have already completed this activity, you may wish to review it at this time.

Teacher's Notes for Response to Literature

This overview for response to literature includes some specific teaching suggestions for this unit.

Writing Focus

Response Paragraph (pages 283–286)

The sample response paragraph in this chapter distills the essential features of the main character. Of course, the author has written much more, but this paragraph highlights the important aspects of the protagonist. By writing such paragraphs, students learn to write succinct book reviews, a handy skill for future class work. Also, students develop the talent to share with each other the central themes and characters of a book.

Interpreting a Story (pages 287–322)

Every English class will expect students to interpret what they have read or are reading. The point of that expectation is to get readers to think. Is the material well written or worthwhile? Does it have some insight about living? Is it good enough to recommend to a friend? By raising those questions, students will find their reading becomes even more valuable.

Poetry Review (pages 323–328)

Since poetry is written to express thoughts, feelings, and insights about life, readers often wrestle with what the poet is saying. That's because poets tend to use a phrase or a word in an unexpected way. There is more to a poem than mere words would suggest. Encouraging your students to think about what a poem means is a good start. A sample poetry review is included.

Grammar Focus

For support with this unit's grammar topics, consult the resource units (Basic Grammar and Writing, A Writer's Resource, and Proofreader's Guide).

Academic Vocabulary

Read aloud the academic terms, as well as the descriptions and questions. Model for students how to read one question and answer it. Have partners monitor their understanding and seek clarification of the terms by working through the meanings and questions together.

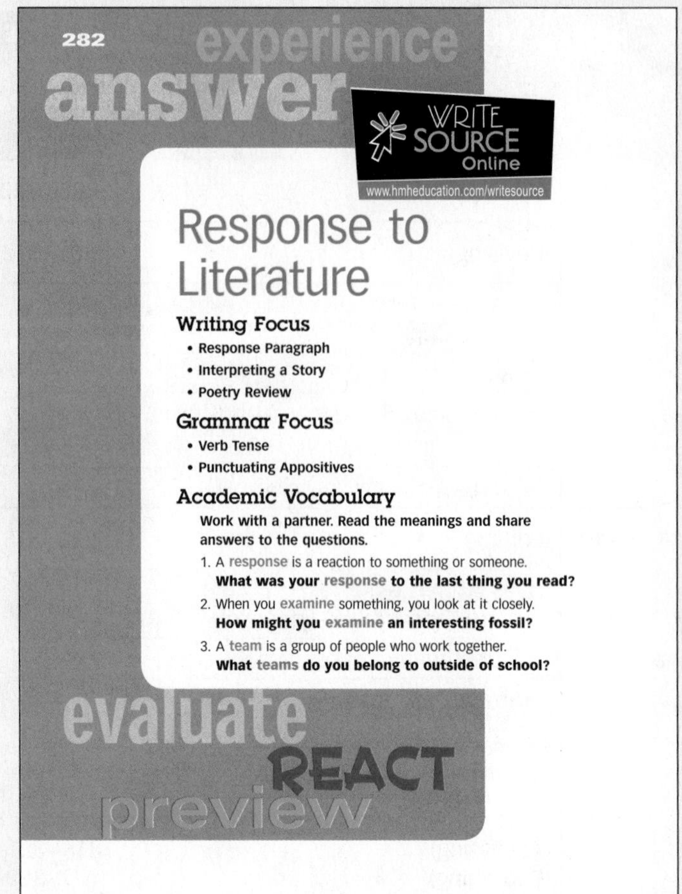

Minilessons

Peanut Butter? — Response Paragraph

- Often a character in a story can be described using behavior cues. **READ** the essay on pages 76–77 in your textbook. **USE** cues from the essay and **DESCRIBE** the author of the essay. What do you think his room at home is like?

What to Include — Interpreting a Story

- **READ** the response essay on pages 289–290 in your textbook. **WRITE** down what you think are important pieces of information about the main character and the story. Briefly explain why those are important points. **SHARE** your thoughts with the class.

Thunder — Poetry Review

- **READ** the poem on page 354 in your textbook. **CHOOSE** three dramatic images. **WRITE** a paragraph explaining why you chose them and what they mean to you.

Response to Literature

Response Paragraph

A typical jar of spaghetti sauce holds ten tomatoes, two stalks of celery, an onion, a green pepper, four cloves of garlic, and five other spices. How can one jar hold so much? All the ingredients in spaghetti sauce get boiled down until only the best parts remain.

A typical novel contains more than a thousand paragraphs about the main character. Even so, you can capture that same character in just one paragraph. All you need to do is "boil down" the information.

On the next page, you will read a sample paragraph about Moon Shadow, a boy who leaves China to find a new home in America. Then you will write a response paragraph of your own.

Writing Guidelines

Subject: An important character in a book or short story
Form: Response paragraph
Purpose: To carefully examine a character
Audience: Classmates

Response Paragraph

Objectives

- understand the content and structure of a response paragraph
- choose a topic (a character from a novel) to write about
- plan, draft, revise, and edit a response paragraph

A **response paragraph** is a summary or a reaction to something the writer has read. Paragraphs have a topic sentence, the body, and a closing sentence.

Read aloud or invite volunteers to read aloud the introduction to this section. Ask students to think about how *they* can describe a character in just one paragraph, when the author has used many pages to develop the character.

- Point out that the important word here is *capture*.
- Explain that the goal is to "boil down" the information by describing only the basic qualities that make the character interesting and to show how the character changes. This is how students can capture the character in just one paragraph.

Technology Connections

Use this unit's Interactive Whiteboard Lesson to introduce literature response writing.

Interactive Whiteboard Lessons

Response Paragraph

Invite students to describe a time when they had a totally different reaction to a book or story character than their friends had. Explain that because readers' life experiences and tastes differ, their responses to literature often differ as well.

Students may have a difficult time recognizing the difference between a response paragraph and a book summary.

- Explain that the sample response paragraph focuses on the development of one character, Moon Shadow.
- Point out that a book summary would provide more information about the setting, other characters in the story, and key events in the plot.

Respond to the reading.

Answers

Ideas **1.** how to live in America
2. He's suspicious of Americans with their strange language. His braid makes him a target of bullies.

Organization **3.** time

Voice & Word Choice **4.** bravely keeps going, overcome his fears, learn the ways of his new country, learns how important family and friends are

284

Response Paragraph

When you write a paragraph about something you've read, you may be asked to focus on one character. The **topic sentence** of your paragraph identifies the title, the author, and the character. The **body** sentences tell about the character, and the **closing sentence** tells how the character changed. In the following response, Keira writes about a character named Moon Shadow.

Topic Sentence

Body

Closing Sentence

Moon Shadow

In the book *Dragonwings* by Laurence Yep, a young Chinese boy named Moon Shadow learns how to live in America. Moon Shadow is eight years old when he leaves his mother and grandmother in China and sails to America to be with his father, Wind Rider. Together the two of them work long, hard days at a laundry in San Francisco. They send money back to China. At first, Moon Shadow is suspicious of Americans with their strange language. He knows that his long braid of hair makes him a target for neighborhood bullies. Moon Shadow also faces many frightening situations, including an earthquake, but he bravely keeps going. Later, he makes two American friends, Miss Whitlaw and Robin. They help him overcome his fears and learn the ways of his new country. He learns how important family and friends are in pursuing lifelong dreams.

Respond to the reading. On your own paper, answer each of the following questions.

- ☐ **Ideas** (1) What main problem does the character face? (2) What details about the problem does the writer include? Name two.
- ☐ **Organization** (3) Is this paragraph organized by time, by order of importance, or by logical order?
- ☐ **Voice & Word Choice** (4) What words or phrases near the end show how the writer feels about the character?

Prewriting Selecting a Topic

Your first step in writing a response to literature is selecting a book or short story to write about. Keira began by listing books she had read. Then she wrote down the names and descriptions of characters that interested her.

Topics Chart

Books or Stories	Characters	Descriptions
Dragonwings	Moon Shadow	young boy from China
No More Dead Dogs	Wallace Wallace	eighth-grade football hero
"Flowers for Algernon"	Charlie Gordon	a mentally challenged man

Choose a book or short story. Make a chart like the one above. Circle the character that interests you most.

Gathering Details About the Character

After you have chosen a character that you would like to write about, gather details about her or him. A cluster like the one below can help you.

Details Cluster

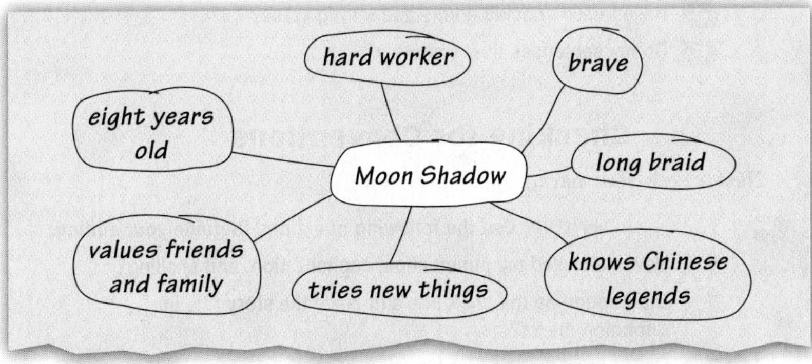

Create a cluster. First write the name of the character and circle it. Around the name, write details about the character's appearance, personality, hopes, and fears.

Prewriting Selecting a Topic

Have students work together to brainstorm a list of titles from previous reading assignments and independent reading. Students can refer to their reading logs and **reader-response journals** *(see below)* for ideas. Remind them to follow the conventions for punctuating titles in their charts.

* For punctuating titles, see SE pages 600 and 602.

Prewriting

Gathering Details About the Character

Encourage students to gather details that will help them explain how the character changes. Ask the following questions:

- What is important to the character as the story begins?
- What makes the character unique?
- Who (or what) causes problems for the character?
- What are the character's feelings at the end of the story (happy, relieved, sad, accepting)?

Teaching Tip: Reader-Response Journals

While this unit provides step-by-step instruction for writing literature responses, students should be encouraged to reflect often in a reader-response journal as they read (see SE page 434).

In a reader-response journal, students can

- explore their feelings while they read and after they read,
- connect characters and events in a story to people and events in their own lives, and
- express their opinions about writing style, main ideas, and themes.

Grammar Connection

Punctuating Titles

- **Proofreader's Guide** pages 600 (+), 602–603
- ***SkillsBook*** pages 33–34

Janelle leaned toward her and patted her back. "Maria, pull yourself together. Somebody's staring at us."

Maria looked across the coffee shop and saw an elderly lady sitting at another table. Her big brown eyes didn't blink as she stared at the two girls. The woman seemed to scowl.

Maria looked away and coughed into a napkin. "I wish she'd leave."

The woman pushed herself up with her stainless steel cane and shuffled away from the table. Instead of walking out the door, though, she walked to the counter and ordered. "A cappuccino and six biscotti."

"She must have worked up an appetite from all that staring," Maria whispered to Janelle, and they laughed quietly.

The woman turned around. In one hand, she held a tray with coffee and six slices of crunchy pastry. She stared at the girls. Then, ambling with her cane, the woman came right up to their table.

"Those cappuccinos are the best in the city," she said with a thick Italian accent. "But these biscotti are the best in the world. I should know. I brought this recipe with me from Rome."

The girls stared at her. Maria said, "You must be Chiara." *

"I must be," she said, pulling up a chair and sitting down. She lifted a piece of biscotti, dunked it into her coffee, and then raised it slowly to her mouth. "Here's how you learn to like cappuccino." She crunched on the pastry and slid the other biscotti toward the girls.

Each of them took a piece and dunked it into the coffee. Nervously, they bit in. The bitterness of the coffee somehow tasted right with the mild sweetness and crunch of the biscotti.

"Did you grow up in Rome?" Maria asked. "My great-grandma came from Italy."

"Yes. I even had children there—two daughters.* They were your age when we moved to America." As Chiara spoke, Maria could picture the places she described: the Colosseum, the Pantheon, and the fountains of Rome. The woman's voice carried Maria back 60 years, back to when Chiara had been her age. They connect.

Half an hour later, "the girls' coffee cups were empty, and their minds were full."

"Is there always biscotti?" Maria asked as Janelle got up to go. "I mean, every Saturday?"

Chiara said, "Sure. Always biscotti and cappuccino and stories."

"Then we'll be back," Maria pledged, and Janelle agreed. They'd acquired the taste. not just for coffee

LITERATURE

After students read the story and the comments in blue, ask them if there are any additional comments or marks they would have made if they were taking the test.

English Language Learners

Make sure students understand the events of the story before you ask them to study the sample response to the prompt. First, read aloud the story to students. Then, as you reread it, have students create a sequence chain to summarize the story.

- To make the chain, have students draw a series of horizontal rectangles down the center of their paper. Tell them to draw arrows pointing downward to connect the rectangles.
- As you slowly reread the story, students should record words and phrases in each box of the chain, to show the events in the order in which they happened.

Struggling Learners

Explain that if a time limit is imposed for their writing, students can organize their time by using guidelines such as the following:

- **10 minutes:** Read and plan
- **25 minutes:** Write
- **10 minutes:** Proofread and correct

Ask students to look for these traits as they read the sample response.

Ideas
a statement of the theme and an insight into how the characters change

Organization
- a beginning that contains a focus statement that introduces the main characters and the theme
- middle paragraphs that describe key events from the story, support the focus statement, and help develop the insight
- an ending that explains the change in the character(s), shows how the writer feels about the character(s), and summarizes the theme
- transitions that connect ideas in and between paragraphs

Voice
use of a knowledgeable voice that shows interest in the characters

Student Response

The following essay is a student's response to the story "Acquiring the Taste." Notice how the student uses details from the story to support the focus.

Beginning
The first paragraph states the focus of the essay.

The story "Acquiring the Taste" is about two seventh-grade girls who want to be grown-up. Maria and Janelle think that changing the posters on their walls and learning to drink coffee will make them more grown-up. These changes are just on the surface, though. When the girls meet a woman named Chiara, they find out that there's a lot more to growing up than just coffee.

Middle
The middle paragraphs support the focus with examples from the story.

Maria and Janelle go to Chiara's Coffee Shop because they feel like they need "to learn how to drink coffee." They order cappuccinos and get drinks that are bitter. Maria even starts to choke. The girls are acting pretty immature at this point.

Then Chiara comes to their table, gives them biscotti, and shows them how to dunk the pastry in their coffee. The sweet biscotti and the bitter coffee taste good together. Chiara also tells the girls stories about her life. She grew up in Rome and had daughters like Maria and Janelle before she moved to America. The girls like Chiara's stories

Advanced Learners

Before reading the sample response, invite students to write their own response essay, following the directions and the prompt on SE page 336. Then give them time to compare and contrast their ideas with those in the sample response.

evaluate answer experience react 339
Writing for Assessment

more than they like the coffee. In the end, "the girls' coffee cups were empty, and their minds were full."

By the end of the story, Maria and Janelle are more grown-up than when the story started. They've gone from having posters of rock stars in their bedrooms to actually meeting a person from Rome and learning about her life. The story "Acquiring the Taste" is about learning to like coffee, but it is also about developing an appreciation for the lives of other people and the stories they have to tell.

Ending

The final paragraph explains how the characters have changed. It also discusses the overall meaning of the story.

Respond to the reading. Answer the following questions about the sample prompt and student response.

- ☐ **Ideas** (1) What is the focus of the student's response? (2) What changes in the characters does the student note?
- ☐ **Organization** (3) How did the underlining and comments on pages 336–337 help the student organize the response?
- ☐ **Voice & Word Choice** (4) Is the student's voice objective or personal? (5) What words tell you so?

LITERATURE

Respond to the reading.

Answers

Ideas 1. When Maria and Janelle meet a woman named Chiara, they find out that there's a lot more to growing up than just drinking coffee.
2. They change the posters on their walls. They try to learn how to drink coffee by ordering cappuccinos. They meet Chiara, a woman from Rome, who shows them how to dunk biscotti in their coffee.

Organization 3. The underlining and comments helped the writer keep track of the order of key events and details related to these key events.

Voice & Word Choice 4. objective, but caring and interested
5. Students should note that the writer keeps the voice objective by not expressing personal feelings about the characters. Possible choices: The story "Acquiring the Taste" is about two seventh-grade girls; The girls are acting pretty immature at this point; In the end, "the girls' coffee cups were empty and their minds were full"; . . . it is also about developing an appreciation for the lives of other people . . .

English Language Learners

Reinforce the idea that the sample response to the prompt includes details from the story as well as comments about the lesson the characters learned.

- Place the student response on an overhead transparency. After reading it one or more times with students, guide them in analyzing it.
- Have students identify details from the story that the writer included in the sample response. Underline these in a colored transparency pen.
- Then help students identify the writer's ideas about what the girls in the story learned. Underline these in a different color pen.

Practice Writing Prompt

Point out that students must approach writing-on-demand assignments differently from open-ended writing assignments.

Allow students the same amount of time to write their response essay as they will be allotted on school, district, or state assessments. Break down each part of the process into clear chunks of time. For example, you might give students

- 10 minutes for reading, note-taking, and planning,
- 25 minutes for writing, and
- 10 minutes for editing and proofreading.

Tell students when time is up for each section. Start the assignment at the top of the hour or at the half-hour to make it easier for students to keep track of the time.

Practice Writing Prompt

Practice a response to literature. Carefully read the directions to the practice writing prompt on the next two pages. Use about 10 minutes at the beginning to read the story, make notes, and plan your writing. Also leave time at the end to proofread your work.

Directions:

- Read the following story.
- As you read, make notes on your own paper.
- After reading the story, write an essay. You have 40 minutes to read, plan, write, and proofread your work.

When you write, focus on the main character. Show your insight into how he changes over the course of the story. Use clear organization, and support your focus with examples from the text.

The Mute King

From February through April, the school auditorium became Yan's second home. It wasn't that he liked drama. He hadn't even tried out for the spring production of *Once Upon a Mattress* because he was terrified of being onstage. Yan didn't like drama, but his girlfriend Kallie did. So he camped in the school auditorium every afternoon, his glossy black hair hanging over his face as he bent above algebra homework. Yan sat and worked, waiting for the times when Kallie came onstage and started to sing.

And could she sing! Kallie was playing Princess Winnifred the Woebegone, and whenever she came onstage, she owned the whole auditorium. Everybody stopped and just stared in amazement. Yan would lift his eyes from his algebra paper and let his pencil drop to the page and just soak in the sound of her voice. Those moments made all the waiting worthwhile. But the best moment of all was when play practice was done and Yan got to walk Kallie home.

"You should have tried out, you know," Kallie said to him one day as they strolled past the park.

English Language Learners

If necessary, replace "The Mute King" with a story at the students' reading level. Have them prepare for writing by quickly listing main events. Then have them write a sentence telling how the character(s) changed. Tell students to circle the events that were most important in causing the change. Explain that they can use these notes to write a response.

Struggling Learners

Students who are not easily able to gain insights when reading fiction may resort to writing a summary of the story. Adapt the exercise as needed, in one or more of the following ways:

- Have students refer to Keys to Effective Prewriting (SE page 291) as they write their response.
- Have students work in a small group with you.
- Have students work in pairs.
- Allow students to discuss their plans for their responses with one another.
- Lengthen the time frame to allow deeper exploration of the characters and how they change.

Yan looked at her and shrugged. "You know I couldn't talk in front of all those people."

"I know, but you could've tried out for the part of the mute king," Kallie shot back with a laugh.

Kallie hadn't meant anything by it, but the comment stung Yan. The king in the play was under a spell that kept him from talking. Yan felt like he was under a spell, too. He knew this play as well as anybody. He'd watched it a hundred times. He could have recited the lines and sung every song. Instead, stage fright kept him where he was, in the seats instead of onstage. He was like the mute king, just waiting for his chance to speak.

Dress rehearsal came. Kallie looked great in her princess getup, and everybody buzzed with excitement. Still, by 3:15, the rehearsal hadn't begun.

Suddenly, Kallie burst onstage and shuffled down the aisle. Behind her walked Mrs. Spejewski, who was in charge of music. Kallie approached Yan and pointed at him. "He can do it. He's our only hope. He knows the whole play."

"What? What?" Yan asked, standing up to protest.

"Our drummer Tony's got the flu," Mrs. Spejewski explained, "and Kallie says you know how to play drums."

"Yeah, I do, but—"

"You're hired," Kallie said, grabbing Yan's hand and pulling him toward the stage.

A moment later, Yan sat in the pit with the other musicians. He held drumsticks in his hand and stared at the printed music—but he knew every song by ear. Mrs. Spejewski lifted her baton, and the overture began. Yan played as if he'd always been behind those drums.

Out came the actors, and they sang, and Yan kept up the beat. Even when Kallie appeared to belt out her first solo, Yan didn't give in to the old spell.

He smiled. At last, he had found his place in the play, and the mute king had found his voice.

Encourage students to practice writing responses to books, stories, and articles they read in class or on their own. The more opportunities they have to practice, the better writers on demand they will become. In addition, writing responses to literature will encourage them to become careful, more involved readers.

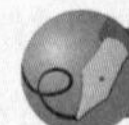

Writer's Craft

Literary devices: Whenever responding to literature, students should think about the craft of the writer. For example, "The Mute King" includes a story within a story. The real-life story of Yan parallels the fictional story of the mute king.

Student who comment on these sorts of literary devices demonstrate a deeper understanding of the literature than those who simply recount the events. They also score higher.

Advanced Learners

Have students research periodicals and Web sites that feature literature reviews (such as *Book Links* or *Amazon*) and select one response they feel is particularly well written to share with the class. Encourage students to explain why they think the review is well written by pointing out specific details.

Creative Writing Overview

Common Core Standards Focus

Writing 3: Write narratives to develop real or imagined experiences or events using effective technique, relevant descriptive details, and well-structured event sequences.

Language 2: Demonstrate command of the conventions of standard English capitalization, punctuation, and spelling when writing.

Writing Forms

- Writing Stories
- Writing Poems

Focus on the Traits

- **Ideas** Using sensory details, action, and dialogue
- **Organization** Following a plot line as a writing plan
- **Voice** Keeping the reader's interest and showing the writer's personality
- **Word Choice** Using figures of speech and other techniques to enliven poems
- **Sentence Fluency** Creating rhythm in poems with line breaks
- **Conventions** Checking for errors in punctuation, capitalization, spelling, and grammar

Literature Connections

- **"Hum"** by Naomi Shihab Nye
- **"Arithmetic"** by Carl Sandburg

Technology Connections

Write Source Online
www.hmheducation.com/writesource

- ***Net-text***
- ***Bookshelf***
- ***GrammarSnap***
- ***Portfolio***
- ***Writing Network features***
- ***File Cabinet***

Interactive Whiteboard Lessons

Suggested Creative Writing Units (Three Weeks)

	Day	Writing and Skills Instruction	*Student Edition* Creative Writing Unit	*Student Edition* Resource Units*	*SkillsBook*	*Daily Language Workouts*	*Write Source Online*
Week 1	1	**Writing Stories: Short Stories** (Model) Literature Connections "Hum"	343–345			56–57, 103	*Interactive Whiteboard Lessons*
	2–3	(Prewriting)	346–347				*Net-text*
	4–5	(Writing)	348				*Net-text*

* These units are also located in the back of the Teacher's Edition. Resource Units include "Basic Grammar and Writing," "A Writer's Resource," and "Proofreader's Guide."
(+) This activity is located in a different section of the *Write Source Student Edition.* If students have already completed this activity, you may wish to review it at this time.

Week	Day	Writing and Skills Instruction	Student Edition: Creative Writing Unit	Student Edition: Resource Units*	SkillsBook	Daily Language Workouts	Write Source Online
Week 2	6–7	(Revising)	348			58–59, 104	*Net-text*
		Skills Activities: • Punctuating Dialogue		588 (+), 598 (+), 600 (+)			*GrammarSnap*
		• Rambling Sentences		507	87		
		• Verbs		484, 724 (+)	71–72		*GrammarSnap*
		• Sentences Combining (compound subjects and predicates)		515	117–118		
	8–9	(Editing, Publishing)	349				*Portfolio, Net-text*
		Skills Activities: • Sentence Problems (review)		504, 506 (+), 507	85		*GrammarSnap*
		• Commas		582 (+)	9–10		
	10 opt.	*Other Story Patterns* and *Elements of Fiction*	350–352				
Week 3	11–12	**Writing Poems: Free Verse Poem** (Model) Literature Connections "Arithmetic"	353–354			60–61, 105	
		(Prewriting)	355–356				*Net-text*
		(Writing)	356				*Net-text*
		Skills Activities: • Prepositional Phrases		494, 519 (+), 742 (+)			
	13–14	(Revising)	357				*Portfolio, Net-text*
		Skills Activities: • Parts of Speech Review		702–748 (+), 749	199–200		
		• Apostrophes		604 (+), 606 (+)	38, 39–40		
		• Hyphens		608–609, 610–611, 732 (+)	41–42		
	15	(Editing)	357				*Portfolio, Net-text*
		Skills Activities: • Spelling		642 (+)			
	opt.	*Writing a Parts of Speech Poem*	358				
	opt.	*Other Forms—(concrete, acrostic, 5 W's)*	359	519 (+)			

* These units are also located in the back of the Teacher's Edition. Resource Units include "Basic Grammar and Writing," "A Writer's Resource," and "Proofreader's Guide."
(+) This activity is located in a different section of the *Write Source Student Edition.* If students have already completed this activity, you may wish to review it at this time.

Teacher's Notes for Creative Writing

This overview for creative writing includes some specific teaching suggestions for the unit.

Writing Focus

Writing Stories (pages 343–352)

Although writing a short story is a good starting point for young writers, a good short story is not an easy task. Encourage your students to limit the number of characters in their stories while focusing on one problem or challenge those characters must overcome. Students can write an adaptation of something they have experienced, or they can use their imaginations to form a plausible story line.

Writing Poems (pages 353–361)

Story writing is challenging, but writing poetry doesn't seem possible for some students. At least that is what they believe. You will need to encourage your students to try. Fortunately, there are some poem types that can give even the beginner a feeling of satisfaction. Students should be able to fashion a good poem using free verse, parts of speech, or concrete, acrostic, or 5 W's poetry. Examples of each of these forms are found in this chapter. To help get them started, guide your students through SE pages 360–361 dealing with poetry techniques.

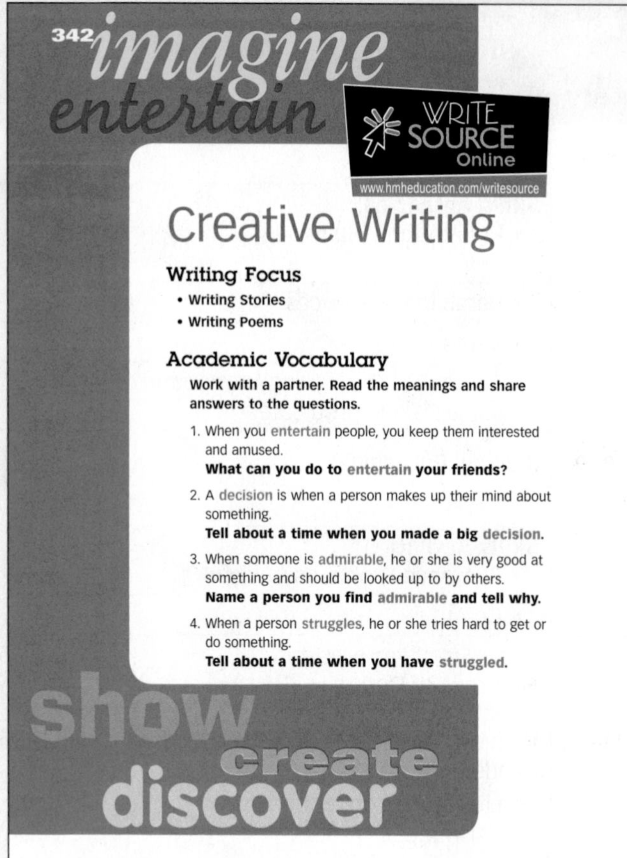
342 imagine entertain

WRITE SOURCE Online

www.hmheducation.com/writesource

Creative Writing

Writing Focus

- Writing Stories
- Writing Poems

Academic Vocabulary

Work with a partner. Read the meanings and share answers to the questions.

1. When you entertain people, you keep them interested and amused.
   What can you do to entertain your friends?
2. A decision is when a person makes up their mind about something.
   Tell about a time when you made a big decision.
3. When someone is admirable, he or she is very good at something and should be looked up to by others.
   Name a person you find admirable and tell why.
4. When a person struggles, he or she tries hard to get or do something.
   Tell about a time when you have struggled.

show create discover

Academic Vocabulary

Read aloud the academic terms, as well as the descriptions and questions. Model for students how to read one question and answer it. Have partners monitor their understanding and seek clarification of the terms by working through the meanings and questions together.

Minilessons

You Don't Say — Writing Stories

- **WRITE** a short dialogue between two children who are bragging about how great their parents are. **SHIFT** gears to write a short dialogue between two teenagers who are complaining about their parents.

Rap-A-Tap-Tap — Writing Poems

- **WRITE** a short rap (rhythmic, rhyming poem) on a favorite topic or a pet peeve. **SHARE** your rap with the class.

343

Creative Writing

Writing Stories

Have you ever seen a movie with amazing special effects but no story? What a disappointment! On the other hand, a movie with an amazing story may not need special effects.

What makes a story amazing or wonderful? Usually, it has *people* in a *place* where a *conflict* occurs. If readers or viewers care about the people and the conflict, they will care about the story.

In this chapter, you will read a sample story about a tough decision at a school dance. Then you will develop a decision story of your own to share.

Writing Guidelines

Subject: A decision
Form: Short story
Purpose: To entertain
Audience: Classmates

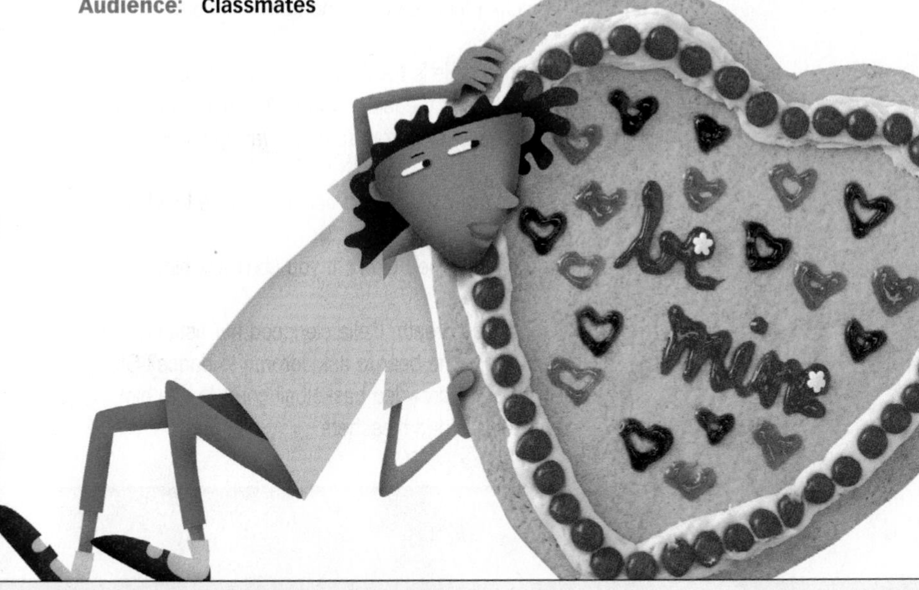

Copy Masters

Time Line (TE pp. 344, 347)

Sensory Chart (TE p. 347)

Writing Stories

Objectives

- understand the content and structure of a short story
- choose a topic (character, conflict, and setting) to write about
- plan, draft, revise, and edit a short story

A **short story** has these characteristics:

- It is a short piece of literature with only a few characters.
- It usually concerns just one problem or conflict.

A short story has

- a setting,
- characters, and
- a plot with a beginning, rising action, a high point, and an ending.

Point out that one of the greatest challenges in writing a short story is its short length. Everything in a short story must happen over a relatively limited amount of time and space. Students should keep this in mind as they write their short stories.

Technology Connections

Use this unit's Interactive Whiteboard Lesson to introduce creative writing.

 ***Interactive Whiteboard Lessons***

Short Story

Work through this sample story with the class, pointing out the elements that make it a good short story and a strong decision story.

Ideas

- The main character finds the confidence she needs to act on a decision she makes.
- Action and dialogue clearly show the different personalities of three characters.

Organization

Suspense is created by a plot line that has a strong beginning, a rising action that builds to the high point, and an ending that quickly follows the high point.

Voice and Word Choice

- Interest is created by characters who speak in natural voices using contemporary language.
- Action words and phrases such as *Celia clenched her fists* and *teetering on a tightrope* capture the character, conflict, and setting.

Short Story

One type of story is based on a tough decision that the main character must make. In the beginning, the character wonders what to do. Tension builds until he or she makes the decision, and the ending tells how that decision changes the character. The following story is about a girl named Celia who faces a tough decision at a school dance.

Beginning

The beginning introduces the characters, the setting, and the decision.

Rising Action

The rising action adds a conflict for the characters.

Just Keep Going . . .

"Why don't you take a break, Celia?" Shaundra shouted above the pounding beat of the dance music. "You've been serving punch all night. Aren't you going to dance?"

"No," Celia shot back. "I mean, sure. Of course I'm going to dance." She ran her thumb up the stack of party napkins. "But we've been really busy. People get thirsty, dancing."

"Yeah, and people who aren't dancing need something to do."

Celia watched the ice bob in the bowl. "Nobody's asked me."

"Girl, you think this is the '90s? You've got to do the asking." Shaundra took the ladle from Celia's hand and nodded across the gym. "Jerome's been waiting for you all night."

Celia's eyes grew wide. "You better not have told him I like him!"

"Maybe I did. Maybe I didn't. If you don't ask him, you'll never know."

Drawing a deep breath, Celia clenched her fists beside her hips. How could she bear to ask Jerome to dance? She stared out across the crowded basketball court to see him leaning against the folded bleachers.

English Language Learners

To develop students' comprehension of the story, help them make a time line showing changes in Celia's feelings.

- Draw a horizontal line on the board.
- Have students recall the events of the story.
- Use simple sketches, words, or phrases to record the events in sequential order above the line.
- Encourage students to identify words from the story that reveal Celia's feelings about each event.
- Record those words below the appropriate events on the time line.

Struggling Learners

Before discussing the sample short story, have student groups analyze their favorite movies to identify setting, characters, and conflict. Encourage students to discuss how these elements contribute to the appeal of these movies. Make the connection that, similarly, writers use these elements to create excitement in their stories.

Jerome's hair was shaved short, and he wore a button-down shirt with khaki pants. He was more dressed up than Celia had ever seen him.

"Well," Shaundra said, "what's your decision?"

Celia began to walk. The first step was the hardest. She felt like she was teetering on a tightrope. The music pounded in her chest. Halfway there, she wondered if she should veer off to the restroom, but something inside her said, "Just keep going." Suddenly, she stood in front of Jerome.

He looked up, saw her, and smiled. "What's up, Celia?" He was wearing cologne.

High Point
The high point is when the main character makes her decision.

Celia shrugged, and she couldn't think of a single thing to say. How was she going to get out of this one? Taking a deep breath, she blurted, "You don't want to dance, do you?"

Jerome's smile grew broader. "Sure." They walked together out to the free-throw line. Then the beat stopped. Celia and Jerome were left standing there, facing each other in dead silence. She wanted to sink into the floor. At last, the DJ started a slow song.

Ending
The ending suggests that the main character changes.

Jerome murmured, "So, I guess Shaundra told you I like you."

Celia relaxed and smiled. "Maybe she did, and maybe she didn't."

CREATIVE

Respond to the reading. Answer the following questions.

- ☐ **Ideas (1) What decision is Celia struggling to make?**
- ☐ **Organization (2) How does the writer build the suspense that leads up to Celia's decision?**
- ☐ **Voice & Word Choice (3) What words or phrases keep your interest? List at least three.**

Literature Connections: For another example of a short story, read "Hum" by Naomi Shihab Nye.

Respond to the reading.

Possible responses:

Ideas 1. Celia can't decide whether or not to ask Jerome to dance.

Organization 2. The writer builds suspense by not revealing what Shaundra has told Jerome, by describing in detail Celia's thoughts and feelings as she walks across the gym to talk to Jerome, and by having the music stop abruptly just as Celia and Jerome start to dance.

Voice & Word Choice 3. Possible choices (accept any three): eyes grew wide, Drawing a deep breath, clenched her fists, teetering on a tightrope, pounded in her chest, Taking a deep breath, the beat stopped, facing each other in dead silence, sink into the floor

Literature Connections

In Naomi Shihab Nye's short story "Hum," a boy named Sami Salsaa and his family move to the United States from Palestine to escape the dangers of their homeland. However, Sami and his family must overcome new fears and unjust treatment after the attacks of September 11, 2001.

Discuss the theme of the short story, as well as lessons each character learns. Also discuss the story's strengths, including: natural voice, vivid details, and organization. For additional short story models, see the Reading-Writing Connections beginning on page TE-36.

English Language Learners

Be sure that students understand colloquial language and idioms used in the story. Review the meanings of the following phrases:

- take a break (stop what you are doing and rest)
- shot back (answered quickly)
- ice bob in the bowl (ice moved up and down in the bowl)
- What's up? (What are you doing? What is happening?)
- sink into the floor (disappear, be someplace else)

Struggling Learners

Creative writers use specific verbs as speaker tags, too.

- Have students identify the verbs the writer of the sample story used instead of the word *said* (shouted, shot back, blurted, murmured).
- Challenge students to use a thesaurus to find five more synonyms for *said*. (Possible responses: whispered, announced, promised, warned, yelled)

Prewriting Selecting a Topic

Point out to students that no one in real life is perfect. Other than in fairy tales, story characters are not usually all good or all bad. Believable characters have weaknesses or flaws that make them more interesting and realistic.

To help students choose a topic and develop ideas for their table diagram, discuss the strengths and weaknesses of several characters in stories they have read.

Prewriting Creating a Conflict

Recalling the kinds of decisions young people have to make in real life or in books may spark an idea for writing. Ask students to think of books they've read where the main character had to make a decision. List the different decisions on the board, and ask the following questions:

- Why was the decision so tough for the character? Was it because of a personality trait? Was it because of the possible consequences? Was it both?
- What finally helped the character decide what to do?
- What happened afterward?

Encourage students to keep these questions in mind as they try to choose a conflict.

Technology Connections

Students can use the added features of the Net-text as they explore this stage of the writing process.

***Write Source Online* Net-text**

Prewriting Selecting a Topic

A strong decision story starts with an interesting character. One way to create a character that readers will care about is to give the person one main strength and one main weakness. The strength makes the character admirable, and the weakness primes the character for a tough decision. A table diagram like the one below can help.

Table Diagram

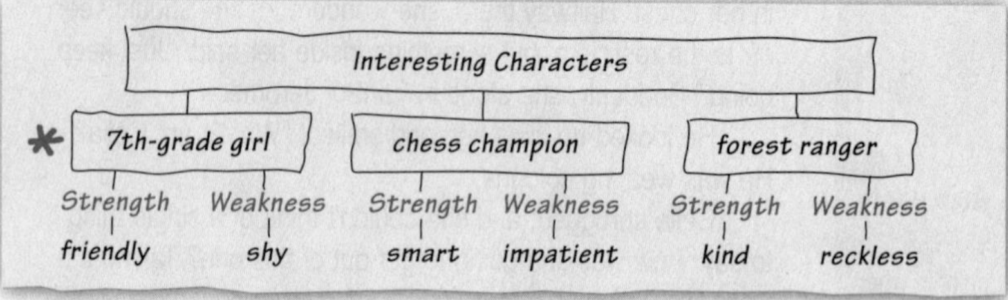

Create a table diagram. List three characters you find interesting. Under each, list one strength to make your character likable and a weakness to challenge him or her. Choose one character to write about in a story.

Creating a Conflict

The difficult decision your character will face will create the conflict in your story. The writer of the sample story listed decisions that would be tough for her character.

Decisions List

Character weakness:

— Celia is shy.

Tough decisions:

— Whether to throw a surprise party for her best friend.

— Whether to make friends with a new girl from Japan.

— Whether to talk to a boy she likes.

Choose a conflict. Think about the character you chose and his or her weakness. List decisions that would be tough for the person to make. Choose one decision for your story.

Struggling Learners

Provide support for students who have difficulty thinking of interesting characters for the table diagram. Suggest that students list the following kinds of fictional characters:

- a person with whom they can easily empathize (e.g., a new student, a boy/girl trying out for a team)
- someone they admire (e.g., a blind gymnast, a firefighter)
- a professional whose career the student finds intriguing (e.g., a private investigator, an author)

Setting the Scene and Gathering Details

You have discovered the character and the conflict for your story. Now it's time to think about the place, or setting, where your story happens. Think of a place that would make the decision especially difficult.

For the main character of the sample story, the setting is a school dance. The author used a sensory chart to gather details about the setting.

CREATIVE

Sensory Chart

Setting: School dance in a gymnasium

See	Hear	Smell	Taste	Touch/Feel
punch bowl	hip-hop	cologne	punch	cold ice
khaki pants	advice	cookies	pretzels	pounding beat
shaved hair	awkward silence			dizzy
				shaky

Set the scene. Choose the place where your story will occur. Then use a sensory chart to gather details about the place. Try to come up with at least two details for each sense.

Focus on the Traits

Organization

The actions that take place during a story make up the plot line. Each part of the plot plays an important role in the story.

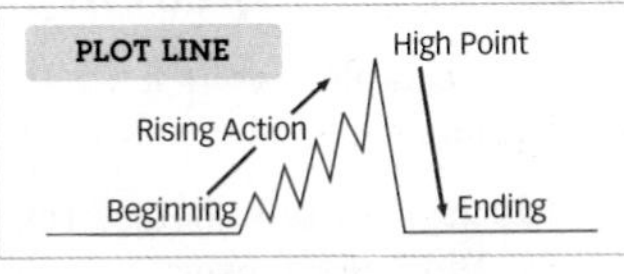

- The **beginning** introduces the characters and setting.
- The **rising action** adds a conflict—a problem for the characters.
- The **high point** is the moment when the conflict is strongest, and a decision is made.
- The **ending** tells how the main character has changed.

Prewriting

Setting the Scene and Gathering Details

Provide photocopies of the reproducible sensory chart (TE page 793). Students who have chosen a conflict that automatically suggests a setting can get right to work on their chart. For example, if the conflict is whether or not to try out for the school swim team, the setting is likely to be a pool.

Have other students work in groups to brainstorm ideas for a setting. Suggest that they begin by listing all the places they usually go during the week and on weekends.

Some students may still be trying to choose a conflict. Thinking about a setting may help them make their choice.

Focus on the Traits

Organization

Draw a plot line on the board and ask students to help you fill it out using details from "Just Keep Going . . ." on SE pages 344–345. Then encourage students to create a detailed plot line for their own story. They can use their filled-in plot line as a plan for writing.

Struggling Learners

As an alternative to creating a plot line, have students create a time line of events in their story. Provide photocopies of the reproducible time line (TE page 790), and have students use words, phrases, or drawings to show the sequence of events. Have them determine which event is the high point and highlight it.

Writing Developing Your First Draft

Encourage students to experiment with different story beginnings before they actually start to write. Students can share their ideas in small groups for immediate feedback. Tell students to

- fold a piece of paper into thirds to create three rows,
- write a different story beginning at the top of each row, and
- pass their paper around the group.

Each group member can put a check mark under the beginning he or she likes best.

Revising Improving Your Writing

As students revise, tell them to make sure they have used details and dialogue that **show, not tell** (*see below*) the reader what is happening.

* For more about using dialogue, see SE page 556.

Technology Connections

Have students use the Writing Network features of the Net-text to comment on each other's drafts.

Write Source Online ***Net-text***

Writing Developing Your First Draft

Now that you have created a character, a conflict, and a setting, you are ready to write your story. As you write, use the following tips.

1. **Start strong.** In your first sentence, focus on the character, the conflict, or the setting.
   - *Character:* Celia smiled shyly as she ladled punch from the bowl.
   - *Conflict:* Celia had watched Jerome all evening, but he didn't seem to know she even existed.
   - *Setting:* The gymnasium of Cleveland Junior High was hopping.
2. **Describe the action.** Describe the action using a variety of specific details.

   Celia began to walk. The first step was the hardest. She felt like she was teetering on a tightrope. The music pounded in her chest.
3. **Include dialogue.** Let your characters speak in their natural voices.

   Jerome murmured, "So, I guess Shaundra told you I like you."
   Celia relaxed and smiled. "Maybe she did, and maybe she didn't."

Write your first draft. Tell the story of your character's big decision. Start strong and include action and dialogue to build up to the decision point. Think about the strength and weakness of your main character.

Revising Improving Your Writing

Once you complete your first draft, take a break. Later, you can return to your story and revise it by looking at the following traits.

- ☐ **Ideas** Do I tell about a tough decision for my main character? Do I include sensory details, action, and dialogue?
- ☐ **Organization** Do I start strong? Do I build to the decision point? Do I resolve, or end, the story quickly after the high point?
- ☐ **Voice** Does my voice (including dialogue) keep the reader's interest?
- ☐ **Word Choice** Have I chosen words that capture the character, conflict, and setting?
- ☐ **Sentence Fluency** Do my sentences flow well?

Revise your story. Use the questions above as a guide when you revise your first draft.

Grammar Connection

Punctuating Dialogue

- ***Proofreader's Guide*** pages 588 (+), 598 (+), 600 (+)
- ***GrammarSnap*** Punctuating Dialogue

Rambling Sentences

- ***Write Source*** page 507
- ***SkillsBook*** page 99

Verbs

- ***Proofreader's Guide*** page 724 (+)
- ***Write Source*** page 484
- ***SkillsBook*** pages 71–72
- ***GrammarSnap*** Past Tense and Past Perfect Tense Verbs

Sentences Combining (Compound Subjects and Verbs)

- ***Write Source*** page 515
- ***SkillsBook*** pages 117–118
- ***GrammarSnap*** Subject-Verb Agreement with Compound Subjects

Teaching Tip: Show, Don't Tell

Suggest that students apply one or more of these strategies:

- Add details that help the reader see, hear, smell, taste, and feel what's happening.
- Add details about a character's movements, gestures, and facial expressions.
- Give each character her or his own voice by using dialogue.

* For more about showing, not telling, see SE page 557.

entertain create imagine discover show
Writing Stories 349

CREATIVE

Editing Checking for Conventions

After you finish revising your story, you should edit it for *conventions*.

- ☐ **Conventions** Have I punctuated dialogue correctly? Have I checked my spelling and grammar?

Edit your story. Use the questions above to guide your editing. When you finish, use the tips below to write a title. Then create a clean final copy and proofread it.

Creating a Title

Your title is your first opportunity to hook the reader, so make it memorable. Here are some tips for writing a strong title.

- Use a metaphor: **Teetering on a Tightrope**
- Borrow a line from the story: **Just Keep Going . . .**
- Be creative: **The Punch-Bowl Predicament**

Publishing Sharing Your Story

Stories are meant to be shared. Here are three publication ideas.

- **Recite your story.**
  Read your story out loud to friends or family, or recite it from memory. Be dramatic with your voice, your facial expressions, and your gestures.
- **Create a skit.**
  Ask classmates to help you act out your story. If you can, gather costumes and props. Then perform the story for your class.
- **Submit your story.**
  Check the library for youth publications that accept stories. Format your work according to the submission guidelines and send your story in.

Present your story. Choose one of the ideas above or make up one of your own. Then share your story with the world.

Editing Checking for Conventions

If possible, take the time to review conventions for using end punctuation inside and outside quotation marks in dialogue (see SE page 600).

✱ For more help with end punctuation, see SE pages 579–580.

Creating a Title

A metaphor is a figure of speech that compares two things without using the word *like* or *as*. For example, "Teetering on a Tightrope" compares the events in the story to walking unsteadily on a tightrope.

Publishing Sharing Your Story

Provide these additional publishing ideas for students:

- Create a series of drawings that depict the main events in the story to go with the final draft.
- Use a computer to print the story. Bind it with the drawings and a creative cover and place it in the school library.

Technology Connections

Remind students that they can use the Writing Network features of the Portfolio to share their work with peers.

Write Source Online ***Portfolio***

Write Source Online ***Net-text***

Advanced Learners

Have students create illustrated board books of their stories to share with an elementary school class.

- If the stories students have written for this lesson are inappropriate, encourage them to write an additional story. This will give students experience in writing with a sound sense of purpose for an intended audience.
- Before students select the topic, suggest that they study a variety of picture books to determine what types of topics might be appropriate for younger readers.

Grammar Connection

Sentence Problems (Review)

- ***Write Source*** pages 504, 506 (+), 507
- ***SkillsBook*** page 97
- ***GrammarSnap*** Complete Sentences and Sentence Fragments

Commas in a Series

- **Proofreader's Guide** page 582 (+)
- ***SkillsBook*** pages 9–10

Story Patterns

Ask volunteers to read aloud the descriptions of the different story patterns.

- As each description is read, invite students to identify stories they have read that fit each pattern.
- Ask students to give a one-sentence summary of the story.

Alternately, ask students to name stories they have read in class. As each title is mentioned, ask which pattern the story fits.

For the **Try It** activity, students may create a summary sentence for an original story (as in the samples provided with each pattern) or they may choose to summarize a story that is already in print.

 **Answers**

Answers will vary.

After students complete the **Try It** activity, invite them to share their original story ideas in small groups.

- Ask groups to record the ideas for each story.
- Compile the ideas into one master list of story ideas to share with the class, either as a poster or a printed handout.

Students can refer to the list for story ideas for future writing assignments.

Story Patterns

You just finished writing a decision story, but there are many other story patterns to choose from.

The Initiation	In an *initiation* story, a young person has to overcome a test of his or her abilities or beliefs. The way the person deals with the test will influence the rest of her or his life. **Sarah struggles to adjust to a new school.**
The Surprise	In a *surprise* story, the main character and the reader misunderstand what is happening around them. The high point reveals a surprise that explains everything. **Jack thinks his friends are gossiping about him, but really they are planning a party for him.**
The Union	The *union* pattern features two main characters who are attracted to each other. Usually, they have to overcome obstacles to be together. **Haleh meets a handsome young runner from a rival school's track team.**
The Quest	In the *quest* pattern, the main character goes on a journey into the unknown, often to search for an object or reach a goal. The person usually gains the prize—or learns something in the process of losing it. **Drew journeys into the rain forest to find his father, who has been lost there for three weeks.**
The Mystery	In a *mystery* story, the main character must follow a series of tantalizing clues to discover a secret. **Jessica stays up one night to discover who is leaving flowers on her front step.**

 Choose one of the story patterns above. Think of a story that would fit that pattern. Write a single sentence that sums up the story.

Struggling Learners

To help students become more familiar with the story patterns, share with them, over time, a series of very short stories. Ask students to identify the pattern that each story follows.

Advanced Learners

To extend the **Try It** activity, have students expand their story summary into a story.

- Allow students to work with a partner, if they choose.
- Invite students to share their completed story with the class, and challenge the class to identify which pattern it represents.

Elements of Fiction

The following list includes many terms used to describe the elements or parts of literature. This information will help you discuss and write about the novels, poetry, essays, and other literary works you read.

CREATIVE

Action: Everything that happens in a story

Antagonist: The person or force that works against the hero of the story (See *protagonist.*)

Character: A person or an animal in a story

Characterization: The way in which a writer develops a character, making him or her seem believable

Here are three methods:

- Sharing the character's thoughts, actions, and dialogue
- Describing his or her appearance
- Revealing what others in the story think or say about this character

Conflict: A problem or clash between two forces in a story

There are five basic conflicts:

- **Person Against Person** A problem between characters
- **Person Against Himself or Herself** A problem within a character's own mind
- **Person Against Society** A problem between a character and society, the law, or some tradition
- **Person Against Nature** A problem with some element of nature, such as a blizzard or a hurricane
- **Person Against Destiny** A problem or struggle that appears to be beyond a character's control

Dialogue: The words spoken between two or more characters

Foil: The character who acts as a villain or challenges the main character

Mood: The feeling or emotion a piece of writing creates in a reader

Moral: The lesson a story teaches

Narrator: The person or character who tells the story, giving background information and filling in details between portions of dialogue

Plot: The action that makes up the story, following a plan, or plot line

Plot Line: The planned action or series of events in a story (The basic parts are the beginning, the rising action, the high point, and the ending.)

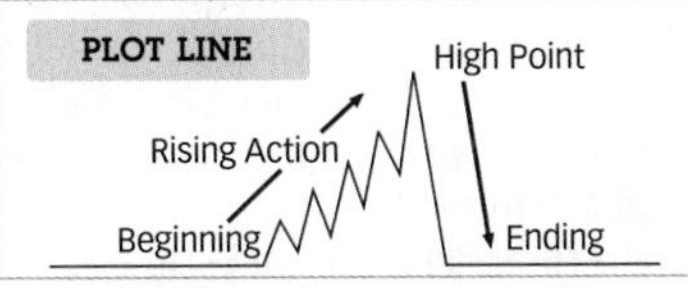

- The **beginning** introduces the characters and the setting.
- The **rising action** adds a conflict—a problem for the characters.
- The **high point** is the moment when the conflict is strongest.
- The **ending** tells how the main characters have changed.

Elements of Fiction

Take time to clarify for students any element that they don't completely understand. For example, they might be confused about the differences between

- an antagonist,
- a foil, and
- a protagonist.

As practice, have students look at the sample short story on SE pages 344–345 and identify

- the protagonist (Celia),
- the foil (Shaundra), and
- the antagonist (Celia's shyness).

Struggling Learners

To reinforce students' understanding of the term *conflict*, write the types of conflict as headings across the board. Encourage students to name familiar stories and to identify the type of conflict involved in each. List the titles under the headings.

Possible titles:

- Person against person—*The Lion King* (Scar vs. Simba)
- Person against himself—*Finding Nemo* (Marlin vs. his fear of the open sea)
- Person against society—*A Christmas Carol* (Ebenezer Scrooge vs. the tradition of Christmas)
- Person against nature—*Moby Dick* (Captain Ahab vs. the whale)
- Person against destiny—"Cinderella" (Cinderella's chance to become a princess vs. a lifetime of servitude to members of her stepfamily)

Share examples from literature to

- help students distinguish between the different points of view, and
- guide students to understand how each point of view affects what readers learn about story characters.

Point out the difference between the main idea of a story (what it's mostly about) and the **theme** (*see below*). Have students identify the main idea and theme of the sample story on SE pages 344–345. (Main Idea: A girl is too shy to ask a boy to dance until a friend urges her to take a chance. Theme: Taking action is sometimes an act of courage.)

Have students work on the **Try It** independently or in pairs.

 **Answers**

Answers will vary. Responses should show that students

- recognize the conflict that drives the story plot,
- know when and where the story takes place, and
- can identify the main character.

Point of View: The angle from which a story is told (The angle depends upon the narrator, or person telling the story.)

- **First-Person Point of View** This means that one of the characters is telling the story: "We're just friends—that's all—but that means everything to us."
- **Third-Person Point of View** In third person, someone from outside the story is telling it: "They're just friends—that's all—but that means everything to them." There are three third-person points of view: *omniscient, limited omniscient,* and *camera view.* (See the illustrations on the right.)

Protagonist: The main character or hero in a story (See *antagonist.*)

Setting: The place and the time period in which a story takes place

Theme: The message about life or human nature that is "hidden" in the story that the writer tells

Tone: The writer's attitude toward her or his subject (can be described by words like *angry* and *humorous*)

Total Effect: The overall influence or impact that a story has on a reader

Third-Person Points of View

Omniscient point of view allows the narrator to tell the thoughts and feelings of all the characters.

Limited omniscient point of view allows the narrator to tell the thoughts and feelings of only one character at a time.

Camera view (objective view) allows the story's narrator to record the action from his or her own point of view without telling any of the characters' thoughts or feelings.

 Select a story that you have read that fits one of the five basic conflicts on page 351. In one sentence, describe its conflict. In another sentence, describe the setting for this story. Add a sentence that describes the protagonist.

Advanced Learners

Point out that the sample story on SE pages 344–345 is written from the third-person point of view. Ask students if it is told from the omniscient, limited omniscient, or camera point of view (limited omniscient). Challenge students to rewrite the story from either the first-person point of view or the third-person omniscient point of view.

Teaching Tip: Conveying Theme

To make it easier for students to write fiction, help them become familiar with the strategies authors use to "hide" the theme, or message about life or human nature, in a story. Point out to students that once they have decided on the message they want readers to get from their story, they can convey that message through

- what the main character says, does, feels, and thinks;
- what happens as a result of what the main character says, does, feels, or thinks;
- and what other story characters say and think about the main character.

Have students find examples of each of these points in "Just Keep Going . . ." on SE pages 344–345.

Response to Literature

Poetry Review

Poetry uses sounds and images to reach beyond your mind and grab your heart. Other forms of writing may inform or entertain, but a poem's purpose is to make you feel and respond—and sometimes even soar!

One great way to respond to a poem is to write a poetry review. Like a book review, a poetry review tells what the poem is about. It also explains what makes the poem work so well. In this chapter, you will learn how to write your own poetry review.

Writing Guidelines

Subject: A poem that you enjoy
Form: A review
Purpose: To analyze and explain what is good about the poem
Audience: Family and classmates

Poetry Review

Objectives

- understand what a poetry review is
- use what was learned about responding to literature to create a poetry review
- plan, draft, revise, edit, and share a poetry review

A **poetry review** interprets the meaning of a poem and tells what makes the poem work well.

Analyzing poetry can be a challenge for readers of all ages.

- As you work through the steps of writing a poetry review, provide extensive modeling and examples.
- Depending on the ability of your students, consider having the class write the poetry review as a group activity.
- Or have students work in pairs or small groups to discuss a poem, share interpretations, and then write individual reviews. Even if the essays are similar, students will have accomplished the task and realized the benefits of working cooperatively in a group.

Poetry Review

Give students a few moments to read "The Hawk" silently and think about its meaning.

- Ask students to tell what the poem is about and describe how it makes them feel.
- Invite volunteers to take turns reading aloud the poem. Encourage them to read it expressively, to convey the feelings they had while reading the poem to themselves.
- Then ask students who didn't understand the poem when they read it silently if hearing it read aloud helped.

As you introduce each element at the bottom of the page (meaning, imagery, sound, thoughts), have students read the paragraph focusing on that element in the sample review on SE page 325.

Do not go on until you are satisfied that students understand how each element is treated in the review.

Provide time for students to review the poetry terms explained on SE pages 360–361.

Poetry Review

For her response to poetry, Teresha chose to write a review of the following poem about a hawk. You will find Teresha's review on the next page.

The Hawk

Keen yellow eyes
fly high. Sharp shrieks
pierce the clouds.

He is lord of height and
gusting wind,
master of green valleys
and harvest fields.

A songbird trembles.
A mouse
hides as the winged
shadow passes.

The hungry hunter glides
alone
through autumn's
cloudy gray sky.

— Doug Niles

Writing the Review

When Teresha wrote her review of "The Hawk," she focused on the following elements of poetry:

- **Meaning:** The first paragraph describes the topic of the poem.
- **Imagery:** The second paragraph focuses on images, or word pictures.
- **Sound:** The third paragraph deals with the sounds in the poem.
- **Thoughts:** The final paragraph tells what Teresha thought of the poem.

See pages **360–361** for poetry terms you may want to use in your review. Each term has a definition and an example to make it easy to understand.

Struggling Learners

You can streamline the assignment if necessary by having students write about *imagery* or *sound* (rather than both) in the middle part of the essay.

Beginning
The beginning identifies the poet and tells about the **meaning** of the poem.

Middle
The middle paragraphs focus on **imagery** and **sound**.

Ending
The ending reflects on the reviewer's **thoughts**.

Flying with "The Hawk"

Doug Niles's poem, "The Hawk," is about a hawk flying high on a fall day. The poem describes the bird as a hunter, gliding far above the ground as it watches for prey. The poem does a good job of making the reader feel the greatness of this hunting bird.

One way the poet expresses this greatness is with exciting imagery. He includes sights like the hawk's yellow eyes, its passing shadow, and the cloudy gray sky. The poem also mentions the trembling of a songbird as the hawk passes overhead.

The poem includes some interesting sounds as well. There's a little alliteration in the poem, in "sharp shriek" and "hungry hunter." The poem also uses words that make interesting sounds. The cry of a hawk is a "shriek," the word "gusting" sounds like wind, and the word "trembles" seems to shake with fear.

This poem captures the feeling of watching a hawk flying high in the air. The reader feels as if he or she were actually gliding with the hawk, trembling with the songbird, and hiding with the mouse.

Respond to the reading. Think about how Teresha uses the following traits in her review; then answer the questions that follow.

- ☐ **Ideas** (1) Did Teresha notice anything about the poem that you did not? Explain.
- ☐ **Organization** (2) What is the main purpose for each of the paragraphs in Teresha's review?
- ☐ **Voice & Word Choice** (3) What words show Teresha's feelings about this poem?

Literature Connections: You can read another type of response-to-literature writing in "Three Essays on *Barrio Boy*."

LITERATURE

Respond to the reading.

Answers

Ideas 1. Possible choices:

- meaning—idea of the hunter searching for prey
- imagery—hawk's yellow eyes, passing shadows, green land, cloudy gray sky, trembling songbird, hiding mouse
- sound—alliteration (sharp shrieks, hungry hunter); interesting sounds (shrieks, gusting)

Organization 2. The first paragraph identifies the poem and the poet and tells the meaning of the poem. The second paragraph describes imagery in the poem. The third paragraph focuses on the sounds in the poem. The fourth paragraph tells what Teresha thinks about the poem and how it makes her feel.

Voice & Word Choice 3. The reader feels as if he or she were actually gliding with the hawk, trembling with the songbird, and hiding with the mouse.

Literature Connections

In Ernesto Galarza's poem "Barrio Boy," the main character adapts to a new school after moving to the United States from Mexico. Discuss "Three Essays on *Barrio Boy*," noting that the first includes well-supported details that make it a stronger poetry review than the other two essays.

Discuss and compare the strengths and weaknesses of each review. For additional response-to-literature models, see the Reading-Writing Connections beginning on page TE-36.

Advanced Learners

Invite students to locate additional poems about hawks or other birds.

Have students choose one poem and compare and contrast the meaning, imagery, and sounds they identify in that poem with those in "The Hawk."

Students should then

- tell which poem they like best and why, and
- explain how that poem makes them feel.

Prewriting Understanding a Poem

Spend time as a class reading and rereading "Never Out of Mind" and discussing the questions.

Meaning

- It's about a waterfall that the speaker cannot forget.
- The writer imagines seeing and hearing the waterfall in the most ordinary things. He seems to be comforted by this.
- The ideas are imaginative and surprising.

Imagery

- Sensory details: quiet pool, rain on bus windows, parking lot puddles, foam in storm drains, clock-radio static, hissing strips of bacon, moans of traffic, shower steam, spray from a hydrant, slick door handle
- The details about ordinary familiar things make readers feel as if the waterfall is part of their memory.

Sound

- Alliteration: not, never; parking, puddles; static, strips, steam, spray, slick; look, listen
- Onomatopoeia: static, hissing, moans

Technology Connections

Students can use the added features of the Net-text as they explore this stage of the writing process.

***Write Source Online* Net-text**

Prewriting Understanding a Poem

The first step to understanding a poem is reading it—several times. Read the following poem and then consider the questions below.

Meaning: Poems are full of meaning. To understand the meaning of a poem, ask yourself three questions.

- What is the poem's subject?
- How does the writer feel about the subject?
- How do I feel about the writer's ideas?

Imagery: Poems contain images, or word pictures. Ask yourself the following questions to focus on imagery.

- What sensory details (things you can see, hear, smell, taste, or touch) does the writer include?
- What feelings do those sensory details create?

Sound: Poems play with the way words sound. Focus on the sound of the poem by asking yourself the following questions. (See pages 360–361.)

- Does the poem include words that sound alike *(rhyme)* or words that repeat beginning consonant sounds *(alliteration)*?
- Does the poem include words that sound like the noise they name *(onomatopoeia)*?

Never Out of Mind

My favorite place
is not far away,
is never out of mind—
a waterfall above a quiet pool.
I look for my waterfall
in rain on bus windows
and parking lot puddles
and foam in storm drains.
I listen for my waterfall
in clock-radio static
and hissing strips of bacon
and distant moans of traffic.
I reach for my waterfall
in steam from the shower
or spray from a hydrant
or the slick handle on my front door.
My favorite place
is not far away
is never out of mind—
as long as I look and listen and reach.

—Luke Regan

Prewrite

Review the poem. Reread "Never Out of Mind." Ask yourself the questions above and think about the meaning, imagery, sound, and overall thoughts and feelings about the poem.

Advanced Learners

Students who would like to select a different poem to review should be encouraged to do so. Provide a variety of poetry books from which to choose.

Gathering Details

Teresha used a chart to help her gather answers about the meaning, imagery, and sound of the poem she reviewed—"The Hawk."

Gathering Chart

Meaning	Imagery	Sound
The hawk is - alone - feared - a hunter	Word pictures - yellow eyes - green valleys - harvest fields - winged shadow - gray sky	Rhymes - hides/glides Alliteration - sharp shrieks - hungry hunter Onomatopoeia - "shriek" - "gusting"

Create a poem chart. Use the chart above as a guide to gather details about your poem. Fill in information about your poem's meaning, imagery, and sound.

Writing Creating Your First Draft

With your chart in hand, you are ready to write the first draft of your poetry review. Take it one paragraph at a time.

- **Beginning Paragraph** In your first paragraph, name the poem (in quotation marks) and the poet. Then summarize the poem's *meaning* by using information from your gathering chart. End with a focus statement that sums up how you feel about the poem.
- **Middle Paragraphs** Use the second and third columns of your chart to write the middle paragraphs of your review. In the first middle paragraph, describe the *imagery* of the poem. In the second middle paragraph, focus on the *sound*.
- **Ending Paragraph** In your last paragraph, explain your *feelings* about the poem. Leave the reader with a final thought about it.

Create your first draft. Write the beginning, middle, and ending of your poetry review. Follow the guidelines above.

Prewriting Gathering Details

After students look over the sample gathering chart, suggest that they look back at "Flying with 'The Hawk' " on SE page 325 to see how Teresha incorporated these ideas into her review.

- Students can use the answers from the class discussion and analysis of "Never Out of Mind," along with any new ideas they have, to fill in the gathering chart.

Writing Creating Your First Draft

Read aloud the guidelines for creating a first draft of a poetry review.

- Stress that students should follow the guidelines closely.
- Encourage students to refer frequently to Teresha's sample poetry review on SE page 325 and to use it as a model whenever possible.

Remind students that poem titles, like those of short stories, belong in quotation marks.

✱ For more about punctuating titles, see SE page 600.

Technology Connections

Students can use the added features of the Net-text as they explore this stage of the writing process.

Write Source Online ***Net-text***

English Language Learners

Complete the gathering chart as a classroom or group activity. Have each student draw a gathering chart on a piece of paper. Then help students identify words and phrases in the poem that relate to meaning, imagery, and sound.

Revising Improving Your Writing

Suggest that students work with a partner to revise their papers.

- Have partners exchange papers and use the questions as a guide as they read each other's papers.
- Then have responders list the traits (ideas, organization, voice, word choice, and sentence fluency) and answer the questions for each trait.
- If the answer to any question is "no," have responders suggest how their partner might make revisions.

Editing Checking for Conventions

Suggest that students read backward from the end of their essay to look for spelling errors. When they are not distracted by the meaning of the words, they are more likely to find spelling mistakes.

* See SE page 642 for help with common spelling errors.

Publishing Sharing Your Writing

Provide time for students to share their finished reviews with each other.

Technology Connections

Have students use the Writing Network features of the Net-text to comment on each other's drafts.

Write Source Online ***Net-text***

Revising Improving Your Writing

Once you finish the first draft of your poetry review, set the draft aside for a while. Then return to it and revise it by looking at the first five traits.

- ☐ **Ideas** Have I summed up the meaning of the poem? Have I included specific details about the imagery and sound?
- ☐ **Organization** Do I follow the plan from page 327 for my beginning, middle, and ending?
- ☐ **Voice** Does my interest show? Is my review enjoyable to read?
- ☐ **Word Choice** Are my words clear and accurate?
- ☐ **Sentence Fluency** Do my sentences read smoothly?

Revise your editorial. Using the questions above as a guide, revise your work until it flows smoothly and is clear and interesting throughout.

Editing Checking for Conventions

Now that you have revised your work, it's time to check it for any errors in conventions.

- ☐ **Conventions** Is my review free of errors in spelling, punctuation, capitalization, and grammar?

Edit your editorial. Check your review carefully and correct any errors you may find in spelling, punctuation, and so on.

Publishing Sharing Your Writing

By letting other people read your review, you encourage them to read and think about the poem. Here are some ideas for publishing your review.

- Submit your review to the school paper.
- Post your review on a bulletin board where classmates can read it.
- Mail a copy of the poem and your review to a relative. Ask the person to respond with an opinion of the poem and of your review.
- Send your review to the poet (perhaps in care of the publisher). Let him or her know why you enjoyed the poem.

Share your opinion. Let other people see your review. Their responses may give you new insights into the poem, and they may recommend other poems for you to read.

Grammar Connection

Complex Sentences with Relative Pronouns

- **Proofreader's Guide** pages 706 (+)
- ***Write Source*** page 514
- ***SkillsBook*** pages 129–130
- ***GrammarSnap*** Simple, Compound, Complex, and Compound-Complex Sentences

Using the Right Word

- **Proofreader's Guide** pages 658–659

Subject-Verb Agreement

- ***Write Source*** pages 508 (+), 509 (+)
- ***SkillsBook*** page 109
- ***GrammarSnap*** Subject-Verb Agreement with Compound Subjects, Subject-Verb Agreement with Prepositional Phrases

Advanced Learners

Invite students to read and review other poems. Encourage them to type, print, and compile the poems and their reviews in a class book. Some students might like to illustrate the book and create a cover for it. Display the book in the classroom or in the school library for all students to read.

Response to Literature

Across the Curriculum

Imagine that you could travel back in time and interview a historical figure. Whom would you choose? Joan of Arc? Galileo? King Arthur? Imagine that you could travel to another planet. Where would you go? Mars, Neptune, or some undiscovered world? Literature allows you to make these journeys.

This chapter shows you how you might respond to literature in a number of classes. For example, you will learn how to interview a historical figure and summarize a scientific article. The chapter will also help you prepare for a writing assessment.

What's Ahead

- **Social Studies:** Interviewing a Person from History
- **Science:** Summarizing a Science Article
- **Practical Writing:** Evaluating a Book

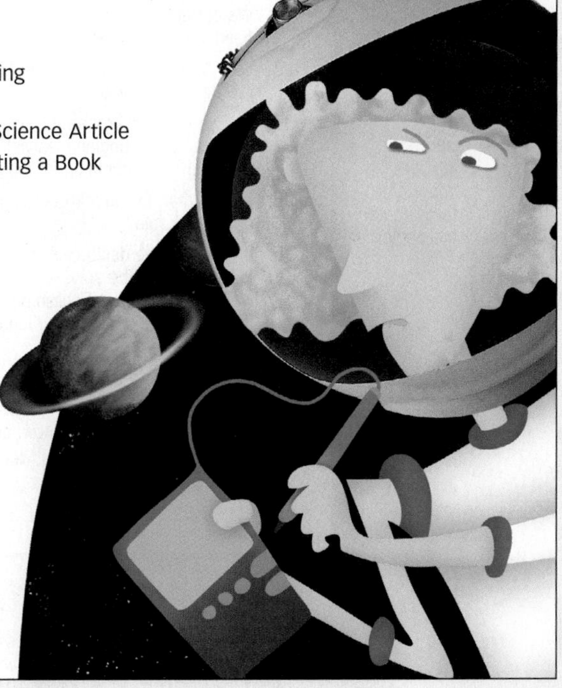

Across the Curriculum

Objectives

- apply what students have learned about responding to literature to other curriculum areas
- practice writing for assessment

The lessons on the following pages provide samples of response writing students might do in different content areas. The particular form used in one content area may also be used in another content area (for example, students can interview a person from science just as well as they can interview someone from social studies).

Assigning these forms of writing will depend on

- the skill level of your students,
- the subject matter they are studying in different content areas, and
- the writing goals of your school, district, or state.

Social Studies: Interviewing a Person from History

Ask students to recall the insight that they developed for their story interpretation and how it guided their writing. Help students recognize that the sample writer has used a similar strategy to organize and guide this interview.

- The beginning introduces the character (Queen Elizabeth), the setting (England, 1600), and gives an insight into her importance. (She was one of the greatest rulers of all time.)
- The middle provides more background information. The writer chooses an important event, specifically the defeat of the Spanish Armada, to support the insight.
- The ending adds a new insight into the kind of entertainment the queen might have enjoyed.

Social Studies: Interviewing a Person from History

One way to bring the past to life is to imagine interviewing an important person you have read about. In the following interview, one student asks Queen Elizabeth I of England about her reign.

The Interview of a Lifetime

The **beginning** answers the questions *when, where,* and *who.*

JB: This is Johnny Babcock, time-traveling reporter for Time Travel Network News. I'm in Windsor, England. It's 1600, and I have been granted an interview with Queen Elizabeth herself. Your Majesty, would you mind answering a few questions?

QE: It would be our pleasure. What do you want to know?

JB: Well, I'm interested in your place in history. Some would say that you are one of the greatest rulers in English history. Do you think so?

QE: We certainly would never state it quite so bluntly, but our reign has been long, and it has been marked by significant achievements.

JB: Your Majesty, why do you say "our" instead of "my" reign? You don't have a king, do you?

The **middle** includes important facts about the person.

QE: No, we have never married. But since we represent the people and the land of England, as well as ourselves—the person named Elizabeth—it is common for the monarch to use "we," not "I."

JB: I see. What do you think is the greatest accomplishment of England under your rule?

QE: It has to be the destruction of the Spanish Armada. If our fleet had failed to defeat the ships of Phillip II, England would have lost the war with Spain. The English people's freedom would have ended then and there. Instead, our lands prospered, and we became a great world power.

The **ending** shows the person in her time in history.

JB: What do you do for fun?

QE: We are very interested in the plays of that Shakespeare fellow. In fact, we are going to one now, and we must not be late.

JB: You've been very generous with your time, Your Majesty. Thank you, and enjoy the play!

English Language Learners

Role-play an interview situation.

- If possible, have the students' social studies teacher play the role of the historical figure studied in that class.
- Encourage students to offer suggestions for interview questions based on what they know about the historical figure.
- The teacher should answer the questions as that person.
- Afterward, discuss the interview.
- Students should prepare for the **Try It** activity on SE page 331 using the kinds of questions that are asked during the interview.

Writing Tips

Before you write . . .

- **Do your research.**
  Learn a lot about the person you are going to interview. Check several different sources: an encyclopedia, a book, Web sites, and perhaps even a historically accurate movie.
- **Take notes.**
  Jot down plenty of facts that you can use to write questions for the interview.
- **Organize your thoughts.**
  Plan how you will begin your interview. Then think about your purpose and consider which facts you will use in the middle. Finally, decide on a dramatic detail that you can use in your conclusion.

During your writing . . .

- **Let your questions guide you.**
  Ask questions that require more than a yes or no answer. Ask about the person's place in history, as well as his or her successes and failures.
- **Let the character speak in his or her true voice.**
  Learn a little about the manner of speech the person might have used and let that show in the interview.

After you've written a first draft . . .

- **Get feedback.**
  Ask one of your classmates or someone from your family to read your interview. See if the reader has any suggestions for revision.
- **Proofread carefully**
  Go over your interview to make sure that there are no mistakes in spelling, punctuation, or other conventions.

Choose a real person from history and imagine a fictional interview with her or him. Research your subject and write an imaginary conversation with that person. Then share your interview with your teacher and classmates.

Writing Tips

Review the writing tips, which provide a sound and thorough approach for researching a subject and writing the interview.

- Consult with social studies teachers for a list of people students have been studying and might enjoy writing about.
- If possible, provide examples of interviews with other historical figures for students to read and discuss.
- Explain that the sample interview on SE page 330 is informative and factual (except for the imaginary dialogue), but it also shows that the writer had fun with the subject. For example, point out the queen's use of *we,* not *I,* and her reference to "that Shakespeare fellow."

Encourage students to be creative and to have fun with their subjects as they plan and write their interviews for the **Try It** activity.

Answers

Interviews will vary but should tell who the person is and provide an insight into why the person is important.

English Language Learners

Have students select a person whom they have recently studied in social studies class and about whom they can readily find information at the appropriate reading level.

If you did a role-play interview (TE page 330), remind students to refer to the notes they took at that time.

Advanced Learners

Invite students who enjoy performing to do an interview with a partner, taking either the role of interviewer or interviewee, and to present the report to the class.

Science: Summarizing a Science Article

Remind students that a summary

- focuses on the main idea of an article,
- retells only the most important ideas,
- is in the writer's own words, and
- is much shorter in form than the original article.

Emphasize that when students summarize information, they need to write the main ideas **in their own words** (*see below*).

Science: Summarizing a Science Article

A summary paragraph "boils down" the information in a longer piece of writing. The article on this page describes the excitement in the scientific community as new discoveries are made about the planet Mars. The paragraph is a student's summary of the article.

An Exciting New Era of Planetary Exploration

Mars, named for the Roman god of war, has always been an intriguing spark of color in the night sky. With its faint reddish hue and unusual brightness, it stands out among the field of stars. Mars is considered the most likely planet to have life forms. For thousands of years, humans have studied and pondered the Red Planet. Beginning with crude probes that reached the planet in the 1970s, scientists have progressed until we now have three satellites—two American and one from the European Union—in orbit around Mars.

By far the most detailed information on Mars has reached us through the Martian rover project. Two robots, named *Spirit* and *Opportunity*, were launched in 2003 and landed on the Red Planet early in 2004. Unlike some earlier probes, these robots landed perfectly and went to work studying the planetary surface. Their primary mission was to look for signs of water, and they recorded much data from each of the landing sites, which were on opposite sides of Mars.

Spirit landed in Gusev Crater, an area about the size of Connecticut. *Spirit* soon began to move around, dig in the sandy ground, and grind away at nearby rocks. On the other side of the planet, *Opportunity* rolled right into a small crater—a cosmic "hole in one." It went to work studying bedrock that was exposed when the crater was formed. Both rovers have added much new evidence to support the hypothesis that Mars was once a much wetter, warmer place than it is today. In 2007, *Spirit* took pictures of stones revealing an explosive past on Mars. Scientists hope the two vehicles will continue operating.

A Good Year for Mars

Topic Sentence — ***Mars has been watched throughout history and is being closely studied today.***

Body — *It is the planet most likely to have life and was named for the Roman god of war. Humans have launched satellites that are in orbit around Mars. In 2004, two rovers, named Spirit and Opportunity, found out a lot about Mars. The rovers landed on two different sides of the planet. Their main mission was to look for signs of water, and both rovers found evidence that water was once there. One set of pictures reveal significant past explosions.*

Closing Sentence — ***Together, the rovers have sent much useful information back to Earth.***

Teaching Tip: In Their Own Words

Many students have difficulty with summarizing ideas in their own words. Provide opportunities for students to practice paraphrasing.

- Hand out short newspaper articles or articles from age-appropriate science or social studies magazines. (Ask your school librarian for these.)
- Have students work with a partner to summarize an article in their own words.

Tell students to

- find the main idea in each paragraph, and
- write the main idea in their own words by thinking about how they would explain it to a student in a lower grade.

English Language Learners

Select a simpler article from a science magazine.

- Put the article on an overhead transparency.
- Use a table organizer (see SE page 447) to help students identify and record the main idea and supporting details.
- Ask volunteers to give an oral summary.

Writing Tips

Before you write . . .

- **Read the article carefully.**
  Review the material to make sure you know it well. Use a dictionary to look up any words you don't understand.
- **Take notes.**
  Write down the main point of the article. Then write down important details you will want to use in the summary. For example, the main point of the article on page 332 is the history of Mars exploration. The names of the two rovers are important details that support the main point.
- **Organize your thoughts.**
  Plan a good topic sentence to begin your paragraph. Then consider which facts you will use in the body. Finally, decide on a strong concluding sentence.

During your writing . . .

- **Stick to important facts.**
  Try to write a summary that is about one third the length of the original—or shorter. Focus on the main point of the article and the most important details to support the point.
- **Use your own words.**
  Think of ways to paraphrase or summarize information. Avoid copying phrases and sentences from the article.

After you've written a first draft . . .

- **Review your paragraph.**
  Make sure that you have captured the main point of the article. Check to see that you have included the most important details.
- **Proofread carefully.**
  Check your paragraph to make sure that there are no mistakes in spelling, punctuation, or other conventions.

Try It Read a brief article that you find (in a newspaper or magazine) or one that your teacher hands out to you. Using the tips above, write a single paragraph that summarizes the article.

LITERATURE

Writing Tips

Provide students with a variety of science articles from which to choose. Ask a science teacher to suggest suitable topics or choose an appropriate article.

Before assigning the **Try It** activity, review the writing tips with students.

Answers

Summaries will vary but should be shorter than the original article, contain a clear topic sentence that states the article's main point, use only the most important details to support the main point, and have a strong concluding sentence.

Struggling Learners

It will be easier for some students to write a summary if they can underline or highlight the important details as they read.

- Provide newspaper and magazine articles that students may mark up.
- Students may find it easier to highlight or underline the important details first and then determine the main point of the article.

Practical Writing: Evaluating a Book

Invite students who have read *The Black Cauldron* to tell whether they agree or disagree with the sample evaluation.

- Next, ask how many students would consider reading *The Black Cauldron* based on the evaluation. Have them explain why.
- Then ask how many would *not* read it because of the evaluation. Have them explain why.

Point out that when students evaluate a book, much of the evaluation

- will be subjective and
- will depend on their own taste and preferences.

However, the evaluation should reflect serious, careful thought about the book.

Practical Writing: Evaluating a Book

A book evaluation form gives readers a quick way to write about literature. It also allows other students to decide if they would like to read the book. The following evaluation was filled out by a student who had just finished reading *The Black Cauldron*.

Talk Back to Books: Reader Reaction Form

Please answer the questions below by circling the appropriate number or writing a brief response.

Book and Author *The Black Cauldron by Lloyd Alexander*

Rate your reaction to the following:

Setting	1 Dull	2 Interesting	(3) Exciting
Plot	1 Boring	(2) Engaging	3 Thrilling
Characters	1 Shallow	(2) Believable	3 Fascinating
Author's Voice	1 Hard to recall	2 Interesting	(3) Unforgettable

What was the best part of the book? *I liked the part where Taran and his friends were arguing with Orwen, Orgoch, and Orddu about the Black Cauldron.*

Who was your favorite character, and why? *I liked Taran because he was confused about what to do but really tried to do the right thing. I think it was funny that he was called an "Assistant Pig-Keeper."*

List any criticisms of the book. *I didn't like the way Prince Ellidyr was unkind to Taran and that Taran could never fight back.*

Writing Tips

Before you write . . .

- **Consider the questions you will need to answer.** Review the evaluation form before you read the book, if possible. Pay special attention to the items on the form.
- **Read the book carefully.** Take your time as you read. Notice how the story is developing, what the characters are like, and how the writer chooses words and puts them together.
- **Take notes.** Jot down any reactions that strike you as important. If you really like something, are puzzled by something, or dislike something about the book, make a note of your reaction so you'll remember it later.

During your writing . . .

- **Be honest.** Share what you liked and didn't like about the book. Provide reasons for your opinions.
- **Use complete sentences.** If a question requires more than a short answer, write out your response as a complete sentence.

After you've written a first draft . . .

- **Check all the questions.** Make sure you haven't misread a question. Double-check your answers to make sure they represent your true opinions.
- **Proofread carefully.** Review your evaluation form to make sure that there are no mistakes in spelling, punctuation, or other conventions.

LITERATURE

Try It Think of a book you have recently read. Then, on your own paper, re-create and complete the form on the bottom of page 334.

If you supply a standard book evaluation form for students to use to do the **Try It** activity, review the directions with them now. After students complete the activity, invite them to share their ratings, comments, and recommendations.

Answers

Answers will vary.

Many Internet booksellers provide an option for customers to review books. Students may enjoy submitting their evaluations to one of these sites.

English Language Learners

Create a form similar to the one on SE page 334, but adjust the format and language to suit the needs of your students. For example, you can change *List any criticisms of the book* to *What didn't you like about the book?* Make a photocopy of the form for each student.

Advanced Learners

Invite interested students to read and evaluate other selections in *The Chronicles of Prydain* series or any other book by Lloyd Alexander.

- Suggest that each student read a different book.
- Have students meet to share and discuss their evaluations.
- Encourage students to use their evaluations as a basis to discuss the author's work in general.

Writing for Assessment

If your students must take a school, district, or state assessment this year, focus on the form of writing on which they will be tested.

Read through the instruction and the directions for the sample with students. Ask them which words and phrases in the directions they would underline or highlight as key words to remember if they were taking the test. (Possible choices: 40 minutes, focus on the main characters, show your insight, support focus with examples from the text)

Make sure students understand that the marks and words in blue are the student reader's notes.

Test Prep!

On-demand writing tests often feature responses to literature. A response to literature prompt ensures that all students start with the same material. It also makes grading easier, because graders can be familiar with the literary work and can check citations. Response to literature prompts are also popular because they test reading and writing ability at the same time.

Response to Literature

Writing for Assessment

On some state and school tests, you may be asked to read a story and write a response to it. The next two pages give you an example of such a test. Read the directions, the story, and notice the student's underlining and comments (**in blue**). Then read the student's response on pages 338–339.

Response to Literature Prompt

Directions:

- Read the following story.
- As you read, make notes. (Your notes will not be graded.)
- After reading the story, write an essay. You have 40 minutes to read, plan, write, and proofread your work.

When you write, focus on the main characters in the story. Show your insight into how the characters change as they interact with each other. Use clear organization, and support your focus with examples from the text.

Acquiring the Taste

When Maria and Janelle became seventh graders, they thought they were pretty grown-up. They had graduated from Franklin Elementary and now attended Westmore Junior High. The old posters of cats and koalas had come down from their bedroom walls, and new posters of rock stars had gone up. Maria and Janelle decided they even "needed to learn how to drink coffee." One Saturday morning, they met at Chiara's Coffee Shop and ordered cappuccinos.

"Bleck!" Maria said, letting the coffee dribble out of her mouth and back into the cup. "How can adults drink this stuff?"

Janelle laughed. "Cappuccino is an acquired taste." She took a sip and winced.

"If *acquired* means *awful*, I have to agree," Maria said. She took another taste. The stuff was bitter and burning. She gasped and started to choke.

Struggling Learners

Many students experience stress at the idea of timed writing tests. If your class participates in timed assessments, tell students the actual time limit for the test, and reassure them that they will have ample opportunity during the year to practice reading, planning, writing, and proofreading more quickly.

Jerome's hair was shaved short, and he wore a button-down shirt with khaki pants. He was more dressed up than Celia had ever seen him.

"Well," Shaundra said, "what's your decision?"

Celia began to walk. The first step was the hardest. She felt like she was teetering on a tightrope. The music pounded in her chest. Halfway there, she wondered if she should veer off to the restroom, but something inside her said, "Just keep going." Suddenly, she stood in front of Jerome.

He looked up, saw her, and smiled. "What's up, Celia?" He was wearing cologne.

High Point

The high point is when the main character makes her decision.

Celia shrugged, and she couldn't think of a single thing to say. How was she going to get out of this one? Taking a deep breath, she blurted, "You don't want to dance, do you?"

Jerome's smile grew broader. "Sure." They walked together out to the free-throw line. Then the beat stopped. Celia and Jerome were left standing there, facing each other in dead silence. She wanted to sink into the floor. At last, the DJ started a slow song.

Ending

The ending suggests that the main character changes.

Jerome murmured, "So, I guess Shaundra told you I like you."

Celia relaxed and smiled. "Maybe she did, and maybe she didn't."

CREATIVE

Respond to the reading. **Answer the following questions.**

- ☐ **Ideas (1) What decision is Celia struggling to make?**
- ☐ **Organization (2) How does the writer build the suspense that leads up to Celia's decision?**
- ☐ **Voice & Word Choice (3) What words or phrases keep your interest? List at least three.**

Literature Connections: **For another example of a short story, read "Hum" by Naomi Shihab Nye.**

Respond to the reading.

Possible responses:

Ideas 1. Celia can't decide whether or not to ask Jerome to dance.

Organization 2. The writer builds suspense by not revealing what Shaundra has told Jerome, by describing in detail Celia's thoughts and feelings as she walks across the gym to talk to Jerome, and by having the music stop abruptly just as Celia and Jerome start to dance.

Voice & Word Choice 3. Possible choices (accept any three): eyes grew wide, Drawing a deep breath, clenched her fists, teetering on a tightrope, pounded in her chest, Taking a deep breath, the beat stopped, facing each other in dead silence, sink into the floor

Literature Connections

In Naomi Shihab Nye's short story "Hum," a boy named Sami Salsaa and his family move to the United States from Palestine to escape the dangers of their homeland. However, Sami and his family must overcome new fears and unjust treatment after the attacks of September 11, 2001.

Discuss the theme of the short story, as well as lessons each character learns. Also discuss the story's strengths, including: natural voice, vivid details, and organization. For additional short story models, see the Reading-Writing Connections beginning on page TE-36.

English Language Learners

Be sure that students understand colloquial language and idioms used in the story. Review the meanings of the following phrases:

- take a break (stop what you are doing and rest)
- shot back (answered quickly)
- ice bob in the bowl (ice moved up and down in the bowl)
- What's up? (What are you doing? What is happening?)
- sink into the floor (disappear, be someplace else)

Struggling Learners

Creative writers use specific verbs as speaker tags, too.

- Have students identify the verbs the writer of the sample story used instead of the word *said* (shouted, shot back, blurted, murmured).
- Challenge students to use a thesaurus to find five more synonyms for *said*. (Possible responses: whispered, announced, promised, warned, yelled)

Prewriting Selecting a Topic

Point out to students that no one in real life is perfect. Other than in fairy tales, story characters are not usually all good or all bad. Believable characters have weaknesses or flaws that make them more interesting and realistic.

To help students choose a topic and develop ideas for their table diagram, discuss the strengths and weaknesses of several characters in stories they have read.

Prewriting Creating a Conflict

Recalling the kinds of decisions young people have to make in real life or in books may spark an idea for writing. Ask students to think of books they've read where the main character had to make a decision. List the different decisions on the board, and ask the following questions:

- Why was the decision so tough for the character? Was it because of a personality trait? Was it because of the possible consequences? Was it both?
- What finally helped the character decide what to do?
- What happened afterward?

Encourage students to keep these questions in mind as they try to choose a conflict.

Technology Connections

Students can use the added features of the Net-text as they explore this stage of the writing process.

***Write Source Online* Net-text**

Prewriting Selecting a Topic

A strong decision story starts with an interesting character. One way to create a character that readers will care about is to give the person one main strength and one main weakness. The strength makes the character admirable, and the weakness primes the character for a tough decision. A table diagram like the one below can help.

Table Diagram

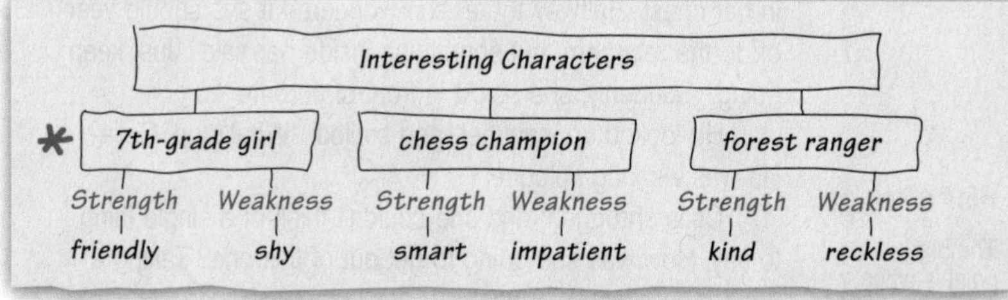

Create a table diagram. List three characters you find interesting. Under each, list one strength to make your character likable and a weakness to challenge him or her. Choose one character to write about in a story.

Creating a Conflict

The difficult decision your character will face will create the conflict in your story. The writer of the sample story listed decisions that would be tough for her character.

Decisions List

Character weakness:
- *Celia is shy.*

Tough decisions:
- *Whether to throw a surprise party for her best friend.*
- *Whether to make friends with a new girl from Japan.*
- *Whether to talk to a boy she likes.*

Choose a conflict. Think about the character you chose and his or her weakness. List decisions that would be tough for the person to make. Choose one decision for your story.

Struggling Learners

Provide support for students who have difficulty thinking of interesting characters for the table diagram. Suggest that students list the following kinds of fictional characters:

- a person with whom they can easily empathize (e.g., a new student, a boy/girl trying out for a team)
- someone they admire (e.g., a blind gymnast, a firefighter)
- a professional whose career the student finds intriguing (e.g., a private investigator, an author)

Setting the Scene and Gathering Details

You have discovered the character and the conflict for your story. Now it's time to think about the place, or setting, where your story happens. Think of a place that would make the decision especially difficult.

For the main character of the sample story, the setting is a school dance. The author used a sensory chart to gather details about the setting.

CREATIVE

Sensory Chart

Setting: School dance in a gymnasium

See	Hear	Smell	Taste	Touch/Feel
punch bowl	hip-hop	cologne	punch	cold ice
khaki pants	advice	cookies	pretzels	pounding beat
shaved hair	awkward			dizzy
	silence			shaky

Set the scene. Choose the place where your story will occur. Then use a sensory chart to gather details about the place. Try to come up with at least two details for each sense.

Focus on the Traits

Organization

The actions that take place during a story make up the plot line. Each part of the plot plays an important role in the story.

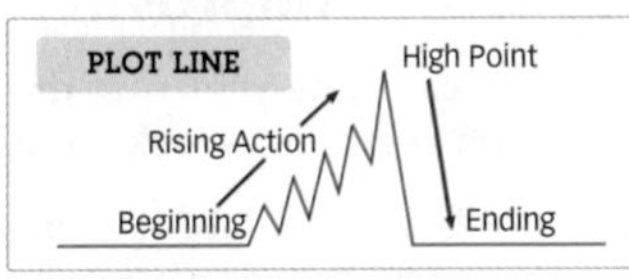

- The **beginning** introduces the characters and setting.
- The **rising action** adds a conflict—a problem for the characters.
- The **high point** is the moment when the conflict is strongest, and a decision is made.
- The **ending** tells how the main character has changed.

Prewriting

Setting the Scene and Gathering Details

Provide photocopies of the reproducible sensory chart (TE page 793). Students who have chosen a conflict that automatically suggests a setting can get right to work on their chart. For example, if the conflict is whether or not to try out for the school swim team, the setting is likely to be a pool.

Have other students work in groups to brainstorm ideas for a setting. Suggest that they begin by listing all the places they usually go during the week and on weekends.

Some students may still be trying to choose a conflict. Thinking about a setting may help them make their choice.

Focus on the Traits

Organization

Draw a plot line on the board and ask students to help you fill it out using details from "Just Keep Going . . ." on SE pages 344–345. Then encourage students to create a detailed plot line for their own story. They can use their filled-in plot line as a plan for writing.

Struggling Learners

As an alternative to creating a plot line, have students create a time line of events in their story. Provide photocopies of the reproducible time line (TE page 790), and have students use words, phrases, or drawings to show the sequence of events. Have them determine which event is the high point and highlight it.

Writing Developing Your First Draft

Encourage students to experiment with different story beginnings before they actually start to write. Students can share their ideas in small groups for immediate feedback. Tell students to

- fold a piece of paper into thirds to create three rows,
- write a different story beginning at the top of each row, and
- pass their paper around the group.

Each group member can put a check mark under the beginning he or she likes best.

Revising Improving Your Writing

As students revise, tell them to make sure they have used details and dialogue that **show, not tell** (*see below*) the reader what is happening.

* For more about using dialogue, see SE page 556.

Technology Connections

Have students use the Writing Network features of the Net-text to comment on each other's drafts.

Write Source Online ***Net-text***

Writing Developing Your First Draft

Now that you have created a character, a conflict, and a setting, you are ready to write your story. As you write, use the following tips.

1. **Start strong.** In your first sentence, focus on the character, the conflict, or the setting.
   Character: Celia smiled shyly as she ladled punch from the bowl.
   Conflict: Celia had watched Jerome all evening, but he didn't seem to know she even existed.
   Setting: The gymnasium of Cleveland Junior High was hopping.
2. **Describe the action.** Describe the action using a variety of specific details.
   Celia began to walk. The first step was the hardest. She felt like she was teetering on a tightrope. The music pounded in her chest.
3. **Include dialogue.** Let your characters speak in their natural voices.
   Jerome murmured, "So, I guess Shaundra told you I like you."
   Celia relaxed and smiled. "Maybe she did, and maybe she didn't."

Write your first draft. Tell the story of your character's big decision. Start strong and include action and dialogue to build up to the decision point. Think about the strength and weakness of your main character.

Revising Improving Your Writing

Once you complete your first draft, take a break. Later, you can return to your story and revise it by looking at the following traits.

- ☐ **Ideas** Do I tell about a tough decision for my main character? Do I include sensory details, action, and dialogue?
- ☐ **Organization** Do I start strong? Do I build to the decision point? Do I resolve, or end, the story quickly after the high point?
- ☐ **Voice** Does my voice (including dialogue) keep the reader's interest?
- ☐ **Word Choice** Have I chosen words that capture the character, conflict, and setting?
- ☐ **Sentence Fluency** Do my sentences flow well?

Revise your story. Use the questions above as a guide when you revise your first draft.

Grammar Connection

Punctuating Dialogue

- **Proofreader's Guide** pages 588 (+), 598 (+), 600 (+)
- ***GrammarSnap*** Punctuating Dialogue

Rambling Sentences

- ***Write Source*** page 507
- ***SkillsBook*** page 99

Verbs

- **Proofreader's Guide** page 724 (+)
- ***Write Source*** page 484
- ***SkillsBook*** pages 71–72
- ***GrammarSnap*** Past Tense and Past Perfect Tense Verbs

Sentences Combining (Compound Subjects and Verbs)

- ***Write Source*** page 515
- ***SkillsBook*** pages 117–118
- ***GrammarSnap*** Subject-Verb Agreement with Compound Subjects

Teaching Tip: Show, Don't Tell

Suggest that students apply one or more of these strategies:

- Add details that help the reader see, hear, smell, taste, and feel what's happening.
- Add details about a character's movements, gestures, and facial expressions.
- Give each character her or his own voice by using dialogue.

* For more about showing, not telling, see SE page 557.

entertain create imagine discover show
Writing Stories 349

Editing Checking for Conventions

After you finish revising your story, you should edit it for *conventions*.

☐ **Conventions** Have I punctuated dialogue correctly? Have I checked my spelling and grammar?

Edit your story. Use the questions above to guide your editing. When you finish, use the tips below to write a title. Then create a clean final copy and proofread it.

Creating a Title

Your title is your first opportunity to hook the reader, so make it memorable. Here are some tips for writing a strong title.

- Use a metaphor: **Teetering on a Tightrope**
- Borrow a line from the story: **Just Keep Going . . .**
- Be creative: **The Punch-Bowl Predicament**

CREATIVE

Publishing Sharing Your Story

Stories are meant to be shared. Here are three publication ideas.

- **Recite your story.**
  Read your story out loud to friends or family, or recite it from memory. Be dramatic with your voice, your facial expressions, and your gestures.
- **Create a skit.**
  Ask classmates to help you act out your story. If you can, gather costumes and props. Then perform the story for your class.
- **Submit your story.**
  Check the library for youth publications that accept stories. Format your work according to the submission guidelines and send your story in.

Present your story. Choose one of the ideas above or make up one of your own. Then share your story with the world.

Editing Checking for Conventions

If possible, take the time to review conventions for using end punctuation inside and outside quotation marks in dialogue (see SE page 600).

✱ For more help with end punctuation, see SE pages 579–580.

Creating a Title

A metaphor is a figure of speech that compares two things without using the word *like* or *as*. For example, "Teetering on a Tightrope" compares the events in the story to walking unsteadily on a tightrope.

Publishing Sharing Your Story

Provide these additional publishing ideas for students:

- Create a series of drawings that depict the main events in the story to go with the final draft.
- Use a computer to print the story. Bind it with the drawings and a creative cover and place it in the school library.

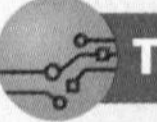

Technology Connections

Remind students that they can use the Writing Network features of the Portfolio to share their work with peers.

Write Source Online ***Portfolio***

Write Source Online ***Net-text***

Advanced Learners

Have students create illustrated board books of their stories to share with an elementary school class.

- If the stories students have written for this lesson are inappropriate, encourage them to write an additional story. This will give students experience in writing with a sound sense of purpose for an intended audience.
- Before students select the topic, suggest that they study a variety of picture books to determine what types of topics might be appropriate for younger readers.

Grammar Connection

Sentence Problems (Review)

- ***Write Source*** pages 504, 506 (+), 507
- ***SkillsBook*** page 97
- ***GrammarSnap*** Complete Sentences and Sentence Fragments

Commas in a Series

- **Proofreader's Guide** page 582 (+)
- ***SkillsBook*** pages 9–10

Story Patterns

Ask volunteers to read aloud the descriptions of the different story patterns.

- As each description is read, invite students to identify stories they have read that fit each pattern.
- Ask students to give a one-sentence summary of the story.

Alternately, ask students to name stories they have read in class. As each title is mentioned, ask which pattern the story fits.

For the **Try It** activity, students may create a summary sentence for an original story (as in the samples provided with each pattern) or they may choose to summarize a story that is already in print.

 **Answers**

Answers will vary.

After students complete the **Try It** activity, invite them to share their original story ideas in small groups.

- Ask groups to record the ideas for each story.
- Compile the ideas into one master list of story ideas to share with the class, either as a poster or a printed handout.

Students can refer to the list for story ideas for future writing assignments.

350

Story Patterns

You just finished writing a decision story, but there are many other story patterns to choose from.

The Initiation	In an *initiation* story, a young person has to overcome a test of his or her abilities or beliefs. The way the person deals with the test will influence the rest of her or his life. **Sarah struggles to adjust to a new school.**
The Surprise	In a *surprise* story, the main character and the reader misunderstand what is happening around them. The high point reveals a surprise that explains everything. **Jack thinks his friends are gossiping about him, but really they are planning a party for him.**
The Union	The *union* pattern features two main characters who are attracted to each other. Usually, they have to overcome obstacles to be together. **Haleh meets a handsome young runner from a rival school's track team.**
The Quest	In the *quest* pattern, the main character goes on a journey into the unknown, often to search for an object or reach a goal. The person usually gains the prize—or learns something in the process of losing it. **Drew journeys into the rain forest to find his father, who has been lost there for three weeks.**
The Mystery	In a *mystery* story, the main character must follow a series of tantalizing clues to discover a secret. **Jessica stays up one night to discover who is leaving flowers on her front step.**

 Choose one of the story patterns above. Think of a story that would fit that pattern. Write a single sentence that sums up the story.

Struggling Learners

To help students become more familiar with the story patterns, share with them, over time, a series of very short stories. Ask students to identify the pattern that each story follows.

Advanced Learners

To extend the **Try It** activity, have students expand their story summary into a story.

- Allow students to work with a partner, if they choose.
- Invite students to share their completed story with the class, and challenge the class to identify which pattern it represents.

Elements of Fiction

The following list includes many terms used to describe the elements or parts of literature. This information will help you discuss and write about the novels, poetry, essays, and other literary works you read.

CREATIVE

Action: Everything that happens in a story

Antagonist: The person or force that works against the hero of the story (See *protagonist.*)

Character: A person or an animal in a story

Characterization: The way in which a writer develops a character, making him or her seem believable

Here are three methods:

- Sharing the character's thoughts, actions, and dialogue
- Describing his or her appearance
- Revealing what others in the story think or say about this character

Conflict: A problem or clash between two forces in a story

There are five basic conflicts:

- **Person Against Person** A problem between characters
- **Person Against Himself or Herself** A problem within a character's own mind
- **Person Against Society** A problem between a character and society, the law, or some tradition
- **Person Against Nature** A problem with some element of nature, such as a blizzard or a hurricane
- **Person Against Destiny** A problem or struggle that appears to be beyond a character's control

Dialogue: The words spoken between two or more characters

Foil: The character who acts as a villain or challenges the main character

Mood: The feeling or emotion a piece of writing creates in a reader

Moral: The lesson a story teaches

Narrator: The person or character who tells the story, giving background information and filling in details between portions of dialogue

Plot: The action that makes up the story, following a plan, or plot line

Plot Line: The planned action or series of events in a story (The basic parts are the beginning, the rising action, the high point, and the ending.)

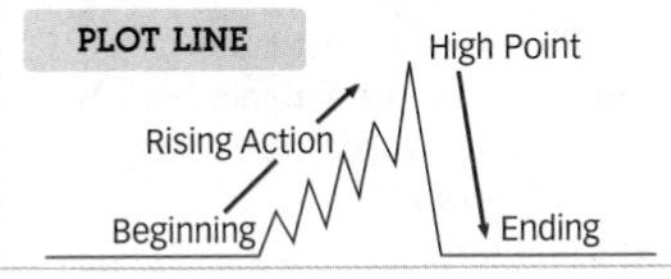

- The **beginning** introduces the characters and the setting.
- The **rising action** adds a conflict—a problem for the characters.
- The **high point** is the moment when the conflict is strongest.
- The **ending** tells how the main characters have changed.

Elements of Fiction

Take time to clarify for students any element that they don't completely understand. For example, they might be confused about the differences between

- an antagonist,
- a foil, and
- a protagonist.

As practice, have students look at the sample short story on SE pages 344–345 and identify

- the protagonist (Celia),
- the foil (Shaundra), and
- the antagonist (Celia's shyness).

Struggling Learners

To reinforce students' understanding of the term *conflict*, write the types of conflict as headings across the board. Encourage students to name familiar stories and to identify the type of conflict involved in each. List the titles under the headings.

Possible titles:

- Person against person—*The Lion King* (Scar vs. Simba)
- Person against himself—*Finding Nemo* (Marlin vs. his fear of the open sea)
- Person against society—*A Christmas Carol* (Ebenezer Scrooge vs. the tradition of Christmas)
- Person against nature—*Moby Dick* (Captain Ahab vs. the whale)
- Person against destiny—"Cinderella" (Cinderella's chance to become a princess vs. a lifetime of servitude to members of her stepfamily)

Share examples from literature to
- help students distinguish between the different points of view, and
- guide students to understand how each point of view affects what readers learn about story characters.

Point out the difference between the main idea of a story (what it's mostly about) and the **theme** (*see below*). Have students identify the main idea and theme of the sample story on SE pages 344–345. (Main Idea: A girl is too shy to ask a boy to dance until a friend urges her to take a chance. Theme: Taking action is sometimes an act of courage.)

Have students work on the **Try It** independently or in pairs.

Answers

Answers will vary. Responses should show that students
- recognize the conflict that drives the story plot,
- know when and where the story takes place, and
- can identify the main character.

Point of View: The angle from which a story is told (The angle depends upon the narrator, or person telling the story.)
- **First-Person Point of View** This means that one of the characters is telling the story: "We're just friends—that's all—but that means everything to us."
- **Third-Person Point of View** In third person, someone from outside the story is telling it: "They're just friends—that's all—but that means everything to them." There are three third-person points of view: *omniscient, limited omniscient,* and *camera view.* (See the illustrations on the right.)

Protagonist: The main character or hero in a story (See *antagonist.*)

Setting: The place and the time period in which a story takes place

Theme: The message about life or human nature that is "hidden" in the story that the writer tells

Tone: The writer's attitude toward her or his subject (can be described by words like *angry* and *humorous*)

Total Effect: The overall influence or impact that a story has on a reader

Third-Person Points of View

Omniscient point of view allows the narrator to tell the thoughts and feelings of all the characters.

Limited omniscient point of view allows the narrator to tell the thoughts and feelings of only one character at a time.

Camera view (objective view) allows the story's narrator to record the action from his or her own point of view without telling any of the characters' thoughts or feelings.

Select a story that you have read that fits one of the five basic conflicts on page 351. In one sentence, describe its conflict. In another sentence, describe the setting for this story. Add a sentence that describes the protagonist.

Advanced Learners

Point out that the sample story on SE pages 344–345 is written from the third-person point of view. Ask students if it is told from the omniscient, limited omniscient, or camera point of view (limited omniscient). Challenge students to rewrite the story from either the first-person point of view or the third-person omniscient point of view.

Teaching Tip: Conveying Theme

To make it easier for students to write fiction, help them become familiar with the strategies authors use to "hide" the theme, or message about life or human nature, in a story. Point out to students that once they have decided on the message they want readers to get from their story, they can convey that message through
- what the main character says, does, feels, and thinks;
- what happens as a result of what the main character says, does, feels, or thinks;
- and what other story characters say and think about the main character.

Have students find examples of each of these points in "Just Keep Going . . ." on SE pages 344–345.

Creative Writing

Writing Poems

"A poem begins with a lump in the throat," says Robert Frost, but that's not where poetry ends. Poetry doesn't tell readers what they should feel. It leads them to discover the feeling for themselves. Along the way, a poem also entertains them with carefully chosen words, phrases, and rhythms.

Most modern poems are written in free-verse style, which means they do not have to rhyme. In this chapter, you will write your own free-verse poem about a weather event. If all turns out well, people will be able to hear raindrops on their windows or feel the wind whirling around them when they read your poem.

Writing Guidelines

Subject: A type of weather
Form: Free-verse poem
Purpose: To entertain
Audience: Family and classmates

Copy Masters

Sensory Chart (TE p. 355)

Writing Poems

Objectives

- understand the form and content of a free-verse poem
- understand the use and effect of poetry techniques
- choose a topic (a weather memory) for a free-verse poem
- plan, draft, revise, and edit a free-verse poem

A **free-verse poem** does not follow any set pattern of rhythm or rhyme, but it does use imagery and other poetic techniques to create its own pleasing sound and vivid images.

Help students become familiar and comfortable with poetry.

- Begin class every day by reading aloud a new poem.
- To encourage students to settle down as quickly as possible, suggest that as they listen carefully, they write down one question they have about the poem.
- Use students' questions to briefly discuss the poem.

Free-Verse Poem

Read aloud traditional poems to help students hear distinct patterns of rhythm and rhyme.

Ask students to read "Lightning's Song" silently and to think about its meaning. Then invite volunteers to read it aloud, using good oral expression that reflects the meaning of the poem.

Explain that the poet uses personification—the lightning speaks as if it's a person.

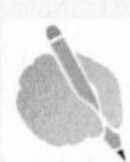

Respond to the reading.

Answers

Ideas & Organization

1. sounds:
- crackle
- boom
- grumbling

sights:
- branch across the sky
- giant, fiery tree
- flame
- flash
- beneath the clouds
- brighter than the sun

2. Indented lines form the shape of a bolt of lightning.

Voice & Word Choice 3. Look at me! I branch across the sky, I stalk across the musty earth, I flash beneath the clouds, brighter than the sun! These words show that lightning is bold and has a big ego.

Literature Connections

Each of the seven stanzas in Carl Sandburg's poem "Arithmetic" offers a unique way of thinking about arithmetic. Explain to students that "Arithmetic" is a catalogue poem, or a type of free-verse poem in which writers use a list of examples and details to convey their subject and message.

Discuss the organization and strengths of the poem. Then encourage students to brainstorm a detail or stanza that shows what they think of the subject. For additional models, see the Reading-Writing Connections beginning on page TE-36.

Free-Verse Poem

Traditional poems follow a strict pattern of rhythm and rhyme, but each free-verse poem creates its own form. Even so, when poets write free-verse poetry, they consider each word and line. They want to make sure their poems sound good and create effective images (word pictures) in the reader's mind. Hector wrote this free-verse poem to convey his feelings about lightning.

Lightning's Song

I am lightning!
I crackle and I boom,
"Look at me! Look at me!"
I branch across the sky,
like a giant, fiery tree!
I stalk across the earth
on legs of crackling flame.
I flash beneath the clouds,
brighter than the sun!
But when the sun returns,
the clouds carry me,
grumbling,
away.

Respond to the reading. Reflect on the traits in the poem above.

- ☐ **Ideas & Organization** (1) What sounds and sights does the writer include? List two of each. (2) Why are the lines of the poem staggered on the page?
- ☐ **Voice & Word Choice** (3) What words show the personality of the lightning?

Literature Connections: For another example of a free-verse poem, read "Arithmetic" by Carl Sandburg.

English Language Learners

After several volunteers have read aloud the poem with expression, invite students to read the poem chorally with you, imitating your expressiveness.

Prewriting Selecting a Topic

Like Hector, you will be writing a poem about a memory of some type of weather. To generate possible topics, Hector made a list of weather memories.

Listing

Weather Memories

- *Riding home in my uncle's car during a lightning storm*
- *Wind rattling the windows of our apartment*
- *My bare feet on hot sand at the beach*
- *Rain from one little cloud on a sunny day*
- *Wading through deep snow in the park*
- *Feeling fog's mist on my face on the way to school*

Make a list. Write the words "weather memories" as a heading on a blank piece of paper. Then start listing experiences you remember about weather until you have at least six memories. Select one as your topic.

CREATIVE

Gathering Details

An encyclopedia explains; a poem usually describes. Hector created the following sensory chart to gather details about a lightning storm before writing his poem. These details helped create effective images in his poem.

Sensory Chart

See	Hear	Smell	Taste	Touch/Feel
bright flashes	crackle	dampness	moist air	mist or rain
jagged lines	rumble	ozone		heart thumping
branching fingers	boom			
dark clouds				
sun breaking through				

Create a sensory chart. Gather sensory details about your own weather memory, using the chart above as a guide. Include specific details from the image in your mind.

Prewriting Selecting a Topic

To spark students' weather memories, have them work as a class to brainstorm a list of times when weather affected their plans. List ideas on the board as students suggest them. If students have trouble getting started, ask them these questions:

- Have you ever had a vacation, picnic, or sports event ruined because of the weather?
- Have you ever taken a picture of or wished you had a camera so you could take a picture of a weather event?
- What is your favorite kind of weather during the spring? summer? fall? winter?

Prewriting Gathering Details

Provide photocopies of the reproducible sensory chart (TE page 793). Some students may have an easier time generating sensory details if they first explore a weather memory through freewriting. Have students write for five minutes to describe their memory in as much detail as possible. Afterward, have them list sensory details they used in their writing in appropriate columns of their chart.

* For more about using sensory details, see SE page 488.

Technology Connections

Students can use the added features of the Net-text as they explore this stage of the writing process.

Write Source Online **Net-text**

Struggling Learners

- Discuss a weather memory experienced by the entire class (for example, a stormy field trip adventure, a snowstorm that began during the school day), and make a quick sketch on the board, or ask a volunteer to sketch it. Then record on the sensory chart (TE page 793) details shown in the sketch.
- Have students do the same, using their own drawing to list sensory details on their chart.

Prewriting Using Poetry Techniques

Discuss the poetry techniques here and on SE pages 360–361.

- Encourage volunteers to offer their own example of each technique.
- As students look over their sensory charts, encourage them to look for words or details that they might use to incorporate a variety of these poetry techniques into their poem.

Writing Developing Your First Draft

Read aloud the tips for writing the first draft. Then, if students have trouble getting started, suggest that they follow the same or a similar pattern as the sample weather poem on SE page 354.

Before students begin writing, discuss the boxed information about line breaks.

- Emphasize that a line break often indicates a slight pause in reading, as a comma does, even when there is no punctuation.
- Point out the line *I stalk across the earth* in the poem on SE page 354.
- Read it and the next line aloud, pausing slightly after *earth*.

Technology Connections

Students can use the added features of the Net-text as they explore this stage of the writing process.

***Write Source Online* Net-text**

Prewriting Using Poetry Techniques

Poets play with the sounds of words. **Onomatopoeia** *(ŏn′ə-mat′ə-pē′ə)* is one example. It means using words that sound like the noises they name.

I crackle and I boom.

Sometimes poets use **personification** *(pər-sŏn′ə-fĭ-kā′shən)*, which means treating a nonhuman subject as if it were human. Hector's lightning poem personifies lightning as a bold personality who speaks directly to the reader.

"Look at me! Look at me!"

Use special techniques. On your sensory chart, underline words that sound like noises. Circle words or details that could be used as personification. (For a list of other special poetry techniques, turn to pages 360–361.)

Writing Developing Your First Draft

The following tips will help you as you write your first draft.

- **Think** about the weather memory you have chosen. Scan your sensory chart again for details about it.
- **Recall** your feelings as you think about that memory.
- **Write** the first sentence or phrase that comes to mind. Don't worry about getting it perfect. Just get the words flowing. Hector started by writing, "I am lightning."
- **Keep writing** until you run out of ideas and sensory details.

Shaping Poetry

Poets also play with the way words are placed on the page. **Line breaks,** for instance, help control the rhythm of a poem. In the following example, line breaks cause pauses that emphasize the word "grumbling" and represent the storm fading in the distance.

The clouds carry me,
grumbling,
away.

Write your first draft. Use the tips above to guide your writing. Experiment with onomatopoeia, personification, and line breaks.

Grammar Connection

Prepositional Phrases

- **Proofreader's Guide** page 742 (+)
- ***Write Source*** pages 494, 519 (+)
- ***GrammarSnap*** Prepositions and Prepositional Phrases

Struggling Learners

Some students may need explicit help organizing their ideas.

- Display a skeleton framework of part or all of the sample poem on SE page 354 for students to copy (see second column).
- Leave blanks for them to fill in with their own images and details.
- These hints will give structure to students who need it.

I am ______ (kind of weather)!

I _____ (sound) and I ____ (sound),

"_____! _____!" (repeat a command or statement)

I _____ (an action) like _____ (create a simile)

I _____ (another action) on _____ . . .

Using the Library

Libraries hold a wide range of resources for your research. Besides books, you'll find periodicals (like magazines and newspapers), CD's, and a lot more. Check your school's library and the local public library to see what sorts of things are available there.

1. Books are usually divided into three sections.
   - The **fiction** section includes stories and novels. These books are arranged in alphabetical order by the authors' last names.
   - The **nonfiction** section contains books that are based on fact. They are usually arranged according to the Dewey decimal system. (See page 370.)
   - The **reference** section has encyclopedias, atlases, dictionaries, directories, and almanacs.

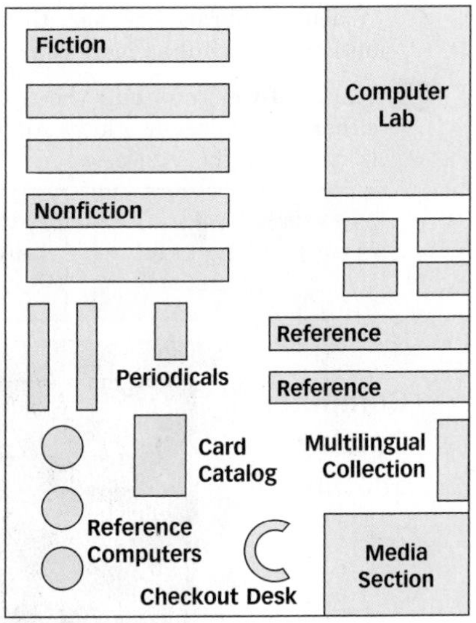

2. The periodicals section includes magazines and newspapers.
3. The computer lab has computers, often connected to the Internet. You usually sign up to use a computer.
4. The media section includes music CD's, cassettes, DVD's, videotapes, and CD-ROM's. Computer software (encyclopedias, games, and so on) may be found in this section as well.

Try It Write the following list of words down the left side of a piece of paper: *fiction books, nonfiction books, reference section, periodicals section, computer lab, media section.* Then visit your school library and look for each of these sections. When you find a section, write a short description of what is there.

Using the Library

To familiarize students with your school library, schedule a mini field trip.

- As they walk around the library, tell them to take note of the layout of the library and about what is in the various sections. They can also make quick sketches.
- Then have each student make a map similar to the one on this page, showing where resources are located in your school library.

Ask students to check with their local public library to see if a map of its layout is available.

- If so, have them bring the map to class, along with any other handouts on the library's resources.
- Discuss how to make good use of the public library.

Try It Answers

Answers will vary.

Searching a Computer Catalog

Ask your school librarian to give your class an overview of your school's computer catalog. Give students plenty of time to get comfortable with the system.

Some students may have difficulty determining which keywords to use. Give students practice by having them use keywords to research the following topics:

- how to play the **guitar**
- traveling to **Asia**
- how to design **Web pages**
- the history of **soccer**
- who the **Impressionist painters** were

Answers

Answers will vary.

Searching a Computer Catalog

Every computer catalog is a little different. Therefore, the first time you use a particular computer catalog, it's a good idea to check the instructions for using it or to ask a librarian for help. With a computer catalog, you can find information on the same book in three ways:

1. If you know the book's **title**, enter the title.
2. If you know the book's **author**, enter the author's name. (When the library has more than one book by the same author, there will be more than one entry.)
3. Finally, if you know only the **subject** you want to learn about, enter either the subject or a keyword. (A keyword is a word or phrase that is related to the subject.)

If your subject is . . .	your keywords might be . . .
constructing kites,	kite design, kite history, kite festivals and exhibitions.

Computer Catalog Screen

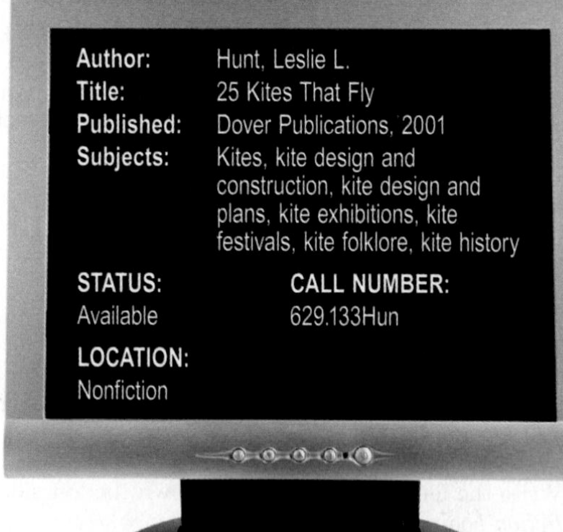

Create a computer catalog screen like the one above for a book you have read or one you are reading.

Struggling Learners

Assist students not only in determining keywords but also in narrowing the search. For example, to research traveling to Asia, students would

- choose one country as a keyword,
- then choose one city as a keyword,
- then choose keywords such as *hotels, tourist attractions,* and so on.

Searching a Card Catalog

If your library has a card catalog, it will most likely be located in a cabinet full of drawers. The drawers contain title, author, and subject cards, which are arranged in alphabetical order.

1. To find a book's **title card**, ignore a beginning *A, An,* or *The* and look under the next word of the title.
2. To find a book's **author card**, look under the author's last name. Then find the author card with the title of the book you want.
3. To find a book's **subject card**, look up an appropriate subject.

All three cards will contain important information about your book—most importantly, its call number. This number will help you find the book on the library's shelves.

RESEARCH

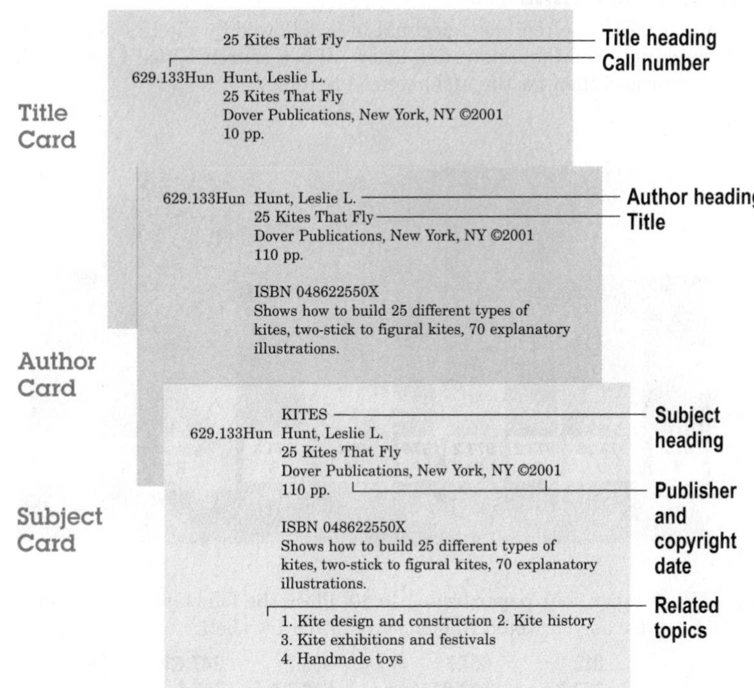

Searching a Card Catalog

Discuss the information on each of the types of catalog cards shown on the page. Point out the following items especially:

- The title card for this book will be under *T*, as if the number 25 were spelled out.
- The letters following the Dewey decimal number are the first three letters of the author's last name.
- The publisher, city, and copyright date are important details for a works-cited page.
- Related topics on the subject card are helpful if students need to make a broader search.

If your school library has a card catalog, have each student choose a topic of interest (for example, the topic they chose on TE page 364) and find the author, subject, and title cards for one book related to that topic. Have students find the information you discussed on each card.

Finding Books

Have students create a flap booklet as a study guide to the Dewey decimal system. Give each student a sheet of white 8½" x 11" paper. Read aloud the following directions (see diagram below):

1. Fold the paper in half the long way, then twice more, until there are eight sections.
2. Open the sheet. Then fold it in half from top to bottom.
3. Turn the folded paper sideways, so the fold is on the left. On the top half of the paper (the "cover"), cut out each of the eight sections to the fold.
4. Select eight Dewey decimal categories. Write one category number on each front flap.
5. On the inside left-hand flap, record the category heading.
6. On the inside right-hand (folded) section, write down one book title from the library.

Use the school library so students can find actual book titles for this activity.

Answers

1. 347 Gil
2. 546.44 C
3. 636.7
4. 636.7 B
5. 637.7
6. 793 Ka
7. 797.5
8. 797.52
9. 812
10. 822.82 Kam

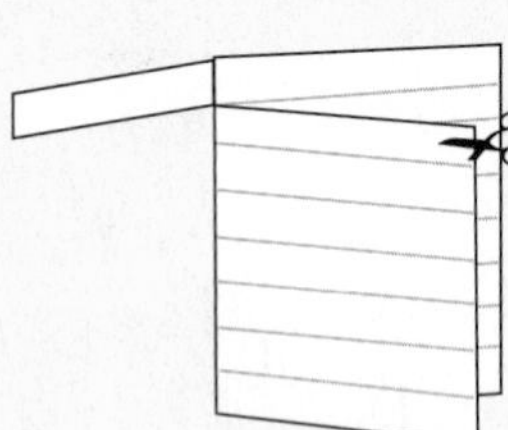

370

Finding Books

Each catalog entry for a book includes a **call number**. You can use this number to find the book you are looking for. Most libraries use the Dewey decimal classification system to arrange books. This system divides nonfiction books into 10 subject categories.

000–099	General Works	500–599	Sciences
100–199	Philosophy	600–699	Technology
200–299	Religion	700–799	Arts and Recreation
300–399	Social Sciences	800–899	Literature
400–499	Languages	900–999	History and Geography

Using Call Numbers

A call number often has a decimal in it, followed by the first letters of the author's name. (See the illustration below.) When searching for a book, look for the number and then for the alphabetized letters.

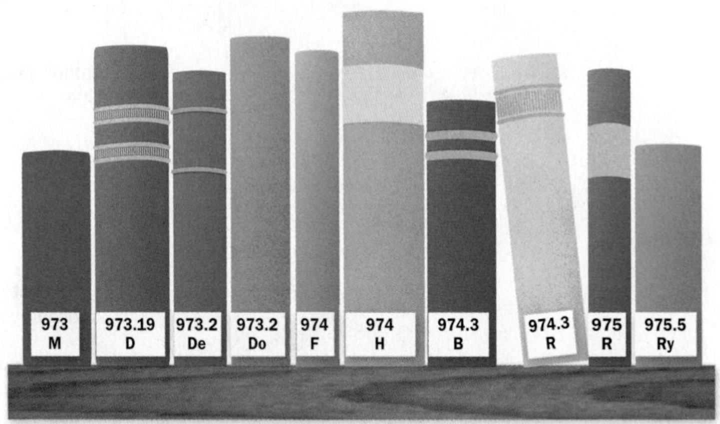

Try It: Number your paper from 1 to 10. Place the following call numbers in order as you would find them on a library shelf.

812	637.7	636.7	347 Gil	797.52
793 Ka	822.82 Kam	636.7 B	797.5	546.44 C

Understanding the Parts of a Book

Understanding the parts of a nonfiction book can help you to use that book efficiently.

- The **title page** is usually the first page. It tells the title of the book, the author's name, the illustrator's name, and the publisher's name and city.
- The **copyright page** comes next. It tells the year the book was published. This can be important because some information in an old book may no longer be correct.
- A **preface**, a **foreword**, or an **introduction** may follow. It may tell what the book is about, why it was written, and how to use it.
- The **table of contents** shows how the book is organized. It gives the names and page numbers of the sections, chapters, and major topics. (See illustration.)
- A **cross-reference** sends the reader to another page for more information. *Example:* (See page 372.)
- An **appendix** has extra information, such as maps, tables, lists, and so on.
- A **glossary** explains special words used in the book. It's like a mini-dictionary.
- A **bibliography** lists books, articles, and other sources that the author used while writing the book. To learn more about the topic, read the materials listed in the bibliography.
- The **index** is an alphabetical list of all the topics in the book. It gives the page numbers where each topic is located.

RESEARCH

Find the following information in this book.

1. Who is the illustrator of the book?
2. What are the page numbers of the table of contents?
3. What is the first entry under H in the index?

Understanding the Parts of a Book

Pass out sticky notes or small strips of paper. Write the list below on the board. Then tell students they will have five minutes to find the following items in the *Write Source* book. Have them bookmark each item and quietly raise their hands when they are finished.

- the first page of the index (SE page 751)
- credits (SE page 750)
- copyright page (SE page ii)
- the first page of the table of contents (SE page iv)
- the first page of the Proofreader's Guide (SE page 578 or 579)
- the first page of the section on Expository Writing (SE page 156 or 157)
- the first page of "The Basic Elements of Writing" section (SE page 468 or 469)

Answers

1. Chris Krenzke
2. iv–xviii
3. Habits, good writing, 6

If you have not had students do the Getting Started activities (TE 794–797), you could use them now.

Advanced Learners

Have students create their own Scavenger Hunt of the *Write Source* student edition for classmates.

- Ask students to create a list of questions such as the ones in the **Try It** activity. Encourage them to write questions that cover all sections of the book.
- Direct students to create a separate answer key and to check it for accuracy.
- Distribute the Scavenger Hunt as a class activity.

This activity provides opportunities for all students to spend time becoming familiar with the student edition.

Using Reference Materials

Because reference books cannot always be checked out, remind students to come prepared for **taking notes** (*see below*). Sometimes a library has an older edition of a reference book that can be checked out, but students must be wary in case the information is out of date.

Using Encyclopedias

Because of students' growing dependence on the Internet, many may not be familiar with an actual hardbound set of encyclopedias. After reading this page, take your class to the library to use an encyclopedia. Have each student choose a topic to research, such as the one they chose on TE page 364, and write the topic on a piece of paper. Then have students note the following items:

- the volume and page number where they found information
- a few of the subheadings in the article
- two resources listed at the end of the article
- related topics listed in the index

 **Answers**

1. C: 301
2. P: 14 and P: 21
3. C: 90

Using Reference Materials

The reference section in a library contains materials such as encyclopedias, atlases, and dictionaries.

Using Encyclopedias

An **encyclopedia** is a set of books, a CD, or a Web site with articles on almost every topic you can imagine. The topics are arranged alphabetically. The tips below can guide your use of encyclopedias.

- If the article is long, skim any subheadings to find specific information.
- Encyclopedia articles are written with the most basic information first, followed by more detailed information.
- At the end of an article, you may find a list of related topics. Use them to learn more about your topic.
- The index lists all the places in the encyclopedia where you will find more information about your topic. (See the sample below.) The index is usually in the back of the last volume of a printed set.

Encyclopedia Index

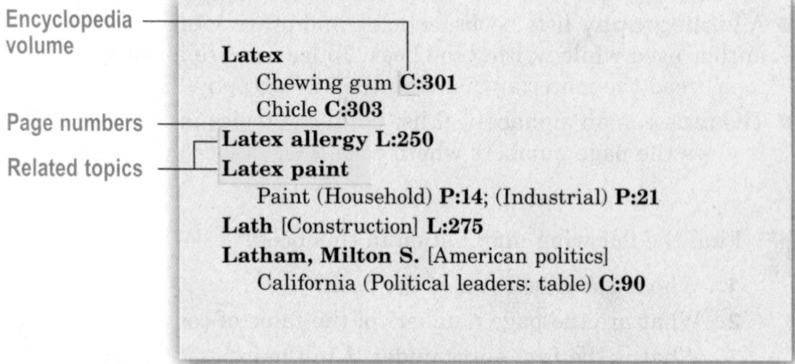

 Using the index entries above, list the volume and page or pages where you might find the following information.

1. A description of chewing gum.
2. An explanation of the difference between house paint and industrial paint.
3. A list of political leaders of California.

Teaching Tip: Taking Notes

Review with students some general guidelines for taking notes.

- Skim the article or book chapter to see what is most important. Note the heads and subheads.
- Take notes in your own words. It will help you to understand ideas better and avoid plagiarizing.
- Summarize the information in pictures, charts, or maps.
- List the key words, and look up the definitions of any that are new to you.
- Go through your notes, and write down any questions you have.
- See SE pages 441–448 for more information.

Finding Magazine Articles

Periodical guides are found in the reference section of the library and list magazine articles about many different topics.

- **Locate the right edition** of the *Readers' Guide to Periodical Literature* (or a similar guide). The latest edition will have the newest information, but you may need information from an older edition.
- **Look up your subject.** Subjects are listed alphabetically. If your subject is not listed, try another word related to it.
- **Write down the information** about the article. Include the name of the magazine, the issue date, the name of the article, and its page numbers.
- **Find the magazine.** Ask the librarian for help if necessary.

RESEARCH

Readers' Guide Format

PEROXIDES — Subject Entry
Cosmetic and skin protective compositions. — Title of Article
Soap, Perfumery & Cosmetics v77 no2 p57 F 2008.
See also — Cross-Reference
Hydrogen peroxide
PEROXISOMES
Treating a mystery malady. M. Egan. *Forbes* v173 no2 p38–39 F 2 2008. — Name, Volume, and Number of Magazine
Unloading dock. G. Chin. *Science* v303 no5666 p1947–1948 Mr 26 2008.
PERPETUAL MOTION
McKeon, 73, continues to be one for the ages. H. Bodley. — Name of Author
USA Today Ja 16 2008.
Perpetual motion, almost. K. Smith. *Motor Trend* v56 no1 p24 Ja 2008. — Page Number/Date
PERRIN, PAT — Author Entry
What happened next? P. Perrin. *Appleseeds* v6 no6 p24–27 F 2008.

Internet-based databases are online subscription services that allow you to search for and read periodicals on the Internet.

Using the sample entries above, write answers to these questions.

1. Under what additional heading can you find more articles about peroxides?
2. Who wrote the article "Unloading Dock"?
3. What month is listed most often in the entries above?

Finding Magazine Articles

Now that an electronic version of the *Readers' Guide to Periodical Literature* is available, many libraries subscribe to that edition—called InfoTrac—instead of purchasing the hardbound version.

- Find out which version your students have used.
- Especially if your students are not familiar with the electronic version of the *Readers' Guide,* ask the school librarian to give them a short lesson on how to use it and on how to locate the magazines to which it refers.

Answers

1. Hydrogen peroxide
2. G. Chin
3. February

Checking a Dictionary

Tell students that dictionaries reflect the English language, which is constantly changing. Every time a dictionary is reprinted, its staff spends many months deciding which new words to add. If possible, have students compare a very recent dictionary—one published within the last year or two—with one that is at least ten years old. While one student looks for the following words in the new dictionary, have another student look for the words in the older edition.

- chat room
- Chunnel
- latte
- legalese
- polypropylene

Most likely, these words will be found only in the new dictionary. Have the student who finds the definitions read them aloud.

Answers

Answers will vary.

Checking a Dictionary

A dictionary is the most reliable source for learning the meanings of words. It offers the following aids and information.

- **Guide words** are located at the top of every page. They show the first and last entry words on a page, so you can tell whether the word you're looking up is listed on that page.
- **Entry words** are the words that are defined on the dictionary page. They are listed in alphabetical order for easy searching.
- **Parts of speech** labels tell you the different ways a word can be used. For example, the word *Carboniferous* can be used as a noun or as an adjective.
- **Syllable divisions** show where you can divide a word into syllables.
- **Spelling and capitalization** (if appropriate) are given for every entry word. If an entry is capitalized, capitalize it in your writing, too.
- **Spelling of verb forms** is shown. Watch for irregular forms of verbs because the spelling can be a whole new word.
- **Illustrations** are often provided to make a definition clearer.
- **Accent marks** show which syllable or syllables should be stressed when you say a word.
- **Pronunciations** are special spellings of a word to help you say the word correctly.
- **Pronunciation keys** give symbols to help you pronounce the entry word correctly.
- **Etymology** gives the history of a word [in brackets]. Knowing a little about a word's history can make the definition easier to remember.

Remember: Each word may have several definitions. It's important to read all of the meanings to determine if you're using it accurately.

Open a dictionary to any page and find the following information.

1. Write down the guide words on that page.
2. Find a multisyllable word and write it out by syllables. Jot down the word's part of speech. (There may be more than one.)
3. Find an entry that includes spelling of verb forms and write them down.

English Language Learners

Make dictionaries appropriate to various reading levels available to students. Also, meet with students and go over the terms on this page to be sure each student understands them. Ask students to point out each term on a dictionary page themselves.

Advanced Learners

Invite students to add to the list of new words above.

- Challenge students to find as many new technology and general words (such as *schlock* and *punk rock*) as they can and list them with definitions.
- Post the list in the classroom.

Dictionary Page

Guide words
Entry word
Part of speech
Syllable division
Spelling and capitalization
Spelling of verb forms
Accent marks
Pronunciation
Pronunciation key
Etymology

carbon dioxide | carburetor 150

carbon dioxide *n.* A colorless or odorless gas that does not burn, composed of carbon and oxygen in the proportion CO2 and present in the atmosphere or formed when any fuel containing carbon is burned. It is exhaled from an animal's lungs during respiration and is used by plants in photosynthesis. Carbon dioxide is used in refrigeration, in fire extinguishers, and in carbonated drinks.

carbonic acid *n.* A weak acid having the formula H_2CO_3. It exists only in solution and decomposes readily into carbon dioxide and water.

car·bon·if·er·ous (kär′bə-**nĭf′**ər-əs) *adj.* Producing or containing carbon or coal.

Carboniferous *n.* The geologic time comprising the Mississippian (or Lower Carboniferous) and Pennsylvanian (or Upper Carboniferous) Periods of the Paleozoic Era, from about 360 to 286 million years ago. During the Carboniferous, widespread swamps formed in which plant remains accumulated and later hardened into coal. See table at **geologic time.—Carboniferous** *adj.*

car·bon·ize (kär′bə-nīz′) *tr. v.* **car•bon•ized, car•bon•iz•ing, car•bon•iz•es 1.** To change an organic compound into carbon by heating. **2.** To treat, coat, or combine with carbon.—**car′bon•i•za′tion** (kär′be-nī-zā′shən) *n.*

carbon monoxide *n.* A colorless odorless gas that is extremely poisonous and has the formula CO. Carbon monoxide is formed when carbon or a compound that contains carbon burns incompletely. It is present in the exhaust gases of automobile engines.

carbon paper *n.* A paper coated on one side with a dark coloring matter, placed between two sheets of blank paper so that the bottom sheet will receive a copy of what is typed or written on the top sheet.

carbon tet·ra·chlor·ide (tĕt′rə-**klôr′**īd′) *n.* A colorless poisonous liquid that is composed of carbon and chlorine, has the formula CCl_4, and does not burn although it vaporizes easily. It is used in fire extinguishers and as a dry-cleaning fluid.

Car·bo·run·dum (kär′bə-**rŭn′**dəm) A trademark for an abrasive made of silicon carbide, used to cut, grind, and polish.

car·bun·cle (**kär′**bŭng′kəl) *n.* **1.** A painful inflammation in the tissue under the skin that is somewhat like a boil but releases pus from several openings. **2.** A deep-red garnet.

car·bu·re·tor (**kär′**bə-rā′tər *or* **kär′**byə-rā′tər) *n.* A device in a gasoline engine that vaporizes the gasoline with air to form an explosive mixture. [First written down in 1866 in English, from *carburet*, carbide, from Latin *carbō*, carbon.]

ă	pat	ôr	core
ā	pay	oi	boy
âr	care	ou	out
ä	father	ŏŏ	took
ĕ	pet	ŏŏr	lure
ē	be	ōō	boot
ĭ	pit	ŭ	cut
ī	bite	ûr	urge
îr	pier	th	thin
ŏ	pot	*th*	this
ō	toe	zh	vision
ô	paw	ə	about

RESEARCH

Have students search through a dictionary to find an example of each item shown on this page.

- If you have a limited number of dictionaries available, have students work with a partner or in small groups.
- Direct students to label sticky notes with each kind of information they're looking for (guide words, entry word, and so on).
- When students find an example of each of these, have them bookmark the page with the appropriate sticky note.
- If time permits, have partners or groups exchange labeled dictionaries to see what kinds of examples classmates found.

Evaluating Sources

Ask students to explain how they decide whether a source will be useful for their research. Discuss the validity of their criteria.

- Then pick a high-interest class topic, such as skateboarding or popular music, and have each student find one source on that topic in the library.
- If resources are limited, have students work in pairs or small groups.
- Tell students to copy the six questions for evaluating sources from SE page 376. Then have them answer those questions, based on the source they found.

Evaluating Sources

Before you use any information in your writing, you must decide if it is trustworthy. Ask yourself the following questions to help judge the value of your sources.

Is the source a primary or a secondary source?

Firsthand facts are often more trustworthy than secondhand facts. However, many secondary sources are also trustworthy. (See page 364.)

Is the source an expert?

An expert is an authority on a certain subject. You may need to ask a teacher, parent, or librarian for help when deciding how experienced a particular expert is.

Is the information accurate?

Sources that are well respected are more likely to be accurate. For example, a large city newspaper is much more reliable than a supermarket tabloid.

Is the information complete?

If a source of information provides some facts about a subject, but you still have questions, find an additional source.

Is the information current?

Be sure you have the most up-to-date information on a subject. Check for copyright dates of books and articles and for posting dates of online information.

Is the source biased?

A source is biased when it presents information that is one-sided. Some organizations, for example, have something to gain by using only some of the facts. Avoid such one-sided sources.

English Language Learners

Students will find it easier to evaluate sources if they have narrowed their topic sufficiently.

For example, if they know how to skateboard but want to learn more about it, they can research

- the history of skateboarding,
- how to build their own skateboard, and
- advanced techniques.

Research Writing

Summary Paragraph

After you see a movie, someone may ask, "What was it about?" You don't tell them the whole thing. Instead, you share with them the main idea and a few important facts.

When you write a summary paragraph of an article, you also share the main idea and some key facts. You want the reader to get an overview of the article. You will find that summary writing is a useful skill whenever you are asked to do research or report writing.

In this chapter, you'll learn how to find the main idea and most important information in an article. Then you'll learn to write a summary paragraph that clearly presents that information.

Writing Guidelines

Subject: A research article
Form: Summary paragraph
Purpose: To express the main idea
Audience: Classmates

Summary Paragraph

Objectives

- identify the main idea of a paragraph
- choose an article to summarize
- write a summary paragraph

A **summary paragraph** states the main idea and the most important information from its source.

Give each student a 4" × 6" index card. Ask students to create a recipe for writing a summary paragraph. Tell them to list the ingredients first, followed by a numbered list of directions. Discuss their recipes. Here is an example:

Ingredients

- 1 pencil with a sharp point
- 1 interesting article
- 1 well-lit desk area
- 1 sheet of clean writing paper

Directions:

1. Place the article on the desk in front of you.
2. Read the article.
3. Write down the main idea.
4. Write down the key facts.
5. Draft a summary paragraph using your own words.

Technology Connections

Use this unit's Interactive Whiteboard Lesson to introduce research writing.

 ***Interactive Whiteboard Lessons***

Copy Masters

5 W's Chart (TE p. 379)

Summary Paragraph

To help students find the main idea in "Portugal's 'Triangle Trade,'" hand out sticky notes and have the students place the notes wherever they think they have found a main idea.

Respond to the reading.

Answers

Ideas 1. The main idea is that the Portuguese "trade triangle" began with Africa and Brazil in the early 1500s.

Organization 2. The paragraph is organized chronologically, explaining the series of events that resulted in the "trade triangle."

Word Choice 3. "However, the native workers soon came down with smallpox and measles, diseases that the Portuguese brought with them. Many of the workers died."

378

Summary Paragraph

The following article, "Portugal's 'Triangle Trade,' " explains how and why Portugal set up trade routes between Brazil, Africa, and Portugal. The paragraph "The Trade Triangle" summarizes that article.

Portugal's "Triangle Trade"

During the 1400s, Portugal was looking for an ocean route to the East Indies. The Portuguese were tired of the Italian merchants controlling the trade of cinnamon, peppercorn, and cloves from the East. To compete with the Italians, they sent ships south along the coast of Africa, seeking a route to India. Along the way, they began to trade with African nations, giving cloth, knives, and guns in exchange for gold and ivory. In 1498, they finally reached India.

At about the same time, Portuguese ships also landed in Brazil and started a colony there. The colonists set up sugar, cotton, and tobacco plantations, using local people as workers. However, the native workers soon came down with smallpox and measles, diseases that the Portuguese brought with them. Many of the workers died. As a result, the plantation owners needed new workers to harvest the sugarcane.

Portuguese merchants began to trade for slaves from Africa to work in the sugarcane fields. Ships would sail from Portugal to Africa with cloth, knives, and guns to trade for slaves. Then they would sail from Africa to Brazil with slaves. Finally, they would sail back to Portugal with sugar, cotton, and tobacco. Their trade routes formed a triangle in the Atlantic Ocean, often referred to as the "Triangle Trade."

The Trade Triangle

Topic Sentence (main idea) *Portugal's "Trade Triangle" began with Africa and Brazil around the beginning of the 1500s.* *Up until that time, the Portuguese traded with African nations for gold and ivory. After they colonized Brazil, however, they soon found that they needed more workers.*

Body *The natives they had been using were dying from smallpox and measles, diseases that were brought in by the Portuguese. They decided to use Africans as replacements and began trading cloth, knives, and guns for human beings. The Portuguese then took the Africans to Brazil to work as slaves.*

Closing Sentence *From Brazil, the traders completed the triangle when they returned to Portugal on ships loaded down with sugar, cotton, and tobacco.*

Respond to the reading. Answer the following questions.

- ☐ **Ideas** (1) What is the main idea of the summary?
- ☐ **Organization** (2) How is the paragraph organized?
- ☐ **Word Choice** (3) What two sentences from the original selection are paraphrased in the fourth summary sentence?

Prewriting Selecting an Article

For this assignment, you must find an article to summarize. Choose an article that . . .

- relates to a subject you are studying,
- discusses an interesting topic, and
- is fairly short (between three and six paragraphs).

Choose an article. **Look through magazines and newspapers for an article to summarize. Choose one that has the three features listed above. Ask your teacher if the article will work for your summary paragraph.**

Reading the Article

If possible, make a photocopy of your article so that you can underline important facts as you read. Otherwise, take brief notes on the article. The writer of the sample summary underlined the key facts.

> Portuguese merchants began to trade for slaves from Africa to work in the sugarcane fields. Ships would sail from Portugal to Africa with cloth, knives, and guns to trade for slaves. Then they would sail from Africa to Brazil with slaves. Finally, they would sail back to Portugal with sugar, cotton, and tobacco. Their trade routes formed a triangle in the Atlantic Ocean, often referred to as the "Triangle Trade."

Read your article. **First, read through the article. Then reread it and take notes or underline the important facts.**

Finding the Main Idea

A summary focuses on the main idea of an article. Look over the facts you noted or underlined. What main idea do those facts present? The writer of the sample summary wrote this main idea: *Portugal's "Trade Triangle" began with Africa and Brazil around the beginning of the 1500s.*

Write the main idea. **Review the facts you identified. What main idea do they suggest? Write the main idea as a single sentence. This sentence (or a version of it) will be the topic sentence for your paragraph.**

Prewriting Selecting an Article

Have students browse a variety of magazines and newspapers as they search for an article. Choose publications geared to a wide range of reading abilities.

Prewriting Reading the Article

Encourage students to use a graphic organizer (see TE pages 789–793), or outline to organize the information in the articles they have selected.

Prewriting Finding the Main Idea

Tell students that a **topic sentence** *(see below)* is often, but not always, the first sentence in a paragraph. Placing that sentence at the beginning of the paragraph will help students focus on the main point before developing it. Starting out with the topic sentence also helps readers, by making it clear what the writer will discuss.

✱ Additional information about writing a topic sentence is on SE page 525.

Teaching Tip: Topic Sentence

Students often fall into the trap of writing a topic sentence that begins with "This article is about." Discuss the topic sentence of the summary paragraph on SE page 378 (it contains the title of the article, an active verb, and a big concept or idea). As a class, practice rewriting the topic sentence. Use various verbs and experiment with ways to reword the main idea (for example, In the early 1500s, Portugal created a "trade triangle" among Africa, Brazil, and Portugal). Students will see there is more than one way to write a topic sentence.

Find well-written, high-interest magazine articles, and highlight the topic sentences in the articles. Pass the articles around so students can see some examples of strong topic sentences (see the SE index for models of topic sentences).

Writing Developing the First Draft

Give students these additional pointers on writing topic sentences:

- Don't make your topic sentence too long.
- Use the active voice.
- Make clear statements.
- Give your readers a general idea of what's to come, but don't give away the best details that you will use to support the topic sentence.
- Use specific language.

Editing Checking for Conventions

After students proofread their own summary paragraphs, have partners trade papers and read each other's drafts for errors in capitalization, punctuation, spelling, and grammar.

* Additional information about proofreading is on SE pages 578–749.

Writing Developing the First Draft

A summary paragraph includes a topic sentence, a body, and a closing sentence. As you write each part, follow these tips.

- **Topic sentence:** Introduce the main idea of the article.
- **Body:** Include just enough important facts to support or explain the main idea. As much as possible, use your own words and phrases to share these facts.
- **Closing sentence:** Restate the main idea of the summary in a different way.

Write the first draft of your summary paragraph. Complete your topic sentence based on the main idea of the article. Add facts that support the main idea. Then end your paragraph with a closing sentence.

Revising Reviewing Your Writing

As you revise, check your first draft for the following traits.

- ☐ **Ideas** Does the topic sentence correctly identify the main idea? Do I include only the most important facts to support it?
- ☐ **Organization** Is all of the information in a logical order?
- ☐ **Voice** Does my voice sound confident and informative?
- ☐ **Word Choice** Do I use my own words? Do I define any difficult terms?
- ☐ **Sentence Fluency** Do I use a variety of sentence types and lengths?

Revise your paragraph. First, reread the article and your summary. Then use the questions above as a guide for your revising.

Editing Checking for Conventions

Focus on conventions as you edit your summary.

- ☐ **Conventions** Have I checked the facts against the article? Have I checked for errors in punctuation, spelling, and grammar?

Edit your work. Use the questions above as your editing guide. Make your corrections, write a neat final copy, and proofread it for errors.

Grammar Connection

Pronouns (indefinite)
- **Proofreader's Guide** pages 710–711
- ***Write Source*** pages 474–475
- ***SkillsBook*** pages 151–152

Complex Sentences
- **Proofreader's Guide** page 590 (+)
- ***Write Source*** page 517 (+)
- ***SkillsBook*** pages 125–126
- ***GrammarSnap*** Simple, Compound, and Complex Sentences

Sentence Problems Review
- ***Write Source*** pages 504 (+), 506 (+), 507 (+)
- ***SkillsBook*** page 97

Subject-Verb Agreement
- ***Write Source*** pages 508 (+), 509 (+)
- ***SkillsBook*** pages 110, 111
- ***GrammarSnap*** Subject-Verb Agreement with Compound Subjects

Using the Right Word
- **Proofreader's Guide** pages 684–685, 686–687

Research Writing

Research Report

History is full of stories of amazing people—whether ancient kings and queens who lived long ago or heroes who are still living today. We can learn a lot by finding out how these people grew from childhood to adulthood, what obstacles they faced along the way, and how they overcame them. Their stories can inspire us to accomplish great things ourselves.

In this chapter, you will write a report about a person who inspires you. You will use the research skills you learned about in "Building Skills" (pages **363–376**) to uncover important information about this person. You will then compile the information in a research report to share with your classmates. Along the way, you're sure to learn a lot about your subject—and about yourself.

Writing Guidelines

Subject: A person who inspires you
Form: Research report
Purpose: To present research about a person's accomplishments
Audience: Classmates

Research Report

Objectives

- select an inspiring person to write about
- gather details and keep track of sources
- write a well-researched report

To stimulate topics, have students play the "Famous People A-B-C" game.

- Beginning with the letter *A*, have students go through the alphabet naming famous people whose first or last names begin with each letter of the alphabet. These may be historical or present-day people.
- Play the game orally or make up a copy master of word boxes for each letter. Group some of the challenging letters (*Q* and *R; X, Y,* and *Z*) together.

Research Report

Read aloud the first paragraph. Then have students take turns reading aloud the report as the rest of the class follows along. Choose one student for each paragraph—six students in all. Assist students with the pronunciation of any unfamiliar words.

Point out that the quotation marks around the word *King* in the model report title are purposely used by the writer to set apart a word that is being used in a special way.

Research Report

Miri Mocelin wrote this research report about an important figure in African history. Notice how the information in the report is organized. The side notes point out key features in the report.

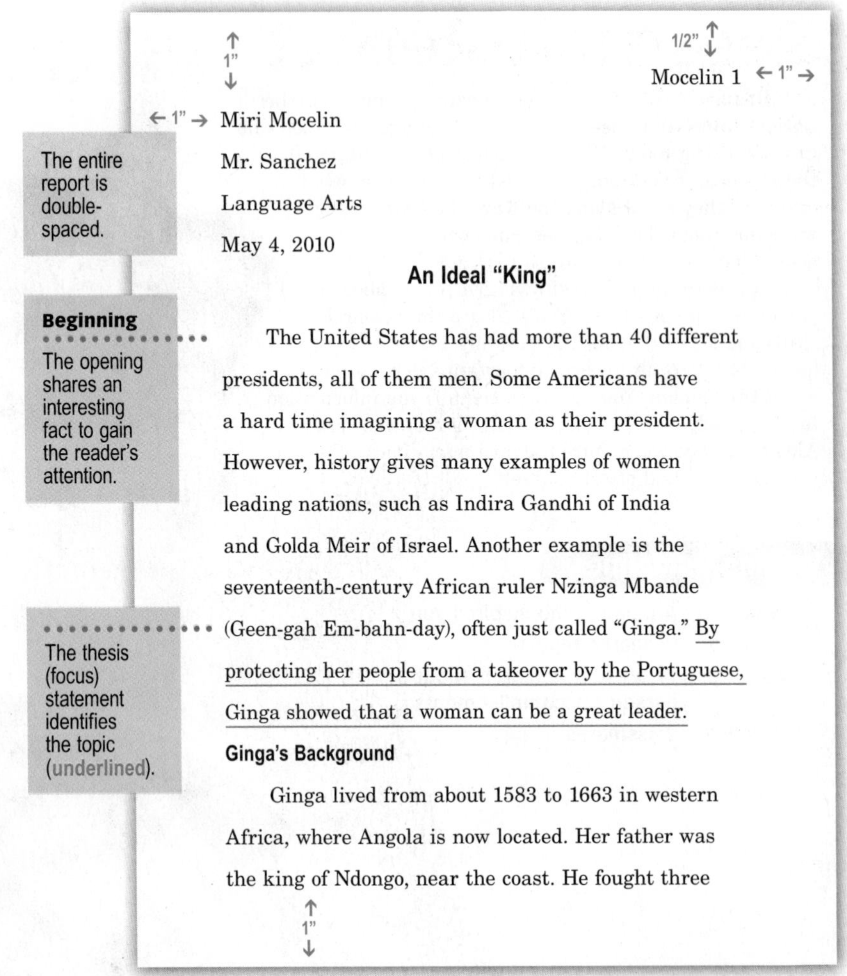

1/2"

Mocelin 1 ← 1" →

1"

← 1" → Miri Mocelin

Mr. Sanchez

Language Arts

May 4, 2010

An Ideal "King"

The United States has had more than 40 different presidents, all of them men. Some Americans have a hard time imagining a woman as their president. However, history gives many examples of women leading nations, such as Indira Gandhi of India and Golda Meir of Israel. Another example is the seventeenth-century African ruler Nzinga Mbande (Geen-gah Em-bahn-day), often just called "Ginga." By protecting her people from a takeover by the Portuguese, Ginga showed that a woman can be a great leader.

Ginga's Background

Ginga lived from about 1583 to 1663 in western Africa, where Angola is now located. Her father was the king of Ndongo, near the coast. He fought three

1"

The entire report is double-spaced.

Beginning

The opening shares an interesting fact to gain the reader's attention.

The thesis (focus) statement identifies the topic (underlined).

English Language Learners

Before students read "An Ideal 'King,'" work with them to create a word web based on their prior knowledge about kings. Ask questions such as the following:

- What is a king?
- What does a king do?
- What skills does a king need?

Use words and phrases to record their ideas on the web. Provide additional information and correct any misunderstandings.

Save the web and use it after reading the sample report to help students understand why Ginga insisted on being called King.

Middle
The first middle paragraph gives background about the person's family and homeland.

Mocelin 2

wars against the Portuguese, who were invading the region and capturing people for slavery. He won the first two wars, but he lost the third. Her father died in 1617, and Ginga's younger brother became king. Her brother was not a strong king, so Ginga began to take on his responsibilities (Grayson 47). Through negotiation, leadership, warfare, and alliances with other nations, Ginga worked to protect her people from the Portuguese.

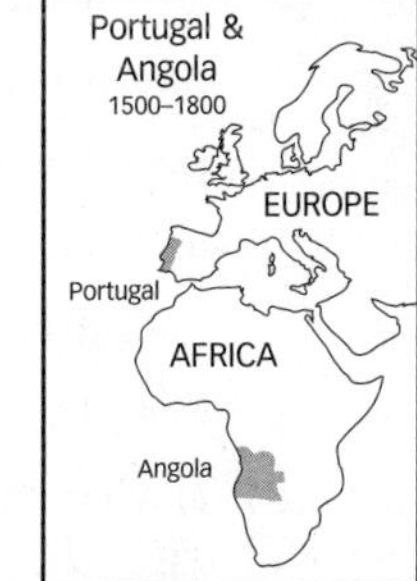

Headings help the reader to understand the paper's organization.

Ginga's Accomplishments

Ginga showed her skill for negotiation when her brother first became king. Because he knew she was a good negotiator, he sent her in his place to make a treaty with the Portuguese. Ginga went to meet the Portuguese governor in the city of Luanda, where he ruled. The governor met Ginga in a room with only one chair, his official seat, to make her feel like his subject. To show that she was his equal, Ginga gestured to one of her followers. That follower knelt on the ground to become a seat for her. Having shown her authority,

Each of the next four middle paragraphs starts with a topic sentence that covers one main accomplishment.

Point out the map, and ask students whether it helps them visualize what they are reading.

Discuss how the writer illustrates Ginga's strong sense of self in the first paragraph under "Ginga's Accomplishments."

- Can students imagine one of Ginga's followers making himself (or herself) into a seat for her?
- Why is this detail so important?
- What does it reveal about Ginga's personality?

English Language Learners

Be sure students understand vocabulary they will encounter in the report. Discuss the meanings of the following words:

- slavery (owning people and making them work for no money)
- alliance (agreement)
- negotiation (making a deal)
- treaty (formal signed agreement)
- regiment (group of soldiers)
- ambush (attack by surprise)
- retreat (to go away from danger)
- diplomat (person who makes agreements with other countries on behalf of his or her country)

Review the topic sentences for the two paragraphs on this page.

- Examine each paragraph, one at a time. Ask students whether they think the writer did a good job of writing topic sentences and to explain why.
- Discuss how the rest of each paragraph supports the topic sentence.
- For the first paragraph, ask: How does the writer show that Ginga proved her leadership skills?
- For the second paragraph, ask: What evidence supports the idea that Ginga was a capable war leader?

384

Mocelin 3

Ginga was then able to negotiate a good treaty for her people (Diouf 18–20).

A source and page numbers are identified in parentheses.

In 1624, when Ginga's brother died, she took the throne and proved her leadership skills. To get her people's respect, she insisted on being called King instead of Queen. To show that women could be strong, she gathered bodyguards who were all women, and she formed three regiments of women in her army. She and her two sisters each led one of these regiments whenever her army went to war (Grayson 49).

When the Portuguese broke their treaty a few years later, Ginga showed her skill as a war leader. She personally led troops into battle against the invaders. Author Emma Hahn explains some of Ginga's tactics. She says that because the Portuguese had gunpowder and Ginga's people did not, Ginga learned to ambush the invaders on rainy days when their weapons would not fire well. Ginga also used the jungle to hide her warriors from the enemy. Sometimes she would attack and then retreat to lead the enemy into a trap (77). Ginga's warriors respected her leadership and fought fiercely for her.

When the source or author is mentioned in the text, only the page number is listed in parentheses.

English Language Learners

Be sure students understand the following idioms they will encounter in the report:

- have a hard time (find that something is difficult to do)
- take on his responsibilities (do his work for him)
- in his place (instead of him)
- took the throne (became king)
- broke their treaty (did not do what they agreed to do)

The writer's last name and page number go on every page.

Mocelin 4

As the Portuguese gained power in the region, Ginga made deals with other African nations and with the Dutch for help. She even married the chief of a neighboring tribe to gain their aid. Eventually, Ginga moved her people, "every man, woman, and child—including the elderly, sick, and wounded—and their cattle," to the highlands of Matamba in order to save them from the Portuguese (Diouf 22). That long march took five years, but it kept her people from being enslaved.

The exact words of the author are placed in quotation marks.

Ending

The final paragraph sums up the paper and tells the reader one last interesting fact.

Ginga's Legacy

Ginga continued to rule her people until she died at the age of 81. Because of her, the nation remained strong long afterward, and it had many women rulers as well as men. Eventually, it became part of modern Angola. Ginga's struggle against the Portuguese kept them from conquering all of western Africa. Because of that, today she is remembered as a hero in Africa. She is also respected throughout Europe, even in Portugal. People remember her as a great diplomat, a fierce war leader, and a strong ruler ("Kingdom"). By being a great "king," Ginga showed that in a leader, being male or female really doesn't matter.

Examine the first paragraph on this page.

- Ask students how the details support the writer's thesis statement that Ginga was a great leader.
- Discuss how Ginga's commitment to her people's welfare and her fierce determination contributed to her place in history.

Take a close look at the final paragraph. Ask:

- Why does the writer mention the effect of Ginga's actions on the rest of western Africa?
- Why does the writer put quotation marks around the word *king*? Where else in the report did the writer use quotation marks around *king*?

Discuss the closing sentence. Ask:

Do you think this is a successful ending? Explain.

Struggling Learners

Invite students to share one detail from the article that really "jumps out" at them. Together, discuss why these details make such an impression.

- It creates a vivid picture in my mind.
- It seems impossible.
- It makes me respect Ginga even more.

Point out that titles of books and magazines are underscored when handwritten or italicized when typeset, while titles of articles are in quotation marks.

Respond to the reading.

Answers

Ideas **1.** The main idea is that Ginga was an outstanding leader.
2. The writer discusses negotiation, leadership, warfare, and alliances with other nations.

Organization **3.**

- Ginga gradually took on leadership responsibilities because her brother was weak.
- Ginga proved she was a worthy negotiator by showing that she was just as worthy of respect as the Portuguese governor.
- Ginga showed that women could be strong by enlisting other women into her army.
- Ginga was a strategic warrior and outsmarted her enemies.
- Ginga went to great lengths to protect her people from enslavement.

Voice **4.** Possible choices:

- That long march took five years, but it kept her people from being enslaved.
- People remember her as a great diplomat, a fierce war leader, and a strong ruler ("Kingdom").

A separate page alphabetically lists sources cited in the paper.

Mocelin 5

Works Cited

Diouf, Sylviane Anna. *Kings and Queens of Southern Africa.* New York: Franklin Watts, 2000. Print.

Grayson, John. "Nzinga of Ndongo and Matamba." *Legendary Figures* 28 Dec. 2003: 47–50. Print.

Hahn, Emma. *Unlikely Heroes: Historic and Contemporary Figures.* Portland: J. Weston Walch, 2004. Print.

"Kingdom of Ndongo." *About Angola.* Republic of Angola's Embassy in Stockholm and to the Nordic Countries, n.d. Web. 1 May 2010.

Respond to the reading. After you have finished reading the sample research report, answer the following questions about the traits of writing.

- ☐ **Ideas** (1) What is the main idea of the report? (2) What four aspects of leadership does the writer talk about?
- ☐ **Organization** (3) What is the main idea in each middle paragraph? Make a list.
- ☐ **Voice** (4) How does the author show her admiration for her subject? Choose two sentences from the final paragraphs that show this.

Advanced Learners

Challenge students to use the research tools discussed on pages 364–376 to locate even more information about Nzinga Mbande to share with the class.

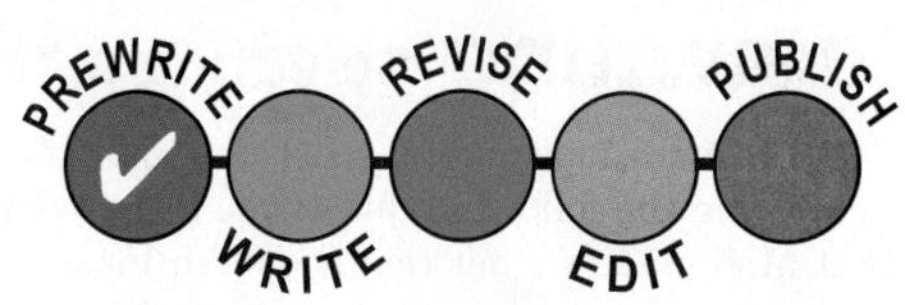

Prewriting

Prewriting is to writing what packing your gear is to traveling. The more prepared you are for the "journey," the more successful you will be. Keep the following points in mind as you prepare.

Keys to Effective Prewriting

1. As a topic, choose an important person who interests you.
2. Make a list of questions you want to have answered about the person.
3. Make sure that there is enough to say about your topic; you need background information and at least three important ideas about the person.
4. Use a gathering grid to organize your research questions and answers.
5. Be careful to credit your sources when paraphrasing ideas or quoting words.
6. Keep track of the publication details for all your sources so you can use them in a works-cited page later.

RESEARCH

Prewriting

Keys to Effective Prewriting

Remind students of the purpose of the prewriting stage in the writing process. (It's when the writer gets ready to write.)

Keys to Effective Prewriting explains the process students will be guided through on SE pages 388–395.

Tell students to put a sticky note on the top of this page, and suggest that they refer to it often as they begin their research. Encourage them to keep these important elements in mind during the prewriting phase.

Technology Connections

Students can use the added features of the Net-text as they explore this stage of the writing process.

Write Source Online **Net-text**

Prewriting Selecting a Topic

Tell students that they don't have to choose a historical figure. They can also consider a present-day famous person they admire. If you played the "Famous People A-B-C" game at the beginning of this section, remind students to review the list of names they compiled.

Prewriting Selecting a Topic

To find a topic, make a list of important people who interest you. Start by answering the following questions. (Also read the list of possible topics below that Miri made for her report on "An Ideal 'King.' ")

- What famous or historical people would I like to know more about?
- What events would I like to research, and who was involved?
- What interesting people does my social studies textbook mention?

Topics List

I'd like to know more about these people . . .
- George Lucas
- J. K. Rowling
- Genghis Khan
- Albert Schweitzer
- Helen Keller

I'd like to learn about the people involved in these events . . .
- finding the Titanic
- building the Great Wall of China
- landing on the moon

My textbook mentions these historical figures . . .
- Nzinga Mbande, 1583–1663 C.E., African hero
- Xuanzang, 600–664 C.E., Chinese traveler
- Timur the Lame, 1336–1405 C.E., Mongol leader

Make your topics list. Try to list at least five people as possible topics. Then choose the one that interests you the most.

English Language Learners

Steer students toward
- a person from a social studies unit they have studied,
- a famous person from their homeland, or
- another person about whom they have substantial prior knowledge.

This approach will ensure that students have a background on which to build.

Struggling Learners

Another way for students to select a topic is to think of someone connected to a career that interests them. For example, a student considering becoming a teacher could write about Annie Sullivan or Christa McAuliffe. A student considering starting a business could write about Henry Ford or Bill Gates.

Advanced Learners

Together, define the word *hero.* Discuss famous people who are considered heroes and compare their accomplishments with the definition. Ask the following:
- Are all accomplished athletes heroes?
- Does overcoming misfortune always make people heroes?
- Can fictional characters be heroes?

Sizing Up Your Topic

A good research report about an important person should include detailed information about the person's background and three or four major points about the person's accomplishments.

Miri decided to write about Nzinga ("Ginga") Mbande, an African leader mentioned in her social studies textbook.

Research Notes

Ginga Mbande

Background

– She lived during the late 1500s and middle 1600s near the western coast of Africa, and she became "King" of her people. (She refused to be called "Queen.")

Major Accomplishments

– She was famous as a negotiator.

– She was also a skilled war leader.

– Her people respected her strength as a ruler.

– She fought against the Portuguese invasion of Africa and against the slave trade.

Legacy

– She kept the Portuguese from conquering western Africa.

– She is a hero for African people today.

From this information, Miri felt confident that she would be able to write a good research paper about Ginga.

Size up your topic. **Look up your chosen topic in an encyclopedia and on the Internet. List background information and the most important points about the person. Are there enough details to write a good research report?**

RESEARCH

Prewriting Sizing Up Your Topic

Clarify the idea of "legacy" in the model. Explain that a legacy can be the long-lasting (into future generations) effects of a person's accomplishments.

Advanced Learners

Based on the explanation of the word *legacy,* discuss instances where historical figures have been remembered for their misdeeds, positive accomplishments, or a combination of the two.

Prewriting Gathering Details

Have students select their **sources** *(see below)* before they begin to fill in the gathering grid.

The gathering grid is a great way to show students how manageable the research process can be. Going straight to note cards can be overwhelming for some students.

As students write their questions, tell them to pose each question in an open-ended way so that the answers won't be "yes" or "no." Suggest that students use the words *how, what, where, why,* and *when* in their questions.

Prewriting Gathering Details

A gathering grid can help you organize the information from your research. Miri made the following grid during her research about Ginga. Down the left-hand side, she listed her questions. Across the top, she listed sources she found. For answers too long to fit in the grid, Miri used note cards. (See page 391.)

Gathering Grid

"Ginga" Mbande	Kings and Queens of Southern Africa	Unlikely Heros	Grayson article	Angola Web site
What is her background?		Lived 1583 to 1663 in what is now Angola	See note card number 1.	Daughter of an African king
How was she great?	Protected her people from Portuguese invasion			
What were her major deeds?	Negotiated a treaty with the Portuguese governor	Led troops into battle See note card number 2.	Took over as "King" when her brother died	
What has been her effect on the world?				Kept Portuguese from conquering western Africa

Create a gathering grid. Make a list of questions in the left-hand column of your grid. Across the top, list the sources you will use. Fill in the squares with answers you find. Use note cards for longer, more detailed answers.

Teaching Tip: Sources

To help students choose appropriate sources, discuss the importance of screening a variety of sources.

- Students should aim to use at least a few books, including biographies, in addition to Web sites, magazine articles, and an encyclopedia or two.
- Students need to look at the copyright dates of all of their sources to make sure that they are using up-to-date information.
- Students should use several sources to confirm factual information. Whenever they find specific information in one source that is contradicted in another source, they need to find a third or fourth source to clarify the information.

English Language Learners

If students select a subject with whom they already have some familiarity, a KWL chart is an alternative organizer for gathering details. Have students create three-column charts to record what they already **K**now about the subject, what they **W**ant to know, and what they **L**earn—the notes from their research, including source information.

Creating Note Cards

While a gathering grid is a great way to see all your research at one glance, sometimes you need more space for an answer. You can use note cards to keep track of longer answers and the details from your research.

When using note cards, number each card and write a question at the top. Then answer the question by writing a paraphrase (see page 392), a list, or a quotation. At the bottom, identify the source of the information (including a page number if appropriate). Here are three sample cards Miri made for her report on Ginga.

Card number — 1. What is Ginga's background?
Question
Answer (paraphrase) — Her father fought three wars against the Portuguese. He lost the last one. When he died, her brother became king but was weak. Ginga had to help him. When he died, she became "king."
Source — Grayson article page 47

2. How did she fight the Portuguese?
- Attacked on rainy days, when their gunpowder wouldn't work.
- Retreated to lead them into ambushes.
- Used the jungle to hide her warriors.

Answer (list)

Unlikely Heroes

3. Who did Ginga take on the retreat to Matamba?
"every man, woman, and child—including the elderly, sick, and wounded—and their cattle"
Kings and Queens of Southern Africa page 22

Answer (quotation)

RESEARCH

Create note cards. Make note cards like the examples above whenever your answers are too long to fit on your gathering grid.

Prewriting Creating Note Cards

Make a copy master for each of the three sample note cards. Provide students with photocopies to use as models as they take notes during research.

Review each of the sample note cards.

- When you discuss **paraphrasing** *(see below)*, stress that students need to be careful to rewrite material in their own words.
- When you talk about writing a list, emphasize the importance of not picking up phrases right from the text, an approach some students might use inadvertently when writing their reports.
- When addressing the quotation model, tell students that they must be careful to copy down every word and every punctuation mark exactly as it appears in the original text.

Teaching Tip: Paraphrasing

Most students need to practice paraphrasing. Tell them that when they take notes, they must get into the habit of rewriting information, unless they are going to pull a quotation from a text. You cannot overemphasize the importance of paraphrasing. Many students fall into the habit of writing entire phrases from a text word for word, without even realizing what they're doing.

- Give students two or three reading passages to take notes on.
- When they are finished, review their notes carefully and point out places where they have copied material verbatim.
- Have students rewrite their notes until you are satisfied that they understand what it means to paraphrase.

Prewriting Avoiding Plagiarism

Tell students that using their own words to restate information from a source has another advantage besides avoiding plagiarism. It is a good way to ensure that they understand the information.

 **Answers**

Possible choices:

Quote: "She was more than strong, however; she was also flexible."

Summary (Paraphrasing):
Nzinga was a strong and flexible leader. Her good negotiation skills led her to bargain with both Jaga warriors and European leaders to form alliances against the Portuguese.

Prewriting Avoiding Plagiarism

You must be careful to give credit for the facts and ideas you find in your sources. Using other people's words and ideas without giving them credit is called plagiarism, and it is stealing. Here are two ways to avoid plagiarism.

- **Quote exact words:** When a source states something so perfectly that it makes sense to use those exact words, you may include them in quotation marks and give credit to the source. (See page **385**.)
- **Paraphrase:** However, it's usually best to put the ideas from a source in your own words. This is called paraphrasing. Remember, though, to give credit to the source of the idea. (See pages **383–384**.)

Quoting Exact Words

4. How did Ginga show leadership?
"Nzinga Mbande understood that leadership required both strength and flexibility. She knew how to earn respect and when to demand it. She knew when to parley, when to fight, and when to retreat to fight another day."
Grayson article page 50

Paraphrasing

4. How did Ginga show leadership?
Ginga knew that a leader must sometimes show strength, sometimes use diplomacy, and sometimes retreat.
Grayson article page 50

 Read the following passage from the article "Nzinga of Ndongo and Matamba" by John Grayson. On a note card, quote the sentence that best sums up the passage. On another note card, paraphrase the entire passage. (Use the note cards above as a guide.)

Nzinga impressed the Portuguese governor with her powerful personality. She was more than strong, however; she was also flexible. She could negotiate as well with the warlike Jaga tribes as with "sophisticated" European leaders. In allying against the Portuguese with both the Jaga and the Dutch, Nzinga showed strength and flexibility.

English Language Learners

The **Try It** passage is particularly challenging for students with limited vocabulary. Find short passages from nonfiction trade books or magazines at a lower reading level for students to use to practice paraphrasing.

Advanced Learners

Challenge students to be investigative reporters by having them use the research tools discussed on SE pages 364–376 to uncover court cases involving plagiarism, including the resulting consequences.

Keeping Track of Your Sources

As you research, keep careful track of your sources so that you can cite them correctly in your final report. You'll need to write down the following information.

- **Encyclopedia entry:** Author's name (if listed). Entry title. Encyclopedia title. Edition (if given). Publication date.
- **Book:** Author's name. Title. Publisher and city. Copyright date.
- **Magazine:** Author's name. Article title. Magazine title. Date published. Page numbers.
- **Internet:** Author's name (if listed). Page title. Site title. Date posted or copyright date (if listed). Name of sponsor. Date found.

My Source Notes

Encyclopedia: "Angola." Columbia Encyclopedia. 2001.

Book: Sylviane Anna Diouf. Kings and Queens of Southern Africa. Franklin Watts. New York. 2000.

Magazine: John Grayson. "Nzinga of Ndongo and Matamba." Legendary Figures December 28, 2003. Pages 47–50.

Internet: No author. "Kingdom of Ndongo." About Angola. Republic of Angola's Embassy in Stockholm and to the Nordic Countries. No posting date. May 1, 2010.

List sources. Keep a list of all your sources, recording the information listed above. Whenever you find a new source, add it to the list.

Prewriting Keeping Track of Your Sources

To give students practice with the format of citations, provide a variety of books and magazines, as well as some reference books.

- Have each student select three sources and write a mini-bibliography for those sources.
- Check each student's list or have them trade papers with partners to make sure that each entry follows the sample citations.

Struggling Learners

To help students record the correct citation information, provide photocopies of templates for each type of source and have students fill in the blanks.

Prewriting Writing Your Thesis Statement

To give students more practice writing thesis statements, prepare a copy master like the model at the top of this page.

- Fill in the first two boxes with information about a famous person.
- Then distribute photocopies and tell students to write a thesis statement based on the information you have provided.
- Have each student read aloud her or his thesis statement. Discuss how students came up with variations on the same information.

Prewriting Writing Your Thesis Statement

After your research is done, you need to develop a thesis (focus) statement to guide your writing. The thesis is the main point or idea you want to emphasize. It serves as the focus for your report so that all the parts work together. Use the following formula to help you write your thesis statement.

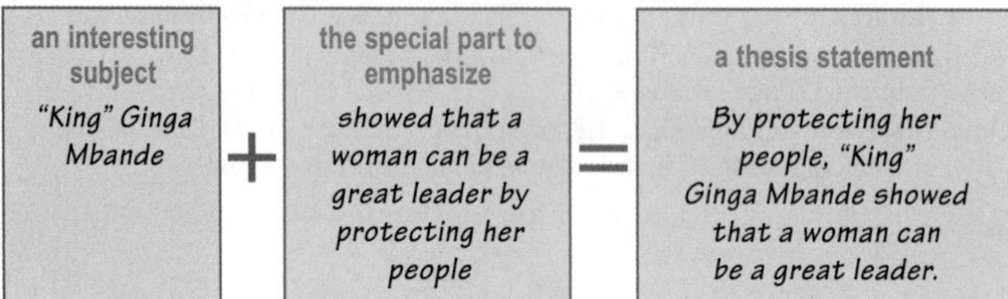

Sample Thesis Statements

Ginga Mbande, a seventeenth-century African ruler (an interesting topic), *protected her people from the Portuguese invasion* (the part to emphasize).

Robert Ballard, the man who found the Titanic (an interesting topic), *is both an ocean scientist and an explorer* (the part to emphasize).

Donna Shirley, who had been told, "Girls can't be engineers," (an interesting topic) *went on to lead NASA's Mars exploration program* (the part to emphasize).

Form your thesis statement. Review your research notes on page 389 and choose one main point you could make about your topic. Using the formula above, write a thesis statement.

Struggling Learners

Pair each student with a competent and supportive partner who can help him or her locate the "special part to emphasize" in their research notes. Have partners ask one another questions such as these:

- What is the most important thing you learned from your notes?
- What idea best ties all the details together?

Outlining Your Ideas

An outline is one way to organize your thinking and plan your report. You can use either a topic outline or a sentence outline to list the main ideas of your report. A **topic outline** lists ideas as words or phrases; a **sentence outline** lists them as full sentences. (Also see page 550.)

Sentence Outline

Below is the first part of a sentence outline for the report on pages 382–386. Notice that the outline begins with the thesis statement and then organizes ideas below it. Compare this partial outline with the opening paragraph and first middle paragraph of the report.

Thesis statement	*THESIS STATEMENT: By protecting her people from a takeover by the Portuguese, Ginga showed that a woman can be a great leader.*
I. Topic Sentence (for first middle paragraph)	*I. Ginga lived from about 1583 to 1663 in western Africa, where Angola is now located.*
A. B. C. D. Supporting Ideas	*A. Her father was the king of Ndongo.* *B. He fought three wars against the Portuguese slave trade, winning two but losing the third.* *C. When he died, Ginga's brother became king, and she carried some of his responsibilities.* *D. Ginga used negotiation, warfare, and alliances with other nations to protect her people.*
II. Topic Sentence (for second middle paragraph)	*II. Ginga showed her skill for negotiation when her brother first became king.* *A. . . .* *B. . . .*

Remember: In an outline, if you have a I, you must have at least a II. If you have an A, you must have at least a B.

Create your outline. Write a sentence outline for your report, using the details from your research. Be sure that each topic sentence (I, II, III, . . .) supports the thesis statement and that each detail (A, B, C, . . .) supports the topic sentence above it. Use your outline as a guide when you write the first draft of your report.

RESEARCH

Prewriting Outlining Your Ideas

To help students create an outline, have them spread out all of their note cards on a desk or table and then follow these steps.

1. Arrange the note cards into two categories: background details and accomplishments.
2. Put the note cards in sequential order within each category.
3. Place a rubber band or paper clip around each group of note cards.
4. Students can then record the information off each index card in an orderly fashion onto the outline.

This method of organizing details will help students understand the importance of good organization.

* Additional information about organizing details is on SE page 550.

Review the correct form of an outline. Discuss proper indentation and the correct progression of numerals and letters. If time permits, create an outline with mistakes. Provide photocopies. Have students mark the errors and indicate corrections.

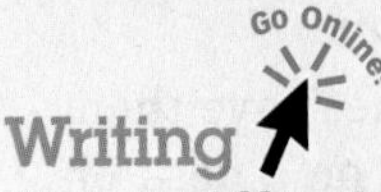

Writing

Keys to Effective Writing

Remind students that the writing stage is when they get to write, or draft, their ideas on paper.

Keys to Effective Writing explains the process students will be guided through on SE pages 397–404.

Remind students that a first draft isn't supposed to be flawless. After writing a strong thesis statement that expresses the focus clearly, the most important goal is to organize the supporting information in a logical, cohesive way.

Technology Connections

Students can use the added features of the Net-text as they explore this stage of the writing process.

***Write Source Online* Net-text**

396

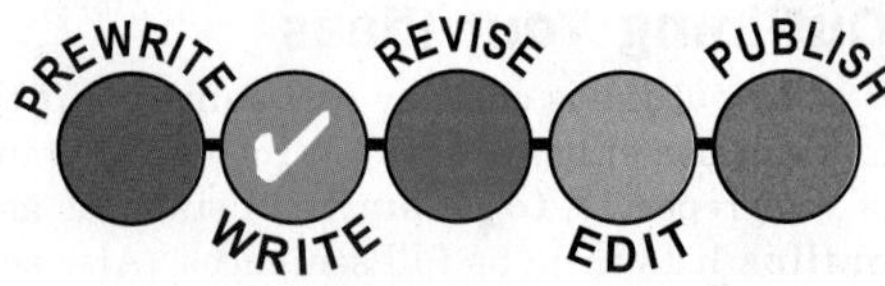

Writing

With your research and planning finished, it's time to write the first draft of your paper. This is your chance to share your information and thoughts with other people. As you write, keep the following points in mind.

Keys to Effective Writing

1. Use your first paragraph to grab your reader's attention, introduce your topic, and present your thesis statement.
2. In the second paragraph, give the background for the person's accomplishments.
3. In the next paragraphs, give details about those accomplishments. Start each paragraph with a topic sentence.
4. In your ending paragraph, explain how the person has contributed to history.
5. Remember to cite the sources of any ideas you paraphrase or quote. List your sources alphabetically on a works-cited page.

Struggling Learners

Suggest that students use a new sheet of paper for each paragraph. This makes it easier to rearrange the middle paragraphs and provides more room for revising and editing.

Citing Sources in Your Report

As you write, remember to give credit to the sources you quote directly or paraphrase in your report.

When You Have All the Information

- The most common type of credit (citation) lists the author's last name and the page number in parentheses.

  She and her two sisters each led one of these regiments whenever her army went to war (Grayson 49).

- If you already name the author in your report, just include the page number in parentheses.

  Author Emma Hahn explains . . . Sometimes she would attack and then retreat to lead the enemy into a trap (77).

When Some Information Is Missing

- Some sources do not list an author. In those cases, use the title and page number. (If the title is long, use only the first word or two.)

  The Sahara Desert made it difficult for people in North Africa to communicate with people in South Africa ("History" 39).

- Some sources (especially Internet sites) do not use page numbers. In those cases, list just the author.

  In 1635, Ginga formed an alliance with the kingdoms of Kongo and Kassange (O'Shaughnessy).

- If a source does not list the author or page number, use the title.

  People remember her as a great diplomat, a fierce war leader, and a strong ruler ("Kingdom").

Notice that in each of the examples above, the period comes after the parentheses that include the title or author credit.

Copy the following sentence by Rachel Buchholz from page 31 of *Legendary Figures*, and then cite the source.

The Portuguese encouraged the Jaga people to war upon their peaceful neighbors.

Writing Citing Sources in Your Report

Remind students to give credit to the sources that they quote or paraphrase. It may feel unnatural to them to include this information in their draft, but if they wait until the revising and editing stages, they are likely to forget to include some of the necessary citations.

Answers

"The Portuguese encouraged the Jaga people to war upon their peaceful neighbors." (Buchholz 31)

Struggling Learners

Students may omit source citations because it's too much work. Make it easier for them by showing them how to use "shorthand" to quickly write citations in their first draft.

- Have students locate source citations in the model report on SE pages 382–385.
- Then have students look at the model Works Cited page on SE page 386.
- Point out that each author or article name begins with a different letter. Suggest that the "shorthand" the writer of the model report could use is the first letter of the name and the page number. For example, G49 instead of Grayson 49.
- Have students check the list of sources they made for their own report to see if this shorthand method works for them. If not, they can adapt it by using the first two letters of names that begin with the same letter.
- Explain that during the revision process, they should change the shorthand to the full name.

Writing Starting Your Research Report

Have students practice each of the three suggested openers.

- Tell them to make a three-column chart.
- At the top of the columns, write *Interesting Fact, Interesting Question,* and *Quotation*.
- Then write an opening sentence of each type in the appropriate column.

After they finish writing the three sentences, students can decide which one would make the strongest and most appealing opener.

Writing Starting Your Research Report

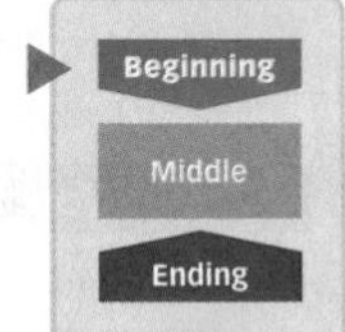

The opening paragraph of your report should grab the reader's attention, introduce your topic, and present your thesis statement. To start your opening paragraph, try one of these three approaches.

- **Start with an interesting fact.**
  The United States has had more than 40 different presidents, all of them men.
- **Ask an interesting question.**
  How many people know that one of the most powerful leaders in African history was a woman?
- **Start with a quotation.**
  "Sometimes the best man for the job is a woman," it has been said.

Miri decided to begin her opening paragraph with an interesting fact.

Beginning Paragraph

The beginning paragraph starts with an interesting fact and ends with the thesis (focus) statement (underlined).

The United States has had more than 40 different presidents, all of them men. Some Americans have a hard time imagining a woman as their president. However, history gives many examples of women leading nations, such as Indira Gandhi of India and Golda Meir of Israel. Another example is the seventeenth-century African ruler Nzinga Mbande (Geen-gah Em-bahn-day), often just called "Ginga." By protecting her people from a takeover by the Portuguese, Ginga showed that a woman can be a great leader.

Write your opening paragraph. Use one of the three strategies listed above to start your paragraph. After you grab the reader's attention, be sure to introduce your topic. End your paragraph with a clear thesis statement.

Developing the Middle Part

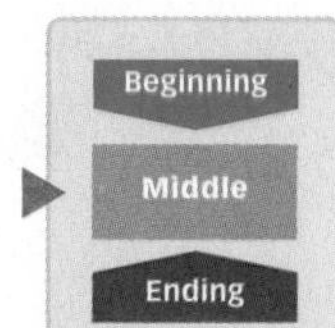

Begin the middle part of your report with background information, starting with where and when your subject lived, and how that person became involved in her or his work. After that, provide details about the work and its importance to the world.

Start each middle paragraph with a topic sentence that covers one main idea. The other sentences in each paragraph should support that main idea. Remember to use your sentence outline as a guide when writing.

RESEARCH

Middle Paragraphs

The first middle paragraph explains the subject's background.

All the details support the topic sentence (underlined).

Ginga's Background

Ginga lived from about 1583 to 1663 in western Africa, where Angola is now located. Her father was the king of Ndongo, near the coast. He fought three wars against the Portuguese, who were invading the region and capturing people for slavery. He won the first two wars, but he lost the third. Her father died in 1617, and Ginga's younger brother became king. Her brother was not a strong king, so Ginga began to take on his responsibilities (Grayson 47). Through negotiation, leadership, warfare, and alliances with other nations, Ginga worked to protect her people from the Portuguese.

Writing Developing the Middle Part

Good headings

- reveal the organization of a piece of research writing,
- make it easier for readers to preview an article,
- help readers find information they may be looking for.

Review the headings in "An Ideal 'King'" on SE pages 382–385, and ask students how these headings help them as readers.

Review how to use transition words to make paragraphs flow from one to the other. Using the paragraphs on SE page 384 and the top of SE page 385, ask:

- What words does the writer use at the beginning of each paragraph? (in 1624, when the Portuguese, as the Portuguese)
- What do these words show? (chronological, or time, order)

English Language Learners

Have students use questions for their headings. Explain that

- a topic sentence will answer the question posed in each heading, and
- the details will support the answer given in the topic sentence.

Struggling Learners

Have students count the number of sentences in each middle paragraph of the sample research report (7, 7, 4, 7, 4).

- Suggest that they follow this example and use four to seven sentences in each of their middle paragraphs as well.
- Assist students in organizing at least three middle paragraphs.

Review the side notes to generate ideas for how students can organize their middle paragraphs.

- Tell students to include colorful stories that reveal their subject's personality and leadership.
- Remind them to write about accomplishments that illustrate their person's strengths and prove why she or he is an important figure.

Ginga's Accomplishments

Ginga showed her skill for negotiation when her brother first became king. Because he knew she was a good negotiator, he sent her in his place to make a treaty with the Portuguese. Ginga went to meet the Portuguese governor in the city of Luanda, where he ruled. The governor met Ginga in a room with only one chair, his official seat, to make her feel like his subject. To show that she was his equal, Ginga gestured to one of her followers. That follower knelt on the ground to become a seat for her. Having shown her authority, Ginga was then able to negotiate a good treaty for her people (Diouf 18–20).

In 1624, when Ginga's brother died, she took the throne and proved her leadership skills. To get her people's respect, she insisted on being called King instead of Queen. To show that women could be strong, she gathered bodyguards who were all women, and she formed three regiments of women in her army. She and her two sisters each led one of these regiments whenever her army went to war (Grayson 49).

When the Portuguese broke their treaty a few years later, Ginga showed her skill as a war leader.

The second middle paragraph reveals an interesting event that illustrates Ginga's negotiation skills.

In the third middle paragraph, the writer tells of Ginga's leadership skills.

Struggling Learners

Read aloud the second middle paragraph above. Discuss how this "scene" creates a vivid picture for the reader. Invite students to tell a real-life story about their subject. Discuss how they can incorporate the story as a middle paragraph.

The fourth middle paragraph describes Ginga as a skilled leader.

She personally led troops into battle against the invaders. Author Emma Hahn explains some of Ginga's tactics. She says that because the Portuguese had gunpowder and Ginga's people did not, Ginga learned to ambush the invaders on rainy days when their weapons would not fire well. Ginga also used the jungle to hide her warriors from the enemy. Sometimes she would attack and then retreat to lead the enemy into a trap (77). Ginga's warriors respected her leadership and fought fiercely for her.

In the fifth middle paragraph, Ginga's alliances with others are explained.

As the Portuguese gained power in the region, Ginga made deals with other African nations and with the Dutch for help. She even married the chief of a neighboring tribe to gain their aid. Eventually, Ginga moved her people, "every man, woman, and child—including the elderly, sick, and wounded—and their cattle," to the highlands of Matamba in order to save them from the Portuguese (Diouf 22). That long march took five years, but it kept her people from being enslaved.

RESEARCH

Write your middle paragraphs. Keep these tips in mind as you write.

1. Support the topic sentence for each paragraph with details.
2. Refer to your outline for help with your organization. (See page 395.)
3. Give credit to your sources in your paper. (See page 397.)

As students write their reports, tell them not to be overwhelmed by the length of the assignment.

- Encourage them to consider one paragraph at a time.
- By concentrating on making each paragraph work and not worrying about all the writing to come, students will create better paragraphs and will find their papers unfolding more quickly than they expected.

English Language Learners

Tell students to cross out or put an *X* next to each part of their outline as they finish writing about it. This will help them stay on track and will keep them from skipping important ideas and details.

Advanced Learners

* As students finish their middle paragraphs, ask them to analyze the order in which the information is presented—by time, location, or importance; as a comparison; or in logical order—referring to the descriptions on SE page 551.

Writing Ending Your Research Report

Show students how to reword their thesis in order to write their conclusion.

- Explain that a good ending relates back to the beginning in some way.
- Although the ending may repeat the idea stated in the thesis, it should restate the main idea in a different way.

Have students work in pairs to review each other's first and last paragraphs to see if the thesis statement is restated in the final paragraph. If it isn't, partners can suggest ways to do so.

As students look over their reports, provide them with a paragraph checklist.

* Additional information on using a paragraph checklist is on SE page 541.

Writing Ending Your Research Report

Your ending paragraph should bring your report to a thoughtful close. Try one or more of the following ideas in your closing paragraph.

- Remind the reader about the overall point or thesis of the report.
- Tell one last interesting fact about the topic.
- Explain the person's contribution to history.

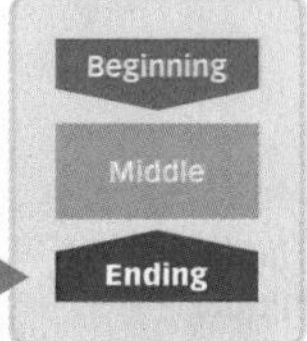

Ending Paragraph

Ginga's Legacy

Ginga continued to rule her people until she died, when she was 81 years old. Because of her, the nation remained strong long afterward, and it had many women rulers as well as men. Eventually, it became part of modern Angola. Ginga's struggle against the Portuguese kept them from conquering all of western Africa. Because of that, today she is remembered as a hero in Africa. She is also respected throughout Europe, even in Portugal. People remember her as a great diplomat, a fierce war leader, and a strong ruler ("Kingdom"). By being a great "king," Ginga showed that in a leader, being male or female really doesn't matter.

The ending paragraph explains the person's contribution to history.

The thesis statement is repeated (underlined).

Write your final paragraph. Draft your final paragraph using one or more of the strategies listed above.

Look over your report. Read your report, looking over your notes and outline to see whether you have included all the necessary details. Make notes about possible changes.

Struggling Learners

If students have difficulty wrapping up their research reports, have them ask themselves this question:

> What might have happened if my topic person had NOT taken action?

Creating Your Works-Cited Page

The first step in creating a works-cited page is to set up or "format" your sources. The following two pages show the proper format for common types of sources. Notice that the second line and additional lines for each source are indented one-half inch, about five letters or spaces.

Encyclopedia

Author (if available). Article title (in quotation marks). Title of the encyclopedia (underlined or in italics if typed). Edition (if available). Date published. Medium of publication ("Print").

"Angola." Columbia Encyclopedia. 2001. Print.

Books

Author or editor (last name first). Title (underlined or in italics if typed). City where the book was published: Publisher, copyright date. Medium of publication.

Diouf, Sylviane Anna. Kings and Queens of Southern Africa. New York: Franklin Watts, 2000. Print.

Magazines

Author (last name first). Article title (in quotation marks). Title of the magazine (underlined or in italics if typed) Date (day, month, year): Page numbers of the article. Medium of publication.

Grayson, John. "Nzinga of Ndongo and Matamba." Legendary Figures 28 Dec. 2003: 47–50. Print.

RESEARCH

Writing Creating Your Works-Cited Page

Point out the way the citations under "Books" and "Magazines" are indented in the examples. Tell students to indent all the lines that follow the first line of a citation.

* Review capitalization of titles. Refer students to SE page 624. Then have them check their list of sources for accuracy before creating their works-cited page.

Remind students that titles of books, magazines, and Web sites are underscored in a handwritten works-cited page. Point out that the titles would be italicized if done on a computer, however.

* Additional information on italics and underlining is on SE page 602.

Titles of magazine articles and individual pages from Web sites are placed in quotation marks.

* Additional information on quotation marks is on SE pages 598 and 600.

Have students check their punctuation of titles before creating their works-cited page.

Internet

Author (if available). Page title (if available, in quotation marks). Site title (underlined or in italics if typed). Name of sponsor (if available; use "N.p." if not), date published (if available; use "n.d." if not). Medium of publication ("Web"). Date accessed.

"Kingdom of Ndongo." About Angola. Republic of Angola's Embassy in Stockholm and to the Nordic Countries, n.d. Web. 1 May 2010.

Format your sources. Check your report and your list of sources (from page 393) to see which sources you actually used. Then follow these directions.

1. Write your sources using the guidelines above and on the previous page. You can write them on a sheet of paper or on note cards.
2. Alphabetize your sources.
3. Create your works-cited page. (See the example below.)

Works Cited

Diouf, Sylviane Anna. Kings and Queens of Southern Africa. New York: Franklin Watts, 2000. Print.

Grayson, John. "Nzinga of Ndongo and Matamba." Legendary Figures 28 Dec. 2003: 47-50. Print.

Hahn, Emma. Unlikely Heroes: Historic and Contemporary Figures. Portland: J. Weston Walch, 2004. Print.

"Kingdom of Ndongo." About Angola. Republic of Angola's Embassy in Stockholm and to the Nordic Countries, n.d. Web. 1 May 2010.

Advanced Learners

Have students create a poster for each type of citation, listing the required information and modeling the correct form. Display the poster in the classroom or school library for students' reference.

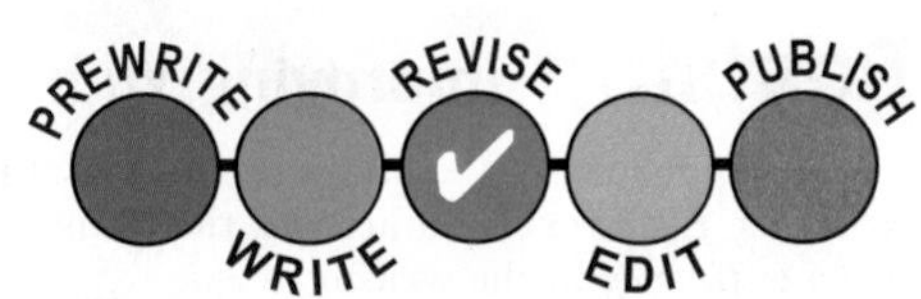

Revising

A good research report needs more than one draft. The first time through, you work mainly with organization and ideas. In the second draft, you fill in missing information, rearrange ideas for clarity, and polish your word choice. Take the time to make your report as good as it can be.

Keys to Effective Revising

1. *Read your entire draft to get an overall sense of your report.*
2. *Review your thesis statement to be sure that it clearly states your main point about the topic.*
3. *Make sure your beginning draws readers in. Then check that your ending brings your report to an interesting close.*
4. *Make sure you sound knowledgeable and interested in the topic.*
5. *Check for correct, specific words and complete sentences.*
6. *Use the editing and proofreading marks in the back cover of this book.*

Revising

Keys to Effective Revising

Keys to Effective Revising explains the process students will go through with their research report. Help students recognize how it follows the traits of good writing.

Give students plenty of time to revise their research reports. Set aside at least three days for revising. Break down the revising process into distinct tasks.

- On Day 1 of revising, have students revise just the introduction.
- On Day 2 of revising, have them focus on revising the middle paragraphs.
- On Day 3 of revising, have them work on the final paragraph and their works-cited page.

Having students focus on one section at a time can make the revising process more manageable.

Technology Connections

Have students use the Writing Network features of the Net-text to comment on each other's drafts.

Write Source Online ***Net-text***

Revising Improving Your Writing

Remind students to consider each writing trait separately as they revise. This approach helps students look at their work carefully and thoughtfully, without being overwhelmed by the revision process.

Revising Improving Your Writing

In the following sample page, the writer makes several important revisions. Each revision improves the *ideas, organization, voice, word choice,* or *sentence fluency* in the writing.

The United States has had more than 40 different presidents, all of them men. Some Americans ~~think it would be crazy to have~~ [have a hard time imagining] a woman as their president. However, history gives many examples of women leading nations, such as Indira Gandhi of India and Golda Meir of Israel. Another example is the seventeenth-century African ruler Nzinga Mbande [(Geen-gah Em-bahn-day)], often just called "Ginga." By protecting her people from a takeover by the Portuguese, Ginga showed that a woman can be a great leader.

A phrase is reworded for better voice.

A helpful pronunciation is added.

Ginga's Background

Ginga lived from about 1583 to 1663 in western Africa [where Angola is now located]. ~~The Portuguese~~ were invading the region and capturing people for slavery. Her father was the king of Ndongo, near the coast. He fought three wars against the Portuguese [who]. He won the first two wars, but he . . .

Details are added for clarity.

A sentence is moved for better organization.

Grammar Connection

Active and Passive Verbs

- **Proofreader's Guide** page 726 (+)

Sentence Variety and Ellipses

- **Proofreader's Guide** pages 614–615
- ***SkillsBook*** pages 137–138
- ***GrammarSnap*** Simple, Compound, and Complex Sentences

Sentence Expanding

- ***Write Source*** pages 511, 521–522
- ***SkillsBook*** pages 81–82, 131–132, 129–130
- ***GrammarSnap*** Adjectival Phrases

Pronouns

- **Proofreader's Guide** pages 708–709
- ***Write Source*** page 476
- ***SkillsBook*** pages 153–154

Wordiness

- ***SkillsBook*** page 100

Struggling Learners

Have students whisper-read aloud their research reports, highlighting any name or place words that are difficult to pronounce. Next, they can have two other students try to say the highlighted proper nouns. If those students are unsure how to pronounce the words as well, the writer needs to look up the pronunciation and add it to the report.

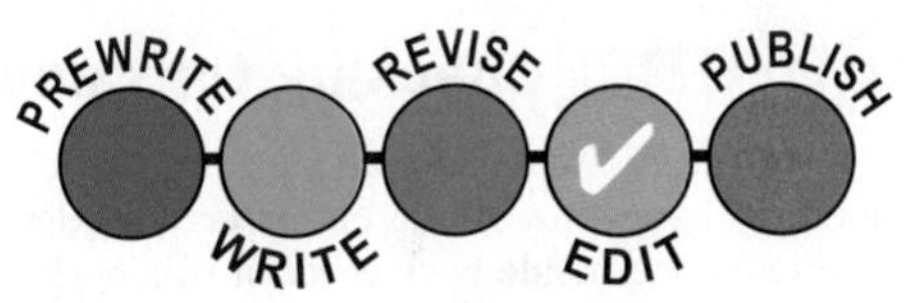

Editing

Once you have finished revising your report, edit your work for conventions like spelling, punctuation, capitalization, and grammar.

Keys to Effective Editing

1. Use a dictionary, a thesaurus, your computer's spell-checker, and the "Proofreader's Guide."
2. Read your essay out loud and listen for words or phrases that may be incorrect.
3. Look for errors in punctuation, capitalization, spelling, and grammar.
4. Check your report for proper formatting. (See pages 382–386 and 403–404.)
5. If you use a computer, edit on a printed computer copy. Then enter your changes on the computer.
6. Use the editing and proofreading marks inside the back cover of this book.

RESEARCH

Editing

Keys to Effective Editing

Keys to Effective Editing explains the process students will go through with their research report.

Warn students not to rely too heavily on a computer's spell-checker.

- Explain that a computer doesn't know the difference between the usage of *there* and *their* or *it's* and *its*. Computers will spot words that don't exist, but they don't know when a word is missing or when the wrong word has been used.
- Guide students in using a computer spell-checker. Encourage them to double-check the suggestion for correction against the Proofreader's Guide at the back of the pupil edition before making changes.

Technology Connections

Students can use the added features of the Net-text as they explore this stage of the writing process.

Write Source Online **Net-text**

Editing Checking for Conventions

Have students exchange reports with a partner.

- Partners can use the Editing Checklist on SE page 22 to check each other's writing for conventions.
- Suggest that students use a different colored pencil for marking corrections for each convention.

Editing Checking for Conventions

In the following sample page, editing changes have been made to correct spelling, usage, and punctuation errors. (See the editing and proofreading marks on the inside back cover of this book.)

Ginga's Accomplishments

Ginga showed her skill for negotiation when her brother first became king. Because he knew she was a good negotiator, he sent her in his place to make a treaty with the Portuguese. Ginga went to meet the Portuguese ~~governer~~ governor in the city of Luanda, where he ruled. The ~~govener~~ governor met Ginga in a room with only one chair, his official seat, to make her feel like his subject. To show that she was his equal, Ginga gestured to one of her followers. That follower knelt on the ground to become a seat for her. Having shown her authority, Ginga was then able to negotiate a good treaty for her people (Diouf 18–20).

In 1624, when Ginga's brother died, she took the throne and proved her leadership skills. To get her people's respect, she insisted on being called King instead of Queen. To show that women could be . . .

A spelling error is corrected.

A run-on sentence is corrected.

A period is moved to its proper place.

Capitalization errors are corrected.

Grammar Connection

Commas Review

- **Proofreader's Guide** pages 582–591 (+)
- ***SkillsBook*** pages 25–26

Misplaced Modifiers

- **Proofreader's Guide** page 694 (+)
- ***Write Source*** page 505
- ***SkillsBook*** pages 103–104
- ***GrammarSnap*** Misplaced and Dangling Modifiers

Sentence Problems Review

- ***Write Source*** pages 511, 506–509 (+), 510 (+)
- ***SkillsBook*** pages 98, 112

Pronoun-Antecedent Agreement

- **Proofreader's Guide** pages 706–707
- ***Write Source*** pages 477, 478
- ***SkillsBook*** pages 149–150, 161–162
- ***GrammarSnap*** Pronoun-Antecedent Agreement

Parts of Speech Review

- **Proofreader's Guide** pages 702–748 (+)
- ***SkillsBook*** pages 201–202

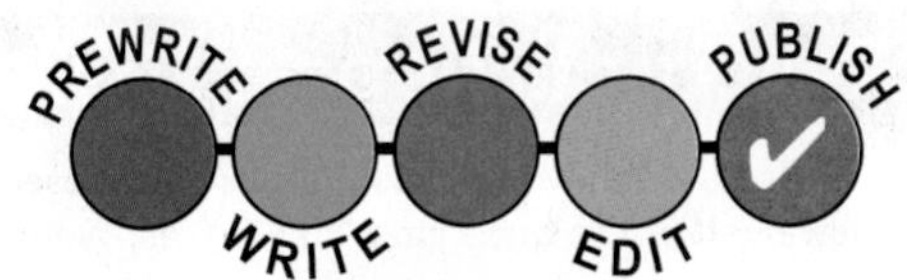

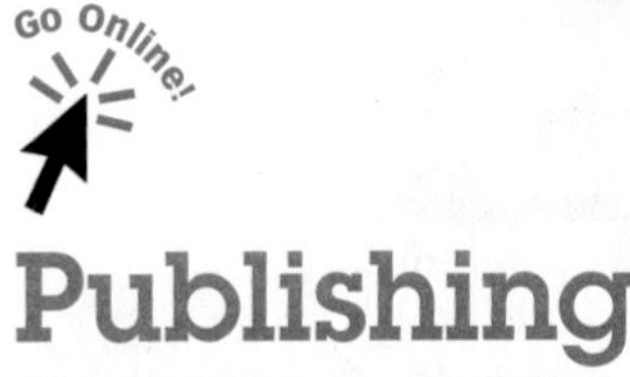

Publishing

Sharing Your Report

After you have worked so hard to write and improve your report, you'll want to make a neat-looking final copy to share. You may also decide to prepare your report as an electronic presentation, an online essay, or an illustrated report.

Make a final copy. Use the following guidelines to format your report. (If you are using a computer, see page 60.) Create a clean final copy and carefully proofread it.

RESEARCH

Focus on Presentation

- Use blue or black ink and double-space the entire paper.
- Write your name, your teacher's name, the class, and the date in the upper left corner of page 1.
- Skip a line and center your title; skip another line and start your writing.
- Indent every paragraph and leave a one-inch margin on all four sides.
- For a research paper, you should write your last name and the page number in the upper right corner of every page of your report.

Creating a Title Page

If your teacher requires a title page, follow his or her requirements. Usually you center the title one-third of the way down from the top of the page. Then go two-thirds of the way down and center your name, your teacher's name, the name of the class, and the date. Put each piece of information on a separate line.

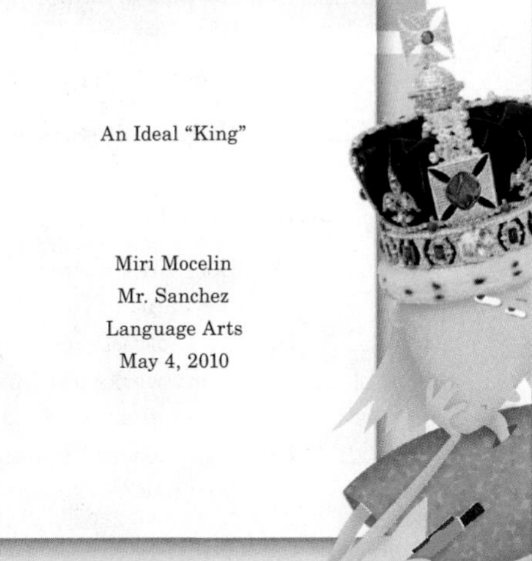
An Ideal "King"

Miri Mocelin
Mr. Sanchez
Language Arts
May 4, 2010

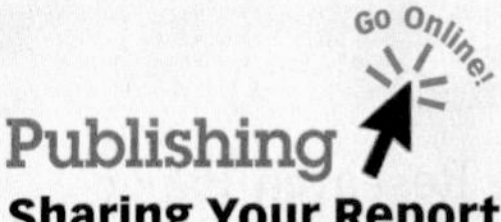

Publishing

Sharing Your Report

If students prepare their reports on a computer, they may want to add graphics to clarify information in their reports. Maps, charts, and diagrams all add interest while providing important details that help readers understand what they are reading about.

* Additional information on adding graphics is on SE page 574.

Technology Connections

Remind students that they can use the Writing Network features of the Portfolio to share their work with peers.

Write Source Online **Portfolio**

Write Source Online **Net-text**

Research Report Checklist

Tell students that using the Research Paper Checklist is a good way to catch any mistakes before turning in their paper for a final grade.

- Students shouldn't be afraid to make corrections at this point.
- They can use this time to assess their papers and make certain that they have fulfilled all the criteria on the checklist.

Research Report Checklist

Use the following checklist for your research report. When you can answer all of the questions with a "yes," your report is ready to hand in.

Ideas

_____ **1.** Is my research report interesting and informative?

_____ **2.** Are my sources current and trustworthy?

Organization

_____ **3.** Does my paper have a thesis statement in the opening paragraph and a topic sentence in each middle paragraph?

_____ **4.** Does my ending paragraph bring my report to an interesting close?

Voice

_____ **5.** Do I sound knowledgeable and interested in my topic?

Word Choice

_____ **6.** Have I explained any technical terms or unfamiliar words?

_____ **7.** Do I use quotations and paraphrasing effectively?

Sentence Fluency

_____ **8.** Do my sentences flow smoothly from one to another?

Conventions

_____ **9.** Does my first page include my name, my teacher's name, the name of the class, the date, and a title? (See page 382.)

_____ **10.** Do I correctly cite my sources? (See pages 383–385 and 397.)

_____ **11.** Is my works-cited page set up correctly? Are the sources listed in alphabetical order? (See pages 386 and 403–404.)

_____ **12.** If my teacher requires a title page, is mine done correctly? (See page 409.)

Research Writing

Multimedia Presentations

If you've just written your best report or essay ever, you may want to share it with a larger audience. To reach a larger audience, you may have to shift from being the writer to being the director. As director, you can write a multimedia presentation complete with special effects, which a wide range of viewers can enjoy.

There are several kinds of software that you can use to produce multimedia presentations. Just add a little imagination, and you'll be connecting with your audience in a new, dynamic way.

What's Ahead

- Creating Interactive Reports
- Interactive Report Checklist

Multimedia Presentations

Objectives

- select a piece of writing for a multimedia presentation
- create a storyboard

Discuss multimedia presentations in one or more of these ways:

- Ask students whether they have made multimedia reports. If they have, ask them to discuss some of the steps that they took in preparing their presentations.
- Discuss what kinds of computers and software students know and may have used for doing multimedia work.
- Ask students who have prepared multimedia presentations how long it took them to develop the presentations and what steps they would like to learn more about.
- Have students watch a multimedia presentation. What aspects do they like, and why?

Advanced Learners

Have students use the research tools discussed on SE pages 364–376 to locate information on how to become a film director. Then have them report back to the class.

Creating Interactive Reports

Prewriting Selecting a Topic and Details

As students begin to consider possible topics, tell them to think about whether the topic easily lends itself to visual images and sounds.

- For example, an abstract scientific theory would not be a good topic because it would be too difficult to illustrate with concrete examples.
- A report on a favorite sports figure, musician, or artist would be better, because students probably could locate video clips, audio clips, and still photos of these real people.
- Suggest that students consider using the research report they've just written.

 **Answers**

Answers will vary.

Creating Interactive Reports

With the help of a computer, you can design a report that others can interact with. Your computer-generated slides, graphics, and sound effects will make the important parts of your report clearer and more interesting.

Prewriting Selecting a Topic and Details

For your interactive report, you will want to use something you've already written, something that interests both you and your audience. After you've chosen your piece of writing, make a list of its main ideas. Then find or create one or more of the following graphics or sound effects:

- **Pictures** such as photos or "clip art"
- **Animations** that show a process or tell a story
- **Videos** of something you've filmed yourself
- **Sounds and music** to use as background or to make a point

 Make a plan and organize your ideas by creating a list or media grid like the one below.

Media Grid

Main Ideas	Pictures or Videos	Animations or Music	Sounds
1. Ginga was a great African leader in the seventeenth century.	portrait of Ginga	background music	
2. She took her brother's throne when he died.	picture of a throne		cheers of a crowd

 **Gather details.** Select ideas from your list or media grid for graphics and sounds to include with each slide. Create the graphics or sounds yourself or find them on the Internet. Save the images (credit the source if necessary) and sounds on your computer in a special folder created for this report.

Advanced Learners

Have students interview the school library media specialist and make a classroom poster listing recommended safe Internet sites from which clips and photos can be downloaded.

LISTEN speak clarify observe respect 421
Listening and Speaking

Group Skills

It's a pleasure to work in a group when the members respect each other, because the group will get more done. A few specific skills will improve a group's effectiveness: observing, cooperating, encouraging, and clarifying.

Observe the speaker by . . .

- watching body language, including facial expressions, gestures, and posture.
- listening to the tone of voice—excited, nervous, or shy.

Cooperate by . . .

- staying positive and waiting your turn.
- avoiding put-downs.
- being respectful when you disagree.

Encourage others by . . .

- complimenting them on their ideas.
- asking them for their opinions.

Clarify by . . .

- asking if there are any questions you can answer.
- restating a speaker's idea to be sure you understand it.

Try It Observe, cooperate, encourage, and clarify. Read the situations and questions below and discuss your answers with a classmate.

1. When Jim speaks, he talks too fast and looks out the window of the classroom.
   What impression will Jim's listeners get from the way he speaks?
2. Juana is shy about speaking in the group.
   What can group members do to encourage Juana to participate?
3. Yolanda notices that group members sometimes seem confused about what she is saying.
   What should Yolanda do when her listeners appear to be puzzled?

LEARNING

Group Skills

Divide the class into four groups. Assign each group one of the following topics:

- observing
- cooperating
- encouraging
- clarifying

Have each group make a poster that illustrates the skill. Students may create an icon that represents the skill and a slogan that captures the skill's essence.

When the groups have finished their posters, have members present them to the class. Hang the posters in the classroom so that students can refer to them when they are working in groups.

Many students are uncomfortable **giving encouragement** *(see below)* to their classmates. Encourage students to praise each other when they are impressed by a classmate's ideas or presentation.

Answers

Answers will vary.

Teaching Tip: Giving Encouragement

Explain that specific praise is a way to encourage a peer. Present some examples (see bulleted list that follows).

- "You expressed your idea so clearly that you convinced me."
- "That was a great point. I hadn't thought of it."

English Language Learners

In order to use the second tip under "Clarify by . . . ," students need to be able to paraphrase. Review that paraphrasing means putting the ideas of others into their own words, or restating the meaning of something heard or read. Provide practice in the skill by having students turn sentences you have read aloud into questions that clarify the meaning.

- For example, you say, "Sun, soil, and water are necessary for plants to grow."
- Then students use paraphrasing to ask, "Do you mean that plants will die without sun, soil, and water?"

Speaking in Class

Make a paper "speak-o-meter" to indicate speaking volume.

- Cut a semicircle from a piece of cardboard.
- Cut out a red arrow and place it vertically in the middle of the straight edge of the semicircle.
- Attach the bottom of the arrow to the cardboard with a brad so the arrow can move.
- Write 1 through 9 around the edges of the curve. Place the 5 at the top of the curve.

Use the speak-o-meter to show students when they are speaking loudly and clearly.

- Ask students, one at a time, to read aloud a short passage from a favorite book.
- Use the speak-o-meter to indicate the student's volume (1 for a whisper—9 for a yell).
- Restart any student who speaks at level 1 or 2 until the volume is a 5—loud enough for everyone to hear and comfortable enough for everyone to continue listening.

Speaking in Class

Speaking in class is sometimes like playing a sport—it's a team effort. You can only speak effectively in the classroom or have a good discussion when the group is working well together. These basic strategies will help you and your classmates become better speakers.

Before you speak . . .

- listen and take notes.
- think about what others are saying.
- wait until it's your turn to speak.
- plan how you can add something positive to the discussion.

When you speak . . .

- speak loudly and clearly.
- stick to the topic.
- avoid repeating what's already been said.
- support your ideas with examples.
- look at others in the group or class.

Play "Twenty-Question Who Am I?" In your group or class, select one person to play the part of the mystery guest. The mystery guest is a famous person whose identity everyone else has to guess by asking "yes" or "no" questions. As you play this game, practice using the strategies listed above.

1. Each player takes a turn asking one question until someone guesses who the famous person is.
2. The player who guesses correctly becomes the next mystery guest.
3. If no one guesses correctly within 20 questions, the mystery guest reveals his or her identity and becomes a new famous person.

English Language Learners

Students will gain confidence about speaking to a group by using the Think-Pair-Share technique before speaking.

Ask a key question.

- Give students time to think about their response.
- Have students share their answer with a partner.

Then ask students to share their answers with the class.

Struggling Learners

Students can use a tape recorder to assess their speaking skills. They can learn to improve the quality of their public speaking by making changes after listening to themselves.

Record students as they read aloud, give an opinion, or explain an answer. As they listen to themselves, they should focus on such questions as:

- How well can a listener understand what I am saying? How do I speak? Do I talk too quickly? Do I mumble?
- How many times do I use fillers, such as *um, like*, or *you know?*

Help students recognize and overcome difficulties. Record them again and ask whether they think they have improved their skills.

Making Oral Presentations

"The world famous Flying Ling has just crawled into the loudspeaker. He gives the signal. The fuse is lit. This is one oral presentation that should start off with a bang. . . ."

Luckily, when you make an oral presentation, you won't have to crawl into a loudspeaker, but you might feel like crawling under a rock. "Stage fright" happens to everyone. Careful preparation is the key to overcoming this feeling and creating an effective oral presentation. This chapter will lead you through the process. With a little work, your presentation will be a big hit!

What's Ahead

- Preparing Your Presentation
- Using Visual Aids
- Organizing an Informative Speech
- Delivering Your Speech
- Overcoming Stage Fright

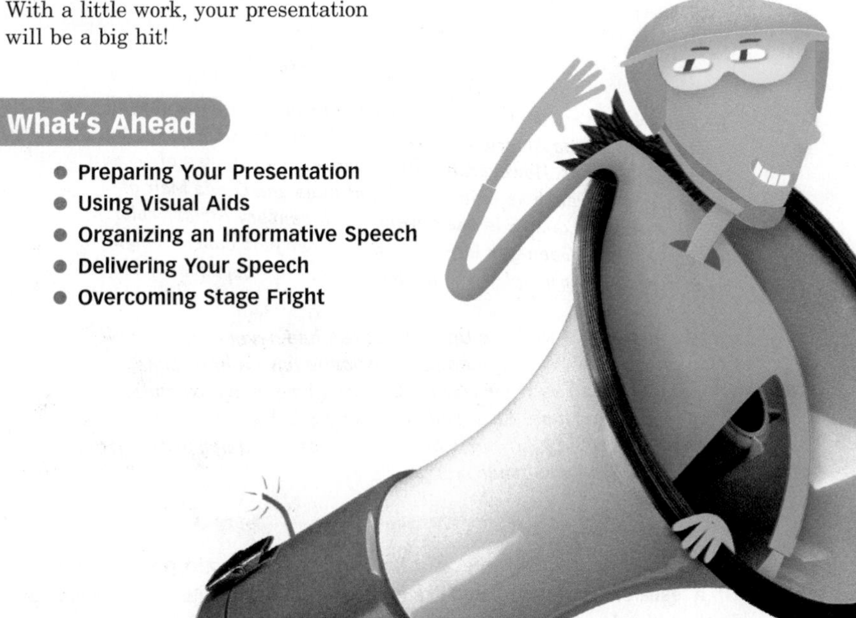

Making Oral Presentations

Objectives

- prepare an oral presentation that incorporates visual aids
- use note cards to create an organized speech
- present a speech to the class using appropriate volume, tone, and speed

Students have many opportunities across the curriculum to prepare and deliver oral presentations. They will find that the more they prepare, the better the presentation.

Ask students to describe the best speech they ever heard.

- What made it memorable?
- What did the speaker do to help the listener understand and remember the speech?

Discuss students' experiences with oral presentations. Ask:

- What do you enjoy about speaking in front of a group?
- What aspects of public speaking do you dislike?
- How do you prepare for an oral presentation?
- In what ways would you like to improve your oral presentation skills?

Preparing Your Presentation

If students do not have a research report to rework into an oral presentation, help them choose a topic. Generate a list of ideas on the board. Possible topics might be related to

- a personal hobby
- a favorite sport
- a historical or contemporary figure

Rewriting in Action

If students use their own research report as the basis of their oral presentation, suggest the following ideas for revising the beginning of the report:

- To grab the listener's attention, rework the opening to make the language more conversational. Imagine you are speaking to a classmate.
- Decide on the most important details.
- Make sentences shorter and simpler so listeners can easily follow what they hear.
- Choose words that are not too complicated or sophisticated.
- Keep your audience in mind as you rewrite.

424

Preparing Your Presentation

Preparing an informative speech from a research report is different than writing a speech from scratch. You already have a topic, you've gathered lots of information, and you know the type of speech you will make. Here are some tips to help you shape the information from your report into a good speech.

- Grab your listeners' attention with an opening question or a surprising fact.
- Know how much time you have to give your presentation.
- Emphasize your most important points and cut unneeded information.
- Mark your paper for visual aids or gestures.

Rewriting in Action

Below is the opening of the research report on pages **382–386**. Notice that the new beginning (on gold paper) has been revised to better fit the requirements of an oral presentation and get the listeners' attention.

An Ideal "King"

The United States has had more than 40 different presidents, all of them men. Some Americans have a hard time imagining a woman as their president. However, history gives many examples of women leading nations, such as Indira Gandhi of India and Golda Meir of Israel. Another example is the seventeenth-century African ruler Nzinga Mbande (Geen-gah Em-bahn-day), often just called "Ginga." By protecting her people from a takeover by the Portuguese, Ginga

Do you ever wonder why the United States has never elected a woman president? Although some Americans have a hard time imagining a woman as their leader, history gives many examples of women leading nations. An excellent example is Nzinga Mbande, a seventeenth-century African woman who protected her people from being taken over by another country.

Rework your beginning and think about the main points. Choose a research report you would like to present orally. Rewrite your opening so that it grabs your audience's attention. Then think about which important details you want to emphasize in your report.

Using Visual Aids

After you finish rewriting the beginning of your informative speech and choosing the most important details, it's time to gather visual aids for your presentation. Visual aids like those listed below are informative and will hold your listeners' interest.

Posters	show words, pictures, or both.
Photographs	help your audience "see" who or what you are talking about.
Charts	compare ideas or explain main points.
Transparencies	highlight key words, ideas, or graphics.
Maps	show specific places being discussed.
Objects	allow your audience to see the real thing.

Here are some tips for preparing your visual aids.

1. **Bigger is better.** Be sure your visual aids can be seen by the people in the back row.
2. **Keep the wording simple.** Sentences and paragraphs are out. Labels are in.
3. **Make your visual aids eye-catching.** Colorful and attractive designs are the key.

List visual aids. List a number of possible visual aids you could use in your presentation. Then select two that you think will work best. Jot down notes about how you will use them.

Map	*show a map of Africa and Europe*
Photograph	*show a picture of Ginga*

Using Visual Aids

Students may find materials on the Internet to use in preparing their visual aids. Remind them that they must cite sources.

- Tell students to keep their visual materials clear, neat, and simple.
- The goal is to create visuals that clarify and illustrate the main points of their oral presentation.

Struggling Learners

Help students focus on how visual aids in their textbooks are used to organize and clarify information. Ask:

- How do visual aids help in a social studies or science text? (Examine examples of visual aids in their textbooks.)
- What visual aids could you make that will help your audience to understand your topic more clearly?

Organizing an Informative Speech

Emphasize the importance of opening an informative speech with something that will intrigue the audience. Students can start strong with one of several approaches:

- a surprising fact
- a question
- a strong opinion

Using Note Cards

By writing the introduction and the conclusion on separate, single cards, students will be forced to keep these parts concise and distinct.

Give students these additional note-card reminders:

- Do not write on the backs of the note cards.
- Number or color-code note cards to keep them in order.
- Keep sentences short and simple to help listeners absorb the information.

Organizing an Informative Speech

Now that you've written an exciting beginning and have gathered visual aids, you're ready to organize your speech. *Remember:* An informative speech is meant to teach your audience something. Clear organization is the key. Use the following tips.

1. **Start strong.** Grab the listeners' attention and keep it.
2. **Organize your details logically.** Put your details in the best order and use transitions to guide listeners from one idea to another.
3. **End even stronger.** Make sure that the last thing your audience hears is memorable.

Using Note Cards

Putting information on note cards is a simple and an effective way to organize your speech. The cards can contain your main points and are easier to handle during a presentation than sheets of notepaper. By using note cards, you also have more opportunity for eye contact.

For example, the student who developed an informative speech from her research report on pages 382–386 put her main ideas and details on note cards. She gave her speech using the note cards as a guide.

Note-Card Guidelines

- Write out your entire introduction on the first note card.
- Use a separate card for each of the main ideas that follow.
- Number each card and write the main idea at the top. Add specific details for that idea underneath.
- Note your visual aids on appropriate cards, with instructions for what to do with each one.
- Write out your entire ending on the last note card.

Create your note cards. Look over the note cards on the next page. Then create a note card for each step in your presentation. Be sure to add notes to yourself about visual aids. Also write a memorable ending.

English Language Learners

Students can use a colored pen or a highlighter on note cards to do the following:

- Mark key points and details, such as dates. Highlighting enables students to quickly identify what is important.
- Write a simple phonetic spelling of new names or words (for example, GEEN-gah) to help students pronounce them correctly.

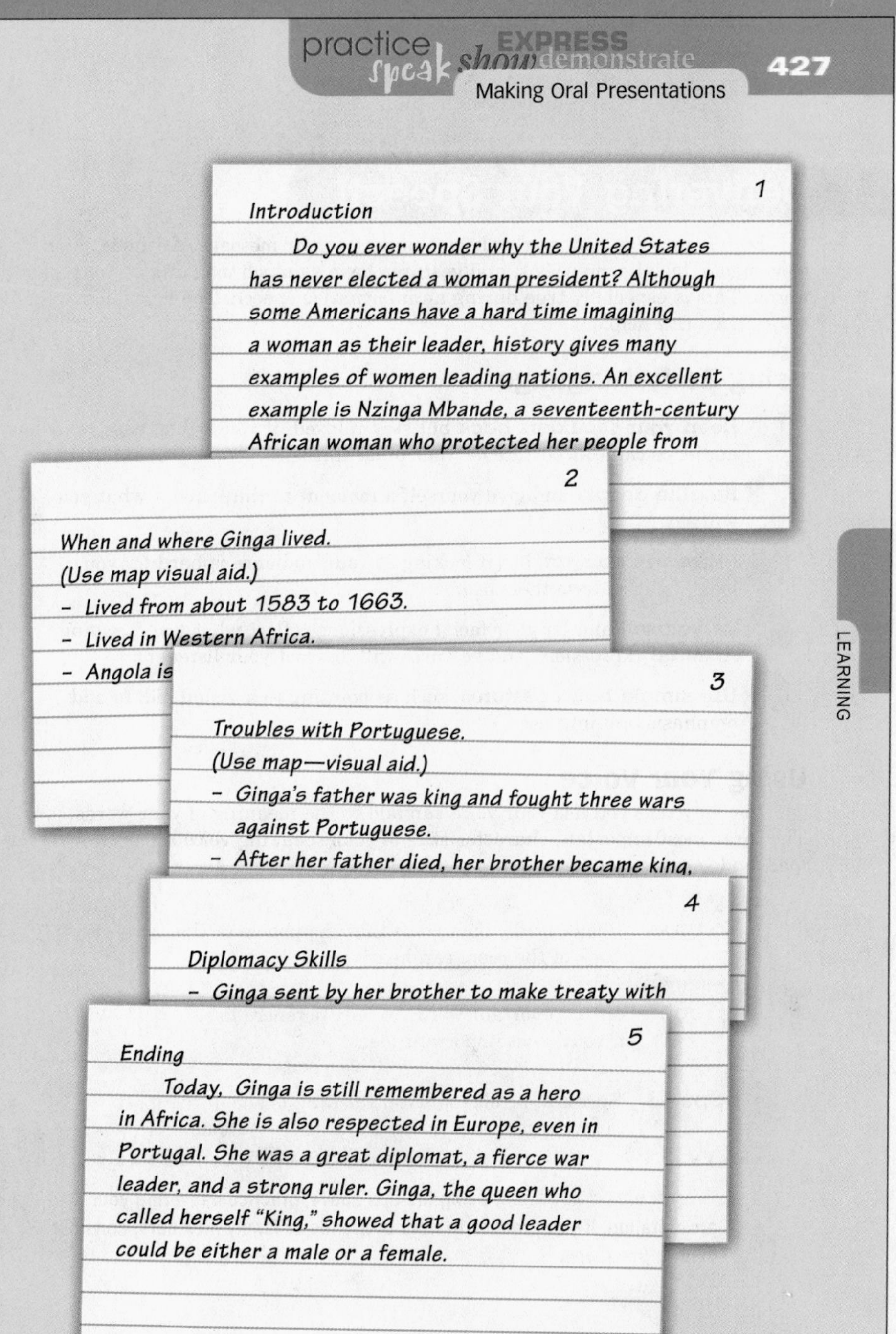

Discuss the transition from phrases on the note cards to full sentences in the presentation.

- Point out that the information on note cards 2 through 4 is not written in full sentences.
- Remind students that although they will use phrases on some note cards, they should speak in complete sentences when they give their presentations.
- Encourage students to practice using their note cards so that they become comfortable turning phrases into sentences when they speak.

Delivering Your Speech

Have students discuss the special skills they need in order to make a good presentation.

Using Body Language

As they make a presentation, students must focus on posture, facial expression, and gestures, as well as on the content of their speech. They should practice their delivery before a mirror or ask a family member to watch for body language as they practice the speech.

Using Your Voice

Students should work to eliminate fillers, such as *um* and *you know,* that they use while speaking.

- Have students present their speeches to a partner.
- Let the partner tally the number of fillers they hear.

Students will benefit from taping their speech and then listening to the recording. They can assess their clarity, pacing, volume, and expression. They should then modify and improve their delivery.

Delivering Your Speech

Both your voice and your body communicate your message. At times, your movements, facial expressions, and gestures have as much meaning as your words. This is especially true during an informative speech. The following suggestions can help.

Using Body Language

1. **Keep your shoulders back** but stay relaxed. If you look at ease, your audience can concentrate on your presentation.
2. **Breathe deeply** and give yourself a moment to think about what you will say.
3. **Make eye contact**, but if looking at your audience is hard for you, look slightly above their heads.
4. **Be yourself** and let your facial expressions reflect what you're saying. Artificial expressions and gestures will distract your listeners.
5. **Use simple hand gestures**, such as pointing to a visual aid, to add emphasis and interest.

Using Your Voice

The way that you use your voice can add to the meaning of your words. The three most important characteristics of your speaking voice are *volume, tone,* and *speed.*

Volume	Speak loudly enough so that the people at the back of the room can hear you.
Tone	Stress important words to help listeners focus on your most important ideas.
Speed	Speak at a relaxed pace. Rushing is one of the most common faults in making oral presentations.

Practice and present. Using the tips above, practice delivering your presentation. If you practice in front of friends or family members, consider their suggestions.

English Language Learners

Play a body-language game to clarify the given tips.

- Read aloud something from a book or an article.
- Ignore one of the tips. For example, you might look down (avoid eye contact) as you read.
- Have students discuss how to improve your delivery.
- Repeat, ignoring a different tip each time.

Struggling Learners

Help students learn to project.

- Have the speaker repeat, "Testing, testing 1 – 2 – 3," until the entire audience can hear.
- Have a friend of the speaker sit at the back of the audience and use agreed-upon hand signals to let the speaker know whether to increase or decrease volume. Encourage students to choose hand signals that won't distract the speaker.

Overcoming Stage Fright

If you think you're the only one who feels nervous speaking in front of a group, you're wrong. Everyone feels that way at one time or another. There are things that you can do to relax and reduce "stage fright."

1 Practice, practice, practice.

Preparation is the key. The more often you rehearse your speech, the more relaxed you will be. Practicing in front of friends or family will also help you get used to having an audience.

2 Take a deep breath.

Arrange your notes. Look around before you begin. Don't rush into your speech.

3 Focus.

Concentrate on what you are doing and on what comes next. Visualize the steps in your presentation.

Using a Checklist

Practice your presentation using the checklist below. If possible, videotape yourself so that you can see what you do well and what you can improve. Also consider having someone else watch your presentation and make suggestions.

_____ **1.** I stand up straight, and I look relaxed.

_____ **2.** I maintain eye contact with my audience instead of staring at my notes.

_____ **3.** My voice is loud and clear.

_____ **4.** My voice and appearance show that I am interested in my topic.

_____ **5.** I speak at a natural pace (not too fast or too slow).

_____ **6.** I avoid "stalling" words like *um, er,* and *like.*

_____ **7.** My visual aids are large and easy to understand.

_____ **8.** I make gestures for emphasis, and I point out my visual aids.

Overcoming Stage Fright

Many students tend to speak quickly when they are nervous. To give students a more precise idea of appropriate speed,

- model the introduction and ending paragraphs on SE page 427.
- first use normal pacing and then use "fast forward" pacing.

Exaggerating the speed will inject humor into the lesson and remind students to slow down.

Presentation Tips

Provide as much class time for practice as possible.

- Once students have timed their speeches and adjusted the length, they should practice repeatedly.
- If possible, each student should present his or her speech to an audience (a friend, a relative, and so on).
- The more students familiarize themselves with the speech, the less often they will need to refer to their notes.
- Each practice session will make them more fluent, which, in turn, will make them more comfortable.

Presentation Tips

Before your presentation . . .

- **Get everything organized.** Put the main points of your speech on note cards and make your visual aids.
- **Time your speech.** If it's too long or too short, adjust the length by adding or removing note cards.
- **Practice.** The more you remember without looking at your notes, the easier it will be to give the presentation.

During your presentation . . .

- **Project your voice.** Be sure everyone can hear you.
- **Speak clearly and slowly.** Don't rush through your speech.
- **Maintain eye contact.** Make a connection with your audience.
- **Hold visual aids so that everyone can see them.** Point out the things that you are talking about.

After your presentation . . .

- **Answer questions.** Clarify any information that your listeners ask about.
- **Make closing comments.** Summarize the listeners' questions and concerns.

Practice and present. Have a final practice with a friend or someone at home. After you make your speech in the classroom, listen for suggestions from your teacher and classmates. You can try out these ideas in your next speech.

Struggling Learners

Before the presentations, write these quotes on the board.

- Everything that can go wrong will go wrong.
- The show must go on.

Relieve some student anxiety by engaging in a light discussion, opening with a question that begins with, "What can a speaker do if . . . ?"

Invite students to think of possible problems. Encourage serious and silly potential issues (dropping note cards, cracking voice, coughing spasm, surprise fire drill, and so on). Then brainstorm solutions that would help a speaker make the best of the situation.

Keeping Journals and Learning Logs

Every day, amazing thoughts go through your mind. Journals and learning logs can capture and organize these thoughts and can also help you to become a better writer and thinker.

A journal lets you reflect on your daily experiences. In the same way, a learning log lets you reflect on classroom experiences. When you write learning-log entries, you think about what you are learning and gain a deeper understanding of the material.

This chapter will teach you more about journals, learning logs, and other writing-to-learn activities.

What's Ahead

- **Writing in a Travel Journal**
- **Writing in Other Journals**
- **Writing in a Learning Log**
- **Writing-to-Learn Activities**

Teaching Tip: Journals vs. Learning Logs

To help students understand the difference between a journal and a learning log, explain the following:

- Journals provide a quiet space to organize thoughts, clarify opinions, and think through courses of action.
- Learning logs are a place for students to record what they are learning in school as they are learning it.

Keeping Journals and Learning Logs

Objectives

- write in a travel journal
- learn about the purpose of keeping other kinds of journals
- make entries in other kinds of journals
- create a learning log

Writing in a journal gives students opportunities to reflect on their daily experiences and observations. Writing in a learning log helps students reinforce what they have learned in school.

To generate discussion on **journals and learning logs** *(see below)*, ask the following questions:

- How often do you write in a journal at home?
- What kinds of things do you write about in your journal?
- For what subject(s) have you kept a learning log?
- Was the learning log helpful?
- What did you learn from keeping a learning log?

Writing in a Travel Journal

Explain that students don't have to go to a distant, exotic place in order to write a travel journal. They might write a travel journal entry about a day trip to a(n)

- local museum,
- nearby zoo,
- baseball park,
- amusement park.

The key objective is for students to record their observations. They can record thoughts about any experience that takes them away from their everyday life. Being someplace new should awaken their senses and create memories and observations to write about.

Getting Started

To help students warm up, tell them to draw or tell something about their trip. Drawing may generate ideas they can translate into writing. Telling may trigger details that they had forgotten.

Provide 5–10 minutes for students to freewrite. When time is up, ask students to count the number of words they have written. As they discover how much they have written, they will see how easy it is to write about something they experienced directly.

Writing in a Travel Journal

When you travel, you have new experiences. Perhaps you sleep in a tent in the woods, touch a porpoise at an aquarium, or see trees that have turned to stone. A travel journal can help you think about such experiences. You don't have to organize your thoughts into an essay—you just record them.

Getting Started

To get started on your own travel journal, follow these steps:

1 Gather the proper tools.

All you need is some paper and your favorite pen or pencil. You can buy a special journal or a blank book, or an ordinary school notebook—whatever you wish. You can even use a portable computer if you have one available.

2 Establish a regular routine.

Choose a time of day for journaling. Maybe you'll write at night, just before going to sleep, or first thing in the morning. When you write, find a comfortable place where you won't be interrupted.

3 Write for at least 5 to 10 minutes at a time.

Write freely. This may seem hard at first, but you'll relax as time goes on. After several days, look back at your earlier efforts. You'll probably notice a big improvement in the length and quality of your writing.

4 Write about things that are important to you.

Here are some topic ideas to consider:

- interesting things you see and hear,
- personal thoughts and feelings,
- daily happenings, or
- funny or surprising stories

5 Return to your writing.

Go back and read your travel journal from time to time. Mark ideas and entries that you would like to write more about in the future. Watch for possible story or poem ideas.

Start your journal writing. Write in a journal the next time you go somewhere. Review your entries a week or two later and explain how you might develop one of them into a longer piece.

English Language Learners

Provide practice in writing in a travel journal.

- Take students on a "trip" in or around the school.
- Tell them to think about at least five things that they do not ordinarily notice.
- Back in the classroom, review the five steps on this page.
- Then have students write a journal entry.

Struggling Learners

Invite students to start an imaginary travel journal of a place they would like to visit.

- Begin by showing students a travelogue.
- Have students create a drawing of a favorite place on the cover of their journal.
- Remind students to think about what makes the place special and to include lots of visual details as they make notes.
- Encourage them to use their five senses and their imaginations as they tell a partner about the real or imagined experience.
- They should write about the place as if they've recently visited there.

CLUSTER record draw learn freewrite 433
Keeping Journals and Learning Logs

Travel Journal Entry

In the journal entry below, a student writes about her first airplane trip. She went to her cousin's wedding in Los Angeles with her parents and her brother Eric.

June 16

When we got on the plane to Los Angeles this morning, I couldn't believe how big it was! I was worried that the pilots wouldn't get the thing off the ground with the hundreds of people in it, but at 9:00 we took off with no problems. Later, the flight attendants brought us a snack. Eric complained there wasn't enough to eat, but he always says that at home, too. I liked the little bags of pretzels.

I fell asleep, and later I woke up when a pilot announced we were over the Pacific Ocean. Eric told me they had missed LA and we were flying to Japan, but pretty soon the plane swung around and we headed down to our landing at Los Angeles International Airport.

We waited at the baggage claim for a long time, because Eric's bag didn't show up. After about a half hour, we went to the office where you report lost luggage. When the man in the office asked Eric what his bag looked like, Eric got a blank look on his face. He finally told Mom and Dad that he thought his bag was still sitting in his bedroom in Chicago. I told him I thought that it was probably on its way to Japan. I didn't know that flying could be so funny.

When you write a journal entry about an experience, focus on the most important details. The following two questions will help you.

What was most surprising or interesting about the experience?

What did I learn from the experience?

Travel Journal Entry

Tell students that writing freely and quickly usually won't produce a perfect journal entry, such as the model on this page. The student who wrote this entry must have revised it to achieve such a polished piece of writing. Most journal entries are not so carefully edited. There may not be distinct paragraphs, complete sentences, or correct spelling, among other things.

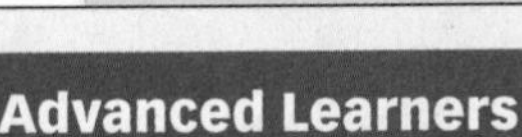

Advanced Learners

Challenge students to write a travel journal entry based on the journey or experience of a character in a book they've read. Tell them to

- write in the voice of the character
- show the character's personality through their word choices.

Writing in Other Journals

Incorporate into the classroom setting assignments in keeping

- specialized journals and
- reader-response journals.

Some school districts discourage teachers from using diaries and personal journals in the classroom. If this is the case, remind students that they may keep personal journals at home if they wish.

Make a connection to literature by providing a list of books that use journal writing as a basis for the plot, for example:

- *Anne Frank: Diary of a Young Girl* by Anne Frank
- *Don't You Dare Read This, Mrs. Dunphrey* by Margaret Haddix
- *The Adrian Mole Diaries* by Sue Townsend

Writing in Other Journals

Travel journals can help you reflect on school trips, vacations, and other journeys. Here are some other types of journals for you to try.

Personal Journal

A personal journal contains thoughts and observations about your life and experiences. Certain entries may inspire you to create longer pieces of writing. Sometimes personal journals contain poems, stories, and jokes.

Diary

A diary is like a personal journal, but a diary focuses more on daily events and experiences. The entries are often shorter, and the details are more specific. A diary is a history of your day-to-day life.

Specialized Journal

A specialized journal focuses on an ongoing activity or experience. It can be a separate journal or a section set aside in your regular journal or diary. You may want to use a specialized journal to explore your thoughts while practicing for a school play, participating in a team sport, or working on a group project.

Reader-Response Journal

A reader-response journal is an excellent way for you to reflect about the content of a book, magazine, or textbook chapter you're reading. Here are some questions that will help you write about what you read.

1. What were my main impressions after reading the opening? After reading half of the selection? After finishing?
2. Did the reading change my understanding or feelings about anything? In what way?
3. Does the reading connect with my life?
4. What is most important about the reading? An idea? A theme? A character?
5. Would I recommend this reading to others? Why?

Write in a specialized journal. The next time you are involved in an ongoing activity or experience, set aside a section of your notebook to write about your thoughts. Use the explanation above to help you get started with your specialized journal.

English Language Learners

Reader-response journals can be effective in helping students understand fiction and nonfiction reading assignments. Provide some guided practice.

- Read aloud a passage of fiction.
- Discuss with students each of the questions listed on this page under the heading Reader Response Journal.
- Have students write a brief answer to each question.
- On another occasion, repeat the process using a textbook or a nonfiction book that students are required to read.

Writing in a Learning Log

Learning logs are outstanding tools for students. They can be made to fit any school subject and are especially useful for making sense out of new or difficult material.

1. **Create a learning log for any subject.** Difficult subjects are made easier when you write about them.
2. **Keep your learning log in good order.** Either keep a separate notebook or make a learning-log entry after each day's class notes in your regular notebook. Date each entry and leave margins to add information later.
3. **Make charts and drawings.** Illustrations and graphic organizers can help you understand difficult concepts.
4. **Write freely about any of the following:**
   - the key idea from a reading assignment or lecture,
   - your questions, or
   - how the material relates to your experience.

LEARNING

English Class Mar. 23

Key words about plot:

beginning = The setting, characters, and conflict are introduced.
rising action = A character struggles to try to solve a problem.
high point = The most important or exciting part of the story—the turning point.
ending = The problem is solved, and the story ends.

In the beginning of Langston Hughes's story "Thank You, Ma'am," I thought Roger's treatment of Mrs. Washington was very rude. This was not a conflict that I would have handled well. Then she talked to him and

Writing in a Learning Log

Science, math, and social studies teachers may ask students to keep a learning log.

- This task will help students see a purpose for writing in all classes.
- Check that content-area teachers rotate the assignments so that students are not overwhelmed by requirements to make daily entries in multiple logs.

English Language Learners

Direct students' attention to the fourth tip. Show students how to organize the information to make it more manageable and useful, by following these tips:

- Draw a vertical line in the middle of their log page.
- Write key ideas from the assignment or lecture in the left column.
- Write questions about the material and thoughts about how the material relates to their experiences on the right.

This method helps students distinguish between ideas they must learn and questions they want to ask or thoughts that help them remember key concepts.

Struggling Learners

Ask students to consider how learning logs can help them keep track of what they learn. Ask them how applying the technique in each subject area could help them learn more effectively.

Science Log

Science class learning logs are a great way for students to observe changes in nature. For example, students might be assigned to

- choose a tree on the school property,
- visit their tree once a week and write down observations and make sketches showing what they see, and
- keep a log of all the changes that take place over the course of the school year.

Tell students that in reviewing their science logs, they may find themselves **questioning** *(see below)* some of the material. This is a good way to identify gaps in their understanding.

Science Log

The entry below was written after a science class discussion about how heat flows from one object to another. Learning logs work best if you put ideas into your own words and include drawings and other graphic aids.

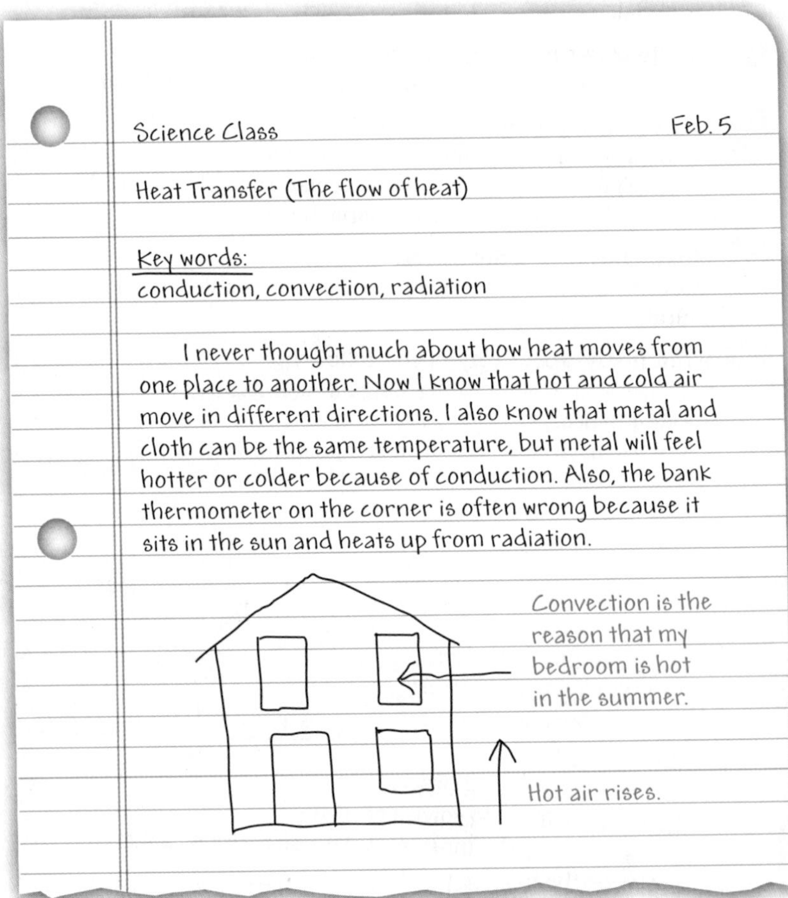

Log on in science. On your own paper, write down the subject of the science unit you are currently studying. Then write a learning-log entry about something that you find interesting, surprising, or confusing.

Teaching Tip: Questioning

Keeping a science learning log enables students to review information written in their own words. They may find that they don't understand something they wrote or that they left a question mark about a certain key point. Offer these tips on what to do:

- Students should highlight parts they don't understand in their log and write a question about it.
- Ask the teacher, using a question format such as, "I understand that . . . , but I don't understand what happens when . . . ."
- Once they get the answer, students should add it to their log.

Students help themselves learn by identifying confusing material, questioning, and getting answers.

Math Log

Keeping a math log is a good way to focus on the concepts taught in your math class. One way to set up a math log is to use a question-answer pattern. Write a question related to the day's lesson and then answer that question. Two examples are shown below.

Math Class Sept. 22
Question: Who invented zero?
Answer: I couldn't understand why somebody had to invent zero. Wasn't it always there? It all became clear when Ms. Jackson told us that Hindus in India worked out a number system based on ten places. In about 200 C.E., they used a dot that meant "empty" as the tenth numeral. Later, the dot became a small circle—zero.

Sept. 23
Question: How does zero work together with the other numerals?
Answer:
Any number + or – 0 = the original number.
If I have five cookies and add none or take none away, I still have five cookies. Simple.

Any number x 0 = 0. I think of multiplying by 0 as the opposite of adding 0. I end up with 0 instead of the number. I can't multiply or divide something that's not there in the first place, right?

Log on in math. On your own paper, write a learning-log entry for math. First write down a question about a math concept you are studying. Then answer that question. (Use the samples above as a guide.)

Math Log

Students may use a math log to think through concepts they are currently studying.

Encourage students to view their math logs as a place to
- practice new concepts and
- make personal connections between concepts.

If possible, suggest that students use their math logs at home, where they have unstructured time in which to think and write freely about what they are learning in school.

Struggling Learners

Invite students to brainstorm a list of questions about a math concept they're learning that could be written in a math log. Then form small groups for the following activity.
- Assign a different question to each small group.
- Have students work together to record an answer on chart paper, using the sample math-log entry as a model.
- Have groups take turns explaining their work to the class.
- Assess the clarity of the written explanations.

Social Studies Log

A social studies log gives students an opportunity to

- connect with the historical era that they are learning about,
- bring history alive,
- reflect on people's lives in a different time and place,
- deepen their understanding of what was going on in the world during a different time period, and
- take the facts from a social studies textbook and transform them into a more meaningful personal experience.

438

Social Studies Log

In the following sample, the student writes about a period of history that was introduced in her social studies class. She reflects on how her life might be different today if events had happened differently back then.

Social Studies Nov. 17

Magna Carta

Mr. Simpson was telling us about how the feudal lords in England forced bad King John to sign the Magna Carta in 1215. Mr. S. said that the Magna Carta was the basis for our Constitution and Declaration of Independence. What really hit me was that the king basically agreed to obey the same laws as everyone else.

More than 500 years later, Americans rebelled because they were being treated poorly under different laws than the people in England had. So here's the part I think is amazing. If John had been a better king, he might not have been forced to sign the Magna Carta. If George III had been a better king, there might not have been an American Revolution. It's hard for me to believe we have all this freedom because of two bad kings. The M.C. was really important to us and to everybody in the world who has a government like ours.

Last summer, Uncle Bill was in England and visited the place where King John signed the Magna Carta.

Log on in social studies. On your own paper, write the subject of the unit you are now studying in social studies. Then write an entry about something in the unit that you can relate to in a personal way.

English Language Learners

Have students incorporate charts and drawings in their logs, as recommended on SE page 435. Social studies logs often contain facts that are related by cause and effect, comparison and contrast, and chronological order. Therefore, the following organizers are effective in clarifying information about social studies topics (and they're a shortcut to writing):

- cause-effect organizers or charts
- comparison-contrast diagrams
- time lines

Refer students to SE pages 548–549 and discuss what organizers they could have used with the text on the Magna Carta (a cause-effect organizer or T-chart, a time line).

Writing-to-Learn Activities

There are many different ways to write in a learning log. Three basic ways are described below, and five additional approaches are discussed on the next page.

The Basic Three

1. **Freewriting** When you freewrite in a learning log, you write quickly about a subject you are studying. Writing freely and rapidly allows you to explore a subject from many different angles. Don't stop to correct your writing—just keep writing. Try to write for at least 5 to 10 minutes at a time.
2. **Clustering** Clustering works well in a learning log because the cluster actually gives you a picture of how ideas fit together. Place the subject you are studying in the center of the page and circle it. Then write words and phrases about the subject. Circle each one and draw a line connecting it to the closest related word. (See page **544**.)
3. **Listing** Listing is another way to discover how ideas relate to each other. As you think about a subject, make a list of ideas, feelings, and questions that come to mind.

Stopping the Use of Tobacco

- *nicotine and carbon monoxide in blood drop the first day*
- *heart rate and blood pressure get lower the first week*
- *heart disease and cancer risk lower within a few years*
- *stop wasting money on bad habit*
- *Why is it so hard to quit smoking?*
- *Which method of stopping is the most successful? (Nicotine patch, hypnosis, and so on)*

After listing for 3 or 4 minutes, you may find it helpful to freewrite about the subject using one or more of the ideas in your list.

Make a list like the one above for a subject you are studying in one of your classes. *Remember:* Write the subject at the top of your list. Keep listing until you run out of ideas.

LEARNING

Struggling Learners

To give students additional practice in using the three basic writing-to-learn activities, show a short content-area video. Then ask each student to respond to the video by freewriting, clustering, or listing. As a class, discuss and compare the results.

Writing-to-Learn Activities

Emphasize that students may use a variety of these approaches in a single learning log.

Answers

Answers will vary.

Special Writing Activities

Tell students to examine the sample personal summary at the bottom of the page.

- Discuss how comparing the diagram of a leaf to a layer cake helps the student relate the diagram to something familiar and appealing. Point out that this is one good way to remember new material.
- Discuss how in the second paragraph, the writer likens the leaf to a glass jar filled with marbles. This image will help the writer recall what he or she learned about chlorophyll.
- Encourage students to use their imagination when writing personal summaries in their learning logs. Emphasize that they will remember new information better when they write about it in a personal way.

Answers

Answers will vary.

Special Writing Activities

The learning-log activities on this page are quite different from each other and can be used for special purposes. As you read about them, try to think of a class in which each one would help you.

First Thoughts When you begin a new unit in one of your classes, write about your first impressions. Does the new material sound difficult or easy? Can you connect it with something you've learned before?

Stop 'n' Write After you get into the middle of new material, stop and write down what you are thinking, including any questions that you may have. This will help you understand what you are studying.

Picture Outlining A picture can help you "see" what you're learning. Make a drawing to help you understand and remember a set of ideas. Your drawing can be a diagram that the teacher has put on the board, or your drawing can be of your own "mental picture."

Role-Playing Imagine yourself as an eyewitness to some important event. Write about what happened as if you were a reporter or bystander at the time of the event.

Personal Summary Summarize a reading assignment or a lecture and put the information in your own words. Adding your own thoughts and experiences will help you understand and remember the material. The sample below is about a biology lesson.

> Mr. Petrie's leaf diagram looks like a big layer cake. In the middle of the leaf "cake" are plastids—little structures that have lots of green chlorophyll in them. They also contain yellow and orange, but in summer the chlorophyll blocks those colors. The sap has reds and purples, which are also blocked by the green. I think the leaf is like a big glass jar filled with yellow, red, orange, and purple marbles. But you can't see the marbles because someone has put dark green food coloring in water and then poured it into the jar.

Write a personal summary of a recent class lesson. Try to recall the main points from memory rather than looking at your class notes.

Advanced Learners

Ask students to choose a strategy they have used from the eight different writing-to-learn activities. Have students make a classroom poster or an overhead transparency for their strategy. Guidelines include the following:

- Make the display for your strategy colorful and clever.
- Include a logo and a slogan.
- Include a visual example.

Display the posters around the classroom or make the overhead transparency available for students to refer to as they complete their writing assignments.

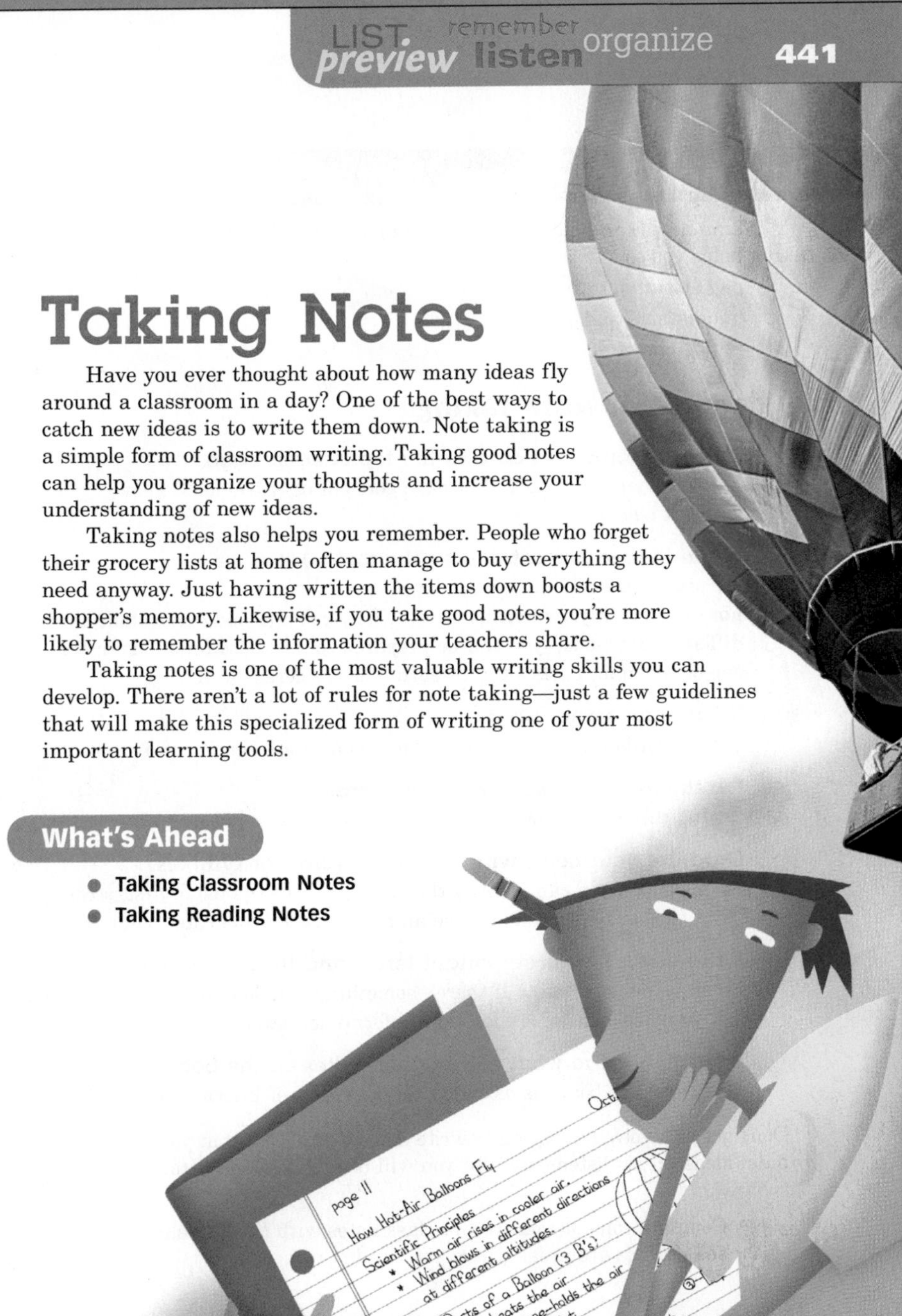

LIST preview remember listen organize 441

Taking Notes

Have you ever thought about how many ideas fly around a classroom in a day? One of the best ways to catch new ideas is to write them down. Note taking is a simple form of classroom writing. Taking good notes can help you organize your thoughts and increase your understanding of new ideas.

Taking notes also helps you remember. People who forget their grocery lists at home often manage to buy everything they need anyway. Just having written the items down boosts a shopper's memory. Likewise, if you take good notes, you're more likely to remember the information your teachers share.

Taking notes is one of the most valuable writing skills you can develop. There aren't a lot of rules for note taking—just a few guidelines that will make this specialized form of writing one of your most important learning tools.

What's Ahead

- Taking Classroom Notes
- Taking Reading Notes

Taking Notes

Objectives

- learn how to take good classroom notes
- learn how to take reading notes
- learn various organizers for taking notes while reading

Discuss the methods students use for taking notes. Ask the following questions:

- In what form do you write your notes? (In complete sentences? In phrases? In abbreviations?)
- How do you arrange your notes? (lists? clusters? outlines?)
- What kinds of visual aids do you include? (drawings? diagrams? charts?)
- How do you use your notes as a studying and learning tool?

Pass out a short nonfiction reading passage, or you may use an excerpt from the student edition or a student textbook. Have students take notes as they read. Then arrange students into small groups. Tell each group to pass around their notes to share different methods of note taking.

Taking Classroom Notes

After students examine the Guidelines for Note Taking, read aloud the nonfiction article on SE page 378.

- Have students take notes as you read.
- After the reading, have students exchange notes with a partner.
- Ask partners to read each other's notes and compare them with the Guidelines for Note Taking.
- Encourage students to give each other tips on how to improve their note taking.

Students may find it difficult to take clear and comprehensive notes while listening to and following what is going on in class. Remind them that they can fill in the gaps after class. (Encourage them to do this later the same day, while their memory is still fresh.) Reassure them that their ability to do this will improve as they learn how taking good notes will help them in all their classes.

Taking Classroom Notes

Taking notes can help you learn new material and prepare for tests. Note taking helps you . . .

- pay attention,
- understand, and
- remember.

Guidelines for Note Taking

1. **Write the topic and date at the top of each page.** Also number your pages. If a page gets out of order, you'll know where it belongs.
2. **When the teacher introduces the topic, listen for the main ideas.** For example, if your teacher says, "The cerebrum and cerebellum have different functions," you can be prepared to list those functions under one of the main parts—the cerebrum or the cerebellum.
3. **Be alert for signal words.** Signal words include *most important, as a result, finally,* and so on.
4. **Put the main ideas in your own words.** Saying things your own way can help you understand new ideas.
5. **Organize your notes with numbers, words, or symbols.** For example, you can identify the steps in a process using *first, second, third,* and so on, or you can use an asterisk (*) to indicate a main idea.
6. **Write down new or important terms and their meanings.** Be sure to make a note if there's something you don't understand. Then ask your teacher or look for more information later.
7. **Pay attention to what the teacher writes on the board.** What's on the board is often the most important information.

Don't get so involved in trying to write down every word that you miss the main ideas. If you listen carefully, you will be able to fill in details later.

Try It Compare some of your recent class notes with the guidelines above to see if there are areas where you can improve.

English Language Learners

Students may find it challenging to comprehend spoken English and record ideas at the same time. Provide support by suggesting these strategies:

- Whenever possible, draw a table, diagram, sequence chain, or web as you take notes. The graphic will provide automatic organization.
- Do not worry if you miss writing down an important point. Place a question mark at that place and keep taking notes. Later, you can ask your teacher or another student to help you figure out what information is missing.

Struggling Learners

Read aloud a short passage.

- Have students listen for main ideas without taking notes.
- Discuss the main idea and important supporting details.
- During a second reading, have students take notes and compare them with a partner.
- Ask students to assess whether their notes are effective, using the Guidelines for Note Taking.

Setting Up Your Notes

Keep your notes in a notebook, preferably one for each subject. (Follow your teacher's instructions for the type and size of each notebook.) Keep your notes neat and leave wide margins. This makes your notes easier to read and illustrate. The side notes below give additional tips.

page 11

How Hot-Air Balloons Fly Oct. 27

Scientific Principles
* Warm air rises in cooler air.
* Wind blows in different directions at different altitudes.

Three Parts of a Balloon (3 B's)
1. Burner—heats the air
2. Balloon envelope—holds the air
3. Basket—carries pilot

Steps in Launching a Balloon
1. Attach propane burner to basket and then attach basket to balloon.
2. Unroll balloon.
3. Inflate balloon with huge fan.
4. Ignite burner flame to heat air in balloon.
5. Climb into basket.
6. Ground crew lets the balloon go.

Flying the Balloon
1. Blast large flame to heat air and ascend.
2. Open parachute valve at top of balloon to let hot air out and descend.

Leave wide margins.

Make sketches.

Skip a line between ideas.

LEARNING

Setting Up Your Notes

Emphasize the importance of creating a personal note-taking style that is clear and readable.

- If students forget their notebook, they should take notes on white, lined paper and then staple those pages into their notebook so they don't lose them.
- If students are absent, encourage them to borrow a classmate's notes, read them, and rewrite them in their own note-taking style.
- Or, have students take turns taking notes each day that can be utilized by students who have missed class.

Reviewing Your Notes

Most students find it easier to study from their own notes than to study from a textbook.

- Students' notes should include main points and should be easy to follow. Clear, organized notes are a sign that students understand the material.
- Confusing notes may indicate a lack of understanding, or they may show a need for a better note-taking strategy.
- Stress the importance of rewriting or adding to notes after students have received answers to any questions about the lesson.

Reviewing Your Notes

Review your notes each day.

- **In the margins, briefly note any questions that you have.** Ask your teacher or a classmate to help you understand any difficult concepts; then add the explanation to your notes.
- **Follow up on any words you don't understand.** Look up unfamiliar terms in a dictionary and add the correct spelling and meaning to your notes.
- **Rewrite your notes if they are confusing or unreadable.** Keep your notes organized so that you will be able to understand them later.
- **Read your notes before the next class.** Then you'll be ready for a class discussion or a test.

page 11

How Hot-Air Balloons Fly — Oct. 27

Scientific Principles
- * Warm air rises in cooler air.
- * Wind blows in different directions at different altitudes.

envelope: the balloon before it is filled with hot air

Three Parts of a Balloon (3 B's)
1. Burner—heats the air
2. Balloon envelope—holds the air
3. Basket—carries pilot

Steps in Launching a Balloon
1. Attach propane burner to basket and then attach basket to balloon.
2. Unroll balloon.
3. Inflate balloon with huge fan.
4. Ignite burner flame to heat air in balloon.
5. Climb into basket.
6. Ground crew lets the balloon go.

Find out if this is dangerous. Does balloon ever catch on fire?

Review your work. How well does your note taking compare with the suggestions on this page? Which suggestion would improve your notes the most?

Taking Reading Notes

If you take notes when you read, you will understand and remember the information better. As you read, pause to jot down important ideas. Here are some tips for taking reading notes.

1 Skim an assignment before reading it.

Preview the title, introduction, headings, and chapter summaries. Study the pictures, charts, or other graphics. These steps can give you many of the main ideas before you start reading.

2 Take notes while you read.

Concentrate on what you are reading and write down only what is important.

- **Note each heading or subtopic.** Write down the heading and all the important facts you find there.
- **Write your notes in your own words.** Rewording the text will help you to understand and remember the material.
- **Summarize the information in pictures, charts, or maps.** Making your own drawings is another option.
- **Read challenging material out loud.** *Hearing* what you are reading will help you understand the information better.
- **List words that are new to you.** Find definitions in a dictionary or glossary and write them down. Be sure you understand how the words fit into the reading before you move on.
- **Go through your notes.** Review your notes and write down any questions you have.

3 Add graphic organizers to your notes.

Use any of the helpful organizers on the next three pages for taking notes.

Try It The next time you have a reading assignment, take reading notes. Use the tips from this page.

LEARNING

Taking Reading Notes

To provide students with additional practice, find high-interest magazine articles.

- Share the articles with your students.
- Tell them to take notes as they read each article.
- When they finish taking notes, have students reread the tips on this page and check to see whether they have followed the guidelines for taking good notes.
- Suggest that students work in groups to compare notes.

Answers

No answers are required.

Struggling Learners

Work on a short magazine article, paragraph by paragraph. Guide students through the process of reading and taking notes. Review these steps:

- Think about what you already know about the topic while skimming the article.
- Read the title and the first sentence of each paragraph, and make predictions about what you expect to read.
- Slow your pace when reading more difficult material or encountering unfamiliar words or technical terms.
- Reread difficult passages.
- Think about what each section tells you before taking notes.
- Find the important details that support what you determine is the main idea.
- Use phrases and abbreviations, not sentences.
- Write any questions you have in the margins of your paper next to your notes on the topic or subtopic.

Using a Cause-Effect Organizer

After students read the article and the cause-effect organizer, discuss the organizer with them to make sure they understand the multiple causes and their effect. Work with students to answer these questions.

- What is the effect listed in the chart? (southwestern U.S. changed hands three times in less than 50 years)
- What caused the Spanish people to move north? (wanted more land and gold, wanted to spread Christianity, needed food)
- What caused the southwestern U.S. to change hands three times in less than 50 years? (the Spanish people moving north)

Answers

Students should identify the effect that the Spanish claimed part of the southwestern United States.

Causes include these facts:

- Coronado found a Zuni pueblo in New Mexico.
- His men found the Rio Grande and the Grand Canyon.
- Coronado traveled to Kansas.

The Spanish claimed the areas that Coronado and his men explored.

Using a Cause-Effect Organizer

Cause-and-effect writing shows how or why things happen. It may be one cause that has many effects, several causes and several effects, or lots of causes for one effect. The article "Northward Ho!" below tells about one effect that has several causes. The **cause-effect organizer** to the right of the article is an example of a good way to chart this type of writing.

Northward Ho!

For many reasons, the people of the Middle Americas were urged to move to the north. Some Spaniards moved north because they wanted more land or gold, and some wanted to spread Christianity. The Spanish also ventured north because there was not much food in the south.

In less than 50 years, the land that is now the southwestern part of the United States had changed hands three times. This all began when the Spanish moved.

Cause-Effect Organizer

The Move North

Spanish people from the Middle Americas moved north.

wanted more land

▽

wanted gold

▽

wanted to spread Christianity

▽

needed food

The land that is now the southwestern U.S. changed hands three times in less than 50 years.

Read the following paragraph about Spanish claims to the Southwest. Then create an organizer that shows the causes and their effect.

The Spanish felt they could claim part of the southwestern United States because Coronado had explored it. He was looking for the golden city of Cibola. First Coronado went to New Mexico looking for the golden city but found only a Zuni pueblo. He sent men east and west, but they found only the Rio Grande and the Grand Canyon. Then Coronado went north to Kansas, but he didn't find the city of gold there, either. He returned to Mexico a failure, but his travels allowed the Spanish to claim the desert Southwest.

English Language Learners

Explain that Middle America includes Mexico, Central America, and sometimes the Caribbean.

If the reading level of the **Try It** passage is too challenging for students, try using the sample on SE pages 200–201. Do the same for the **Try It** passages on SE pages 447–448.

Using a Table Organizer

Some types of writing are organized around a main idea. Each main idea is supported by details, the way a tabletop is supported by legs. Essays, articles, feature stories, and textbook chapters are usually organized in this way.

Read the following paragraph, "Don't Hold Your Breath." Then look at the **table organizer** to see how one student took notes on this reading.

Don't Hold Your Breath

Marine mammals can stay under the water longer than we can because their bodies are built differently. When a marine mammal dives, its heart rate drops dramatically—to as low as four to six beats per minute! In addition, marine mammals such as seals and whales have more oxygen-carrying cells in their blood than humans do. Finally, they have more blood. For example, a seal can have two to three times more blood than a man. It can even store oxygen-rich blood in its huge spleen.

Table Organizer

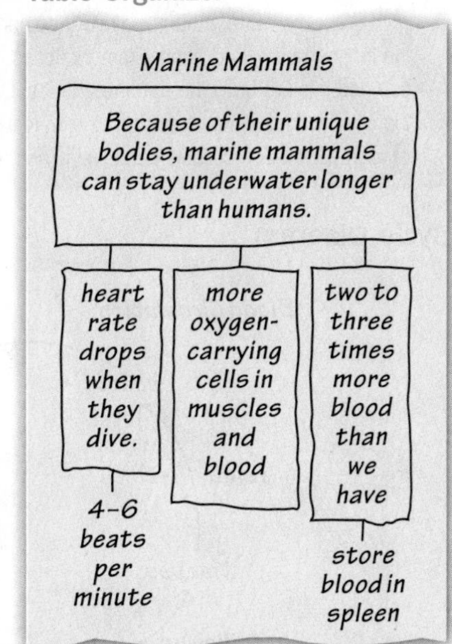

Try It Read the following paragraph about marine mammals. Then take notes on it using a table organizer. Put the main idea in the top box (the tabletop). Under it, put supporting details (the table legs).

There are three main orders of marine mammals: carnivora, cetacea, and sirenia. Carnivora are meat eaters that live on land or in the sea. This group includes seals, sea lions, otters, and even polar bears! Cetacea are meat eaters that live in the open ocean. This group includes whales, dolphins, and porpoises. Finally, sirenia are plant eaters that live in warm tropical waters near shorelines. This group includes dugongs and manatees.

LEARNING

Using a Table Organizer

After students read the paragraph and the table organizer, discuss the organizer with them to make sure they understand the entries and how they are set up. Ask these questions:

- Where is the main idea in the organizer?
- What are the three details that support the main idea?
- Why is there something else written under two of those details?
- How is the organizer like a table?

Answers

Answers will vary. Students' table organizers should say that the main idea is that marine mammals can be broken down into three main orders. The table "legs" should give details about the three orders: Carnivora, Cetacea, and Sirenia.

Struggling Learners

Ask students to bring to class their science textbook. Read a short selection from the text aloud to the students. During a second reading, fill in a table organizer that you put on the board or an overhead. Discuss the results; then assign students to take notes with a table organizer from another short section in the textbook.

Using a Cycle Diagram

Ask a student to try to describe the flow of blood through the body just by looking at the diagram. Then have students read the paragraph. Ask these questions.

- What do +O and –O in the diagram refer to? (oxygen-rich and oxygen-poor blood)
- Are abbreviations helpful when taking notes?
- What other processes have you studied in science that could be shown in a cycle diagram? (Answers will vary.)
- In which of your classes might you use a cycle diagram to take reading notes?

Answers

The order of events within the cycle diagram should be as follows: nebula → star → red giant → supernova → nebula. On the outside of the circle, the following can be written in the appropriate locations: gas and dust, heat and light.

448

Using a Cycle Diagram

Science writing often describes various processes that are repeated. A **cycle diagram** is an effective way to record the steps or details in such a process. Read the paragraph below. Then look at the cycle diagram one student made to remember the details.

The Blood Circle

Blood flows from the veins into the heart. The heart pumps the blood into the lungs to pick up oxygen. From the lungs, the blood returns to the heart and is pumped into the body through the arteries. Capillaries are little vessels between the arteries and veins where the oxygen leaves the blood to feed the tissues. The oxygen-poor blood collects in the veins and returns to the heart.

Cycle Diagram

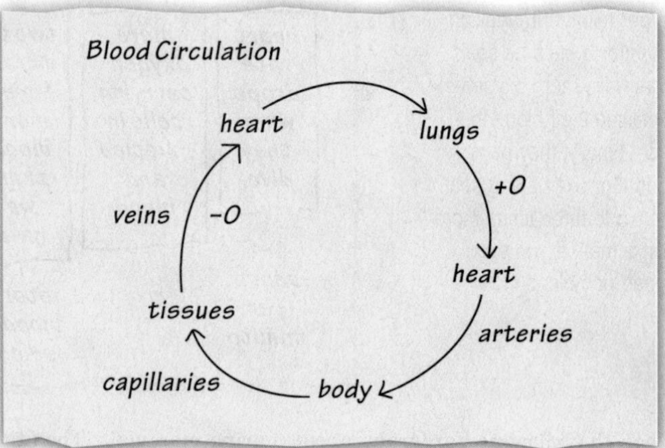

Try It Read the following brief paragraph about the birth of the stars. Then create a cycle diagram that shows the process.

Some stars eventually produce more stars. A nebula of gas and dust is pulled together by gravity. It gets very hot and forms a star that gives off heat and light. The star gradually runs out of fuel and turns into a red giant. The red giant may explode into a supernova. Gas and dust fly away from the supernova and form a nebula, which can form a new star.

Advanced Learners

Ask students to find excerpts of text on which they could take notes using one of the three organizers discussed on SE pages 446–448. They can look in

- content-area textbooks,
- magazines, and
- nonfiction books.

Use these excerpts with the class for additional practice with the organizers.

Completing Writing Assignments

Have you ever gotten lost in a writing assignment? You thought you knew where you were going, but you reached the second paragraph and hit "the wall." You couldn't move forward, you couldn't move backward, and there was no end in sight. What a frustrating "place" to be!

This chapter is your writing compass, and it will help you navigate through even the most difficult writing assignments. By plotting your course before you head out and by checking for milestones along the way, you'll soon reach your writing goal.

What's Ahead

- Understanding the Assignment
- Thinking Through Each Assignment
- Setting Up an Assignment Schedule

Copy Masters

T-chart (TE p. 456)

Completing Writing Assignments

Objectives

- understand what a writing assignment is asking
- learn how to set up a schedule for completing a writing assignment

Ask students how they organize themselves before they begin a writing assignment. Discuss the various approaches that teachers and students take. Be careful not to make any judgments; at this point, you just want to learn how students keep themselves on schedule while working on a writing assignment.

Understanding the Assignment

As a class, discuss each kind of writing assignment: open-ended, specific, and combination.

- Ask students to talk about the experiences they have had with the various kinds of assignments.
- Have the class decide which type of writing assignment is being suggested in the **Try It** activity.

 **Answers**

1. specific
2. open-ended
3. combination

Understanding the Assignment

There are three basic kinds of writing assignments.

Open-Ended
An open-ended assignment allows you to select your own topic. (Write a story about your most embarrassing moment.)

Specific
A specific assignment provides the topic for you. (Explain why the sky is blue.)

Combination
A combination assignment gives one part of the topic but allows you to select another part. (Compare today's teen fashion with teen fashion from another era.)

 Decide if each of the assignments below is open-ended, specific, or a combination. Write your answers on your own paper.

1. *Tell how a cell phone works.*
2. *Persuade others to watch your favorite TV show.*
3. *Compare jogging with some other form of exercise.*

Assignment Checklist

Make sure that you understand everything about your writing assignment before you begin. Use the following checklist as a guide.

_____ 1. **Plan ahead** so that you have enough time to do a good job.
_____ 2. **Know what is expected** in the assignment.
_____ 3. **Follow the directions** and ask questions.
_____ 4. **Focus on key words**—*persuade, explain, recall*—so you know exactly what your writing should do.
_____ 5. **Revise and improve** your writing.

Struggling Learners

Assist students who are having trouble recognizing different kinds of writing assignments.

- Review the descriptions of open-ended, specific, and combination writing.
- Provide samples of each type of writing prompt.
- Guide students in sorting the assignments into the correct category.

Thinking Through Each Assignment

Your brain thinks in a lot of different ways, including *recalling, understanding, applying, analyzing, synthesizing,* and *evaluating.* Different writing assignments ask you to use different kinds of thinking. The chart below briefly describes these thinking tasks, and the next six pages give you a closer look at each one.

Recalling means remembering information. Use recalling when you are asked to . . .

- fill in the blanks
- define terms
- list facts or words
- label parts of something

Understanding means knowing what information means. Use understanding when you are asked to . . .

- explain something
- choose the best answer
- tell if something is true or false
- summarize something

Applying means using information. Use applying when you are asked to . . .

- follow directions
- solve a problem

Analyzing means breaking information down into different parts. Use analyzing when you are asked to . . .

- compare things
- divide things into groups
- give reasons for something
- tell why something is the way it is

Synthesizing means using information to create something new. Use synthesizing when you are asked to . . .

- create something
- add new ideas
- combine things
- predict something

Evaluating means using information to tell the value of something. Use this advanced level of thinking when you are asked to . . .

- assess something
- give your opinion of something

Thinking Through Each Assignment

Have each student make a booklet to describe the thinking tasks:

- Place a sheet of paper on the desk horizontally. Put three sheets on top of the first, placing the right edge of each sheet about three-quarters of an inch to the left of the sheet below it (see the illustration).

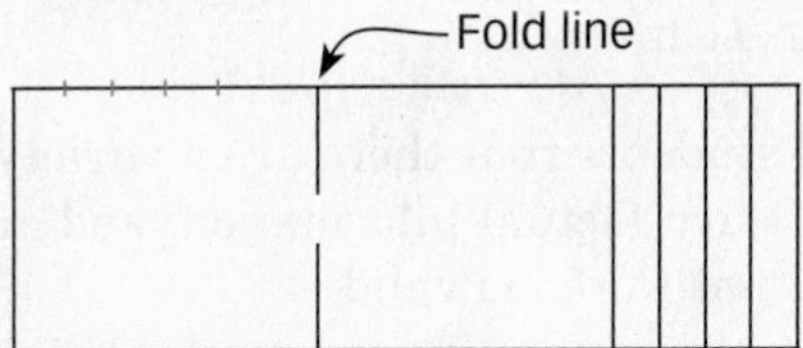

- When the layers are in place, fold the left side of the four papers over to form a book, with the edges of all the pages visible (see the illustration).

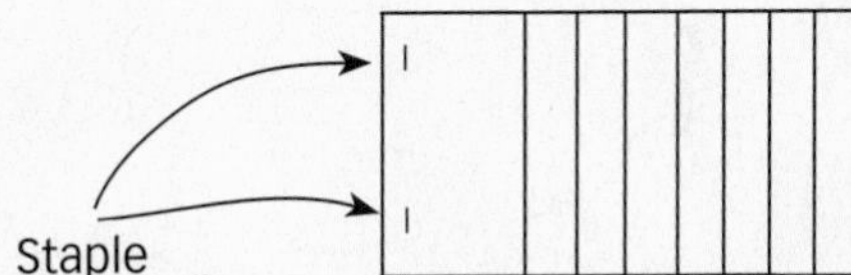

- Staple along the fold line.
- Design a cover with the title *Six Kinds of Thinking.*
- Label the next six layers: *Recalling, Understanding, Applying, Analyzing, Synthesizing,* and *Evaluating.* Have students add notes as they read SE pages 452–457.

Recalling

Have students read this page and then take notes about **recalling** *(see below)* by following these steps:

- Record information under the heading *Recalling* in the booklet they made (TE page 451).
- Write a reflection on their personal approach to recalling information.
- Write about an experience in which they discovered a helpful way to remember new information.

Remind students that there are a variety of ways to learn factual information, and any method that works is valid.

 **Answers**

Answers will vary.

Recalling

Recalling is remembering what you have learned. To prepare for this type of thinking, listen carefully in class, read your assignments, and take careful notes.

You recall when you . . .

- **study the information until you can remember it.**
- **write down facts, terms, and definitions.**

The following test questions ask the student to recall.

DIRECTIONS: Fill in the blanks below with the correct answers.

1. The Middle Ages in Europe lasted about ___________ (number) years.
2. Kings awarded land to their nobles under the ___________ system.

DIRECTIONS: Define each term by completing the sentence.

1. A lord's *manor* was his ____.
2. Guilds were ____.

recall

 Work with a classmate to review your notes on a topic that you are studying. Then ask each other questions to see how many details the two of you can *recall* from the notes.

Teaching Tip: Recalling

Most middle school students are studying a foreign language, social studies, and science. All of these subjects require memorization. Since students learn differently, they will benefit from the variety of techniques for recalling in the following list. They can . . .

- make a list of factual material, study it, hide it, and then try to rewrite it.
- put information in a graphic organizer.
- visualize, or picture in their mind, the new information or concepts.
- connect new information to what they already know.
- write a poem about what they have learned.

English Language Learners

Help students find examples of recall questions in textbooks or on handouts or tests in other subject areas. They can use the sample questions on this page and the description on SE page 451 to identify recall questions.

Ask them to write one example on the "Recalling" page in the booklet they are creating. Follow the same procedure with SE pages 453–457.

Understanding

Understanding information is knowing what it means. If you are able to accurately put the information in your own words, then you clearly understand it.

You understand when you . . .

- explain something in your own words.
- tell how something works.
- summarize information.

The following question asks the student to show understanding, and the answer does that.

DIRECTIONS: Explain how the feudal system worked in the European Middle Ages.

During the Middle Ages, a king gave land to his nobles. In return, the nobles supplied soldiers for the king's army. Peasants worked the land in return for protection from thieves and invading armies. The peasants had to give most of what they produced to the noble and got to keep only as much as they needed to survive. The lives of the peasants, also known as serfs, were controlled by the noble. That noble, lord of the manor, even made the laws and enforced them.

understand

LEARNING

Try It Write a paragraph explaining your *understanding* of something you've recently learned in social studies class.

Understanding

After students read the page, have them

- take notes on *Understanding* on their booklet page with that heading, and
- write about their personal approach to understanding information.

There is often a gap between what students are expected to understand and what they do understand.

- The first step in **closing the gap** *(see below)* is to recognize what they don't know that would help them understand the concept.
- Then they can review material or ask questions to enhance their understanding.

Answers

Answers will vary.

Teaching Tip: Closing the Gap

Sometimes progress toward understanding is impeded by misconceptions or lack of background knowledge. Give students the following tips for getting the help they need. They should

- give themselves credit for the parts they do understand.
- make notes to organize their thinking.
- identify where they need help by asking questions as they read. (This will open communication with the teacher.)
- explain what they already know, and ask the person who is helping them to explain what they need to know next.

Applying

After students read the page, have them

- take notes on *Applying* on their booklet page with that heading, and
- write about their personal approach to applying information.

When students apply information, they use a more advanced level of thinking. Applying information may involve

- the ability to prioritize important points, and
- transferring material to a different context.

These skills can be challenging for some students. Give students practice by providing short reading passages and then asking students to identify the most important points in the material. Ask students under what circumstances they might use the information.

Answers

Answers will vary.

Applying

When you *apply* information, you understand it well enough to use it.

You apply when you . . .

- **use information to solve problems.**
- **select the most important facts or details.**

In this assignment, the writer reviews information and chooses the most important details.

ASSIGNMENT: Why did the feudal system last so long in medieval Europe? Give the most important reason.

The feudal system lasted for a long time in medieval Europe because the family was its basic unit. These were not the families of the peasants, but of the nobles who controlled the land. Huge estates remained in these upper-class families for hundreds of years. The reason for this was that all across Europe, laws were passed so that only the oldest son in the family could inherit the property. Under these laws, the property was never broken up, and the original families continued the feudal system.

Write a journal entry about an important reason for a problem in today's world or in your school.

Struggling Learners

To reinforce the meaning of applying information, help students recognize the connection between learning math procedures and using them to solve word problems relating to the real world.

- For example, 4 x 3 = 12 is a number fact; it involves multiplication.
- How would they apply this information to solve the following word problem? *Judy wants to buy four books at the school book fair. Each book costs three dollars. How much money does she need in all?*
- Have students think up additional word problems that apply math facts and procedures in their own words.

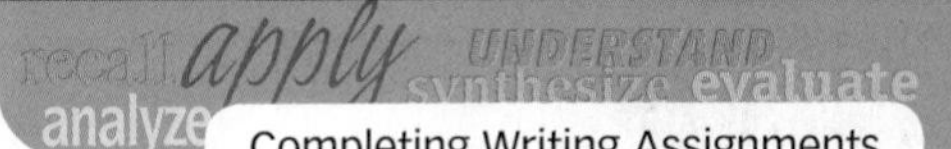

Analyzing

Analyzing information is breaking it down into parts. There are many different ways to analyze information.

You analyze when you . . .

- tell how things are alike or different.
- tell which parts are most important.
- divide things into different groups.
- give reasons for something.

In this assignment, the writer tells how two periods of time are alike and different.

ASSIGNMENT: How is life today both better and worse than it was for a serf in the Middle Ages?

Life today is better than the life of a serf in the Middle Ages. People have more freedoms. No one controls their lives like the nobles did back then. They can own property, change jobs, and move to new places. Also, they have the right to a fair trial, unlike the peasants.

In one way, the serfs seemed to have it better than people do today. Serfs' lives were simpler. They knew what they were supposed to do, and they knew that someone would take care of them. Knowing that they would be protected must have been a good feeling.

analyze

LEARNING

Try It Give reasons why cell phones or some other recent technology has become so popular.

Analyzing

Ask students to read this page. Then have them

- use their booklet page marked *Analyzing* to take notes on what they have just read,
- write about their own experiences in analyzing information, and
- use illustrations and diagrams to show how they have broken down material in order to analyze it.

Analyzing *(see below)* information requires students to make judgments.

- When they analyze, they decide which parts are more important than others and determine how the parts are related to each other.
- They must be able to back up their analysis with reasons.

Answers

Answers will vary.

Teaching Tip: Analyzing

For additional practice, analyze the following topics as a class:

- Decide whether school hours should be changed and why.
- Give reasons for or against leash laws in cities.
- Describe how ATMs have changed the way people access money today compared to 10 years ago.

Synthesizing

After students read this page, tell them to

- take notes about synthesizing on their booklet page marked *Synthesizing,* and
- include personal anecdotes related to synthesizing.

 **Answers**

Answers will vary.

Synthesizing

When you *synthesize*, you create something new using information you have already learned.

You synthesize when you . . .

- add some new ideas to existing information.
- use information to make up a story or other creative writing.
- predict the future based on this information.

In this assignment, the writer uses information to imagine living in medieval times.

ASSIGNMENT: Imagine that you and a friend live in another time and place. Write a short narrative that describes how you each would live.

My friend Hob leaves today. He is the squire to Sir Nicolet. Lord Halfdome promised Sir Nicolet to the king for his wars against France, so Hob has to leave, too. I will probably never see him again because these French wars seem to go on forever. Hob will ride away wearing a shirt embroidered with spring flowers. I wear the plain-colored tunic of the household. That's only the beginning of how different our lives will be. I will be trained to be the next bailiff of the manor. Hob will visit foreign lands and see wonders, while I will spend my life on the lord's estate. Oh well, we must do as we are told.

synthesize

 Write your own narrative about how you and a friend would live in a time or place you are studying in social studies.

Struggling Learners

Suggest that students use a T-chart (TE page 789) for the **Try It** activity. They should . . .

- label the two columns *Facts* and *Observations.*
- list historical events and details about the place or time period under *Facts.*
- imagine what it would be like to experience each detail and write an observation in the chart.

Advanced Learners

Ask students to think about how historical fiction and science fiction use synthesis.

- Brainstorm a list of books and movies under the two headings: *historical fiction* and *science fiction*
- Form small groups; each group chooses a movie or book under one of the headings.
- Each group discusses how synthesis was used in their selection and answers the question, "Which parts of the story are factual and which are imaginary?"

recall apply UNDERSTAND analyze synthesize evaluate 457 Completing Writing Assignments

Evaluating

When you *evaluate*, you tell the value of something. Before you can evaluate something, you must know a lot about it.

You evaluate when you . . .

- **tell your opinion about something.**
- **tell the good points and bad points about something.**

In this assignment, the writer gives her opinion about a historical event.

ASSIGNMENT: What is your opinion about the importance of the Black Death in the medieval world?

The spread of the Black Death (bubonic plague) was the most important event of the medieval period. It killed about one out of three people in Europe and Asia. It was a horrible, disgusting way to die, and whole cities fell apart in fear. The Church couldn't explain it, so people lost faith. There weren't enough peasants and laborers alive to work the fields, so the feudal system fell apart. Today people worry about cancer, AIDS, and diseases they will probably never get, like Ebola virus. If contemporary people had a plague like the Black Death, it would change the world.

evaluate

LEARNING

Try It Write a paragraph that explains your opinion about country music, whole-grain bread, or exercise.

Advanced Learners

Have students write about an important decision they made recently and why they made the one they did.

Evaluating

Tell students to

- take notes about what it means to evaluate information on the booklet page marked *Evaluating,* and
- write about any personal experiences related to evaluating.

Answers

Answers will vary.

Have partners exchange paragraphs. Tell them to think about whether the writer has clearly given an opinion and whether she or he has spelled out the good and bad points effectively. If not, suggest more effective ways to support the writer's opinion.

Setting Up an Assignment Schedule

Show students how to organize a multiple-day schedule for a writing assignment.

- Suggest that students use the given schedule as a starting point and adapt it to meet their own deadline.
- Discuss where they might add or subtract days to accommodate a longer or shorter time period.

Scheduling a Timed Writing

Follow the steps below for a timed writing assignment:

- In a 45-minute teaching block, give students 10 minutes to plan, 25 minutes to write, and 10 minutes to proofread and revise.
- Watch the clock throughout the writing session, and announce the end of each section.
- Tell students to move on to the next part, whether or not they think they are ready.
- Using this method from time to time should help get students accustomed to timed writing assignments.

458

Setting Up an Assignment Schedule

Your teacher may give you a schedule to follow for completing your writing assignments. If not, you can set up your own. Let's say that you have been asked to write a persuasive essay, and it is due in two weeks. Here's a suggested schedule.

Day	Week 1	Day	Week 2
1	**Prewriting:** ● Review the assignment and the assessment rubric. ● Begin a topic search.	1	**Revising:** ● Revise the completed draft for ideas and organization.
2	**Prewriting:** ● Choose a writing topic. ● Start gathering details.	2	**Revising:** ● Revise the draft for voice. ● Ask a peer to review it.
3	**Prewriting:** ● Gather and organize details. ● Find a focus for the writing.	3	**Revising:** ● Check for word choice and sentence fluency.
4	**Writing:** ● Begin the first draft.	4	**Editing:** ● Check for conventions. ● Write and proofread the final copy.
5	**Writing:** ● Complete the first draft.	5	**Publishing:** ● Share the final copy.

Change this schedule to fit your assignment. For example, if you have a week to do your work, you could focus on one step in the writing process per day.

Scheduling a Timed Writing

If you must complete a piece of writing in a single class period (for example, 45 minutes), it is very important to plan your work. Try to set aside 5 to 10 minutes at the beginning of the period to plan your writing, 25 to 30 minutes for drafting, and about 5 to 10 minutes at the end to make any necessary changes.

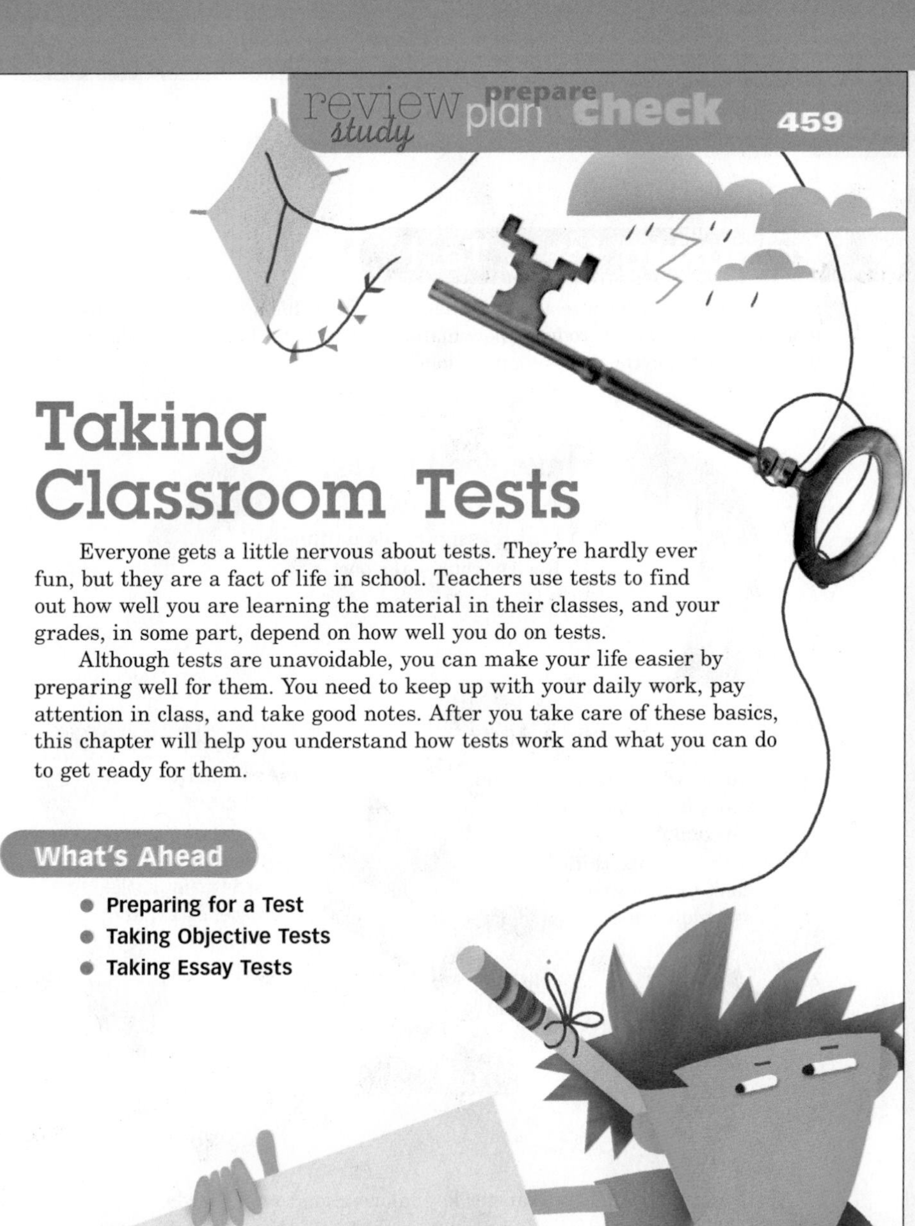

review study prepare plan check 459

Taking Classroom Tests

Everyone gets a little nervous about tests. They're hardly ever fun, but they are a fact of life in school. Teachers use tests to find out how well you are learning the material in their classes, and your grades, in some part, depend on how well you do on tests.

Although tests are unavoidable, you can make your life easier by preparing well for them. You need to keep up with your daily work, pay attention in class, and take good notes. After you take care of these basics, this chapter will help you understand how tests work and what you can do to get ready for them.

What's Ahead

- **Preparing for a Test**
- **Taking Objective Tests**
- **Taking Essay Tests**

Taking Classroom Tests

Objectives

- understand how to prepare for tests
- find out how to take objective tests
- learn how to take essay tests

Testing *(see below)* is an inevitable fact of school life. While most students get nervous before taking a test, those who are well prepared will have greater confidence in themselves.

Have students do a 5-minute freewrite in which they tell their feelings about taking tests. When they finish, have them read their paragraphs aloud. Hearing each other's thoughts about tests should help students realize that they are all in the same boat.

Discuss ways to help students work on relaxation during tests.

- Before beginning a test, have students stretch to remove tension from their muscles.
- Make sure students clear off their desks so that they have room to work comfortably.

Teaching Tip: Testing with Pop Quizzes

Tell students that one way teachers test students is by giving a "pop" quiz. Explain that often pop quizzes are used to find out if students have studied the assigned materials. As long as students pay attention in class and keep up with assignments, they should be prepared for any pop quiz.

Preparing for a Test

Effective **studying for a test** *(see below)* does not come naturally to many students. Ask students to share their study methods and discuss which seem most effective.

Explain that students can use previous tests as learning tools. Stress the need to follow up on errors they make on their tests.

- Encourage students to ask the teacher questions about tests that have been returned to them so that they learn from their mistakes.
- They should also review the tested material so that they understand what they left out in an answer or where they went wrong when solving a problem.

Preparing for a Test

Getting ready for a test isn't a one-night effort. It's a cycle that begins the moment the teacher introduces new material. The chart below will help you understand the cycle of test preparation.

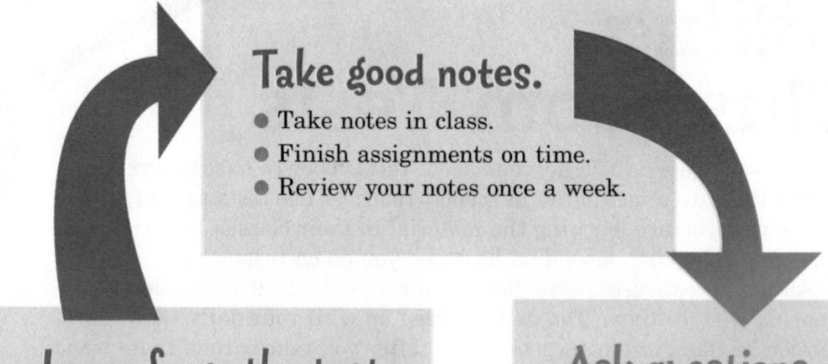

Take good notes.
- Take notes in class.
- Finish assignments on time.
- Review your notes once a week.

Ask questions.
- Ask what the test will cover.
- Ask what types of questions will be on the test (multiple-choice, essay, and so on).

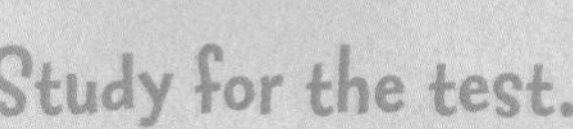

Study for the test.
- Transfer key information to note cards.
- Read your note cards aloud.
- Picture the information in your mind.
- Explain the information to someone else.

Learn from the test.
- Notice what you do well and think about how you can improve.
- If there's something you don't understand, ask a question.

Teaching Tip: Studying for a Test

There is no foolproof formula for effective test preparation. Students must discover which study methods work best for them.

- Spend time with each student, discussing how he or she prepares for a test.
- Before a test, offer a study session for students who want to improve their test preparation skills.
- Review the key information that students should have in their notes.
- Have pairs of students quiz each other, and encourage students to have a family member quiz them also.

Struggling Learners

Advise students who find they are having difficulty with new material to do the following:

- They should ask for a peer tutor immediately; they should not wait until right before test time, when there is too much to learn.
- They should also ask if a study guide is available that outlines important elements and lists vocabulary.

Test-Taking Tips

Before you begin . . .

- **Listen** carefully to the instructions.
- **Write** your name on your paper.
- **Check the clock** to see how much time you have.

During the test . . .

- **Skim the whole test quickly** so that you can plan your time.
- **Read and answer each question carefully.**
- **Skip difficult questions** and come back to them later.
- **Watch the time** so that you can finish the whole test.

After you've finished the test . . .

- **Go back and check your answers,** if you have time.
- **Be sure that you have put your name on the test.**

One of the most important ways to prepare for a test is to get a good night's sleep beforehand. Also make sure to eat a good breakfast. If your body is rested and fed, your mind is free to work.

Write a paragraph about an upcoming test. In your paragraph, answer the following questions.

1. What information will the test cover, and what types of questions will appear on the test?
2. What will be the most difficult area for you?
3. Would it be helpful to study with someone else for this test? Why or why not?

Test-Taking Tips

If students are allowed to make additional marks on a test, tell them they can make pencil marks in the margins of their test. Suggest that they use symbols, such as a star, a question mark, or an exclamation point, to remind themselves to return to a question in order to review or answer it more fully.

Emphasize the importance of leaving at least five minutes to

- revisit test items,
- proofread essays for spelling and grammatical errors.

Make sure students know what to do when they have completed the test.

- Some tests require remaining in one's seat with test answers hidden.
- Other tests require students to turn in their answers as soon as they are completed.
- If students are taking a classroom test, be sure to tell them what you'd like them to do when they finish.

Answers

Answers will vary.

Taking Objective Tests

One practical way to develop understanding about test-taking is to create a test. Have students read SE pages 462 and 463. Then ask them to create a test on a chapter in a book that they have read in class or another unit of study that they have all completed.

- Place four boxes at the front of the room, and label them *True/False, Matching, Multiple-Choice, and Fill-in-the-Blanks.*
- Students write at least one of each type of question, and its answer, on a strip of paper. They put their name on each and drop it in the correct box.
- Students write as many questions as they want but place only one question on each slip of paper.
- Make up a class test using questions from as many students as possible.

 **Answers**

1. No.
2. If you know most of the answers but are unsure of two, you can use the process of elimination to figure out the last couple of matches.

462

Taking Objective Tests

Objective tests have four common types of questions: true/false, matching, multiple-choice, and fill-in-the-blanks. Depending upon what type of question you're answering, you'll want to keep certain tips in mind.

True/False

On this type of test, you decide whether a statement is true or false.

- Remember that if any part of the statement is false, the answer is "false."

  False **A barometer measures humidity in the air.**
  (A barometer measures air pressure.)

- Look carefully at words like *always, all, every, never, none,* or *no*. Few things are always or never true.

  False **Lightning never strikes twice in the same place.**
  (The word "never" makes this statement false.)

- Be aware of words containing the contraction for "not", such as *doesn't, don't, isn't, wasn't*. Make sure that you understand what the statement means.

  True **Precipitation isn't always rain.**

Matching

Matching is connecting an item in one list to an item in another.

- Read both lists and then match the items you are sure of. Next, match the more difficult items using the process of elimination. Cross out the answers as you use them.

B	**1.** Some people are allergic to this.	A. bacteria
A	**2.** Antibiotics kill them.	B. pollen
C	**3.** They cause the common cold.	C. viruses

- Think carefully about items in a list that seem to mean about the same thing. They can be the hardest to match.

 On your own paper, answer each of the following questions.

1. Are questions containing words like "never" always false?
2. How do you use the process of elimination in matching tests?

Struggling Learners

As they design test questions, suggest that students include some of the potentially confusing words mentioned in the True/False section of the page. Learning how those words affect an answer will improve their ability to answer such questions.

Multiple-Choice

Multiple-choice questions ask you to choose from several possible answers. Follow the tips below.

- Check the directions carefully to see if you are allowed to choose just one answer or more than one.

1. Which of the following were important during the Renaissance?
A. Mark Twain **C. Julius Caesar**
(B.) Michelangelo **(D.) Shakespeare**

- Pay special attention to words like *never, except,* and *unless.*

2. All of the following were important during the Renaissance except
A. art **(C.) the steam engine**
B. literature **D. the printing press**

- The hardest questions often include possible answers like "both A and B" or "None of the above."

3. Renaissance writers wrote about
A. philosophy **C. patriotism**
B. the Civil Rights Movement **(D.) both A and C**
E. none of the above

Narrow your choices by eliminating answers you know are incorrect. Then focus on the remaining answers.

Fill-in-the-Blanks

On a fill-in-the-blanks test, you supply key terms that are missing.

- A blank usually stands for one missing answer. Therefore, three blanks would mean you will be filling in three answers.

1. All cells have a membrane**,** cytoplasm**, and a** nucleus**.**

- Sentences sometimes give you clues about answers. If the word before a blank is *an*, the word you have to fill in will begin with a vowel sound.

2. An extinct **species no longer exists.**

Discuss the following statement with a classmate: Some students say that multiple-choice questions are easier than fill-in-the-blank questions. Do you agree? How would you study differently for the two kinds of questions?

LEARNING

As students write their multiple-choice and fill-in-the-blanks questions, emphasize how important it is that they word their questions carefully. Also have students reread their questions several times to make sure that they are clear and contain information that the class has studied.

Answers

Answers will vary.

Taking Essay Tests

Discuss with students their experiences in writing essays on tests. Ask:

- What do you do before you begin writing?
- What clues do you look for in the questions?
- How do you plan your time?
- Do you prefer essay or objective tests? Why?

1 Understand the Question

Understanding the essay question is one key to writing a good essay.

- Students should carefully read all directions before they begin to write.
- They should note the key words in the directions, and if they are permitted to write on the test, they should highlight or underscore key words.
- They should look back at the directions and think about what the essay question is asking them to do as they write.

Answers

1. explain
2. illustrates
3. define
4. contrasts
5. diagrams

Taking Essay Tests

An essay-test question asks you to give a written response. Your response may be one paragraph or longer, and your time is usually limited. The information below will help you write effective essay-test answers.

1 Understand the Question

- Read the question very carefully.
- Identify the key word that explains what you have to do. Here are some key words and an explanation of what each asks you to do.

Compare	. . . tell how things are alike.
Contrast	. . . tell how things are different.
Define	. . . give a clear, specific meaning of a word or an idea.
Describe	. . . tell how something looks, sounds, and feels.
Diagram	. . . explain using lines, a web, or other graphic organizer.
Evaluate	. . . give your opinion about the value of something.
Explain	. . . tell what something means or how something works.
Identify	. . . answer the 5 W's about a topic.
Illustrate	. . . show how something works by using examples.
Prove	. . . present facts that show something is true.
Review	. . . give an overall picture of a topic.
Summarize	. . . tell just the key information about a topic.

Read the following essay questions. For each one, identify the key word. Write your answers on your own paper.

1. Explain how a thunderstorm forms.
2. Write a paragraph that illustrates condensation.
3. In a paragraph, define the term "super cell."
4. Write an essay that contrasts cumulonimbus clouds with cirrus clouds.
5. Draw a meteorological map that diagrams a cold front and a warm front.

Struggling Learners

Use Think-Pair-Share to examine the key words in essay questions.

- Ask students to separate the easy key words in the list above from the difficult ones.
- Have them compare lists with a partner and discuss why some words are more difficult.
- Finally, open the discussion to the whole class.

Using current curriculum topics, write some sample questions together and organize the answers. Help students find and underline the key word in each question. Discuss how changing a key word affects the question.

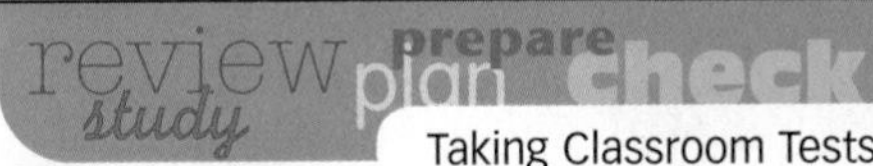

2 Plan a One-Paragraph Answer

Some essay-test questions require a one-paragraph answer. The following guidelines will help you with this type of question.

- Study the essay-test question and the key word used.
- Write a focus (topic sentence) to start your answer.
- Use a list, an outline, or a graphic organizer to arrange your details.

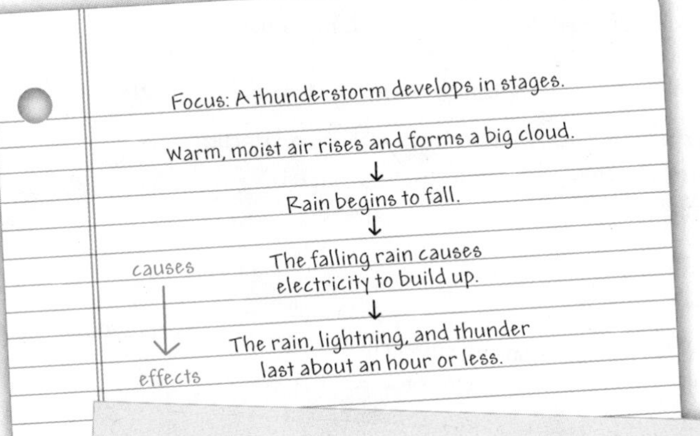

Science Test

Explain how a thunderstorm forms.

A thunderstorm develops in stages. It all begins when warm air and moisture come together. Then the warm air rises rapidly and carries the moisture up into colder air. If there is enough moisture, a huge cloud forms. As the cloud gets full, rain begins to fall. This movement causes electricity to build up in the air, and lightning jumps from one place to another, making thundering noises. The whole process is usually over in less than an hour because the cloud runs out of moisture.

LEARNING

2 Plan a One-Paragraph Answer

Give students practice in writing one-paragraph answers.

- Write three essay-test questions related to a book they have recently read.
- Allow students to choose which question to answer.
- Tell students that in order to answer in one paragraph, they need to organize their details in a clear, step-by-step manner.
- Have students use a graphic organizer to arrange the details.

English Language Learners

Call students' attention to the guideline about using lists, outlines, or graphic organizers to plan essay-test answers. Point out that specific organizers work best with certain kinds of questions:

- Venn diagram—compare/contrast
- Web—describe
- Cause-effect—explain
- Main-idea table—review, summarize
- Sequence chain—process

Using copy masters (TE pages 789–793) and referring students to SE pages 548–549, show students examples of different organizers. Help them decide which organizer works best for each topic in the **Try It** activity on SE page 464.

Advanced Learners

Challenge students to use key words from SE page 464 to write essay questions on science and social studies topics.

- Have students answer the questions on a separate sheet of paper.
- They exchange questions with a partner and answer the partner's question.
- They compare answers and evaluate what they learned.

3 Plan an Essay Answer

Many essay questions ask students to define, explain, or describe. Some questions require students to do a combination of all three. Tell students to take the following steps as they prepare their essay answer:

- Define the subject.
- Analyze the subject by breaking it down into several parts.
- Explain each of the parts.
- Describe how the parts work together.

In writing an essay that explains a process, students should break down their explanation into the steps in the process. Then they should explain the steps in the order in which they occur.

Answers

Answers will vary.

3 Plan an Essay Answer

Some essay-test questions require you to write an answer longer than one paragraph. For example, the question below asks you to explain how weather forecasters predict thunderstorms. The question needs an essay-length answer, not just one paragraph.

- Study the essay-test question and write a focus statement.
- Make a "quick list" of the main points of your essay, leaving room under each point for details.
- Add your specific details under each main point.

Science Test:

Explain how weather forecasters can predict thunderstorms.

Quick List

Focus Statement: Forecasters look at many factors to predict thunderstorms.

1. Relative humidity
   - -air can hold only so much water
   - -high humidity means storms can develop
2. Temperature
   - -hotter air holds more water
   - -hot air rises and cools
   - -loses water and forms storms
3. Wind
   - -carries moisture and heat
   - -direction tells where a storm will hit

Try It Think of a scientific process that you can explain. Make a quick list of main points and details for your explanation.

Essay Answer

The essay below uses the main points and details from the quick list on page 466.

Wind, the movement of air that carries moisture and heat, is important in forecasting whether an ... t, ... erts ... ght ... n if a ... tning, ... ud

Science Test: The Weather

Explain how weather forecasters can predict thunderstorms.

Forecasters look at many factors to predict thunderstorms. Moisture, temperature, and air movement are a few of these factors. Each one plays an important part in severe weather.

People hear about "relative humidity" quite often in weather reports. Relative humidity tells how much water vapor the air has in it. Air can hold only a certain amount of water vapor, so 50 percent humidity indicates that the air contains half as much water as it can hold. Weather forecasters know that high humidity can mean that it may rain and that thunderstorms can develop.

Temperature is the amount of heat in the air. Hot air can hold more water vapor than cold air can. Hot air also rises, carrying water vapor up into the colder air. Forecasters know that when warm air full of water vapor rises and is suddenly cooled, violent storms can happen.

LEARNING

Essay Answer

Tell students to review the quick list they made about a scientific process for the **Try It** activity on SE page 466. Then ask them to write an in-class essay about that process using the model on SE page 467 as their guide.

- Give students a reasonable time period—between 30 and 40 minutes—to write their essay.
- Ask students to underline or highlight their focus statement.
- Have them put a check mark in the margin where each detail is given.
- Invite students to read aloud their essays to the class.

Struggling Learners

Help students examine differences between the quick list on SE page 466 and the essay answer by comparing

- the focus statement with the first paragraph and
- the notes on supporting details with the essay sentences and paragraphs.

Ask: What do you think the last paragraph might say, based on the existing text?

Advanced Learners

When writing an explanatory essay, the writer should assume that the reader doesn't know much about the topic. This strategy helps a writer to organize the details clearly and include helpful definitions related to the topic.

Ask students to discuss answers to these questions:

- Did this writer follow this advice? What supports your opinion?
- How will using this advice help you to organize your essay?

Suggested Writing Paragraphs Unit (One Week)

	Day	Writing and Skills Instruction	*Student Edition* Basic Grammar and Writing Unit	*Student Edition* Resource Units*	*SkillsBook*
Week 1	1	**Writing Paragraphs** (Models)	523–524, 526–529		
		(topic sentences)	525		
	2	(guidelines and details)	530–533		
		(models and order)	534–537		
	3–4	(unity)	538–539		
		Revising Skills: • Voice			
		• Kinds of sentences		518	109–110, 111–112
		Editing Skills: • End punctuation		500 (+), 579–581	3–4, 5–6
		• Capitalization		620–623	
		• Plurals		630–633	47–48
		• Numbers		638–641	49–50
	5 *opt.*	**Paragraph to Essay**	540		

* These units are also located in the back of the Teacher's Edition. Resource Units include "Basic Grammar and Writing," "A Writer's Resource," and "Proofreader's Guide."

(+) This activity is located in a different section of the Write Source Student Edition. If students have already completed this activity, you may wish to review it at this time.

Constructing Strong Paragraphs (pages 523–541)

A paragraph is a group of sentences focusing on one specific topic or idea. Students can develop paragraphs as stories, descriptions, explanations, or opinions. The type of paragraph depends upon the topic, the kinds of details the writer is able to gather, and the audience. A paragraph must contain enough details to give the reader a complete picture of the topic. Paragraphs have three basic parts: the topic sentence, the body, and the closing sentence.

Paragraphs are building blocks of stories, essays, and articles. Sentences within paragraphs, and paragraphs within longer texts, require linking words and transitions. Paragraphs help readers make sense of longer pieces of writing, so learning to write and identify paragraphs is important.

Academic Vocabulary

Read aloud the academic terms, as well as the descriptions and questions. Model for students how to read one question and answer it. Have partners monitor their understanding and seek clarification of the terms by working through the meanings and questions together.

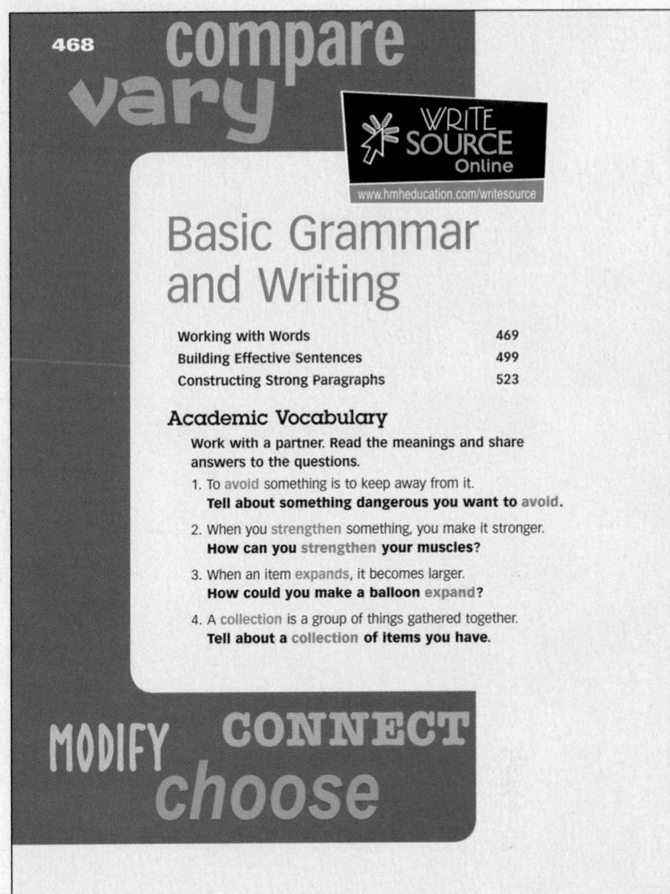

468

compare vary

WRITE SOURCE Online
www.hmheducation.com/writesource

Basic Grammar and Writing

Academic Vocabulary

Work with a partner. Read the meanings and share answers to the questions.

1. To avoid something is to keep away from it.
   Tell about something dangerous you want to avoid.
2. When you strengthen something, you make it stronger.
   How can you strengthen your muscles?
3. When an item expands, it becomes larger.
   How could you make a balloon expand?
4. A collection is a group of things gathered together.
   Tell about a collection of items you have.

MODIFY CONNECT choose

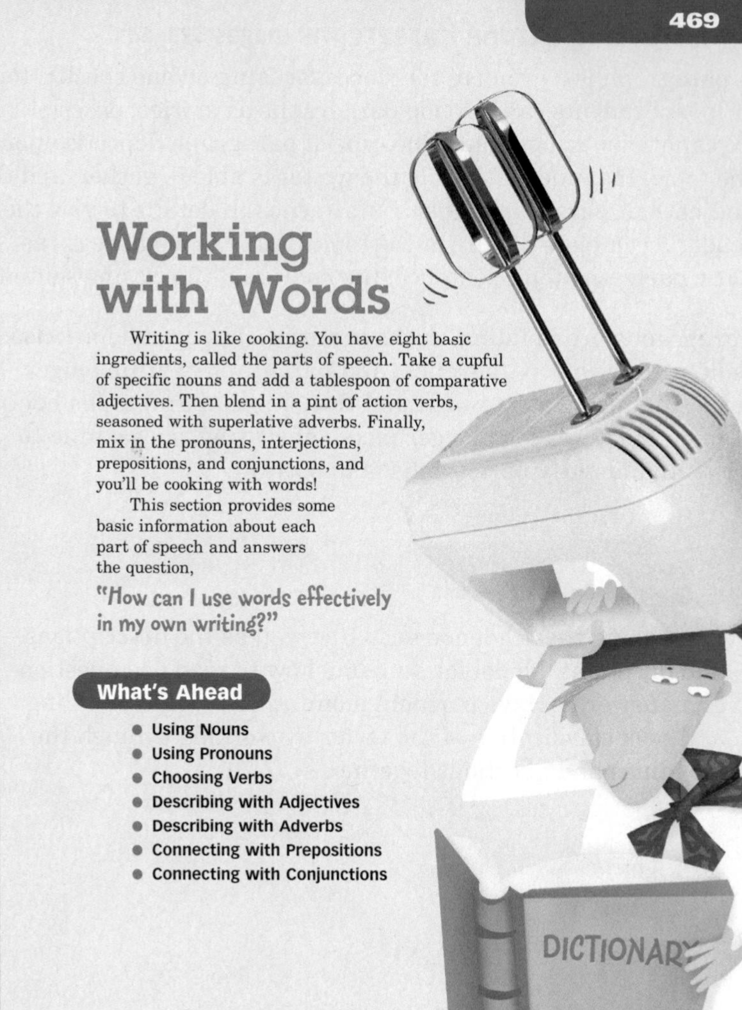

Working with Words

Writing is like cooking. You have eight basic ingredients, called the parts of speech. Take a cupful of specific nouns and add a tablespoon of comparative adjectives. Then blend in a pint of action verbs, seasoned with superlative adverbs. Finally, mix in the pronouns, interjections, prepositions, and conjunctions, and you'll be cooking with words!

This section provides some basic information about each part of speech and answers the question,

"How can I use words effectively in my own writing?"

What's Ahead

- Using Nouns
- Using Pronouns
- Choosing Verbs
- Describing with Adjectives
- Describing with Adverbs
- Connecting with Prepositions
- Connecting with Conjunctions

Using Nouns

A noun is a word that names a person, a place, a thing, or an idea in your writing. (See page 702.)

Person	athlete, Bonnie Blair, students, President Taft
Place	country, Canada, gymnasium, Tampa, middle school
Thing	dog, Irish setter, kayaks, stopwatch
Idea	holiday, Fourth of July, strength, freedom

Number from 1 to 10 on a piece of paper. For each of the 10 underlined nouns in the paragraph below, write whether it is a person, a place, a thing, or an idea.

Volleyball is one of the fastest-growing team **(1)** sports. Team **(2)** members play the **(3)** game on a **(4)** court divided by a net. To get started, the **(5)** players on team A serve the ball over the **(6)** net to team B. Players on team B can then hit the ball three **(7)** times on their **(8)** side of the net before returning the ball to team A's side. If team B is not able to return the **(9)** ball, team A scores a **(10)** point.

Concrete, Abstract, and Collective Nouns

Concrete nouns name things that can be seen or touched.

Abstract nouns name things that you can think about but cannot see or touch.

Concrete	food	snow	storm	heart
Abstract	hope	December	fear	love

On your own paper, write three more concrete nouns and three more abstract nouns. Use each pair of nouns in a separate sentence.

Collective nouns name a collection of persons, animals, or things.

Persons	class	team	family	troop	crew
Animals	herd	flock	pack	pod	school

List at least five additional collective nouns of your own. Use each of these nouns in a separate sentence.

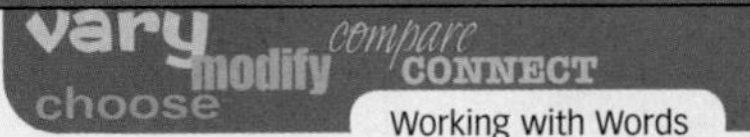

Proper and Common Nouns

Proper nouns name specific people, places, things, or ideas. Proper nouns are always capitalized. A **common noun** is any noun that is not a proper noun.

	Person	Place	Thing	Idea
Common	catcher	stadium	bat	league
Proper	Rachel	Yankee Stadium	Louisville Slugger	American League

Common nouns: The man toured the stadium on the holiday.

Proper nouns: Randy Williams toured Yankee Stadium on Labor Day.

Make a chart like the one above. Add four of your own common and four of your own proper nouns. Be sure to capitalize the proper nouns.

General and Specific Nouns

When you use specific nouns in your writing, you give the reader a clear picture of people, places, things, and ideas. The following chart shows the difference between **general nouns** and **specific nouns**.

General	coach	field	hat	principle
Specific	Frank Bender	Wrigley Field	baseball cap	fairness

Read the facts below about Sammy Sosa. Then write a brief paragraph about him, using as many specific nouns as possible.

Full Name:	Samuel Sosa
Born:	November 12, 1968
Birthplace:	San Pedro de Macoris, Dominican Republic
Family:	wife Sonia, children Keysha, Kenia, Sam, and Michael
Employed by:	Chicago Cubs
Position:	right field
Accomplishments:	has hit more than 500 home runs; in 1998 named Most Valuable Player by the National Baseball League

BASIC GRAMMAR

Answers

1. idea
2. person
3. idea
4. place
5. person
6. thing
7. idea
8. place
9. thing
10. idea

Answers

Answers will vary.

Answers

Answers will vary.

Possible Answers

common nouns	sister	dog	country	team
proper nouns	Jessica	Rover	France	Red Sox

Answers

Answers will vary.

What can I do with nouns in my writing?

Show Possession

You can make your writing more specific by naming who (or what) possesses something. See the guidelines below. (Also see 604.4 and 606.1.)

Forming the Singular Possessive

- Add an apostrophe and an *s* to a singular noun: **Pat's ball.**
- For multi-syllable nouns ending in an *s* or a *z* sound, the possessive may be formed in two ways: **Cletus' glove** or **Cletus's glove.**

Forming the Plural Possessive

- Add an apostrophe for most plural nouns ending in *s*: **the boys' bats.**
- Add an apostrophe and an *s* for plural nouns not ending in s: **the men's lockers.**

List five singular nouns in one column and five plural nouns in another column. (Include at least one or two singular nouns that end in an *s* or a *z* sound.) Then exchange papers with a classmate and write a sentence for each noun, using the possessive form of the word. Discuss the results with your partner.

Rename the Subject

Whenever you use a noun after a linking verb *(am, is, are, was, were, be, been, being)*, the noun renames the subject and is called a **predicate noun**.

Dad was a pitcher for his high school team, but he was never a catcher.

List the 10 predicate nouns in the paragraph below.

Gita is not just any soccer player; she is the best scorer in the league. When she was a young girl, her mother was the coach of the local soccer team. Gita often tagged along with her mother to the matches. She must have been a keen observer because she learned very quickly when she started playing. Although her teammates were good players, Gita was a standout. She has been a top-rated player for the last three years. Gita has also been an excellent role model for youngsters, and someday she may be an excellent coach.

Make the Meaning of the Verb Complete

Some sentences are not complete with just a subject and a verb.

Reggie threw. (*What* did Reggie throw?)
Nell trusts. (*Whom* does Nell trust?)

When you use a transitive verb like "threw" or "trusts" in a sentence, you need to include a **direct object** to make the meaning of the verb complete. The direct object is a noun (or pronoun) that answers the question *what* or *whom*.

Reggie threw the football. **Nell trusts her teammates.**

To add further information, you might include a noun (or pronoun) that answers the question *to whom* or *for whom*. This type of noun is called an **indirect object**. In order for a sentence to have an indirect object, it must also have a direct object.

Wayne tossed Raj the ball. (Wayne tossed the ball *to Raj.*)
I made my sister a pom-pom. (I made a pom-pom *for my sister.*)

Write the direct object in each of the following sentences. If there is an indirect object as well, write it and underline it.

Example: Tennis can give you a strong body.
body, <u>you</u>

1. This sport burns calories, too.
2. Aunt Sheryl gave me a racquet.
3. I play tennis regularly.
4. Yesterday, I sent Ruth a powerful serve.

Add Specific Information

Another kind of object noun is the **object of a preposition** (see 704.7). A prepositional phrase begins with a preposition and ends with an object. You can use prepositional phrases to add specific information to sentences. The object of each prepositional phrase below is highlighted in blue. (Also see pages 494–495.)

I do some stretches <u>before a game</u> <u>of tennis</u>.
I also drink lots <u>of water</u> <u>during a game</u>.

Write a brief sports-related paragraph that includes at least five prepositional phrases. Underline the object of each prepositional phrase. Here are some prepositions to choose from: *over, under, before, after, during,* and *against*. (See page 742 for more.)

BASIC GRAMMAR

Answers

Answers will vary.

Answers

line 1: player
scorer
line 2: girl
coach
line 4: observer
line 5: players
line 6: standout
player
line 7: role model
line 8: coach

Answers

1. calories
2. racquet, <u>me</u>
3. tennis
4. serve, <u>Ruth</u>

Answers

Answers will vary.

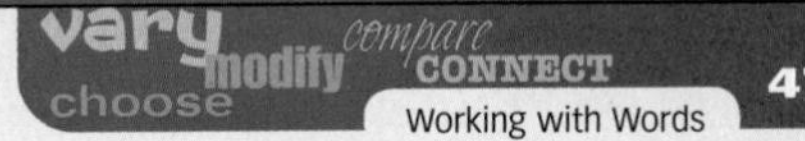

Using Pronouns

A pronoun is a word used in place of a noun. The noun replaced, or referred to, by the pronoun is called the pronoun's **antecedent**. The arrows below point to each pronoun's antecedent. (Also see 706.1.)

The volleyball team was determined, so it won the match.

Coach Johnson said that she never saw a team work so hard.

The **personal pronouns** listed below are the most common pronouns used by writers. (For a complete list of personal pronouns, see page 710.)

Personal Pronouns

I	you	he	she	it	we	they
me		him	her		us	them

Person and Number of a Pronoun

Pronouns show "person" and "number" in writing. The following chart shows which pronouns are used for the three different persons *(first, second, third)* and the two different numbers *(singular or plural)*.

		Singular	Plural
First Person	(The person speaking)	I called.	We called.
Second Person	(The person spoken to)	You called.	You called.
Third Person	(The person spoken about)	He called. She called. It called.	They called.

Number your paper from 1 to 4. Write sentences that use the pronouns described below as subjects.

Example: first-person singular pronoun *(I)*

I want to join the basketball team.

1. third-person singular pronoun
2. third-person plural pronoun
3. second-person singular pronoun
4. first-person plural pronoun

Indefinite Pronouns

An **indefinite pronoun** refers to people or things that are not named or known. The chart below lists which indefinite pronouns are singular, which are plural, and which can be singular or plural.

Indefinite Pronouns

Singular				Plural	Singular or Plural
another	either	nobody	someone	both	all
anybody	everybody	no one	something	few	any
anyone	everyone	nothing		many	most
anything	everything	one		several	none
each	neither	somebody			

When you use a singular indefinite pronoun as a subject, the verbs and the other pronouns that refer to the subject all must be singular. If the indefinite pronoun is plural, the verbs and other pronouns that refer to the subject must all be plural.

Singular

Everybody does her or his **stretches before practice.**

Plural

Several **of the boys** do their **sit-ups after warming up.**

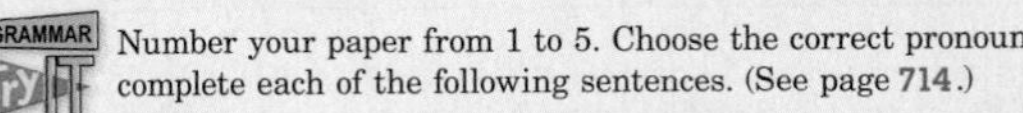

Singular or Plural

Most **of the time** is spent **on drills.** (singular)

Most **of the players** are looking **forward to the match.** (plural)

Number your paper from 1 to 5. Choose the correct pronoun to complete each of the following sentences. (See page 714.)

1. Someone left *(their, his* or *her)* racquet on the tennis court.
2. None of the girls were happy about losing *(their, her)* match.
3. Most of the match would be remembered for *(their, its)* intensity.
4. Has everyone turned in *(their, her* or *his)* gear?
5. Several of the coaches will drive *(their, his* or *her)* own cars.

If using *her* or *his* is clumsy, try changing the singular pronoun to a plural pronoun. For example, the first sample sentence above could be rewritten like this: **All** *of the players* **do their** *stretches before practice.*

BASIC GRAMMAR

GRAMMAR Try It Answers

Answers to item 1 will use one of the pronouns listed. Possible answers are provided.

1. he, she, it; He loves to play soccer.
2. they; They went to the movies.
3. you; Do you know what time it is?
4. We went out for ice cream.

GRAMMAR Try It Answers

1. his or her
2. their
3. its
4. his or her
5. their

How can pronouns improve my writing?

Avoid Repeating Nouns

You can use pronouns in your writing to avoid repeating the same nouns over and over again. (See pages 706–714.) Read the sample paragraph below. How many times did the writer use "Lance Armstrong"?

Without Pronouns

Lance Armstrong, a champion cyclist, was born in 1971. Lance Armstrong's competitive nature led Lance Armstrong to win the Iron Kids Triathlon when Lance Armstrong was only 13 years old. Armstrong became a member of the United States Olympic Team in 1992. Despite getting cancer at age 25, Lance Armstrong went on to win the Tour de France seven times by 2005.

Now read the revised sample below. The writer has replaced some of the nouns with pronouns. Which pronouns refer to Lance Armstrong?

With Pronouns

Lance Armstrong, a champion cyclist, was born in 1971. His competitive nature led him to win the Iron Kids Triathlon when he was only 13 years old. Armstrong became a member of the United States Olympic Team in 1992. Despite getting cancer at age 25, he went on to win the Tour de France seven times by 2005.

On your own paper, rewrite the following paragraph, changing some of the underlined nouns to pronouns so that the paragraph reads more smoothly.

At the start of Lance Armstrong's professional career, Lance Armstrong spent eight months a year racing in Europe. Lance Armstrong became very popular with European fans, and Lance Armstrong had to learn how to deal with the fans. Very quickly, Lance Armstrong gained recognition as a world-class cyclist. In many events, Lance Armstrong was the only American racer. During Lance Armstrong's first professional year, Lance Armstrong won 10 races.

How can I use pronouns properly?

Avoid Agreement Problems

You can make your writing clear by using pronouns properly. You must use pronouns that agree with their antecedents. (An antecedent is the noun or pronoun that a pronoun replaces or refers to.) Pronouns must agree with their antecedents in number, person, and gender. (See 712.1–712.4.)

When Mom and Dad go golfing, they usually rent a golf cart.

Uncle Carl didn't know how to golf, so Dad taught him.

Agreement in Number

The **number** of a pronoun is either singular or plural. The pronoun must match the antecedent in number.

- A singular pronoun refers to a singular antecedent.

Dad has had his own golf clubs since he was 18 years old.

- A plural pronoun refers to a plural antecedent.

All of the woods have their own protective covers.

Select the correct pronouns from the following list to complete the sentences below.

his	its	their	he	them	her	they	it

Example: Dad plays golf whenever ________ gets a chance.
he

1. Golfers try to keep ________ scores as low as possible.
2. The pitted surface of a golf ball helps ________ fly smoothly.
3. A putting green is different from the rest of the golf course because ________ grass is very short.
4. People lose ________ golf balls when ________ hit ________ into the water.
5. Golfers usually bring an umbrella along with ________ .
6. Babe Didrikson Zaharias, one of the most famous female golfers, did not let fame go to ________ head.

BASIC GRAMMAR

Possible Answers

1. no change
2. he
3. He
4. no change
5. he
6. them
7. no change
8. he
9. his
10. he

Answers

1. their
2. it
3. its
4. their, they, them
5. them
6. her

Agreement in Person

When you use pronouns, you must choose either first, second, or third **person** pronouns. If you start a sentence in one "person," don't shift to another "person" later in the sentence.

Pronoun shift: **I have learned a lot about Babe, and with all that knowledge you can write an interesting report.**

Correct: **I have learned a lot about Babe, and with all that knowledge I can write an interesting report.**

For each sentence below, change the underlined pronoun so it doesn't cause a shift in person.

1. We are studying famous athletes in their social studies class.
2. If golfers knew how many sports Babe shined in, you would be amazed.
3. She was an incredible athlete, and we won 13 straight golf tournaments in 1946.
4. Babe won 82 golf tournaments in all, and you became famous on both sides of the Atlantic.
5. Babe qualified for five Olympic events in 1932, but, as a woman, you could compete in only three.

Agreement in Gender

The **gender** of a pronoun *(her, his, its)* must be the same as the gender of its antecedent. Pronouns can be feminine (female), masculine (male), or neuter (neither male nor female).

Babe Didrikson's father required his children to take part in a sport.

Babe Didrikson excelled in nearly every sport she tried.

Number your paper from 1 to 5. Correct each underlined pronoun so that it agrees with its antecedent in gender.

Babe challenged some old-fashioned ideas about his role in sports. Although best known for golf, she did not limit himself to that sport. He played basketball, tennis, and softball. Its participation in the 1932 Olympics led to three medals in track and field. The Associated Press named him Athlete of the Year six times.

What else should I know about pronouns?

Make Your References Clear

When you use a pronoun, don't confuse your reader by making its antecedent unclear. Make sure that the word your pronoun refers to is obvious; it should plainly refer to only one noun.

Confusing Pronoun Reference

Ancient Egyptian drawings show some people playing handball. They were found in tombs.

(Which noun—*drawings* or *people*—does the pronoun *they* refer to?)

There are two ways to fix this error. The first way is to reword the sentences to clarify your meaning.

In ancient Egyptian tombs, drawings were found. They show some people playing handball.

The second way to fix the error is to reword the sentences without using a pronoun.

Ancient Egyptian drawings show some people playing handball. The drawings were found in tombs. (or)

Ancient Egyptian drawings found in tombs show some people playing handball.

Correctly rewrite the passages below that contain confusing pronoun references. (There are five.)

People played many games long before they were included in the Olympics. Field hockey, for example, is one of the oldest competitive sports in the world. It began with the ancient civilizations of Egypt, Greece, and Rome.

Today, players use field hockey rules that were developed in the mid-1800s in England. They say that there are 11 people per team. Each team tries to advance the ball down the field to the other team's goal cage. Players can hit it only with the flat side of their sticks. Players can shoot at the goal only from within the "striking circle," which extends 16 feet from the goal.

Now, every four years, field hockey teams vie for the World Cup. When the 2002 World Cup competition was held in Perth, Australia, more people became aware of it. In fact, field hockey has gained in popularity every year.

BASIC GRAMMAR

Answers

1. our
2. they
3. she
4. she
5. she

Answers

1. her
2. herself
3. She
4. Her
5. her

Possible Answers

1. People played many games long before those games were included in the Olympics.
2. For example, field hockey, which began with the ancient civilizations of Egypt, Greece, and Rome, is one of the oldest competitive sports in the world.
3. Players today use the rules developed in the mid-1800s in England. There are 11 people per team, and the team tries to advance the ball down the field to the other team's goal cage.
4. The players can hit the ball only with the flat side of their sticks.
5. When the 2002 World Cup competition was held in Perth, Australia, more people became aware of field hockey, which gains in popularity every year.

Choosing Verbs

Writers must constantly make choices, and one of their most important choices is which verb to use to express their thoughts clearly.

Action Verbs

An **action verb** tells what the subject is doing. Action verbs help bring your writing to life.

A luge zooms down ice-covered canals.

Lugers race at high speeds through the frozen canals.

Linking Verbs

A **linking verb** connects (links) a subject to a noun or an adjective in the predicate.

Common Linking Verbs	
Forms of "be"	be are were been is was am being
Other linking verbs	appear become feel grow look remain seem smell sound taste

A luge is a type of sled.
(The linking verb *is* connects the subject *luge* to the noun *type*. *Type* is a **predicate noun**.)

The rider must be brave.
(The linking verb *be* connects the subject *rider* to the adjective *brave*. *Brave* is a **predicate adjective**.)

For the sentences below, write the subject, the linking verb, and the predicate noun or predicate adjective that follows the verb. (One of the sentences does not include a linking verb.)

One kind of luge track is natural, following the contours of a snowy mountain. The other kind (used in the Olympics) is a frozen ice canal built for speed. The luger lies on the luge, faceup and feetfirst. During a run, she or he remains still to increase speed. Obviously, speed is very important. The luger with the fastest run becomes the leader in a competition.

Helping Verbs

The simple predicate may include a **helping verb** plus the main verb. The helping verb makes the verb more specific.

Valerie will attempt a luge run.
(The helping verb *will* helps express future tense.)

She may need special clothing. (*May* helps express a possibility.)

The track, which was destroyed, had been built for the 1984 Olympics in Sarajevo. (*Had been* helps express past perfect tense and passive voice.)

Select a helping verb from the following list to complete each sentence in the paragraph below.

would	does	will	could	should

I **(1)** _____ like to ride a luge, but Mom **(2)** _____ not think that's a good idea. Dad thinks that I **(3)** _____ learn more about luges first. Are there any luge schools that I **(4)** _____ attend? I **(5)** _____ research that on the Internet, and perhaps I **(6)** _____ find an instructor nearby.

Irregular Verbs

Most verbs in the English language are regular. A writer adds *ed* to regular verbs to show a past action. A writer can also use *has, have,* or *had* with the past participle to make other verb tenses. **Irregular verbs** do not follow the *ed* rule. Instead of adding *ed* to show past tense, the word might change. (See the list of irregular verbs on page 722.)

Present	I speak.	She runs.
Past	Yesterday I spoke.	Yesterday she ran.
Past Participle	I have spoken.	She has run.

On your own paper, write five sentences using the irregular verbs listed below.

1. took
2. make
3. has seen
4. went
5. ride

Answers

line 1: kind is natural
lines 2–3: kind is canal
line 4: he or she remains still
line 4: speed is important
line 5: luger becomes leader

Answers

1. would
2. does
3. should
4. could
5. could
6. will

Possible Answers

1. I took dance lessons for five years.
2. I make brownies every Sunday.
3. Who has seen this movie?
4. Carla went to her grandmother's house.
5. We all ride the bus to school.

How can I use verbs effectively?

Show Powerful Action

You can use **action verbs** to show the reader exactly what is happening (or has happened).

Ordinary Action Verbs

Vashon shot the basketball through the hoop.
Dave got the rebound and ran up the court.

Powerful Action Verbs

Vashon flipped the basketball through the hoop.
Dave grabbed the rebound and dashed up the court.

Try to avoid using linking verbs *(is, are, was, were)* too much. Often, a stronger (action) verb can be made from another word in the same sentence.

Kristy is a good basketball player. (linking verb)
Kristy plays basketball well.
(The action verb *plays* is made from the word *player.*)

Create Active Voice

A verb is in the **active voice** if the subject in the sentence is doing the action. (See page 726.) A verb is passive if the subject is not doing the action. Try to use active verbs as much as possible because they make your writing sound more direct and action packed.

The ball was passed from Kristy to Tamika. (passive)
Kristy passed the ball to Tamika. (active)

Rewrite each of the following sentences so that the verb is in the active voice rather than the passive voice.

Example: A basket was made by Will.
Will made a basket.

1. Thirteen points were scored by Yao in the first half.
2. A layup was attempted by me, but I missed the basket.
3. Most of the fouls were called by one referee.
4. A zone defense was played by the opposing team.
5. Basketball games at my school are attended by many people.

Show When Something Happens

You can use different verb tenses to "tell time" in sentences. The three **simple tenses** are *present, past,* and *future.* (See page 720.)

At times, you might need to use different tenses in the same sentence to show that one action happened before another action.

The Harlem Globetrotters is a basketball team that began in the 1920s.

Both a present tense verb and a past tense verb appear in the sentence, and it makes sense. However, you need to avoid a shift in verb tense if it is unnecessary.

Shift in tense:
They tour the country and played any team that will take them on.
(The verb tense shifts from *present* to *past*, confusing the reader.)

Corrected:
They tour the country and play any team that will take them on.

For each blank in the sentences below, write a verb that is the same tense as the first verb in the sentence.

1. When the Globetrotters play another team for the first time, their opponents ______ surprised.
2. Early on, the Globetrotters recruited players from many places, and they ______ a long time to play together as a team.
3. One cannot deny the skill of these team members; they ______ superior athletes.
4. The Globetrotters will play at the arena next week, and I ______ there.

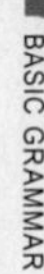

Rewrite each sentence below that has an unnecessary shift in verb tense. (You should find three tense-shift errors.)

(1) Players for the Harlem Globetrotters have always been truly talented athletes. **(2)** In a 1939 game, however, the Globetrotters led by more than 100 points, so they start clowning around. **(3)** From then on, the team included comedy routines in their games.

(4) Since the Globetrotters regularly entertain sold-out crowds around the world, they were the most-recognized team on earth. **(5)** The team's 76-year record for 21,236 games includes only 336 losses, and there was no doubt that they will continue to win. **(6)** The Globetrotters will delight fans around the globe for years to come.

Answers

1. Yao scored 13 points in the first half.
2. I attempted a layup, but I missed the basket.
3. One referee called most of the fouls.
4. The opposing team played a zone defense.
5. Many people attend basketball games at my school.

Possible Answers

1. seem/are/act
2. practiced
3. are
4. will be

Answers

2. In a 1939 game, however, the Globetrotters led by more than 100 points, so they started clowning around.
4. Since the Globetrotters regularly entertain sold-out crowds around the world, they are the most-recognized team on earth.
5. The team's 76-year record for 21,236 games includes only 336 losses, and there is no doubt that they will continue to win.

How else can I use verbs?

Show Special Types of Action

You need **perfect tense verbs** to express certain types of action. (See page 724 in the "Proofreader's Guide.") There are three perfect tenses.

play, played	Singular	Plural
Present perfect tense states an action that *began in the past but continues or is completed in the present.*		
Present perfect (use *has* or *have* + past participle)	I have played. You have played. He or she has played.	We have played. You have played. They have played.
Past perfect tense states an action that began in the past and was completed in the past.		
Past perfect (use *had* + past participle)	I had played. You had played. He or she had played.	We had played. You had played. They had played.
Future perfect tense states an action that *will begin in the future and will be completed by a specific time in the future.*		
Future perfect (use *will have* + past participle)	I will have played. You will have played. He or she will have played.	We will have played. You will have played. They will have played.

Identify the tense of each underlined verb in the following paragraphs. The first one has been done for you.

1. past perfect

At the end of last summer, our local bowling alley **(1)** had burned down. Since then our bowling league **(2)** has moved to another bowling alley across town. I hope the owners of the old alley **(3)** will have rebuilt our bowling alley by the start of the next season. We **(4)** have missed bowling there.

I **(5)** have owned my bowling ball for one year. Up until three months ago, my fingers **(6)** had fit the holes perfectly. Now the thumb hole is getting a bit tight because I **(7)** have grown so much. By the end of the season, I'm sure the local sports store **(8)** will have redrilled the holes for me.

Form Verbals

Verbals are words that are made from verbs but are used as other parts of speech. Verbals are used as nouns, adjectives, and adverbs, and they are often used in phrases. (See 730.2–730.4.)

Gerunds

A **gerund** is a verb form that ends in *ing* and is used as a noun.

Bowling is an enjoyable activity.
(The gerund *bowling* acts as a subject noun.)
You should try bowling in our league.
(The gerund phrase *bowling in our league* acts as a direct object.)

Participles

A **participle** is a verb form used as an adjective. A participle ends in *ing* or *ed.*

Regina had a bowling party on her birthday.
(The participle *bowling* describes what kind of party; *bowling* acts as an adjective.)
A ball spinning down the next alley hit the pocket perfectly.
(The participial phrase acts as an adjective describing *ball.*)

Infinitives

An **infinitive** is a verb with "to" before it. An infinitive can be used as a noun, an adjective, or an adverb.

My goal for today is to get three strikes.
(The infinitive phrase *to get three strikes* acts as a predicate noun.)
Our plan to go bowling is still a "go."
(*To go bowling* acts as an adjective modifying the noun *plan.*)
Please watch me carefully to evaluate my form.
(*To evaluate my form* acts as an adverb modifying the verb *watch.*)

Write a sentence for each of the verbals listed below.

1. knocking down the pins *(gerund phrase)*
2. to earn a good score *(infinitive phrase)*
3. spinning *(participle)*
4. taking a few long strides *(participial phrase)*
5. to make a spare *(infinitive phrase)*

BASIC GRAMMAR

Answers

2. present perfect
3. future perfect
4. present perfect
5. present perfect
6. past perfect
7. present perfect
8. future perfect

Possible Answers

1. The best thing about bowling is knocking down the pins.
2. Everyone wants to earn a good score.
3. My sister watched the spinning ball move down the lane.
4. I saw my brother taking a few long strides.
5. If he can't get a strike, then his goal is to make a spare.

Describing with Adjectives

Adjectives are words that describe or modify nouns or pronouns. Sensory adjectives help the reader see, hear, feel, smell, and taste what writers are describing. (Also see pages 732 and 734.)

Without Adjectives

Leroy dived into the water. He swam along the lane markers to the end of the pool. His coach held up a stopwatch.

With Adjectives

Leroy dived into the cold, blue water. He swam along the red, white, and blue lane markers to the end of the Olympic-sized pool. His cheering coach held up an oversized stopwatch.

Adjectives answer three questions: *what kind? how many (much)?* or *which one? Remember:* Proper adjectives can be made from proper nouns (England, *English;* Italy, *Italian*) and are capitalized.

What Kind?	French **bread**	sour **lemon**	black **cat**
How Many (Much)?	two **puppies**	few **friends**	some **milk**
Which One?	this **chair**	these **students**	those **caps**

For each blank in the sentences below, write an adjective of the type called for in parentheses.

1. There are *(how many?)* students on the swim team.
2. Marla just got a *(what kind?)* swimsuit.
3. She has swum on the team for *(how many?)* years.
4. Marla always swallowed *(how much?)* water during practice.
5. Last year, she injured her *(which one?)* elbow during a race.
6. During the conference meet, Marla's relay team won a *(what kind?)* medal.
7. Altogether, Marla won *(how many?)* medals during the meet.
8. The *(which one?)* meet was the highlight of last season.
9. This year's *(what kind?)* swim team will be as good as last year's.
10. Marla accepts *(how much?)* responsibility for her performances.

Comparative and Superlative Forms

You can use comparative adjectives to compare two things. For most one-syllable adjectives, add *er* to make the **comparative form**. To compare three or more things, add *est* to make the **superlative form**.

Positive	Comparative	Superlative
large	larger	largest

Comparative: A volleyball is larger than a baseball.
Superlative: The largest ball in professional team sports is a basketball.

Add *er* and *est* to some two-syllable words and use *more* or *most* (or *less* or *least*) with others. Always use *more* or *most* with three-syllable adjectives.

Positive	Comparative	Superlative
joyful	more joyful	most joyful

Comparative: Swimming is a more strenuous sport than golf is.
Superlative: I think that gymnastics is the most strenuous of all sports.

NOTE Some adjectives use completely different words to express comparison—for example, *bad, worse, worst.* (See 734.6.)

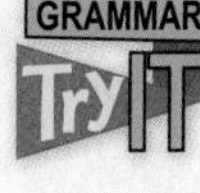

Write the positive, comparative, or superlative form of the underlined adjective to fill in the blanks in each of the following sentences.

1. You will see some fast balls in baseball, but a golf ball hit from a tee is a ________ ball. The ________ of all balls in sports is a jai-alai ball.
2. The soccer practices are ________, but the games are more difficult than the practices are. I had the ________ of all my games when I was sick.
3. Student athletes do some amazing feats. Of course, professional athletes can do things that are ________ than what the students can do. However, participants in extreme sports can do the ________ feats of all.
4. While Angela is a ________ runner, Lee is a better runner, and Takeisha is the ________ runner of all.
5. For a few players, spiking a volleyball is easy. For many other players, serving is ________ than spiking the ball. Then there are those who find setting up the ________ part of the game.

BASIC GRAMMAR

GRAMMAR Try It Possible Answers

1. fourteen
2. new
3. three
4. some
5. right
6. silver
7. two
8. last
9. girls'
10. full

GRAMMAR Try It Answers

1. faster, fastest
2. difficult, most difficult
3. more amazing, most amazing
4. good, best
5. easier, easiest

How can I strengthen my writing with adjectives?

Use Sensory Details

Writers use adjectives to help create **sensory details**. Sensory details help readers experience something with all their senses. Note how the sensory adjectives add effective details in the following paragraph.

> **The sweet aroma of fresh-mown grass floated off the baseball diamond. Bright white lines had been carefully painted on it. The buzzing crowd waited in anticipation. Food and drink vendors began hawking their mouth-watering treats as the first blaring notes of "The Star-Spangled Banner" tumbled out of the band's shiny instruments.**

Draw a chart like the one below and list two or three adjectives for each sense.

sight	sound	smell	taste	feeling (texture)
golden	*humming*	*rich*	*salty*	*smooth*

Form Extra-Strength Modifiers

Compound adjectives are made of two or more words. Some are spelled as one word; others are hyphenated. (Use a dictionary to check spelling.)

> **Some baseball fields feature man-made grass.**

For each of the following sentences, write a compound adjective to fill in the blank. Make your compound adjectives by combining words from the following list. (All of them should be hyphenated.)

front	high	filled	row	flying	third	fan	base

Example: We entered the noisy, __________ stadium just as the game started.
fan-filled

1. Our tickets were for __________ seats.
2. Santiago hit a __________ ball toward the bleachers.
3. The __________ umpire shouted, "Foul ball!"

Include Adjectives in the Predicate

Most adjectives are placed before the nouns they describe. A **predicate adjective** comes after a linking verb and describes the noun or pronoun before it.

> **The worn mitt is ancient, and it smells musty.**
> **Darnell remains confident about the mitt's supposed "luck."**

GRAMMAR Try It — Write a predicate adjective to fill in each blank in the paragraph below. The linking verbs are underlined.

> When Mom dropped me off at baseball practice, I was **(1)** ______ . Our opening game was only three days away. The whole team seemed **(2)** ______ . Our fielders were **(3)** ______ , and some of the batters were really **(4)** ______ . Carl, our main pitcher, looked **(5)** ______ . We didn't know how the other team would play, but we felt **(6)** ______ . We couldn't wait!

Write a brief paragraph about a personal experience related to your favorite sport. In your paragraph, use at least five linking verbs, such as *become, feel, seem, appear,* and *sound*, that link to predicate adjectives.

Be General or Specific

You can use **indefinite adjectives**, such as *few, many, more,* and *some,* to give the reader approximate information. (*Approximate* means "general" rather than "specific.")

> **Some neighborhood kids picked teams for baseball.**
> **Gina and Sandy decided to play another game.**

A **demonstrative adjective** points to a specific noun. The demonstrative adjectives are *this, that, these,* and *those*.

> **Those kids over there want to play, too.**
> **I want to use this bat when it's my turn.**

Note that both indefinite and demonstrative adjectives must come before the nouns they modify. If they appear alone, they are pronouns.

Write two sentences that use indefinite adjectives and two that use demonstrative adjectives. Exchange papers with a classmate and underline each other's indefinite and demonstrative adjectives.

BASIC GRAMMAR

Possible Answers

Answers will vary.

Answers

1. front-row or third-row
2. high-flying
3. third-base

Answers

1. excited
2. confident
3. excellent
4. strong
5. incredible
6. prepared

Answers

Answers will vary.

Answers

Answers will vary.

Describing with Adverbs

Adverbs describe or modify verbs, adjectives, or other adverbs. You can use adverbs to answer *how? when? where?* or *how much?* (See pages 736 and 738.)

How?	gracefully	Deena did a backflip gracefully on the beam.
When?	yesterday	She was in the semifinals yesterday.
Where?	indoors	The events were all held indoors.
How Much?	barely	Mark barely met the time limit on his routine.

For each of the following paragraphs, write the adverbs you find. (The number of adverbs in each paragraph is shown in parentheses.)

I. I went with Darla to a gymnastics competition today. She told me about the men who perform gymnastic routines on a pommel horse. These athletes must practice regularly. The most basic skills are extremely difficult to master because only the hands can touch the horse. The athlete spends most of the time carefully balancing on one arm as his free hand reaches to begin the next skill. There are no stops or pauses allowed. At the end of his routine, the gymnast's dismount is a landing without any steps or hops afterward. That's a challenge! (5)

II. Although Darla really liked the uneven bars when she started gymnastics, her favorite event now has become the balance beam. She fearlessly leaps, jumps, and does handsprings on a four-foot high, four-inch-wide beam! The hard ground lies below. Her dance moves are expertly completed. Of course, she is very flexible, but she must concentrate totally for the 90 seconds of her routine. (7)

Comparative and Superlative Adverbs

You can use adverbs to compare two things. The **comparative form** of an adverb compares two people, places, things, or ideas. The **superlative form** of an adverb compares three or more people, places, things, or ideas.

For most one-syllable adverbs, add *er* to make the comparative form and *est* to make the superlative form.

Positive	Comparative	Superlative
soon	sooner	soonest

While you add *er* and *est* to some two-syllable adverbs, you need to use *more* or *most* (or *less* or *least*) with others. Always use *more* or *most* with adverbs of three or more syllables.

Positive	quickly	importantly
Comparative	more quickly	more importantly
Superlative	most quickly	most importantly

Comparative: I ran faster than my guard did.
Ed plays basketball more frequently than I do.

Superlative: Kayla ran fastest of all and grabbed the jump ball.
Of all of us, Ed plays basketball most frequently.

Make sure that you write a complete comparison: *I ran faster than my guard did* rather than *I ran faster than my guard.*

In each sentence below, change the adverb (underlined) twice: first to compare two things and then to compare three (or more) things. Reword the sentences as needed.

Example: Delia quickly put on her uniform.
I put my uniform on more quickly than Delia did.
Of the three of us, Beryl put hers on most quickly.

1. She would be on the soccer field soon.
2. Rolando kicked the ball powerfully.
3. Joe skillfully set up his teammates.

BASIC GRAMMAR

Answers

I. today, regularly, extremely, carefully, afterward

II. really, now, fearlessly, below, expertly, very, totally

Possible Answers

1. She would be on the soccer field sooner than I would. Jasmine was ready first, so she was on the soccer field the soonest of us all.
2. Leif kicked the ball more powerfully than Rolando. Out of all the team members, Juan kicked the most powerfully.
3. Joe set up his teammates more skillfully than Roger did. Of all the team, however, Carole set up her teammates the most skillfully.

How can I use adverbs effectively?

Describe Actions

You can make your writing more descriptive by using adverbs. Since they can appear just about anywhere in a sentence, experiment to find the best place to include them. *Remember:* Changing an adverb's location may slightly change the meaning of the sentence.

Greg smoothly rowed his kayak through the water.
Greg rowed his kayak smoothly through the water.
Greg rowed his kayak through the water smoothly.
Smoothly, Greg rowed his kayak through the water.

GRAMMAR Try It Rewrite the following sentences, placing the adverb (in parentheses) where you think it fits best.

1. I decided to try kayaking myself. *(finally)*
2. I will have to practice. *(definitely)*
3. I don't want to go where the current is fast. *(really)*
4. A kayak has a low probability of capsizing. *(surprisingly)*
5. Kayakers should learn how to flip themselves back up again if they do capsize. *(actually)*

Add Emphasis

You can stress the importance of something with adverbs. Generally, use adverbs of degree (those that answer *how much?*) for this job. (See 736.4.)

We paddled extremely fast in the river rapids.
Rapids can be awfully dangerous.

Write a short paragraph about this picture that shows kayakers in calm water. Use a few adverbs to add emphasis.

Express Frequency

With adverbs, you can describe how often something happens or how often something is done in a certain way. Adverbs that tell how often include *often, sometimes, usually, occasionally, always,* and so on.

Dwight has always enjoyed track-and-field events.
He is rarely disappointed in the athletes' performances.

Use three of the following "how often" adverbs in sentences about your attitude toward a specific sport.

regularly	never	occasionally	always	seldom	frequently

When you use a negative adverb such as *hardly, barely,* or *scarcely* in a sentence, avoid using another negative term *(no, not, neither)* to express the same idea. Using two negative words together results in a **double negative**, which is an error.

I can't hardly fit this skateboard in my backpack.

To correct a double negative, remove one of the negative terms:

I can't fit this skateboard in my backpack.
I can hardly fit this skateboard in my backpack.

Be Precise

With adverbs, you can tell the readers exactly when *(then, yesterday, now, right away)* or where *(here, there, nearby, inside)* something happens.

Leila then invited me to jump on her trampoline.
"Will you stay close while I jump?" I asked.

For each blank, write an adverb that tells "when" or "where."

When I went to Leila's house **(1)** ______, I saw her trampoline. Other families who lived **(2)** ______ also had trampolines. I asked Leila if we could try out her tramp **(3)** ______. **(4)** ______ we jumped for a long time. Leila's friend next door called to us. "Come **(5)** ______ and jump on our tramp, too!" she said.

Answers

Answers will vary.

Answers

Answers will vary.

Answers

Answers will vary.

Possible Answers

1. yesterday
2. nearby
3. right away
4. Then
5. here

Connecting with Prepositions

A preposition is a word (or words) that show how one word or idea is related to another. A preposition is the first word of a prepositional phrase, a phrase that acts as an adjective or an adverb in a sentence. (See page 742 for a complete list of prepositions.)

The Astrodome is located in Houston, Texas.
(The preposition *in* shows the relationship between the verb *is located* and the object of the preposition *Houston, Texas.* The prepositional phrase acts as an adverb telling "where.")

When the panels in the roof **were painted, the grass died.**
(The preposition *in* shows the relationship between the noun *panels* and the object of the preposition *roof.* The prepositional phrase acts as an adjective telling "which ones.")

Preposition or Adverb?

If a word that sometimes is used as a preposition appears alone in a sentence, that word is probably an adverb, not a preposition.

Two students lagged behind the group.
(*Behind the group* is a prepositional phrase.)

Two students lagged behind, **so we waited.**
(*Behind* is an adverb that modifies the verb *lagged.*)

"To" as a Preposition or Part of an Infinitive Phrase

If the words that follow *to* do not include the object of the preposition (a noun or pronoun), then *to* is not a preposition. When a verb or verb phrase follows *to, to* is considered an infinitive, a kind of verbal. (See page 485.)

We are going to the stadium.
(*To the stadium* is a prepositional phrase.)

We are going to watch **a football game.**
(*To watch* is an infinitive.)

Write four sentences about a place where people play a sport. Use the word *around* as a preposition in one sentence and as an adverb in another. Use the word *to* as a preposition in one sentence and as part of an infinitive in another.

How can I use prepositional phrases?

Add Information

You can use a prepositional phrase as an adjective to describe either a noun or a pronoun. Adjectives answer *what kind? how many?* or *which one?*

The Major League Baseball park on Chicago's north side [*Which one?*], **Wrigley Field, is a stadium just** for baseball [*Which kind?*].

Write a prepositional phrase that could modify each of the subjects below. Your phrases should answer *what kind? how many?* or *which one?* Use a variety of prepositions to introduce your prepositional phrases.

Example: the players
the players on our team

1. the most exciting game
2. the sports arena
3. the locker room
4. several days
5. that camera
6. the referee
7. those basketballs
8. a shrill whistle
9. spectators
10. the scoreboard

You can also use a prepositional phrase as an adverb to describe a verb, an adjective, or another adverb. Adverbs answer *how? when? where? how long? how often?* or *how much?*

The team will play at Green Field [*Where?*] on Tuesday afternoon [*When?*].

On a piece of paper, list each prepositional phrase that is used as an adverb in the following paragraph. (You should find nine.) Tell what question each one answers.

Team Members:

We will be going to a tournament on Saturday. If you can attend, let me know before Friday. We will meet in the school parking lot at 8:00 a.m., and we'll get there by bus. We will return between 8:00 and 9:00 p.m., and the bus will drop us at the school. Please note: All team members must wear uniforms during the tournament.

Coach Marty

BASIC GRAMMAR

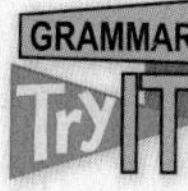

Possible Answers

1. The cross-country team ran around the track.
2. We knew they were around, but we weren't sure where.
3. We went to the gym and looked for them.
4. Now we are going to look for them outside.

Possible Answers

1. the most exciting game of this season
2. the sports area in the city's downtown
3. the locker room in the gym
4. several days after the game
5. that camera by the ball
6. the referee on the right side
7. those basketballs on the shelf
8. a shrill whistle from the stands
9. spectators from the opposing side
10. the scoreboard at the end of the field

Answers

line 2: to a tournament (where) on Saturday (when)
line 3: before Friday (when)
in the school parking lot (where)
line 3: at 8:00 a.m. (when)
line 4: by bus (how) between 8:00 and 9:00 p.m. (when)
line 5: at the school (where)
line 6: during the tournament (when)

Connecting with Conjunctions

Conjunctions connect words, groups of words, and sentences. There are three kinds of conjunctions: *coordinating, subordinating,* and *correlative*. The following sentences show some of the ways to use conjunctions. (See page 744 for a list of common conjunctions.)

Coordinating Conjunctions

Connect Words

Should I play basketball or volleyball this winter?

I am good at dribbling and shooting the ball.

Connect Compound Subjects and Predicates

All the coaches and current team members attend tryouts.

The coaches will test our skills and make the final decisions.

Connect Sentences

I hope I make the team, but I am not worried about it.

The team has practice every day, and that's a big commitment.

Subordinating Conjunctions

Connect Dependent Clauses to Independent Clauses

Players remain on the team as long as their grades are satisfactory.

When the team goes to the playoffs, students seem to have more school spirit.

Correlative Conjunctions

Connect Noun Phrases and Verb Phrases

Our team neither wins all the time nor loses all the time.

Being part of a team can help you improve not only your physical abilities but also your mental skills.

Choose three of the sentences above to use as models. Write three sentences of your own imitating the three you've chosen. (Make sure to use your own words.) Underline the conjunctions you use.

How can I use conjunctions?

Connect a Series of Ideas

You can use a conjunction to connect a series of three or more words or phrases in a row. Place commas between the words or phrases, and place a conjunction before the final item.

Blind athletes compete in skiing, swimming, and football.
(The conjunction *and* connects three nouns.)

They also ride bikes, lift weights, or shoot targets.
(The conjunction *or* connects three verb phrases.)

Copy the following sentence beginnings. Include a series of three or more ideas to finish each one.

1. My favorite sports are . . .
2. I admire how the players . . .
3. A few sports I'd like to try include . . .

Expand Sentences (with Coordinating Conjunctions)

You can use **coordinating conjunctions** *(and, but, or, nor, for, so, yet)* to make compound subjects and predicates and to write compound sentences.

Blind individuals and visually impaired people are able to participate in sports, but they don't always have the necessary equipment.
(The conjunction *and* creates a compound subject, and *but* creates a compound sentence.)

For each blank below, write a coordinating conjunction. Tell whether it connects a compound subject, a compound predicate, or a compound sentence.

An athlete may be blind, **(1)** _______ that doesn't mean he or she is less talented than any other athlete. In fact, some blind athletes have competed against sighted individuals **(2)** _______ won medals. The International Blind Sports Association conducts sports programs for blind people, **(3)** _______ it changes negative ideas about them in the process. The organization wants to spread its message, **(4)** _______ it runs public service campaigns. A blind person **(5)** _______ a sighted individual can be a successful athlete.

BASIC GRAMMAR

Possible Answers

1. Should I make soup <u>or</u> sandwiches for lunch?
2. <u>When</u> I lend books to my friend, she never seems to give them back.
3. This game was <u>neither</u> too long <u>nor</u> too short.

Possible Answers

1. My favorite sports are field hockey, basketball, and tennis.
2. I admire how the players are determined, hard-working, and always practicing.
3. A few sports I'd like to try include soccer, fencing, skiing, and track.

Answers

1. but (compound sentence)
2. and (compound predicate)
3. and (compound sentence)
4. so (compound sentence)
5. or (compound subject)

Expand Sentences (with Subordinating Conjunctions)

You can use a **subordinating conjunction** to connect a dependent clause to another sentence. A dependent clause (one that *cannot* stand alone as a sentence) must be connected to an independent clause (one that *can* stand alone as a sentence). In the expanded sentences below, the dependent clause is underlined, and the subordinating conjunction is in blue.

> Although martial arts teach self-defense, they also provide benefits to the body, mind, and spirit. Students improve themselves as they make progress in these three areas.

Choose a subordinating conjunction from the following list to fill in each blank below: *until, because, when, since, even though.* Try to fill in each blank with a different conjunction.

> Many martial arts are linked to the Far East **(1)** ______ that is where they were first practiced. Martial arts means "arts of war" **(2)** ______ people used them in actual combat. **(3)** ______ the martial arts are considered sports, people have discovered the health benefits they offer. Students still learn self-defense **(4)** ______ they learn a chosen "art." **(5)** ______ a person becomes really skilled, she or he stays out of competitions.

Show a Relationship

You can use **correlative conjunctions** to show a relationship between two words, phrases, or clauses. Correlative conjunctions are always used in pairs: *both/and, not only/but also, neither/nor, either/or, whether/or.*

> While performing martial arts, people use not only their bodies, but also their minds.
>
> Both tai chi and jujitsu are forms of martial art.

For each of the blanks in the sentences below, write the correlative conjunctions that make the most sense. (More than one answer may be correct.)

1. The martial arts stress ______ aggression ______ domination.
2. Practicing martial arts can help improve ______ your health ______ your self-esteem.
3. A bow to an instructor can express ______ gratitude ______ respect.

Building Effective Sentences

Imagine eating the same thing every day, at every meal. Eventually, you would dislike even the cheesiest pizza or the most scrumptious ice cream. People just naturally like variety.

The same is true with writing. A story with one long sentence after another, or one short sentence after another, would soon become boring. Sometimes a short sentence expresses feeling in a way that a long sentence cannot, and a long sentence does a better job of explaining a complicated idea. One key to clear writing is sentence variety.

What's Ahead

You will learn about . . .

- writing complete sentences.
- fixing sentence problems.
- improving your sentence style.
- combining sentences.
- adding variety to your sentences.
- using different types of sentences.
- expanding and modeling sentences.

GRAMMAR Try It Answers

1. since
2. because
3. Even though
4. when
5. Until

GRAMMAR Try It Possible Answers

1. neither, nor
2. not only, but also
3. either, or

Writing Complete Sentences

A sentence is a group of words that forms a complete thought. Writers use complete sentences in order to communicate clearly. The following group of words does not form a complete thought:

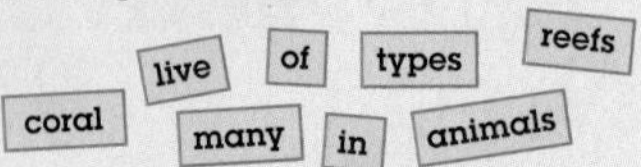

The jumble of words above does not make sense. When these same words are rearranged into a sentence, however, they do make sense. They communicate a clear, complete thought:

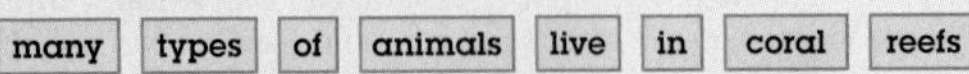

On your own paper, unscramble the word groups below to create complete sentences. (See the helpful clues in parentheses.) Remember to capitalize and punctuate each sentence correctly.

Example: in corals clear live shallow water *(equal adjectives)*

Corals live in clear, shallow water.

1. they simple creatures without are eyes *(pronoun subject)*
2. tiny animals corals the in eat floating ocean *(prepositional phrase)*
3. form limestone reefs huge of coral ridges under water *(appositive)*
4. fish sharks and eat seals *(compound direct objects)*
5. some hundreds grow very slowly for corals and live of years *(compound verb)*
6. the Reef is about Barrier 1,250 Great long miles *(prepositional phrase)*
7. shrimp and on live fish coral reefs *(compound subject)*
8. purple can red be yellow coral green or *(a series)*
9. pollution can and hurt garbage coral oil *(appositive)*

Write NOW **Write three sentences about the animals living on a coral reef. On another sheet, mix up the words and leave out punctuation and capitalization. Ask a classmate to rearrange the words so they form complete sentences.**

Basic Parts of a Sentence

Every sentence has two basic parts: a complete subject (which tells who or what is doing something) and a complete predicate (which tells what the subject is doing).

Complete Subject	Complete Predicate
Who or what did something?	*What did the subject do?*
Jacques Cousteau and Emile Gagnan	invented modern scuba gear.
Cousteau, a famous ocean explorer,	was also a film producer.

Divide a piece of paper into two columns. For each of the sentences below, write the complete subject in the left column and write the complete predicate in the right column.

In the following sentences, the words that come before the verb are the *complete subject.* The verb and all the words that follow it are the *complete predicate.*

Example: People have always explored under the sea.

People | have always explored under the sea.

1. The first piece of diving equipment was a snorkel made of a hollow reed.
2. The ancient Greeks used diving bells to walk underwater.
3. The English astronomer Edmond Halley discovered a comet and invented a diving bell.
4. Scuba stands for self-contained underwater breathing apparatus.
5. Diving suits with heavy helmets appeared for the first time in the 1800s.
6. Harry Houdini, the famous magician, invented a diving suit.
7. Plastic or rubber swim fins help a diver swim through the water.
8. The first team of women divers to live underwater for weeks was led by Sylvia Earle.
9. Earle, who spent more than 6,000 hours underwater, continues to work on saving oceans.

Answers

1. They are simple creatures without eyes.
2. Corals eat tiny animals floating in the ocean.
3. Coral reefs, huge limestone ridges, form underwater
4. Sharks eat fish and seals.
5. Some corals grow very slowly and live for hundreds of years.
6. The Great Barrier Reef is about 1,250 miles long.
7. Shrimp and fish live on coral reefs.
8. Coral can be red, purple, yellow, or green.
9. Pollution, oil and garbage, can hurt coral.

Answers

1. The first piece of diving equipment | was a snorkel make of a hollow reed.
2. The ancient Greeks | used diving bells to walk underwater.
3. The English astronomer Edmond Halley | discovered a comet and invented a diving bell.
4. Scuba | stands for self-contained underwater breathing apparatus.
5. Diving suits with heavy helmets | appeared for the first time in the 1800s.
6. Harry Houdini, the famous magician, | invented a diving suit.
7. Plastic or rubber swim fins | help a diver swim through the water.
8. The first team of women divers to live underwater for weeks | was led by Sylvia Earle.
9. Earle, who spent more than 6,000 hours underwater, | continues to work on saving oceans.

Subjects and Predicates

Every sentence has a subject and a predicate. A simple subject consists of the subject without the words that modify it. A simple predicate is the verb without the words that modify it or complete the thought. In the sentences below, the simple subjects are orange and the simple predicates are blue.

Complete Subject	Complete Predicate
Octopuses	have the most complex brain of all invertebrates.
Their acute sense of touch	also aids in their survival.

A compound subject includes two or more subjects that share the same predicate (or predicates). A compound predicate includes two or more predicates that share the same subject (or subjects).

Complete Subject	Complete Predicate
Lobsters and crabs	scatter and hide from preying octopuses.

Number a piece of paper from 1 to 5, skipping a line between numbers. For each sentence below, write the simple subject on one line and the simple predicate on the next line. (Remember to look for compound subjects and predicates.)

Example: A female octopus lays between 200,000 and 400,000 eggs at one time and dies shortly after laying her eggs.
octopus
lays, dies

1. Newborn octopuses float to the surface for about a month and then sink to live on the bottom of the ocean.
2. Crustaceans and mollusks are the main sources of food for newborn octopuses.
3. Moray eels eat octopuses.
4. Octopuses change color and squirt ink to protect themselves.
5. Sometimes, in calm water, the cloud of ink harms or kills the octopus.

Write one sentence with a single subject and a compound predicate. Then write another sentence with a compound subject and a compound predicate.

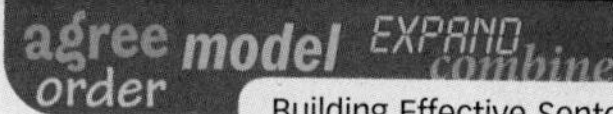

How can I make sure my sentences are complete?

Check Your Subjects and Predicates

Incomplete thoughts are called fragments. Fragments may be missing a subject, a predicate, or both. Study the fragments below. Then read the complete sentences made from them. Notice that a subject, a predicate, or both have been added to make the corrections.

Fragment	Sentence
Are lurking in Monterey Bay.	Strange creatures are lurking in Monterey Bay. (A subject is added.)
Battery-powered robots deep to gather data.	Battery-powered robots dive deep to gather data. (A simple predicate is added.)
Part of a $10 million study of the ocean's climate.	Underwater robots are part of a $10 million study of the ocean's climate. (A subject and a simple predicate are added.)

Number your paper from 1 to 5. Read each group of words below. If the group of words is a complete sentence, write "C" next to the number. If it is a fragment, write "F" and tell if you need to add a subject, a predicate, or both to make it a complete sentence.

Example: Can operate for days or weeks on lithium flashlight batteries.
F-subject

1. They can gather ocean data cheaper than research ships can.
2. According to scientist Francisco Chavez, "We to predict undersea weather."
3. Can affect surface weather, shoreline recreation, and fishing.
4. Monterey Bay once the largest sardine fishery in the world.
5. Scientists think many sardines may have died because of a change in underwater weather.

Correct any fragments above by adding the missing parts to form complete sentences. Exchange papers with a classmate and check each other's sentences.

BASIC WRITING

Answers

1. octopuses
   float, sink
2. crustaceans, mollusks
   are
3. eels
   eat
4. Octopuses
   change, squirt
5. cloud
   harms, kills

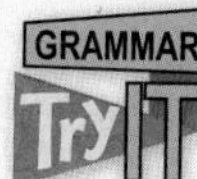

Answers

1. C
2. F: predicate
3. F: subject
4. F: predicate
5. C

Edit Your Writing Carefully

A sentence must express a complete thought. A sentence fragment does not do this even though it may look like a sentence with a capital letter and end punctuation. Reading a sentence out loud, however, can help a writer figure out whether a sentence is expressing a complete thought.

In the example below, the writer found and underlined a number of fragments. Then she turned the fragments into complete sentences by adding information to finish each thought.

Some Fragments	All Sentences
Before a newly hatched lobster looks like a real lobster. The newborn must shed its shell three times. When baby lobsters are 15 days old. They live within three feet of the surface of the ocean. Called "bugs" during this stage.	**Before a newly hatched lobster looks like a real lobster, the newborn must shed its shell three times. When baby lobsters are 15 days old, they live within three feet of the surface of the ocean. They are called "bugs" during this stage.**

Read the following paragraph and check for fragments. Then, on your own paper, tell how many fragments you found. Rewrite the paragraph, correcting each of the fragments.

Before lobsters become a favorite food of many people. The animals begin life as tiny creatures swimming near the surface of the ocean. When the baby lobsters are about a month old. They begin looking for a hiding place on the ocean's floor. After they settle into this spot or find another safe habitat. They spend their first year hiding in small tunnels. Because they have so many enemies. The young lobsters usually eat just the food that floats through their little tunnels.

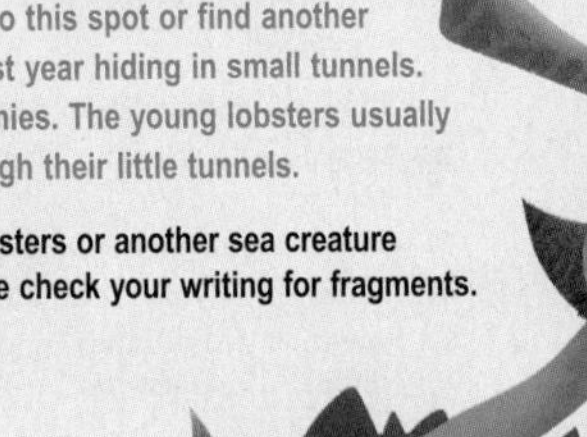

Write NOW **Write a short paragraph about lobsters or another sea creature you know about. Have a classmate check your writing for fragments.**

Move Misplaced Modifiers

A misplaced modifier can make a sentence very confusing. You can avoid this problem by making sure that modifiers are placed next to the words they modify. This is especially important when using descriptive phrases.

Misplaced Modifiers	Corrected Sentences
Looking like a balloon with fins, the predator lets the puffer fish escape. (It sounds as though the predator looks like a balloon.)	**Looking like a balloon with fins, the puffer fish escapes from the predator.** (or) **The puffer fish, looking like a balloon with fins, escapes from the predator.** (Move the word being modified closer to its modifying phrase.)
We set out to observe fish in a glass-bottom boat. (It sounds like the fish are in a glass-bottom boat.)	**We set out in a glass-bottom boat to observe fish.** (or) **To observe fish, we set out in a glass-bottom boat.**

Rewrite each of the sentences below so that the proper word is modified.

Example: Hiding in deep sea grasses, you can find the puffer fish.
You can find the puffer fish hiding in deep sea grasses.

1. Camouflaged by the seaweed, predators can't always see the fish.
2. Prized for superb flavor, many people want a puffer fish for dinner.
3. Although it is tasty, poison makes the puffer fish dangerous to eat.
4. When properly trained, puffer fish can be prepared by careful chefs.
5. Swimming in an aquarium, I saw a puffer fish and its cousin, a porcupine fish.

Using the facts below, write two sentences containing misplaced modifiers. (Hint: Separate your modifying phrase from the thing it is describing.) Then exchange sentences with a classmate and correct each other's work.

A Porcupine Fish

- normally swims around with spikes lying flat
- when threatened, spikes stick out and body inflates
- inflates by taking in tiny gulps of water
- sends a jet spray into sand, looking for mollusks
- has large teeth

BASIC WRITING

Answers

Four fragments

Although lobsters are a favorite food of many people, these animals begin life as tiny creatures swimming near the surface of the ocean. When the baby lobsters are about a month old, they begin looking for a hiding place on the ocean's floor. After they settle into this spot or find another safe habitat, they spend their first year hiding in small tunnels because they have so many enemies. The young lobsters usually eat just the food that floats through their little tunnels.

Answers

1. Predators can't always see the fish camouflaged by the seaweed.
2. Prized for superb flavor, a puffer fish is the dinner choice of many people.
3. Although it's tasty, the puffer fish contains poison that makes it dangerous to eat.
4. When properly trained, careful chefs can prepare a puffer fish.
5. Once I saw a puffer fish and its cousin, a porcupine fish, swimming in an aquarium.

Fixing Sentence Problems

Avoid Run-On Sentences

Sometimes you may accidentally write a run-on sentence by putting together two or more sentences. One type of run-on is called a *comma splice,* in which the sentences are connected with a comma only. Another type of run-on has no punctuation at all.

One way to fix run-on sentences is to add a comma and a coordinating conjunction (*and, so, or, for, but, yet,* and *nor*). Another way is to connect the two sentences with a semicolon.

Run-On Sentence	Corrected Sentences
Manta rays are similar to sharks they both have skeletons made of cartilage.	**Manta rays are similar to sharks**, for **they both have skeletons made of cartilage.**
	Manta rays are similar to sharks; **they both have skeletons made of cartilage.**

On your own paper, correct the run-on sentences below by adding a comma and a coordinating conjunction.

Example: Manta rays live in warm oceans these fish have fins that look like giant wings.

Manta rays live in warm oceans, and these fish have fins that look like giant wings.

1. These huge creatures look ferocious they are really quite gentle.
2. Mantas use their wings to "fly" through the water they look like great floating triangles.
3. Manta rays that weigh more than 3,000 pounds can leap out of the water they can also gracefully avoid divers underwater.
4. Manta rays do not have a stinging barb they do not have sharp teeth.
5. These unique fish often swim near the surface they sometimes swim in deeper lagoon water, too.

Now rewrite each run-on sentence above, correcting each with a semicolon.

Eliminate Rambling Sentences

A rambling sentence occurs when you use too many *and's* to combine your ideas. You can eliminate rambling sentences by checking for extra *and's*. Here are two ways to correct the same rambling sentence.

Rambling Sentences	Corrected Sentences
The number of North Atlantic right whales has been reduced by heavy whaling and only about 300 whales are left and efforts to increase their numbers are starting to bring results.	**The number of North Atlantic right whales has been reduced by heavy whaling; therefore, only about 300 whales are left. Efforts to increase their numbers are starting to bring results.** (Replace the first *and* with a semicolon and a conjunctive adverb to connect two related thoughts. Drop the second *and* to make two sentences.)
	The number of North Atlantic right whales has been reduced by heavy whaling. There are only about 300 whales left, although efforts to increase their numbers are starting to bring results. (Drop the first *and* to make two sentences. Combine thoughts by using a subordinating conjunction to create a subordinate clause.)

Some *and's* are needed in sentences to connect compound subjects, compound predicates, items in a list, and so on.

Correct the following rambling sentences on your own paper. Try using a subordinating conjunction where possible. (See 746.1.)

1. Right whales were prized by whalers and they were easy to hunt and the whales were almost hunted to extinction and then, 100 years ago, laws were made to protect them.
2. Female whales give birth and they nurse their babies, called calves, for 13 months, sometimes carrying them on their backs, and then the mothers keep the babies close to them for another year and a female may have a calf every three to five years.
3. The northern right whale was almost extinct and the species is now making a comeback and scientists are finding that more babies are being born each year and last year 14 whale calves were born and that was the most calves born in one year recently.

BASIC WRITING

Possible Answers

1. These huge creatures look ferocious, yet they are really quite gentle.
2. Mantas use their wings to "fly" through the water, so they look like great floating triangles.
3. Manta rays that weigh more than 3,000 pounds can leap out of the water, and they can also gracefully avoid divers underwater.
4. Manta rays do not have a stinging barb, nor do they have sharp teeth.
5. These unique fish often swim near the surface, or they sometimes swim in deeper lagoon water, too.

Possible Answers

1. Right whales were prized by whalers. Because they were easy to hunt, the whales were almost hunted to extinction. Then, 100 years ago, laws were made to protect them.
2. After female whales give birth, they nurse their babies, called calves, for 13 months, sometimes carrying them on their backs. Then the mothers keep the babies close to them for another year. A female may have a calf every three to five years.
3. Although the northern right whale was almost extinct, the species is now making a comeback. Scientists are finding that more babies are being born each year. Last year, 14 whale calves were born, the most calves born in one year recently.

What can I do to write clear sentences?

Make Subjects and Verbs Agree

Writers must be careful to make the subjects and verbs in each of their sentences agree. That means a singular subject needs a singular verb, and a plural subject needs a plural verb. (Also see 728.1.) Indefinite pronouns used as subjects can be tricky because some of them can be singular or plural. (See the chart on page 475.)

Singular or Plural Subjects

A verb must agree with its subject in number.

- If a subject is singular, the verb must be singular, too.
  A pod is a group of dolphins.
- If a subject is plural, the verb must be plural.
  Bottleneck dolphins live in pods.

Don't forget that most nouns ending in *s* or *es* are plural, and most verbs ending in *s* are singular.

- If an indefinite pronoun is singular, its verb must be singular, too.
  Nobody wants to be left behind for the dolphin tour.
- If an indefinite pronoun is plural, its verb must be plural also.
  Many like watching the playful dolphins.

GRAMMAR Try It Number your paper from 1 to 7. For each of these sentences, write the form of the verb (or verbs) that agrees with its subject.

Example: Bottlenose dolphins sometimes swims with whales.
swim

1. Like humans, both is mammals.
2. A dolphin are not a porpoise.
3. Dolphins hunts and plays together.
4. Everybody know that dolphins does not chew their food.
5. Using its tail, a dolphin often flip a fish out of the water and then eat it.
6. Dolphins fears sharks.
7. Many people swims with and feeds dolphins.

Write Now **Write one sentence using the subject "dolphins" and another using the subject "all." Make sure your subjects and verbs agree.**

Compound Subjects Connected by "And"

A compound subject connected by the word *and* usually needs a plural verb.
Our guide and our chaperones take us on a tour.

Compound Subjects Connected by "Or"

A compound subject connected by the word *or* needs a verb that agrees in number with the subject nearest to the verb.
Tour guides or the boat's captain talks about the dolphins.
(*Captain*, the subject nearer the verb, is singular, so the singular verb *talks* is used.)

GRAMMAR Try It Number your paper from 1 to 8. Write the correct verb choice for each of these sentences.

Example: Manatees and a dolphin pod *(is, are)* fun to watch.
are

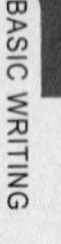

1. Large tours or small private boats *(let, lets)* people view dolphins in harbor areas.
2. A telescope and an observation deck *(offer, offers)* clear views of the marine life.
3. Passengers or a crew member *(report, reports)* interesting sights.
4. Electronic games and cell phones *(is, are)* not affected by the ship's magnetic navigation equipment.
5. Either a dolphin or manatees *(like, likes)* to swim in a boat's wake.
6. Sometimes, dark skies or rain *(spoil, spoils)* the outings.
7. My brothers and Mom *(enjoy, enjoys)* boat rides more than I do.
8. Dockside shopkeepers and restaurant owners *(wait, waits)* impatiently for the tour to be over.

Write Now **Rewrite sentence 5 above so that a singular verb is correct. Rewrite sentence 6 so that a plural verb is correct. (Do not add or change anything—except the word order.)**

BASIC WRITING

GRAMMAR Try It Answers

1. are
2. is
3. hunt, play
4. knows, do
5. flips, eats
6. fear
7. swim, feed

GRAMMAR Try It Answers

1. let
2. offer
3. reports
4. are
5. like
6. spoils
7. enjoy
8. wait

What should I do to avoid nonstandard sentences?

Avoid Double Negatives

Two negative words used together in the same sentence form a double negative *(not no, barely nothing, not never)*. Double negatives also happen if you use contractions ending in *n't* with a negative word *(can't hardly, didn't never)*. Your writing will not be accurate if you use double negatives.

Negative Words

nothing nowhere never not barely hardly nobody none no

Negative Contractions

don't can't won't shouldn't wouldn't couldn't didn't hadn't

Number your paper from 1 to 5. List the double negatives you find in the sentences below and then correctly rewrite each sentence. *Remember:* There is usually more than one way to correct a double negative.

Example: My family never has no time to go to the ocean.

never has no

My family never has any time to go to the ocean.

1. Just yesterday, Dad said, "I can't hardly find time to watch TV."
2. I wonder why we aren't going nowhere for a vacation this year.
3. Maybe it's because Mom and Dad don't barely get any time off.
4. Or maybe it's because my brother and I wouldn't hardly want to miss any baseball games.
5. I don't want nothing to keep us from taking an ocean-side vacation.

Avoid Using "Of" for "Have"

Do not use "of" in a sentence when you mean "have." When *have* is said quickly it can sound like *of.*

Incorrect: We could of gone to the beach together.

Corrected: *We could have gone to the beach together.*
We could've gone to the beach together.

Write four sentences. In two of them use double negatives. In the other two use "of" when you really mean "have." Exchange papers with a classmate, rewrite each other's sentences correctly, and then check each other's work.

Improving Your Sentence Style

There are a number of ways to add variety to your sentences and improve your writing style. Here are four of the most common ways.

1. **Combine short sentences.**
2. **Use different types of sentences.**
3. **Expand sentences by adding words and phrases.**
4. **Model sentences of other writers.**

What happens when too many sentences in a paragraph are the same length or follow the same pattern? Read the following paragraph to find out.

Little Variety

Eelgrass is a flowering saltwater plant. It grows along the coasts of the Atlantic, Pacific, and Indian Oceans. Eelgrass helps the environment in two ways. It uses photosynthesis and puts oxygen into our water and air. Many fish and marine animals live at least part of their lives in eelgrass. Eelgrass is home to crustaceans, sea stars, clams, and young salmon.

Using different types of sentences would keep this paragraph from sounding choppy. Read the following version, which has a better variety of sentences.

Good Variety

Eelgrass, a flowering saltwater plant, grows along the coasts of the Atlantic, Pacific, and Indian Oceans. Eelgrass helps the environment in two ways. First, through photosynthesis, eelgrass puts oxygen into our water and air. Second, eelgrass is "home" to many fish and marine animals. Crustaceans, sea stars, clams, and young salmon live at least part of their lives in eelgrass.

Read the paragraph below. Then, on your own paper, rewrite the paragraph by creating more sentence variety.

Eelgrass along the Atlantic coast was almost destroyed during the hot weather in 1930–1931. The water temperature rose. The eelgrass died out. Fish and animals that lived in the eelgrass died. Then the fishing industry ran into trouble. There were fewer fish. This made a bad economy worse. It took nearly 20 years for the eelgrass to grow back. Today, boat engines destroy eelgrass. Coastal construction and oil spills also kill eelgrass. People need to protect this valuable plant.

Possible Answers

1. can't hardly
   Just yesterday, Dad said, "I can hardly find time to watch TV."
2. aren't going nowhere
   I wonder why we aren't going anywhere for a vacation this year.
3. don't barely
   Maybe it's because Mom and Dad barely get any time off.
4. wouldn't hardly
   Or maybe it's because my brother and I wouldn't want to miss any baseball games.
5. don't want nothing
   I don't want anything to keep us from taking an ocean-side vacation.

Possible Answers

Answers will vary.

Eelgrass was almost destroyed along the Atlantic coast during the hot weather in 1930–1931. When the water temperature rose, the eel grass and the fish and animals that lived in it died out. Because there were fewer fish, the fishing industry ran into trouble, making a bad economy worse. It took nearly 20 years for the eelgrass to grow back. Today, boat engines, coastal construction, and oil spills destroy eelgrass. People need to protect this valuable plant.

How can I make my sentences flow more smoothly?

Writers often combine sentences to help their writing flow more smoothly. Too many short sentences can make writing sound choppy. Combining some of the sentences will add variety to your writing and improve your overall writing style.

Combine with Phrases

Combining Using Two or More Phrases

Short Sentences	*Combined Sentences*
Seals don't have hands. Seals have short front flippers.	**Seals have short front flippers** instead of hands.

Combining Using an Appositive Phrase

Elephant seals sometimes weigh more than 5,000 pounds. Elephant seals are the largest seal species.	**Elephant seals,** the largest seal species, **sometimes weigh more than 5,000 pounds.**

Combining Using a Prepositional Phrase

Seals are able to stay submerged at great depths. Seals can do this for long periods of time.	For long periods of time, **seals are able to stay submerged at great depths**

Combine each of the following sets of sentences by using the method given in parentheses.

1. Seals can lift their bodies off the ground. Seals do this with their flippers. *(prepositional phrase)*
2. Sea lions can swim at the top speed of 25 mph. Sea lions are the fastest seals. *(appositive phrase)*
3. Antarctic seals eat krill. These are tiny shrimp-like creatures. *(appositive phrase)*
4. Baby harp seals are born with white fur. The white fur is a natural camouflage. *(appositive phrase)*
5. The stout-bodied walrus is a unique-looking mammal. It has wrinkled skin and long tusks. *(prepositional phrase)*

Write a pair of sentences for a classmate to combine. Model your sentences after one of the sentence pairs above.

Combine with a Series of Words

You can combine sentences using a series of words, phrases, or clauses.

Combining with a Series

Short Sentences	*Combined Using a Series of Words*
Moray eels eat shrimp and small fish. They also eat crabs and octopuses.	**Moray eels eat** shrimp, small fish, crabs, **and** octopuses**.**
Short Sentences	*Combined Using a Series of Phrases*
Eels make good aquarium pets if they have plenty of room to swim. They also need a place to hide. They need plenty of food to eat, too.	**Eels make good aquarium pets if they have** plenty of room to swim, a place to hide, **and** plenty of food to eat**.**

The items in any series must be alike (or parallel). For example, if the first item is a phrase, all the items must be phrases. The same is true for series containing words or clauses. (See 582.1.)

Using a series of parallel words or phrases, combine each of the following groups of sentences. (You may change some words to make the sentences work.)

Example: Moray eels are related to American eels and conger eels. Worm eels and wolf eels are also related to moray eels.
American, conger, worm, and wolf eels are all related to moray eels.

1. Eels have long, thin bodies. They have snake-like heads. They have large mouths.
2. Some moray eels can weigh up to 100 pounds. Some can grow to 10 feet long. They can look like prehistoric monsters.
3. Moray eels live in caves. They live in coral reefs. Some also live in shallow waters.
4. Would you like to keep an eel for a pet? Would you like to see an eel in the wild? Would you like to eat "eel surprise" for dinner?

Write one sentence about another animal in which you use three or more words in a series. Then write another sentence about the same or a different animal in which you use three or more phrases in a series.

BASIC WRITING

Answers

1. Seals can lift their bodies off the ground with their flippers.
2. Sea lions, the fastest seals, can swim at the top speed of 25 mph.
3. Antarctic seals eat krill, tiny shrimp-like creatures.
4. Baby harp seals are born with white fur, a natural camouflage.
5. The stout-bodied walrus is a unique-looking mammal with its wrinkled skin and long tusks.

Answers

1. Eels have long, thin bodies, snake-like heads, and large mouths.
2. Some moray eels can weigh up to 100 pounds, grow to 10 feet long, and look like prehistoric monsters.
3. Moray eels live in caves, in coral reefs, and in shallow waters.
4. Would you like to keep an eel for a pet, see an eel in the wild, or eat "eel surprise" for dinner?

Combine with Relative Pronouns

You can combine two short sentences by using a relative pronoun to make a complex sentence. A complex sentence contains one independent, or main, clause and one dependent clause. (See 698.2–698.3 for more information.)

Relative pronouns include words such as *who, which, that, whose, whom,* and so on.

Combining with Relative Pronouns

Two Short Sentences	*Combined Using a Relative Pronoun*
The Bay of Fundy has the world's highest tides. The bay is in Nova Scotia.	**The Bay of Fundy, which is in Nova Scotia, has the world's highest tides.** or **The Bay of Fundy, which has the world's highest tides, is in Nova Scotia.**

Combine each set of sentences below by using the relative pronoun in parentheses. (A dependent clause beginning with the relative pronoun "which" is always set off by commas.)

Example: At high tide, the water rises as much as 53 feet. This is as high as a four-story building. *(which)*

At high tide, the water rises as much as 53 feet, which is as high as a four-story building.

1. Many people love exploring tidal pools. These people enjoy viewing sea creatures close-up. *(who)*
2. Tide-pool creatures can survive the varying temperatures of water and air. These temperatures may be as hot as 86 degrees Fahrenheit in summer or –22 degrees Fahrenheit in winter. *(which)*
3. Many animals and plants thrive in tidal zones. These animals and plants need constant moisture. *(that)*
4. At around mid-tide, you can hear what is called the "voice of the moon." This "voice" is actually the roar of the tidal currents. *(which)*

Write freely for 5 minutes about a water-related experience. Afterward, underline any sentences containing relative pronouns. Also find two shorter sentences in your writing that you can combine using a relative pronoun.

What can I do to add variety to my writing?

Writers use different types of sentences to add variety to their writing and make it sound interesting. The three common types of sentences are **simple**, **compound**, and **complex**. By learning to write these three types of sentences effectively, you can create sentence variety in your writing.

Write Simple Sentences

A **simple sentence** is one independent clause. (An independent clause is a group of words that can stand alone as one sentence.) A simple sentence may contain a single or compound subject and a single or compound predicate.

Simple Sentence = One Independent Clause

Single Subject with a Single Predicate

Icebergs are a hazard to shipping.

Single Subject with a Compound Predicate

Usually ships avoid icebergs but sometimes collide with one.

Compound Subject with a Single Predicate

"Growlers" and "bergy bits" are two names for small Arctic icebergs.

Write the paragraph below on your own paper. In each sentence, underline the simple subject once and the simple predicate twice. (*Remember:* Watch for compound subjects and verbs.)

Icebergs come from glaciers and float in the ocean. Antarctic icebergs are the largest type of iceberg. Antarctic icebergs and Arctic icebergs have only a small portion showing above the water. Most of an iceberg remains below the water. Tall castle bergs and pinnacle icebergs are found in the Arctic. Huge tabular icebergs with vertical sides and flat tops form in the Antarctic.

Write three simple sentences about something in nature that interests you. Give the first sentence a single subject and predicate, the second one a compound subject, and the third one a compound predicate.

BASIC WRITING

Answers

1. Many people who enjoy viewing sea creatures close-up love exploring tidal pools.
2. Tide-pool creatures can survive the varying temperatures of water and air, which may be as hot as 86 degrees Fahrenheit in summer or -22 degrees Fahrenheit in winter.
3. Many animals and plants that need constant moisture thrive in tidal zones.
4. At around mid-tide, you can hear what is called the "voice of the moon," which is actually the roar of the tidal currents.

Answers

Icebergs come from glaciers and float in the ocean. Antarctic icebergs are the largest type of iceberg. Antarctic icebergs and Arctic icebergs have only a small portion showing above the water. Most of an iceberg remains below the water. Tall castle bergs and pinnacle icebergs are found in the Arctic. Huge tabular icebergs with vertical sides and flat tops form in the Antarctic.

Create Compound Sentences

A **compound sentence** is made up of two or more simple sentences (independent clauses) joined by a comma and a coordinating conjunction (*and, for, but, or, so, nor,* and *yet*) or by a semicolon.

Compound Sentence = Two Independent Clauses

Pacific manta rays are the largest in the ray family, and some of them have wingspans of 20 feet. (A comma and the conjunction *and* join the two independent clauses.)

Mobilla rays are smaller than the Pacific rays; Mobilla rays seem to enjoy swimming with and being touched by humans. (Here, the two independent clauses are joined by a semicolon.)

GRAMMAR Try It On your own paper, join the following sets of independent clauses (simple sentences) using either a semicolon or a comma and a coordinating conjunction.

Example: Stingrays are known as "birds" of the sea. Manta rays are called the "gigantic birds" of the sea.

Stingrays are known as "birds" of the sea, but manta rays are called the "gigantic birds" of the sea.

1. Manta rays sometimes swim in tropical waters close to shore. They really prefer to roam in the open sea.
2. A manta ray is one of the gentlest creatures in the sea. For many years, the manta ray was known as a "devil fish."
3. Growths on either side of the manta's head look like horns. These "horns" help the ray to herd plankton into its mouth.
4. Female rays give birth to one or two babies at a time. Each "pup" may weigh as much as 25 pounds.
5. Baby manta rays learn to avoid predators. The babies spend much of their time on the sea floor, flapping their fins to throw sand over their bodies.

Write Now **Write two compound sentences explaining how you would feel about swimming with a giant manta ray. Make sure to punctuate your sentences correctly.**

Develop Complex Sentences

When you join a dependent clause to an independent clause, you form a **complex sentence**. Complex sentences may contain a relative pronoun such as *that, which,* and *who.* (See page 710 for more information.) They may also contain a subordinating conjunction such as *after, although, because, before, until, when,* and *while.* (See page 744 for more subordinating conjunctions.)

Complex Sentence =

A Dependent Clause	+	An Independent Clause
Because the *Atlantis* is equipped for research,		it carries a submersible called *Alvin*.
An Independent Clause	+	**A Dependent Clause**
Alvin is a white and orange sub		that is used to explore underwater mountains.

GRAMMAR Try It Number your paper from 1 to 5. Then write the dependent clause in each of the following complex sentences.

Example: Because scientists were exploring undersea mountains south of Kodiak Island in Alaska, *National Geographic Today* sent a reporter along on the expedition.

Because scientists were exploring undersea mountains south of Kodiak Island in Alaska

1. Chad Cohen, a reporter, joined the crew researching a world that contains bizarre spider crabs, exotic corals, and squiggly rockfish.
2. Alvin is launched by a giant A-frame, which first lifts the sub off of *Atlantis'* deck and then sets the sub into the water.
3. When the sub is cut loose, it falls below the ocean's surface and starts to descend into the darkness.
4. As soon as the sub reaches the ocean floor, *Alvin's* lights reveal millions of tiny jellyfish and bacteria glowing like stars.
5. *Alvin* maneuvers around on the lunar-like seafloor and gathers crabs and coral until the engine runs out of power and has to resurface.

Write Now **Write a short paragraph about some undersea exploring that you would like to do. Underline any complex sentences that you used. Also try to find two shorter sentences that you could combine into a complex sentence.**

BASIC WRITING

GRAMMAR Try It Answers

1. Manta rays sometimes swim in tropical waters close to shore, but they really prefer to roam in the open sea.
2. A manta ray is one of the gentlest creatures in the sea, yet for many years it was known as a "devil fish."
3. Growths on either side of the manta's head look like horns; these "horns" help the ray to herd plankton into its mouth.
4. Female rays give birth to one or two babies at a time, and each "pup" may weigh as much as 25 pounds.
5. Baby manta rays learn to avoid predators; they spend much of their time on the sea floor, flapping their fins to throw sand over their bodies.

GRAMMAR Try It Answers

1. that contains bizarre spider crabs, exotic corals, and squiggly rockfish
2. which first lifts the sub off of *Atlantis'* deck and then sets the sub into the water
3. When the sub is cut loose
4. As soon as the sub reaches the ocean floor
5. until the engine runs out of power and has to resurface

Use Questions and Commands

Writers use a variety of sentences to make statements, ask questions, give commands, or show strong emotion. See the chart below.

Kinds of Sentences

Declarative .	Makes a statement about a person, a place, a thing, or an idea	**An adult loggerhead sea turtle weighs 200 to 350 pounds.**	This is the most common kind of sentence.
Interrogative ?	Asks a question	**Do you know where they nest?**	A question gets the reader's attention.
Imperative .	Gives a command	**Find out what a loggerhead looks like.**	Commands often appear in dialogue or directions.
Exclamatory !	Shows strong emotion or feeling	**Wow, its head is 10 inches wide!**	Use these sentences for occasional emphasis.

On a piece of paper, write the numbers 1 to 5. Identify each of the sentences below by writing "D" for declarative, "INT" for interrogative, "IMP" for imperative, or "EX" for exclamatory.

1. Can you imagine not living to be 12 years old?
2. Only one in ten thousand loggerhead sea turtles lives that long!
3. Every year, on certain beaches from the eastern coast of the United States through Central and South America, female loggerheads lay their eggs.
4. Using their rear flippers, the turtles dig egg chambers that are about 20 inches deep.
5. Count the number of threats they have to face: humans, raccoons, skunks, shorebirds, sharks, fishing nets, and motorboats.

Write four sentences—one of each kind—about a sea creature you find interesting.

What can I do to add details to my sentences?

Expand with Prepositional Phrases

Writers use prepositional phrases to add details and information to their sentences. The chart below shows how this is done. Prepositional phrases function as adjectives or adverbs. *Remember:* A prepositional phrase includes a preposition, the object of a preposition, and the modifiers of the object. (See page **742** for a list of prepositions.)

Prepositional Phrase	Use in a Sentence
Some fish have beaklike mouths of fused teeth.	The phrase acts as an **adjective** to describe the noun *mouths.*
Parrot fish live on coral reefs.	The phrase acts as an **adverb** to modify the verb *live.*

- Prepositional phrases used as adjectives answer the questions *How many? Which one? What kind?*
- Prepositional phrases used as adverbs answer the questions *When? How? How often? How long? Where? How much?*

Write the prepositional phrases that you find in the following sentences. (There are 10 phrases in sentences 1 through 5.)

Example: Parrot fish can be a variety of colors and patterns.
of colors and patterns

1. These fish swim between coral formations.
2. Their beaklike teeth scrape algae-covered coral from the reef.
3. After swallowing pieces of algae-covered coral, the parrot fish spits out the bits of coral.
4. At night, parrot fish sleep along the bottom of the reef.
5. Some types of parrot fish bury themselves in the sand until morning.

Use one or two prepositional phrases to add information to each of the sentences below.

1. City aquariums have huge tanks of water.
2. One of my favorite tanks contains freshwater fish.
3. A new exhibit presents tropical fish.

BASIC WRITING

Answers

1. INT
2. EX
3. D
4. D
5. IMP

Answers

1. between coral formations
2. from the reef
3. of algae-covered coral, of coral
4. At night, along the bottom, of the reef
5. of parrot fish, in the sand, until morning

Expand with Participial Phrases

Writers sometimes make their sentences more interesting by adding participial phrases. A participial phrase includes a participle and its modifiers. (A participle is a verb form usually ending in *ed* or *ing.*) A participial phrase serves as an adjective in a sentence.

Participial Phrases

Sea horses have a body encased in hard armor.
(This participial phrase modifies the noun *body.*)

Drifting from one coral to another, **sea horses are beautiful to watch.**
(The participial phrase modifies the noun *sea horses.*)

Write the participial phrase in each of the following sentences. Also identify the noun that it modifies.

Example: Adapting their color to their surroundings, some sea horses depend on camouflage for protection.
adapting their color to their surroundings, sea horses

1. Reaching the length of 10 inches, sea horses swim slowly among seaweed.
2. Depending on the size of its brooding pouch, a sea horse hatches between 10 and 100 eggs.
3. The bottom of a large aquarium or reef tank covered in a layer of sand is a good home for sea horses.
4. A sea horse likes certain types of structures, including colorful coral branches.
5. An adult sea horse maintained in good health may live more than three years.

Write a brief paragraph about the sand dollar or another interesting sea creature of your own choosing. Include at least two participial phrases in your writing.

A Sand Dollar

- missing its cover of little spines when washed up on a beach
- related to sea lilies and starfish
- pores, or little holes, used to move seawater for movement
- lives on top or just beneath the surface of sandy or muddy areas
- eats organic particles
- no real predators
- when alive, often found with other sand dollars

How can I make my sentences more interesting?

Model Sentences

You can learn a great deal about writing by studying the sentences of other writers. When you come across sentences that you like, practice writing some of your own that use the same pattern. This process is called *modeling.*

Professional Models	Student Models
I walked along the sandy beach, inhaling the smell of salty surf and dried seaweed.	I ate at the carnival, devouring the huge sour pickles and salty French fries.
Manatees have blimpy bodies, giant beaver tails, and rubbery faces bristling with whiskers. —*Muse*	My tabby cat has a fat tummy, huge tiger paws, and soft fur marked by dark orange stripes.

Guidelines for Modeling

- Find a sentence or a short passage that you like and write it down.
- Think of a topic for your practice writing.
- Follow the pattern of the sentence or passage as you write about your own subject. (You do not have to follow the model exactly.)
- Build each sentence one part at a time and check your work when you are finished. (Take your time.)
- Review your work and change any parts that seem confusing or unclear.
- Share your new sentences with your classmates.
- Find other sentences to model and keep practicing.

On your own paper, model the following sentences. Remember: You do not have to follow the model sentence exactly.

1. The sun was dropping into the dark ocean, but I kept wandering down the beach.
2. Ocean waves pounded the beach, washing away Tegan's sand castle.
3. I wanted to dive into the water, swim out to the nearest island, and hide away for a day or two.

Answers

1. reaching the length of 10 inches, sea horses
2. Depending on the size of its brooding pouch, sea horse
3. covered in a layer of sand, bottom
4. including colorful coral branches, structures
5. maintained in good health, sea horse

Develop a Sentence Style

Modeling sentences can help you make your writing more exciting, lively, and appealing. The following writing techniques will also help you improve your style. (Also see page 42.)

Varying Sentence Beginnings

To add variety to the common subject-verb pattern, try beginning a sentence with a phrase or a dependent clause.

In his hand he held a whip.

—*Black Stallion* by Walter Farley

As winter drew on, Mollie became more and more troublesome.

—*Animal Farm* by George Orwell

Moving Adjectives

Usually, you write adjectives before the nouns they modify. You can also emphasize adjectives by placing them after the nouns.

I would come in from a day of progging for crab, sweating and filthy.

—*Jacob Have I Loved* by Katherine Paterson

Repeating a Word

You can repeat a word to emphasize a particular idea or feeling.

Little by little, the wind died down.

—*The Count of Monte Cristo* by Alexandre Dumas

Creating a Balanced Sentence

You can write a sentence that uses parallel words, phrases, or clauses for emphasis.

The wind in our ears drove us crazy and pushed us on.

—*Rogues to Riches* by Rob King

Study the sample sentences above. Then write your own sentences that follow each sample pattern. Share your sentences with your classmates.

Constructing Strong Paragraphs

One thing that can help you gain control of your writing is learning to write a good paragraph. Think of the paragraph as an important building block for all of your writing. If you can create strong, well-organized paragraphs, you can also create effective essays, book reviews, and reports.

A paragraph is made up of a group of sentences focused on one topic. Each sentence should add something to the overall picture. A paragraph can be developed to explain a process, share an opinion, describe something, or tell a story.

What's Ahead

You will learn about . . .

- **the parts of a paragraph.**
- **types of paragraphs.**
- **writing effective paragraphs.**
- **adding details to paragraphs.**
- **gathering details.**
- **organizing your details.**
- **refining your details.**
- **turning paragraphs into essays.**
- **using a checklist.**

The Parts of a Paragraph

Most paragraphs have three main parts: a topic sentence, a body, and a closing sentence. Paragraphs usually begin with a **topic sentence** that tells what the paragraph is about. The sentences in the **body** share details about the topic, and the **closing sentence** brings the paragraph to a close.

Adventure Sports

Topic Sentence: Many outdoor enthusiasts are looking for more adventure in their sports. Why else would a sane person jump out of an airplane, do some acrobatic tricks on a skyboard, and then parachute to the ground? People seek adventure by water, too. They navigate the same rivers and shoot the same rapids that early Native Americans, fur traders, and explorers did. They travel by canoe, kayak, or raft. On land, adventurers backpack and camp in the wilderness, in areas where they might meet bear, moose, and mountain lions. After climbing mountains, some outdoor enthusiasts ski, snowboard, or even bike down to the bottom. Closing Sentence: Today, an adventure sport is out there for just about anyone, and more sports are being invented all the time.

Body

Respond to the reading. How many types of adventure sports are mentioned? What do they all have in common?

A Closer Look at the Parts

The Topic Sentence

The topic sentence tells the reader what a paragraph is going to be about. A good topic sentence (1) names the topic and (2) states a specific detail or a feeling about it. Here is a simple formula for writing a topic sentence.

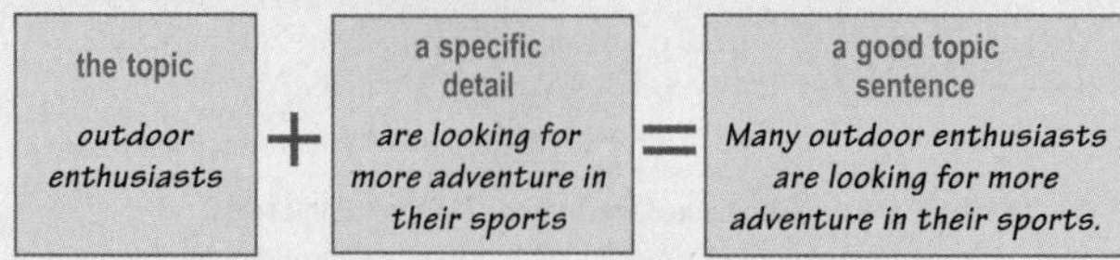

The topic sentence is usually the first sentence in a paragraph, although sometimes it comes later. It guides the direction of the sentences in the rest of the paragraph.

Many outdoor enthusiasts are looking for more adventure in their sports.

The Body

The sentences in the body of the paragraph include the details needed to understand the topic.

- **Use specific details to make your paragraph interesting.** The specific details below are shown in red.

  People seek adventure by water, too. They navigate the same rivers and shoot the same rapids that early Native Americans, fur traders, and explorers did.

- **Organize your sentences in the best possible order.** Five common ways to organize sentences are chronological (time) order, order of location, order of importance, comparison, and logical order. (See page 551.)

The Closing Sentence

The closing sentence comes after all the details in the body. It will often restate the topic, give the reader something to think about, or provide a transition into a following paragraph.

Today, an adventure sport is out there for just about anyone, and more sports are being invented all the time.

Answers

Respond to the reading.

There are 10 types of adventure sports mentioned. (skyboarding, canoeing, kayaking, rafting, backpacking, camping, mountain climbing, skiing, snowboarding, mountain biking)

They are all a type of adventure.

Types of Paragraphs

There are four basic types of paragraphs: *narrative, descriptive, expository,* and *persuasive.* Each type requires a different way of thinking and planning.

Write Narrative Paragraphs

In a **narrative paragraph,** you share a personal story or an important experience with the reader. The details in a narrative paragraph should answer the 5 W's (*who? what? when? where?* and *why?*). A narrative is often organized according to time (what happened *first, next, then, finally*).

Topic Sentence

Body

Closing Sentence

My Camping Adventure

Camping in the wilderness can be a real adventure, especially if you have a close encounter with a bear. One night while camping, my mom, dad, and younger sister were sound asleep in the tent, but I was wide-awake. Suddenly, I heard snorting noises coming from our campsite. I crept to the door and peered out cautiously. By the light of the moon, I saw a big brown bear munching on a bag of our marshmallows. I wanted to shout a warning, but I was so scared that I couldn't get out one sound. As I crawled across the tent to wake my dad, I must have bumped my sister. She sat up and screamed. Her scream startled me, and I yelled, "It's a bear!" Our shouts must have scared the bear because when we opened the tent, there was no bear. My family said I must have been dreaming about a bear, but they couldn't explain how that bag of marshmallows disappeared.

Respond to the reading. Find the key word repeated in the topic sentence and the closing sentence. Does this paragraph answer the 5 W's?

Write your own paragraph. Write a paragraph that tells about a memorable experience you've had. Be sure to include the 5 W's.

Develop Descriptive Paragraphs

When you write a **descriptive paragraph,** you give a detailed picture of a person, a place, an object, or an event. Descriptive paragraphs include many sensory details (sight, sound, smell, taste, touch).

Topic Sentence

Body

Closing Sentence

Rainbow Rock

Rainbow Rock, a huge man-made wall, helps people learn rock-climbing techniques. Rainbow Rock rises 30 feet above the ground and is covered with purple, green, and red climbing paths. Each path contains a variety of odd-shaped footholds, rough outcroppings, and challenging overhangs. The purple path offers a low-key climbing experience that just about anybody can scratch and scramble up. The green path is more advanced and ends with a very tricky, smooth overhang right at the top. The difficult red path has tiny, slippery toeholds that are only about one inch in diameter. It almost takes a mountain goat to maneuver on this path. If someone missteps and falls, a harness snaps into action and catches the climber. He or she is left groaning and swinging in midair. Rainbow Rock may be just an artificial training ground, but it provides a real test of a rock climber's balance, strength, and courage.

Respond to the reading. Which of the five senses are covered in the paragraph? Which two or three details are especially descriptive?

Write your own paragraph. Write a paragraph that describes a place. Use lots of sights, sounds, and other sensory details in your description.

BASIC WRITING

Answers

Respond to the reading.

Bear

Yes:
Who: narrator and family
What: saw a bear
Where: in the wilderness
When: at night
Why: the bear wanted marshmallows

Answers

Respond to the reading.

sights: colors of climbing paths, odd-shaped footholds, swinging in midair

sounds: harness snaps, groaning

touch: rough outcroppings, smooth overhang, slippery toeholds

Construct Expository Paragraphs

In an **expository paragraph**, you share information. You can explain a subject, give directions, or show how to do something. Transition words like *first, next, then,* and *finally* are often used in expository writing.

Topic Sentence

Body

Closing Sentence

Snowboarding

Today, snowboarding is one of the most popular and exciting winter sports in America. While people have been skiing and ice-skating for centuries, snowboarding has been around for only about 40 years. In 1998, snowboarding became an Olympic sport in Nagano, Japan. By the year 2000, 7.2 million snowboarders, also known as "shredders," were hitting the slopes. Now, both children and adults seem to love snowboarding. Freestyle snowboarders do all sorts of jumps and tricks. These people use a soft boot and a fairly short board. On the other hand, Alpine snowboarders focus on carving turns down the slopes and on racing. Their boots are hard, and their boards are longer and narrower. Snowboarding will probably continue to take the winter sports scene by storm.

Respond to the reading. List the transitions used between sentences in the paragraph above. (See pages 572–573 for a list of transitions.)

Write an expository paragraph. Write a paragraph that explains a sport that you know very well. Be sure to use transitions to connect your ideas.

Build Persuasive Paragraphs

In a **persuasive paragraph**, you share your opinion (or strong feeling) about a topic. To be persuasive, you must include plenty of reasons, facts, and details to support your opinion. Persuasive writing is usually organized by order of importance or by logical order (as in the paragraph below).

Topic Sentence

Body

Closing Sentence

Face the High Ropes Course Challenge

The high ropes course is waiting to help young people build confidence and group cooperation. It's also a lot of fun. Many courses, indoor and outdoor, are available in camps, clubs, and schools across America. Some may think that climbing the high ropes is dangerous, but it isn't. Safety ropes and harnesses are carefully managed by course experts and members of each group to give lots of support. When someone attempts to cross a suspended log or move by rope across an expanse that seems scary, teammates will encourage the climber. Even if someone cannot complete the course, he or she will feel supported and know the accomplishment of having faced the challenge. Why not join a group this summer and experience the true team spirit and the confidence that a high ropes course offers?

Respond to the reading. What is the writer's opinion in the paragraph? Name reasons that support her opinion. When is the most important reason given?

Write an opinion paragraph. Write an opinion about an outdoor activity. Include at least three strong reasons that support your opinion.

Answers

Respond to the reading.

In 1998 . . .
By the year 2000 . . .
Now, both . . .
On the other hand . . .

Answers

Respond to the reading.

A high ropes course builds confidence, group cooperation, and is a lot of fun.

1. Safety ropes and harnesses are carefully managed by course experts and members of your group to give you lots of support.
2. Your teammates will encourage you.
3. It makes you feel great when you can encourage someone else to succeed.
4. Even if you cannot complete the course, you'll know the accomplishment of having faced the challenge.

The most important reason is given last.

Writing Effective Paragraphs

Use the following general guidelines whenever you write paragraphs.

Prewriting Selecting a Topic and Details

- Select a specific topic.
- Collect facts, examples, and details about your topic.
- Write a topic sentence that states what your paragraph is going to be about. (See page 525 for help.)
- Decide on the best way to arrange your details.

Writing Creating the First Draft

- Start your paragraph with the topic sentence.
- Write sentences in the body that support your topic. Use the details you collected as a guide.
- Connect your ideas and sentences with transitions.
- End with a sentence that restates your topic, leaves the reader with a final thought, or (in an essay) leads into the next paragraph.

Revising Improving Your Writing

- Add information if you need to say more about your topic.
- Move sentences that aren't in the correct order.
- Delete sentences that do not support the topic.
- Rewrite any sentences that are not clear.

Editing Checking for Conventions

- Check the revised version of your writing for capitalization, punctuation, grammar, and spelling errors.
- Then write a neat final copy and proofread it.

When you write a paragraph, remember that readers want . . .
- original ideas. *(They want to learn something new and interesting.)*
- personality. *(They want to hear the writer's voice.)*

How can I find interesting details?

Every paragraph needs good supporting details. Here are several types of details you can use in expository and persuasive paragraphs: facts, explanations, definitions, reasons, examples, and comparisons. You might get these details from personal knowledge and memories or from other sources of information.

Use Personal Details

For narrative and descriptive writing, personal details can add interest. Personal details may include sensory, memory, and reflective details.

- **Sensory details** are things that you see, hear, smell, taste, and touch. (These details are important in descriptive paragraphs.)
  He or she is left groaning and swinging in midair.
- **Memory details** are things you remember from experience. (These details are important in narrative paragraphs.)
  Her scream startled me, and I yelled, "It's a bear!"
- **Reflective details** are things you think about or hope for. (These details are often used in narrative and descriptive paragraphs.)
  Rainbow Rock may be just an artificial training ground, but it provides a real test of a rock climber's balance, strength, and courage.

Use Other Sources of Details

To collect details from other sources, use the following tips.

1. **Talk with someone you know.** Parents, neighbors, friends, or teachers may know a lot about your topic.
2. **Write for information.** If you think a museum, a business, or a government office has information you need, send for it.
3. **Read about your topic.** Gather details from books, magazines, and newspapers.
4. **Use the Internet.** The quickest source of information is the Internet. Remember to check Internet sources carefully for reliability. (See page 376.)

What can I do to make my final copy look better?

Add Graphics to Your Writing

You can add information and interest to essays and reports by using diagrams, tables, and graphs.

Diagrams are drawings that show the parts of something.

Picture diagrams show how something is put together. A diagram may leave out some parts to show only the parts you need to learn.

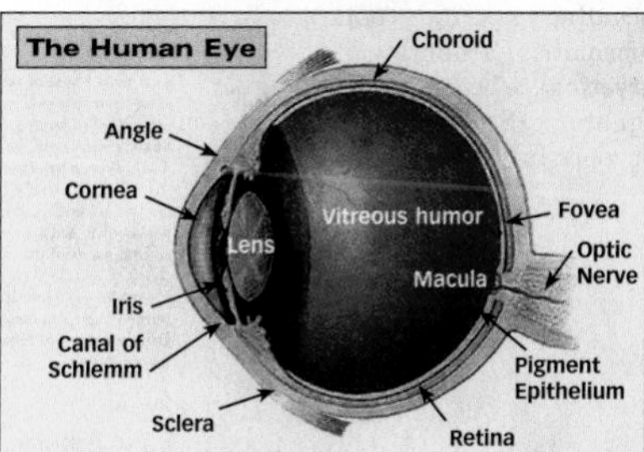

Line diagrams show something you can't really see. Instead of objects, line diagrams show ideas and relationships. This diagram shows how the Germanic languages are related to one another.

Germanic Languages
- West Germanic
  - Dutch
    - Afrikaans
  - English
  - German
- North Germanic
  - Danish
  - Norwegian
  - Icelandic
  - Swedish

Tables are another form of diagram. Tables have two parts: rows and columns. Rows go across and show one kind of information or data. Columns go up and down and show a different kind of data.

To read a table, find where a row and a column meet. In the table below, to compare the size of Canada and the United States, find where the first row meets the first and third columns. Canada is slightly larger than the United States.

Comparing Countries

	Canada	Mexico	United States
Size (Sq. Miles)	3.85 million	759,000	3.8 million
Type of Government	Parliamentary	Republic	Republic
Voting Age	18	18	18
Literacy	99%	87%	98%

Graphs are pictures of information. **Bar graphs** show how things compare to one another. The bars on a bar graph may be vertical or horizontal. (*Vertical* means "up and down." *Horizontal* means "from side to side.") Sometimes the bars on graphs are called *columns.* The part that shows numbers is called the *scale.*

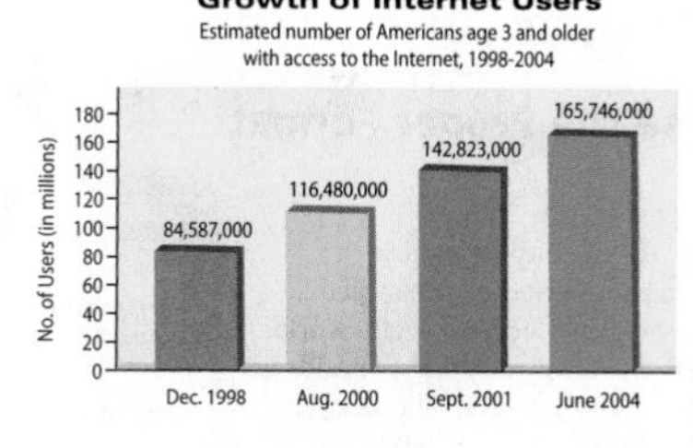

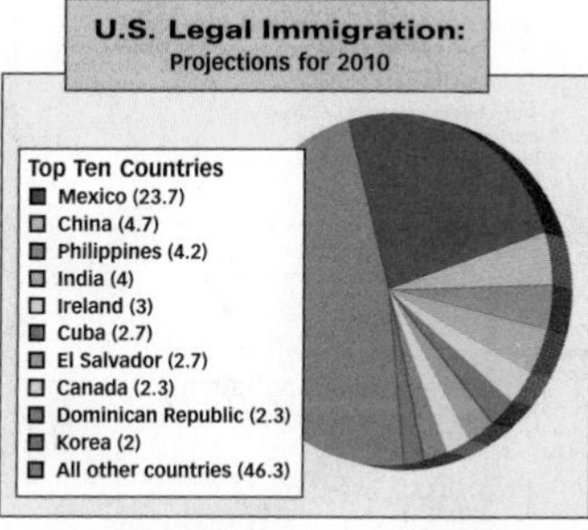

Pie graphs show how all the parts of something add up to make the whole. A pie graph often shows percentages. (A percentage is the part of a whole stated in hundredths: 35% = 35/100.) It's called a pie graph because it is usually in the shape of a pie or circle.

A pie graph begins with the largest segment at the top and moves clockwise around the circle by size. (Notice the example at the left.)

Line graphs show how something changes as time goes by. A line graph always begins with an L-shaped grid. One axis of the grid shows passing time; the other axis shows numbers.

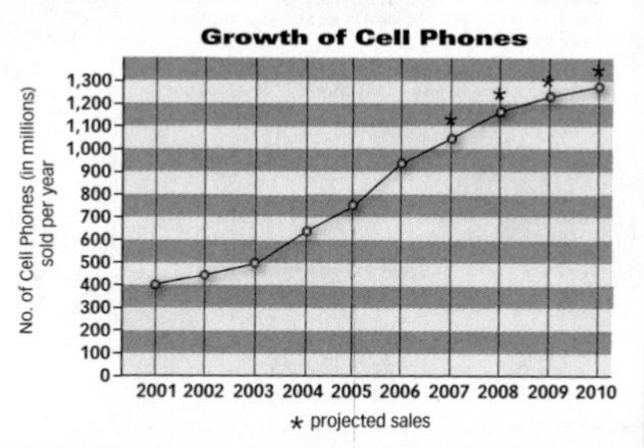

How should I set up my practical writing?

Use the Proper Format

E-Mail Messages

E-mail allows quick communication between people across town or across the world. The heading includes the address and a subject line. The body should be set up in letter format.

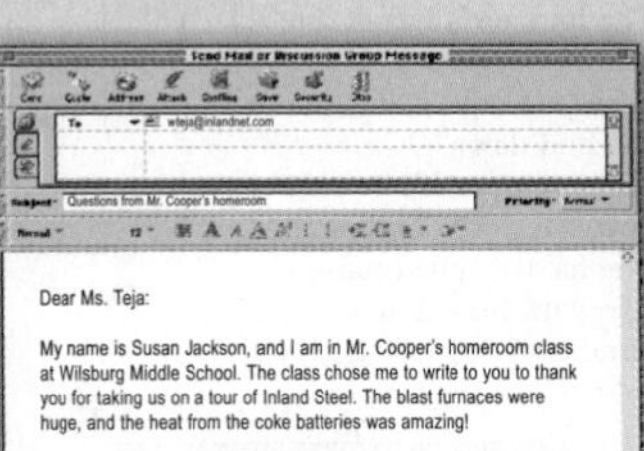

Dear Ms. Teja:

My name is Susan Jackson, and I am in Mr. Cooper's homeroom class at Wilsburg Middle School. The class chose me to write to you to thank you for taking us on a tour of Inland Steel. The blast furnaces were huge, and the heat from the coke batteries was amazing!

In our class discussion, we came up with three more questions for you. We would really appreciate it if you could take a moment to answer them.

1. What is the difference between coal and coke?
2. How does annealing change steel?
3. You showed us how the slag is removed, but is there any use for slag?

Thanks so much for taking us on the tour! We look forward to hearing

Jackson
on@wilsburgmiddleschool.edu

Traction and Four-Wheel Drive

Description: I'd like to test how well a motorized model truck climbs surfaces made of different materials and at different angles. I will create graphs to show how far and how fast the truck climbs in each situation.

Materials: I will use a radio-controlled four-wheel drive model truck, a plank, a protractor, a stopwatch, graph paper, and colored pencils. The different surface materials will include the following: water, aluminum foil, sandpaper, and loose sand.

Schedule: By March 2, I will have the materials collected and assembled. By March 9, I will have performed all my tests for different materials at different angles. By March 16, the total display will be ready for the science fair.

Procedure:
- For each surface, the plank will be pitched at 10°, 20°, 30°, 40°, and 50°.
- First, I will test the plain wooden ramp at each pitch.
- Then I will repeat the experiment with the plank wet, with the plank coated with aluminum foil, coated with sandpaper, and finally coated with loose sand.
- I will create graphs displaying how far and how fast the truck climbed in each situation.

Conclusion: I believe this experiment will show different levels of traction. Please let me know if this proposal is accepted. Any suggestions are welcome.

Proposals

A proposal is a detailed plan for doing a project, solving a problem, or meeting a need.

Follow Guidelines

Business Letters

A letter is a written message sent through the mail. Letters follow a set format, including important contact information, a salutation (greeting), a body, and a closing signature. (See pages 274–277 for more information.)

1212 Maple Park
Voree, IN 46300
March 24, 2011

Bruce Reynolds, Owner
Pet Project Pet Store
341 Jones Street
Voree, IN 46300

Dear Mr. Reynolds:

Last year I bought two long-haired guinea pigs from your store, and this year we have five guinea pigs. Are you interested in buying the three babies? They are all female and six weeks old, and I have included pictures of them. We would like to sell them back to you if you are interested.

Our veterinarian checked the three babies, and they are in fine health. We also had the veterinarian neuter the father so that we won't have more pigs to care for.

Please let me know if you are interested in buying our guinea pigs. You may call me at 555-9770 after 3:30 p.m. Otherwise, I will create fliers to sell them myself. Thanks for your time.

Sincerely,

Jessica Botticini

Jessica Botticini

Envelope Addresses

Place the return address in the upper left corner, the destination address in the center, and the correct postage in the upper right corner.

JESSICA BOTTICINI
1212 MAPLE PK
VOREE IN 46300

BRUCE REYNOLDS
PET PROJECT PET STORE
341 JONES ST
VOREE IN 46300

U.S. Postal Service Guidelines

1. Capitalize everything and leave out ALL punctuation.
2. Use the list of common address abbreviations at 634.1. Use numerals rather than words for numbered streets and avenues (9TH AVE NE, 3RD ST SW).
3. If you know the ZIP + 4 code, use it.

capitalize SPELL punctuate

Proofreader's Guide

Academic Vocabulary

Work with a partner. Read the meanings and share answers to the questions.

1. When a person is **patient**, he or she is willing to wait for something.
   Tell about a time when you were patient at school.
2. Cooperative learning can help students by **facilitating** the learning process.
   Does facilitating something make it easier or harder?
3. When you **improve** something, you make it better.
   Tell about one thing you could improve at school.

improve edit

Marking Punctuation

Periods

Use a **period** to end a sentence. Also use a period after initials, after abbreviations, and as a decimal point.

579.1 At the End of Sentences

Use a period to end a sentence that makes a statement or a request. Also use a period for a mild command, one that does not need an exclamation point. (See page 518.)

The Southern Ocean surrounds Antarctica. (statement)
Please point out the world's largest ocean on a map. (request)
Do not use a laser pointer. (mild command)

NOTE It is not necessary to place a period after a statement that has parentheses around it if it is part of another sentence.

The Southern Ocean is the fourth-largest ocean (it is larger than the Atlantic).

579.2 After Initials

Place a period after an initial.

J. K. Rowling (author)
Colin L. Powell (politician)

579.3 After Abbreviations

Place a period after each part of an abbreviation. Do not use periods with acronyms or initialisms. (See page 636.)

Abbreviations: Mr. Mrs. Ms. Dr. B.C.E. C.E.
Acronyms: AIDS NASA
Initialisms: NBC FBI

NOTE When an abbreviation is the last word in a sentence, use only one period at the end of the sentence.

My grandfather's full name is William Ryan James Koenig, Jr.

579.4 As Decimal Points

Use a period to separate dollars and cents and as a decimal point.

The price of a loaf of bread was $1.54 in 1992.
That price was only 35 cents, or 77.3 percent less, in 1972.

Academic Vocabulary

Read aloud the academic terms, as well as the descriptions and questions. Model for students how to read one question and answer it. Have partners monitor their understanding and seek clarification of the terms by working through the meanings and questions together.

Related Skills Activities

- **Basic Grammar and Writing**
  Writing Complete Sentences, p. 500
  Use Questions and Commands, p. 518
- ***SkillsBook***
  End Punctuation 1 and 2, pp. 3–6

Question Marks

A **question mark** is used after an interrogative sentence and also to show doubt about the correctness of a fact or figure. (See page 518.)

580.1 At the End of Direct Questions

Use a question mark at the end of a direct question (an interrogative sentence).

Is a vegan a person who eats only vegetables?

580.2 At the End of Indirect Questions

No question mark is used after an indirect question. (An indirect question tells about a question you or someone else asked.)

Because I do not eat meat, I'm often asked if I am a vegetarian.
I asked the doctor if going meatless is harmful to my health.

580.3 To Show Doubt

Place a question mark within parentheses to show that you are unsure that a fact or figure is correct.

By the year 2020 (?) the number of vegetarians in the United States may approach 15 percent of the population.

Exclamation Points

An **exclamation point** may be placed after a word, a phrase, or a sentence to show emotion. (The exclamation point should not be overused.)

580.4 To Express Strong Feelings

Use an exclamation point to show excitement or strong feeling.

Yeah! Wow! Oh my!
Surprise! You've won the million-dollar sweepstakes!

Caution: Never use more than one exclamation point in writing assignments.

Incorrect: Don't ever do that to me again!!!
Correct: Don't ever do that to me again!

Grammar Practice

End Punctuation

For each numbered sentence below, write the last word in the sentence and the correct end punctuation after it.

Example: The blue whale is the largest animal that has ever lived
lived.

(1) Whales may look like fish and swim like fish, but did you know that whales are really mammals **(2)** Just like other mammals, they have a heart with four chambers, they are warm-blooded, and they give birth to live young **(3)** They even have some hair

(4) Whales travel in small groups called pods **(5)** They communicate with each other using a series of clicks and whistles **(6)** The sounds are just remarkable **(7)** People think of them as songs and have even recorded them **(8)** Have you heard any of these recordings

(9) Gentle and friendly, many whale species seem to trust people **(10)** Scientists say that whales are very intelligent and that their vision and hearing are excellent **(11)** Would you believe that whales can live for quite a long time **(12)** Just imagine: Some large whales have probably lived for more than 100 years

Next Step: Based on the reading above, write two sentences about whales: one should be a question you would like to ask, and one should be an emotional personal comment. Use the correct end punctuation for each.

Related Skills Activities

- **Basic Grammar and Writing**
  Writing Complete Sentences, p. 500
  Use Questions and Commands, p. 518
- ***SkillsBook***
  End Punctuation 1 and 2, pp. 3–6

Answers

1. mammals?
2. young.
3. hair. (or) hair!
4. pods.
5. whistles.
6. remarkable!
7. them.
8. recordings?
9. people.
10. excellent.
11. time?
12. years. (or) years!

Commas

Use a **comma** to indicate a pause or a change in thought. This helps to keep words and ideas from running together so that the writing is easier to read. For a writer, no other form of punctuation is more important to understand than the comma.

582.1 Between Items in a Series

Use commas between words, phrases, or clauses in a series. (A series contains at least three items.) (See page 513.)

Chinese, English, and Hindi are the three most widely used languages in the world. (words)

Being comfortable with technology, working well with others, and knowing another language are important skills for today's workers. (phrases)

My dad works in a factory, my mom works in an office, and I work in school. (clauses)

582.2 To Keep Numbers Clear

Use commas to separate the digits in a number in order to distinguish hundreds, thousands, millions, and so on.

More than 104,000 people live in Kingston, the capital of Jamaica.

The population of the entire country of Liechtenstein is only 29,000.

NOTE Commas are not used in years.

The world population was 6.1 billion by 2003.

582.3 In Dates and Addresses

Use commas to set off items in an address and items in a date.

On August 28, 1963, Martin Luther King, Jr., gave his famous "I Have a Dream" speech.

The address of the King Center is 449 Auburn Avenue NE, Atlanta, Georgia 30312.

NOTE No comma is placed between the state and ZIP code. Also, when only the month and year are given, no comma is needed.

In January 2029 we will celebrate the 100th anniversary of Reverend King's birth.

Grammar Practice

Commas 1

- Between Items in a Series
- To Keep Numbers Clear
- In Dates and Addresses

For each sentence below, write the series, date, address, or number that should include a comma. Add the commas.

Example: The Civil War was caused by differences in opinion about slavery economics and politics.
slavery, economics, and politics

1. The war officially began on April 12 1861 when Confederate troops fired upon Fort Sumter, South Carolina.
2. Today Fort Sumter is a national monument at 1214 Middle Street Sullivan's Island South Carolina 29482.
3. South Carolina left the Union, and Virginia Arkansas Tennessee and North Carolina soon followed.
4. More than 13000 Union soldiers and 10000 Confederates lost their lives during the Battle of Shiloh.
5. Three other major battles of the war were fought at Wilderness Spotsylvania and Cold Harbor.
6. After four years of fighting, the war officially ended with the Confederates' surrender on April 9 1865 in Appomattox Virginia.
7. The final death toll of the Civil War was more than 620000 soldiers from both the North and the South.
8. You can learn about the Civil War by reading government papers diaries and letters written during that time period.
9. You can read records of soldiers who fought in the Civil War at the National Archives 700 Pennsylvania Avenue Washington DC 20408.

PUNCTUATION

Related Skills Activities

- **Basic Grammar and Writing**
  Combine with a Series of Words, p. 513
- ***SkillsBook***
  Commas Between Items in a Series 1 and 2, pp. 7–10
  Other Comma Uses 1, pp. 11–12

Answers

1. April 12, 1861,
2. 1214 Middle Street, Sullivan's Island, South Carolina 29482
3. Virginia, Arkansas, Tennessee, and North Carolina
4. 13,000
   10,000
5. Wilderness, Spotsylvania, and Cold Harbor
6. April 9, 1865, Appomattox, Virginia
7. 620,000
8. papers, diaries, and letters
9. National Archives, 700 Pennsylvania Avenue, Washington, DC 20408

Commas . . .

584.1 To Set Off Nonrestrictive Phrases and Clauses

Use commas to set off nonrestrictive phrases and clauses—those not necessary to the basic meaning of the sentence.

People get drinking water from surface water or groundwater, which makes up only 1 percent of the earth's water supply. (The clause *which makes up only 1 percent of the earth's water supply* is additional information; it is nonrestrictive—not required. If the clause were left out, the meaning of the sentence would remain clear.)

Restrictive phrases or clauses—those that are needed in the sentence—restrict or limit the meaning of the sentence; they are not set off with commas.

Groundwater that is free from harmful pollutants is rare. (The clause *that is free from harmful pollutants* is restrictive; it is needed to complete the meaning of the basic sentence and is not set off with commas.)

584.2 To Set Off Titles or Initials

Use commas to set off a title, a name, or initials that follow a person's last name. (Use only one period if an initial comes at the end of a sentence.)

Melanie Prokat, M.D., is our family's doctor. However, she is listed in the phone book only as Prokat, M.

NOTE Although commas are not necessary to set off "Jr." and "Sr." after a name, they may be used as long as a comma is used both before and after the abbreviation.

584.3 To Set Off Interruptions

Use commas to set off a word, phrase, or clause that interrupts the main thought of a sentence. These interruptions usually can be identified through the following tests:

1. You can leave them out of a sentence without changing its meaning.
2. You can place them other places in the sentence without changing its meaning.

Our school, as we all know, is becoming overcrowded again. (clause)

The gym, not the cafeteria, was expanded a while ago. (phrase)

My history class, for example, has 42 students in it. (phrase)

There are, indeed, about 1,000 people in my school. (word)

The building, however, has room for only 850 students. (word)

Grammar Practice

Commas 2

- To Set Off Nonrestrictive Phrases and Clauses
- To Set Off Titles or Initials
- To Set Off Interruptions

For each of the following sentences, write the information that should be set off with a comma. Include the word before the information and add the commas.

Example: The ferret which is a cousin of the weasel can make a good pet.

ferret, which is a cousin of the weasel,

1. Ferrets once only wild animals of the Great Plains are now a common tame breed.
2. Victoria Patterson D.V.M. claims they are as smart and loving as dogs and cats.
3. John Carpenter M.D. says he has never had to treat a ferret bite.
4. Ferrets need toys to keep them busy—old socks for instance.
5. Any pet as you know needs a lot of care.
6. Ferrets are known for their active and curious nature which sometimes gets them into trouble.
7. Ferrets on the loose will for example dig in your houseplant dirt.
8. They will "steal" small things and hide them in or under the furniture which could be annoying.
9. Ferrets which are like cats in some ways can be trained to use a litter box.

Next Step: Write two sentences about your favorite pet. Include a nonrestrictive phrase or clause in one and an interruption in the other. Use commas to correctly set off these items.

Related Skills Activities

- ***SkillsBook***

  Commas to Set Off Nonrestrictive Phrases and Clauses 1 and 2, pp. 15–18

  Commas with Interruptions, Direct Address, and Interjections, pp. 19–20

Answers

1. Ferrets, once only wild animals of the Great Plains,
2. Victoria Patterson, D.V.M.,
3. John Carpenter, M.D.,
4. socks, for instance
5. pet, as you know,
6. nature, which sometimes gets them into trouble
7. will, for example,
8. furniture, which could be annoying
9. Ferrets, which are like cats in some ways,

Commas . . .

586.1 To Set Off Appositives

Commas set off an appositive from the rest of the sentence. An appositive is a word or phrase that identifies or renames a noun or pronoun.

The capital of Cyprus, Nicosia, has a population of almost 643,000. (Nicosia renames *capital of Cyprus,* so the word is set off with commas.)

Cyprus, an island in the Mediterranean Sea, is about half the size of Connecticut. (*An island in the Mediterranean Sea* identifies *Cyprus,* so the phrase is set off with commas.)

Do not use commas with appositives that are necessary to the basic meaning of the sentence.

The Mediterranean island Cyprus is about half the size of Connecticut. (*Cyprus* is not set off because it is needed to make the sentence clear.)

586.2 To Separate Equal Adjectives

Use commas to separate two or more adjectives that equally modify the same noun.

Comfortable, efficient cars are becoming more important to drivers. (*Comfortable* and *efficient* are separated by a comma because they modify *cars* equally.)

Some automobiles run on clean, renewable sources of energy. (*Clean* and *renewable* are separated by a comma because they modify *sources* equally.)

Conventional gasoline engines emit a lot of pollution. (*Conventional* and *gasoline* do not modify *engines* equally; therefore, no comma separates the two.)

Use these tests to help you decide if adjectives modify equally:

1. Switch the order of the adjectives; if the sentence is clear, the adjectives modify equally.
   Yes: Efficient, comfortable cars are becoming more important to drivers.
   No: Gasoline conventional engines emit a lot of pollution.
2. Put the word *and* between the adjectives; if the sentence is clear, use a comma when *and* is taken out.
   Yes: Comfortable and efficient cars are becoming more important to drivers.
   No: Conventional and gasoline engines emit a lot of pollution.

Grammar Practice

Commas 3

PUNCTUATION

To Set Off Appositives

For each sentence below, write the appositive phrase as well as the noun it renames. Set off the appositive with commas.

Example: Reginald Fessenden a Scotsman living in Canada made the first voice broadcast on radio in 1906.
Reginald Fessenden, a Scotsman living in Canada,

1. Edwin Armstrong developed FM radio a signal offering clearer sound than AM radio.
2. Lee DeForest the "father of radio" used some of Armstrong's and some of Fessenden's ideas.
3. David Sarnoff another radio pioneer later moved into television, forming NBC.
4. Many other inventors people from all over the world added to the growth of radio.

To Separate Equal Adjectives

For each sentence below, write the adjectives that need commas between them. Add the commas.

Example: Lee DeForest was a vain determined inventor.
vain, determined

1. In the wild crazy years of the 1920s, radios become very popular.
2. During the Depression, even poor jobless people had radios to brighten their lives.
3. Soon, companies were designing radios with beautiful stylish cabinets.
4. A huge powerful radio was often the main piece of furniture in a living room.
5. Now the demand is for smaller lighter radios.

Related Skills Activities

- **Basic Grammar and Writing**
  Combine with Phrases, p. 512
- ***SkillsBook***
  Other Comma Uses 2, pp. 13–14
  Commas to Set Off Explanatory and Appositive Phrases, pp. 21–22
- ***GrammarSnap***
  Commas to Set Off Explanatory Phrases or Clauses

Answers

1. FM radio, a signal offering clearer sound than AM radio
2. Lee DeForest, the "father of radio,"
3. David Sarnoff, another radio pioneer,
4. inventors, people from all over the world,

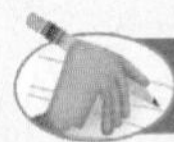

Answers

1. wild, crazy
2. poor, jobless
3. beautiful, stylish
4. huge, powerful
5. smaller, lighter

Commas . . .

588.1 To Set Off Dialogue

Use commas to set off the exact words of a speaker from the rest of the sentence. (Also see page 556.)

The firefighter said, "When we cannot successfully put out a fire, we try to keep it from spreading."

"When we cannot successfully put out a fire, we try to keep it from spreading," the firefighter said.

NOTE Do not use a comma or quotation marks for indirect quotations. The words *if* and *that* often signal dialogue that is being reported rather than quoted.

The firefighter said that when they cannot successfully put out a fire, they try to keep it from spreading. (These are not the speaker's exact words.)

588.2 In Direct Address

Use commas to separate a noun of direct address from the rest of the sentence. (A noun of direct address is a noun that names a person spoken to in the sentence.)

Hanae, did you know that an interior decorator can change wallpaper and fabrics on a computer screen?

Sure, Jack, and an architect can use a computer to see how light will fall in different parts of a building.

588.3 To Set Off Interjections

Use commas to separate an interjection or a weak exclamation from the rest of the sentence.

No kidding, you mean that one teacher has to manage a class of 42 pupils? (weak exclamation)

Uh-huh, and that teacher has other classes that size. (interjection)

588.4 To Set Off Explanatory Phrases

Use commas to separate an explanatory phrase from the rest of the sentence.

English, the language computers speak worldwide, is also the most widely used language in science and medicine.

More than 750 million people, about an eighth of the world's population, speak English as a foreign language.

Grammar Practice

Commas 4

- To Set Off Dialogue
- In Direct Address
- To Set Off Interjections
- To Set Off Explanatory Phrases

For each of the following sentences, write the word or words that should be set off with a comma. Add the commas.

Example: Jenni let's go see a movie.
Jenni,

1. Hey do you want to go see a movie with us?
2. I answered "It depends on what movie."
3. Today's movies especially the computer-animated films are pretty amazing.
4. The earliest films lasting no more than 10 minutes were just brief looks at sports or fashions of the early 1900s.
5. Wow it cost a whole nickel to see one of those movies!
6. Did you know Curtis that movies were silent until 1927?
7. Music usually played on a piano often accompanied films, but they were still called "silent" movies.
8. In the first movie with sound, Al Jolson said "Wait a minute. You ain't heard nothin' yet!"
9. A few silent-film stars including the famous Charlie Chaplin didn't think "talkies" would last.
10. Of course sound movies soon replaced the silent ones.
11. "I'm glad" Jennie said "that I can hear people talk in movies!"

Next Step: Write a brief conversation between yourself and a friend about a movie you've both seen. Include commas where needed in the dialogue and for nouns of direct address and interjections.

Related Skills Activities

- **Basic Grammar and Writing**
  Write Narrative Paragraphs, p. 526
- ***SkillsBook***
  Commas with Interruptions, Direct Address, and Interjections, pp. 19–20
  Commas to Set Off Explanatory and Appositive Phrases, pp. 21–22
- ***GrammarSnap***
  Commas to Set Off Explanatory Phrases or Clauses

Answers

1. Hey,
2. answered,
3. movies,
   films,
4. films,
   minutes,
5. Wow,
6. know,
   Curtis,
7. Music,
   piano,
8. said,
9. stars,
   Chaplin,
10. course,
11. glad,
    said,

Commas . . .

590.1 To Separate Introductory Clauses and Phrases

Use a comma to separate an adverb clause or a long phrase from the independent clause that follows it.

If every automobile in the country were a light shade of red, we'd live in a pink-car nation. (adverb clause)

According to some experts, solar-powered cars will soon be common. (long modifying phrase)

590.2 In Compound Sentences

Use a comma between two independent clauses that are joined by a coordinating conjunction (such as *and, but, or, nor, for, so,* and *yet*), forming a compound sentence. An independent clause expresses a complete thought and can stand alone as a sentence. (Also see page 516.)

Many students enjoy working on computers, so teachers are finding new ways to use them in the classroom.

Computers can be valuable in education, but many schools cannot afford enough of them.

Avoid Comma Splices: A comma splice results when two independent clauses are "spliced" together with only a comma—and no conjunction. (See page 506.)

SCHOOL DAZE

Grammar Practice

Commas 5

- To Separate Introductory Clauses and Phrases
- In Compound Sentences

For each sentence below, write the word that should be followed by a comma. Add the comma.

Example: Often considered a Canadian sport hockey has also grown in popularity in the United States.
sport,

1. To be a good hockey player a person must be an excellent skater and a superb athlete.
2. Hockey players have a lot of gear but their most important pieces of equipment are their skates.
3. Since the skates must be kept clean and sharp every team has an equipment manager to sharpen the skates.
4. Although a skate appears to have one sharp blade each skate actually has two blades along a hollow center.
5. A deeper hollow means two sharp blades and that can mean faster skating.
6. Because they move from side to side a lot goalies prefer the control a flatter blade gives.
7. Regular skating dulls blades but they can be dulled even more quickly by crashing against another skater's blades.
8. The quality of the ice affects skating so stadiums take care to maintain their rinks.
9. While "fast ice" is hard and slick "slow ice" is soft and rough.

Next Step: Write four sentences about your favorite winter sport. Include two sentences with introductory clauses or phrases and two compound sentences. Place commas correctly.

PUNCTUATION

Related Skills Activities

- **Basic Grammar and Writing**
  Avoid Run-On Sentences, p. 506
  Connecting with Conjunctions, pp. 496–497
  Create Compound Sentences, p. 516
  Develop Complex Sentences, p. 517
  Expand with Participial Phrases, p. 520
- ***SkillsBook***
  Commas in Compound Sentences, pp. 23–24
- ***GrammarSnap***
  Commas after Introductory Words, Phrases, and Clauses
  Punctuating Compound Sentences

Answers

1. player,
2. gear,
3. sharp,
4. blade,
5. blades,
6. lot,
7. blades,
8. skating,
9. slick,

Test Prep!

Number your paper from 1 to 12. For each underlined part of the paragraphs below, write the letter (from the next page) of the best way to punctuate it.

Throughout parts of the United States caves (1) have been carved out of thick layers of limestone. Why does this happen Natural acids (2) in water dissolve limestone so the constant (3) trickle of groundwater over thousands of years forms a cave. Sometimes there is enough dripping water and minerals to form a stalactite, a kind (4) of stone icicle hanging from the roof of the cave. A stalagmite is a column built up on the floor of the cave and it (5) is also formed from the dripping water. People have found fantastic odd formations (6) in caves.

Some places in caves are so small that spelunkers cave explorers (7) must stretch their arms out in front of them while squeezing through the tight opening Other places (8) open into huge dark rooms (9) big enough to offer shelter. In fact, birds, animals, and people (10) actually use caves for this reason.

When water stops dripping from the ceiling the cave (11) stops growing. Eventually, an earthquake the weight of the ground above the cave or natural erosion (12) can mean the end of a cave.

1. Ⓐ United States caves, Ⓑ United States' caves Ⓒ United States, caves Ⓓ correct as is
2. Ⓐ happen? Natural acids Ⓑ happen. Natural acids Ⓒ happen; natural acids Ⓓ correct as is
3. Ⓐ limestone, so, the constant Ⓑ limestone so, the constant Ⓒ limestone, so the constant Ⓓ correct as is
4. Ⓐ a stalactite a kind, Ⓑ a stalactite, a kind, Ⓒ a stalactite a kind Ⓓ correct as is
5. Ⓐ the cave and, it Ⓑ the cave, and, it Ⓒ the cave, and it Ⓓ correct as is
6. Ⓐ fantastic, odd formations Ⓑ fantastic, odd formations, Ⓒ fantastic, odd, formations Ⓓ correct as is
7. Ⓐ spelunkers, cave explorers Ⓑ spelunkers, cave explorers, Ⓒ spelunkers cave explorers, Ⓓ correct as is
8. Ⓐ tight opening? Other places Ⓑ tight opening. Other places Ⓒ tight opening, other places Ⓓ correct as is
9. Ⓐ huge, dark, rooms Ⓑ huge dark, rooms Ⓒ huge, dark rooms Ⓓ correct as is
10. Ⓐ birds animals and people Ⓑ birds, animals, and people, Ⓒ birds, animals and people Ⓓ correct as is
11. Ⓐ the ceiling, the cave Ⓑ the ceiling, the cave, Ⓒ the ceiling the cave, Ⓓ correct as is
12. Ⓐ an earthquake, the weight of the ground above the cave, or natural erosion Ⓑ an earthquake the weight of the ground above the cave, or natural erosion, Ⓒ an earthquake, the weight of the ground above the cave or natural erosion Ⓓ correct as is

PUNCTUATION

Related Skills Activities

- ***SkillsBook***
  Comma Rules, pp. 25–26
  Comma Review, pp. 27–28

Answers

1. C
2. A
3. C
4. D
5. C
6. A
7. B
8. B
9. C
10. D
11. A
12. A

Semicolons

Use a **semicolon** to suggest a stronger pause than a comma indicates. A semicolon may also serve in place of a period.

594.1 To Join Two Independent Clauses

In a compound sentence, use a semicolon to join two independent clauses that are not connected with a coordinating conjunction. (See 744.1.)

The United States has more computers than any other country; its residents own more than 164 million of them.

594.2 With Conjunctive Adverbs

A semicolon is also used to join two independent clauses when the clauses are connected by a conjunctive adverb (such as *as a result, for example, however, therefore,* and *instead*). (See 738.1.)

Japan is next on that list; however, the Japanese have fewer than half as many computers as the U.S.

594.3 To Separate Groups That Contain Commas

Use a semicolon between groups of words in a series when one or more of the groups already contain commas.

Many of our community's residents separate their garbage into bins for newspapers, cardboard, and junk mail; glass, metal, and plastic; and nonrecyclable trash.

SCHOOL DAZE

Grammar Practice

Semicolons

For each of the following sentences, write the words on either side of the needed semicolons and insert the semicolons.

Example: Animation has become very popular however, artists actually began animating cartoons in the early 1900s.
popular; however

1. The first cartoons were hand drawn frame by frame as a result, each cartoon took a long time to create.
2. Winsor McCay took his time making his cartoons his five-minute cartoon *Gertie the Dinosaur* took more than a year to make.
3. Early cartoons created by individual artists took a lot of time their quality was very high compared to some later cartoons.
4. Some of the most well-known names in animation include Walt Disney, who led the way Max Fleischer, who thought up Popeye and Walter Lantz, the creator of Woody Woodpecker.
5. Computer-generated animation is now fairly common it can make animation look very real.
6. Computer-animated movies include Disney's *Toy Story, A Bug's Life,* and *Finding Nemo* Dreamworks' *Shrek, Antz,* and *Spirit: Stallion of the Cimarron* and Columbia Tri-Star's *Final Fantasy: The Spirits Within.*
7. Lately, *anime* has caught on in this country it is a Japanese style of animation.
8. Animated movies used to be made for children today, they are just as likely to be aimed at the parents, too.

Next Step: Write two independent clauses (sentences) about a cartoon you like and join them with a semicolon.

PUNCTUATION

Related Skills Activities

- **Basic Grammar and Writing**
  Create Compound Sentences, p. 516
- ***SkillsBook***
  Semicolons and Colons, pp. 29–30
- ***GrammarSnap***
  Semicolons and Colons

Answers

1. frame; as
2. cartoons; his
3. time; their
4. way; Max
   Popeye; and
5. common; it
6. *Nemo;* Dreamworks'
   Cimarron; and
7. country; it
8. children; today

Colons

A **colon** may be used to introduce a list or an important point. Colons are also used in business letters and between the numbers in time.

596.1 To Introduce Lists

Use a colon to introduce a list. The colon usually comes after words describing the subject of the list (as in the first example below) or after summary words, such as *the following* or *these things.* Do not use a colon after a verb or preposition.

Certain items are still difficult to recycle: foam cups, car tires, and toxic chemicals.

To conserve water, you should do the following three things: fix drippy faucets, install a low-flow showerhead, and turn the water off while brushing your teeth.

Incorrect: **To conserve water, you should: install a low-flow showerhead, turn the water off while brushing your teeth, and fix drippy faucets.**

596.2 To Introduce Sentences

A colon may be used to introduce a sentence, a question, or a quotation.

This is why air pollution is bad: We are sacrificing our health and the health of all other life on the planet.

Answer this question for me: Why aren't more people concerned about global warming?

596.3 After Salutations

A colon may be used after the salutation of a business letter.

Dear Ms. Manners: Dear Dr. Warmle: Dear Professor Potter: Dear Captain Elliot: Dear Senator:

596.4 For Emphasis

Use a colon to emphasize a word or phrase.

The newest alternative energy is also the most common element on earth: hydrogen.

Here's one thing that can help save energy: a programmable thermostat.

596.5 Between Numbers in Time

Use a colon between the parts of a number that indicate time.

My thermostat automatically sets my heat to 60 degrees between 11:00 p.m. and 6:00 a.m.

Grammar Practice

Colons

The following letter needs colons placed correctly. Write the line number and the words or numbers that need colons. Then add the colons.

1 March 9, 2011

2 JoAnne White Cloud
3 1315 Wells Road
4 Colfax, WA 99201

5 Dear Ms. White Cloud
6 The Colfax Junior Heritage Club would like you to be the guest
7 speaker at our next meeting on April 6. During the last three months,
8 we have been studying the goals of the Spokane Tribe independence,
9 honesty, and tradition. These goals have inspired many of us with
10 Native American roots.
11 We meet in the large lecture hall at the community center. The
12 meeting will begin at 730 p.m. and end at about 900 p.m. Here is our
13 plan for the evening a short business meeting, your presentation, time
14 for questions, and refreshments.
15 Let me add one final thought Our club's goal is "peace through
16 understanding," and your visit could help us all to learn more about
17 our common history. I hope you will be able to join us in April.

18 Sincerely,

19 Carolyn Mose

Next Step: Write a note to a friend. Ask him or her to meet you at a certain time and place. Include colons after the salutation, between numbers in a time, and to introduce a list.

PUNCTUATION

Related Skills Activities

- ***SkillsBook***
  Semicolons and Colons, pp. 29–30
- ***GrammarSnap***
  Semicolons and Colons

Answers

line 5: Dear Ms. White Cloud:
line 8: Spokane Tribe:
line 12: 7:30 p.m.
9:00 p.m.
line 13: evening:
line 15: thought:

Quotation Marks

Quotation marks are used in a number of ways:

- to set off the exact words of a speaker,
- to punctuate material quoted from another source,
- to punctuate words used in a special way, and
- to punctuate certain titles.

598.1 To Set Off a Speaker's Exact Words

Place quotation marks before and after a speaker's words in dialogue. Only the exact words of the speaker are placed within quotation marks.

> Marla said, "I've decided to become a firefighter."
> "A firefighter," said Juan, "can help people in many ways."

598.2 For Quotations Within Quotations

Use single quotation marks to punctuate a quotation within a quotation.

> Sung Kim asked, "Did Marla just say, 'I've decided to become a firefighter'?"

When titles occur within a quotation, use single quotation marks to punctuate those that require quotation marks.

> Juan said, "Springsteen's song 'The Rising' really inspired her."

598.3 To Set Off Quoted Material

When quoting material from another source, place quotation marks before and after the source's exact words.

> In her book *Living the Life You Deserve*, Tess Spyeder explains, "Choose a job you'll enjoy doing day after day over one that will fatten your bank account."

598.4 To Set Off Long Quoted Material

If more than one paragraph is quoted from a single source, quotation marks are placed before each paragraph and at the end of the last paragraph.

Quotations that are more than four lines are usually set off from the rest of the paper by indenting each line 10 spaces from the left. Quotations that are set off in this way require no quotation marks either before or after the quoted material.

Grammar Practice

Quotation Marks 1

- To Set Off a Speaker's Exact Words
- For Quotations Within Quotations

For each of the following sentences, write the first and last word of each quotation or title, adding the correct quotation marks. Use ellipses as shown.

Example: Bettina said, My science project, which I will call Communicating with Your Pet, is a sure winner.
"My . . . 'Communicating . . . Pet,' . . . winner."

1. I don't know, I said. Are you sure Ms. Lazarus knows about your plans?
2. Sure. She even said, That's a wonderful idea, Bettina stated.
3. I said, That's not what I would have said. I would have told you that it's a crazy idea.
4. Then I asked, What are you going to do for scientific research? We're supposed to show our research for this project, you know.
5. Bettina replied, I'm going to keep track of how my dog, Moose, communicates with me when he wants something. I will record all my information in a chart.
6. Do you think Moose will cooperate? I asked.
7. I already asked him, Bettina replied, and he said, Go for it!
8. Bettina, you are incredible, I said.
9. Woof! Moose joined in from his spot under the table.

Next Step: Write a short conversation you might have with your pet or the pet of a friend. Use quotation marks correctly.

Related Skills Activities

- **Basic Grammar and Writing**
  Write Narrative Paragraphs, p. 526
- ***SkillsBook***
  Punctuating Dialogue, pp. 31–32
- ***GrammarSnap***
  Punctuating Dialogue

Answers

1. "I . . . know,"
   "Are . . . plans?"
2. "Sure. . . . 'That's . . . idea,' "
3. "That's . . . idea."
4. "What . . . know."
5. "I'm . . . chart."
6. "Do . . . cooperate?"
7. "I . . . him,"
   "and . . . 'Go . . . it!' "
8. "Bettina . . . incredible,"
9. "Woof!"

Quotation Marks . . .

600.1 Placement of Punctuation

Always place periods and commas inside quotation marks.

"I don't know," said Lac.

Lac said, "I don't know."

Place an exclamation point or a question mark inside the quotation marks when it punctuates the quotation.

Ms. Wiley asked, "Can you actually tour the Smithsonian on the Internet?"

Place it outside when it punctuates the main sentence.

Did I hear you say, "Now we can tour the Smithsonian on the Internet"?

Place semicolons or colons outside quotation marks.

First, I will read the article "Sonny's Blues"; then I will read "The Star Café" in my favorite music magazine.

600.2 For Special Words

Quotation marks also may be used (1) to set apart a word that is being discussed, (2) to indicate that a word is slang, or (3) to point out that a word or phrase is being used in a special way.

1. **Renny uses the word "like" entirely too much.**
2. **Man, your car is really "phat."**
3. **Aunt Lulu, an editor at a weekly magazine, says she has "issues."**

600.3 To Punctuate Titles

Use quotation marks to punctuate titles of songs, poems, short stories, lectures, episodes of radio or television programs, chapters of books, and articles found in magazines, newspapers, or encyclopedias. (Also see **602.3**.)

"21 Questions" (song)
"The Reed Flute's Song" (poem)
"Old Man at the Bridge" (short story)
"Birthday Boys" (a television episode)
"The Foolish and the Weak" (a chapter in a book)
"Science Careers Today" (lecture)
"Teen Rescues Stranded Dolphin" (newspaper article)

NOTE When you punctuate a title, capitalize the first word, last word, and every word in between—except for articles *(a, an, the)*, short prepositions *(at, to, with,* and so on), and coordinating conjunctions *(and, but, or)*. (See **624.2**.)

Grammar Practice

Quotation Marks 2

- Placement of Punctuation
- To Punctuate Titles

Copy the following sentences and properly place quotation marks, commas, and end punctuation.

Example: We're going on vacation next week Dan said to Chicago

"We're going on vacation next week," Dan said, "to Chicago."

1. He began singing lines from the song My Kind of Town
2. What do you know about Chicago I asked
3. Dan said, I know that Carl Sandburg wrote poems, such as Clark Street Bridge and Skyscraper, about Chicago
4. I know they have an elevated train system he added and it can get you just about anywhere in the city
5. Oprah Winfrey's show is taped there, so Mom wants to get tickets She loved the episode Bargain Shopping with Oprah he said
6. You just said Mom wants to get tickets But what about you What do you want to see I asked
7. I want to see Buckingham Fountain, the Sears Tower, and Navy Pier Dan said
8. Are you going to go shopping for some souvenirs on Michigan Avenue I teased
9. Oh, yeah Dan winked

Next Step: What would be your dream vacation? Write a brief discussion you might have with a friend, explaining your dream vacation. Punctuate it correctly with quotation marks and properly placed commas and end punctuation.

PUNCTUATION

Related Skills Activities

- ***SkillsBook***
  Quotation Marks and Italics, pp. 33–34
- ***GrammarSnap***
  Punctuating Dialogue

Answers

1. He began singing lines from the song "My Kind of Town."
2. "What do you know about Chicago?" I asked.
3. Dan said, "I know that Carl Sandburg wrote poems, such as 'Clark Street Bridge' and 'Skyscraper,' about Chicago."
4. "I know they have an elevated train system," he added, "and it can get you just about anywhere in the city."
5. "Oprah Winfrey's show is taped there, so Mom wants to get tickets. She loved the episode 'Bargain Shopping with Oprah,' " he said.
6. "You just said, 'Mom wants to get tickets.' But what about you? What do you want to see?" I asked.
7. "I want to see Buckingham Fountain, the Sears Tower, and Navy Pier," Dan said.
8. "Are you going to go shopping for some souvenirs on Michigan Avenue?" I teased.
9. "Oh, yeah," Dan winked.

Italics and Underlining

Italics is slightly slanted type. In this sentence, the word *happiness* is typed in italics. In handwritten material, each word or letter that should be in italics is **underlined**. (See an example on page 403.)

602.1 In Printed Material

Print words in italics when you are using a computer.

In *Tuck Everlasting*, the author explores what it would be like to live forever.

602.2 In Handwritten Material

Underline words that should be italicized when you are writing by hand.

In Tuck Everlasting, the author explores what it would be like to live forever.

602.3 In Titles

Italicize (or underline) the titles of books, plays, book-length poems, magazines, newspapers, radio and television programs, movies, videos, cassettes, CD's, and the names of aircraft and ships.

Walk Two Moons (book) *Teen People* (magazine)
Fairies and Dragons (movie) *Everwood* (TV program)
The Young and the Hopeless (CD) U.S.S. *Arizona* (ship)
Columbia (space shuttle) *Daily Herald* (newspaper)

Exception: Do not italicize or put quotation marks around your own title at the top of your written work.

A Day Without Water (personal writing: do not italicize)

602.4 For Scientific and Foreign Words

Italicize (or underline) scientific and foreign words that are not commonly used in everyday English.

Spinacia oleracea is the scientific term for spinach.

Many store owners who can help Spanish-speaking customers display an *Hablamos Español* sign in their windows.

602.5 For Special Uses

Italicize (or underline) a number, letter, or word that is being discussed or used in a special way. (Sometimes quotation marks are used for this same reason.)

Matt's hat has a bright red *A* on it.

Grammar Practice

Italics and Underlining

For each of the following sentences, write the word or words that should be italicized and underline them.

Example: Ancient Greek drama grew from dithyrambs, choral songs honoring the god Dionysus.
dithyrambs

1. One book about early drama in ancient Greece is I Came, I Saw, I Applauded.
2. Plays were acted out on a stage called a skene, the source of our modern words scene and scenery.
3. The book Ancient Greek Drama explains the interesting special effects used back then.
4. One of the most famous writers of Greek theater was Sophocles, who wrote the two plays Oedipus Rex and Antigone.
5. Another Greek writer, Homer, wrote a book-length poem called The Odyssey.
6. A recent article in the New York Times said that all modern drama stems from the early Greek tragedies.
7. Obviously confused, Ted thought the '60s movie Zorba the Greek was based on a 2,000-year-old play.
8. He had missed the day the class watched the video Ancient Greece: A Journey Back in Time.
9. Ted thinks he can prove his point if he brings in Imiskoubria 2030, a CD of Greek hip-hop he found at a resale shop.

Next Step: What special words are used in a hobby or an activity that you enjoy? Write a brief paragraph explaining the activity, correctly underlining the special words.

PUNCTUATION

Related Skills Activities

- **Basic Grammar and Writing**
  Use Order of Location, p. 535
- ***SkillsBook***
  Quotation Marks and Italics, pp. 33–34

Answers

1. I Came, I Saw, I Applauded
2. skene, scene, scenery
3. Ancient Greek Drama
4. Oedipus Rex, Antigone
5. The Odyssey
6. New York Times
7. Zorba the Greek
8. Ancient Greece: A Journey Back in Time
9. Imiskoubria 2030

Capitalization . . .

622.1 Geographic Names

Capitalize the following geographic names.

Planets and heavenly bodies . . . . **Venus, Jupiter, Milky Way**

Lowercase the word "earth" except when used as the proper name of our planet, especially when mentioned with other planet names.

What on earth are you doing here?

Sam has traveled across the face of the earth several times.

Jupiter's diameter is 11 times larger than Earth's.

The four inner planets are Mercury, Venus, Earth, and Mars.

Continents . . . . **Europe, Asia, South America, Australia, Africa**
Countries . . . . **Morocco, Haiti, Greece, Chile, United Arab Emirates**
States. . . . . . **New Mexico, Alabama, West Virginia, Delaware, Iowa**
Provinces . . . .**Alberta, British Columbia, Quebec, Ontario**
Counties. . . . . **Sioux County, Kandiyohi County, Wade County**
Cities . . . . **Montreal, Baton Rouge, Albuquerque, Portland**
Bodies of water . . . . **Delaware Bay, Chickamunga Lake, Indian Ocean, Gulf of Mexico, Skunk Creek**
Landforms . . . . **Appalachian Mountains, Bitterroot Range**
Public areas . . . . **Tiananmen Square, Sequoia National Forest, Mount Rushmore, Open Space Park, Vietnam Memorial**
Roads and highways . . . . **New Jersey Turnpike, Interstate 80**
Buildings. . . . **Pentagon, Paske High School, Empire State Building**
Monuments . . . . **Eiffel Tower, Statue of Liberty**

622.2 Particular Sections of the Country

Capitalize words that indicate particular sections of the country. Also capitalize proper adjectives formed from names of specific sections of a country.

Having grown up on the hectic East Coast, I find life in the South to be refreshing.

Here in Georgia, Southern hospitality is a way of life.

Words that simply indicate a direction are not capitalized; nor are adjectives that are formed from words that simply indicate direction.

The town where I live, located east of Memphis, is typical of others found in western Tennessee.

Grammar Practice

Capitalization 3

- Geographic Names
- Particular Sections of the Country

Write the answer to each of the following questions.

Example: What is the name of the country located just south of the United States?
Mexico

1. What are the two continents not listed on the facing page?
2. Which four planets are closest to the sun?
3. What section of the country is famous for cowboys?
4. If you flew from New York to London, England, what body of water would you fly over?
5. What is the name of a mountain range in Colorado?
6. Which state is completely surrounded by an ocean, and what ocean is it?
7. What is the large, centrally located park in New York City?
8. What are two European countries?
9. What is the capital of Canada, and which province is it located in?
10. Which city is the second largest in the United States?
11. What is the name of the street where you live?
12. In what part of the country is Alabama located?
13. What is the name of the building in which the U.S. president lives?
14. What large canyon is located in Arizona?

Next Step: Write two sentences about your favorite place. Include geographic names in both sentences.

MECHANICS

Answers

1. North America, Antarctica
2. Mercury, Venus, Earth, Mars
3. the West
4. Atlantic Ocean
5. Rocky Mountains
6. Hawaii, Pacific Ocean
7. Central Park
8. Possible answers: France, England
9. Ottawa, Ontario
10. Los Angeles
11. Answers will vary.
12. the South
13. White House
14. Grand Canyon

Capitalization . . .

624.1 **First Words**

Capitalize the first word of every sentence and the first word in a direct quotation.

In many families, pets are treated like people, according to an article in the *Kansas City Star*. (sentence)

Marty Becker, coauthor of *Chicken Soup for the Pet Lover's Soul*, reports, "Seven out of ten people let their pets sleep on the bed." (direct quotation)

"I get my 15 minutes of fame," he says, "every time I come home." (Notice that *every* is not capitalized because it does not begin a new sentence.)

"It's like being treated like a rock star," says Becker. "Now I have to tell you that feels pretty good."

Do not capitalize the first word in an indirect quotation.

Becker says that in the last 10 years, pets have moved out of kennels and basements and into living rooms and bedrooms. (indirect quotation)

624.2 **Titles**

Capitalize the first word of a title, the last word, and every word in between except articles *(a, an, the)*, short prepositions, and coordinating conjunctions. Follow this rule for titles of books, newspapers, magazines, poems, plays, songs, articles, movies, works of art, pictures, stories, and essays. (See 600.3.)

Locked in Time (book)

Boston Globe (newspaper)

Dog Fancy (magazine)

"Roses Are Red" (poem)

The Phantom of the Opera (play)

Daddy Day Care (movie)

"Intuition" (song)

Mona Lisa (work of art)

Grammar Practice

Capitalization 4

- First Words
- Titles

For each of the following sentences, correctly write any word that is incorrectly capitalized.

Example: Kai bought four tickets to the play *the Phantom Of the Opera.*
The, of

1. He said, "as long as I can get the tickets I want, I really don't mind waiting in line."
2. The *New York times* had a fantastic review of the play in an article called "Phantom appears; Here to stay."
3. Shar read the poem "the Road not Taken" by Robert Frost.
4. "That poem," said Shar, "Really makes me think."
5. it is one of his best-known poems.
6. Danté enjoys the electronic magazine *EEK!: Environmental education for Kids.*
7. "I learned about the careers of park rangers," he said, "And wildlife biologists."
8. after we saw the movie *The Cat In The Hat*, Bruce got a hat just like the cat's.
9. He said that It made him look cool.

Next Step: Write a sentence for each of the following: a name of a book, a song, and a movie. Make sure you capitalize correctly.

MECHANICS

Related Skills Activities

- ***SkillsBook***
  Capitalization 2, pp. 51–52

Answers

1. As
2. Times, Appears, Stay
3. The, Not
4. really
5. It
6. Education
7. and
8. After, in the
9. it

Capitalization . . .

626.1 Abbreviations

Capitalize abbreviations of titles and organizations.

Dr. (Doctor) **M.D.** (Doctor of Medicine)
Mr. (Mister) **UPS** (United Parcel Service)
SADD (Students Against Destructive Decisions)

626.2 Organizations

Capitalize the name of an organization, an association, or a team.

New York State Historical Society	**the Red Cross**
General Motors Corporation	**the Miami Dolphins**
Republicans	**the Democratic Party**

626.3 Letters

Capitalize the letters used to indicate form or shape.

T-shirt U-turn A-frame T-ball

Capitalize	Do Not Capitalize
American	**un-American**
January, February	**winter, spring**
Missouri and Ohio Rivers	**the rivers Missouri and Ohio**
The South is humid in summer.	**Turn south at the stop sign.**
Duluth Middle School	**a Duluth middle school**
Governor Bob Taft	**Bob Taft, our governor**
President Luiz Lula Da Silva	**Luiz Lula Da Silva, Brazil's president**
Nissan Altima	**a Nissan automobile**
The planet Earth is egg shaped.	**The earth on Grandpa's farm is rich.**
I'm taking World Cultures.	**I'm taking social studies.**

Grammar Practice

Capitalization 5

- Abbreviations
- Organizations
- Letters

Capitalize the words that need to be capitalized in the following sentences.

Example: The construction crew carefully lowered the i-beam onto the foundation.
I-beam

1. The green bay packers won the first two Super Bowls.
2. Our substitute teacher, ms. Lukas, will complete her m.a. degree this spring.
3. After I fell off the bleachers and broke my arm, mr. Stevenson took me to see dr. Bell at the clinic.
4. One of the largest ships in the United States Navy is the u.s.s. *Enterprise.*
5. Over the years, the smithsonian institution has become a world-famous museum.
6. The city council passed a new ordinance outlawing u-turns on Davis Avenue.
7. Most politicians seek public office as either a republican, a democrat, or an independent.
8. Did you see the new a-frame picnic shelter in Franklin Park?
9. The Northwest High School panthers' football games are broadcast on radio station kyxx.
10. Engineers at General motors corporation changed the angle of the b-pillar on their new sedan.
11. On the last day of school, the entire seventh-grade science class wore t-shirts with the words "mr. Kall is the coolest."

Related Skills Activities

- ***SkillsBook***
  Capitalization 2, pp. 51–52
  Abbreviations and Numbers, pp. 53–54

Answers

1. Green Bay Packers
2. Ms., M.A.
3. Mr., Dr.
4. U.S.S.
5. Smithsonian Institution
6. U-turns
7. Republican, Democrat, Independent
8. A-frame
9. Panthers', KYXX
10. Motors Corporation, B-pillar
11. T-shirts, Mr.

Test Prep!

For each underlined part of the paragraphs below, choose the letter on the next page that shows the correct capitalization. If the underlined part is correct, choose "D."

In Science Class (1), we talked about the invention of the windchill chart. Mr. Land said That (2) two scientists in antarctica, Paul Sipel (3) and P. F. Passel, noticed how wind speed affected people and animals. they developed (4) a formula in the 1940s to measure the "windchill factor." Why do low temperatures feel even colder in the wind—especially in january and february (5)? It's because wind removes any heated air around your body. It also evaporates moisture from your skin.

Every Winter here in chicago (6), we get a lot of windchill warnings. Mom and dad (7) have a membership with aaa (8) that helps them if their ford Focus (9) sedan won't start in the bitter cold. And they're always telling me, "Don't forget chapstick (10) lip balm, and make sure you wear a hat!"

Even in states like Florida, Texas, and California (11), the wind can make temperatures seem colder than they actually are. A windy day in the gulf of Mexico (12) might trick people into thinking they won't get a sunburn. (When Ms. Huang, our Principal (13), returned from a vacation in New Orleans, her fair skin was all pink.) Windchill factors, however, are not usually printed in the *Miami herald* (14) or the *Brownsville Sun.* Perhaps such cities should publish a "sun warmth factor" instead!

1. Ⓐ In Science class Ⓑ In science class Ⓒ in science class Ⓓ correct as is
2. Ⓐ Mr. Land said that Ⓑ Mr. land said That Ⓒ mr. Land said that Ⓓ correct as is
3. Ⓐ antarctica, Paul sipel Ⓑ Antarctica, paul sipel Ⓒ Antarctica, Paul Sipel Ⓓ correct as is
4. Ⓐ Animals. they developed Ⓑ animals. They developed Ⓒ Animals. They developed Ⓓ correct as is
5. Ⓐ January and february Ⓑ January and February Ⓒ january and February Ⓓ correct as is
6. Ⓐ winter Here in Chicago Ⓑ Winter here in Chicago Ⓒ winter here in Chicago Ⓓ correct as is
7. Ⓐ mom and dad Ⓑ Mom and Dad Ⓒ mom and Dad Ⓓ correct as is
8. Ⓐ membership with Aaa Ⓑ Membership with AAA Ⓒ membership with AAA Ⓓ correct as is
9. Ⓐ Ford focus Ⓑ Ford Focus Ⓒ ford focus Ⓓ correct as is
10. Ⓐ Don't forget Chapstick Ⓑ don't forget chapstick Ⓒ don't forget Chapstick Ⓓ correct as is
11. Ⓐ florida, Texas, and california Ⓑ Florida, Texas, and california Ⓒ Florida, texas, and California Ⓓ correct as is
12. Ⓐ the Gulf of Mexico Ⓑ The gulf of Mexico Ⓒ The Gulf Of Mexico Ⓓ correct as is
13. Ⓐ Ms. Huang, Our Principal Ⓑ Ms. huang, our Principal Ⓒ Ms. Huang, our principal Ⓓ correct as is
14. Ⓐ *miami herald* Ⓑ *Miami Herald* Ⓒ *miami Herald* Ⓓ correct as is

Related Skills Activities

- ***SkillsBook***
  Capitalizations and Abbreviations Review, pp. 55–56
  Capitalization Mixed Reviews, pp. 57–58

Answers

1. B
2. A
3. C
4. B
5. B
6. C
7. B
8. C
9. B
10. A
11. D
12. A
13. C
14. B

Plurals

630.1 Most Nouns

The **plurals** of most nouns are formed by adding *s* to the singular.

cheerleader — **cheerleaders** wheel — **wheels**
bubble — **bubbles**

630.2 Nouns Ending in *ch, sh, s, x,* and *z*

The plural form of nouns ending in *ch, sh, s, x,* and *z* is made by adding *es* to the singular.

lunch — **lunches** dish — **dishes** mess — **messes**
buzz — **buzzes** fox — **foxes**

630.3 Nouns Ending in *o*

The plurals of nouns ending in *o* with a vowel just before the *o* are formed by adding *s*.

radio — **radios** studio — **studios** rodeo — **rodeos**

The plurals of most nouns ending in *o* with a consonant just before the *o* are formed by adding *es*.

echo — **echoes** hero — **heroes** tomato — **tomatoes**

Exceptions: Musical terms and words of Spanish origin always form plurals by adding *s*.

alto — **altos** banjo — **banjos** taco — **tacos**
solo — **solos** piano — **pianos** burro — **burros**

630.4 Nouns Ending in *ful*

The plurals of nouns that end with *ful* are formed by adding an *s* at the end of the word.

three platefuls **six tankfuls** **four cupfuls** **five pailfuls**

630.5 Nouns Ending in *f* or *fe*

The plurals of nouns that end in *f* or *fe* are formed in one of two ways: If the final *f* sound is still heard in the plural form of the word, simply add *s*; if the final sound is a *v* sound, change the *f* to *ve* and add *s*.

roof — **roofs** chief — **chiefs** belief — **beliefs**
(plural ends with *f* sound)

wife — **wives** loaf — **loaves** leaf — **leaves**
(plural ends with *v* sound)

Grammar Practice

Plurals 1

- Nouns Ending in *ch, sh, s, x,* and *z*
- Nouns Ending in *o, ful, f,* or *fe*

For each of the following sentences, write the plural form of the underlined word or words.

Example: The class collected five box of books for the book drive.
boxes

1. Before the final bell rang, eight bus lined up in front of the school.
2. Several coral reef form a natural barrier for the chain of island off the South American coast.
3. Farmer in Idaho have a history of raising huge potato.
4. Jill likes two spoonful of sugar in her tea.
5. Clear the ash out of the fireplace before building a new fire.
6. Our school's music teacher wants 10 more soprano in the choir.
7. We saw 30 calf during our field trip to the Pell dairy farm.
8. Salid and Jerry decided to rent three video for the weekend.
9. After eating just one jalapeño pepper, Frank needed five mouthful of milk to cool his tongue.
10. Diego loves to play the bongo.
11. The drawing board in Mom's office faces a row of four window.
12. She enjoys watching the leaf change every fall.
13. Zack packed three lunch for the family's day of hiking.

Next Step: Write three sentences using the plurals of *radio, capful,* and *life.*

Related Skills Activities

- ***SkillsBook***
  Spelling and Plurals, pp. 59–60

Answers

1. buses
2. reefs, islands
3. Farmers, potatoes
4. spoonfuls
5. ashes
6. sopranos
7. calves
8. videos
9. mouthfuls
10. bongos
11. windows
12. leaves
13. lunches

Plurals . . .

632.1 Nouns Ending in *y*

The plurals of common nouns that end in *y* with a consonant letter just before the *y* are formed by changing the *y* to *i* and adding *es*.

fly — **flies** baby — **babies** cavity — **cavities**

The plurals of common nouns that end in *y* with a vowel before the *y* are formed by adding only *s*.

key — **keys** holiday — **holidays** attorney — **attorneys**

The plurals of proper nouns ending in *y* are formed by adding s.

There are three Circuit Citys in our metro area.

632.2 Compound Nouns

The plurals of some compound nouns are formed by adding *s* or *es* to the main word in the compound.

brothers-in-law **maids of honor** **secretaries of state**

632.3 Plurals That Do Not Change

The plurals of some words are the same in singular and plural form.

deer **sheep** **trout** **aircraft**

632.4 Irregular Spelling

Some words (including many foreign words) form a plural by taking on an irregular spelling; others are now acceptable with the commonly used *s* or *es* ending.

child — **children** woman — **women** man — **men**
goose — **geese** mouse — **mice** ox — **oxen**
tooth — **teeth** octopus — **octopuses** or **octopi**
index — **indexes** or **indices**

632.5 Adding an *'s*

The plurals of letters, figures, symbols, and words discussed as words are formed by adding an apostrophe and an *s*.

Dr. Walters has two Ph.D.'s.

My dad's license plate has three *2's* between two *B's*.

You've got too many *but's* and *so's* in that sentence.

For information on forming plural possessives, see 606.1.

Grammar Practice

Plurals 2

- Nouns Ending in *y*
- Compound Nouns
- Plurals That Do Not Change
- Irregular Spelling
- Adding an *'s*

For each of the following sentences, write the correct form of any underlined plural that is not correct. If an underlined plural is correct, write "C."

Example: Aaron's mother said one of her sister-in-laws worked in a circus for three years.
sisters-in-law

1. The circus announcer shouted out, "Ladys and gentlemans, welcome to the finest show on earth!"
2. For the next five days, people entered the Fair Wing Circus Grounds through several archwaies set up near the roads.
3. Flags full of Fs and Ws flew above the tents.
4. Elaine expected to see elephants, but she did not expect to see mooses!
5. Faleena wondered if there were many mouses running around the circus grounds that might scare the elephants.
6. When a little girl saw the lion's sharp tooths, she started to cry.
7. The three clowns with donkies were so funny!
8. We could see the acrobats doing their warm-ups before climbing the ladder.
9. After the evening's performance, both Jane and Camille wrote in their diarys.

Related Skills Activities

- ***SkillsBook***
  Spelling and Plurals, pp. 59–60

Answers

1. Ladies and gentlemen
2. C, archways
3. F's and W's
4. moose
5. mice
6. teeth
7. donkeys
8. C
9. diaries

Abbreviations

634.1 Abbreviations

An **abbreviation** is the shortened form of a word or phrase. The following abbreviations are always acceptable in any kind of writing:

Mr. **Mrs.** **Ms.** **Dr.** **a.m., p.m.** (A.M., P.M.)
B.C.E. (before the Common Era) **C.E.** (Common Era)
B.A. **M.A.** **Ph.D.** **M.D.** **Sr.** **Jr.**

Caution: Do not abbreviate the names of states, countries, months, days, or units of measure in formal writing. Also, do not use signs or symbols (%, &) in place of words.

Common Abbreviations

AC alternating current
a.m. ante meridiem
ASAP as soon as possible
COD cash on delivery
DA district attorney
DC direct current
etc. and so forth
F Fahrenheit
FM frequency modulation
GNP gross national product
i.e. that is (Latin id est)
kg kilogram
km kilometer
kW kilowatt
l liter
lb. pound
m meter
M.D. doctor of medicine
mfg. manufacturing
mpg miles per gallon
mph miles per hour
oz. ounce
pd. paid
pg. (or p.) page
p.m. post meridiem
ppd. postpaid, prepaid
qt. quart
R.S.V.P. please reply
tbs., tbsp. tablespoon
tsp. teaspoon
vol. volume
vs. versus
yd. yard

Address Abbreviations

	Standard	Postal		Standard	Postal		Standard	Postal
Avenue	Ave.	AVE	Lake	L.	LK	Route	Rt.	RTE
Boulevard	Blvd.	BLVD	Lane	Ln.	LN	South	S.	S
Court	Ct.	CT	North	N.	N	Square	Sq.	SQ
Drive	Dr.	DR	Park	Pk.	PK	Station	Sta.	STA
East	E.	E	Parkway	Pky.	PKY	Street	St.	ST
Expressway	Expy.	EXPY	Place	Pl.	PL	Terrace	Ter.	TER
Heights	Hts.	HTS	Plaza	Plaza	PLZ	Turnpike	Tpke.	TPKE
Highway	Hwy.	HWY	Road	Rd.	RD	West	W.	W

Grammar Practice

Abbreviations 1

Write out the words that the abbreviations in the following sentences stand for.

Example: The field is 50 m wide, not 50 yd. wide.
meters, yards

1. There are 16 oz. in a lb.
2. The article is on pg. 345 of vol. 2.
3. This item is COD, so the bill must be pd. when you get it.
4. The DA needs an M.D. ASAP!
5. TicTec is a mfg. company located near the Virginia Tpke.
6. If this car gets 32 mpg, how far will it go on a qt. of gas?

Write the standard abbreviations of the following addresses.

Example: 2103 East Fremont Court
2103 E. Fremont Ct.

1. 7828 West Greentree Road
2. 697 Samson Highway
3. 992A Ryan Avenue
4. 5 South Elm Lane
5. 1218 North Adobe Terrace
6. 22223 Maple Parkway
7. 250 High Street

Next Step: Create an imaginary address for a place you would like to live some day.

MECHANICS

Answers

1. ounces, pound
2. page, volume
3. cash on delivery, paid
4. district attorney, doctor of medicine, as soon as possible
5. manufacturing, Turnpike
6. miles per gallon, quart

Answers

1. 7828 W. Greentree Rd.
2. 697 Samson Hwy.
3. 992A Ryan Ave.
4. 5 S. Elm Ln.
5. 1218 N. Adobe Ter.
6. 22223 Maple Pky.
7. 250 High St.

Abbreviations . . .

636.1 Acronyms

An **acronym** is an abbreviation that can be pronounced as a word. It does not require periods.

WHO — World Health Organization
ROM — read-only memory
FAQ — frequently asked question

636.2 Initialisms

An **initialism** is similar to an acronym except that it cannot be pronounced as a word; the initials are pronounced individually.

PBS — Public Broadcasting Service
BLM — Bureau of Land Management
WNBA — Women's National Basketball Association

Common Acronyms and Initialisms

AIDS	acquired immune deficiency syndrome	**ORV**	off-road vehicle
CETA	Comprehensive Employment and Training Act	**OSHA**	Occupational Safety and Health Administration
CIA	Central Intelligence Agency	**PAC**	political action committee
FAA	Federal Aviation Administration	**PIN**	personal identification number
FBI	Federal Bureau of Investigation	**PSA**	public service announcement
FCC	Federal Communications Commission	**ROTC**	Reserve Officers' Training Corps
FDA	Food and Drug Administration	**SADD**	Students Against Destructive Decisions
FDIC	Federal Deposit Insurance Corporation	**SSA**	Social Security Administration
FHA	Federal Housing Administration	**SUV**	sport-utility vehicle
FTC	Federal Trade Commission	**SWAT**	special weapons and tactics
HTML	Hypertext Markup Language	**TDD**	telecommunications device for the deaf
IRS	Internal Revenue Service	**TMJ**	temporomandibular joint
MADD	Mothers Against Drunk Driving	**TVA**	Tennessee Valley Authority
NAFTA	North American Free Trade Agreement	**VA**	Veterans Administration
NASA	National Aeronautics and Space Administration	**VISTA**	Volunteers in Service to America
		WAC	Women's Army Corps
NATO	North Atlantic Treaty Organization	**WAVES**	Women Accepted for Volunteer Emergency Service
OEO	Office of Economic Opportunity		
OEP	Office of Emergency Preparedness		

Grammar Practice

Abbreviations 2

- Acronyms
- Initialisms

In each sentence below, write what the abbreviation stands for. (Be careful; some abbreviations can stand for more than one thing!) Choose from the list at the bottom of the page.

Example: Rachel's family makes a yearly donation to CARE.
Cooperative for American Relief to Everywhere

1. The newest model of this car has an ABS.
2. Grandma always writes "P.S. I love you" at the end of the letters that she sends to me.
3. Is this toothpaste approved by the ADA?
4. Jake's car stereo has AFT.
5. The awards program begins at seven o'clock CST.
6. Mom said that she has to get some cash from the ATM.
7. The HVAC technician came to our house to fix the furnace.
8. I used to go to PS 106 in Far Rockaway, New York.
9. Each of the math instructors is a member of the AFT.

American Dental Association
American Federation of Teachers
antilock braking system
automatic fine tuning
automatic teller machine
Central Standard Time
Cooperative for American Relief to Everywhere
heating, ventilation, and air conditioning
postscript
public school

Next Step: Use your imagination to write what these acronyms might stand for: *COMB, SMED,* and *TRIK.*

MECHANICS

Answers

1. antilock braking system
2. postscript
3. American Dental Association
4. automatic fine tuning
5. Central Standard Time
6. automatic teller machine
7. heating, ventilation, and air conditioning
8. public school
9. American Federation of Teachers

Numbers

638.1 Numbers Under 10

Numbers from one to nine are usually written as words; all numbers 10 and over are usually written as numerals.

two seven nine 10 25 106

638.2 Numerals Only

Use numerals to express any of the following forms:

- money $2.39
- decimals 26.2
- percentages .... 8 percent
- chapters .... chapter 7
- pages .... pages 287–289
- time (with "a.m." or "p.m.") .... 4:30 p.m.
- telephone numbers 1-800-555-1212
- dates .... 44 B.C.E.; July 6, 1942
- identification numbers .... Highway 36
- addresses .... 2125 Cairn Road
- ZIP codes 60004
- statistics .... a vote of 23 to 4

When abbreviations and symbols are used (for instance, in science or math), always use numerals with them.

12° C 7% 33 kg 9 cm 55 mph

638.3 Very Large Numbers

You may use a combination of numerals and words for very large numbers.

Of the 17 million residents of the three Midwestern states, only 1.3 million are blondes.

You may spell out a large number that can be written as two words. If more than two words are needed, use the numeral.

More than nine thousand people attended the concert.

About 3,500 people missed the opening act.

Grammar Practice

Numbers 1

- Numbers Under 10
- Numerals Only
- Very Large Numbers

If a number in the sentences below is written incorrectly, write the correct form. Otherwise, write "correct."

Example: Yesterday morning at five-fifteen, Mom's cell phone rang once and stopped.
5:15

1. My family has 2 phone numbers: one for the regular telephone and one for the cell phone.
2. The cell phone number, 555-989-9889, is easy to remember.
3. Since we got the cell phone, our other phone bill has gone down nine percent.
4. Some businesses have ten or more phone numbers.
5. Alpha International, a company at Ten-Twenty Visible Lane, has 66 phone numbers.
6. Area codes were introduced in the United States about fifty years ago, when there were 87 of them.
7. As of June First, 1999, there were 215 area codes in use.
8. Each area code has almost eight million phone numbers.
9. With one point three billion phone numbers currently available, when will the United States run out of phone numbers?
10. In the United States, people make 30 million long-distance calls a day.
11. They make 1.5 billion local calls, which is a twenty-five percent increase since 1990.

Next Step: Write a sentence about the number of times you talk on the phone in a week. Write another sentence that includes the page numbers of the pages you're reviewing.

MECHANICS

Related Skills Activities

- ***SkillsBook***
  Abbreviations and Numbers, pp. 53–54

Answers

1. two
2. correct
3. 9
4. 10
5. 1020
6. 50
7. 1
8. 8 (or) correct
9. 1.3
10. correct
11. 25

Numbers . . .

640.1 Comparing Numbers

If you are comparing two or more numbers in a sentence, write all of them the same way: as numerals or as words.

Students from 9 to 14 years old are invited.

Students from nine to fourteen years old are invited.

640.2 Numbers in Compound Modifiers

A compound modifier may include a numeral.

The floorboards come in 10-foot lengths.

When a number comes before a compound modifier that includes a numeral, use words instead of numerals.

We need eleven 10-foot lengths to finish the floor.

Ms. Brown must grade twenty 12-page reports.

640.3 Sentence Beginnings

Use words, not numerals, to begin a sentence.

Nine students had turned in their homework. Fourteen students said they were unable to finish the assignment.

640.4 Time and Money

When time or money is expressed with a symbol, use numerals. When either is expressed with words, spell out the number.

6:00 a.m. (or) **six o'clock**

$25 (or) **twenty-five dollars**

SCHOOL DAZE

Grammar Practice

Numbers 2

- Comparing Numbers
- Numbers in Compound Modifiers
- Sentence Beginnings
- Time and Money

For each of the following sentences, write the correct form of the number, word, or phrase that is incorrect.

Example: There were 18 15-pound babies at the audition for the diaper commercial.
eighteen

1. 12 of the babies were less than a year old.
2. Those selected would be paid 500 dollars for their "work."
3. The director said, "Will the people sitting in rows eight through 15 please stand up?"
4. 25 people stood up.
5. "Go to soundstage B at 10 o'clock," she said.
6. "The audition should be over by two p.m.," she added.
7. After almost 20 10-minute auditions, the director had to make a decision.
8. She whispered, "I can't decide between Baby Six and Baby 11."
9. 16 of the babies were sent home, and the two remaining babies were in the commercial together.

Next Step: Write a sentence comparing your age and the age of a baby you know. In another sentence, tell how much money you might get to baby-sit that baby.

MECHANICS

Related Skills Activities

- ***SkillsBook***
  Abbreviations and Numbers, pp. 53–54

Answers

1. Twelve
2. $500 (or) five hundred
3. 8 through 15 (or) eight through fifteen
4. Twenty-five
5. ten o'clock (or) 10:00
6. 2:00 p.m.
7. twenty
8. Baby 6 and Baby 11 (or) Baby Six and Baby Eleven
9. Sixteen

Improving Spelling

642.1
i before e

Write *i* before *e* except after *c*, or when sounded like *a* as in *neighbor* and *weigh*.

Some Exceptions to the Rule: *counterfeit, either, financier, foreign, height, heir, leisure, neither, science, seize, sheik, species, their, weird.*

642.2
Silent e

If a word ends with a silent *e*, drop the *e* before adding a suffix that begins with a vowel. There are exceptions, for example, *knowledgeable* and *changeable.*

state—stating—statement	**use—using—useful**
like—liking—likeness	**nine—ninety—nineteen**

NOTE You do not drop the *e* when the suffix begins with a consonant. Exceptions include *truly, argument,* and *ninth.*

642.3
Words Ending in y

When *y* is the last letter in a word and the *y* comes just after a consonant, change the *y* to *i* before adding any suffix except those beginning with *i.*

fry—fries—frying	**happy—happiness**
hurry—hurried—hurrying	**beauty—beautiful**
lady—ladies	

When forming the plural of a word that ends with a *y* that comes just after a vowel, add *s.*

toy—toys **play—plays** **monkey—monkeys**

642.4
Consonant Endings

When a one-syllable word ends in a consonant (*bat*) preceded by one vowel (*bat*), double the final consonant before adding a suffix that begins with a vowel (*batting*).

sum—summary **god—goddess**

When a multisyllable word ends in a consonant preceded by one vowel (*control*), the accent is on the last syllable (*contról*), and the suffix begins with a vowel (*ing*)—the same rule holds true: double the final consonant (*controlling*).

prefer—preferred **begin—beginning**

Grammar Practice

Spelling 1

- *i* before *e*
- Silent *e*

For each of the following sentences, write the correct choice from each set of words in parentheses.

Example: Our *(nieghbor, neighbor)* Esteban bought his *(nineth, ninth)* wrench yesterday; soon he'll have a complete set.
neighbor, ninth

1. The *(cheif, chief)* reason he buys these tools is that he likes *(useing, using)* them for home-improvement projects.
2. Manuel, Esteban's seventh-grade son, is *(hopeful, hopful)* he will own his father's tools someday.
3. A tool *(reveiw, review)* in *Popular Mechanics* magazine rated his father's new scroll saw first out of 20 models.
4. Manuel and Esteban showed some of the tools to Mrs. Gomez, who shares *(thier, their)* enthusiasm for home improvement.
5. She likes to watch that *(fameous, famous)* TV show about fixing up old houses.
6. Mrs. Gomez was impressed with the *(variety, vareity)* of tools and asked Manuel to lend her a saw.
7. Using his best *(judgement, judgment)*, Manuel said he would have to ask his father if she could borrow the scroll saw.
8. After practicing for a while, Mrs. Gomez successfully cut a difficult design out of a *(peice, piece)* of oak.
9. She could not *(believe, beleive)* how smoothly the saw worked.
10. With great *(excitment, excitement)*, she ordered the same scroll saw for herself.

Next Step: Add a suffix to the words *arrive, care,* and *true*; then use each word in a sentence.

SPELLING

Answers

1. chief, using
2. hopeful
3. review
4. their
5. famous
6. variety
7. judgment
8. piece
9. believe
10. excitement

Grammar Practice

Spelling 2

- Words Ending in *y*
- Consonant Endings

For each sentence below, write the correct spelling of any underlined word that is misspelled.

Example: The boys bought three bags of frys for lunch.
fries

1. Mrs. Bock enjoys going to each of the six librarys in our city.
2. When the hurricane occured, it seemed that people were running everywhere.
3. Relief workers knew the food supplies would be greeted with happyness by the storm victims.
4. Samuel's father keeps busy repairing antique toies at his shop and shipping them back to their owners.
5. Workers' salaries could be droping since business is slow.
6. February's blizzard buryed Springfield under two feet of snow—even more in the valleys.
7. Students must stay within the school's boundaries during school dayes.
8. Phil trys to walk two miles every evening, and last week, he saw several rabbits hoping all over the city park.
9. Ms. Stanton needs three students to help her buy groceries for the retreat that our class is planing.
10. We beged the teacher to give us more time to write our essays.
11. The journies of Lewis and Clark led them through beautiful and dangerous territorys.
12. All the canaries took off at once, flaping their yellow wings.

Next Step: Write sentences using the plurals of the following words: *memory, chimney,* and *city*.

Yellow Pages Guide to Improved Spelling

Be patient. Becoming a good speller takes time.

Check your spelling by using a dictionary or list of commonly misspelled words (like the list that follows). And, remember, don't rely too much on computer spell-checkers.

Learn the correct pronunciation of each word you are trying to spell. Knowing the correct pronunciation of a word will help you remember how it's spelled.

Look up the meaning of each word as you are checking the dictionary for pronunciation. (Knowing how to spell a word is of little use if you don't know what it means.)

Practice spelling the word before you close the dictionary. Look away from the page and try to see the word in your mind's eye. Write the word on a piece of paper. Check the spelling in the dictionary and repeat the process until you are able to spell the word correctly.

Keep a list of the words that you misspell.

Write often. As noted educator Frank Smith said, "There is little point in learning to spell if you have little intention of writing."

A

abbreviate
aboard
about
above
absence
absent
absolute (ly)
abundance
accelerate
accident
accidental (ly)
accompany
accomplice
accomplish
according
account
accurate
accustom (ed)
ache
achieve (ment)
acre
across
actual
adapt
addition (al)
address
adequate
adjust (ment)
admire
adventure
advertise (ment)
advertising
afraid
after
afternoon
afterward
again
against
agreeable
agree (ment)
ah
aid
airy
aisle
alarm
alcohol
alike
alive
alley
allowance
all right
almost
already
although
altogether
aluminum
always
amateur
ambulance
amendment
among
amount
analyze
ancient
angel
anger
angle
angry
animal

Answers

1. libraries
2. occurred
3. happiness
4. toys
5. dropping
6. buried
7. days
8. tries, hopping
9. planning
10. begged
11. journeys, territories
12. flapping

anniversary
announce
annoyance
annual
anonymous
another
answer
Antarctic
anticipate
anxiety
anxious
anybody
anyhow
anyone
anything
anyway
anywhere
apartment
apiece
apologize
apparent (ly)
appeal
appearance
appetite
appliance
application
appointment
appreciate
approach
appropriate
approval
approximate
architect
Arctic
aren't
argument
arithmetic
around
arouse
arrange (ment)
arrival
article
artificial

asleep
assassin
assign (ment)
assistance
associate
association
assume
athlete
athletic
attach
attack (ed)
attempt
attendance
attention
attitude
attorney
attractive
audience
August
author
authority
automobile
autumn
available
avenue
average
awful (ly)
awkward

B

baggage
baking
balance
balloon
ballot
banana
bandage
bankrupt
barber
bargain
barrel

basement
basis
basket
battery
beautiful
beauty
because
become
becoming
before
began
beggar
beginning
behave
behavior
being
belief
believe
belong
beneath
benefit (ed)
between
bicycle
biscuit
blackboard
blanket
blizzard
bother
bottle
bottom
bough
bought
bounce
boundary
breakfast
breast
breath (n.)
breathe (v.)
breeze
bridge
brief
bright
brilliant

brother
brought
bruise
bubble
bucket
buckle
budget
building
bulletin
buoyant
bureau
burglar
bury
business
busy
button

C

cabbage
cafeteria
calendar
campaign
canal
cancel (ed)
candidate
candle
canister
cannon
cannot
canoe
can't
canyon
capacity
captain
carburetor
cardboard
career
careful
careless
carpenter
carriage

carrot
cashier
casserole
casualty
catalog
catastrophe
catcher
caterpillar
catsup
ceiling
celebration
cemetery
census
century
certain (ly)
certificate
challenge
champion
changeable
character (istic)
chief
children
chimney
chocolate
choice
chorus
circumstance
citizen
civilization
classmates
classroom
climate
climb
closet
clothing
coach
cocoa
cocoon
coffee
collar
college
colonel
color

colossal
column
comedy
coming
commercial
commission
commit
commitment
committed
committee
communicate
community
company
comparison
competition
competitive (ly)
complain
complete (ly)
complexion
compromise
conceive
concerning
concert
concession
concrete
condemn
condition
conductor
conference
confidence
congratulate
connect
conscience
conscious
conservative
constitution
continue
continuous
control
controversy
convenience
convince
coolly

cooperate
corporation
correspond
cough
couldn't
counter
counterfeit
country
county
courage
courageous
court
courteous
courtesy
cousin
coverage
cozy
cracker
cranky
crawl
creditor
cried
criticize
cruel
crumb
crumble
cupboard
curiosity
curious
current
custom
customer
cylinder

D

daily
dairy
damage
danger (ous)
daughter
dealt

deceive
decided
decision
declaration
decorate
defense
definite (ly)
definition
delicious
dependent
depot
describe
description
desert
deserve
design
desirable
despair
dessert
deteriorate
determine
develop (ment)
device (n.)
devise (v.)
diamond
diaphragm
diary
dictionary
difference
different
difficulty
dining
diploma
director
disagreeable
disappear
disappoint
disappprove
disastrous
discipline
discover
discuss
discussion

disease
dissatisfied
distinguish
distribute
divide
divine
divisible
division
doctor
doesn't
dollar
dormitory
doubt
dough
dual
duplicate

E

eager (ly)
economy
edge
edition
efficiency
eight
eighth
either
elaborate
electricity
elephant
eligible
ellipse
embarrass
emergency
emphasize
employee
employment
enclose
encourage
engineer
enormous
enough
entertain
enthusiastic
entirely
entrance
envelop (v.)
envelope (n.)
environment
equipment
equipped
equivalent
escape
especially
essential
establish
every
evidence
exaggerate
exceed
excellent
except
exceptional (ly)
excite
exercise
exhaust (ed)
exhibition
existence
expect
expensive
experience
explain
explanation
expression
extension
extinct
extraordinary
extreme (ly)

F

facilities
familiar
family
famous
fascinate
fashion
fatigue (d)
faucet
favorite
feature
February
federal
fertile
field
fierce
fiery
fifty
finally
financial (ly)
foliage
forcible
foreign
forfeit
formal (ly)
former (ly)
forth
fortunate
forty
forward
fountain
fourth
fragile
freight
friend (ly)
frighten
fulfill
fundamental
further
furthermore

G

gadget
gauge
generally
generous
genius
gentle
genuine
geography
ghetto
ghost
gnaw
government
governor
graduation
grammar
grateful
grease
grief
grocery
grudge
gruesome
guarantee
guard
guardian
guess
guidance
guide
guilty
gymnasium

H

hammer
handkerchief
handle (d)
handsome
haphazard
happen
happiness
harass
hastily
having
hazardous
headache
height

hemorrhage
hesitate
history
hoarse
holiday
honor
hoping
hopping
horrible
hospital
humorous
hurriedly
hydraulic
hygiene
hymn

I

icicle
identical
illegible
illiterate
illustrate
imaginary
imaginative
imagine
imitation
immediate (ly)
immense
immigrant
immortal
impatient
importance
impossible
improvement
inconvenience
incredible
indefinitely
independence
independent
individual
industrial
inferior
infinite
inflammable
influential
initial
initiation
innocence
innocent
installation
instance
instead
insurance
intelligence
intention
interested
interesting
interfere
interpret
interrupt
interview
investigate
invitation
irrigate
island
issue

J

jealous (y)
jewelry
journal
journey
judgment
juicy

K

kitchen
knew
knife
knives
knock
knowledge
knuckles

L

label
laboratory
ladies
language
laugh
laundry
lawyer
league
lecture
legal
legible
legislature
leisure
length
liable
library
license
lieutenant
lightning
likable
likely
liquid
listen
literature
living
loaves
loneliness
loose
lose
loser
losing
lovable
lovely

M

machinery
magazine
magnificent
maintain
majority
making
manual
manufacture
marriage
material
mathematics
maximum
mayor
meant
measure
medicine
medium
message
mileage
miniature
minimum
minute
mirror
miscellaneous
mischievous
miserable
missile
misspell
moisture
molecule
monotonous
monument
mortgage
mountain
muscle
musician
mysterious

N

naive
natural (ly)
necessary
negotiate
neighbor (hood)
neither
nickel
niece
nineteen
nineteenth
ninety
ninth
noisy
noticeable
nuclear
nuisance

O

obedience
obey
obstacle
occasion
occasional (ly)
occur
occurred
offense
official
often
omission
omitted
operate
opinion
opponent
opportunity
opposite
ordinarily
original
outrageous

P

package
paid
pamphlet
paradise
paragraph
parallel
paralyze
parentheses
partial
participant
participate
particular (ly)
pasture
patience
peculiar
people
perhaps
permanent
perpendicular
persistent
personal (ly)
personnel
perspiration
persuade
phase
physician
piece
pitcher
planned
plateau
playwright
pleasant
pleasure
pneumonia
politician
possess
possible
practical (ly)
prairie
precede
precious
precise (ly)
precision
preferable
preferred
prejudice
preparation
presence
previous
primitive
principal
principle
prisoner
privilege
probably
procedure
proceed
professor
prominent
pronounce
pronunciation
protein
psychology
pumpkin
pure

Q

quarter
questionnaire
quiet
quite
quotient

R

raise
realize
really
receipt
receive
received
recipe
recognize
recommend
reign
relieve
religious
remember
repetition
representative
reservoir
resistance
respectfully
responsibility
restaurant
review
rhyme
rhythm
ridiculous
route

S

safety
salad
salary
sandwich
satisfactory
Saturday
scene
scenery
schedule
science
scissors
scream
screen
season
secretary
seize
sensible
sentence
separate
several

sheriff
shining
similar
since
sincere (ly)
skiing
sleigh
soldier
souvenir
spaghetti
specific
sphere
sprinkle
squeeze
squirrel
statue
stature
statute
stomach
stopped
straight
strength
stretched
studying
subtle
succeed
success
sufficient
summarize
supplement
suppose
surely
surprise
syllable
sympathy
symptom

T

tariff
technique
temperature
temporary
terrible
territory
thankful
theater
their
there
therefore
thief
thorough (ly)
though
throughout
tired
tobacco
together
tomorrow
tongue
touch
tournament
toward
tragedy
treasurer
tried
tries
trouble
truly
Tuesday
typical

U

unconscious
unfortunate (ly)
unique
university
unnecessary
until
usable
useful
using
usual (ly)
utensil

V

vacation
vacuum
valuable
variety
various
vegetable
vehicle
very
vicinity
view
villain
violence
visible
visitor
voice
volume
voluntary
volunteer

W

wander
wasn't
weather
Wednesday
weigh
weird
welcome
welfare
whale
where
whether
which
whole
wholly
whose
width
women
worthwhile
wouldn't
wreckage
writing
written

Y

yellow
yesterday
yield

Using the Right Word

652.1 **a, an**

A is used before words that begin with a consonant sound; *an* is used before words that begin with any vowel sound except long "u."

a heap, a cat, an idol, an elephant, an honor, a historian, an umbrella, a unicorn

652.2 **accept, except**

The verb *accept* means "to receive"; the preposition *except* means "other than."

Melissa graciously accepted defeat. (verb)

All the boys except Zach were here. (preposition)

652.3 **affect, effect**

Affect is almost always a verb; it means "to influence." *Effect* can be a verb, but it is most often used as a noun that means "the result."

How does population growth affect us?

What are the effects of population growth?

652.4 **allowed, aloud**

The verb *allowed* means "permitted" or "let happen"; *aloud* is an adverb that means "in a normal voice."

We aren't allowed to read aloud in the library.

652.5 **allusion, illusion**

An *allusion* is a brief reference to or hint of something (person, place, thing, or idea). An *illusion* is a false impression or idea.

The Great Dontini, a magician, made an allusion to Houdini as he created the illusion of sawing his assistant in half.

652.6 **a lot**

A lot is not one word, but two; it is a general descriptive phrase meaning "plenty." (It should be avoided in formal writing.)

652.7 **all right**

All right is not one word, but two; it is a phrase meaning "satisfactory" or "okay." (Please note, the following *are* spelled correctly: *always, altogether, already, almost.*)

Grammar Practice

Using the Right Word 1

■ accept, except; affect, effect; allowed, aloud; a lot

For each of the following sentences, write the correct choice from each set of words in parentheses.

Example: When Josie reads her writing *(allowed, aloud)*, she hears the mistakes she needs to fix.
aloud

1. Sari's gentle touch and her soft voice had a calming *(affect, effect)* on the frightened collie.
2. Everyone at the school assembly stood and cheered when Franklin went forward to *(accept, except)* the community service award.
3. The use of pocket calculators is not *(allowed, aloud)* during the final exam.
4. That quiz won't *(affect, effect)* my grade *(a lot, alot).*
5. Marlyn put all the wood *(accept, except)* the heaviest piece in his pickup truck.
6. Oil spills around the world *(affect, effect)* future generations of wildlife.
7. Greta volunteers at a senior center, reading the residents' mail *(allowed, aloud)* for them.
8. "Please *(accept, except)* our late report," we begged Mr. Potter.
9. Matthew's little brother is not *(allowed, aloud)* to cross the street unless his mom or dad is there.
10. Troy was upset when everyone *(accept, except)* him was able to walk to the playground.
11. The rule can have a bad *(affect, effect)* on him, it seems.

Next Step: Read the text about "a lot" on the opposite page. Think of a type of writing where you might use this phrase, and write two sentences using it.

Related Skills Activities

- ***SkillsBook***
  Using the Right Word 1, pp. 61–62

Answers

1. effect
2. accept
3. allowed
4. affect, a lot
5. except
6. affect
7. aloud
8. accept
9. allowed
10. except
11. effect

654.1 **already, all ready**

Already is an adverb that tells when. *All ready* is a phrase meaning "completely ready."

We have already eaten breakfast; now we are all ready for school.

654.2 **altogether, all together**

Altogether is always an adverb meaning "completely." *All together* is used to describe people or things that are gathered in one place at one time.

Ms. Monces held her baton in the air and said, "Okay, class, all together now: sing!"

Unfortunately, there was altogether too much street noise for us to hear her.

654.3 **among, between**

Among is used when speaking of more than two persons or things. *Between* is used when speaking of only two.

The three friends talked among themselves as they tried to choose between trumpet or trombone lessons.

654.4 **amount, number**

Amount is used to describe things that you cannot count. *Number* is used when you can actually count the persons or things.

The amount of interest in playing the tuba is shown by the number of kids learning to play the instrument.

654.5 **annual, biannual, semiannual, biennial, perennial**

An *annual* event happens once every year. A *biannual* (or *semiannual*) event happens twice a year. A *biennial* event happens once every two years. A *perennial* event happens year after year.

The annual PTA rummage sale is so successful that it will now be a semiannual event.

The neighbor has some wonderful perennial flowers.

654.6 **ant, aunt**

An *ant* is an insect. An *aunt* is a female relative (the sister of a person's mother or father).

My aunt is an entomologist, a scientist who studies ants and other insects.

654.7 **ascent, assent**

Ascent is the act of rising or climbing; *assent* is agreement.

After the group's ascent of five flights of stairs to the meeting room, plans for elevator repairs met with quick assent.

Grammar Practice

Using the Right Word 2

■ already, all ready; altogether, all together; among, between; amount, number; ascent, assent

For each of the following sentences, write the word "correct" if the underlined word is used correctly. If it is incorrect, write the right word.

Example: The amount of professional football teams has grown over the last 30 years.
number

1. In a "draft," the teams choose new players from between the hundreds who want to join the NFL.
2. A team might think it already has the best players possible.
3. In that case, it is altogether possible they will be the champions.
4. When the team is altogether in the locker room, the coach encourages the players to do their best.
5. A good running back can dash between two defenders and avoid being tackled.
6. A quarterback needs the ascent of all the players to make a successful play.
7. Some players are on the field for a greater amount of time than other players.
8. On the day of the game, professionals must be already to play.
9. If they play well, their team's ascent in the rankings may mean a trip to the Super Bowl.

Next Step: Show that you understand the words *between* and *assent* by using them in a sentence. Then write another sentence using the words *amount* and *already*.

RIGHT WORD

Answers

1. among
2. correct
3. correct
4. all together
5. correct
6. assent
7. correct
8. all ready
9. correct

656.1 **bare, bear**

The adjective *bare* means "naked." A *bear* is a large, heavy animal with shaggy hair.

Despite his bare feet, the man chased the polar bear across the snow.

The verb *bear* means "to put up with" or "to carry."

Dwayne could not bear another of his older brother's lectures.

656.2 **base, bass**

Base is the foundation or the lower part of something. *Bass* (pronounced like "base") is a deep sound or tone.

The stereo speakers are on a base so solid that even the loudest bass tones don't rattle it.

Bass (rhymes with "mass") is a fish.

Jim hooked a record-setting bass, but it got away . . . so he says.

656.3 **beat, beet**

The verb *beat* means "to strike, to defeat," and the noun *beat* is a musical term for rhythm or tempo. A *beet* is a carrot-like vegetable (often red).

The beat of the drum in the marching band encouraged the fans to cheer on the team. After they beat West High's team four games to one, many team members were as red as a beet.

656.4 **berth, birth**

Berth is a space or compartment. *Birth* is the process of being born.

We pulled aside the curtain in our train berth to view the birth of a new day outside our window.

656.5 **beside, besides**

Beside means "by the side of." *Besides* means "in addition to."

Besides a flashlight, Kedar likes to keep his pet boa beside his bed at night.

656.6 **billed, build**

Billed means either "to be given a bill" or "to have a beak." The verb *build* means "to construct."

We asked the carpenter to build us a birdhouse. She billed us for time and materials.

656.7 **blew, blue**

Blew is the past tense of "blow." *Blue* is a color and is also used to mean "feeling low in spirits."

As the wind blew out the candles in the dark blue room, I felt more blue than ever.

Grammar Practice

Using the Right Word 3

■ bare, bear; base, bass; berth, birth; beside, besides; billed, build

For each of the following sentences, write the correct choice from each set of words in parentheses.

Example: In rural areas, families *(billed, build)* small shelters so that students who have to wait for the bus can stay out of the cold wind.
build

1. Julian claims that even on a cold, windy day, his *(bare, bear)* hands stay very warm.
2. *(Beside, Besides)* the strong north winds, last year's big storm brought a great deal of snow.
3. In only an hour, the snow completely covered the flagpole's stone *(base, bass)*.
4. A small tree *(beside, besides)* the library was bent over by the weight of the snow.
5. During that storm, Jake wore a hat that looked like it was made out of *(bare, bear)* fur.
6. Rena knew that the rumbling *(base, bass)* sound she heard meant a snowplow was coming down the street.
7. An ambulance with a woman about to give *(berth, birth)* was able to get through to the hospital.
8. My dad, who has a plow on his truck, *(billed, build)* his customers for plowing their driveways.
9. A passenger traveling through the storm by train was very happy to be in a comfortable *(berth, birth)*.
10. Incredibly, the storm didn't bother the people who were ice fishing for fresh *(base, bass)*.

Next Step: Write two sentences that show your understanding of the two meanings of the word *bass*.

RIGHT WORD

Related Skills Activities

- ***SkillsBook***
  Using the Right Word 1, pp. 61–62

Answers

1. bare
2. Besides
3. base
4. beside
5. bear
6. bass
7. birth
8. billed
9. berth
10. bass

658.1 **board, bored**

A *board* is a piece of wood. *Board* also means "a group or council that helps run an organization."

The school board approved the purchase of 50 pine boards for the woodworking classes.

Bored means "to become weary or tired of something." It can also mean "made a hole by drilling."

Dulé bored a hole in the ice and dropped in a fishing line. Waiting and waiting for a bite bored him.

658.2 **borrow, lend**

Borrow means "to *receive* for temporary use." *Lend* means "to *give* for temporary use."

I asked Mom, "May I borrow $15 for a CD?"

She said, "I can lend you $15 until next Friday."

658.3 **brake, break**

A *brake* is a device used to stop a vehicle. The verb *break* means "to split, crack, or destroy"; as a noun, *break* means "gap or interruption."

After the brake on my bike failed, I took a break to fix it so I wouldn't break a bone.

658.4 **bring, take**

Use *bring* when the action is moving toward the speaker; use *take* when the action is moving away from the speaker.

Grandpa asked me to take the garbage out and bring him today's paper.

658.5 **by, buy, bye**

By is a preposition meaning "near" or "not later than." *Buy* is a verb meaning "to purchase."

By tomorrow I hope to buy tickets for the final match of the tournament.

Bye is the position of being automatically advanced to the next tournament round without playing.

Our soccer team received a bye because of our winning record.

658.6 **can, may**

Can means "able to," while *may* means "permitted to."

"Can I go to the library?"

(This actually means "Are my mind and body strong enough to get me there?")

"May I go?"

(This means "Do I have your permission to go?")

Grammar Practice

Using the Right Word 4

■ board, bored; borrow, lend; brake, break; bring, take; by, buy, bye

For each of the following sentences, write a word from the list above to fill in the blank. Use each word once.

Example: Students who enjoy working with tools almost never complain about being __________ in shop class.
bored

1. Protective glasses are required for a student driving a nail into a __________.
2. Lucinda said, "Mr. Johnson, I will need to __________ my uncle's band saw to cut this wood."
3. Brenda __________ five evenly spaced holes into the top of the trunk she is building.
4. The emergency __________ on the high-speed drill quickly stops its motor.
5. Mr. Johnson asked Lyle to __________ the extra plywood sheet back to the storage room.
6. Esai, the football team's quarterback, was able to finish his project because the team had a __________ last weekend.
7. Curtis said he could not afford to __________ the wood he wanted for his project.
8. As Lawrence walked __________ the pile of lumber, it fell over and hit his left leg.
9. Mr. Johnson asked the school nurse to __________ an ice bag to the classroom.
10. Lawrence was glad he didn't __________ his leg in the accident, but he did require crutches for a few days.
11. Angela said her family had some crutches that they could __________ to Lawrence.

Related Skills Activities

■ ***SkillsBook***
Using the Right Word 1, pp. 61–62

Answers

1. board
2. borrow
3. bored
4. brake
5. take
6. bye
7. buy
8. by
9. bring
10. break
11. lend

660.1 **canvas, canvass**

Canvas is a heavy cloth; *canvass* means "ask people for votes or opinions."

Our old canvas tent leaks.

Someone with a clipboard is canvassing the neighborhood.

660.2 **capital, capitol**

Capital can be either a noun, referring to a city or to money, or an adjective, meaning "major or important." *Capitol* is used only when talking about a building.

The capitol building is in the capital city for a capital (major) reason: The city government contributed the capital (money) for the building project.

660.3 **cell, sell**

Cell means "a small room" or "a small unit of life basic to all plants and animals." *Sell* is a verb meaning "to give up for a price."

Today we looked at a human skin cell under a microscope.

Let's sell those old bicycles at the rummage sale.

660.4 **cent, sent, scent**

Cent (1/100 of a dollar) is a coin; *sent* is the past tense of the verb "send"; *scent* is an odor or a smell.

After our car hit a skunk, we sent our friends a postcard that said, "One cent doesn't go far, but skunk scent seems to last forever."

660.5 **chord, cord**

Chord may mean "an emotion or a feeling," but it is more often used to mean "the sound of three or more musical tones played at the same time." A *cord* is a string or rope.

The band struck a chord at the exact moment the mayor pulled the cord on the drape covering the new statue.

660.6 **chose, choose**

Chose (chōz) is the past tense of the verb *choose* (chōōz).

This afternoon Mom chose tacos and hot sauce; this evening she will choose an antacid.

660.7 **coarse, course**

Coarse means "rough or crude." *Course* means "a path" or "a class or series of studies."

In our cooking course, we learned to use coarse salt and freshly ground pepper in salads.

Grammar Practice

Using the Right Word 5

■ capital, capitol; cell, sell; cent, sent, scent; chose, choose; coarse, course

For each of the following sentences, write the correct choice from each set of words in parentheses.

Example: Last month, the entire seventh-grade class went to our state's *(capital, capitol)* city to watch a debate.
capital

1. Ben began sanding the *(coarse, course)* wood on the old desk.
2. Every student in science class gets a chance to look through a microscope at a single skin *(cell, sell)*.
3. After looking carefully at each toy, Darien *(chose, choose)* the model car kit.
4. Will opened the door and immediately smelled the *(cent, sent, scent)* of a burning candle.
5. Ms. Jur said that José, Cana, Fran, and Carmen could *(chose, choose)* the next film for the class to watch.
6. Senators from every state meet regularly in the *(Capital, Capitol)* building in Washington, D.C.
7. Julian will *(cell, sell)* candy for the school's fund-raiser.
8. The art class students picked the best drawings of the city and *(cent, sent, scent)* them to the mayor's office.
9. Teachers of each *(coarse, course)* expect that students will complete homework assignments on time.
10. Julio saw that the "sale" price of the CD was $9.99, which was only one *(cent, sent, scent)* less than its regular price of $10.

Next Step: Using the pairs of words in this exercise, write two sentences that offer a choice (as in the sentences above). Exchange papers with a partner and pick the right words for each other's sentences.

Answers

1. coarse
2. cell
3. chose
4. scent
5. choose
6. Capitol
7. sell
8. sent
9. course
10. cent

662.1 complement, compliment

Complement means "to complete or go with." *Compliment* is an expression of admiration or praise.

Aunt Athena said, "Your cheese sauce really complements this cauliflower!"

"Thank you for the compliment," I replied.

662.2 continual, continuous

Continual refers to something that happens again and again; *continuous* refers to something that doesn't stop happening.

Sunlight hits Peoria, Iowa, on a continual basis; but sunlight hits the earth continuously.

662.3 counsel, council

When used as a noun, *counsel* means "advice"; when used as a verb, *counsel* means "to advise." *Council* refers to a group that advises.

The student council asked for counsel from its trusted adviser.

662.4 creak, creek

A *creak* is a squeaking sound; a *creek* is a stream.

I heard a creak from the old dock under my feet as I fished in the creek.

662.5 cymbal, symbol

A *cymbal* is a metal instrument shaped like a plate. A *symbol* is something (usually visible) that stands for or represents another thing or idea (usually invisible).

The damaged cymbal lying on the stage was a symbol of the band's final concert.

662.6 dear, deer

Dear means "loved or valued"; *deer* are animals.

My dear, old great-grandmother leaves corn and salt licks in her yard to attract deer.

662.7 desert, dessert

A *desert* is a barren wilderness. *Dessert* is a food served at the end of a meal.

In the desert, cold water is more inviting than even the richest dessert.

The verb *desert* means "to abandon"; the noun *desert* (pronounced like the verb) means "deserving reward or punishment."

A spy who deserts his country will receive his just deserts if he is caught.

Grammar Practice

Using the Right Word 6

- complements, compliments; counsel, council; creak, creek; cymbal, symbol; desert, dessert

For each sentence below, write a word from the list above to fill in the blank.

Example: I would offer this __________ to any visitor to my city: Visit Becker Park.
counsel

1. Although my city is located in the __________, Becker Park is full of green trees and colorful flowers.
2. What I like most about the park is the little __________ that runs through it.
3. I like to hear the __________ of the boards when I walk on the bridge over the water.
4. Every six months, the city __________ organizes a day for volunteers to pick up trash and work in the gardens.
5. Last time, the cleanup day followed a parade, and someone found a __________ from the marching band!
6. The volunteer work __________ the work done by city employees.
7. On the day of the cleanup, each participant receives a T-shirt with a huge oak tree on the back, a __________ of Becker Park.
8. A local restaurant offers free coffee and __________ to the volunteers.
9. The city newspaper always __________ the volunteers' work in the next day's issue.

Next Step: Write two sentences that show your understanding of the words *complement* and *compliment*.

Related Skills Activities

- ***SkillsBook***
  Using the Right Word 2, p. 63

Answers

1. desert
2. creek
3. creak
4. council
5. cymbal
6. complements
7. symbol
8. dessert
9. compliments

Understanding Sentences

Sentences

A **sentence** is a group of words that expresses a complete thought. A sentence must have both a subject and a predicate. A sentence begins with a capital letter; it ends with a period, a question mark, or an exclamation point.

I like my teacher this year.
Will we go on a field trip?
We get to go to the water park!

Parts of a Sentence

690.1 Subjects

A subject is the part of a sentence that does something or is talked about.

The kids on my block play basketball at the local park.
We meet after school almost every day.

690.2 Simple Subjects

The simple subject is the subject without the words that describe or modify it. (Also see page 502.)

My friend Chester plays basketball on the school team.

690.3 Complete Subjects

The complete subject is the simple subject and all the words that modify it. (Also see page 501.)

My friend Chester plays basketball on the school team.

690.4 Compound Subjects

A compound subject has two or more simple subjects. (See page 502.)

Chester, Malik, and Meshelle play on our pickup team.
Lou and I are the best shooters.

Grammar Practice

Parts of a Sentence 1

■ Simple, Complete, and Compound Subjects

For each numbered sentence in the paragraphs below, write the complete subject. Then circle the simple subject or the compound subject. (*Remember:* Compound sentences have two subjects.)

Example: Car problems made me late for school.
Car (problems)

(1) I was on my way to school in my dad's car. **(2)** Suddenly, a light mist came from the vents, and an odd, sweet smell filled the car. **(3)** Dad pulled over and called a tow truck. **(4)** Thinking about yet another trip to the repair shop, he sighed deeply.

(5) A mechanic at the repair shop took a look at the engine. **(6)** Cars are so complex these days! **(7)** How does the mechanic know what to look for? **(8)** In most cases, training programs prepare mechanics for their work. **(9)** A two-year degree from a technical college is required for employment at many automobile dealerships. **(10)** Today's cars call for special training on computerized shop equipment. **(11)** Additionally, mechanics need some knowledge of electronics. **(12)** Of course, they must also work with traditional hand tools. **(13)** Besides a complete knowledge of automobiles, a good mechanic also needs the ability to solve problems.

(14) Dad's mechanic gave him the news. **(15)** "The problem is probably with the heater core." **(16)** Poor, stressed-out Dad had the repair shop fix his car . . . again.

Next Step: Write two sentences about a career that interests you. Exchange papers with a classmate. Underline your partner's complete subjects and circle the simple (or compound) subjects.

SENTENCES

Related Skills Activities

- **Basic Grammar and Writing**
  Writing Complete Sentences, pp. 500–501
  Subjects and Predicates, p. 502
  Make Subjects and Verbs Agree, p. 509
- ***SkillsBook***
  Subjects and Predicates 1, pp. 69–70
  Subjects and Predicates 2, pp. 71–72
  Compound Subjects and Predicates, pp. 73–74
- ***GrammarSnap***
  Complete Sentences and Sentence Fragments

Answers

1. (I)
2. a light (mist)
   an odd, sweet (smell)
3. (Dad)
4. Thinking about yet another trip to the repair shop, (he)
5. A (mechanic) at the repair shop
6. (Cars)
7. the (mechanic)
8. training (programs)
9. A two-year (degree) from a technical college
10. Today's (cars)
11. (mechanics)
12. (they)
13. a good (mechanic)
14. Dad's (mechanic)
15. The (problem)
16. Poor, stressed-out (Dad)

Parts of a Sentence . . .

692.1 Predicates

The predicate, which contains the verb, is the part of the sentence that shows action or says something about the subject.

Hunting has reduced the tiger population in India.

692.2 Simple Predicates

The simple predicate is the predicate (verb) without the words that describe or modify it. (See page 502.)

In the past, poachers killed too many African elephants.
Poaching is illegal.

692.3 Complete Predicates

The complete predicate is the simple predicate with all the words that modify or describe it. (See page 501.)

In the past, poachers killed too many African elephants.
Poaching is illegal.

692.4 Direct Objects

The complete predicate often includes a direct object. The direct object is the noun or pronoun that receives the action of the simple predicate—directly. The direct object answers the question *what* or *whom*. (See page 570.)

Many smaller animals need friends who will speak up for them.

The direct object may be compound.

We all need animals, plants, wetlands, deserts, and forests.

692.5 Indirect Objects

If a sentence has a direct object, it may also have an indirect object. An indirect object is the noun or pronoun that receives the action of the simple predicate—indirectly. An indirect object names the person *to whom* or *for whom* something is done. (See page 570.)

I showed the class my multimedia report on endangered species. (*Class* is the indirect object because it says *to whom* the report was shown.)

Remember, in order for a sentence to have an indirect object, it must first have a direct object.

692.6 Compound Predicates

A compound predicate is composed of two or more simple predicates. (See page 502.)

In 1990 the countries of the world met and banned the sale of ivory.

Grammar Practice

Parts of a Sentence 2

- Simple, Compound, and Complete Predicates
- Direct and Indirect Objects

For each numbered sentence below, write the complete predicate. (*Remember:* Compound or complex sentences will have two.) Underline any direct objects once and indirect objects twice.

Example: Some people innocently plant weeds.
innocently plant weeds

(1) Kudzu is a vine found in the southern states. **(2)** The climate there encourages the vine's rapid growth—as much as a foot per day! **(3)** The vine climbs trees, signposts, and barns. **(4)** It covers anything in its way. **(5)** Giant kudzu-covered trees that look like monsters are pretty scary!

(6) Although kudzu grows so well in the Southeast, it is not a native plant in the United States. **(7)** For Philadelphia's 1876 U.S. Centennial Exposition, the Japanese government created a delightful garden. **(8)** Plants from Japan, including kudzu, gave Americans ideas. **(9)** Japanese gardeners sold people the lush, sweet-smelling vine.

(10) Kudzu helped prevent soil erosion, so people planted the vine throughout the South. **(11)** Kudzu now covers seven million acres of land in the region. **(12)** Unfortunately, the thick vines prevent trees from getting sunlight, and valuable forests are dying as a result.

Next Step: Now go back and circle the simple or compound predicates within the complete predicates you wrote down.

SENTENCES

Related Skills Activities

- **Basic Grammar and Writing**
  Make the Meaning of the Verb Complete, p. 473
  Writing Complete Sentences, pp. 500–501
  Subjects and Predicates, p. 502
  Make Subjects and Verbs Agree, p. 509
- ***SkillsBook***
  Subjects and Predicates 1, pp. 69–70
  Subjects and Predicates 2, pp. 71–72
  Compound Subjects and Predicates, pp. 73–74
- ***GrammarSnap***
  Direct and Indirect Object

Answers

1. is a vine found in the southern states
2. encourages the vine's rapid growth—as much as a foot per day
3. climbs trees, signposts, and barns
4. covers anything in its way
5. look like monsters
   are pretty scary
6. grows so well in the Southeast
   is not a native plant in the United States
7. For Philadelphia's 1876 U.S. Centennial Exposition
   created a delightful garden
8. gave Americans ideas
9. sold people the lush, sweet-smelling vine
10. helped prevent soil erosion
    planted the vine throughout the South
11. now covers seven million acres of land in the region
12. Unfortunately
    prevent trees from getting sunlight
    are dying as a result

Parts of a Sentence . . .

694.1 Understood Subjects and Predicates

Either the subject or the predicate (or both) may not be stated in a sentence, but both must be clearly understood.

[You] **Get involved!** (*You* is the understood subject.)

Who needs your help? Animals [do]. (*Do* is the understood predicate.)

What do many animals face? [They face] **Extinction.** (*They* is the understood subject, and *face* is the understood predicate.)

694.2 Delayed Subjects

In sentences that begin with *there* followed by a form of the "be" verb, the subject usually follows the verb. (See page 570.)

There are laws **that protect endangered species.** (The subject is *laws; are* is the verb.)

The subject is also delayed in questions.

How can we **preserve the natural habitat?** (*We* is the subject.)

694.3 Modifiers

A modifier is a word (adjective, adverb) or a group of words (phrase, clause) that changes or adds to the meaning of another word. (See pages 486–493.)

Many North American **zoos and aquariums** voluntarily **participate** in breeding programs that help prevent extinction.

The modifiers in this sentence include the following: *many, North American* (adjectives), *voluntarily* (adverb), *in breeding programs* (phrase), *that help prevent extinction* (clause).

Grammar Practice

Parts of a Sentence 3

■ Understood Subjects and Predicates

For the answer to each question below, write the word or words that are not stated but are understood. Identify them as "subject," "predicate," or "both."

Example: *How do we get to Turner Road?*
Turn right at the first stoplight. *You (subject)*

1. *Who is the substitute teacher today?*
Mr. Ross.
2. *When is our next test?*
Friday.
3. *May I go outside after lunch?*
Yes.
4. *How do I cut this?*
Use a pair of scissors.
5. *What has been added to this popcorn?*
Oil, butter, and salt.
6. *What did Marva get from Johnny?*
A box of chocolates.

■ Delayed Subjects

Rewrite each of the following sentences so that the subject is not delayed.

Example: Would you like to go for a walk?
You would like to go for a walk.

1. Is that a Siamese cat?
2. May I ride my bike to the arcade?
3. Are we having dinner with the Thorsens tonight?
4. After the movie, will Marcus need a ride home?

SENTENCES

Related Skills Activities

- **Basic Grammar and Writing**
Describing with Adjectives, p. 486
Describing with Adverbs, p. 490
- ***GrammarSnap***
Adjectives and Adverbs

Answers

1. is the substitute teacher today (predicate)
2. Our next test is on (both)
3. You may go outside after lunch (both)
4. You (subject)
5. have been added (predicate)
6. Marva got (both)

Answers

1. That is a Siamese cat.
2. I may ride my bike to the arcade.
3. We are having dinner with the Thorsens tonight.
4. Marcus will need a ride home after the movie.

Test Prep!

Number your paper from 1 to 20. For each underlined part in the following paragraphs, choose the letter or letters from the list below that best describe it. (Some answers will have two letters.)

(A) simple subject	(D) simple predicate
(B) complete subject	(E) complete predicate
(C) compound subject	(F) compound predicate

In 1883, a volcano in eastern Indonesia (1) erupted. As a result, 100-foot ocean waves traveling at 400 miles per hour crashed (2) onto some nearby islands. More than 36,000 people (3) died. The disaster was a *tsunami*, a series of huge ocean waves. Usually an earthquake or a volcanic eruption (4) causes a tsunami.

A tsunami's waves (5) are vast amounts of water pushed by a sudden movement of the earth. These incredible waves can travel great distances without losing power (6). Near shore, the shallow seafloor makes (7) the first wave slow down. Meanwhile, the waves behind it are still coming in fast. They all start to pile up and, therefore, become a high wall of water (8). The waves are so powerful that, when they finally do come ashore, they can go inland for half a mile.

Although a tsunami (9) can travel 450 miles per hour along the ocean floor, it may not be noticed in the open ocean. Though these gigantic waves extend thousands of feet deep, they may be only three feet higher than usual on the surface (10). For this reason, it may be impossible to see an approaching tsunami. The terrible aftermath of the December 2004 tsunami in the Indian Ocean (11) revealed (12) the incredible power and destruction of these waves. However, the International Tsunami Warning System (13) was set up in 1965. This organization tries to predict tsunamis (14). The workers detect earthquakes on the ocean floor and use tsunami detection buoys (15). They (16) record and study (17) data from satellite measurements of sudden sea-level changes.

Once a tsunami is set in motion, it can't be stopped. However, areawide alerts (18) allow people to get away from the coast. Loss of life and damage to property (19) can be reduced thanks to the early warnings. After 2004, national leaders and officials (20) began an international effort to extend the early warning system to all vulnerable areas of the Pacific.

Answers

1. B
2. D
3. B
4. B and C
5. A
6. E
7. D
8. E and F
9. A
10. E
11. B
12. D
13. B
14. E
15. E and F
16. A
17. F
18. A
19. B
20. B and C

Parts of a Sentence . . .

698.1 Clauses

A clause is a group of related words that has both a subject and a verb. (Also see pages 513–515.)

a whole chain of plants and animals is affected
(*Chain* is the subject, and *is affected* is the verb.)

when one species dies out completely
(*Species* is the subject; *dies out* is the verb.)

698.2 Independent Clauses

An independent clause presents a complete thought and can stand alone as a sentence.

This ancient oak tree may be cut down.

This act could affect more than 200 different species of animals!

Why would anyone want that to happen?

698.3 Dependent Clauses

A dependent clause does not present a complete thought and cannot stand as a sentence. A dependent clause *depends* on being connected to an independent clause to make sense. Dependent clauses begin with either a subordinating conjunction (*after, although, because, before, if*) or a relative pronoun (*who, whose, which, that*). (See pages 710 and 744 for complete lists.)

If this ancient oak tree is cut down, it could affect more than 200 different species of animals!

The tree, which experts think could be 400 years old, provides a home to many different kinds of birds and insects.

698.4 Adverb Clauses

An adverb clause is a clause that acts as an adverb. It contains a subject and a verb and modifies a verb.

Samuel gave me a call when he arrived at the airport.

698.5 Adjective Clauses

An adjective clause is always introduced by a relative pronoun—*who, whom, which, whose,* or *that.*

The car that she is driving is brand new.

Grammar Practice

Parts of a Sentence 4

■ Clauses

Some "sentences" in the following paragraphs are actually dependent clauses. Combine these clauses with a nearby independent clause to form a complex sentence.

Example: Before a bee is able to make a pound of beeswax. It must eat about 10 pounds of honey.
Before a bee is able to make a pound of beeswax, it must eat about 10 pounds of honey.

(1) There are three types of bees in a colony, including the queen. Who produces the eggs. **(2)** The male bees are called drones. **(3)** The thousands of female worker bees gather nectar, build the cells of a honeycomb, and make and store honey. **(4)** Worker bees also feed the larvae. **(5)** Until they reach mature size.

(6) Bees know where to find food. **(7)** Because they communicate with each other by "dancing" in a certain pattern. **(8)** Most bees get all of their food from flowers. **(9)** Which provide pollen and nectar. **(10)** The nectar is converted to honey. **(11)** When it reaches the bee's digestive tract.

(12) A beekeeper knows how to care for honeybees so that they produce and store more honey than they need. **(13)** The beekeeper collects the excess honey. **(14)** After the bees have been made sleepy with smoke. **(15)** The bees can then refill the honeycombs, or the beekeeper might melt the honeycomb. **(16)** If she or he wants to use the beeswax.

Next Step: In two columns labeled "relative pronouns" and "subordinating conjunctions," write all of the words that begin the dependent clauses in the paragraphs above.

Related Skills Activities

■ **Basic Grammar and Writing**
Combine with a Series of Words, p. 513
Combine with Relative Pronouns, p. 514
Write Simple Sentences. p. 515
Create Compound Sentences, p. 515
Develop Complex Sentences, p. 516

■ ***SkillsBook***
Clauses, pp. 75–76
Adverb Clauses, pp. 77–78
Adjective Clauses, pp. 79–80

■ ***GrammarSnap***
Adjectival Clauses
Adverbial Clauses

Answers

1. There are three types of bees in a colony, including the queen, who produces the eggs.
2. Worker bees also feed the larvae until they reach mature size.
3. Bees know where to find food because they communicate with each other by "dancing" in a certain pattern.
4. Most bees get all of their food from flowers, which provide pollen and nectar.
5. The nectar is converted to honey when it reaches the bee's digestive tract.
6. The beekeeper collects the excess honey after the bees have been made sleepy with smoke.
7. The beekeeper can then refill the honeycombs, or the beekeeper might melt the honeycomb if he or she wants to use the beeswax.

Parts of a Sentence . . .

700.1 Phrases

A phrase is a group of related words that lacks either a subject or a predicate (or both). (See pages 519–520.)

guards the house (The predicate lacks a subject.)

the ancient oak tree (The subject lacks a predicate.)

with crooked old limbs (The phrase lacks both a subject and a predicate.)

The ancient oak tree with crooked old limbs guards the house. (Together, the three phrases form a complete thought.)

700.2 Types of Phrases

Phrases usually take their names from the main words that introduce them (prepositional phrase, verb phrase, and so on). They are also named for the function they serve in a sentence (adverb phrase, adjective phrase).

The ancient oak tree (noun phrase)

with crooked old limbs (prepositional phrase)

has stood its guard, (verb phrase)

very stubbornly, (adverb phrase)

protecting the little house. (verbal phrase)

For more information on verbal phrases, see page 730.

Grammar Practice

Parts of a Sentence 5

■ Phrases

Combine each of the following groups of phrases to write a sentence that forms a complete thought.

Example: of water and land / are creatures / animals called amphibians

Animals called amphibians are creatures of water and land.

1. belong in this classification / salamanders, toads, frogs, and newts
2. to the water / on land / is clear / but their connection / spend most of their lives / these animals
3. will slowly dry out / without a moist environment / any amphibian
4. in addition, they / need water / to lay their eggs
5. in body shape / go through a change / most amphibians
6. is probably / the everyday frog / the best-known example
7. a frog / in the water / as a tadpole / begins life
8. develops legs and lungs / and the tail / eventually disappears / during its growth period / the tadpole
9. onto land / a fully developed frog / will crawl / at last

Next Step: Label each of the phrases in numbers 5, 7, and 9 above as a "noun phrase," "verb phrase," or "prepositional phrase."

SENTENCES

Related Skills Activities

■ **Basic Grammar and Writing**
Expand with Prepositional Phrases, p. 519
Expand with Participial Phrases, p. 520

■ ***SkillsBook***
Phrases, pp. 81–82

■ ***GrammarSnap***
Prepositions and Prepositional Phrases
Participles and Participial Phrases
Adjectival Phrases

Answers

1. Salamanders, toads, frogs, and newts belong in this classification.
2. These animals spend most of their lives on land, but their connection to the water is clear.
3. Any amphibian will slowly dry out without a moist environment.
4. In addition, they need water to lay their eggs.
5. Most amphibians go through a change in body shape.
6. The best-known example is probably the everyday frog.
7. A frog begins life in the water as a tadpole.
8. The tadpole develops legs and lungs during its growth period, and the tail eventually disappears.
9. A fully developed frog will crawl at last onto land.

Using the Parts of Speech

Nouns

A **noun** is a word that names a person, a place, a thing, or an idea.

Person: **John Ulferts** (uncle) Thing: **"Yankee Doodle"** (song)
Place: **Mississippi** (state) Idea: **Labor Day** (holiday)

Kinds of Nouns

702.1 Common Nouns

A common noun is any noun that does not name a specific person, place, thing, or idea. These nouns are not capitalized.

woman museum book weekend

702.2 Proper Nouns

A proper noun is the name of a specific person, place, thing, or idea. Proper nouns are capitalized.

Hillary Clinton Central Park *Maniac McGee* Sunday

702.3 Concrete Nouns

A concrete noun names a thing that is physical (can be touched or seen). Concrete nouns can be either proper or common.

space station pencil Statue of Liberty

702.4 Abstract Nouns

An abstract noun names something you can think about but cannot see or touch. Abstract nouns can be either common or proper.

Judaism poverty satisfaction illness

702.5 Collective Nouns

A collective noun names a group or collection of persons, animals, places, or things.

Persons: **tribe, congregation, family, class, team**
Animals: **flock, herd, gaggle, clutch, litter**
Things: **batch, cluster, bunch**

702.6 Compound Nouns

A compound noun is made up of two or more words.

football (written as one word)
high school (written as two words)

Grammar Practice

Nouns 1

■ Kinds of Nouns

Write the answers to the questions following each paragraph.

After 300 years of Spanish rule, Mexico gained its independence in 1810. Like the United States, Mexico is a federal republic headed by a president. The country is divided into 31 states.

Which of the underlined nouns is . . .

1. a common, concrete noun?
2. a common, abstract noun?
3. a proper, concrete noun?

The population of the entire country is nearly 105 million. A full 89 percent of the people are Roman Catholics. The country's official language is Spanish.

Which of the underlined nouns is . . .

4. a collective noun?
5. a proper, abstract noun?
6. a proper, concrete noun?

Mexico's geography ranges from mountains to desert to low coastal plains. As a result, its climate also varies; there are hot, temperate, and cool regions. Mexico can be an enjoyable place for a family to vacation.

Which of the underlined nouns is . . .

7. a proper, concrete noun?
8. a collective noun?
9. a common, abstract noun?
10. a common, concrete noun?

Related Skills Activities

- **Basic Grammar and Writing**
  Using Nouns, pp. 470–471
- ***SkillsBook***
  Common and Proper Nouns, pp. 141–142
  Concrete and Abstract Nouns, pp. 143–144
- ***GrammarSnap***
  Nouns Overview

Answers

1. president
2. independence
3. United States
4. population
5. Spanish
6. Roman Catholics
7. Mexico
8. family
9. result
10. mountains

Nouns . . .

Number of Nouns

The number of a noun is either singular or plural.

704.1 Singular Nouns

A singular noun names one person, place, thing, or idea.

boy group audience stage concert hope

704.2 Plural Nouns

A plural noun names more than one person, place, thing, or idea.

boys groups audiences stages concerts hopes

Gender of Nouns

704.3 Noun Gender

Nouns are grouped according to gender: *feminine, masculine, neuter,* and *indefinite.*

Feminine (female): **mother, sister, women, cow, hen**
Masculine (male): **father, brother, men, bull, rooster**
Neuter (neither male nor female): **tree, cobweb, closet**
Indefinite (male or female): **president, duckling, doctor**

Uses of Nouns

704.4 Subject Nouns

A noun that is the subject of a sentence does something or is talked about in the sentence.

The roots of rap can be traced back to West Africa and Jamaica.

704.5 Predicate Nouns

A predicate noun follows a form of the *be* verb *(am, is, are, was, were, being, been)* and renames the subject.

In the 1970s, rap was a street art.

704.6 Possessive Nouns

A possessive noun shows possession or ownership.

Early rap had a drummer's beat but no music.

704.7 Object Nouns

A noun is an object noun when it is used as the direct object, the indirect object, or the object of the preposition.

Some rappers tell people their story about life in the city. (indirect object: *people;* direct object: *story*)

Rap is now a common music choice in this country. (object of the preposition: *country*)

Grammar Practice

Nouns 2

Number and Gender of Nouns

Draw a chart like the one below. Classify the underlined nouns in the following paragraph by writing them in the correct box.

Gender	Singular	Plural
feminine		
masculine		*men*
neuter		
indefinite		

Antarctica was a continent without men or women until explorers and researchers from other parts of the world arrived. Only penguins and seals lived on the land. In December 1911, Roald Amundsen and four other men made their way across Antarctica using skis and dogsleds. They were the first people to reach the South Pole, which is the point in the earth's southern hemisphere where all the lines of longitude start. The group traveled quickly across snow and mountains. When they reached the pole, they set up the Norwegian flag. A month later, a team led by British explorer Robert Scott arrived at the South Pole. It wasn't until 1969, however, that the first woman reached the pole.

Uses of Nouns

Number your paper from 1 to 4. List each underlined noun from the following paragraph and identify it as a "subject noun," a "predicate noun," a "possessive noun," or an "object noun."

Example: Twelve nations signed the International Antarctic Treaty in 1961.
nations, subject noun

The treaty's rules say that people can use Antarctica only for peaceful purposes. The rules also promise freedom to do scientific study. Today, many countries have permanent research stations in Antarctica, and about 4,000 people are full-time residents during its summer months.

PARTS OF SPEECH

Related Skills Activities

- **Basic Grammar and Writing**
  Show Possession, p. 472
  Make the Meaning of a Verb Complete, p. 473
- ***SkillsBook***
  Subject and Object Nouns, pp. 145–146
- ***GrammarSnap***
  Nouns Overview

Answers

Gender	Singular	Plural
feminine	woman	women
masculine	Roald Amundsen	men
neuter	flag	mountains
indefinite	group	researchers

Answers

1. treaty's, possessive noun
2. freedom, object noun
3. countries, subject noun
4. residents, predicate noun

Pronouns

A **pronoun** is a word used in place of a noun. Some examples are *I, you, he, she, it, we, they, his, hers, her, its, me, myself, us, yours,* and so on.

Without pronouns: **Kevin said Kevin would be going to Kevin's grandmother's house this weekend.**

With pronouns: **Kevin said he would be going to his grandmother's house this weekend.**

706.1 Antecedents

An antecedent is the noun that the pronoun refers to or replaces. All pronouns (except interrogative and indefinite pronouns) have antecedents. (See page 474.)

Jamal and Rick tried out for the team, and they both made it.
(*They* refers to *Jamal* and *Rick; it* refers to *team.*)

NOTE Pronouns must agree with their antecedents in number, person, and gender. (See pages 477–478.)

Types of Pronouns

There are several types of pronouns. The most common type is the personal pronoun. (See the chart on page 710.)

706.2 Personal Pronouns

A personal pronoun takes the place of a specific person (or thing) in a sentence. Some common personal pronouns are *I, you, he, she, it, we,* and *they.*

Suriana would not like to live in Buffalo, New York, because she does not like snow.

706.3 Relative Pronouns

A relative pronoun is both a pronoun and a connecting word. It connects a dependent clause to an independent clause in a complex sentence. Relative pronouns include *who, whose, which,* and *that.* (See page 514 and 684.6.)

Buffalo, which often gets more than eight feet of snow in a year, is on the northeast shore of Lake Erie.

The United States city that gets the most snow is Valdez, Alaska.

706.4 Interrogative Pronouns

An interrogative pronoun helps ask a question.

Who wants to go to Alaska?
Which of the cities would you visit?
Whom would you like to travel with?
What did you say?

Grammar Practice

Pronouns 1

■ Personal, Relative, and Interrogative Pronouns

For each of the following sentences, identify the underlined pronouns as "personal," "relative," or "interrogative."

Example: Great horned owls, which are the second-largest owls in North America, rely on their night vision to find prey in the dark.
relative

1. An owl near Madison, Wisconsin, was starving in the wild because it had gone blind.
2. Who was brave enough to capture the creature?
3. Sue Theys, the woman who netted the owl, suspected that it had cataracts.
4. She and her husband took the owl to the veterinarian.
5. What does a vet do when an owl can't see?
6. Dr. Chris Murphy, a veterinary eye doctor, decided that he could perform surgery on the bird.
7. Dr. Murphy supervised two other doctors, and they implanted a pair of contact lenses into the bird's eyes.
8. Whose were they?
9. The lenses were originally made for another owl that ended up not having the surgery.
10. The Theyses gave the bird antibiotics and fed it mice during its recovery.
11. The great horned owl, whose wingspan can reach 55 inches, eats a variety of other animals.

Next Step: Go back to the previous sentences and write the antecedent for each of the personal and relative pronouns.

Related Skills Activities

■ **Basic Grammar and Writing**
Using Pronouns, pp. 474, 476, 477, 478, 479
Combine with Relative Pronouns, p. 514

■ ***SkillsBook***
Pronouns and Antecedents, pp. 149–150
Types of Pronouns 2, pp. 153–154
Pronoun-Antecedent 1 and 2, pp. 159–162

■ ***GrammarSnap***
Pronoun-Antecedent Agreement

Answers

1. personal (owl)
2. interrogative
3. relative (woman)
4. personal (Sue Theys)
5. interrogative
6. personal (Dr. Chris Murphy)
7. personal (doctors)
8. interrogative
9. relative (owl)
10. personal (bird)
11. relative (owl)

Pronouns . . .

Types of Pronouns

708.1 Demonstrative Pronouns

A demonstrative pronoun points out or identifies a noun without naming the noun. When used together in a sentence, *this* and *that* distinguish one item from another, and *these* and *those* distinguish one group from another. (See page 710.)

This is a great idea; that was a nightmare.

These are my favorite foods, and those are definitely not.

NOTE When these words are used before a noun, they are not pronouns; rather, they are demonstrative adjectives.

Coming to this picnic was fun—and those ants think so, too.

708.2 Intensive Pronouns

An intensive pronoun emphasizes, or *intensifies*, the noun or pronoun it refers to. Common intensive pronouns include *itself, myself, himself, herself,* and *yourself.*

Though the chameleon's quick-change act protects it from predators, the lizard itself can catch insects 10 inches away with its long, sticky tongue.

When a chameleon changes its skin color—seemingly matching the background—the background colors themselves do not affect the chameleon's color changes.

NOTE These sentences would be complete without the intensive pronoun. The pronoun simply emphasizes a particular noun.

708.3 Reflexive Pronouns

A reflexive pronoun refers back to the subject of a sentence, and it is always an object (never a subject) in a sentence. Reflexive pronouns are the same as the intensive pronouns—*itself, myself, himself, herself, yourself,* and so on.

A chameleon protects itself from danger by changing colors. (direct object)

A chameleon can give itself tasty meals of unsuspecting insects. (indirect object)

I wish I could claim some of its amazing powers for myself. (object of the preposition)

NOTE Unlike sentences with intensive pronouns, these sentences would *not* be complete without the reflexive pronouns.

Grammar Practice

Pronouns 2

■ Demonstrative Pronouns

Write whether the underlined word is a demonstrative adjective or a demonstrative pronoun. *Extra Challenge:* Rewrite any sentence that contains a demonstrative adjective, changing the sentence so that the word is used as a pronoun instead.

Example: This cave is deep and dark.
demonstrative adjective
This is a deep and dark cave.

1. That concert was awful.
2. This is my absolute favorite meal!
3. Those are some of the birds I told you about.
4. This diagram is very confusing.
5. That was an unusual discovery.

■ Intensive Pronouns
■ Reflexive Pronouns

For each sentence below, write whether the underlined pronoun is "intensive" or "reflexive."

Example: Have you yourself ever tried inventing something?
intensive

1. Many famous inventors have found themselves doing unusual things to prove their points.
2. Even Benjamin Franklin himself, a remarkable inventor, took risks.
3. I myself would be afraid to fly a kite during a lightning storm.
4. A metal wire on the kite drew the lightning's electricity to itself.
5. Mr. Franklin just wanted to prove something to himself.

Related Skills Activities

- ***SkillsBook***
  Types of Pronouns 1, pp. 151–152
  Types of Pronouns 2, pp. 153–154

Answers

1. demonstrative adjective
   That was an awful concert.
2. demonstrative pronoun
3. demonstrative pronoun
4. demonstrative adjective
   This is a very confusing diagram.
5. demonstrative pronoun

Answers

1. reflexive
2. intensive
3. intensive
4. reflexive
5. reflexive

Pronouns . . .

Types of Pronouns

710.1 Indefinite Pronouns

An indefinite pronoun is a pronoun that does not have a specific antecedent (the noun or pronoun it replaces). (See page 475.)

Everything about the chameleon is fascinating.

Someone donated a chameleon to our class.

Anyone who brings in a live insect can feed our chameleon.

Types of Pronouns

Personal Pronouns

I, me, mine, my, we, us, our, ours, you, your, yours, they, them, their, theirs, he, him, his, she, her, hers, it, its

Relative Pronouns

who, whose, whom, which, what, that, whoever, whomever, whichever, whatever

Interrogative Pronouns

who, whose, whom, which, what

Demonstrative Pronouns

this, that, these, those

Intensive and Reflexive Pronouns

myself, himself, herself, itself, yourself, yourselves, themselves, ourselves

Indefinite Pronouns

all	both	everything	nobody	several
another	each	few	none	some
any	each one	many	no one	somebody
anybody	either	most	nothing	someone
anyone	everybody	much	one	something
anything	everyone	neither	other	such

Grammar Practice

Pronouns 3

■ Indefinite Pronouns

Number your paper from 1 to 3. Write the indefinite pronouns that appear in each of the three paragraphs below.

Example: "Neither of my sisters will believe me," I thought.
neither

"Marisol," I said, "you are someone who is trustworthy. I couldn't tell this to just anyone."

"You have nothing to worry about," Marisol said. "No one will hear a word from me."

I explained, "Something happened last night. I had one of those strange dreams again."

Pronoun Review

For each sentence below, identify the underlined pronoun as "relative," "demonstrative," or "indefinite."

Example: The neighbors have a parrot that talks.
relative

1. Anthony, whose family lives in the blue house, borrowed my bike.
2. Everyone was looking at a stereo in the cafeteria.
3. It was there for the dance, which would take place that evening.
4. Delia pointed and said, "I want to get that for my room."
5. If you asked any of the other kids, they'd say the same thing.
6. This is my favorite song of the CD!

Related Skills Activities

- **Basic Grammar and Writing**
  Indefinite Pronouns, p. 475
- ***SkillsBook***
  Types of Pronouns, pp. 151–152

Answers

1. someone, anyone
2. nothing, no one
3. something, one

Answers

1. relative
2. indefinite
3. relative
4. demonstrative
5. indefinite
6. demonstrative

Pronouns . . .

Number of a Pronoun

712.1 Singular and Plural Pronouns

Pronouns can be either singular or plural in number.

Singular: I, you, he, she, it Plural: we, you, they

NOTE The pronouns *you, your,* and *yours* may be singular or plural.

Person of a Pronoun

The person of a pronoun tells whether the pronoun is speaking, being spoken to, or being spoken about. (See page 474.)

712.2 First Person Pronouns

A first-person pronoun is used in place of the name of the speaker or speakers.

I am speaking. We are speaking.

712.3 Second Person Pronouns

A second-person pronoun is used to name the person or thing spoken to.

Eliza, will you please take out the garbage?

You better stop grumbling!

712.4 Third Person Pronouns

A third-person pronoun is used to name the person or thing spoken about.

Bill should listen if he wants to learn the words to this song.

Charisse said that she already knows them.

They will perform the song in the talent show.

Uses of Pronouns

A pronoun can be used as a subject, as an object, or to show possession. (See the chart on page 714.)

712.5 Subject Pronouns

A subject pronoun is used as the subject of a sentence *(I, you, he, she, it, we, they).*

I like to surf the Net.

A subject pronoun is also used after a form of the *be* verb *(am, is, are, was, were, being, been)* if it repeats the subject. (See "Predicate Nouns," 704.5.)

"This is she," Mom replied into the telephone.

"Yes, it was I," admitted the child who had eaten the cookies.

Grammar Practice

Pronouns 4

- Number of a Pronoun
- Person of a Pronoun

Write the antecedent for the missing pronoun in each sentence. Is it singular or plural? Is it first, second, or third person? Then, for each blank, write the correct pronoun.

Example: The first time Maggie and I saw the movie *Bambi,* __________ cried.

Maggie and I (plural, first person) we

1. Carlota bought a new leash for __________ dog.
2. Since the leash is leather, __________ will last a long time.
3. Franklin and John have soccer practice, so __________ will be late for dinner.
4. "Boys, you will have to make __________ own meal," Mom said.
5. I don't wake up in the morning until my cat licks ________ nose.
6. Theo isn't very tall, but __________ can really shoot hoops.
7. Grandpa gave this book to Kyle and me, and it is now ________ most prized possession.
8. Darcy, when you grab luggage off the carousel at the airport, make sure it's really __________.
9. Mr. and Mrs. Gunderson are trying to sell __________ house.
10. The towering maple tree has lost all of __________ leaves early this year.
11. I asked Jason to give __________ a ride to school.
12. Jessi and I don't like brussels sprouts, and __________ won't eat lima beans, either.

Next Step: Write a sentence in which you use a singular, second-person pronoun. Write a second sentence using a plural, first-person pronoun.

Related Skills Activities

- **Basic Grammar and Writing**

- ***SkillsBook***

Answers

1. Carlota (singular, third person), her
2. leash (singular, third person), it
3. Franklin and John (plural, third person), they
4. you (plural, second person), your
5. I (singular, first person), my
6. Theo (singular, third person), he
7. Kyle and me (plural, first person), our
8. you (singular, second person), yours
9. Mr. and Mrs. Gunderson (plural, third person), their
10. tree (singular, third person), its
11. I (singular, first person), me
12. Jessi and I (plural, first person), we

Pronouns . . .

Uses of Pronouns

714.1 Object Pronouns

An object pronoun *(me, you, him, her, it, us, them)* can be used as the object of a verb or preposition. (See 692.4, 692.5, and 742.1.)

I'll call her as soon as I can. (direct object)

Hand me the phone book, please. (indirect object)

She thinks these flowers are from you. (object of the preposition)

714.2 Possessive Pronouns

A possessive pronoun shows possession or ownership. These possessive pronouns function as adjectives before nouns: *my, our, his, her, their, its,* and *your.*

School workers are painting our classroom this summer. Its walls will look much better.

These possessive pronouns can be used after verbs: *mine, ours, hers, his, theirs,* and *yours.*

I'm pretty sure this backpack is mine and that one is his.

NOTE An apostrophe is not needed with a possessive pronoun to show possession.

Uses of Personal Pronouns

	Singular Pronouns			Plural Pronouns		
	Subject Pronouns	Possessive Pronouns	Object Pronouns	Subject Pronoun	Possessive Pronouns	Object Pronouns
First Person	I	my, mine	me	we	our, ours	us
Second Person	you	your, yours	you	you	your, yours	you
Third Person	he	his	him	they	their, theirs	them
	she	her, hers	her			
	it	its	it			

Grammar Practice

Pronouns 5

■ Uses of Pronouns

For each numbered sentence below, write the underlined pronoun or pronouns and identify each as a "subject pronoun," an "object pronoun," or a "possessive pronoun."

Example: Are you aware of the strange creatures of the sea?
you (subject pronoun)

(1) It is home to lobsters, octopuses, and jellyfish, but one of its most unusual inhabitants has to be the squid. Squid range in size from a few inches to more than 50 feet. **(2)** Ten arms help them swim. **(3)** They move—always backward—by forcing water through a special valve that acts like a jet engine. **(4)** This backward motion probably confuses any fish that might want to eat them. **(5)** A squid can also release an inky cloud that covers its escape.

(6) Even though giant squid live in deep, dark water, their eyes are the largest in the animal kingdom, and they have excellent eyesight. **(7)** This allows them to find food easily. Their one great natural enemy is the sperm whale; however, people also catch tons of squid. **(8)** We use them as bait for other fish and, of course, as food for us, too. **(9)** (My dad loves to eat squid at restaurants.)

Steve O'Shea is a New Zealand zoologist and an expert on squid. **(10)** He and his team of researchers recently caught what they call a "colossal" squid—even larger than the 50-foot giant squid. **(11)** He says, "You are not going to want to meet these in the water." **(12)** I have to believe him!

Next Step: Write two or three sentences about a sea creature. Use the pronoun it in its subject, object, and possessive forms.

Related Skills Activities

■ ***SkillsBook***
Uses of Pronouns, pp. 157–158

Answers

1. it (subject pronoun)
2. them (object pronoun)
3. they (subject pronoun)
4. them (object pronoun)
5. its (possessive pronoun)
6. their (possessive pronoun)
7. this (subject pronoun)
8. we (subject pronoun), us (object pronoun)
9. my (possessive pronoun)
10. he (subject pronoun), his (possessive pronoun)
11. you (subject pronoun)
12. him (object pronoun)

Prepositions

Prepositions are words that show position, direction, or how two words or ideas are related to each other. Specifically, a preposition shows the relationship between its object and some other word in the sentence.

Raul hid under the stairs. (*Under* shows the relationship between *hid* and *stairs*.)

742.1 Prepositional Phrases

A preposition never appears alone; it is always part of a prepositional phrase. A prepositional phrase includes the preposition, the object of the preposition, and the modifiers of the object. (See pages 494–495.)

Raul's friends looked in the clothes hamper. (preposition: *in;* object: *hamper;* modifiers: *the, clothes*)

A prepositional phrase functions as an adjective or as an adverb.

They checked the closet with all the winter coats. (*With all the winter coats* functions as an adjective modifying *closet*.)

They wandered around the house looking for him. (*Around the house* functions as an adverb modifying *wandered*.)

NOTE If a word found in the list of prepositions has no object, it is not a preposition. It is probably an adverb.

Raul had never won at hide 'n' seek before. (*Before* is an adverb that modifies *had won*.)

Prepositions

aboard	apart from	beyond	from	like	outside	under
about	around	but	from among	near	outside of	underneath
above	aside from	by	from between	near to	over	until
according to	at	by means of	from under	next to	over to	unto
across	away from	concerning	in	of	owing to	up
across from	back of	considering	in addition to	off	past	up to
after	because of	despite	in front of	on	prior to	upon
against	before	down	in place of	on account of	regarding	with
along	behind	down from	in regard to	on behalf of	since	within
along with	below	during	in spite of	on top of	through	without
alongside	beneath	except	inside	onto	throughout	
alongside of	beside	except for	inside of	opposite	to	
amid	besides	excepting	instead of	out	together with	
among	between	for	into	out of	toward	

Grammar Practice

Prepositions

Write each prepositional phrase that appears in the following paragraphs. Underline the preposition and circle the object of the preposition.

Example: Spiders live everywhere, even in the finest houses.
in the finest houses

Although many people cringe at the sight of spiders, even dangerous spiders don't look for people as prey. Spiders prefer insects, and they eat billions of these pests.

Spiders capture different kinds of insects in the air and on the ground. Sticky spiderwebs trap insects. Some spiders jump out of special burrows to catch grasshoppers. Other spiders stand very still, just waiting for insects that run into their waiting jaws. All spiders have powerful venom that paralyzes their victims. Fortunately, spiders do not prey on humans. They simply go about their business looking for their next insect meal, and people can be glad about that.

For each of the following sentences, write whether the underlined word is a preposition or an adverb.

Example: When I see a spider in my room, I scoop it up and throw it outside.
adverb

1. When my mom sees a spider, she runs around the house, yelling for someone to get rid of it.
2. In the garden, there are quite a few spiders walking about.
3. Yesterday I found a big yellow one under the watering can.
4. Another one was crawling down a sunflower stalk.
5. I wanted to look around for more.
6. However, I had to cut the grass, and I was running behind.

PARTS OF SPEECH

Related Skills Activities

- **Basic Grammar and Writing**
  Connecting with Prepositions, pp. 494–495
  Expand with Prepositional Phrases, p. 519
- ***SkillsBook***
  Prepositions, pp. 191–192
- ***GrammarSnap***
  Prepositions and Prepositional Phrases

Answers

1. at the sight
2. of spiders
3. for people
4. as prey
5. of these pests
6. of insects
7. in the air
8. on the ground
9. out of special burrows
10. for insects
11. into their waiting jaws
12. on humans
13. about their business
14. for their next insect meal
15. about that

Answers

1. preposition
2. adverb
3. preposition
4. preposition
5. adverb
6. adverb

Conjunctions

A **conjunction** connects individual words or groups of words. There are three kinds of conjunctions: *coordinating, correlative,* and *subordinating.* (See pages 496–498.)

744.1 Coordinating Conjunctions

A coordinating conjunction connects a word to a word, a phrase to a phrase, or a clause to a clause. The words, phrases, or clauses joined by a coordinating conjunction must be equal, or of the same type.

Polluted rivers and streams can be cleaned up. (Two nouns are connected by and.)

Ride a bike or plant a tree to reduce pollution. (Two verb phrases are connected by or.)

Maybe you can't invent a pollution-free engine, but you can cut down on the amount of energy you use. (Two equal independent clauses are connected by but.)

NOTE When a coordinating conjunction is used to make a compound sentence, a comma always comes before it.

744.2 Correlative Conjunctions

Correlative conjunctions are conjunctions used in pairs.

We must reduce not only pollution but also excess energy use.

Either you're part of the problem, or you're part of the solution.

Conjunctions

Coordinating Conjunctions
and, but, or, nor, for, so, yet

Correlative Conjunctions
either, or   neither, nor   not only, but also   both, and   whether, or   as, so

Subordinating Conjunctions
after, although, as, as if, as long as, as though, because, before, if, in order that, provided that, since, so, so that, that, though, till, unless, until, when, where, whereas, while

Grammar Practice

Conjunctions 1

■ Coordinating Conjunctions

Do this activity with a partner. Each of you must follow the directions in one of the two columns. Then put the columns together to make some funny sentences!

COLUMN A	COLUMN B
1. Write a compound subject connected with the conjunction *or*.	**1.** Write a compound predicate connected with the conjunction *and*.
2. Write one sentence followed by a comma and the conjunction *yet*.	**2.** Write one sentence.
3. Write a compound subject connected with the conjunction *and*.	**3.** Write a compound predicate connected with the conjunction *or*.
4. Write one sentence followed by a comma and the conjunction *but*.	**4.** Write one sentence.

■ Correlative Conjunctions

Write the correlative conjunctions that make the most sense in the following sentences.

Example: We are going to the beach _______ it's sunny _______ cloudy.
whether, or

1. _______ whales _______ dolphins are fish.
2. Dad put up a basketball hoop for _____ my brother _____ me.
3. Josh can _______ shoot three-pointers _______ get nothing but net!
4. Because of his busy schedule, he will join _______ the school team _______ a local league team.

Related Skills Activities

- **Basic Grammar and Writing**
  Connecting with Conjunctions, pp. 496–498
  Compound Subjects, p. 509
  Create Compound Sentences, p. 516
- ***SkillsBook***
  Coordinating and Correlative Conjunctions, pp. 197–198
- ***GrammarSnap***
  Coordinating Conjunctions

Answers

1-4. Answers will vary.

Answers

1. Neither, nor
2. both, and
3. not only, but also
4. either, or

Conjunctions . . .

746.1 Subordinating Conjunctions

A subordinating conjunction is a word or group of words that connects two clauses that are not equally important. A subordinating conjunction begins a dependent clause and connects it to an independent clause to make a complex sentence. (See page 517 and the chart on page 744.)

Fuel-cell engines are unusual because they don't have moving parts.

Since fuel-cell cars run on hydrogen, the only waste products are water and heat.

As you can see in the sentences above, a comma sets off the dependent clause only when it begins the sentence. A comma is usually not used when the dependent clause follows the independent clause.

NOTE Relative pronouns and conjunctive adverbs can also connect clauses. (See 706.3 and 738.1.)

Interjections

An **interjection** is a word or phrase used to express strong emotion or surprise. Punctuation (a comma or an exclamation point) is used to separate an interjection from the rest of the sentence.

Wow, would you look at that! **Oh no! He's falling!**

SCHOOL DAZE

Grammar Practice

Conjunctions 2

■ Subordinating Conjunctions

Use a subordinating conjunction from the following list and write one complex sentence out of each pair of sentences below.

if while since although when

Example: Ancient people looked at the sky. They saw shapes of animals, people, or objects in the stars.

When ancient people looked at the sky, they saw shapes of animals, people, or objects in the stars.

1. They mapped out the sky as early as 2000 B.C.E. The constellations in the zodiac were named only 2,000 years ago.
2. There are almost 90 known constellations. There are only 12 in the zodiac.
3. People can use the zodiac. They want to find a particular star in one of its constellations.
4. The zodiac is divided into 12 parts. It's easy to divide a 360-degree circle into 30-degree "slices."

Interjections

Use an appropriate interjection in each of the following sentences. Punctuate it with a comma or an exclamation point.

Example: ______ That was some race!

Wow!

1. ______ I dropped the cake.
2. You passed the test? ______
3. ______ I need you here right now!
4. ______ I've discovered the cure for the common cold!

PARTS OF SPEECH

Related Skills Activities

- **Basic Grammar and Writing**
  Develop Complex Sentences, p. 517
- ***SkillsBook***
  Subordinating Conjunctions, pp. 195–196
  Interjections, pp. 193–194
- ***GrammarSnap***
  Subordinating Conjunctions

Possible Answers

1. Although they mapped out the sky as early as 2000 B.C.E., the constellations in the zodiac were named only 2,000 years ago.
2. While there are almost 90 known constellations, there are only 12 in the zodiac.
3. People can use the zodiac if they want to find a particular star in one of its constellations.
4. The zodiac is divided into 12 parts since it's easy to divide a 360-degree circle into 30-degree "slices."

Possible Answers

1. Oh no!
2. Great!
3. Help!
4. Eureka!

Quick Guide: Parts of Speech

In the English language, there are eight parts of speech. Understanding them will help you improve your writing skills. Every word you write is a part of speech—a noun, a verb, an adjective, and so on. The chart below lists the eight parts of speech.

Noun	A word that names a person, a place, a thing, or an idea Alex Moya Belize ladder courage
Pronoun	A word used in place of a noun I he it they you anybody some
Verb	A word that shows action or links a subject to another word in the sentence sing shake catch is are
Adjective	A word that describes a noun or a pronoun stormy red rough seven grand
Adverb	A word that describes a verb, an adjective, or another adverb quickly today now bravely softer
Preposition	A word that shows position or direction and introduces a prepositional phrase around up under over between to
Conjunction	A word that connects other words or groups of words and but or so because when
Interjection	A word (set off by commas or an exclamation point) that shows strong emotion Stop! Hey, how are you?

Grammar Practice

Parts of Speech Review

For each numbered sentence below, write whether the underlined word is a "noun," a "pronoun," a "verb," an "adjective," an "adverb," a "preposition," a "conjunction," or an "interjection."

Example: Wow, an Eastern diamondback rattlesnake at Brookfield Zoo gave birth to nine babies last week!
interjection

(1) Our class went on a field trip to the Brookfield Zoo last week. **(2)** This zoo features natural settings for the animals. **(3)** The zoo's designers wanted people to be able to get close to the animals, but they didn't want to use cages or bars. **(4)** So the exhibits are separated from visitors with a high wall and a deep ditch or moat.

(5) We enjoyed looking at all the wonderful animals from around the world. **(6)** We saw Amur tigers, Indian rhinoceroses, Siberian ibexes, orangutans, blue poison frogs, Galapagos tortoises, and giant anteaters. **(7)** We stopped at the elephant house and talked about the amazing size of these animals.

(8) Suddenly Peter yelled, "Watch out! That elephant is going to spray us with water." **(9)** Before any of us could move, the elephant blasted us. **(10)** Those closest to the fence got hit the worst.

(11) "Oh, I'm so sorry," said the guide. **(12)** "She meant no harm."

(13) "Does she always do that?" Jill asked.

(14) The guide answered, "No. I guess she thought that the bunch of you needed to cool off!" **(15)** It *was* a hot day, so no one really complained. **(16)** Later, on the bus, we all laughed about our morning shower.

Next Step: Write a few sentences about a time you visited the zoo. Include all the parts of speech.

Related Skills Activities

- ***SkillsBook***
  Parts of Speech Review 1, pp. 199–200
  Parts of Speech Review 2, pp. 201–202

Answers

1. pronoun
2. adjective
3. noun
4. preposition
5. noun
6. verb
7. conjunction
8. adverb
9. conjunction
10. adverb
11. interjection
12. pronoun
13. adverb
14. verb
15. adjective
16. preposition

Copy Masters

RUBRICS

BENCHMARK PAPERS

GRAPHIC ORGANIZERS

GETTING STARTED

6-Point

Rubric for Narrative Writing

Ideas

6 The narrative tells about an unforgettable experience. The details make the story truly memorable.
5 The writer tells about an interesting experience. Details help create the interest.
4 The writer tells about an interesting experience. More details are needed.
3 The writer needs to focus on one experience. Some details do not relate to the story.
2 The writer needs to focus on one experience. Details are needed.
1 The writer needs to tell about an experience and use details.

Organization

6 The organization makes the narrative enjoyable and easy to read.
5 The narrative is well organized, with a clear beginning, middle, and ending. Transitions are used well.
4 The narrative is well organized. Most of the transitions are helpful.
3 The order of events needs to be corrected. More transitions need to be used. One part of the narrative is weak.
2 The beginning, middle, and ending all run together. The order is unclear.
1 The narrative needs to be organized.

Voice

6 The writer's voice creates an unforgettable experience for the reader.
5 The writer's personal voice creates interest in the story. Dialogue is used.
4 The writer's voice creates interest in the story. More dialogue is needed.
3 A voice can usually be heard. More dialogue is needed.
2 The voice is weak. Dialogue is needed.
1 The writer has not gotten involved in the story. Dialogue is needed.

Word Choice

6 The writer's exceptional word choice captures the experience.
5 Specific nouns, strong verbs, and well-chosen modifiers create vivid pictures and express clear feelings.
4 Specific nouns and strong verbs are used. Modifiers are needed to create a clearer picture.
3 Strong nouns, verbs, and modifiers are needed to create a clear picture.
2 General and overused words do not create a clear picture.
1 The writer has not yet considered word choice.

Sentence Fluency

6 The sentences are skillfully written and original. They keep the reader's interest.
5 The sentences show variety and are easy to read and understand.
4 The sentences are varied, but some should flow more smoothly.
3 A better variety of sentences is needed. Sentences do not read smoothly.
2 Many short or incomplete sentences make the writing choppy.
1 Few sentences are written well. Help is needed.

Conventions

6 Grammar and punctuation are correct, and the writing is free of spelling errors.
5 The narrative has a few minor errors in punctuation, spelling, or grammar.
4 The narrative has several errors in punctuation, spelling, or grammar.
3 Some errors confuse the reader.
2 Many errors make the narrative confusing and hard to read.
1 Help is needed to make corrections.

6-Point

Rubric for Expository Writing

Ideas

6 The topic, focus, and details make the essay truly memorable.
5 The essay is informative with a clear focus and specific details.
4 The essay is informative with a clear focus. More specific details are needed.
3 The focus of the essay needs to be clearer, and more specific details are needed.
2 The topic needs to be narrowed or expanded. Many more specific details are needed.
1 A new topic needs to be selected.

Organization

6 The organization makes the essay informative and easy to read.
5 The beginning interests the reader. The middle supports the focus. The ending works well. Transitions are used.
4 The essay is divided into a beginning, a middle, and an ending. Some transitions are used.
3 The beginning or ending is weak. The middle needs a paragraph for each main point. More transitions are needed.
2 The beginning, middle, and ending all run together. Paragraphs and transitions are needed.
1 The essay should be reorganized.

Voice

6 The writer's voice sounds confident, knowledgeable, and enthusiastic.
5 The writer's voice sounds knowledgeable and confident.
4 The writer's voice sounds well-informed most of the time.
3 The writer sometimes sounds unsure.
2 The writer sounds unsure.
1 The writer needs to learn about voice.

Word Choice

6 The word choice makes the essay very clear, informative, and fun to read.
5 Specific nouns and action verbs make the essay clear and informative. Unfamiliar terms are defined.
4 Some nouns and verbs could be more specific. Unfamiliar terms are defined.
3 Too many general words are used. Specific nouns and verbs are needed. Some words need to be defined.
2 General or missing words make this essay hard to understand.
1 The writer needs help finding specific words.

Sentence Fluency

6 The sentences flow smoothly, and people will enjoy reading them.
5 The sentences read smoothly. A variety of sentences is used.
4 Most of the sentences read smoothly, but more variety is needed.
3 Many short, choppy sentences need to be combined to make a better variety of sentences.
2 Many sentences are choppy or incomplete and need to be rewritten.
1 Most sentences need to be rewritten.

Conventions

6 Punctuation and grammar are correct. Spelling is correct.
5 The essay has a few minor errors in punctuation, spelling, or grammar.
4 The essay has several errors in punctuation, spelling or grammar.
3 Some errors confuse the reader.
2 Many errors make the essay confusing and hard to read.
1 Help is needed to make corrections.

6-Point

Rubric for Persuasive Writing

Ideas

6 The clear reasoning informs and convinces the reader.
5 The essay has a clear opinion statement. Persuasive details support the writer's opinion.
4 The opinion statement is clear, and most details support the writer's opinion.
3 The opinion statement is clear. More persuasive details are needed.
2 The opinion statement is unclear. Persuasive details are needed.
1 An opinion statement, reasons, and details are needed.

Organization

6 The organization presents a smooth flow of ideas from beginning to end.
5 The beginning contains the opinion statement. The middle provides clear support. The ending reinforces the writer's opinion.
4 The beginning contains the opinion statement. The middle provides support. The ending needs work.
3 The beginning has an opinion statement. The middle and ending need more work.
2 The beginning, middle, and ending run together.
1 The organization is unclear. The reader is easily lost.

Voice

6 The writer's voice is confident, positive, and completely convincing.
5 The writer's voice is confident and helps persuade the reader.
4 The writer's voice is confident. It needs to persuade the reader.
3 The writer's voice needs to be more confident and persuade the reader.
2 The writer's voice rambles on without any confidence.
1 The writer's voice can't be heard.

Word Choice

6 Precise words create a clear message to engage and persuade the audience.
5 Precise words create a clear message and fit the purpose.
4 Accurate words create a message. More persuasive words are needed.
3 More precise and accurate words are needed to create a clear message.
2 The words do not create a clear message.
1 Word choice has not been considered.

Sentence Fluency

6 The sentences flow smoothly, and people will enjoy reading the variety of sentences.
5 Variety is seen in both the types of sentences and their beginnings.
4 Varied sentence beginnings are used. Sentence variety would make the essay more interesting to read.
3 Varied sentence beginnings are needed. Sentence variety would make the essay more interesting.
2 Most of the sentences begin the same way. Most sentences are simple. Compound and complex sentences are needed.
1 Sentence fluency has not been established. Ideas do not flow smoothly.

Conventions

6 The grammar and punctuation are correct, and all the words are spelled correctly.
5 Grammar and punctuation errors are few. The reader is not distracted by the errors.
4 Grammar and punctuation errors are seen in a few sentences. They distract the reader in those areas.
3 There are a number of errors that may confuse the reader.
2 Frequent errors make the essay difficult to read.
1 Nearly every sentence contains errors.

6-Point

Rubric for Response to Literature

Ideas

6 The focus statement and the meaningful details show knowledge of the reading.
5 The essay has a clear focus statement and all the necessary details.
4 The essay has a clear focus statement. Unnecessary details need to be cut.
3 The focus statement is too broad. Unnecessary details need to be cut.
2 The focus statement is unclear. More details are needed.
1 The essay needs a focus statement and details.

Organization

6 The opening, middle, and ending lead the reader smoothly through the essay.
5 The organization pattern fits the topic and purpose. All parts of the essay are well developed.
4 The organization pattern fits the topic and purpose. A part of the essay needs better development.
3 The organization fits the essay's purpose. All the parts need more development.
2 The organization doesn't fit the purpose.
1 A plan needs to be followed.

Voice

6 The voice expresses interest and complete understanding. It engages the reader.
5 The voice expresses interest and complete understanding.
4 The voice expresses interest, but needs to show more understanding.
3 The voice needs to be interesting and express an understanding.
2 The voice is uninteresting and does not express an understanding.
1 The writer needs to understand how to create voice.

Word Choice

6 Clear word choice creates a response that engages the reader.
5 Connotative words and literary terms create a clear message.
4 Literary terms create a clear message, but connotative words would add feeling.
3 Too many general words are used. More clear, concise words are needed.
2 General or overused words make this essay hard to understand.
1 The writer needs help finding specific words.

Sentence Fluency

6 All sentences are skillfully written and keep the reader's interest.
5 No sentence problems exist. Sentence variety is evident.
4 No sentence problems exist. More sentence variety is needed.
3 Sentence problems are found in a few places.
2 The essay has many sentence problems.
1 The writer needs to learn how to construct sentences.

Conventions

6 Grammar and punctuation are correct, and words are spelled correctly.
5 The essay has minor errors that do not interfere with the reader's understanding.
4 The essay has some errors in punctuation, spelling, or grammar.
3 The essay has errors that may confuse the reader.
2 The number of errors confuses the reader and makes the essay hard to read.
1 Help is needed to make corrections.

5-Point

Rubric for Narrative Writing

Ideas

5 The writer tells about an interesting experience. Details help create the interest.
4 The writer tells about an interesting experience. More details are needed.
3 The writer needs to focus on one experience. Some details do not relate to the story.
2 The writer needs to focus on one experience. Details are needed.
1 The writer needs to tell about an experience and use details.

Organization

5 The narrative is well organized, with a clear beginning, middle, and ending. Transitions are used well.
4 The narrative is well organized. Most of the transitions are helpful.
3 The order of events needs to be corrected. More transitions need to be used. One part of the narrative is weak.
2 The beginning, middle, and ending all run together. The order is unclear.
1 The narrative needs to be organized.

Voice

5 The writer's personal voice creates interest in the story. Dialogue is used.
4 The writer's voice creates interest in the story. More dialogue is needed.
3 A voice can usually be heard. More dialogue is needed.
2 The voice is weak. Dialogue is needed.
1 The writer has not gotten involved in the story. Dialogue is needed.

Word Choice

5 Specific nouns, strong verbs, and well-chosen modifiers create vivid pictures and express clear feelings.
4 Specific nouns and strong verbs are used. Modifiers are needed to create a clearer picture.
3 Strong nouns, verbs, and modifiers are needed to create a clear picture.
2 General and overused words do not create a clear picture.
1 The writer has not yet considered word choice.

Sentence Fluency

5 The sentences show variety and are easy to read and understand.
4 The sentences are varied, but some should flow more smoothly.
3 A better variety of sentences is needed. Sentences do not read smoothly.
2 Many short or incomplete sentences make the writing choppy.
1 Few sentences are written well. Help is needed.

Conventions

5 The narrative has a few minor errors in punctuation, spelling, or grammar.
4 The narrative has several errors in punctuation, spelling, or grammar.
3 Some errors confuse the reader.
2 Many errors make the narrative confusing and hard to read.
1 Help is needed to make corrections.

5-Point

Rubric for Expository Writing

Ideas

5 The essay is informative with a clear focus and specific details.

4 The essay is informative with a clear focus. More specific details are needed.

3 The focus of the essay needs to be clearer, and more specific details are needed.

2 The topic needs to be narrowed or expanded. Many more specific details are needed.

1 A new topic needs to be selected.

Organization

5 The beginning interests the reader. The middle supports the focus. The ending works well. Transitions are used.

4 The essay is divided into a beginning, a middle, and an ending. Some transitions are used.

3 The beginning or ending is weak. The middle needs a paragraph for each main point. More transitions are needed.

2 The beginning, middle, and ending all run together. Paragraphs and transitions are needed.

1 The essay should be reorganized.

Voice

5 The writer's voice sounds knowledgeable and confident.

4 The writer's voice sounds well-informed most of the time.

3 The writer sometimes sounds unsure.

2 The writer sounds unsure.

1 The writer needs to learn about voice.

Word Choice

5 Specific nouns and action verbs make the essay clear and informative. Unfamiliar terms are defined.

4 Some nouns and verbs could be more specific. Unfamiliar terms are defined.

3 Too many general words are used. Specific nouns and verbs are needed. Some words need to be defined.

2 General or missing words make this essay hard to understand.

1 The writer needs help finding specific words.

Sentence Fluency

5 The sentences read smoothly. A variety of sentences is used.

4 Most of the sentences read smoothly, but more variety is needed.

3 Many short, choppy sentences need to be combined to make a better variety of sentences.

2 Many sentences are choppy or incomplete and need to be rewritten.

1 Most sentences need to be rewritten.

Conventions

5 The essay has a few minor errors in punctuation, spelling, or grammar.

4 The essay has several errors in punctuation, spelling, or grammar.

3 Some errors confuse the reader.

2 Many errors make the essay confusing and hard to read.

1 Help is needed to make corrections.

5-Point

Rubric for Persuasive Writing

Ideas

5 The essay has a clear opinion statement. Persuasive details support the writer's opinion.
4 The opinion statement is clear, and most details support the writer's opinion.
3 The opinion statement is clear. More persuasive details are needed.
2 The opinion statement is unclear. Persuasive details are needed.
1 An opinion statement, reasons, and details are needed.

Organization

5 The beginning contains the opinion statement. The middle provides clear support. The ending reinforces the writer's opinion.
4 The beginning contains the opinion statement. The middle provides support. The ending needs work.
3 The beginning has an opinion statement. The middle and ending need more work.
2 The beginning, middle, and ending run together.
1 The organization is unclear. The reader is easily lost.

Voice

5 The writer's voice is confident and helps persuade the reader.
4 The writer's voice is confident. It needs to persuade the reader.
3 The writer's voice needs to be more confident and persuade the reader.
2 The writer's voice rambles on without any confidence.
1 The writer's voice can't be heard.

Word Choice

5 Precise words create a clear message and fit the purpose.
4 Accurate words create a message. More persuasive words are needed.
3 More precise and accurate words are needed to create a clear message.
2 The words do not create a clear message.
1 Word choice has not been considered.

Sentence Fluency

5 Variety is seen in both the types of sentences and their beginnings.
4 Varied sentence beginnings are used. Sentence variety would make the essay more interesting to read.
3 Varied sentence beginnings are needed. Sentence variety would make the essay more interesting.
2 Most of the sentences begin the same way. Most sentences are simple. Compound and complex sentences are needed.
1 Sentence fluency has not been established. Ideas do not flow smoothly.

Conventions

5 Grammar and punctuation errors are few. The reader is not distracted by the errors.
4 Grammar and punctuation errors are seen in a few sentences. They distract the reader in those areas.
3 There are a number of errors that may confuse the reader.
2 Frequent errors make the essay difficult to read.
1 Nearly every sentence contains errors.

5-Point

Rubric for Response to Literature

Ideas

5 The essay has a clear focus statement and all the necessary details.
4 The essay has a clear focus statement. Unnecessary details need to be cut.
3 The focus statement is too broad. Unnecessary details need to be cut.
2 The focus statement is unclear. More details are needed.
1 The essay needs a focus statement and details.

Organization

5 The organization pattern fits the topic and purpose. All parts of the essay are well developed.
4 The organization pattern fits the topic and purpose. A part of the essay needs better development.
3 The organization fits the essay's purpose. All the parts need more development.
2 The organization doesn't fit the purpose.
1 A plan needs to be followed.

Voice

5 The voice expresses interest and complete understanding.
4 The voice expresses interest, but needs to show more understanding.
3 The voice needs to be interesting and express an understanding.
2 The voice is uninteresting and does not express an understanding.
1 The writer needs to understand how to create voice.

Word Choice

5 Connotative words and literary terms create a clear message.
4 Literary terms create a clear message, but connotative words would add feeling.
3 Too many general words are used. More clear, concise words are needed.
2 General or overused words make this essay hard to understand.
1 The writer needs help finding specific words.

Sentence Fluency

5 No sentence problems exist. Sentence variety is evident.
4 No sentence problems exist. More sentence variety is needed.
3 Sentence problems are found in a few places.
2 The essay has many sentence problems.
1 The writer needs to learn how to construct sentences.

Conventions

5 The essay has minor errors that do not interfere with the reader's understanding.
4 The essay has some errors in punctuation, spelling, or grammar.
3 The essay has errors that may confuse the reader.
2 The number of errors confuses the reader and makes the essay hard to read.
1 Help is needed to make corrections.

4-Point

Rubric for Narrative Writing

Ideas

4 The writer tells about an interesting experience. Details help create the interest.
3 The writer tells about an interesting experience. More details are needed.
2 The writer needs to focus on one experience. Some details do not relate to the story.
1 The writer needs to focus on one experience. Details are needed.

Organization

4 The narrative is well organized, with a clear beginning, middle, and ending. Transitions are used well.
3 The narrative is well organized. Most of the transitions are helpful.
2 The order of events needs to be corrected. More transitions need to be used. One part of the narrative is weak.
1 The beginning, middle, and ending all run together. The order is unclear.

Voice

4 The writer's personal voice creates interest in the story. Dialogue is used.
3 The writer's voice creates interest in the story. More dialogue is needed.
2 A voice can usually be heard. More dialogue is needed.
1 The voice is weak. Dialogue is needed.

Word Choice

4 Specific nouns, strong verbs, and well-chosen modifiers create vivid pictures and express clear feelings.
3 Specific nouns and strong verbs are used. Modifiers are needed to create a clearer picture.
2 Strong nouns, verbs, and modifiers are needed to create a clear picture.
1 General and overused words do not create a clear picture.

Sentence Fluency

4 The sentences show variety and are easy to read and understand.
3 The sentences are varied, but some should flow more smoothly.
2 A better variety of sentences is needed. Sentences do not read smoothly.
1 Many short or incomplete sentences make the writing choppy.

Conventions

4 The narrative has a few minor errors in punctuation, spelling, or grammar.
3 The narrative has several errors in punctuation, spelling, or grammar.
2 Some errors confuse the reader.
1 Many errors make the narrative confusing and hard to read.

4-Point

Rubric for Expository Writing

Ideas

4 The essay is informative with a clear focus and specific details.

3 The essay is informative with a clear focus. More specific details are needed.

2 The focus of the essay needs to be clearer, and more specific details are needed.

1 The topic needs to be narrowed or expanded. Many more specific details are needed.

Organization

4 The beginning interests the reader. The middle supports the focus. The ending works well. Transitions are used.

3 The essay is divided into a beginning, a middle, and an ending. Some transitions are used.

2 The beginning or ending is weak. The middle needs a paragraph for each main point. More transitions are needed.

1 The beginning, middle, and ending all run together. Paragraphs and transitions are needed.

Voice

4 The writer's voice sounds knowledgeable and confident.

3 The writer's voice sounds well-informed most of the time.

2 The writer sometimes sounds unsure.

1 The writer sounds unsure.

Word Choice

4 Specific nouns and action verbs make the essay clear and informative. Unfamiliar terms are defined.

3 Some nouns and verbs could be more specific. Unfamiliar terms are defined.

2 Too many general words are used. Specific nouns and verbs are needed. Some words need to be defined.

1 General or missing words make this essay hard to understand.

Sentence Fluency

4 The sentences read smoothly. A variety of sentences is used.

3 Most of the sentences read smoothly, but more variety is needed.

2 Many short, choppy sentences need to be combined to make a better variety of sentences.

1 Many sentences are choppy or incomplete and need to be rewritten.

Conventions

4 The essay has a few minor errors in punctuation, spelling, or grammar.

3 The essay has several errors in punctuation, spelling, or grammar.

2 Some errors confuse the reader.

1 Many errors make the essay confusing and hard to read.

4-Point

Rubric for Persuasive Writing

Ideas

4 The essay has a clear opinion statement. Persuasive details support the writer's opinion.

3 The opinion statement is clear, and most details support the writer's opinion.

2 The opinion statement is clear. More persuasive details are needed.

1 The opinion statement is unclear. Persuasive details are needed.

Organization

4 The beginning contains the opinion statement. The middle provides clear support. The ending reinforces the writer's opinion.

3 The beginning contains the opinion statement. The middle provides support. The ending needs work.

2 The beginning has an opinion statement. The middle and ending need more work.

1 The beginning, middle, and ending run together.

Voice

4 The writer's voice is confident and helps persuade the reader.

3 The writer's voice is confident. It needs to persuade the reader.

2 The writer's voice needs to be more confident and persuade the reader.

1 The writer's voice rambles on without any confidence.

Word Choice

4 Precise words create a clear message and fit the purpose.

3 Accurate words create a message. More persuasive words are needed.

2 More precise and accurate words are needed to create a clear message.

1 The words do not create a clear message.

Sentence Fluency

4 Variety is seen in both the types of sentences and their beginnings.

3 Varied sentence beginnings are used. Sentence variety would make the essay more interesting to read.

2 Varied sentence beginnings are needed. Sentence variety would make the essay more interesting.

1 Most of the sentences begin the same way. Most sentences are simple. Compound and complex sentences are needed.

Conventions

4 Grammar and punctuation errors are few. The reader is not distracted by the errors.

3 Grammar and punctuation errors are seen in a few sentences. They distract the reader in those areas.

2 There are a number of errors that may confuse the reader.

1 Frequent errors make the essay difficult to read.

4-Point

Rubric for Response to Literature

Ideas

4 The essay has a clear focus statement and all the necessary details.
3 The essay has a clear focus statement. Unnecessary details need to be cut.
2 The focus statement is too broad. Unnecessary details need to be cut.
1 The focus statement is unclear. More details are needed.

Organization

4 The organization pattern fits the topic and purpose. All parts of the essay are well developed.
3 The organization pattern fits the topic and purpose. A part of the essay needs better development.
2 The organization fits the essay's purpose. All the parts need more development.
1 The organization doesn't fit the purpose.

Voice

4 The voice expresses interest and complete understanding.
3 The voice expresses interest, but needs to show more understanding.
2 The voice needs to be interesting and express an understanding.
1 The voice is uninteresting and does not express an understanding.

Word Choice

4 Connotative words and literary terms create a clear message.
3 Literary terms create a clear message, but connotative words would add feeling.
2 Too many general words are used. More clear, concise words are needed.
1 General or overused words make this essay hard to understand.

Sentence Fluency

4 No sentence problems exist. Sentence variety is evident.
3 No sentence problems exist. More sentence variety is needed.
2 Sentence problems are found in a few places.
1 The essay has many sentence problems.

Conventions

4 The essay has minor errors that do not interfere with the reader's understanding.
3 The essay has some errors in punctuation, spelling, or grammar.
2 The essay has errors that may confuse the reader.
1 The number of errors confuses the reader and makes the essay hard to read.

Six-Trait Checklist

Ideas

- ☐ focuses on a specific topic
- ☐ has a clear focus statement
- ☐ contains specific details

Organization

- ☐ has a beginning, a middle, and ending
- ☐ has a topic sentence for each paragraph
- ☐ has enough details to develop each topic sentence
- ☐ uses transitions to connect paragraphs

Voice

- ☐ speaks in an engaging way that keeps readers wanting to hear more
- ☐ shows that the writer really cares about the subject

Word Choice

- ☐ contains specific nouns and action verbs
- ☐ presents an appropriate level of language (not too formal or too informal)

Sentence Fluency

- ☐ flows smoothly from sentence to sentence
- ☐ shows variety in sentence beginnings and lengths
- ☐ uses transitions to connect sentences

Conventions

- ☐ follows the basic rules of grammar, spelling, capitalization, and punctuation

Narrative Writing

Lost Trust

My older sister keeps a diary. Every night before she goes to bed she writes in it. Sometimes she writes for only a few minutes, sometimes for a lot longer. When she's done, she slides it back into the drawer of her nightstand, turns off the light, and goes to bed. Every night I go to sleep wondering what she writes in there.

One day we got in a fight. I teased her about a boy she liked at school. She got really mad at me. Then she ran to her room and slammed the door. She didn't come out until it was time for supper. When she was in her room, I was sure she had started writing in her diary, and I was sure she was writing about me.

The next day after school I got home as fast as I could and went right to her room. I found her diary, took it to my room, shut the door, and started to read.

A lot of it was really boring, things like "Amy said Trisha is stupid and Trisha found out so now they're not talking. I hate being in the middle of all this. Why can't they just be friends?!" I flipped ahead to what she had written the night before.

The writing was all really big and had an angry look to it. I think you really have to be mad to make your writing look angry. She wrote all about what I had said and how mean I had been, but then she said she wouldn't have been that upset except that she really liked this Kevin guy. She'd even talked to him a few times after school, and she was pretty sure he liked her, too. But it really made her angry to be teased about it because she was so nervous about the whole thing.

Right then my bedroom door opened and she walked in. "Can I borrow your . . ." She stopped when she saw me move quickly to try to hide her diary, but it was too late. "What are you doing? Why do you have that? Where'd you get that?" she asked faster than I could answer. Each question got louder. I was scared and couldn't really talk. "Give that back!" she screamed. "Give it here! Now! You jerk!" She grabbed it out of my hand and stomped out of the room.

My dad heard all the yelling and came to check. They talked in her room for a few minutes. Then he came in by me and closed the door. He was pretty calm but I could tell he wasn't happy with me. He told me I had no right to take her personal property and read it—that she was more angry with me than ever before and I deserved it. He said more, but he didn't have to. I felt like a real jerk.

I apologized, but my sister didn't talk to me for days. I had to be extra nice to her for her to even look at me. Eventually she started to talk to me again, but it wasn't the same as before. She wouldn't tell me certain things because I'm sure she felt she couldn't trust me. If only I hadn't read her diary. What a stupid thing to do.

Assessment Sheet

Title *Lost Trust*

6 Ideas

- *The topic you chose makes a very good story.*
- *You include all the emotion and drama that help your audience share your personal experience.*

6 Organization

- *This narrative is well organized and makes the order of events clear.*
- *The story builds to a high point and keeps the reader's interest.*

6 Voice

- *The dialogue shows the most tense moments. This technique helps you make these moments sound natural.*
- *Your voice helps you create a tone for this narrative.*

5 Word Choice

- *Strong verbs help readers create images (see lines 3, 6, 8, and 32).*
- *Find words to replace "really" and "pretty" or cut them.*
- *Some of your expressions are too informal (see lines 33 and 37).*

6 Sentence Fluency

- *You use sentences of many different lengths. This gives a natural flow to your writing.*
- *You also use a variety of simple, compound, and complex sentences. This adds interest to your writing.*
- *Using simple sentences for the important events adds tension, a sense that something is going to happen (see lines 1, 6, and 27).*

6 Conventions

- *You have edited and proofread your paper well.*
- *There are a few minor comma errors (see lines 2, 14, and 34).*

Narrative Writing

My Summer in Michigan

Last summer, when I went to visit my aunt in Michigan. She took me to her cabin in the wilderness. I taught it was going to be boring but actually it was fun.

When we got to the cabin she told me where everything is. I saw many interesting things. Lots of birds and plants that I have never seen before. I took my compass, so I wouldn't get lost, and went exploring. Still, I didn't see any animals. So I went back to the cabin, and told my aunt Barbara about my trip through the woods. My aunt advised me that the next day, when I'm going to explore the woods again, I should stay for a longer time and the animals would come out.

The next day, when I woke up, I took my camera and went to the woods. I waited a long time and there still were no animals around me. When I was about to go back to the cabin, I saw a porcupine. He was very close to me! I wanted to take a picture of him. I got up and took some pictures. As I walked toward him, to get a even closer look, I slipped on a rock and fell on the porcupine. I had his quills in my hands. I was in a lot of pain. I pick up my camera with my mouth and go to the cabin.

As I walked to the cabin my aunt saw me and ran up with help. She took me to the closest town to see a doctor. Dr. Johnson took out

23 quills out of my hands. He said I was lucky that we got to him so fast. The doctor also said that for a month or a little longer, I wouldn't be able to do anything with my hands.

On the first day of school we talked about our vacation. My story was definitely the funniest! I had the pictures and the quills to prove that it was the truth.

Assessment Sheet

Title *My Summer in Michigan*

4 **Ideas**

- *You focus on one astonishing experience well.*
- *Use sensory details to describe what you saw and heard in the woods.*
- *A more intriguing title would spark your reader's curiosity.*

3 **Organization**

- *Most, but not all, of your events seem to be in order.*
- *Try starting in the middle of the action to effectively grab the reader's attention.*

2 **Voice**

- *The last paragraph shows your sense of humor.*
- *Share more of your feelings, especially when you fell on the porcupine.*
- *Add dialogue to "show" the personalities of your aunt, Dr. Johnson, and yourself.*

2 **Word Choice**

- *Some of your words and phrases are dull or awkward (see lines 5, 11–12, and 19).*
- *More specific action verbs would add drama. "Walk" could be "bolted" or "sprinted" and "took" could be "rushed" (see lines 19–20).*

2 **Sentence Fluency**

- *Using the short sentence, "He was very close to me!" adds drama (see lines 13–14).*
- *Avoid sentence fragments (see lines 1 and 5–6).*
- *Combine choppy sentences or cut short sentences that aren't needed (see lines 14–15 and 16–17).*

3 **Conventions**

- *You have spelled difficult words well: advised, porcupine, definitely. Check other words.*
- *Review comma rules (see lines 2, 6, 7, 10, 12, 19, and 24).*
- *Be aware of verb tenses (see lines 4, 9, and 17–18).*

Expository Writing

Bikes for Everyone

Whether you are young or old, there's a bike for you. From road bikes to mountain bikes to hybrid bikes, now everyone can choose a bike to match his or her goals. Which kind of bike should you choose? It all depends on where and how you want to travel.

If you're interested in speed and want to travel long distances on paved roads then look at road or touring bikes. Generally, they are constructed of lightweight metals and carbon fiber. Thanks to their narrow tires, skinny seats, or saddles, and 'turned-down" handlebars you can now travel farther and benefit from more of a workout. However, beware, their slim tires tend to go flat more often than wider tires.

Do you prefer leaving the pavement and tackling off-road terrain? If that sounds more like you, then you may want to purchase the strong-framed mountain bike. This bike, equipped with its very low gears, is a perfect companion for climbing steep hills. Its knobby tired provide enough traction to tackle rocks and rough going along the way. You'll experience a pleasant ride on the trails with the mountain bike's comfortable seating. Some models even offer the option of adding shock absorbers. Save your energy though, because this bike is much harder to ride on paved roads.

If you'd like a bike that you can use both on and off the road then consider a hybrid or "cross" bike. It combines the popular features of both mountain and touring bikes. Serious and casual riders enjoy the comfortable seating, flat handlebar position, medium-wide tires, and a light frame. First introduced in the 1980's, they hybrid bike has become popular with the average bike rider.

Road, mountain, and hybrid bikes are only a few of the many choices you'll have when you visit your local bike shop. Know what you want to do on your bike and then talk to an expert to help make the best choice when you're ready to purchase your bike.

Assessment Sheet

Title *Bikes for Everyone*

6 Ideas

- *You've written about a topic in a way that will interest a wide audience.*
- *The essay contains exact and useful details about the bikes.*

6 Organization

- *Clearly, you have taken time to plan your essay.*
- *The transitions both within and between paragraphs work well.*
- *The prepositional phrase at the beginning of the second sentence is misplaced (see lines 1–3).*

5 Voice

- *Your knowledge about bikes creates a confident voice.*
- *The two questions that bike buyers would probably ask give the voice a helpful tone (see lines 3 and 12).*
- *You might include a personal anecdote to add a personal voice.*

6 Word Choice

- *Choosing well-known, clear words to describe each type of bike makes it unnecessary to use jargon that a reader may not understand.*
- *You did a fine job defining the hybrid or "cross" bike (see lines 22–26).*

6 Sentence Fluency

- *The variety in your sentence beginnings makes this essay a pleasure to read (see lines 1-2, 5-6, 14 and additional sentences).*
- *The questions also contribute to the sentence variety (see lines 3 and 12).*

4 Conventions

- *You need to proofread better (see lines 8, 15, 25, and 30).*
- *Study the use of commas (see lines 6, 8, and 29).*
- *You could use dashes around "or saddles" (see line 8).*

Expository Writing

Nature's Powerhouses

If you think about dangerous things in nature you might think about tornadoes and earthquakes. Both are powerful.

A tornado is the most powerful windstorm. It is formed out of violent thunderstorms. These storms happen when two air masses meet. When they meet, they begin mixing together. When this happens a funnel forms. Then it might reach down to the ground. Maybe houses fall down or trees fall over.

An earthquake is also powerful Earthquakes start underground by fault lines. The plates start moving and one slips. When this happens there are vibrations. About 500,000 are detected around the world each year but only 100,000 can be felt and only about 100 of them cause damage and most happen where there aren't many people.

Radar is improving. It makes it easier for scientists to predict tornadoes. Most tornadoes last less than 10 minutes. Sirens warn people to take cover. People who have been in tornadoes say it sound like a train is coming toward them.

It's hard to tell when earthquakes will happen and they happen so far below the ground. Scientists haven't yet found a good way to warn people. Some people say that there is a low rumbling sound that happens when there's an earthquake. They last less than 1 minute.

There are rating scales for tornadoes and earthquakes. The Fujita-Peterson scale is used to rate tornadoes. Tornadoes are rated from F-0 to F-5. Earthquakes are rated by the Richter scale. Any rating over 5.0 can cause damage. 7l0 earthquakes cause major damage.

Assessment Sheet

Title *Nature's Powerhouses*

3 Ideas

- *Choosing two widely researched topics provides an abundance of details.*
- *Capture your reader's interest with more specific and amazing details.*
- *You could expand your focus statement to make it clear that you intend to compare your topics and why you are doing so.*

3 Organization

- *Expand the first paragraph to get your reader's interest and explain what you will say.*
- *You do not have an ending.*

2 Voice

- *You sound interested in these topics, but general details don't help you create a knowledgeable voice (see lines 4–10).*
- *Show more of your feelings about tornadoes and earthquakes, or use a more scientific-sounding voice.*

3 Word Choice

- *You do a good job describing the two different rating scales (see lines 21–25).*
- *Be sure to use precise and accurate terms when you write about scientific topics with a scientific voice.*

2 Sentence Fluency

- *Both short, choppy sentences and run-on sentences confuse readers (see lines 3–7, 8, and 10–12).*
- *Some of your paragraphs do not have clear topic sentences (see paragraphs 4 and 5).*

3 Conventions

- *Your spelling is perfect.*
- *Check that you use the right pronouns and that it is clear to what they refer.*

Persuasive Writing

Support Our Animal Shelter

Imagine that you are lost. You don't know where you are or how to get home, and you can't ask anybody because you can't talk. You are probably hungry and thirsty, and your feet are really tired. If that sounds scary, think about how a stray dog or cat must feel. Dozens of cats and dogs get lost in our city every day. They wander helplessly through the streets looking for home. If they are lucky, they find their way home. They are also lucky if someone finds them and takes them to the local animal shelter. The shelter in our city is the largest in the county, and it keeps every animal until someone takes it home. Lately, though, the shelter has been unable to raise the funds it needs to stay open. Our city can't afford to lose the service this helter provides. Everyone—even people without pets—should support the shelter in every way possible.

The most important reason the shelter needs to stay open is that it takes care of hundred of lost and sick animals. The records at the shelter show that as many as 10 animals show up every week at the shelter. The shelter presently has 50 dogs and 30 cats as well as some other animals. These animals would have no place to go if the shelter were not open. They would wander in the streets, at risk of getting hit by cars. Life at the shelter is so much more better for the animals.

In addition, the shelter is important to the people of our city, too—not just the animals. Every day people at the shelter feed and clean up after the animals. Shelter workers also walk and groom the dogs. The shelter provides jobs for 15 people. People really love working there. Janice Pao has worked there for five years. She loves taking care of the animals and has brought home a few to live with her.

The final reason we need to keep the shelter open is that it is a good reflection on our city. The fact that we can maintain a first-rate shelter shows that the people of our city care about animals. It gives us a good reputation. It makes people want to live here.

In conclusion, we need to keep the city animal shelter open and running as long as there are animals who need it. In an ideal world, no pet would ever stray from home. But because animals need our help, we should provide it. Help the shelter stay in business by making a donation or by donating needed supplies such as dog and cat food, kitty litter, chew toys, paper towels, and plastic garbage bags. Animals can't always take care of themselves, so let's help them as much as we can.

Assessment Sheet

Title *Support Our Animal Shelter*

5 **Ideas**

- *You make excellent use of facts and examples, using specific numbers and a person.*
- *You should address a possible objection to strengthen your argument even more.*

6 **Organization**

- *Your transitions are clear.*
- *I especially like the fact that you show how the shelter affects animals, people, and the city, moving from smallest to largest.*
- *Your call to action is strong and specific.*

6 **Voice**

- *You have excellent confidence, which adds to your persuasive voice.*
- *Your compassion for the animals comes shining through.*

6 **Word Choice**

- *Try to avoid repeating the same word "shelter" over and over.*
- *Your words are appropriate to your audience and properly neutral.*
- *You might be a little more specific by naming the other types of animals the shelter helps.*

5 **Sentence Fluency**

- *Your flow would be improved if you combined some of the shorter groups of sentences for greater sentence variety.*
- *Try to avoid beginning sentences with a coordinating conjunction, such as the "But" in line 34. Combine those instead.*
- *Your opening paragraph has strong sentence variety.*

5 **Conventions**

- *You might want to review the use of comparatives in line 20.*
- *Be sure to proofread carefully to avoid simple errors like the missed plural in line 15 and a redundant phrase in lines 21–22.*

Persuasive Writing

Baby-Sitting Isn't for the Untrained

Should baby sitters be required to take courses? Then they should be made to get a license? I think so. Some friends and me baby-sit to earn money to buy new clothes. We like new clothes. We learned how to baby-sit two ways. We just do it. Or we remember what our baby sitters did. This works often. Most baby-sitting jobs don't have an emergency. Some of the kids are normal. And all goes well. Then I heard glass breaking in the bathroom.

The boy got up to get a drink of water. The glass broke when a very big blast of air came out of the water pipe with the water. All I saw was blood, blood, blood everywhere. Jake began a howl that would have scared the ghosts in the attic if there was an attic or if there was ghosts up there. I grabbed a towel and wrapped it around his arm and carried him to the telephone and called my mother. She is a nurse. Then I needed new clothes.

I did a research paper about emergencies. I got the number of times a rescue squad went to a house with a baby sitter. It showed that during a 3-month period of time, this happens 48 times. Twelve times the child was dying—couldn't breath. The next most times a child had a cut that had a lot of blood. Next in this lineup are times when the baby sitter thought the child may have eaten something poisonous like bath oil. The next most trips that the rescue squad made was for nosebleeds and the baby sitter didn't know what to do and two times were for broken bones and one time was when a child fell and had the wind knocked out of him. And one time was for hiccups and hurling. If you don't know what hurling is you may know what throwing up your kaputties is. Same thing. Only my grandpa says the last one.

Looks like baby sitters need to take a course and after taking the course they can get a license, a piece of paper filled out by some big shots, so that people hiring them know that they have taken a course.

Assessment Sheet

Title *Baby-Sitting Isn't for the Untrained*

3 **Ideas**

- *Your audience will want to read this essay because of the topic and details.*
- *You don't state clearly why you take the position you do.*
- *The information about clothes and ghosts should be cut, since it doesn't directly relate to your focus (see lines 3, 11, 12, and 14).*

3 **Organization**

- *Using a question is a good way to start a persuasive essay.*
- *The first paragraph is confusing and has two unrelated ideas.*
- *Your ending is weak.*

2 **Voice**

- *You have good information to create a strong, confident voice.*
- *Some of the casual words and sentences you use affect your voice.*

3 **Word Choice**

- *You use words that your audience can understand.*
- *Since you are tuned in to your audience, you may have included inappropriate words like "hurling," "kaputties," and "big shots."*

2 **Sentence Fluency**

- *You need to work on your sentences so your audience can enjoy reading them. For example, the second needs clarity (see lines 1–2).*
- *Use a series when possible: "I grabbed a towel, wrapped it around his arm, and carried him to the telephone" (see lines 12 and 13).*
- *Use a complex sentence: "Then I called my mother, who is a nurse" (see line 13).*
- *Listing the emergencies in the third paragraph caused you trouble. Possibly you could use bullets to make a list.*

3 **Conventions**

- *You know how to spell "baby-sit" and "baby sitter."*
- *Learn when to use "I" and when to use "me" (see line 2).*
- *Make the sentence's subject agree with the predicate (see line 22).*
- *Watch for confusing words (breath/breathe in line 18).*

Response to Literature

Blue Heron

At the beginning of Avi's book, *Blue Heron,* 12-year-old Maggie is worried. Usually she lives with her mother in Seattle, but now she is traveling to the East Coast, where she is going to visit her father and his new family. Maggie has always been close with her father, but she is worried about how the birth of her new half-sister will change things During her visit she learns that she can handle a less-than-perfect reality.

Maggie's stepmother, Joanna, picks her up and is friendly, but as Maggie settles into the cabin, she realizes that something is wrong. Her father spends most of his time doing business, on the phone, ignoring not only Maggie but also Joanna and the baby, Linda. Joanna reveals that Maggie's father has had a heart attack, and that he has changed. She is very worried about him, and she and Maggie develop a deep bond of mutual love and trust.

During her stay, Maggie spots a blue heron in a nearby marsh. Her father tells her "The heron is thought to be an omen for two things. . . . Life, but also, death. You take your pick according to your desire." Believing the heron is magical, Maggie begins visiting it every morning. She discovers she is not the only one watching the bird—someone is trying to kill it! She meets the would-be iller, a young boy named Tucker, who simply wants to use the bow and arrow he owns. Maggie tries to convince him not to kill the heron. He doesn't understand her strong need to keep the bird alive, but despite their differences, the two develop a strange kind of friendship.

One day Maggie discovers her father has not been taking his medicine. She tells Joanna, who ask Maggie to confront her father about not taking his medicine when they go out to dinner. She does so, and he becomes enraged. We learn that he has lost his job, and has been frantically trying to find a new one. He doesn't want to take his pills because he doesn't want to face the fact he is getting old. He angrily drops Maggie off and drives away A short while later Joanna receives a call and is told that he suffered a heart attack while driving and had a terrible accident.

Joanna and Maggie discuss the future. Maggie realized the marriage is in trouble, and is surprised to find she feels worse for Joanna than for her father. Maggie is bothered by the new discovery that you don't always like people you love. Joanna helps her understand that it is okay to feel that way, and tells her it wasn't Maggie's fault her father got hurt.

The bird symbolizes Maggie's growth from a little girl who believes in magic to an adult who believes in herself. When she discovers that Tucker has decided not to kill the bird, she realizes that the magic she had been seeking was really within herself.

Assessment Sheet

Title *Blue Heron*

5 **Ideas**

- *The focus statement tells your readers what your main character learns without giving the story away (see lines 6–7).*
- *The key events support your focus, and you manage to work them all into your essay by relating them to each other (see lines 8–14 and 25–33.)*
- *Readers will want to know why the heron symbolizes Maggie's growth (see lines 40–41).*

6 **Organization**

- *The beginning paragraph introduces the main character, and the four middle paragraphs all concentrate on key events.*
- *The organization shows how one event leads to another.*

5 **Voice**

- *The formal voice you have created fits the serious events and the intense feelings that the characters have.*
- *The tone is very objective. You might want to show more feeling.*

5 **Word Choice**

- *You have selected words carefully, finding the right words for the task.*
- *The reference to "a less-than-perfect reality" builds reader interest (see lines 6–7). More words that would engage the reader would result in a stronger essay.*

6 **Sentence Fluency**

- *You use a beautiful variety of sentences.*
- *Your ability to write compound and complex sentences is why you can show how the events relate to one another.*

5 **Conventions**

- *Review your use of commas. Don't mix up compound predicates and compound sentences (see lines 6, 10, 12, 16, 28, and 35).*
- *A dash should not be used to connect sentences (see line 20).*
- *Check for clear pronoun references (see lines 13 and 27).*
- *Check verb tenses and agreement (see lines 26 and 34).*

Response to Literature

Sal Tree Hiddle

The author Sharon Creech creates Sal Tree Hiddle as the main character in *Walk Two Moons*. She is thirteen years old. Sal moves from Kentucky to Ohio with her father. The mother has gone to Idaho. Sal learns you "walk two moons" in another person's moccasins if you want to get to know another person. Sometimes you cry, sometimes you laugh, and sometimes you are scared. Sal feels all these emotions. Readers will, too.

Sal meets many different kinds of people. Phoebe, her new friend, uses a wild imagination to label a young man a lunatic and Mrs. Cadaver an ax murderer. At Phoebe's house, messages in envelopes create mystery. Sal's Grandpa and Grandma, who drive her to Idaho, talk to each other. Sal can see that they have walked in each other's shoes.

She wants to arrive in Idaho for her mother's birthday. Her unusual grandparents slow down the trip. A snake and a stranger make it impossible for Sal to get to her mother. She drives herself the last 90 miles. I won't tell you what happens because I think you should read this book.

Finally, she and her dad move back to Kentucky. Her mother's blackberry kiss, birds singing in a tree, and a chicken that Ben, another friend, gives her as a gift are the noticeable things that prove to Sal that real people find many ways to walk in each other's shoes and to love one another. Sal learns that after walking two moons in another's moccasins, one does not judge other people. One accepts.

Assessment Sheet

Title *Sal Tree Hiddle*

2 **Ideas**

- *You need to explain the phrase "walk two moons" because your whole essay depends on your readers understanding this (see line 4).*
- *You need a statement that clearly turns your idea about walking in another's moccasins into the focus of your essay (see your excellent conclusion in lines 22–24).*

2 **Organization**

- *A clear focus statement and a topic sentence in each paragraph will help you organize this essay.*
- *Instead of listing everything that happens, which is confusing, choose key events that support the focus.*

3 **Voice**

- *Your voice shows interest in the story and the main character.*
- *The voice could be called "matter of fact" since you state the facts and don't show much feeling.*

3 **Word Choice**

- *Your audience will understand the words you use. Ordinary words help make writing clear.*
- *Try to find ways to use common words to create more feeling. For example, you could write, "Mysterious letters frighten Phoebe and Sal" (see lines 10–11).*

3 **Sentence Fluency**

- *A beautiful, balanced sentence shows your potential (see lines 5–6).*
- *Combine the many short, choppy sentences (see lines 2–3 and 14–17).*
- *The 2-word sentence at the end is very effective because it emphasizes the message in the sentence that comes before (see line 24).*

6 **Conventions**

- *You do not have any errors.*
- *When you start combining sentences and adding words to express feelings, you may need to learn more about punctuation. Challenge yourself!*

Assessment Sheet

Use one of the rubrics listed below to rate a piece of writing. Circle the rubric your teacher tells you to use. If you need information about assessing with a rubric, see pages 52 and 55 in your *Write Source* book.

Narrative Rubric (pages 130–131)
Expository Rubric (pages 194–195)
Persuasive Rubric (pages 256–257)
Response to Literature (pages 318–319)

Title ____

____ **Ideas**

____ **Organization**

____ **Voice**

____ **Word Choice**

____ **Sentence Fluency**

____ **Conventions**

Evaluator ____________________

Editing and Proofreading Marks

Use the symbols and letters below to show where and how your writing needs to be changed. Your teachers may also use these symbols to point out errors in your writing.

Symbol	Meaning	Example	Corrected Example
≡	**Capitalize a letter.**	Lorraine Hansberry wrote *A Raisin in the sun.*	Lorraine Hansberry wrote *A Raisin in the Sun.*
/	**Make a capital letter lowercase.**	Her play tells the story of the Younger Family.	Her play tells the story of the Younger family.
⊙	**Insert (add) a period.**	This play focuses on racial attitudes It also...	This play focuses on racial attitudes. It also...
⬭ or *sp.*	**Correct spelling.**	Lena Younger, the family leader, is very religous.	Lena Younger, the family leader, is very religious.
⌐ഠ	**Delete (take out) or replace.**	Lena she makes a down payment on a nice house.	Lena makes a down payment on a nice house.
∧	**Insert here.**	The family wants to escape ∧ life. (ghetto)	The family wants to escape ghetto life.
∧ ∧ ∧ (, : ;)	**Insert a comma, a colon, or a semicolon.**	Her son, Walter Lee, Jr. wants to buy a business.	Her son, Walter Lee, Jr., wants to buy a business.
∨ ∨ ∨ (' " ")	**Insert an apostrophe or a quotation mark.**	Walter Lees wife hopes for a larger apartment.	Walter Lee's wife hopes for a larger apartment.
? ! ∧ ∧	**Insert a question mark or an exclamation point.**	What would Beneatha do with the money	What would Beneatha do with the money?
¶	**Start a new paragraph.**	¶The direction of the play clearly changes when...	The direction of the play clearly changes when...
∽	**Switch words or letters.**	Walter gets the possible worst news.	Walter gets the worst possible news.

T-Chart

Subject:

Time Line

Subject:

(Chronological Order)

1

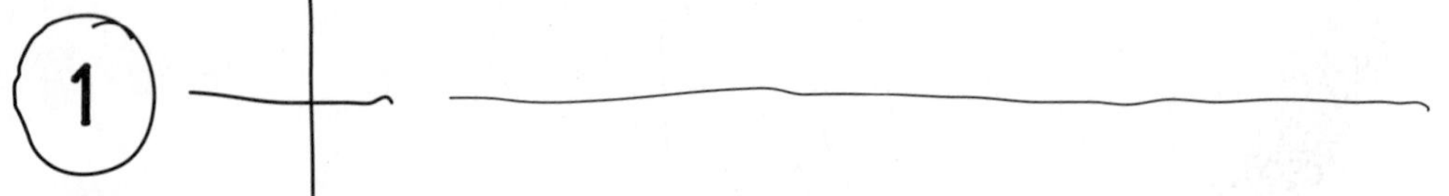

2

3

4

5

6

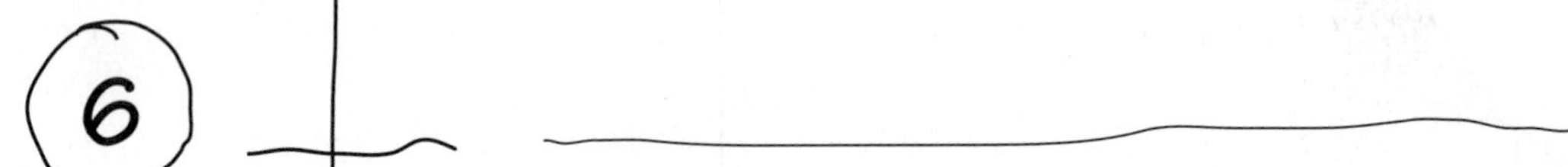

7

8

Venn Diagram

Subject A

Differences

Subject B

Similarities

5 W's Chart

Subject:

Who?	What?	When?	Where?	Why?

Sensory Chart

Subject:

Sights	Sounds	Smells	Tastes	Feelings

Scavenger Hunt 1: Find the Fours

Directions Find the following "fours" in your book by turning to the pages listed in parentheses.

1. **Four** reasons to write (page 2)

____

____

2. **Four** on a rubric means ________________ (page 46)

____

3. **Four** ways to publish in school (page 58)

____

____

4. **Four** sentence starters that can help you select a topic (page 102)

____

____

____

5. **Four** tips to remember as you write middle paragraphs (page 110)

____

____

____

6. **Four** types of fuzzy thinking to avoid (page 231)

____

____

7. **Four** questions that an adverb can answer (page 490)

____

8. **Four** parts of a plot line (page 347 or 351)

____

9. **Four** good listening habits (page 418)

____

10. **Four** ways to improve sentence style (page 511)

____

____

____

Scavenger Hunt 2: What Is It?

Directions Find the answers to the following questions using the index in the back of the book. The underlined words below tell you where to look in the index.

1. What two kinds of details does a writer collect with an action-sensory chart?

2. What is the definition for an abstract noun?

3. What book part is like a mini-dictionary?

4. What is the comparative form for the irregular adverb *badly*?

5. What is a first-person point of view?

6. What are four kinds of sentences?

7. What is a cycle diagram?

8. What is an anecdote?

9. What kind of a verb does a predicate adjective follow?

10. What are some publishing options for a story you have written?

11. What is a simile?

12. What types of visual aids can you use when giving a speech?

Getting to Know *Write Source*

Directions Locate the pages in *Write Source* where answers to the following learning tasks can be found. Both the index and the table of contents can help you.

_____________ **1.** You are requesting information about Harry S. Truman from the Truman Library in Missouri. You need to know how to format a business letter.

_____________ **2.** You are analyzing a story that has an "omniscient point of view." You need to know what that means.

_____________ **3.** Your social studies teacher asks you not to use inflammatory words in your speech about capital punishment. You need to know what words to avoid.

_____________ **4.** Your teacher has asked you to demonstrate using commas between equal adjectives. You need to check the rules about commas with equal adjectives.

_____________ **5.** You often spell *commit* incorrectly. You need to look up the correct spelling before turning in your final copy of an essay.

_____________ **6.** Your teacher says you have "balanced sentences." You want to know if this is a good writing skill or a poor writing skill.

_____________ **7.** You want to win the short story contest, so your teacher says you will need to "create a conflict." You need to learn how to create a conflict.

_____________ **8.** You don't like to make an outline, but one of your friends says it's easy, just use an organized list. You want to know how to make an organized list.

_____________ **9.** When the teacher talked about unity and coherence, you were not in class. Now you need to find out what unity and coherence are.

_____________ **10.** Your younger sister comes to you because she is confused about subject-verb agreement with compound subjects. You want to give her some clear rules.

Getting Started Activity Answers

Scavenger Hunt 1: Find the Fours

1. Four of the most important reasons for writing are to review your experiences, to learn, to show your understanding, and to share ideas.
2. A *4* means that the writing is good and meets most of the requirements for a trait.
3. Some ways to publish in school include school newspapers, school literary magazines, classroom collections, and writing portfolios.
4. These sentence starters can help select a topic: *I was being helpful when . . . ; I was inspired when . . . ; I was exhausted when . . . ; I was excited when . . .*
5. As you write middle paragraphs, remember to put your events in the order in which they happened; appeal to your reader's senses; create a clear picture with action words; and use dialogue to show a speaker's personality, to keep the action moving, or to add information.
6. Avoid these types of fuzzy thinking: jumping to conclusions, bandwagoning, misleading comparisons, and appealing only to emotion.
7. An adverb can answer the questions *how, when, where,* and *how much.*
8. The parts of a plot line are the beginning, rising action, high point, and ending.
9. You can become a better listener if you figure out your purpose for listening, listen carefully, listen for the main ideas and take notes, and condense information.
10. You can improve your sentence style if you use different types of sentences, combine short sentences, expand sentences by adding words and phrases, and model the sentences of other writers.

Scavenger Hunt 2: What Is It?

1. A writer collects action details and sensory details for descriptive and narrative writing. (p. 548)
2. An abstract noun names something that you can think about but cannot see or touch. (p. 470)
3. A glossary is like a mini-dictionary. (p. 371)
4. The comparative form is *worse.* (p. 738.5)
5. First-person point of view is when one of the characters tells the story. (p. 352)
6. The kinds of sentences are declarative, interrogative, imperative, and exclamatory. (p. 518)
7. A cycle diagram shows the steps or details in a process that is repeated. (p. 448)
8. An anecdote is a brief story that makes a point. (p. 554 or 558)
9. A predicate adjective follows a linking verb. (p. 480 or 718.2)
10. Three publication ideas are to recite your story, create a skit, or submit your story. (p. 349)
11. A simile is a comparison that uses the word *like* or *as.* (p. 79, 360, or 559)
12. Some visual aids to use are posters, photographs, charts, transparencies, maps, and objects. (p. 425)

Getting to Know *Write Source*

1. 276–277
2. 352
3. 246
4. 586
5. 647
6. 522 or 513
7. 346
8. 170
9. 538–539
10. 509

Unit Planning

Writing Form

PARAGRAPH

____ days

- **Focus**
- **Skills**

ESSAY 1

____ days

Prewriting

- **Focus**
- **Skills**

Writing

____ days

- **Focus**
- **Skills**

Revising

____ days

- **Ideas**
- **Organization**
- **Voice**
- **Word Choice**
- **Sentence Fluency**

See the Yearlong Timetable beginning on page TE-32.

Unit Planning (continued)

Editing

____ days

- Punctuation
- Capitalization
- Spelling
- Grammar

Publishing

____ days

- Options

Evaluating

____ days

- Self-Assessment
- Benchmark Papers

ESSAY 2

____ days

- Focus
- Skills

ACROSS THE CURRICULUM

____ days

- Social Studies
- Science
- Math
- Practical

Index

G

S

T

V

W

Credits

Student Edition

Photos:

Cover (blue/green coral) ©Digital Vision/Getty Images; Cover (red coral), endsheet, v, xvi, 68, 75, 77, 83, 143, 199, 219, 229, 229 center right, 267, 283, 287, 317, 323, 324, 360 bottom, 363 top right and bottom left, 368, 376, 381, 409, 431, 441 top, 445, 459 top, 460 center, 461, 492, 524, 547, 547 center, 555 center right and background ©Photodisc/Getty Images. vi, viii, 1 bottom left, 27, 36, 63, 71, 93, 97, 101, 106, 107, 113, 125, 129, 157, 165, 171, 177, 189, 227, 233, 239, 251, 291, 295, 301, 305, 313, 329, 387, 396, 405, 407, 423, 430, 469, 474, 476, 499, 501 bottom, 509, 531, 750 center ©Comstock/Getty Images. 135, 161, 193, 261, 343, 354, 359 top, 360 top, 361 bottom, 377 center, 471, 555 bottom, back cover(coral) ©Corbis; back cover (shark), xviii center, 5, 9, 173 left ©Ingram/Getty Images; xii, 417, 419, 422 ©Gaertner/Alamy; 205, 223, 255, 539 ©Getty Images; 10 ©PhotoObjects.net/Jupiter; 11, 16 ©SuperStock RF/SuperStock; 29 ©Jupiter/Brand X/Alamy; 57, 60-61 ©Hemera Technologies/Jupiter; 65 top ©Eyewire/Getty Images; 65 bottom ©Stockbyte/Getty Images; back cover (light) ©Stockbyte/Getty; 105 ©Photos.com/Jupiter; 173 right ©JupiterImages/Getty Images; 359 bottom ©Design Pics/Jupiter; 363 bottom right Courtesy of NASA; 441 bottom, 445 bottom ©Alamy; 521, 533 ©Artville/Getty Images; 523 ©Brownstock Inc./Alamy.

Text:

Page 375: Copyright © 2010 by Houghton Mifflin Company, Adapted by permission from *The American Heritage Student Dictionary.*

Teacher's Edition

Photos:

Cover (blue bandanna) Harcourt; cover (blue/green coral) ©Digital Vision/Getty Images; cover (red bandanna, yellow coral) HMH Collection; cover (red coral), TE-37, TE-39 ©Photodisc/Getty Images; TE-8 ©Bruce Laurance/Blend Images/Getty Images; TE-10-11 ©Andrzej Tokarski/Alamy; TE-12 ©Image Source/Getty Images; TE-16-17 ©Blend Images/Alamy; 812 ©Comstock/Getty Images; back cover (shark) ©Ingram/Getty Images.

Text: